ECONOMIC SCIENCE AND POLITICAL ECONOMY

Also by Susan Howson

BRITISH MONETARY POLICY, 1945–51
DOMESTIC MONETARY MANAGEMENT IN BRITAIN, 1919–38
THE COLLECTED PAPERS OF JAMES MEADE (*editor*)
THE ECONOMIC ADVISORY COUNCIL 1930–1939 (*with Donald Winch*)
THE WARTIME DIARIES OF LIONEL ROBBINS AND JAMES MEADE, 1943–45 (*co-editor*)

Economic Science and Political Economy

Selected Articles

Lionel Robbins

Edited by Susan Howson

Professor of Economics
University of Toronto

Softcover reprint of the hardcover 1st edition 1997

First published 1997 by
MACMILLAN PRESS LTD
Houndmills, Basingstoke, Hampshire RG21 6XS
and London
Companies and representatives
throughout the world

ISBN 978-1-349-12763-4 ISBN 978-1-349-12761-0 (eBook)
DOI 10.1007/978-1-349-12761-0

A catalogue record for this book is available from the British Library.

This book is printed on paper suitable for recycling and made from fully managed and sustained forest sources.

10 9 8 7 6 5 4 3 2 1
06 05 04 03 02 01 00 99 98 97

Contents

Editor's Introduction

Lionel Robbins (1898–1984) was the foremost British economist of his generation. He was appointed Professor of Economics at the London School of Economics in 1929, when he was thirty years of age; from then until his retirement from his Chair in 1961 he dominated the Economics Department at LSE and built it up to its pre-eminent position in British economics. Robbins was not only an academic economist. He was important and influential in the shaping of economic policy in Britain and the international economy in and after the Second World War, in the expansion of British higher education, and in the administration of the arts in Britain. He was created one of the first four life peers in 1959. In the last two decades of his life Lord Robbins was most widely known as the author of the Report of the Committee on Higher Education published in 1963, but this was only the most conspicuous of his several major contributions to British public life. Nonetheless, as James Meade has emphasized, 'the richness of his other lives and of his personality must not be allowed to overshadow the fact that he was by profession an economist and an economist of the first rank'.[1]

In 1926 Edwin Cannan, describing the staff of the London School of Economics to his successor as Professor of Political Economy, Allyn Young, told him that Robbins was 'the most promising young economist in England'.[2] Robbins was then a young assistant lecturer in economics at LSE, about to be promoted to lecturer. After seeing active service in the First World War as an artillery officer in France in 1917–18, he had taken a first class honours degree at the London School of Economics in 1923. The following year he had worked as research assistant to William Beveridge, then Director of the School, compiling employment data and studying business cycle theory, and in 1924–5 he had held a temporary lectureship at New College, Oxford. In 1927 Robbins returned, with Beveridge's encouragement, to New College as Fellow and Lecturer in Economics, but Beveridge also asked him to continue to give a course of lectures on economic theory at LSE.[3] When Allyn Young

1. *The Economist* (8 December 1984), p. 19.
2. Cannan to Young (11 June 1926), Allyn Young Papers, Nathan Marsh Pusey Library, Harvard University.
3. Beveridge to H.A.L. Fisher (28 March and 2 May 1927), Robbins Personal File A, London School of Economics.

died suddenly of pneumonia in March 1929, the reader in economics (and Labour MP), Hugh Dalton, who regarded Robbins 'as quite certainly the most brilliant student who has passed through the School since the War', lobbied hard and successfully to have Robbins appointed as a junior Professor of Economics. And, as Robbins pointed out in his autobiography, 'The Young chair was never filled'.[1] Robbins became and remained the senior professor of economics at LSE until his retirement.

Soon after his appointment as professor Robbins was invited by Keynes to join a select and distinguished group of economists as the youngest member of a Committee of Economists, which Keynes had persuaded the Prime Minister, J. Ramsay MacDonald, to set up under the auspices of the second Labour government's Economic Advisory Council. With the world slump gathering momentum and unemployment in Britain rapidly rising Keynes hoped his committee would demonstrate the unanimity of professional economists on policy questions, by producing 'an agreed diagnosis of our present problems, and a reasoned list of possible remedies'.[2] Keynes was incensed when the young Robbins objected to his 'perfectly monstrous' draft report, with its qualified support for protection and for public works. Robbins refused to sign the final version, even though it incorporated some of his own ideas on the causes of the slump, and insisted on a minority report of his own. There he made clear his 'complete disagreement' with his colleagues on the question of tariffs.[3] He made his opposition to protection more public in talks, articles and newspaper pieces, especially over the next twelve months until a coalition government introduced a tariff in October 1931 after the fall of the Labour government. He also encouraged, though with misgivings, Beveridge to set up another 'Committee of Economists' to produce a book expounding the free trade case (*Tariffs: the Case Examined*, 1931).

At the time of his professorial appointment, Robbins had published only a handful of academic articles, two of which were review articles. He had also written a small textbook on wages, published in 1926. In the next ten years he was to publish some 20 articles and five books and edit three others. (For the details of his publications see the Bibliography p. 429 below.) The first of these books is his most famous: *An Essay on the Nature and Significance of*

1. Dalton, 'Statement by Head of Department' (2 November 1926) Robbins Personal File A, London School of Economics; Ben Pimlott (ed.), *The Political Diary of Hugh Dalton 1918–40, 1945–60* (1986), p. 53; Robbins, *Autobiography of an Economist* (1971), pp. 121–2.

2. Keynes to MacDonald (10 July 1930), quoted in Susan Howson and Donald Winch, *The Economic Advisory Council 1930–1939* (Cambridge, 1977), p. 47.

3. Robbins to Cannan (17 October and 5 November 1930), Cannan Papers 1030, British Library of Political and Economic Science; 'Report by Professor L. Robbins', reprinted in Howson and Winch, *The Economic Advisory Council 1930–1939*, pp. 227–31.

Economic Science, first published in 1932, which is still in print and widely read in the 1990s. It introduced the 'scarcity' definition of economics – 'Economics is the science which studies human behaviour as a relationship between ends and scarce means which have alternative uses'[1] – now so well established as to be cited usually without attribution. In adopting this definition Robbins explicitly rejected the 'materialist' definitions of Cannan, whose lectures he had attended as an undergraduate, and of Marshall and his pupils at Cambridge, and took over some of the ideas of the Austrian economists Menger and von Mises. He acknowledged his 'especial indebtedness' to the works of Ludwig von Mises – whose *Die Gemeinwirtschaft* (1922) he read in his first years of lecturing at LSE – and to *The Common Sense of Political Economy* of the English economist Philip Wicksteed.[2]

In January 1931 Friedrich Hayek came to LSE to give a series of lectures. This led to Hayek's appointment as Tooke Professor of Economic Science and Statistics at the School later the same year. By 1939 Robbins had expanded the small LSE economics department to rival that of Cambridge, effectively encouraging the research and careers of younger economists such as J.R. Hicks, Nicholas Kaldor, Abba Lerner, Evan Durbin and A.K. Dasgupta, as well as developing and organizing the teaching of economics, especially at the postgraduate level. He was involved in all the major controversies in economics, theoretical and practical, microeconomic and macroeconomic, both through the famous LSE seminar which he chaired and in his own professional and public writings.

His interest in the work of Viennese economists, especially in capital theory, which had led him to invite Hayek to lecture at the School in 1931, influenced his second major book, *The Great Depression* (1934). This expanded on the views of the causes of the worldwide slump which he had propounded in the Committee of Economists in 1930, using a monetary theory of the trade cycle derived from Wicksell and Hayek. However, he later repudiated Austrian macroeconomic analysis and this book because of its negative attitude to countercyclical economic policy in the face of a severe deflation. When his publisher reported a revival of interest in the book, which had gone out of print in 1945, he responded that he would prefer it not to be reissued. 'It is very readable, but ... I am sure that it is a pretty good example of a premature and over-simple synthesis ... It sold very well when it was first issued and enabled me, as a young married man, to buy an expensive grand piano. But I would rather that that was the end of it.'[3].

1. *An Essay on the Nature and Significance of Economic Science*, 1st edn, p. 15.
2. *Nature and Significance*, 1st edn, pp. viii–ix; *Autobiography of an Economist*, pp. 105–7.
3. *Autobiography of an Economist*, pp. 154–5; Robbins to Rex Allen (25 March 1963), Robbins Papers.

His early articles had been on microeconomic issues (see Chapters 1 and 2 below). In the 1930s he increasingly wrote on current macroeconomic policy issues, while continuing to write on microeconomics and methodology (see below). Parts of the more applied papers found their way into his 1937 book, *Economic Planning and International Order*, which was based on lectures he had given at the Institute Universitaire des Hautes Etudes Internationales in Geneva in 1935; others he included in his first collection of essays, *The Economic Basis of Class Conflict and Other Essays in Political Economy* (1939). He began to write on the history of economic thought (see Chapters 6 and 11 below), beginning by contributing a chapter on the economic works to the biography of Wicksteed by C.H. Herford (1931). He edited Wicksteed's *The Co-ordination of the Laws of Distribution* (1932) and *The Common Sense of Political Economy* (1933) and Knut Wicksell's *Lectures on Political Economy* (1934–5). He also edited the journal *Economica*, initiated the LSE Series of Reprints of Scarce Tracts on Economics and Political Science and arranged for the translation and publication of several major works of Austrian economists (Mises, Menger, Haberler, Hayek) as well as the Wicksell *Lectures*.

Although LSE became the centre of opposition to Keynesian economics in Britain in the 1930s, Keynes and Robbins were on friendly terms again soon after their clash in the Committee of Economists and remained so for the rest of the decade. Several of the younger LSE economists became Keynesians after the publication of *The General Theory* – with the result, as Robbins later remarked, that the disputes among the LSE and the Cambridge economists were often more acrimonious than those between the two groups.[1] In 1938 Dennis Robertson moved from Cambridge to the more tolerant atmosphere of LSE as Professor of Money and Banking but in the event he was there only a year because of the onset of the Second World War.

On the outbreak of war the School moved to Cambridge for the duration. Robbins taught there for only a few months before he was asked to join the group of economists in the government's Central Economic Information Service. This was split into the Central Statistical Service and the Economic Section in 1941 and Robbins took over the Directorship of the Section in September of that year. He ran it, according to James Meade, as 'a seminar of young academic economists, chaired by their professor'; at the same time he confined their work to manageable and practically useful topics and established good working relations with other government departments.[2] With his deputy director James Meade he was intimately involved in the

1. *Autobiography of an Economist*, p. 134.
2. Meade, *op. cit.*

preparation of the Churchill coalition government's famous white paper on *Employment Policy* published in 1944. He represented the UK government in the Anglo–American official discussions of postwar international economic policy and at the United Nations conferences in Hot Springs, Virginia, in 1943 and Bretton Woods, New Hampshire, in 1944 – the conferences that gave us the Food and Agriculture Organization, the International Monetary Fund and the World Bank. In these activities he worked in close collaboration with Keynes in the Treasury; their prewar doctrinal differences no longer mattered. Robbins was a wholehearted and enthusiastic supporter of Keynes's 'clearing union' plan for the postwar international monetary system and fought hard (and effectively) for it and for Meade's complementary plan for an international 'commercial union' within Whitehall and in the negotiations with American and Canadian officials in Washington and London. His final duty before he was released from government service in January 1946 was to go to Washington as a member of the British team led by Keynes in the bitter and protracted negotiations for a postwar American loan. He wrote of these experiences in his autobiography, utilizing the diaries which he had kept of his missions to North America; the diaries were published in 1990.[1]

Robbins returned to academic life as soon he decently could, to resume his teaching and research and to rebuild the depleted LSE Economics Department. He resurrected the seminar and as in the 1930s he encouraged the research and helped to further the careers of his students and younger colleagues – to mention only a few, William Baumol, Ronald Coase, Frank Hahn, Ralph Turvey, and A.W.H. Phillips. He also recruited James Meade as Professor of Commerce with special reference to international trade when he left government service in 1947.

Robbins did not, of course, publish during most of the war. His last prewar publication had been an essay on *The Economic Causes of War*, which he had to cut short when war arrived. He broke a long silence with an article in January 1947 on 'Economic Prospects' in *Lloyds Bank Review* – which was to be the main outlet for his contributions to contemporary policy as it had been in the 1930s (see the Bibliography). He was critical of the postwar Labour government headed by Clement Attlee in this article, though not as critical as in his next article written after the British balance-of-payments crisis in the summer of 1947, for he feared that the government was, by foolish and misguided policies, frittering away the opportunities provided by the hardwon American loan. The second article was soon notorious since

1. Susan Howson and Donald Moggridge (eds), *The Wartime Diaries of Lionel Robbins and James Meade 1943–45* (London: Macmillan, 1990).

several Liberal and Conservative MPs used it to attack the Chancellor of the Exchequer, Robbins's former teacher Hugh Dalton, in the House of Commons.[1] Although he wished to distance himself from government, he participated vigorously in public policy debate on British economic policy. He was also consulted by at least two Chancellors of the Exchequer on domestic and international monetary policy in the 1950s and served on various semi-official committees at the request of the British government.

Robbins was honoured to be invited to give the Marshall Lectures in Cambridge in May 1947. The lectures, published as *The Economic Problem in Peace and War* later that year, reflected his wartime experiences in government; in his views on the desirable nature and extent of government intervention he was now much closer to Dennis Robertson and the American economist Jacob Viner (who had been a close friend ever since they met in Oxford in 1927) than to Hayek or von Mises.[2] In his comments on the need to use financial policy for the management of aggregate demand he singled out Keynes *and* Robertson as the two economists who had influenced his views.

In his own research Robbins turned to the history of economics, establishing his reputation in this field first with his *The Theory of Economic Policy in English Classical Political Economy* (1952) and then with his work on Robert Torrens (*Robert Torrens and the Evolution of Classical Economics*, 1958 and a new edition of Torrens's *Letters on Commercial Policy*, 1958). He continued to lecture mainly on economic theory until the departure of his younger colleague Terence Hutchison in 1953 led to his taking over the advanced undergraduate course on the history of economic thought which he was to give for the rest of his active life.

In 1952, as a result of his longstanding interest in the arts and his reputation as an effective administrator, Robbins was asked to serve on a Committee on the Export of Works of Art, chaired by his wartime boss Sir John Anderson, now Lord Waverley. In the same year he was invited to become a Trustee of the National Gallery. He served on the reviewing committee recommended by the Waverley Committee until he became Chairman of the Trustees of the National Gallery in 1954. A couple of years later he joined the Board of the Royal Opera House, Covent Garden, becoming chairman of its ballet and finance committees, and remaining on the Board until almost the end of his life.

By 1960 Lionel Robbins, now Baron Robbins, of Clare Market, was chairing the Trustees of the National Gallery, representing the National Gallery on

---

1. In the Debate on the Address on 24 October 1947: *House of Commons Debates*, vol. 443, cols 384–469. The article is reprinted as Chapter 15 below.
2. See his *Autobiography of an Economist*, pp. 219–26, as well as *The Economic Problem in Peace and War*, especially Lecture III.

the Board of the Tate Gallery, a Director of the Royal Opera House and chairman of its finance committee, and chairman of the Committee of Management of the Courtauld Institute of Art. He had also joined the Board of Directors of the *Financial Times* in 1959 at the invitation of Lord Poole, in the expectation that he would succeed Poole as Chairman. Robbins hoped that he could retain his Chair at LSE, at least on a part-time basis, but to his lasting resentment the University of London did not agree. On reaching his first retirement date in September 1961 and having taken over the chairmanship of the *FT* at the beginning of the year, he gave up his professorial title and continued at the school as a part-time lecturer. He was much more reluctant to chair the Committee on Higher Education, for he feared that it would put paid to his long-cherished ambition of writing a book on the principles of economic theory. Asked to consider the assignment by R.A. Butler, the Home Secretary, he was persuaded by one of the senior Treasury officials with whom he had worked in wartime that his book could not be as useful or important as the reform of higher education in Britain.[1] Robbins never wrote his book on economic theory, but he continued to lecture and write and publish on economic policy issues and on the history of economic thought until the 1980s.

Many of the articles, lectures and papers he wrote after the war he gathered together from time to time and published as books. But he did not republish his interwar theoretical papers. They have never been reprinted together, though many have been reprinted in volumes of readings edited by others. They would have been published in the collection his friends William Baumol and Fritz Machlup proposed to edit to celebrate his 65th birthday (on the model of the one prepared for Jacob Viner on Robbins's advice), had Robbins not pointed out to them that he was about to publish one volume of collected papers on policy and already planning another on the history of economic thought.[2]

* * *

In compiling this collection I began with the intention of republishing those academic journal articles published by Robbins before 1939 that he did not republish himself, excluding review articles and his student's recollections

1. *Autobiography of an Economist*, pp. 272–4.
2. Robbins to Baumol (11 February 1963), Robbins Papers (and on the Viner 'festschrift', *The Long View and the Short*, 1958, Robbins to Baumol, 6 January 1954). Robbins was referring to *Politics and Economics: Papers in Political Economy* (1963) and his later *The Evolution of Modern Economic Theory and Other Papers on the History of Economic Thought* (1970).

of Professor Cannan (*Economic Journal*, June 1935). (I have omitted one other article for reasons explained below.) I have excluded chapters in books, such as his contribution to the Cannan *festschrift* (T. Gregory and H. Dalton, (eds), *London Essays in Economics*, 1927), and – with one exception – his more popular articles on interwar policy issues. I then added his major articles on the history of economic thought, which were written both before and after the Second World War; these include at least one review article. For the years after 1945 I have included the major articles he published in academic economics journals and a selection of his writings on economic policy issues, choosing those that made an important contribution to contemporary debate or illustrate Robbins's views particularly clearly. The result is not very different from the selection tentatively made by Baumol and Machlup, except for including later items, and it reflects the wide range of Robbins's interests with economics.

Robbins began to publish in the midst of the contemporary debates on the nature of costs and supply and on the meaning of equilibrium. His first major article, on 'The representative firm' (*Economic Journal*, September 1928; Chapter 1 below), is famous for having succeeded in banishing that Marshallian concept from the discipline. Marshall had introduced the idea in an attempt to reconcile the existence of internal and external economies of scale, and hence increasing returns, with a long-run competitive equilibrium. Robbins showed not just that this attempted reconciliation would not work but that it was redundant. He sent the paper to Keynes as editor of the *Economic Journal* in March 1928. Keynes accepted the paper immediately, as 'a very interesting piece of work, which much wanted doing, and [with which] ... I am in sympathy ... [for] I should like to do away with the representative firm altogether', but he postponed publication until September since he had already accepted an article by Pigou on the same subject for the June issue.[1]

Although Robbins was generally critical of Marshallian partial equilibrium analysis, his two early papers in what now would be called labour economics both use this method of analysis. The first of these, 'The economic effects of variations of hours of labour' (*Economic Journal*, March 1929; Chapter 2 below), shows the influence of his former teacher and colleague, Hugh Dalton, who visited him in Oxford and provided useful critical comments on the paper. (Dalton also suggested that Robbins develop the ideas in the paper with empirical work but admitted that he suspected Robbins would prefer to write on theoretical topics.)[2]

1. Keynes to Robbins (14 March 1928), Keynes Papers EJ/1[1], King's College, Cambridge.
2. Dalton to Robbins (22 October 1928), Robbins Papers.

The second of the pair, 'On the elasticity of demand for income in terms of effort' (*Economica*, June 1930; Chapter 5 below) is notable for an early geometrical presentation of a backward-bending supply curve for labour. On reading the article Pigou wrote to Robbins to object that Robbins had over-simplified an argument in Pigou's *The Economics of Welfare* (3rd edn, 1928); in reply Robbins explained: 'Originally it [his paper] formed part of a course of lectures on general principles & consisted merely of the diagrams & the critique of [F.H.] Knight whose work I use as a supplement to Marshall for teaching purposes. I decided to publish it ... because so many students failed to grasp the diagrammatic exposition that ... I got tired to having to lend out my notes.'[1]

The influence of Knight's work (and Robbins's use of it in his lectures: see p. 60 below) is even more pronounced in his article 'On a certain ambiguity in the conception of stationary equilibrium' (*Economic Journal*, June 1930; Chapter 4 below), as is the influence of Wicksteed. It led to correspondence with Knight (in the Knight Papers in the Regenstein Library of the University of Chicago) and to a lasting friendship. Robbins initiated the republication of Knight's seminal book, *Risk, Uncertainty and Profit* in the LSE Series of Reprints of Scarce Tracts on Economics and Political Science in 1933.

In the meantime Robbins delivered his inaugural lecture as Professor of Economics at LSE in January 1930, taking as his large subject 'The present position of economic science' (Chapter 3 below). Dalton thought it was a 'good performance'; Robbins himself was later somewhat embarrassed by its pretension: 'The only thing I can say in excuse is that it was delivered at a time ... when hardly anyone [in England] knew about the great continental economists, Walras, Pareto, Wicksell, and so on.'[2]

I have omitted 'Notes on some probable consequences of the advent of a stationary population in Great Britain' (*Economica*, 1929) which Robbins gave as a talk to the Oxford Political Economy Club in October 1928. Interesting though it is as exemplifying a concern of many economists at that time, its argument is largely speculative. It also presumes the conclusions of Robbins's chapter on 'The optimum theory of population' in the Cannan *festschrift*, which would therefore have to be included as well.

Chapter 6 reproduces the contribution Robbins made to C.H. Herford's biography of Wicksteed and also published separately in *Economica* (November 1930). Wicksteed's daughter Rebecca was 'quite delighted' with the draft she received in September 1930 and thought it read as though

1. Draft of a letter to Pigou, Robbins Papers.
2. Dalton Diary, vol. 13, British Library of Political and Economic Science; Robbins to P.T. Bauer (26 November 1962), Robbins Papers.

Robbins had known her father in person which she knew he had not.[1] When Robbins subsequently edited Wicksteed's *Common Sense of Political Economy* (1933) he expanded this article into a long Introduction, which he later reprinted in his collection of his essays on the history of economic thought (*The Evolution of Economic Theory*, 1970).

After his clash with Keynes in the Committee of Economists of the Economic Advisory Council in October 1930, one of the several contributions Robbins made to the public debate over protection was a paper attacking current arguments for the introduction of a tariff read to the London Economic Club in November and subsequently published in *Economica* (February 1931; Chapter 7 below). This also indicates Robbins's attitude to Keynes's *Treatise on Money* (1930). A more academic paper given at the meetings of the British Association for the Advancement of Science in York in September 1932 on 'Consumption and the trade cycle' was published in *Economica* in November (Chapter 8 below). This criticised underconsumptionist theories of depression and unemployment and put forward part of the 'Austrian' theory of the trade cycle that Robbins was to use again in his analysis of *The Great Depression*.

It has often been claimed, wrongly, that Robbins on occasion attended von Mises's 'private seminar' in Vienna. He did, however, give a paper to the Nationalökonomische Gesellschaft in Vienna in April 1933 (Chapter 9 below). When it was published as 'Remarks upon certain aspects of the theory of costs' in the *Economic Journal* in March 1934, Gottfried Haberler wrote from Geneva that Jacob Viner, who was visiting Geneva, had just read it and 'was not very pleased'. In Viner's view it underrated the contributions of English classical economists 'before the Austrians were born'. Viner and Robbins were to argue the point in correspondence for several years to come.[2]

Robbins's 'Remarks on the relationship between economics and psychology' (*The Manchester School*, December 1934; Chapter 10 below) also originated in a lecture in 1933, this time at the invitation of Roy Harrod to the Jowett Society at Oxford. His classic paper on Jevons (Chapter 11) was also published in *The Manchester School* (April 1936), having been read before a meeting of the Manchester Statistical Society commemorating the centenary of Jevons's birth. The journal published it again in its own commemorative issue (of its fiftieth anniversary) in December 1982.

Chapter 12, 'How to mitigate the next slump', is the one prewar writing on economic policy from the *Lloyds Bank Review* (May 1937) that I have

1. Rebecca Wicksteed to Robbins (7 September 1930), Robbins Papers.
2. The letter from Haberler is in the Robbins Papers, the correspondence with Viner in the Viner Papers, Seeley G. Mudd Library, Princeton University.

included here. It is on a topic of more lasting interest than Robbins's other more immediately topical contributions to the review in the 1930s and clarifies his attitude to the possibilities of countercyclical economic policy at that time. As he noted himself when republishing the paper in 1939, he took a 'slightly more hopeful view' than he had in his earlier writings.[1]

The remaining prewar papers (Chapters 13 and 14) both published in 1938 return to issues of methodology and his concerns in his *Essay on the Nature and Significance of Economic Science*. The first, 'Live and dead issues in the methodology of economics', appeared in *Economica* in August; the second, a comment on an article by Harrod on 'Interpersonal comparisons of utility' in the *Economic Journal*, Robbins submitted to Keynes in October with the comment that 'I should quite understand if you were to think that the somewhat autobiographical tone rendered it unsuitable. Moreover ... It was written as a distraction at the height of the [Munich] crisis and it may well bear in its quality the marks of that experience'. Keynes immediately sent it to the printer so that it could appear in the December issue.[2]

The first two postwar papers included here were written for *Lloyds Bank Review* (Chapters 15 and 16). The 'Inquest on the crisis', published in October 1947, was written in the aftermath of the 'convertibility crisis' of August 1947 when the Attlee Labour government was forced after only six weeks to suspend the convertibility of sterling into US dollars, a commitment which had been reluctantly agreed to under the Anglo–American Financial Agreement of December 1945. 'The sterling problem' was published exactly two years later, after another British economic crisis had led to the devaluation of the pound sterling by 30 per cent against the US dollar on 18 September 1949. Both attracted considerable attention and (generally) favourable comment in the press. Probably more influential in shaping opinion on British postwar economic policy was Robbins's Stamp Memorial Lecture in the University of London on 20 November 1951 (Chapter 17 below). Robbins was speaking shortly after the general election of 25 October which had returned the first postwar Conservative government, and after the first rise in Bank rate since before the war. He argued for the revival of monetary policy and its assignment to the task of maintaining a fixed exchange rate for the pound sterling.

A couple of months later, in January 1952, Milton Friedman, who had met and become friends with Robbins four years earlier, wrote to Robbins about his 'magnificent' lecture, but, he said, 'I come not to honor but to quibble',

1. *The Economic Basis of Class Conflict*, p. 213.

2. Robbins to Keynes (31 October), and Keynes to Robbins (3 November 1938), Keynes Papers EJ/1[5], King's College, Cambridge.

initiating a prolonged exchange between the two men on the subject of fixed versus floating exchange rates.[1] Robbins also argued the same point with his friends Aaron Director and James Meade. He made his views on the issue clear in his article 'The international economic problem' written for the *Lloyds Bank Review* at the end of the year (Chapter 18).

Robbins reviewed D.H. Robertson's collection of essays *Utility and All That* (1952) for *Economica* (May 1953; Chapter 19 below). As its introduction indicates, it was not a conventional review article. Returning to his early methodological interests Robbins presented an early version of the article to his seminar at LSE in November 1952. Another of Robbins's important review articles is 'Schumpeter's history of economic analysis' (*Quarterly Journal of Economics*, February 1955; Chapter 20 below). As the editor, E.H. Chamberlin, explained, 'the Quarterly Journal of Economics publishes virtually no reviews; only occasional review articles on very important books, with the reviewers in each case very carefully chosen'. Since he 'suspect[ed] that it will be lavishly praised by some and strongly criticized by others ... I am anxious to have in the Journal a really objective evaluation of it from a source of high authority'. Gottfried Haberler, by now at Harvard, also read and commented on the paper before its publication.[2] The third of Robbins's review articles reprinted here is 'Hayek on liberty' (*Economica*, February 1961; Chapter 23 below), which nearly did not get written as Robbins left the review copy of the book, *The Constitution of Liberty* (1960), on a train between Oxford and Paddington.

'Notes on public finance' (*Lloyds Bank Review*, October 1955; Chapter 21 below) was written after the publication of the final report of the Royal Commission on the Taxation of Profits and Income (Cmd. 9474) in 1955. It is interesting as a statement of Robbins's review on the role and effects of the taxation of incomes and wealth. 'Thoughts on the crisis' (*Lloyds Bank Review*, April 1958; Chapter 22 below) had a more complicated, and personal, background. A rapidly developing sterling crisis in the late summer of 1957 had led the Chancellor of the Exchequer, Peter Thorneycroft, who was a friend of Robbins, to announce 'crisis measures' including a rise in Bank rate to 7 per cent. In evidence to the Bank Rate Tribunal set up to investigate an alleged 'leak' of information it came out that Thorneycroft had consulted Robbins on monetary policy shortly before the Bank rate rise. Robbins subsequently told Gottfried Haberler that the article 'was more or less dragged out

---

1. Milton Friedman, 'Robbins Memorial Lecture: Exchange rates in a fiat money world', in Randall Hinshaw (ed.), *The Unstable Dollar: Domestic and International Issues* (1988).
2. Chamberlin to Robbins (10 February 1954), Chamberlin to Robbins, and Haberler to Robbins (25 October 1954), Robbins Papers.

of me by the crudities of the cheaper press which, having formed the erroneous notion that I was continuously associated with the financial policy of the present Government, proceeded to attribute to me all sorts of thoughts and intentions about recent events which I never entertained.'[1]

In the 1960s, after the 'Robbins report' on *Higher Education* (which he did indeed write), he published several papers on issues of higher education, which I have not included. Robbins collected many of them together in his *The University in the Modern World and other papers on higher education* (1966). In economics he was invited to participate in many conferences, at home and abroad, throughout the 1960s and 1970s, often being asked to provide a keynote address or the closing remarks. He continued to review frequently, especially for *Economica.*

At the fifth Conference of [American] University Professors sponsored by the American Bankers Association, to 'facilitate discussion of research in monetary economics and its application to outstanding problems', Robbins was invited to present the opening address (Chapter 24 below). The conference, held at Montauk Point, Long Island NY in September 1967, took place shortly before the IMF Annual Meeting at Rio de Janeiro which was concerned with reform of the Fund, and a few weeks before the long-delayed devaluation of the British pound in November 1967. Robbins took as his subject 'The International monetary problem'; as the editor of the conference proceedings (*Journal of Political Economy*, July–August 1968) reported, 'In the following discussion, the participants were divided on the desirability of maintaining fixed exchange rates and relying on a system of international monetary co-operation'.[2] Robbins spoke on the same subject and on similar lines when he gave the Keynes Lecture in Economics to the British Academy in October 1972, which I have therefore not reprinted here.

Chapter 25, 'On Latsis's *Method and Appraisal in Economics*: a review essay' was written for the *Journal of Economic Literature* in 1979. The book reviewed, Spiro J. Latsis (ed.), *Method and Appraisal in Economics* (Cambridge, 1976), was one of two volumes of proceedings of the Nafplion Colloquium on Research Programmes in Physics and Economics held on 2–14 September 1974, which Robbins had himself attended. William Baumol and Fritz Machlup both commented on the article before its publication, and Robbins expanded the discussion of his own views at the editor's request.[3]

1. Robbins to Haberler (15 May 1958), Robbins Papers.

2. Allan H. Metzler, 'Introduction', *Journal of Political Economy* 76 (July/August 1968), p. 661.

3. Mark Perlman to Robbins (26 February 1979), Baumol to Robbins (2 April 1979), Machlup to Robbins (6 April 1979), Robbins to Perlman (24 April 1979), Robbins Papers.

When William Baumol was elected President of the American Economic Association he asked his former teacher and colleague to give the annual Richard T. Ely Lecture at the 93rd meeting of the Association to be held in Denver, Colorado, in September 1980. Robbins's Lecture (*American Economic Review*, May 1981; Chapter 26 below) was received with a standing ovation. In it Robbins returned again to the methodological issues of the *Essay on the Nature and Significance of Economic Science*, including interpersonal comparisons of utility and welfare economics, on which his position had often been misinterpreted. Robbins's last reflection on the subjects of his *Essay*, Baumol included it in the posthumously published 3rd edition (1984).

* * *

The articles are reproduced as they were first published except for the correction of typographical errors and the correction or completion of publication details for works cited by Robbins. Other editorial additions to the text are enclosed in square brackets; where I have added a footnote not in the original I have indicated it with an asterisk.

In preparing this edition I have made use of unpublished material, including the surviving papers of Robbins himself and of some of his many correspondents. I am especially grateful to Lady Robbins, Anne and Christopher Johnson, and Richard Robbins, for allowing me the access to the Robbins Papers. I should also like to thank the Director of the London School of Economics for allowing me to look at and to quote from material in Lord Robbins's personal file, Dr Angela Raspin and the Librarian of the British Library of Political and Economic Science at LSE for permission to use and to quote from the Beveridge, Cannan and Dalton Papers, and the Provost and Scholars of King's College Cambridge for permission to quote from the Keynes Papers. The Curator of the Pusey Library of Harvard University kindly allowed me to use material in the Allyn Young Papers, which is cited courtesy of the Harvard University Archives.

Last but not least, I should like thank my friend Patricia Wright for tracking down the most obscure references in the Cambridge University Library and my friend, colleague and frequent collaborator Donald Moggridge for helpful critical comment on this introduction.

SUSAN HOWSON
May 1996

1 The Representative Firm

From *The Economic Journal*, vol. 38 (September 1928), pp. 387–404.

I

The Marshallian conception of a Representative Firm has always been a somewhat unsubstantial notion. Conceived as an afterthought – so far as I am able to discover it does not figure at all in the first edition of the *Principles* – it lurks in the obscurer corners of Book V like some pale visitant from the world of the unborn waiting in vain for the comforts of complete tangibility. Mr. Keynes has remarked that, "this is the quarter in which in my opinion the Marshall analysis is least complete and satisfactory and where there remains most to do,"[1] and others have not been lacking to express similar opinions.[2] Marshall himself makes singularly little use of the notion in other writings and, save in one or two instances,[3] it does not appear to have been used much since his day. Nevertheless, as is the way with ghosts, it bids fair to outlast many more virile creations. Not offering the same surface for attack, it tends to pass notice, though continuing indirectly to influence thought, and even to raise up for itself more earthy and tangible descendants. In certain recent discussions of applied economics in particular, its influence has been discernible. For this reason, and for the sake of the intrinsic interest of anything suggested by Marshall,[4] it seems worth while trying to examine it further.

---

1. "Alfred Marshall, 1842–1924", *Economic Journal*, vol. 34 (September 1924), p. 351.

2. E.g. H.J. Davenport, *Value and Distribution: a critical and constructive study* (Chicago, 1908), pp. 374–8.

3. This paper was written and set up before the publication of Professor Pigou's "An analysis of supply", *Economic Journal*, vol. 38 (June 1928), pp. 238–57. It does not contain, therefore, any comment on the use there made of the almost identical concept of the Equilibrium Firm, but I venture to express the hope that the observations I have made upon Marshall's own construction will not be found to be wholly inapplicable to this interesting and important variation.

4. Is it necessary at this stage to make more explicit the inevitable deference of all serious economists, I wonder? Perhaps it is, for in certain quarters there seems to have arisen a strange myth, which I for one should like publicly to repudiate, that economists of the tradition in which I was trained have a secret grudge against Cambridge and all things Marshallian. In fact, of course, nothing could be more ridiculous. In the friendly rivalry of two great centres of study it is natural that controversy should occasionally arise and that good-humoured gibes should be given and taken. But what London man, sensible of his own debts and alive to the massive contribution of Marshall and his successors, will not willingly yield pride of place to the great fountain head of so much that is most vital and significant in modern economics?

II

Let us first try to get a clear idea of matters as they presented themselves to Marshall.

The first appearance of the concept is in the last chapter of Book IV of the *Principles* – the Book which deals with the agents of production. The chapter is headed "Correlation of the Tendencies to Increasing and Diminishing Return." Marshall opens the discussion by recalling the doctrine of internal and external economies. He indicates certain limits to the former and dwells again on the importance of the latter. In the first edition he then contents himself with saying that "these results will be of great importance" when the supply price of a commodity is studied, and that although new producers of any commodity may labour under special difficulties, "the general rule is the other way" and "extra produce will commonly be got by increasing the output of businesses already established at a less than proportionate cost of extra labour and sacrifice."[1] In the second and subsequent editions, however, the wording is changed.[2] After announcing the importance of what has gone before in relation to the study of supply prices, Marshall goes on to state: "We shall have to analyse carefully the normal cost of producing a commodity relatively to a given aggregate of production; and for this purpose we shall have to study the expenses of a Representative Producer for that aggregate volume. On the one hand we shall not want to select some new producer just struggling into business, who works under many disadvantages and has to be content for a time with little or no profit, but who is satisfied with the fact that he is establishing a connection and taking the first steps towards building up a successful business;[3] nor on the other hand shall we want to take a firm which by exceptionally long-sustained ability and good fortune has got together a vast business and huge, well-ordered workshops that give it a superiority over all its rivals. But our representative firm must be one which has had a fairly long life and fair success, which is managed with normal ability, and which has normal access to the economies, external and internal, which belong to that aggregate volume of production: account being taken of the class of goods produced, and conditions of marketing them, and the economic environment generally."[4]

1. *Principles of Economics*, 1st edn (London, 1890), p. 378.
2. The change was obviously the result of the changes in the parts of Book V dealing with the notion of increasing returns under competitive conditions. It would be interesting if some pupil of Marshall's could supply an exact history of these changes.
3. It is interesting to observe that when he comes to study the subject in question this is precisely what he does, safeguarding himself only by depicting the producer as asking whether in time he may hope to become representative.
4. *Principles of Economics*, 2nd edn (1891), p. 375, 8th edn (1920), p. 317.

This is the clearest and fullest definition of the concept. When Marshall refers to it again, he always speaks of it as something which has already been made clear – a plan whose nature has been explained fully in other connections.[1] Nevertheless, by piecing together stray pronouncements, it is possible to add a little precision to the notion.

(1) In the first place, it is clear that it is an economic rather than a legal concept. That is to say, when Marshall speaks of a firm, he has in mind a productive unit of one kind or another. He is not referring merely to a particular legal form of business association – the old-fashioned private partnership or the one-man business. This emerges quite clearly in a passage in *Industry and Trade*, in which he says very definitely that whereas until recently the representative firm was a private partnership, now "joint stock control has become … general even in regard to manufacturing and other industries."[2] And in the *Principles* in one place he commences a discussion with the remark, "We may select as representative a firm whether in private or joint stock management."[3] This, I think, is quite clear; although of course it is not so clear that with this change in the organisation of industry the conception retains its suitability for the purpose for which it was devised. If we read between the lines, indeed, we find signs that Marshall himself was troubled about this.[4]

(2) But while we are on firm ground in concentrating attention on economic organisation as such rather than upon particular legal forms of such organisation, it is not so easy to say whether Marshall was thinking of a representative plant or technical production unit or a representative business organisation. In the *Principles* he gives the impression of referring to the latter. For instance, speaking of the cost of building up a trade connection, he depicts the "alert entrepreneur" asking himself whether his undertaking has a fair chance of becoming representative, saying that the investment of capital in a trade "is … governed by estimates on the one hand of the outgoings required to build up and work such a representative firm, and on the other of the incomings spread over a long period of time"[5] to be got by the price estimated to be normal. But against this must be put a passage in *Industry and Trade*, in which he distinctly asserts that the establishment or plant best suggests the "command possessed of the economics of *production*. Economics of marketing are often better represented by statistics of businesses, but on the

1. As, for instance, on pp. 342 and 396. The qualifications with which the term is accompanied are nearly always a mere verbal paraphrase of the passage just quoted.

2. *Industry and Trade*, 4th edn (London, 1921), p. 314.

3. *Principles of Economics*, 8th edn, p. 318.

4. E.g. *Industry and Trade*, p. 316, and *Principles*, p. 316. These and the references that follow are taken from the 4th edn of *Industry and Trade* and the 8th edn of the *Principles*.

5. *Principles*, pp. 377–8.

whole the establishment is doubtless the best unit."[1] This assertion, however, occurs in the course of an analysis of the statistics of the American Census of Production, and may be regarded, perhaps, as special pleading for his data. On the whole, although it would be hard to contend that Marshall was always very clear on this subject, the main drift of his argument, I suggest, points to the business rather than to the establishment as the representative unit.

(3) Finally we may inquire into the relation of this conception to the statistical conception of an average. Is the representative firm to be conceived as a mere average, to be established by applying one or other of the recognised statistical methods to the analysis of any given set of business statistics? On this point, fortunately, Marshall is fairly explicit. It is not an average of this sort. A given set of business statistics will exhibit the results of both short-period and long-period influences, and the representative firm is essentially a long-period conception. Thus, if we like we may regard it as an average firm, but we must regard it as *an average which would only emerge arithmetically under conditions when all present tendencies to change had reached a state of equilibrium*. In no other way can it be regarded as being statistically established.[2] This fact has a double significance. On the one hand, it seems to render irrelevant all objections to the appropriateness of the conception based on an examination of statistics of actual businesses. Mr. Keynes, for instance, discussing Mr. Coates' very interesting analysis of business profits, suggests that the magnitude of the dispersion is such as "to do some damage to the conception."[3] If the foregoing analysis is correct, I am disposed to agree with Mr. Robertson that Marshall would not have been of this opinion.[4] On the other hand, it cuts equally against the practical usefulness of the notion. If the averages obtainable from statistics are not admissible, then the prospect of simplifying the analysis of supply by this method becomes illusory. To those of us who do not possess the childlike faith in unaided statistical induction now prevalent in many quarters, this will not be a great disappointment if the conception can be proved to be theoretically useful in facilitating the comprehension of general relations. But since it seems probable that in this instance Marshall's main intention in devising this plan was the simplification of practical inquiry, it must be admitted that its *raison d'être* is considerably weakened by these considerations.

---

1. *Industry and Trade*, p. 847.
2. See *Principles*, p. 318.
3. "The Colwyn Report on National Debt and Taxation", *Economic Journal*, vol. 37 (June 1927), p. 205.
4. "The Colwyn Committee, the income tax and the price level", *Economic Journal*, vol. 37 (September 1927), p. 571.

III

Such then is the Representative Firm as conceived by Marshall: a long-period average business unit, representative of the organisation of a given line of production. It is now time to ask for what purposes he devised the conception and to what extent it is suited for these purposes.

Fortunately, on this point there is little need for conjecture. The interesting and important article on "The Colwyn Committee, the income tax and the price level" by Mr. Robertson[1] contains a pronouncement on that point which we may regard as authoritative. It was devised, according to Mr. Robertson, to meet the difficulties occurring in the analysis of supply when there is a disparity of efficiency as between different producers.[2] This harmonises so well with what hints we are able to glean from Marshall[3] that it would be otiose to make further inquiries. The way is therefore clear for us to ask, further, to what extent the conception is appropriate for the purpose for which it was devised.

Before we can do this, however, it is necessary to make plain one distinction. The disparities of efficiency as between different producing units in any given industry, to which Mr. Robertson refers, may be due to two analytically separable sets of conditions. Either they may be due to what are, for the period under consideration, ultimate deficiencies of productive factors of the highest order of efficiency – the best lands, the best managers, the best equipment, etc. – deficiencies which theoretically would make themselves felt were all transitory disturbances of tendencies to change absent; or they may arise as phenomena of maladjustment, when changes in demand or the ultimate conditions of supply are necessitating a new equilibrium. If we follow the generally accepted terminology, we may call the former static, the latter dynamic disparities. The former are the disparities which would appear in any given productive situation were all causes of further change to cease. The latter are disparities which emerge as a result of changes in the given

---

1. *Op. cit.*

2. Mr. Robertson's pronouncement is so relevant to the whole of what follows that I venture to transcribe it in full. It occurs in the course of an analysis of Mr. Coates' contention that owing to this disparity net profits have no influence on price. "In real life," says Mr. Robertson, attempting to paraphrase this contention, "production is in the hands of numerous producers of very varying strength and ability, some of whom are so weak that they are making no profits, or even meeting losses. The goods supplied by these producers form part of the total supply of goods by the magnitude of which, taken in conjunction with the conditions of demand, price is determined. Therefore (so the argument appears to run), the magnitude of net profits is irrelevant to the determination of that price.

"It is precisely this type of argument that Marshall's conception of the Representative Firm was designed, as it seems to me, to forestall." *Ibid.*, pp. 570–1.

3. E.g. the passage quoted above. See also *Principles*, p. 342 *et seq.*

productive situation. In real life, of course, the two are almost inextricably entangled; but unless we are willing to resign ourselves to the nirvana of purposeless observation, this does not render it any less desirable to distinguish them for purposes of analysis. In the following examination of the suitability of the Marshallian doctrine I shall endeavour so to distinguish them.

I turn first to what I have called static disparities and the general problem of economic equilibrium. The elements of the problem are simple. Within the various groups of factors of production employed in any branch of industry the constituent factors are unequal in efficiency. There are not enough lands of the first order of quality, there are not enough managers of the first order of ability, there are not enough workmen of the first order of efficiency, to go round. Recourse is therefore had to factors of inferior efficiency. Demand and the ultimate supplies of all kinds of factors remain constant. What are the conditions of equilibrium?

Now if these disparities were not present, if all lands were of equal quality, all managers of equal ability, all workmen of equal efficiency, within their different grades, we should all be agreed as to the answer to this question. Equilibrium would be reached when the net advantages reaped by the employment of any factor in one line of production were at least as great as the net advantages to be reaped by employment in any other line of production; and if we assume that there is only one kind of land, one kind of worker, one kind of entrepreneur, and that the different lines of industry offer equal attractions other than monetary remuneration, then we should conclude that when equilibrium is attained all rents will be equal, all wages will be equal, and – what is more significant from our point of view – the profits of different firms will be equal.

On this point I think there would be general agreement. We might justly question whether such a state of things was possible, either as regards homogeneity of factors or as regards the attainment of final adjustment, but such objections, though valid enough if there were any disposition to accept the hypothesis as a counterpart of reality, would be irrelevant from the point of view of this argument. The important point is that, in the circumstances assumed, such would be the conditions of equilibrium.

But now let us waive the condition of homogeneity of factor efficiency. Let us permit differences of quality of land, differences of ability of entrepreneurs, differences of efficiency of different kinds of workmen, to enter our hypothesis. Under such conditions is it necessary to modify or to complicate the formula for equilibrium?

Surely the answer is, no it is not in any way necessary. So far as land differentials are concerned, the rent analysis has long shown how competition adjusts the return to different pieces of land according to their differential of quality. It is easy, as Marshall himself has shown, to take account of the differing efficiency of wage-earners.[1] Why then, when we come to deal with long-period profit doctrine and the differences of managerial and business ability, should we find it necessary to consider a firm, an entrepreneur, of average or typical efficiency? Just as units of a given supply may be produced on lands of varying efficiency, so their production may be supervised by business men of varying ability. What is normal profit for one will not be normal profit for another, that is all. *There is no more need for us to assume a representative firm or representative producer, than there is for us to assume a representative piece of land,*[2] *a representative machine, or a representative worker.* All that is necessary for equilibrium to prevail is that each factor shall get at least as much in one line of production as it could get in any other: as much, of course, including all advantages and disadvantages of work, hiring or investment.

At this point it is perhaps desirable to remove a possible cause of misapprehension. This formula of equilibrium does *not* imply that ability below a certain level will find remunerative employment in managerial positions in any line of industry. It is sometimes thought that this theory of unequal normal profits implies that any firm of whatever efficiency can get along somehow, even in the long-term equilibrium adjustment. This is a complete mistake, due to a failure to perceive the true nature of the competitive process assumed to be at work under such hypothetical conditions. Of course, if, following Professor Pigou's conception of negative wages,[3] we are willing to contemplate *negative profits* of *any* dimensions, then theoretically we can conceive the absorption of any number of entrepreneurs of any degree of inefficiency in any given industry. But such an abstraction is neither useful nor necessary at this juncture.[4] A glance at the theory of land rents is much more illuminating. Just as under ideal competition the various bits of land are sorted out into *different* uses according to their respective qualities, so, under the conditions we are assuming, human factors of production are sorted out according to their efficiency, not only horizontally as between different industries, but also vertically as between productive grades. If a man is extramarginal as an entrepreneur, he will find employment as a manual labour or

1. *Principles*, p. 547

2. Strangely enough, this has actually been done by J.E. Cairnes in his essay on "Political economy and land" (*Essays in Political Economy, theoretical and applied* [London, 1873], pp. 187–231). But the results there achieved are not such as to recommend the general adoption of the notion.

3. *Industrial Fluctations* (London, 1927), p. 284. Needless to say, my comments on the use of such a conception in this connection imply no strictures of the illuminating uses to which it is put by Professor Pigou in another context.

4. It may be remarked, however, that it is by no means so fantastic as at first it may appear, in the case of 'gentleman farming' and similar hobbies.

as a salaried official. The doctrine of unequal normal profits no more implies that we are likely to find half-wits or incompetents at the head of businesses than the doctrine of unequal normal rents implies that we are likely to find the wilds of Nova Scotia used as the sites of multiple shops.

For all this, of course, there is abundant confirmation in Marshall's own analysis. I have referred above to the passage in which he shows that "competition tends to make the earnings got by two individuals of unequal efficiency in any given time not equal but unequal."[1] If we turn to his treatment of what he calls the law of substitution, we find an even more pregnant allusion to the way in which "society substitutes one undertaker for another who is less efficient *in proportion to his charges*"[2] (my italics) – a perfectly satisfactory account of the conditions of equilibrium which makes, not equal efficiency, but factors rewarded proportionately to efficiency, the ultimate product of the competitive process. All of which makes it all the more surprising when, a few pages further on, we find him reverting to the man of "normal capacity" asking himself whether, if he sets up in a certain line of business, he may hope that in time his concern may become representative. The necessity for such a complication is certainly not obvious.

But now it is necessary to forestall a possible criticism. It is all very well, it may be urged, to discuss equilibrium in terms of these rigid assumptions, but it is not fair to Marshall to judge his conceptions on this plane of analysis. For Marshall, as is notorious, would not admit the ultimate severity of the static assumptions. Either for fear of becoming unintelligible to business men and economic historians, or because of his curious predilection for biological analogies he always shirked these heroic abstractions.[3] And in this particular connection, it is true, he went out of his way to reject the desirability of such an hypothesis. "Of course," he says, "we might assume that in our stationary state every business remained always of the same size and with the same trade connection. But we need not go as far as that: it will suffice to suppose that firms rise and fall, but that the 'representative' firm remains always of the same size as does the representative tree of a virgin forest, and that therefore the economies resulting from its own resources are constant, and since the aggregate volume of production is constant, so also are those economies resulting from subsidiary industries in the neighbourhood."[4] All this may be admitted. No doubt it is true that as, one by one, we remove artificialities from our assumptions it is important that we should take account of the fact

1. *Principles*, p. 547.
2. *Ibid.*, p. 341.
3. See the very interesting letter to J.B. Clark in *Memorials of Alfred Marshall*, ed. A.C. Pigou (London, 1925), p. 415.
4. *Principles*, p. 367.

that, even in conditions where population is stationary, where capital is constant, where demand is unchanging, and where no technical changes are taking place, that individuals and machines will appreciate and depreciate with the passage of time, and that particular firms will wax and wane in prosperity like the "trees of the forest" which Marshall was so fond of introducing. But this necessitates no modification in our general conception of equilibrium. All that is necessary for equilibrium to persist is that at every particular moment producers shall be getting as much where they are as they can get elsewhere – the "as much" including the other advantage or disadvantage of good or bad times to come in the future.

But still, it may be objected, this was not what Marshall had in mind in the passage we have examined. The ultimate object of this assumption of the stationary state, as we know, was to exhibit the influence of cost upon values.[1] What Marshall was here discussing in other words was not the conditions of equilibrium, but the conditions of "stationariness" as a preliminary to examining the influence of cost upon value under stationary conditions. Of course this is true, but it gives no support to the conception we are discussing. The idea of a representative firm is even less essential to the hypothesis of "stationariness" than to the hypothesis of equilibrium. If demand is unchanging, if technique is unaltered, and if the ultimate supply of all factors of production remains of the same dimensions, *then if we believe in economic determinateness at all, it is totally superfluous to add that the average size of firms in different industries will remain the same.* It may be suggested that if Marshall had considered the conditions of "stationariness" in the sense just indicated (which, of course, makes complete allowance for the kind of change he was contemplating[2]), he would never have found it necessary to introduce the representative firm at this juncture. As it was, approaching the conception not from the point of view of the productive situation as a whole, as Davenport calls it, but from the point of view of one line of production at a time, *he was led to define "stationariness" in terms of the constancy of his various averages.* With great deference, I submit that this is a clumsy and unnecessary expedient, and one which may give rise to false ideas of the ultimate processes of causation involved.

Nor is the necessity of the conception any more apparent when we come to deal with problems of dynamic change, changes in demand, changes in technique, changes in the ultimate supplies of different factors of production. Here new disparities of efficiency emerge. Owing to the changes assumed, some factors and combinations of factors are no longer as comparatively

1. This must not be taken to imply that in the writer's estimation Marshall was successful in achieving this object.
2. Just as when we assume that population is constant, we do not exclude births and deaths.

efficient in one line of industry as they were, and it is necessary that they should go elsewhere.[1] We now approach the equilibrium problem from a rather different angle. Granted, that is to say, that the old equilibrium prices are no longer appropriate, how long will disequilibrium persist? When will these disparities disappear? But again no recourse to the conception of a long-period average seems called for. Disequilibrium will persist, and transfer of productive factors will occur, until once more each factor is receiving as much in the shape of net advantages where it is as it could hope to get elsewhere. Or, to put the same thing another way, if any group of factors is receiving more in one line than similar factors are getting elsewhere, there will be a tendency to transfer to that line; if it is receiving less, there will be a tendency for some to transfer elsewhere. I confess that I find it hard to see the necessity for invoking the conception of an average combination of productive factors in this connection. If, to take perhaps the simplest example, owing to a shift in the conditions of demand, an industry is under the necessity of expanding or contracting, there is surely nothing in the nature of things which would lead us to expect that the factors which are transferred are all the same efficiency, and nothing in the requirements of pure equilibrium theory to necessitate the assumption that they are.

So much for general equilibrium theory. So far the necessity for the representative firm has not been in any way apparent. But what about what Pareto has called the theory of *partial equilibria*, the examination of particular cases of value, with which, as we know, the main detail of Book V is concerned?

I confess that here, too, the conception appears to me superfluous. The intersecting curves of supply and demand, which are the main apparatus of this mode of analysis, are capable of construction without resort to this instrument. Putting aside the objections of the equilibrium theorists to the whole assumption that other things remain equal, there is no difficulty in *conceiving* a supply schedule showing variations in amount offered in response to price changes. Marshall seems to have thought that by concentrating on the supply schedule of his representative firm, this conception might be further simplified. But this hope appears to be illusory. In the first place, as has been shown above, no *practical* simplification is involved. The representative firm is not the short-period average. And secondly, and much more important from our point of view, no theoretical simplification which is not misleading is involved. If *all* firms in a given line of industry were representative, and if an increase or a diminution of output were merely met by a simultaneous expansion or contraction on the part of each firm concerned, then no doubt the examination of the account-books of any one of them would tell us all we

1. On all this see H.J. Davenport, *The Economics of Enterprise* (New York, 1913), pp. 64 and 77–83.

wanted about probable variations in price. But we know that this is not a necessary condition of expansion or contraction. As Mr. Robertson points out, a change of this sort may be met *either* by a change in the output of existing firms *or* by a change in their number.[1] And if the latter event is what happens, then it should be quite clear, from what has been said already, that *the representative firm may cease to be representative and its cost curve cease to be significant.* Under such conditions – which, it is submitted, are just as probable as the other – resort to the representative firm is not merely unnecessary, it is positively misleading.

Finally we may briefly examine the special case of diminishing costs under competitive conditions. For it is quite clear that it was here, if anywhere, that Marshall expected the conception to be really significant. The opening chapters of Book V abound with references to the necessity of applying the "plan" in analysis of such conditions, and both Chapter XII and Appendix H do employ the plan continually.

But here again close examination seems to dispose of the necessity for so doing, and even to suggest that much of the obscurity in which this part of the Marshallian theory is undoubtedly enveloped is due to its adoption. It is quite true that if all internal economies were equal, unequal access to external economies, save in so far as it was due to natural limitations of space, might result in the elimination of those firms in a position of manifestly inferior advantage – always assuming that the existence of external economies, suitable for consideration in this relation and sufficiently powerful to produce such a situation, are conceivable.[2] But surely nothing obliges us to conceive of internal economies in this rigid and limited manner. If we are to restrict the term external economies to economies external to a particular firm but internal to the industry as a whole – and I submit that any extension of the term beyond that is illegitimate in this connection, since it assumes to be a function of one variable what is really a function of many – then surely we must recognise that what are internal and external economies for any one firm are,

---

1. *Op. cit.*, p. 572.

2. The existence of such economies has been questioned both by Professor Young and by Mr. Robertson, and so far as practical applications of the doctrine are concerned, there seems much to be said for their scepticism. Most of the economies cited by the apologists of this doctrine – improved transport, the telephone, subsidiary industries, etc. – seem to be inappropriate to the consideration of the supply curve of any one industry and to fall rather into the sphere of population theory (see D.H. Macgregor, *Industrial Combination* [London, 1906], Part I, Chapter I, for a very illuminating discussion of external economies); while it must be remembered that much of the plausibility of Marshall's exposition depends upon his assumption that internal and external economies vary together – an assumption which I submit is quite illegitimate. The whole doctrine of internal and external economies as presented by Marshall seems, indeed, radically in need of revision. But, for purposes of pure theory, it is legitimate to contemplate the situation in question, if only to exhibit the other anomalies of his exposition.

partly at least, a matter of the capacity and opportunities of management. What is an internal economy for one firm may be an external economy for another. And in any case it is surely obvious that, whatever their nature, the internal economies will vary with the nature of the management. The old doctrine which bade us consider the application of equal quantities of capital and labour to different pieces of land is not more artificial and unnecessary than this doctrine which assumes that all management must be of equal efficiency.

IV

So far in this analysis of the Representative Firm it has been suggested merely that the notion is superfluous, that there is no problem in the whole range of value theory which cannot be more satisfactorily treated without it. But now I want to carry the attack a stage further. I want to suggest, that is to say, that it is not only unnecessary, but misleading. Not only that it is possible to be clear and exhaustive without it, but that its use may actually prevent the attainment of clarity and exhaustiveness.

I have suggested already, in passing, certain ways in which, incautiously handled, the conception may give rise to misapprehension, the way in which it may mislead with regard to the construction of supply curves, and the way in which, in discussions of the stationary state, it may lead us to imagine that the average is the condition rather than the result of equilibrium.[1] But it is possible, I think, to condemn it on grounds more general than this. The whole conception, it may be suggested, is open to the general criticism that it cloaks the essential heterogeneity of productive factors – in particular the heterogeneity of managerial ability – just at that point at which it is most desirable to exhibit it most vividly.

I can best explain what I mean by an example drawn from the work of one Marshall's own followers.

According to Mr. Robertson, the true Marshallian doctrine in this respect is admirably expounded by Mr. Henderson in *Supply and Demand*, chapter V, paragraph 4.[2] Personally, I think I should be inclined to question Marshall's whole-hearted approval of this version of his conception; but at least we shall do no violence to the facts if we take Mr. Henderson's treatment as the product of Marshallian influence. In the paragraph cited by Mr. Robertson, Mr. Henderson is assailing the old argument that the marginal analysis leads to the view that the price of a commodity is determined on the supply side by

1. I do not, of course, suggest that Marshall himself *could* commit so gross an error, but I do submit that such may well be the result of this mode of approach to problems of this character.

2. Robertson, *op. cit.*, p. 574.

the cost at which the least efficient concern in the industry at any given time can market its products. What he has to say in this connection is so important for the rest of my argument that I make no apology for quoting it in full.

"Such an argument," he says, referring to the view I have just mentioned, "is a gross caricature of the marginal conception. The half-witted incompetent will, as we know well enough, speedily disappear under the stress of competition, and his place will be taken by more efficient men. There is an essential difference between him and the 'marginal coal mine' of which we spoke above. For the probabilities are that of the coal resources whose existence is clearly known, the more fertile and better situated parts will already be in process of exploitation; and there is not likely, therefore, to be a supply of substantially better seams which can be substituted for the worst of those in actual use. There *is* likely, on the other hand, to be available a supply of decent business capacity which can be substituted for the most inefficient of existing business men. The marginal concern, in other words, must be conceived as that working under the least advantageous conditions in respect of the assistance it derives from the strictly limited resources of nature, but under average conditions as regards managerial capacity and human qualities in general. Thus in agriculture we can speak of a marginal farm, which we should conceive as the least fertile and worst situated farm which it is just worth while to cultivate ... but we must assume it to be cultivated by a farmer of average ability."[1]

Now so far as this may be conceived to be directed against the very crude and silly view of the marginal analysis already mentioned, it is possible to agree with the intention, if not with the argument. As has been shown already, there is nothing in the marginal, or any other sensible form of analysis, which would leave us to suppose that there is room in the long-period adjustment for the half-witted incompetents as controllers of business enterprise. It is the essence of ideal competition that men whose efficiency is below that of the lowest grade which the social demand, acting in a given situation, necessitates being taken into entrepreneurship, are sifted out into other positions in the system of equilibrium, just as lands below the margin in one use are relegated to inferior uses. In attempting to refute a doctrine of this sort, Mr. Henderson has the support of all economists.

But when he goes on to argue that, because of this, we are justified in assuming that in a long-period adjustment all producers are at least of average ability, I for one must enter a most emphatic protest. Even Adam Smith, that discredited *laissez-faire* economist, with his insistence on the original similarity of porters and philosophers,[2] did not go so far as this. How

1. Hubert D. Henderson, *Supply and Demand* (London and Cambridge, 1922), pp. 59–60.

2. *An Inquiry into the Nature and Causes of the Wealth of Nations*, ed. E. Cannan (London; 1904), p. 17.

Mr. Henderson, who has had day by day the job of teaching men whose capacity, even when they are scarcely out of adolescence, demands half the letters of the Greek alphabet for its classification – for I cannot believe that in this respect things are any different at Cambridge from what they are at Oxford and London – how anyone who has had experience of this sort can bring himself to assert such a thing passes my comprehension – or at least it would, did I not believe it to be directly due to this confusing habit initiated by Marshall. It may be perfectly true that if one had a free hand to pick men from other industries, irrespective of the pull of demand, any given industry could be stocked with entrepreneurs of at least average ability. But it is surely absolutely illegitimate to generalise this argument – *unless one disbelieves altogether in the possibility of diminishing returns to managerial ability.* If one views the organisation of production as a whole, surely it is perfectly obvious that, in any given situation, the position in regard to managerial ability is precisely the same as the position in regard to other productive powers. The best lands and the best men are limited. There are not enough Josiah Stamps to go round; and it there is anything at all in the law of diminishing returns, there will come a time when the crowding of more factors under their control will give a less additional product than the utilisation of inferior talent. And there is nothing in the nature of things to lead us to suppose that this successive resort to men of lower abilities will proceed industry by industry – that we shall find all the Stamps in one line, all the ——s in another, and all the ——s in another. On the contrary, probability and general experience lead us to expect a more irregular dispersion. In some industries where technical considerations dictate huge units, we should expect to find a large proportion of the best organisers; in others, where technique permits very small units, few or none. But in a good many we should find some who are very capable, some who are "average," some who are at the margin of entrepreneurship, even in long-period adjustments. Mr. Henderson should reflect that if all entrepreneurs were *at least* of average managerial ability, they would at once cease to be average.

All this, of course, implies no opposition to the general policy, with which Mr. Henderson has more recently identified himself, of taking every reasonable step to ensure the maximum efficiency possible in all spheres of business management. Nothing that I have said about the requirements of long-period adjustment should imply any hostility whatever to the policy of chivvying up employers generally. That is what the business classes exist for – to be chivvied up generally – they are not retained by society for their contributions to general culture. At the same time, even here this notion of a limited fund of business ability is not without its uses. One has a disconcerting vision of some of the less cautious of Mr. Henderson's admirers going round from industry to industry insisting on the installation of the best abilities in each until, coming back to the one from which they first started, they find that there is less of the best there than there was before, it all having been transferred to the one they last reorganised. I submit that even in a sphere where reason is at such a discount as it is in practical politics, there is a very real need for us to recognise that, although any one industry might be considerably improved by the transfer to it of a few more of the best organisers, yet it does not in the least follow that industry as a whole would be any the better organised in consequence. And I submit that any theoretical instrument which blinds us to the ultimate facts demanding this recognition is a very poor tool of economic analysis.[1]

V

So far the argument of this paper has related chiefly to considerations of value and equilibrium. In conclusion it may be worth while to indicate very briefly what bearing it may be conceived to have on other departments of economic theory.

(1) In the first place, it may be claimed that it is finally conclusive against any idea of a tendency of profits to equality – however profits are defined and delimited. Arguing on different lines and treating not so much of the profits of entrepreneurs and business units, but rather of the incomes of dealers in commodity markets, Mr. Hawtrey reaches a somewhat similar conclusion in *The Economic Problem.*[2] When I reviewed this in *Economica*[3] recently, I

1. Of course, this is not all that can be said against the conception. When we turn from the sphere of economic mechanics and examine the problems of change and development – those realms of economic biology which, according to Marshall, should be the Mecca of the economist – it may be urged that it is liable to veil from us the true nature of economic growth. This is not a matter which I wish to enlarge upon here – the idea was first suggested to me by Professor Young, and I gather that he himself is contemplating a more extensive development of it. But for the sake of completeness it may be pointed out that, in a world in which growth in the economic system proceeds just as much by way of differentiation and subdivision as by the expansion and development of particular economic units, the idea of a representative unit which preserves its essential identity while undergoing progressive expansion is apt to be very misleading. An industry commences as a group of units in each of which whole commodities are manufactured. It grows, and, as a result of technical changes and the expansion of markets, subdivision takes place. There is now one group of units carrying through one stage of manufacture; another in which the process is carried to completion. Surely in such a case to continue to speak of *the* representative firm of the industry in question is to suggest a state of affairs having no counterpart in reality – to introduce an economic nominalism which has not even the Knappian excuse of a legal continuity. It is no accident, I suggest, that in *Industry and Trade* where problems of this sort are dealt with, the use made of the Representative Firm is even more nebulous and half-hearted than in the *Principles*.

2. R.G. Hawtrey, *The Economic Problem* (London, 1926), p. 40.

3. 'Mr. Hawtrey on the scope of economics', *Economica*, vol. 7 (June 1927), pp. 172–8.

remarked that I found it hard to think of an economist who had argued the contrary proposition. This statement I do not retract. But I think it right to observe that the idea of a Representative Firm is liable to give rise to a contrary impression. If, in the long-period adjustment, all firms were representative, then clearly in any industry all profits would be equal. I do not contend that Marshall would have argued in this way. It is, indeed, highly significant that in the chapters in the *Principles* which deal with profits the representative firm is conspicuous by its absence. But, as we have seen from the case of Mr. Henderson, it certainly does not require a very incautious use of the conception for a position not dissimilar from this to be arrived at.

(2) Secondly, it may be urged, considerations such as these imply great caution in interpreting the attempts which are made from time to time to establish by statistical analysis the optimal size of business unit for any industry. I do not refer here to the obvious difficulties of eliminating from such statistics the effects of momentary disturbances, serious as these difficulties are. I refer rather to the fact that, if the foregoing observations are correct, then even if, by the elimination of seasonal fluctuations, cyclical disturbances and the like, we can suppose our statistics to exhibit the result of more permanent tendencies, we must still recognise that *there is not one optimal size, but as many optima as there are different kinds of combination*, and that any attempt to conclude that divergencies from any one of these imply inefficiency may lead to serious errors of judgement.

This does not mean, of course, that, in despair of attaining perfection, statisticians should refrain from attempting such investigations at all. Insistence on the theoretical impossibility of obtaining exact results does not imply the need for a self-denying ordinance with regard to approximations; and it does not follow that *where technical considerations are of preponderating importance* investigations of this sort will not yield useful results, *even though other things are not equal*. Statisticians should be like Tertullian: they should be willing to believe in the absurd, lest theoretical scepticism should paralyse their activities. But, unlike Tertullian, they should not complain if subsequently rationalist infidels submit these beliefs to the most vigorous theoretical scrutiny.

(3) Finally, I submit, if the foregoing results are valid, they enable us at once to dispose of the theoretical flaws in the Report of the Colwyn Committee and the very valuable memorandum of Mr. Coates, against which Mr. Robertson has recently mustered so imposing an armoury of weapons. As a theoretical economist, I need hardly say how thoroughly I endorse Mr. Robertson's main conclusions, nor how entirely unacceptable I find the argument he opposes. But to show that the scarcity of the services of business men is on just the same footing as the scarcity of other factors of production, and that taxes on the payments for these services are to be explained in the

light of exactly the same broad theoretical generalisations as apply to other taxes, does not, I submit, necessitate the resurrection of this cumbersome apparatus of representative business units. All that is necessary is to show (1) firstly, that a curve showing the particular receipts of particular firms over a short period is simply a chart of results, and does not represent ultimate causal factors; (2) that, in any given productive situation, different business men and different business units may be expected to earn different profits even in the lower paid; and (3) finally, that taxes on these profits will affect prices more or less according as the conditions of supply are more or less elastic. All this, of course, Mr. Robertson has done with a skill and persuasiveness which render repetition unnecessary. The contention of this note is merely that, the vindication of Marshall apart, a greater economy of theoretical apparatus was possible.

2 The Economic Effects of Variations of Hours of Labour[1]

From *The Economic Journal*, vol. 39 (March 1929), pp. 25–40.

I

The number of hours a man works is not a matter which is determined independently of other circumstances. It depends partly on habit, partly on technical or legal necessity, partly on the relative pulls of product, production and leisure, and these in turn are partly dependent on it. To exhibit the form of this dependence under the complex conditions of industrial civilisation is one of the chief problems of the analysis of economic equilibrium, but it is not a problem with which I wish to deal in this paper.[2] My object here is of rather a different order. Assuming that a variation of hours takes place, I wish to inquire what other changes we should expect to be associated with it. For the purposes of this analysis, that is to say, the change in the length of the working day is to be regarded as the independent variable. What I discuss is not what causes bring it about, but what consequences follow from it. From a philosophical point of view, no doubt, this procedure is more arbitrary than the analysis of the conditions of equilibrium, but from the point of view of social policy it has much to recommend it. The practical problem which we have to decide at any given moment is the problem whether our present distribution of time between work and leisure is satisfactory; and although the final solution, involving as it does an appeal to subjective standards of worth, is outside the scope of scientific inquiry, yet a precise knowledge of the objective consequences of any variation is of material assistance in arriving at a solution. Our valuations are only valid by accident if they are not based on a knowledge of fact. What I have to say is not new. The materials for a

1. A paper read before Section F of the British Association at Glasgow, September, 1928.
2. The matter is dealt with in Sir Sydney Chapman's article on "Hours of labour," *Economic Journal*, vol. 19 (September 1909), pp. 353–73.

solution of this problem are to be found in all reputable handbooks of economic principles; but they are not often deliberately collated with this particular object in view, and in popular discussion they are apt to be ignored. In view, therefore, of the practical urgency of clear thinking on these matters, it has seemed to me to be worth while, even at the risk of repeating things which are familiar, attempting to combine them in one general survey.

II

I turn first to the connection between hours and output – at once the most simple and the most fundamental of the relations we have to examine.

Here fortunately it is possible to be brief. The days are gone when it was necessary to combat the naïve assumption that the connection between hours and output is one of direct variation, that it is necessarily true that a lengthening of the working day increases output and a curtailment diminishes it. Systematic study of the conditions of efficiency has abundantly vindicated the view, which after all is not very sophisticated, that, if we wish to maximise daily output, just as it is possible to work too little, so it is also possible to work too much. Of course it is true that if we start from the beginning of any given job and measure onwards throughout a single day, so long as we continue to work at all without spoiling what we are doing, we add something to the product. But to argue from this to the conclusion that the longer the average working day, the greater the average daily output, is completely to beg the question at issue. For the human frame is not inexhaustible, and the greater part of the work of the world must be done from day to day and not accomplished in isolated spurts. And this means that if a man continually works beyond a certain point, the intensity of his work will be reduced to such an extent that the gain in longer hours will be more than offset by the loss in hourly output, so that if he had worked less his average output would have been greater.[1] This is true of all continuous occupations. A great number of observations have proved it to be true for many kinds of manual labour,[2] and although in the case of mental work of any complexity quantitative measurement is out of the question, there can be no doubt that in a broad way it is true here likewise. We all know the hacks who are always dull because they are always overworking.

---

1. For convenience of exposition, the above argument has been stated in terms of days and hours, but of course there is no special sanctity about these periods, and it is not difficult to state the theory in terms which are of greater generality.

2. See P. Sargant Florence, *The Economics of Fatigue and Unrest* (London, 1925), for an excellent account of this matter.

If, therefore, we are to predict the effect of a given variation in hours we must conceive of it in relation to a working day of maximum productiveness. This day, of course, will vary from man to man and from industry to industry. It will vary in the same industry with variations of technique, distribution of hours within the day and over longer periods, and general working conditions. It will vary, too – and this is a point which has not been sufficiently emphasised – with the length of time over which the maximisation of output is contemplated. A length of day that would maximise output for a month or a year would not necessarily bring it to a maximum if a period of many years was contemplated. A length of day that maximised output during a short war would not necessarily maximise it during a long peace. But if we bear in mind the essential relativity of the conception, we may legitimately speak of a point (or points) of maximum productiveness in connection with a given variation. So long as the variation is towards this point, output will be increased; so long as it is away from it, it will be diminished. That is, output will be increased if a working day longer than the day of maximum productiveness is shortened, or if a day shorter than the day of maximum productiveness is lengthened. It will be diminished by converse variations. How much it will be increased or diminished will depend on the extent of the change and the rates at which productiveness falls away on either side of the maximum – a matter which again will vary with varying circumstances.

One warning only is needed in this connection. Generalisations of the sort I have been making – of the sort I shall be making throughout this paper – are only statements of tendencies. They are only statements of what will happen if other things remain the same. And this means that, if other things are not equal, such statements cannot be refuted by a mere appeal to facts, nor can they necessarily be proved by facts which appear to support them. During the nineteenth century, for instance, the average duration of the working day was considerably curtailed. At the same time there was a fairly continuous increase in output, and from this it is sometimes argued that the length of day actually worked at the outset was beyond the point of maximum productiveness. No deduction could be more illegitimate. A general increase in productivity may make the yield to a shorter day after the change greater than the yield of a longer day before, even if without the reduction output would have been still greater – and of course during the nineteenth century productivity in general was increasing. Other considerations may lead us to believe that hours of labour were excessively long during the earlier part of this period, but from crude statistics of changes in output it is as illegitimate to argue that the curtailment of the working day was the cause of the increase, as that, if the day had not been reduced, productivity would have increased still faster.

III

That is all I have to say at present on variations of hours and output. I now proceed to deal with the opposite aspect of the matter, the relation between hours and incomes – a subtler connection demanding greater delicacy of treatment.

So far as men consume the product of their own labour, of course, income and output are identical. Robinson Crusoe living alone on his island lives exclusively on the product of his labour. So does human society conceived as a whole. External circumstances being given, what is got in the form of produce depends on what is given in the form of effort. In both cases, therefore, there is nothing to add to the simple generalisations which have been made already.

But when we come to consider not individuals working on their own or society conceived as an aggregate, but individuals and groups of individuals working within society and exchanging their products for the products of other individuals and groups of individuals, matters are not so simple. For in such circumstances what men work for is not their own output but the power to acquire by way of exchange little bits of other people's output. That is to say, what they work for is not their own output but the value of their output. Thus we have to examine, not only the effect of variations of hours on output, but also the effect of such variations of output on the income available from its disposal, and on the incomes of those who purchase it. To do this it will be convenient to proceed by stages. First, we may inquire as to variations on the part of single individuals, then as to variations on the part of single industries, then as to variations on the part of a whole society, and finally as to variations on the part of geographical groups or 'nations.'

IV

I turn first to variations on the part of single individuals.

This is the simplest case and need not detain us long. The fact of exchange introduces no important complications. The income of society (which, as we have just seen, *is* its output) will obviously fluctuate with individual output, and in the great majority of cases so will individual income. For so far as the great majority of people are concerned, the value per unit of the work they do is a fixed fact which is unaffected by variations in their individual output. The total work they do is only a tiny fraction of the total supply of the work they are supplying. The effects on value per unit of fractional variations of this tiny fraction, therefore, are so small that they may be disregarded. In a small minority of cases this might not be so – there are certain British etchers, who, I am told, maintain the value of their work by limiting its quantity – in these cases what I shall be saying about group variation will be applicable. But in most markets individual income will tend to fluctuate with quantitative variations in individual work. It is obvious that it must be so in the case of independent producers. It is no less clear in the case of contract wages paid on a piece-work basis. In the case of wages paid on a time-rate basis and weekly, monthly and yearly salaries, disparities may arise, but except where economic friction is very great, they are not likely to persist.

V

I turn next to variations on the part of all the producers engaged in any one line of industry, a question looming larger in public discussions of industrial policy. Suppose all the producers of, say, coal decide to vary their working day, what results are to be expected?

Here matters become more complicated. As before, we may expect the income of society to fluctuate in the same direction as output, but in the absence of further knowledge with regard to the disposition of other members of society and the technical conditions of production, we are no longer justified in predicting the same of the incomes of the producers in question. For now, by hypothesis, the total volume of supply is fluctuating appreciably, and therefore value per unit must be affected – and, of course, must be affected inversely. But until we know *how* it is affected – at what rate it falls for an increase of supply or rises for a diminution – we cannot say how the incomes of the producers in question are going to fluctuate: 9,000 units at 10*d*. (90,000*d*.) are worth more than 8,000 units at 11*d*. (88,000*d*.), but 9,000 units at 6*d*. (54,000*d*.) are worth considerably less.

It is in tackling problems of this sort that we become conscious of the immense debt that we owe to the Marshallian analysis of demand. For, armed with the concept of elasticity, we can assert quite simply that, in the circumstances we are discussing, if the elasticity of demand is greater than unity – in non-technical terms if the change in amount demanded is more than proportionate to the change in price – incomes will vary directly with output; if it is less, they will vary inversely. It is important, of course, to distinguish between elasticity of demand for the ultimate product and elasticity of demand for the labour that helps to produce it. In cases of simple production with free or low-priced raw materials and no complicated organisation or capital equipment, the divergence between the two may not be considerable. But if expensive raw materials and extensive capital equipment are involved, the divergence may be very important. The elasticity of demand for the product will, of course, be one of the factors governing the conditions of demand for labour. But so will the way the prices of the other factors employed react to changes in the scale of output, and the technical possibilities of varying the proportions in which they co-operate. Overhead costs may be increased or diminished, raw materials may become more or less expensive, different technical combinations may become more expedient, and so on. It would be possible to spend much time unravelling the subtleties of these relations;[1] but in the last resort, here, as in the simple breakfast-table examples of the elementary text-books, we may imagine a scale of prices at which given quantities of work will be taken, and the rate at which this change will be all-important in determining the outcome for the wage-earners of any given variation of hours of labour.

Now if wage-rates are freely adjustable and the market for labour is reasonably competitive, that is the end of the matter. Wage-earners whose labour is in relatively elastic demand will increase their income by increasing their output, and diminish their income by diminishing their output. Wage-earners whose labour is in relatively inelastic demand will increase their income by curtailing output, and diminish their income by increasing output. *So long as the group remains intact* – I shall return to this assumption later – and no changes in the technique of production take place, the effects of variation here exhaust themselves in variation of incomes.

But under modern conditions matters are not quite so simple, even if we do not waive the hypothesis of immobility. For wage-rates seldom have the complete flexibility postulated by these generalisations. Rather they are usually fixed in advance by the same apparatus of collective bargaining which is responsible for the regulation of hours. And this means that, until the contract is revised, wages themselves are rigid. By fixing the rate and fixing the length of the working day the daily wage is itself predetermined.[2]

But this does *not* mean that the conditions of demand lose their governing importance. The general disposition of the market to buy, as exhibited in the demand schedules we have been discussing, does not change when the price prevailing ceases to be flexible. All that happens is that the effects of variations of supply exhibit themselves in a different fashion. Instead of the price accommodating itself to the given supply so that the actual quantity demanded clears the market, the amount demanded accommodates itself to the price that is fixed. If this happens to be the price that will clear the market, then all is as if wage-rates had been flexible. If it is less, then unusual

1. Cp. Marshall, *Principles of Economics*, 8th edn (1920), Notes XIV and XV of the Mathematical Appendix and Chapter VI, Book V.

2. It is assumed, of course, that, in the case of work remunerated on a piece-wage basis, the intensity of work only suffers the consequential changes discussed already.

profits are made until more labourers are drawn into employment. If it is more, then some labour is not purchased, and, since hours are fixed, this means that some labourers will be thrown out of employment, or at any rate that there will be unemployment in that industry. It is surprising indeed that this should not be more universally recognised, for of course it is only a simple application of the general theory of monopoly. We all know that if the proprietor of a patent medicine decides to increase his supply, if he does not successfully readjust his price to the prevailing conditions of demand he is liable to be left with unsold bottles. It is time that we realised that *in this respect* the market for labour is not dissimilar from the market for patent medicines.

Given the variation in supply then, everything is still ultimately dependent upon the conditions of demand. We may, therefore, formulate the following generalisation. *For every wage-rate that can be fixed there is an elasticity of demand for labour that will just maintain employment constant for a given variation in supply of labour.** If the actual elasticity is greater than this, then an increase in the work offered will increase employment, and a decrease diminish it. If it is less, then the converse result is to be expected.

We may illustrate this by two cases of great practical significance. Let us assume that the workers in a given industry have agreed to lengthen their working day, such a lengthening being accompanied by an increase in daily output. Let us assume further that, being willing to submit to a downward revision of rates, they insist only on such rates as maintain daily wages constant. In such a case, clearly, if employment is to remain constant, the elasticity of demand for labour must be of the constant outlay order – that is, in Marshallian terms, equal to unity.[1] If it is greater than this, employment will be increased (or profits will rise); if it is less, it will be diminished – the degree of extension or contraction for the given variation depending on the degree in which the elasticity of demand is greater or less than unity.

Let us now reverse the requirements of our policy. In harmony with recent fashions let us regard constancy of employment rather than constancy of wages as the ultimate *desideratum*. It is not difficult to show that in certain cases a lengthening of the working day with increasing output must result in lower wages per head than would have prevailed if the day had not been

* On his own printed copy Robbins amended "supply of labour" to "the length of the working day."

1. If the changes are not relatively small, then, as Dr. Dalton has shown, the Marshallian formula becomes inadequate (see Hugh Dalton, *Some Aspects of the Inequality of Incomes in Modern Communities* [London, 1920], pp. 192–7). For convenience of application, however, I refrain from introducing this complication.

lengthened. For obviously the downward cut in wage-rates, which is necessary to maintain employment constant, must always be greater if output is increased than if it is not. The greater supply of work must necessarily be cleared at a somewhat lower price per unit. But if the elasticity of demand is greater than unity, this greater diminution in wage-rates will not offset the increase in the number of units by which it is multiplied. On the other hand, if the elasticity of demand is less than unity, this will actually happen. The fall in wages will be greater than it would have been if hours had not been lengthened. The popular belief that, if hours are lengthened, a fall in wages can always be averted or at least diminished, is only true when certain conditions are satisfied. If they are not, then it must prove a bitter delusion. It would be pleasant to believe that some day city editors and leader-writers might become aware of this simple proposition.

Clearly we are a long way here from the harmony we found existing between individual income and output. A group which puts more into the common pool may be compelled to take out less, and a group which diminishes the size of the pool may receive an enhanced share. But notice that our generalisations with regard to individuals are not rendered invalid by the fact of group variation. It still remains true that, if a given individual varies his hours of labour, his income tends to vary with his output. The unfortunate miner may see his standards of life being wrecked by an upward variation of hours affecting price more than proportionately. But if he does not vary his hours upward too, he will get even less than he would have done otherwise. On the other hand, if group rates are being raised by a common restrictive policy, each individual would lose if *all* were to abandon restriction, yet *each* will gain if he singly succeeds in evading the regulation. The behaviour of the group moves the target, but the individual score still depends on the marksman.

VI

But this is not the end of group variations. Rather it is only the beginning. For unless we are willing to contemplate only the institutions of a caste society, it is not to be expected that variations in one group should not sometimes at least involve migration to or from others. This, however, is a matter which can be considered more conveniently when we have surveyed the effects of wider variations. I pass, therefore, to changes of hours of labour throughout society as a whole. Suppose all the producers in a given society decide to vary their hours of labour, what results are to be expected?

So far as the real income of society is concerned, what has been said already is sufficient. The real income of society *is* its output, and therefore what has been said about output exhausts this part of the subject. One caution perhaps is necessary. We have seen that the point of maximum productiveness varies from man to man and from industry to industry. It is not to be expected, therefore, that the output of each man and each industry will be similarly affected by similar variations of hours of labour. On the contrary, we must expect not only the *extent* but even the *direction* of variation to vary. It is only, therefore, after striking a balance that we can speak of effects on the social income.

But now let us turn to the incomes of the various individuals and classes within society. Here obviously we have a problem of greater complexity than any we have yet examined, and it is advisable to proceed to its solution by stages.

Let us begin by assuming homogeneity of skill, flexibility of wage-rates and complete mobility of labour. In this way we can ignore the different effects upon the position of different groups which in almost any real world would be produced by the variation we are supposing, and concentrate on the problem of what will happen to the general level of wages.

Viewed thus, the problem is relatively simple. The number of units of work offered has changed. Their value per unit, therefore, will fluctuate inversely. But the change in the supply of work does not mean a change in the number of labourers. Real wages, therefore, will depend on the elasticity of demand for labour. If the elasticity of demand for labour is greater than unity, then wages will vary directly, and if it is less, inversely, with changes in daily output.

This result is a purely formal one. But we need not be content with formality. For it is the almost universal consensus of opinion among economists[1] that, in the modern world at any rate, with its wealth of technical knowledge and its itch for material improvement, the elasticity of demand for labour is greater than unity. Hence we may assert with some confidence that given our assumptions of plastic wage-rates, a competitive labour market and complete mobility of labour, an increase of hours leading to an increase of output will result in increased wages, and *vice versa*. Some of the increase will no doubt go to other factors, but if this opinion with regard to elasticity is true, there is no need to fear that wages will not benefit.

All this, however, rests upon an assumption which enables us to speak as if all wages were similarly affected. But in the world we live in, this assumption is not valid. Workers are not all of the same degree of skill and adaptability, and even within groups which are homogeneous in these respects, for short periods at least, they are not completely mobile. Therefore, unless we are

1. See, e.g., A.C. Pigou, *Economics of Welfare*, 2nd edn (1924), pp. 622–8.

willing to make the unreal assumption that when the output of different groups varies simultaneously, the amounts spent on the new output vary so as to leave the relative position of the groups unchanged, we are not entitled to assume that the effects of a uniform variation will be uniformly distributed among wage-earners in general. Again, everything will depend upon the demand for different kinds of labour. It is true that things are not quite so simple here as in the cases we contemplated when we were considering group variation. For there we assumed that the supply of one commodity only was changing, the social demand at different prices remaining unaltered. Here not only is supply changing in each industry, but the demand arising from other industries is changing also. In technical terms, it is not only a case of a shift of the point *P* along a given demand curve: the position of the curve itself is to be regarded as changing. None the less, the same broad considerations are applicable. Where the demand is relatively inexpansible the position of the workers will be relatively worsened by an increase and bettered by a diminution of output. Where it is relatively expansible the converse effects will follow.

Hence, if the full effects of the change in output are to be diffused to the maximum extent among different classes of wage-earners, there must at the same time be a transfer of workers from the positions of less to the positions of greater comparative advantage. If it is an increase, workers will have to move to the industries of more expansible demands or to new industries. If it is a diminution, *vice versa*. And of course in a world of specialised skill and incomplete mobility, such a uniform diffusion as we contemplated at first is *never* to be expected. All that can be said is that, granted a fair degree of mobility, disharmonies will be reduced to a minimum.

These conclusions sound abstract, but they embody a perfectly commonsense principle. If productive power increases in any way, it is surely most improbable that the increase will be most effectively utilised by uniform application in all directions. If some uniformly efficient robot were invented which increased our powers to do simple manual labour by, say, 25 per cent., we should not expand the production of wheat and motor-cars in equal proportions. And similarly if some cosmic disaster were to reduce productive powers by a quarter, we should not curtail the production of necessities and luxuries uniformly. Progress, in fact – using the word progress in a strictly non-ethical sense – involves the progressive diminution of the relative proportions of productive power applied to the making of things which are in inelastic demand, and a progressive transfer of productive power to the making of things the demand for which is still elastic. And retrogression, the contrary process. That, incidently, is one of the reasons why, in a progressive age, agriculture is in a state of chronic depression. And, of course, rational increases of hours (increases, that is, which do not go beyond the point of maximum productiveness) *are* increases of productive power – as are also those diminutions which increase production.

Considerations of this sort enable us to complete our treatment of the effects of group variation which we had to leave unfinished a little way back. Obviously we must take into account the possibility of movement both into the industry and away from it. If an extension of hours involves an increase of income, or a contraction a diminution, then we may assume that no movement is engendered.[1] For by hypothesis we are considering *voluntary* variations. We are, therefore, entitled to assume that the group concerned prefer the gain in income or leisure to the sacrifice in leisure or income. But if income moves inversely to the variation in hours, clearly *if* movement is possible it will take place. There is now a double loss or a double gain to disturb the equilibrium, and if mobility is possible there will be transfers until those employed in the industry in question do not gain or lose more than, with their given disposition towards work and leisure, they would gain elsewhere, the loss or gain of productive power being diffused more or less equally throughout the area of mobility. Only, therefore, where there is an absence of mobility will the disharmonies we have studied in this connection be permanent.

VII

That is all I have time to say here about variations throughout a whole society. The interesting complications which arise when wage-rates are not flexible can be deduced for the most part as corollaries from what has been said already. I pass, therefore, finally to consider the case of variations on the part of open geographical groups.

Here fortunately it is possible once more to be brief. For the principles we have already investigated can be combined to afford a sufficient solution to the various puzzles that confront us. So far as the inhabitants of the area of variation consume their own products, what has been said about a closed society is applicable. So far as they obtain their income by exchanging their products for products produced abroad, the analysis developed in connection with industrial groups is applicable. This is easy to see if we suppose that the group is sufficiently small to produce only *one* commodity, for the geographical group *is* then an industrial group, and that is the end of the matter. When the group is wider, then matters become more complicated; but when

1. It is, of course, conceivable that persons outside the group might prefer the new situation and seek it. In such a case the assumption made above would be invalid. I am indebted to Dr. Dalton for this suggestion.

allowance has been made for changes in the relative value of different commodities and the reshifting of employment, the same broad generalisations hold. Whether on balance the group gains or loses depends on the conditions of demand and upon the net economies or diseconomies involved by changes in the scale of production.

Here again, therefore, there is a theoretical possibility that the income of the geographical group – the "national" income, that is to say – and the world income may move in different directions, and no doubt areas are conceivable in the world as we know it which might gain or lose by this disharmony. But a little reflection on the causes influencing elasticity should convince us that ours is not one of these areas. For, as is well known, one of the most important circumstances influencing the demand for exports is the possibility of obtaining similar supplies, or supplies sufficiently similar, from elsewhere. If this is present, demand will tend to be very elastic. A slight rise in price per unit will cause the transference of foreign demand to other sources of production. A slight fall will mean a considerable enhancement of foreign purchases. Other things being equal, the smaller the group the more probable the existence of alternative sources of supply, and hence the greater the elasticity of demand for exports. Of course this factor of "economic size" may be offset by the possession of unique facilities for production, but so far as our own position is concerned, it is abundantly clear that Providence has not granted us this substitute for industry.

All this assumes the absence of transfers of labour and capital between the areas whose fortunes we are considering. And so far as we consider the particular geographical groups called nations and concentrate upon short-period tendencies, in the modern world, with its legal and cultural checks on movement, this assumption is not out of touch with reality, as regards the human factor. But so far as capital is concerned, it is altogether too artificial. If man is of all luggage the most difficult to be transported, free capital is the most easy. Now the variation of hours in any area will clearly make the investment of capital more or less profitable there as compared with investment in other areas. Hence so far as new capital is concerned we should expect to see the gains or losses resulting from any variation rapidly diffused over the whole area of capital investment. The main effects of the change, therefore, will be seen in the incomes of the immobile factors, labour and property which is not easily transferable. Thus, suppose a contraction of hours, a shrinkage of the supply of labour not compensated by an enhancement in the total value of the product. The return per unit to capital would fall, and this would mean that, in the absence of restriction, capital would tend to go elsewhere. With less capital the productivity of labour would be less, and consequently wages would fall still further. Here, too, notice that the effects would be more pronounced in an area that was comparatively small than in one that was comparatively extensive.

VIII

That is all I have to say to-day on the broad effects of variations of hours of labour. It is sometimes urged that, beyond this, reductions of hours tend to produce dynamic changes in the general productive situation, in that they tend to evoke new inventions in organisation and technique. Up to a point no doubt this is true, and it is a matter which in any particular situation deserves the most careful consideration of the negotiating parties.[1] But even the most fervent advocate of this view can hardly contend that these improvements in productive efficiency are *invariably* to be associated with changes in hours, in the same way as the tendencies I have been discussing. If a scarcity of coal or labour stimulates entrepreneurs to new inventions under certain conditions, it is certainly a fact to be noted and to be borne in mind when policy is being considered. But it is not a tendency which is logically implicit in *every* variation in every conceivable situation, and having acknowledged the possibility of its appearance, we are justified here, I think, in regarding it as a secondary complication.

It remains, therefore, only for me to draw certain conclusions from what has been stated already. Two facts, I think, stand out clearly from the welter of complications. In the first place is the absence of harmony between group incentives and the interests of the social income. So far as individuals are concerned, this disharmony is not present. What diminishes the prospect of income for society diminishes it also for the individual, and *vice versa.* But when certain conditions are not present, this is not so for groups of individuals acting concertedly. And this has a double implication. (*a*) On the one hand, it suggests that if we are determined to consider the interests of a group as a group – and in the modern world such a choice is from time to time forced upon us – much greater caution than is usually exercised is necessary before we recommend to the group conduct which might be expedient either for an individual or for society. Deliberately to recommend an increase of hours when the conditions of demand are not elastic is either very ignorant or very Machiavellian. (*b*) And on the other hand, it suggests that, from the

1. It is a matter, too, which, together with the parallel argument as regards increases of wages, is, I think, capable of further theoretical treatment than it has received already. Clearly there must be a point of maximum effectiveness for such pressure – it is not to be believed that *any* reduction of hours or *any* rise of wages must necessarily have healthy dynamic consequences – and it would be highly interesting to know something more about the conditions determining the position of this maximum in any particular situation. No doubt absolute precision here is even harder to attain than in the discussion of static problems. But the attempt would be well worth making. So long as there is *no* quantitative element in our dynamic speculations, they must remain the ready instrument of economic obscurantism.

point of view of long-period policy, it is possible that in recent years too much attention may have been given to the interests of groups as such and too little to the importance of movement between groups. In saying this I do not wish to prejudge the tremendous issues of the relative importance of group and social solidarity. But I do suggest that it is well to recognise that exclusive concentration on the interests of a group, as a group, does not necessarily imply a like preoccupation with the interests of society. The right of an industry to remain such and such a size and to secure for itself the maximum income under the given circumstances can only be maintained at the risk of failing to maximise the income of society. This is true of the society in which we live. It is a problem which would be equally insistent in any other state of society. Only a community that had forsworn the criteria of economy could afford to neglect the importance of considerable mobility of labour.

But, on the other hand – and this is my second point – there is nothing in all this which justifies the view that the income of society as a whole fluctuates inversely with fluctuations in efficiency. To argue from the possible success for a group of a policy of restriction to the probable success for society as a whole of a similar policy is to commit the fallacy of composition. Nor can it be urged, I think, that there is any probability that wages in general could benefit from such a policy. This is probably true of society as a whole in the world as we know it. It is *certainly* true in a small area such as Great Britain. There is nothing in general theory to justify the belief that diminutions in hours which do not increase efficiency will tend to raise general wages, or that increases which do not diminish efficiency will tend to lower them. Only those who have never learnt to distinguish the general from the particular can urge the contrary proposition.

But notice finally, that this is not in the least to argue that increases are desirable or that diminutions are undesirable. Those who have become so preoccupied with accumulating the means of a good life that they have forgotten that the end is existent may argue that men *should* work so as to secure the maximum product. There is nothing in economic science which supports them.[1] The relative values which men assign to leisure and the results of production determine indeed the phenomena we have to analyse,

1. It is obvious, of course, that such an arrangement will be economical only if the last increment of product obtainable is valued *more* than the leisure that has to be sacrificed to obtain it. Even the despised classical economists knew this. "Happiness is the object to be desired, and we cannot be quite sure that, provided he is equally well fed, a man may not be happier in the enjoyment of the luxury of idleness than in the enjoyment of the luxuries of a neat cottage and good clothes." *Letters of David Ricardo to Thomas Robert Malthus 1810–1823*, ed. James Bonar (Oxford, 1887), pp. 138–9.

but to pronounce upon the validity of these valuations as such is completely outside our province. All that we can do is to attempt to exhibit clearly what consequences follow from one choice or another, and to do this for one small part of the field of choice is all that has been attempted in this paper.

3 The Present Position of Economic Science[1]

From *Economica*, vol. 10 (March 1930), pp. 14–24.

I

Ladies and Gentlemen,
To assume the responsibilities of teaching in the London School of Economics is not an easy thing for anyone. It is still less easy for one who has had the privilege of working here as a student. Others know our tradition by public repute. He has known it by daily acquaintance: and to have done that is to find the difficulty of living up to it doubled in intensity. It is in that position that I find myself at present; and I must confess that when I think of the great men who taught us when I was a student – of Edwin Cannan who taught us Economics, of Graham Wallas who taught us Political Science – I tremble at the responsibility of maintaining their standards. I think, too, of [Allyn Young] the late occupant of the Chair of Political Economy, of his wide experience, his profound theoretical insight, his scrupulous and extensive scholarship; and I do not find my apprehensions diminished.

II

But I did not come here to burden you with my personal difficulties. The problem rather to which I wish to direct your attention is the impersonal, the perennial question: how goes it with our science? The years since the war have been important years in the history of economics. Much new work has been done. Much old work has been called in question. We have all been so busy that the wider significance of what we have been doing has not always been apparent. At times like these an occasional stocktaking is not without its uses, and it is a survey of this sort that I am asking you to undertake with me this evening. What is the present position of Economic Science?

1. Inaugural lecture delivered at the London School of Economics and Political Science on January 30th, 1930.

The progress of Economics, like the progress of the quantities it studies, is not altogether a straight line. It is very seldom that there is a definite retrogression, but there are periods of greater and less activity. Both entrepreneurs and economists exhibit fluctuating degrees of confidence in future progress. Ricardo clearly thought that Economics was still in its infancy.[1] Marshall said that economists had enough to occupy them for the next three thousand years.[2] But John Stuart Mill, who came after Ricardo, thought that the main work had been done and that little remained but to devise suitable methods of exposition.[3] And in the years following the period of Marshall's ascendancy, in some quarters, I think, there ensued a like degree of complacency. At the present time, however, the contrary mood predominates. All the best indices suggest that we are enjoying a boom in Economic Theory. Everywhere men are attacking new problems or criticising existing solutions of old ones. We have to go back to the days of Jevons and the utility school to find a period in the history of Economic Thought when economists all over the world were so active or so sceptical. No one is satisfied with what has been done already. No one pretends that what is being done today is anything but provisional.

But let me at once guard against a possible misunderstanding. I say that we are dissatisfied and critical. But I do not say that we are at all disposed totally to reject what has been done already. That is not our frame of mind, and I should be very sorry to give rise to any impression that it is. The rational scrutiny of economic phenomena is an inquiry so repellant to many that there are always those who will seize upon the least dispute among economists as a sign that economic science as a whole is worthless, and that economists themselves cannot agree on the simplest propositions of their science. I do not wish to give any countenance to that attitude, and I do not know any economist who would. We do not dispute the great conquests of the past. We do not deny that the economists who have gone before have already forged tools of great power and utility: what we dispute rather is the finality of their analysis. As a first approximation? – Yes. We will defend it against all the attacks of Philistia. But as a final solution? – No. To accept it as that would be a betrayal of the trust which has been handed on to us.

An illustration will make clear what I have in mind. Take the oldest and one of the most respectable of Economic Theories – the Quantity Theory of Money. "This theory," says Mr. Keynes, "is fundamental."[4] And I think that it

1. See the Preface to the first edn of David Ricardo, *On the Principles of Political Economy and Taxation* (London, 1817).

2. *Memorials of Alfred Marshall*, ed. A.C. Pigou (London, 1925), p. 84.

3. *Principles of Political Economy with some of their applications to social philosophy*, ed. W.J. Ashley (London, 1909), p. 436.

4. *A Tract on Monetary Reform* (London, 1923), p. 74.

would be generally admitted that it is an acid test of a man's capacity to become an economist that he should be willing to admit that there does exist an important connection between the general level of prices and the quantity of money in circulation. That this is not a mere theoretical truism but a maxim with a vital bearing on practice, is, I think, borne out by war experience. Roughly speaking it is not untrue to say that the inflationary troubles of the war period and after, were least where this truth was most clearly appreciated and greatest where it had never found general acceptance. But what is the precise nature of this general connection? What exactly is the mechanism through which the general level of prices is affected by fluctuations in the volume of money? What difference is made by changes in the *rate of flow* of money into or out of circulation? These are problems on whose solution agreement is not yet general. And as post-war experience shows, they are problems which are not devoid of significance for those who have the conduct of policy.

Or again, take the general theory of price. Here again war experience is a touchstone. I suppose there can be no question that the various experiments in State control provided the most triumphant laboratory vindication of the broad theories of price and price-fixing that the world has ever seen. As you, sir, have abundantly shown, where policy was devised with due regard to the elementary generalisations of price theory, control was tolerably effective.[1] Where these generalisations were ignored, there was ignominious chaos and disaster. That is now common ground. And yet, who is there among us, who, reading, let us say, Mr. E.M.H. Lloyd's book on *Experiments in State Control*,[2] or the surpassingly interesting accounts of the experiments of the American Price-Fixing Authorities, has not felt that just at those points where finesse and delicacy of policy were most needed, the teaching of Economics was most incomplete and ambiguous. The great test vindicated old theories. But it also put us new questions to answer.

III

Economics, then, has reached a stage at which a desire to pass beyond first approximations is causing economists to turn back once more to the re-examination of its most fundamental problems. May I try, without being too technical, to indicate very briefly some of the main deficiencies of which

---

1. See W.H. Beveridge, *British Food Control* (Oxford, 1928). [Sir William Beveridge was the Director of LSE.]
2. *Experiments in State Control at the War Office and the Ministry of Food* (Oxford, 1924).

we are becoming conscious? Broadly speaking I think they fall into three classes.

(1) Firstly we have what are admittedly gaps in the existing body of theory. There do exist wide problems of general theory upon which as yet very little extensive work has been done. I am not now thinking of the problems of advanced mathematical economics. I am thinking rather of much less remote matters, such as the relation between saving, discount rates, and prices in a modern credit economy. Here is a field in which, apart from isolated efforts by Wicksell and one or two others, little or nothing had been done before the war. The theory of money and the theory of saving were kept in water-tight compartments. Yet no one, I think, can examine the path-breaking work of Mr. D.H. Robertson in this connection, without the conviction that perhaps here, in the future, are to be forged some of the most powerful instruments of policy. Again we may notice the surprising gap which exists between the theories of equilibrium and the theories of fluctuation. I know no work of any importance in which any attempt is made to correlate the theory of short-period price equilibrium with the theory of periodic fluctuations. Yet surely this is a problem of quite first-class importance. There are other problems, too, on which more work has been done, but on which no general agreement has been reached, and these, too, fall under our general heading. Much as has been written on the theory of Interest, for instance, I do not think it would be wrong to say that outside the broadest generalities, there exists little agreement among economists on this fundamentally important matter.

(2) Secondly come deficiencies due to defects in the logical structure of existing theory. Here we come upon the more seamy side of the present position of Economics. There have always been skeletons in the economist's cupboard – links in his arguments of whose weakness he was dimly conscious, although maybe he was convinced that in the interests of progress it was necessary to tolerate their imperfections. For many years it was possible to ignore their existence. But recently they have been dragged out into the daylight and the result has been not a little disconcerting. Take, for instance, the theory of cost – it would not be impossible to take similar examples from the theory of demand. Ever since the time of Marshall, economists have been vaguely aware that certain difficulties attendant on the construction of particular equilibrium cost curves had not been fully surmounted. Yet, in this country, at any rate, we have been content to proceed as if all was well, as if only a little ingenuity of a rather trifling order was necessary to establish complete logical consistency. It is true that from time to time difficulties have appeared. Results were obtained, analysing in this way, which were inconsistent with other generalisations. But these were regarded as incidental curiosities. We went on using our upward and downward sloping cost curves with sublime indifference to these difficulties. Then came Piero Sraffa, with a

very modest paper,* in which he asked certain questions and refused to proceed until they were answered, and the whole structure trembled. I do not think it is any exaggeration to say that to-day the whole theory of costs in particular equilibrium is an entirely open question. To-day it is only the writers of cram textbooks and the examiners in certain elementary examinations who assume that the laws of cost are simple.

If I might become very technical for a moment, I should be inclined to say that what has happened, here as elsewhere in the theory of value, is that the old plan of analysing "one thing at a time" has definitely broken down – outside very narrow limits. The method of analysing the causes determining the value of one commodity, assuming everything else to remain unchanged, seems to lead to inconsistencies which can only be eliminated by the abandonment of this method. It has this effect in the analysis of cost. It has it also, if I am not mistaken, in the analysis of utility. Only by abandoning this assumption of other things remaining the same and contemplating the process of price determination as a whole do we emancipate ourselves from these difficulties. It is a tribute to the theoretical prescience of the School of Lausanne, that from the outset its founders anticipated this *impasse* and urged the adoption of methods which would have prevented its occurrence.

(3) Thirdly come deficiencies, due, not to logical defects, but to an over-simplicity in the *assumptions* of existing theory. A theory may be perfectly consistent in itself and yet not be applicable to the explanation of a given situation, because the assumptions from which it starts are either too simple or not in harmony with the facts. I think we are coming to realise that this is the case in regard to a large body of existing theory which is not subject to the strictures I have mentioned already. In the past economists have not been altogether careful as regards their assumptions. They have been too inclined to generalise as if the circumstances of their own day were permanently given facts of the social economy. It is a great tribute to the steadiness and good behaviour of the economic system that in the last century and a half it has conformed so well to generalisations made on this basis. But the framework of society gradually changes, the forces at work assume different proportions, and theories based on old assumptions lose their value as instruments of explanation. They do not cease to be true. They just cease to be applicable and new theories have to be devised to take their place.

Take, for instance, the theory of wages. Throughout the classical period of our science, economists were apt to assume that within non-competing groups, at any rate, there was fairly effective mobility of labour: and on the

* "The laws of returns under competitive conditions," *Economic Journal*, vol. 36 (December 1926), pp. 535–50.

basis of this assumption they were able to show a tendency for the wage rates of similar grades of labour to approach something like equality *within short periods*. That theory I do not regard as false. But it is abundantly clear that it depended for its applicability on a state of the labour market peculiar to a rapidly-growing population.[1] Remove the element of rapid growth, remove, that is to say, the comparatively high proportion of free recruits to the labour supply already committed to different industries, and the flexibility postulated by the classics tends to disappear. It seems probable, therefore, that in our own day, as the population becomes more and more stationary, this particular theory and theories based upon it will be more and more inapplicable.

Or again, take the theory of international trade: a great part of this theory, particularly that part which relates to tariffs and capital export, was worked out on the assumption of flexibility of wage rates. And, granted this assumption, a great deal of this theory still stands. But substitute rigid wage rates such as have been the rule rather than the exception in the post-war period, and it is clear, I think, that certain modifications are necessary.[2]

And so I could go on. But I think I have said enough to show that for this generation at any rate the belief that 'it's all in Ricardo' or that 'it's all in Marshall' – great figures as we acknowledge Ricardo and Marshall to have been – is not any longer prevalent. We revert rather to the view of these economists themselves that, although much has been done that is valuable, still more remains to be done in the future.

IV

But in what way is progress to be made? How best can we assist the removal of these deficiencies?

In certain quarters, recently, the suggestion has been made that the bulk of our difficulties are due to the use of an erroneous method. Economic Science, it is urged, is too deductive and theoretical. In future these methods are to be discarded and in their place we are to depend on historical and statistical inductions. By the application of the methods of higher statistical analysis to dense masses of statistics, laws of 'economic behaviour' are to be discovered which will put Economic Science on a basis of equality with the Natural Sciences.

Such is the argument of the so-called Institutionalists. I confess that if to refuse to deny oneself the use of one of the main instruments of scientific

1. This view is developed in my "Notes on some probable consequences of the advent of a stationary population in Great Britain," *Economica*, vol. 9 (April 1929), pp. 71–82.

2. See e.g. A.C. Pigou, "Wage policy and unemployment," *Economic Journal*, vol. 37 (September 1927), pp. 335–68.

discovery is to merit the name, I am content in this matter to remain a conservative. I survey the economics of the past and, in so far as it has been fruitful, I find that it has been neither wholly deductive nor wholly inductive. In this country, at any rate, there has been no sterile separation of methods. The great founders of modern economics were not content to walk on one leg. Stanley Jevons, who was a master of statistics, was one of the founders of the abstract theory of utility. Alfred Marshall, the greatest influence in modern theoretical economics, made important contributions to statistical method. And in our own day – and fortunately still actively working with us – Professor Bowley, the foremost statistician of the age, has done more than most men living to advance the progress of pure analysis. Undoubtedly the methods which have been devised for our use by statisticians are methods of great power and utility, but there is no reason to suppose that they will be any more fruitful than the more primitive methods of the past, *unless guided by suitable theory*. The passive observation of facts, unassisted by theoretical hypothesis, must of necessity be sterile. It is not the scientist, it is the village idiot who is content to approach the world in this manner.

For this reason I cannot but regard the attitude of the more uncompromising members of this school as being essentially barren. I am not of the view that economics can ever dispense with the deductive method. Nor do I think that that method has reached the limit of its usefulness. But I am very far from contending that as progress is made we shall not see a vast extension of quantitative investigations. For clearly, quantitative exactitude is the object of all scientific inquiry, and it is only by continually testing our theories by reference to the facts of the situation that we can discover how far they proceed from assumptions that are appropriate. And fortunately there is reason to suppose that in the future the alliance between the economic theorist and the statistician will be even closer than it has been in the past. The *rapprochement* comes from both quarters. On the one hand recent developments of statistical technique have made much more probable the realisation of the hope, long entertained by theoretical economists, of providing numerical values for the abstract quantities of pure theory. Already a considerable body of important work has been done on the investigation of the elasticity of demand for staple agricultural products in America. And there is little doubt that we are only at the beginning of the movement. No doubt the results of such investigations have profound limitations and must be treated with the greatest caution. Still, when Dr. Schultz assures us that if during a certain period there had been a small increase in the sugar tariff, prices would have risen by 86 per cent. of the tariff, we may feel that the precision is dubious, but we must also feel that to have arrived at the roughest approximation to the truth is an important step forward.

At the same time there are important tendencies on the side of pure theory, which give rise to the hope that, in the future, quantitative analysis will be more general. One of the great difficulties of combining theoretical speculation with statistical analysis in the past has been that theory has been preoccupied mainly with what happened when *one* element in a situation is varied, other things remaining the same. One of the most hopeful developments of the present time is the disposition of theoretical economists to release more than one variable from the pound of *ceteris paribus*. The theory becomes more complex, but its application becomes more practicable.

A very simple example will make plain what I have in mind. It was a direct corollary of the old quantity theory that, other things being equal, fixity in the supply of money would ensure fixity in the general price level. This theory, I think, was true. But as other things were seldom equal, its bearing on the interpretation of facts was indirect and subject to misinterpretation. As demand is continually varying, what we prefer to know is what *rate of variation* of supply will keep prices constant, and how deviations of the actual rate from this ideal rate will affect prices. Here, you see, we need a theory which assumes variations of two factors and asks questions about the resultant. As is well known, such a theory has been developed by Professor Cassel, and the results, though open to criticism on points of detail, have made possible a new precision in dealing with problems of gold supply.[1] I am inclined to believe that an investigation of wage fluctuations on lines somewhat similar, given varying degrees of labour mobility and rates of change of demand, might prove to open up new ways of handling the problem of industrial reorganisation.

Thus I do not think that we need worry ourselves overmuch about method in the abstract, though, of course, discussions about the methods of particular investigations will often be fruitful and illuminating. What we have to do rather is to get on with the actual business of discovery – to use what tools are to hand rather than to debate endlessly about which tools are appropriate. Sometimes we shall go fastest by theoretical speculation. Sometimes it will be the study of particular concrete problems which suggest new generalisations. Sometimes we may do well to go back to the origins of existing doctrines and discover the precise intentions with which they were elaborated. Out of all these channels of inquiry the economics of the future will take shape. Personally, I do not think we must expect very sensational developments yet awhile. I think that there is still a long period of spadework before us. But gradually the materials for a new synthesis will accumulate, and one day it will occur to one of us that much that now appears to be discreet and disconnected is really bound together by a common unity. And then will come the

1. See Gustav Cassel, *The Theory of Social Economy* (London, 1923), Vol. II, p. 441 *et seq.*

time for that comprehensive restatement and architectonic generalisation, for the wide sweep and the clear vision for which today we wait so eagerly. It is not out of discussions of method, but out of the day to day labour of attacking new problems that the economics we look for will be born.

V

Ladies and gentlemen, the science which will emerge from the developments I have been indicating will not be a body of knowledge accessible to everyone. The days are gone when Political Economy was a fit subject for a gentleman to study in his moments of relaxation. It is sometimes said that one of the main duties of economists at the present day is to make plain to everyone the main doctrines of their science. This is not a view which I find it possible to accept. It may be agreed that it is highly desirable that economists should ask themselves more frequently than they do what is the ultimate significance of their conclusions, not only in the universe of discourse of their own sometimes narrow postulates, but also in that wider universe of discourse common to all the social sciences. There is not enough of this, and I think it is a task which is particularly incumbent on members of an institution like this where the various branches of social science are studied in intimate unison. If I might be permitted to allude to my personal pre-occupations, I would say that it is one of my own ambitions to make some contribution to this synthesis. As a student here it was my good fortune to study certain branches of political philosophy under Professor Laski. I am not without hope that at some not too far distant date it may be possible to produce evidence that the stimulus of his generous and sympathetic teaching was not altogether wasted.

But it is one thing to make *definite* the implications of one's conclusions. It is another to make either the implications or the conclusions intelligible to the lay public. And in fact, I believe that the hope that Economics will ever become something which the layman can comprehend without training is doomed for ever to frustration. No doubt economists might be more intelligible than they are. It is true that there is a kind of obscurity which springs from confused thinking. But the main fault is not with economists but with the world they study. The world of economic reality is a complicated thing, and it is not to be expected that as we come to understand it better our generalisations should be less complicated. It is no service to knowledge to make things simpler than they are.

And indeed I am inclined to think that if we as economists devote ourselves too much to attempts at popularisation, we shall be doing our science a disservice, and limiting its chances of beneficial influence. The sort of Economics which the Press and the public would like is an Economics which is bound either to be wrong or to be misapprehended. Surely it is better to push ahead with our analysis, embrace technicality with open arms if technicality will help us, and come to be so frequently right that we acquire the respect now given without question to the practitioners of the natural sciences. We are often told that if we do not make clear step by step the road whereby we arrive at our conclusions, our speculations are doomed to academic impotence. But experience, I suggest, seems to prove the contrary. If there is one field in which the man in the street is willing today to accept with deference the opinion of trained economists it is in matters of monetary theory. It is no accident, I suggest, that it is in just this field that economics is at once most precise, most technical, and most unintelligible to the layman.

VI

But when we have done all, what is the utility of our theories? Why study what the ignorant and the pompous have thought the most dismal of sciences? It has been held by some that if we push far enough with our researches we shall discover new values, new ways of living for humanity. That hope I do not share. I do not believe that investigating the consequences of choice can decide the ultimate problems of choosing; that the study of what happens when we do certain things can decide whether these things are worth doing.

But I do believe that the study of how different choices work out can make our choosing much more rational. Economics cannot tell you whether you ought to do a certain thing. But it should be able to tell you what will happen if you do it. Lack of good will it cannot cure. But lack of that understanding without which good will cannot be effective, it can gradually learn to remedy. And surely that is sufficient justification. To those to whom existence shows no values worth the seeking, economic inquiry has indeed nothing to offer. But to those in whom the sap of life is still active, it offers the prospect of discovering instruments for the achievement of their ends more powerful than any that have yet been known.

4 On a Certain Ambiguity in the Conception of Stationary Equilibrium

From *The Economic Journal*, vol. 40 (June 1930), pp. 194–214.

I

The idea of an equilibrium of forces is one which is common to many sciences, but there are few in which it plays a more important part than in theoretical economics. It has been implicit in our discussions since the time of the Physiocrats,[1] and as the methods of economics have become more and more self-conscious it has become, in one shape or other, one of the main instruments of theoretical analysis. We describe the various forces we have to study by reference to their place in our conception of equilibrium. We measure their variations by reference to equilibrating norms. It is not too much to say that in so far as we pretend to enunciate economic laws at all it is the assumption that, within some limits, an equilibrium of some sort is conceivable that is the justification of our procedure.

Now, of course, many conceptions of equilibrium are possible, from the simple notion of a balance between the supply of and demand for one commodity to the sublime conceptions of the mathematical economists, in which all the quantities contemplated move together in orderly change. But hitherto the dominating conception has been one midway between these extremes. We abstract from various causes of change, and conceive the remaining economic quantities as stationary, and inquire as to their mutual relations. Or, we ask what will be the relation of certain given quantities when certain tendencies to change have come to rest. The stationary state and static laws have been the main subject of investigation.

Whatever the imperfections of this method, it cannot be denied that by its aid, in the past, much has been done which does, in some way or other,

1. See Joseph Schumpeter, *Epochen der Dogmen- und Methodengeschichte* (Tübingen, 1914), pp. 45–8, for a very interesting discussion of the Physiocratic contribution viewed in this aspect.

elucidate the working of economic forces. The man who holds that nothing has yet been accomplished may deserve pity but certainly not respect. Nevertheless, at the present day, it would be idle to pretend that, even within this limited sphere, entire finality has been reached. There are still important differences of opinion among economists, both as regards the form and the significance of static analysis. Some of these differences relate to matters of actual *logic* – it is probable that the dispute with regard to consumers' surplus is a difference of this order. But some arise much more because of certain initial differences of *assumption* which are not always clearly realised. The logic is thought to be faulty because the premises are not clearly stated. It is the contention of this paper that the conception of stationary equilibrium, as used in modern "literary economics", itself involves an ambiguity as regards its ultimate assumptions. It is contended further that this ambiguity is responsible for some of the most important doctrinal confusions of the past, and that even at the present day it has led, in at least one instance, to analysis which is definitely erroneous. The nature of the ambiguity is simple. It can be stated in a couple of sentences. But its full significance cannot be grasped until we have traced its origin in the classical system and followed up some of the confusions which arise from its existence. An historical method of approach will therefore be utilised.[1] The history, however, makes no pretension to exhaustiveness. It is used solely in order to elucidate positive analysis.

II

1. The idea of a stationary state is clearly implicit in the *Tableau Economique* of Quesnay and the Physiocrats.[2] The underlying notion of that com-

---

1. The argument of this paper was first developed in lectures on the history of theory which I delivered at New College [Oxford] in the winter 1928–29. At that time I thought that the contrast which I drew between static states according to suppositions concerning the supply schedules of the factors of production, although, of course, obvious to anyone familiar with mathematical economics, had not been made by any "literary economist." Since then, however, I have discovered a footnote in Professor [F.H.] Knight's *Risk, Uncertainty and Profit* [Boston, 1921] (p. 143) in which this is done, and, as I had read that admirable work many times, I suppose I must have been unconsciously influenced by Professor Knight's comment. Professor Knight's note is, however, very brief, and I therefore venture to hope that my historical exegesis and contemporary applications may not be altogether otiose.

2. On the significance of the *Tableau Economique*, see August Oncken, *Oeuvres Economiques et Philosophiques de François Quesnay, fondateur du système physiocratique* (Berner Beiträge zur Geschichte der Nationalokonomie No. 3; Frankfurt and Paris, 1888), pp. 386–402; also E. Cannan, *A Review of Economic Theory* (London, 1929), pp. 25–34.

plicated arithmetical diagram is one of a state of affairs in the body economic in which production and consumption are in a condition of perfect balance. Year in, year out the same processes recur, the same circulation of goods takes place through the same channels. But the use made of this conception is different from the use which has been most customary since that day. Modern economists use the stationary state to exhibit the nature of certain *tendencies*, to show under what conditions certain kinds of change may be expected to cease. Quesnay used it rather as a model of certain *processes* and a demonstration of the conditions under which these processes could be said to be functioning healthily. It is obvious from the variants of the table given by Mirabeau that its main use was conceived to be that of a formulation of the minimum conditions of civic well-being, rather than a hypothetical construction whereby purely causal phenomena could be studied. It was hoped that actual statistics would be collected of the quantities exhibited in the table; and then, by a comparison of their mutual relationships with the ideal relationships of the table, a diagnosis could be made of the prosperity of the area of collection. It would therefore be unwise to attribute very great importance to the Physiocratic contribution to the analysis of equilibrium.

2. So far as I am able to discover, the first use of the conception in its more familiar form, and the first mention of the actual term, the stationary state, occur in the course of the celebrated chapter on wages in the *Wealth of Nations*.[1]

Adam Smith, it will be remembered, commences his treatment of wages in an "advanced society" by laying down what may be called a buyer's monopoly theory of subsistence wages. The unfortunate worker, who, in "that original state of things which precedes both the appropriation of land and the accumulation of stock," secured the whole produce of labour, now finds himself compelled to bargain with the employers for a share of it. In the face of their tacit combination he is helpless. His wages, therefore, are forced down to subsistence level – a wage, that is to say, which will keep him alive and enable him to bring up a family of just such a size as, allowing for the average expectation of life among the children of the working classes, will keep the population constant.

But, no sooner has Smith elaborated this theory, than he at once commences to replace it by another. His strong sense of reality compels him to admit that wages do not behave as such generalisations would lead one to suppose. (In a buyer's monopoly theory of subsistence wages there is, of

1. Ed. E. Cannan (London, 1904), Vol. I, pp. 66–88.

course, no question of a tendency which may be concealed by countervailing tendencies. *So long as the monopoly is operative it can act at once.*) He therefore proceeds to elaborate a new theory, a theory in which, when subsistence wages emerge at all, their emergence is due as much to forces acting on the supply side as to buyers' combinations on the side of demand. On the demand side, this theory anticipates the wage fund theory; on the supply side, the population theory of the first edition of Malthus' *Essay on Population.* And it is in the course of the development of this theory that the conception which is to be analysed in this paper first emerges.

According to this new version of the theory of wages, the demand for labour is conceived to come from certain funds which in some somewhat mysterious fashion have been "destined for the maintenance of labour." When these funds are increasing faster than the increase of labour, the tacit combination of masters breaks up. "The scarcity of hands occasions a competition among masters, who bid against one another in order to get workmen, and thus voluntarily break through the natural combination of masters not to raise wages." In these circumstances, wages rise above subsistence level. This, Smith thought, was what was happening in the England of his own day and also in North America. But if for any reason these funds cease to increase, if, to use the jargon of a later day, the wage-fund becomes stationary, then wages tend to fall. The wretched labourers multiply, and their share per head of this constant fund is reduced until it reaches that level which is sufficient to maintain the labourer and enable him to support a family of the size necessary to keep population constant. This, he thought, was what had happened in China, whose condition, he said, had "long been stationary." Finally, if the fund actually diminished, as, he thought, was happening in Bengal, then wages fall until "want, famine and mortality" have so reduced the number of labourers as once more to make a subsistence wage possible. Wages therefore form, as it were, an index showing whether the state is advancing, stationary or retrogressive. "It is in the progressive state, while the society is advancing to further acquisition, that the condition of the labouring poor seems to be the happiest and most comfortable. It is hard in the stationary and miserable in the declining state. The progressive state is in reality the cheerful and the hearty state for all the different orders of the society. The stationary is dull; the declining melancholy."

3. This then is the stationary state as it first appears in economic theory. Population is constant, capital is constant, wages are constant and profits are constant.[1] There is life, in that, year in year out, the same things are

1. Presumably technical knowledge has ceased to grow. This, however, is an assumption which was not elucidated until much later. It is not until we come to Marshall and Clark that the technical presuppositions of Static analysis are thoroughly and clearly stated.

repeated. But the fundamental conditions of economic activity remain unchanged.

But why is it stationary?

We have to reconstruct the answer from different parts of Smith's analysis. Population is stationary because the funds destined for the maintenance of labour have ceased to increase and wages are down to subsistence level. The funds destined for the maintenance of labour are stationary because the rate of profit has fallen so low that there is no further incentive to accumulate. How low this is, is difficult to say. Smith admits that the level will vary with the current risk of investment. In China he thinks, because of bad government, accumulation has ceased at 12 per cent. But no other possibility of variation is mentioned. There is no suggestion that there are different static rates in different states of society. Risk is the only cause of variation. Compensation for risk apart, the rate "must always be something more than what is sufficient to compensate the occasional losses to which every employment of stock is exposed ... Were it not more, charity or friendship could be the only motive for lending."[1] And it is suggested that where great risk is absent (as in Holland) the rate is so low that only the very wealthiest can live on interest.

4. Superficially, the stationary state which we encounter in Ricardo is much the same sort of conception.[2] Wages are at their "natural level," dictated by the cost of producing labour. Population is constant. Capital is accumulated to such a point that, the rate of profit having fallen to the minimum necessary to induce accumulation, no further saving is being made. And Ricardo equally with Smith regards the prospect of arriving in this condition with feelings of considerable repugnance: – "If we should attain the stationary state, from which I trust we are far distant...."

But, in fact, if we are willing to dig a little beneath the surface, we find a considerable difference. The structure is more complicated, the possibilities of variation more numerous. In the Smithian conception, the rate of profit is the only supply price which admits of any variation. And as we have seen, what variation there is here derives entirely from variations in the risk of investment. So far as wages are concerned the ultimate figure is more or less *objectively* determinate. It is a *physiological* subsistence level – the lowest wage which will keep the labourer alive and enable him to bring

1. *Op. cit.*, pp. 97–8.

2. See, *e.g.*, *The Collected Works of David Ricardo*, ed. J.R. McCulloch (London, 1852), pp. 59, 104, 120. There is an interesting passage in the *Letters of David Ricardo to Thomas Robert Malthus 1810–1823*, ed. James Bonar (Oxford, 1887), p. 188, in which the distinction between stationariness and stagnation is discussed.

up a family. No doubt it will vary according to climate and the death-rate. But there is no suggestion that it may vary with varying *psychological* dispositions.

But by the time Ricardo came to write his *Principles*, crudities of that sort were becoming a thing of the past so far as the inner circle of classical economists was concerned. The second edition of Malthus' *Essay on Population* had made it plain that, if people wished, population could be kept within limits other than the limit of physiological subsistence. And the researches of Torrens[1] had shown that in fact the "conventional subsistence" wage varied greatly from country to country. And therefore, although in one or two parts of his work there is a harking-back to the idea of physiological subsistence wages,[2] in the main chapter on wages, Ricardo makes it clear that for him the "natural wage" is not so much a wage which *enables* the labourer to subsist and bring up the conventional family, as a wage which *induces* him to do so. It is not a physiological so much as a psychological variable. He is clear that it varies from place to place and from time to time. And he hopes that by wise legislation this natural supply price of labour shall be pushed continually upwards. "The friends of humanity cannot but wish that in all countries the labouring classes should have a taste for comforts and enjoyments, and that they should be stimulated by all legal means in their exertion to procure them."[3]

All this means, of course, that at least one of the supply prices, the supply price of labour, is now recognised to be dependent on states of mind. Whatever the rigidity of the "natural" rate of profit, it is clear that in the Ricardian conception stationariness is conceivable at various "natural" levels of wages. There may be stationary equilibrium with a (relatively) large population and a low "natural" rate of wages. Or if the friends of humanity have had their way, it is possible that there may be stationary equilibrium with a (relatively) small population, and a high "natural" level of wages. It means, therefore – although Ricardo did not recognise this – that the stationary state is robbed of many of its terrors. According to the Smithian conception, the stationary state must be "dull" – to put it mildly. But according to Ricardo, as J.S. Mill pointed out in a celebrated passage, it need not be dull at all.[4] It may all be very pleasant and cultivated.

1. R. Torrens, *An Essay on the External Corn Trade* (London, 1820), p. 68.
2. In the chapter on gross and net revenue, for instance.
3. *On the Principles of Political Economy and Taxation*, ed. J.R. McCulloch (London, 1852), p. 55.
4. *Principles of Political Economy*, ed. W.J. Ashley (London, 1909), pp. 248–75.

5. In Mill's work we get still further refinements. With Smith and Ricardo, as we have seen, if we exclude variations due to variations of risk, the supply price of capital is treated as more or less invariable. Mill does not explicitly introduce any refinement of this conception when he is dealing specifically with the stationary state, but, in the chapter on the increase of capital, it is quite clear that he has learned from John Rae[1] the notion of a natural rate of profit which varies according to what Fisher would call the prevalent conditions of time preference, and what Rae called the effective desire of accumulation. Hence there is now the possibility of an infinite diversity of stationary equilibria with natural wages and profits at different levels.

6. All these tendencies to improvement reach what for our purpose we may regard as a culminating point in the work of Marshall. As is well known, Marshall had a certain aversion to the concept. Partly, I think, because of his temperamental dislike of all extreme abstractions, partly because of a not very clearly formulated distrust of certain apparently similar conceptions which were being elaborated on the other side of the Atlantic. "I cannot conceive," he wrote to J.B. Clark, "of a static state which resembles the real world closely enough to form a subject of profitable study ... I could no more write one book about the statical state and another about the dynamical state than I could write one book about a yacht moving three miles an hour through the water which was running against it and another about a yacht moving through still water at five miles an hour."[2] Instead he preferred the "less violent assumptions" of what he said was "not quite accurately called the statical method," by which "we fix our minds on some central point; we suppose it for the time being to be reduced to a *stationary* state; and we then study in relation to it the forces that affect the things by which it is surrounded and any tendency there may be to equilibrium of these forces."[3]

---

1. *Statement of some New Principles of Political Economy, exposing the Fallacies of the System of Free Trade and of some other Doctrines maintained in the "Wealth of Nations"* (Boston, 1834).
2. *Memorials of Alfred Marshall*, ed. A.C. Pigou (London, 1925), p. 415.
3. *Principles of Economics*, 8th edn (London, 1920), p. 369. For an interesting discussion of the contrast between Marshall's "statical method" and Clark's "static analysis" see Redvers Opie, "Die Quasirente in Marshalls Lehrgebäude," *Archiv für Sozialwissenschaft und Sozialpolitik*, vol. 60 (1928), pp. 251–79. I suspect Mr. Opie of the opinion that the aversion from heroic abstraction was a virtue in Marshall in that it made his constructions more realistic. Personally I should be inclined to urge that in certain connections (increasing returns, for example) it was responsible for a good deal of theoretical confusion. This is not to say that Clark's static state is superior to Marshall's statical method, but rather that, as suggested above, the stationary state itself is superior to the more limited conception.

Nevertheless, from time to time a stationary state does make its appearance in the *Principles.*[1] It is employed (very tentatively, it is true) to demonstrate the relationship (or perhaps the absence of a relationship) between real costs and expenses of production. It appears again in certain versions of the preliminary view of distribution, and I should be prepared to argue, in spite of Marshall himself, that it underlies much of what there is of validity in the results achieved by the "statical method." It is no doubt in one sense a much more attenuated instrument than the original conception. Smith thought the stationary state might actually arrive, that it had, in fact, appeared in China and other places. Marshall is quite clear that the stationary state is a fiction, an analytical instrument simply.[2] But the basic conception is there, and that, of course, in a form whose effectiveness is vastly enhanced by all Marshall's own analytical improvements. There is no longer any doubt as to the variability of the various supply functions. There is no longer any question of causal pre-eminence for any one factor in the total equilibrium. It is the stationary state of the classics lifted on to a new plane of scientific precision.

III

1. Meanwhile, there was being developed, on the other side of the Atlantic, a method of analysis apparently similar to the one whose history we have been following, but, in fact, in important respects substantially different. To these developments we must now turn.

The innovation derives from Mill. We have seen already that in his chapter on the stationary state Mill uses a conception not radically dissimilar from that of his predecessors. So too in other passages. But there is one passage

1. To trace the shadowy appearances, disappearances and reappearances of this "famous fiction" in the various editions would demand a paper in itself, and I suspect it would be well worth doing. We shall never understand the real significance of the Marshallian system until a *variorum* edition of the *Principles* is published. The main sections in which it is used relate to the connection between real costs and expenses of production (e.g. 3rd edn [1895], p. 425, and Appendix H, para. 4, 6th edn [1898], p. 810), and to the conception of normal price and the representative firm (e.g. 6th edn, pp. 366 *et seq.*). It appears also in earlier editions of the "Preliminary survey of distribution" at the commencement of Book VI.

Appendix H on the "Limitations of the use of statical assumptions in regard to increasing return" is very important as an indication of Marshall's attitude with regard to equilibrium analysis in general, and shows clearly, I think, the nature of the step which has to be taken if the various disputes now current with regard to the laws of returns are ever to be satisfactorily settled. I hope to return to this in another paper.

2. I am indebted to my friend, Mr. A.W. Stonier of Christ Church [Oxford] for some very valuable comments on this aspect of Marshall's system.

which bears a different interpretation. It occurs at the commencement of the section on the influence of Progress.[1] Mill is reviewing the earlier sections on production, distribution and value, and making plans, as it were, for future developments.

"The three preceding parts," he says, "include as detailed a view as our limits permit, of what, by a happy generalisation of a mathematical phrase, has been called the statics of the subject. We have surveyed the field of economic facts, and have examined how they stand related to one another as causes and effects: what circumstances determine the amount of production, of employment for labour, of capital and population: what laws regulate rent, profits and wages ... We have thus obtained a collective view of the economic phenomena of society, considered as existing simultaneously. We have ascertained, to a certain extent, the principles of their interdependence, and when the state of some of the elements is known, we should now be in a position to infer in a general way the contemporaneous state of most of the others. All this, however, has only put us in possession of the ... laws of a stationary and unchanging society. We have still to consider the economical condition of mankind as liable to change ... We have to consider what these changes are: what are their laws and what their ultimate tendencies; thereby adding a theory of motion to our theory of equilibrium ... the dynamics of political economy to the statics."

Now it is probable that, in writing this passage, Mill had nothing more in mind than the existing notion of the stationary state, and the difference between the phenomena of such a state and the phenomena of a society which is still advancing. That at any rate is what seems to emerge from a study of the actual content of the subsequent chapters of the section.

But it is clear that, taken apart from its general context, it is capable of another interpretation. Taken as it stands, it seems to say, "We have studied what happens when the factors of production are constant. Now we must proceed to ask what causes their numbers to change." That at least is suggested by the passage, "we have still to consider the condition of mankind as liable to change ... we have to consider what these changes are and what are their laws." In fact, as stated earlier in the passage, the laws of change in the numbers of the population and the quantity of accumulated capital were considered in the first part of the book. But it is easy to see how reading this passage, and being impressed perhaps by the verbal distinction, one might come to divide the statics and dynamics of the subject on this plan. The statics should deal with what happens when the factors are given. The dynamics, with the laws of change in the quantity of the factors.

---

1. Ashley's edition of the *Principles of Political Economy*, p. 695.

2. Whether this interpretation of Mill's influence be true or not, it was the plan actually followed by J.B. Clark in his celebrated classification of static and dynamic phenomena in the opening chapters of *The Distribution of Wealth*. And it is usually held that, in the matter of terminology at least, Clark's debt to Mill is obvious.

Clark reaches his conception of what he calls a static state by abstracting the forces of social progress. "In any given society," he says,[1] "five generic changes are going on, every one of which reacts on the structure of society by changing the arrangements of that group system which it is the work of catallactics to study.

1. Population is increasing.
2. Capital is increasing.
3. Methods of production are improving.
4. The forms of industrial establishments are changing.
5. The wants of consumers are multiplying."

These influences he thinks are to be called dynamic. A world from which they were absent would be a static state.

To study this state, therefore, we must consider changes of this sort absent. "We must in imagination sweep remorselessly from the field the whole set of influences that we have called dynamic. We shall ... stop ... every one of the five organic changes that are actually moving and relocating the economic agents ... Population and capital are treated as neither increasing nor diminishing ... inventions are not made, and processes of production do not change."[2]

3. Now at first sight a static state of this sort would appear to be exactly similar to the stationary state we find in the classics and in Marshall. And there can be no doubt that Clark thought it to be similar. "The term natural," he says,[3] "as used by classical economists in connection with standards of wages and interest, was unconsciously employed as an equivalent of the term static ..." And again,[4] "What the Ricardian theory unconsciously and imperfectly accomplished was the separation of static from dynamic forces. It was really studying a static world, but it studied that world with no complete idea of its nature. There was not in the mind of any of these early writers any

1. *The Distribution of Wealth: a Theory of Wages, Interest, and Profits* (New York, 1899), p. 56.
2. *Op. cit.*, p. 71 *et seq.*
3. *Distribution of Wealth*, p. vi.
4. *Ibid.*, p. 69.

connection of the two distinct sets of forces that are really acting together; and there could therefore be no systematic plan for studying them separately. In reality their 'natural prices' were static prices. They were those to which an actual market would conform if dynamic influences were wholly to cease ... Stop all increase of population and wealth ... but let industry go on and perfect competition continue, and you bring the world into a state in which the standard theoretical prices will be the real ones."

But, plausible as this identification may appear at first sight, it is, I believe, completely mistaken. It is perfectly true that in both the Clarkian and the classical construction the quantities of the factors of production are constant. *But* – and this is the fundamental difference which it is desired here to exhibit – *in the one, this constancy is the condition of equilibrium; in the other, it is simply one of the resultants of the equilibrating process*. In the Clarkian state, population and capital are to be constant – they are *not allowed* to vary. In the classical constructions, population and capital are constant, but this is because, together with wages and interest, etc., they have reached a position of rest. You can no more say of such a construction that wages and interest are constant because population and capital are constant, than you can say that population and capital are constant because wages and interest are constant. All that you can say is that, owing to absence of change of consumers' demand and knowledge of the technique of production on the one hand, or fundamental change in the human or material equipment of production on the other,[1] a position of rest has been reached. The Marshallian analogy of the balls in the bowl was designed expressly to elucidate this conception.

There is one passage in the *Distribution of Wealth* in which Clark appears to contemplate this hypothesis. In this passage[2] he allows that "the fixed condition" of capital, assumed in static analysis, "cannot exist ... unless the motive for saving something from incomes is not equal to the motive for spending it. In the static state there is no abstinence, or creation of new capital, because, with the capital now on hand, men would lose more by foregoing pleasure and making their fund larger than they would gain by doing so." This passage is important. It shows that on essentials there is no difference of opinion as to facts – that is to say, tendencies operative in the real world – between the Clarkian and the neo-classical tradition. But it cannot be

1. This rather awkward wording has been chosen in order to make it clear that anything like exhaustion of mineral resources must be excluded from the strict conception of stationary equilibrium. I am not sure that it is always fully realised that this is the case. A conception of equilibrium that is to be fully realistic *must* be a conception of moving equilibrium. But this does not make the remoter construction any less convenient as a first approximation.

2. *Op. cit.*, p. 136.

held to vitiate the interpretation which has just been given of the general Clarkian conception of static laws and static conditions. For in his very next sentence Clark goes on to say that "the whole subject of creating capital belongs to the dynamic division of the science of economics." Now it should be abundantly clear that if as a matter of hypothesis you stop tendencies to change *other than those assumed to be implicit in the form of the supply and demand functions*, then capital creation and population may go on for some time before stationary conditions in the classical sense are ultimately attained. At any given time, if you stop the creation of capital and the increase of population (demand being assumed constant), then static equilibrium in the Clarkian sense is only so far distant as economic friction delays it. But if you merely stop ultimate changes of taste and technique, then, if the effective desire of accumulation is of a certain order, capital increase (to say nothing of the increase of population[1]) may go on for an almost infinitely long period.

Moreover, the whole treatment of the rest of the book is at variance with this particular passage. Again and again we are told that we must stop in imagination the growth of population and the increase of capital if we are to be in a position to examine the working of static laws. But, of course, if you assume stationary conditions as Marshall and the classics assumed them, this degree of hypothetical violence is unnecessary. All that is necessary is that technique and demand of all kinds (including demand for income in terms of effort and abstinence) shall remain unchanged, and, if exhaustible natural resources are not employed, the stationariness desired will then arrive as part of the general equilibrium. This is perfectly clear from the Marshallian treatment. It is no less implied by the constructions of his predecessors. It was the absence of improvements which characterised the stationary state of Ricardo.[2]

Finally, in this connection, we may appeal to Clark's own criterion of static conditions. "The absence of any flow of labour or of capital from one group to another is the sure outward sign," he says, "of the static condition."[3] Is not this insistence on what may be called horizontal adjustment according to demand for different commodities, rather than on such adjustment *combined* with what may be called vertical adjustment according to demand for

1. In the classical and Marshallian constructions there is supposed to be a functional connection between wages and the production of labourers. It is a matter for dispute how far such a supposition is justifiable.

2. Mill in an incautious moment suggested that improvements might continue in a stationary state. Of course if stationary state is used to designate merely a community where population has ceased to grow, this is true. But if it is used in the technical sense we are discussing it is highly improbable. It would be an odd series of inventions which had no influence on the supply of savings.

3. *Op. cit.*, p. 400.

income from work and abstinence, proof sufficient of the contention here urged? It is impossible to conceive that one who held consistently the view that a stationary state of population was a result rather than a pre-established condition of the stationary equilibrium he was contemplating would have failed to mention it at this juncture. Of course it could be argued that stationariness at any one point implies stationariness at any other, so that stationariness between groups is as good an index of stationary equilibrium in its fullest sense as stationariness in the total quantities of factors of production *and* stationariness between groups. And up to a point that argument might be sustained. But it can scarcely be adduced in the interpretation of one who has insisted that, in order to study static conditions, we must keep constant the supply of factors, and watch the resulting equilibrium.[1]

IV

1. If this analysis of the position be correct, then we must recognise not one general class of "static states" and "static laws," but two: the classical conception in which the condition of stationariness is the resultant of the balancing of forces tending to change, and the Clarkian in which the factors of production are stationary by hypothesis, and equilibrium is attained within these conditions. Both rule out inventions and fundamental changes in nature and human beings. But the one admits the possibility of variations of labour and capital, the other excludes these by definition. In an ultimate classification of course the Clarkian conception can be regarded as a limiting case of the wider concept – the supply curves of capital and labour exhibiting absolute inelasticity. But it is clear that this is not how it is conceived by its inventor.

Now in a matter of abstractions of this sort there is no question of rightness or wrongness. If Clark chooses to assume that labour and capital do not increase, and if he calls the description of what happens under such circumstances, static analysis, we cannot gainsay him. In judging such constructions we do not ask whether they are *right or wrong* – that is a question which is only relevant to the logic of the subsequent inferences: we ask only whether they are *appropriate*.

In fact, of course, each construction is appropriate for particular stages of analysis. It is convenient for some purposes to suppose that the supplies of the ultimate factors are given. For other purposes it is more convenient to

1. It could be argued further that unless the interpretation of Clark given above is correct, Clark's static laws of wages, etc. are wrong. If supply is not fixed it is false to say that wages are *determined* by marginal productivity. But on all this see below.

assume that they have a certain flexibility. If we wish to study the short period effects of a change in technique, *e.g.*, the Clarkian hypothesis is sufficient. If we wish to take account of the subtler but more far-reaching effects over time, we do well to have recourse to the wider conception. The modern economist with even the most fleeting acquaintance with the mathematical theory of equilibrium, will recognise in the two constructions we have been examining, *not competing abstractions, but successive stages of exposition.*

None the less it is fundamentally important that they should be kept apart, that the difference should be clearly shown and its implications fully realised. We have seen already, in discussing the significance of the two hypotheses as regards the distance in time from the ultimate equilibrium of any given disequilibrium, how vast this difference may be. We see it still more vividly if we survey a few of the more prominent controversies of modern times in which the distinction has not been clearly recognised. It is arguable, I think, that most of the more respectable disputes of the past hundred years have arisen just because of a failure on the part of the disputants to define clearly their ultimate assumptions with regard to the conditions of equilibrium.

2. We may take as our first example the celebrated disputes of the 'nineties and the first ten years of this century concerning the ultimate nature of real costs. Are the forces limiting the supply of particular commodities to be regarded as being of the same order as the forces limiting demand? Or are we to admit elements of real costs which are not of this nature? Are all costs ultimately resolvable into foregone products, or are labour-pain and abstinence to be regarded as ultimate? Here there was a battle of the giants: on the one side Marshall and Edgeworth, on the other the great Austrians, together with Wicksteed and some of the Americans.[1]

Now I am far from arguing that there was nothing but misunderstanding in this controversy. No doubt it did bring to light fundamental difficulties in the old doctrine of real costs, and pave the way for the now almost universal recognition that even when disutilities are taken into account they are ultimately to be regarded as being the pull of foregone leisure or foregone present income – opportunity costs rather than disutilities in the sense of the

1. See, *e.g.*, [F.Y.] Edgeworth's review of Böhm-Bawerk's *The Positive Theory of Capital*, *Economic Journal*, vol. 2 (June 1892), pp. 328–37 (reprinted in *Papers relating to Political Economy* [London, 1925], Vol. 3, pp. 22–30); E. von Böhm-Bawerk, "Der letzte Masstab des Guterwertes," *Gesammelte Schriften*, ed. F.X. Weiss (Vienna and Leipzig, 1924), pp. 404–70; David I. Green, "Pain-cost and opportunity-cost," *Quarterly Journal of Economics*, vol. 8 (January 1894), pp. 218–29; H.J. Davenport, *Value and Distribution: a critical and constructive study* (Chicago, 1908); P.H. Wicksteed, *The Common Sense of Political Economy* (London, 1910), Chapter IX.

old hedonistic calculus.[1] But, surveyed from the calm distance of a quarter of a century, it is abundantly clear that the main difference of opinion arose not so much from a difference of opinion as to the totality of forces operative in the economic system, but from a failure on the part of the participants to perceive that each was adopting a different assumption with regard to the conditions of equilibrium. As we have seen, Marshall did not greatly favour the use of the Clarkian terminology, and the great Austrians Wieser and Böhm-Bawerk were writing before it had been made known by Schumpeter to continental circles. But close examination of their respective work reveals precisely the difference of assumption we have been examining. Marshall and Edgeworth were assuming the fluidity of supply of capital and labour which was characteristic of the classical conception of equilibrium. Böhm-Bawerk and Wieser were assuming the fixity of supply which is the assumption of the Clarkian statics. Granted this initial difference of assumption, the conclusions were bound to be different. If the supply of factors is fixed, "disutility," whether conceived in the terms of old-fashioned hedonism or in the more modern sense of displaced resistances, is simply a matter of foregone *products*. If, however, flexible supplies are contemplated, clearly it has a wider significance. We tend to regard it as foregone leisure in the case of work, foregone income in the present in the case of the use of capital, whereas Marshall and Edgeworth were still thinking in terms of something more absolute; but the contrast with the narrower hypothesis is the same. Eventually this came to light,[2] but not before much ink had been wasted.

3. Secondly, we may take certain disputes concerning the theory of wages. Clark, as is well known, asserted that in a state of pure competition, wages are *determined* by final productivity. Others, recollecting the variability of labour supply, have insisted that, since until the form of the supply function is known one cannot tell what productivity is to be regarded as final, this cannot be admitted. Wages measure or express final productivity, but the process of determination is multiple. Of course these objections are fully justified in so far as the Clarkian theory pretends to be a complete explanation of wage determination. But in so far as Clark is merely asserting what would happen in his static state

1. Mr. [H.D.] Henderson's *Supply and Demand* (London and Cambridge, 1922) may be regarded as indicating the definite abandonment of the old absolute conception of real costs. Professor Pigou's treatment of the real costs of war (*The Political Economy of War* [London, 1921], Chapter III) also follows the Austrian conception. But Mr. Henderson does not show very clearly how, if the supply of capital and labour are to be taken as variable, the resistances are to be worked into the opportunity cost concept. This, I think, has been more satisfactorily worked out by Professor Knight (*Risk, Uncertainty and Profit*, Chapter III).

2. See F.Y. Edgeworth, "Professor Böhm-Bawerk on the ultimate standard of value", *Papers relating to Political Economy*, Vol. 3, pp. 59–64.

they miss the point. In the Clarkian state the supply of labour is given. There is no need to elaborate this point at length, as it is well known. Carver dealt with this limitation of the productivity theory at a very early stage,[1] and Mr. Dobb has a very elegant discussion of the same matter in his recent work on Wages.[2]

4. Thirdly, we may take the age-long controversies concerning rent and cost. In what sense, if any, is it true to say that rent does not enter into cost of production? Here, too, we have a case in which much of the controversy of recent years is seen to depend on the last analysis upon differences of hypothetical construction rather than differences of actual logic.[3]

If we are considering a state of equilibrium in which the total supplies of the factors of production are fixed by hypothesis – the Clarkian static state – then clearly rent has the same relation to price as any other income. It is true that if we go to the rentless margin we can say that rent does not "enter into" cost there. But it is equally true that if we go to the wageless margin we can say that wages do not "enter into" cost there. But this is a mere tautology, and, of course, proves nothing. In the conditions here contemplated, costs are obviously the outlays which have to be made in order to secure the use of the factors of production for the production of this commodity rather than for the production of that. Neither from the point of view of the entrepreneur, nor from the point of view of society, is there any reason to regard payment for "land," in the Ricardian sense, as being on a footing different from the payment for other agents.

And, so far as the point of view of the entrepreneur is concerned, this is still true when we turn to contemplate the phenomena of a stationary equilibrium, in which the supplies of the technically variable agents are free to vary – the stationary state of the classics. It was Marshall himself who insisted that "land is but a particular form of capital from the point of view of the individual producer. The question whether a farmer has carried his cultivation of a particular piece of land as far as he profitably can, and whether he should try to force more from it or to take in another piece of land, is of the same kind as the question whether he should buy a new plough or try to get a little more work out of his present stock of ploughs ..."[4] But from the point of view of society there is this difference between the payments made for the

1. Thomas N. Carver, *The Distribution of Wealth* (New York, 1904).
2. M.H. Dobb, *Wages* (London and Cambridge, 1928), Chapters IV and V.
3. Of course this is not the whole story. It would be hard to contend that all who have supported the proposition have been alive to the consideration regarding the reversibility of the rent analysis adduced by Clark and Wicksteed, or that all who have opposed it have understood the implications of the idea of the intensive margin. But we are dealing here with the differences of opinion of really capable economists!
4. *Principles*, 8th edn, p. 430.

use of Ricardian "land" and agents in fixed supply in general, and payments for the use of factors in flexible supply, that we must assume that, if prices were different, the supplies of the flexible factors would be different; but we need not make any such assumptions about the supply of the fixed factors. By definition their supply would be unaltered. It is still undesirable to say that rent does not form part of cost. But in the sense in which cost is to be interpreted as the price of keeping supply constant, there is significance of a sort in the Ricardian proposition that rent does not "enter into" this conception. Rent in the Ricardian sense is still a transfer expense. Other costs are stationary supply prices. It was clearly recognition of this which led Marshall to remark that "it is *wisest not* to say that rent does not enter into cost of production, for that will confuse many people. But it is *wicked* to say that rent does enter into cost of production, because that is *sure* to be applied in such a way as to lead to the denial of subtle truths which, in spite of their being subtle, are of the very highest importance scientifically, and also in relation to the practical well-being of the world."[1]

It is improbable that at the present day there would be found many economists who would regard it as "*wicked*" to say that rent does enter into costs of production. But it is true that, if we are contemplating a stationary equilibrium of the kind conceived by the classics, the proposition that it does not, does imply, even if it does not state correctly, subtle truths which we should be ill advised to lose sight of. And it is significant that those who have urged most strongly for its retention have been those who have learnt their analysis from classical sources whereas those who have opposed it have been very largely under the influence of Clark.

5. Finally, we may take a case of more recent interest – the dynamic theory of interest propounded by Professor Schumpeter. This is a theory which, in my view, is quite definitely wrong. It cannot be salvaged by making its assumptions more explicit. Nevertheless, it seems possible that the ambiguity we have been examining may be responsible for what seems to be the flaw in Professor Schumpeter's reasoning.

The theory may be summarised in two propositions.[2] The first is negative. Under static conditions, says Schumpeter, there can be no interest. All costs

1. *Memorials of Alfred Marshall*, p. 436.

2. It is naturally not possible to provide a complete account of Professor Schumpeter's theory here. I hope to do this on some future occasion. This part of his work is not as well known as it should be to English readers, and although I believe his theory of interest to be wrong, it is wrong, I believe, in a way which has positive significance. Certainly no one can read either *Das Wesen und der Hauptinhalt der theoretischen Nationalökonomie* (Munich and Leipzig, 1908) or *Theorie der wirtschaftlichen Entwicklung* (Munich, 1926) without feeling that his outlook on certain parts of economic analysis can never be quite the same again. For a thorough exposition of the theory in question these two works must be consulted.

are to be imputed back to the two ultimate factors of production, Labour and Land. All incomes, therefore, are either wages or "rent." There is no third class of static incomes. It follows – and this is the second and positive proposition – that interest must be a dynamic income. It emerges only when conditions are changing, and if change were to cease it would disappear. Clark urged that profit was essentially a dynamic surplus; Schumpeter goes one further and urges that the same is true of interest.

Now, there are certain features of Schumpeter's theory with which agreement is possible. We may agree, for instance, that in periods of change there are operative certain frictions which may result in more saving being imposed on the community than would have been undertaken voluntarily if these frictions had not been operative. On this point Mr. Robertson's analysis remorselessly drives home one of the main contentions of the Schumpeterian theory of development. We may admit, too, that in so far as interest is defined as the yield of *new* capital in the sense of net additions to the social stock, it is a phenomenon which will be absent from any conception of static conditions, for, by definition, capital is not increasing.

But in so far as interest is considered not as a payment for new accumulation, but as a net return (*reinertrag*) to produced means of production (*produzierte produktionsmitteln*) – and, in spite of some ambiguities, this is, I think, the interpretation which Schumpeter would have us put on the negative part of his theory – the theory does not seem to be acceptable. So long as we assume private property and exchange it is difficult to conceive a static state in which there exists produced means of production which earn no net income. Why should labour and the use of material factors be devoted to the maintenance of the produced means of production if no net remuneration is forthcoming? It is when we encounter a theory of this sort that we realise the unassailable core of truth underlying the old abstinence theory.

But why should Schumpeter have propounded such a theory?

Partly, no doubt, because of a sense of the practical importance of elements of transitory gain in the determination of actual rates of interest. This I should be inclined to say is the element of truth in the background. But partly, I think, because of a curious misunderstanding of the Clarkian analysis and a reliance upon the Clarkian construction in a way which prevents recognition of the existence of 'static tendencies' in the wider sense of this term. Schumpeter's debt to Clark in this matter is obvious. He adopts the terminology. He bases his initial discussion of development on Clark's five-fold classification. And if this diagnosis is correct, in the last analysis, it is the rigidity of the supply of capital in the Clarkian construction which blinds him to the nature of the forces making for the emergence of interest under conditions which are not dynamic.

We can see this quite clearly if we look closely at his argument in the first chapter of the *Entwicklung*. There is no abstinence in the static state, he argues, following a passage of Clark's which we have already examined.[1] And, as we have seen, if abstinence is to be regarded merely as that degree of refraining from present consumption which gives rise to net addition to the supply of capital, we can agree with him. But if abstinence is to be regarded, not only as a refusal to consume in the present in order that the sources of future income may be *enlarged*, but also as a refusal to enhance one's consumption now in order that the income of the future may not be depleted, then it seems to me that he is at fault and the Clarkian terminology is misleading.[2] But Schumpeter has foreseen some such objection as this, and he proceeds to argue that under static conditions there is no reason to alter the distribution of one's income through time. Given constant needs, he argues, as others have argued before him,[3] the maximum satisfaction will be attained by a constant flow through time. Under such conditions, to encroach upon capital, now, to enhance the income of the present at the expense of the income of the future, would be folly. The gain now does not counterbalance the loss then. The argument is valid, but it does not prove that interest is absent when conditions are not changing. On the contrary, it is the most important part of the case for the view that there must be interest in such circumstances. *For if there were no yield to the use of capital* (no *reinertrag*) *there would be no reason to refrain from consuming it*. If produced means of production are not productive of a net product, why devote resources to maintaining them when these resources might be devoted to providing present enjoyment? One would not have one's cake rather than eat it, if there were no gain to be derived from having it. It is, in short, *an* interest rate, which, other things being given, keeps the stationary state stationary – the rate at which it does not pay to turn income into capital or capital into income. If interest were to disappear the stationary state would cease to be stationary. Schumpeter can argue that no *ac*cumulation will be made once stationary equilibrium has been attained. But he is not entitled to argue that there will be no *de*cumulation unless he admits the existence of interest.

What has happened, I think, is this. Schumpeter has based his static analysis upon Clarkian constructions in which the supply of capital is *held* rigid. Then when he comes to argue that there is no interest unless there is dynamic

1. *Entwicklung*, p. 48.

2. Clark himself, of course, held a productivity theory of interest. We have seen that in this one passage he correctly formulates the conditions of stationary equilibrium in the wider sense.

3. E.g. Adolphe Landry, whose *L'Intérêt du Capital* (Paris, 1904) is in many ways the best treatment of this important subject.

change, ignoring the fact that a wider conception of stationary equilibrium is possible, he is blind to the consideration that if things are free to move, stationariness depends *inter alia* upon the interest payment being at a certain level. Such an interpretation may seem fantastic. Yet it is the only reason I am able to conceive for his apparent unawareness of the significance of the possibility of decumulation.[1] It is no accident, I suggest that when he is discussing the distribution of income over time, he chooses a case where the possibility of decumulation in a straightforward way is absent – the income of a pensioner of the state![2]

---

1. There is one passage in the *Entwicklung* (p. 48) in which Schumpeter admits the possibility of abstinence in the sense of refraining from decumulation, but he brushes it aside as irrelevant to his construction: "Von Abstinenz im Sinne von Nichtkonsumption der Ertragsquellen kann nicht die Rede sein, weil es unter unsern Voraussetzungen andre Ertragsquellen als Arbeit und Boden nicht gibt." I confess I find this incomprehensible. Either there exist "produced means of production," or there do not. If they exist, then, if they are to be maintained, other factors of production must provide for their maintenance, and decumulation will consist in using these factors for making provision for present enjoyment. Or they do not exist, in which case to deny the existence of a return to them is merely tautologous and proves nothing whatever. To state dogmatically that "Arbeit und Boden" are the only "Ertragsquellen" in any static conditions is, of course, to beg the question completely.

2. It might be argued – I do not think it would be argued thus by Schumpeter himself, but it might occur to readers unacquainted with his actual theorem – that all he is denying is the existence of interest in what have been here called Clarkian conditions. I do not think that this would save the theory (Professor Knight has shown that even under such conditions a rate of capitalisation is implicit: *Risk, Uncertainty and Profit*, pp. 129–40), but in any case the interpretation cannot be accepted. Schumpeter's main contention is the positive one that interest is only conceivable under dynamic changing conditions. If the argument outlined above is correct, *a* rate of interest would exist if there were no change in the economic system but the factors were free to vary. Such a state of affairs, the stationary state of the classics, cannot by the wildest stretch of terminology be described as dynamic!

5 On the Elasticity of Demand for Income in Terms of Effort

From *Economica*, vol. 10 (June 1930), pp. 123–9.

1. It is a generally accepted proposition of theoretical economics that the effects of a change in the terms on which incomes from work can be obtained depend upon the elasticity of demand for income in terms of effort.[1] If the elasticity of demand for income in terms of effort is greater than unity, then the effects of a tax or a fall in wage rates will be a diminution of work done and the effects of a bounty or a rise in wage rates will be an increase in work done. If it is less than unity, then the opposite movements are to be expected.

2. These propositions are capable of demonstration by the familiar geometrical constructions of either (*a*) unit or (*b*) integral demand curves. The only difference between the constructions relevant here and those of commodity price analysis is that the prices exhibited will be, not money, but effort prices.

(*a*) Thus, if we employ the unit demand apparatus, we measure quantity of income demanded along *OX* and the effort price of income along *OY*. The curve *dd′* exhibits the conditions of demand, and the quantity of work done for any given income will be shown by a rectangle formed by erecting perpendiculars on *OX* and *OY* to cut any point of equilibrium (*P*) in *dd′*. If e.g. the effort price of income is OE_1 then the quantity of income which will be earned will be OI_1, and the amount of work done will be $OE_1 P_1 I_1$.

The effects of a change in the terms on which income can be obtained can be shown by shifting *E*. Let us suppose for instance the imposition of a uniform income-tax which shifts *E* from E_1 to E_2. Then the quantity of income earned will shift to I_2 and the change in the amount of work done will

1. See Hugh Dalton, *Principles of Public Finance*, 2nd edn (London, 1929), pp. 100–8, or D.H. Robertson, *Banking Policy and the Price Level* (London, 1926), Chapters I and II *passim*. It is possible, of course, to reformulate this proposition in terms of the elasticity of supply of effort, and for some purposes it is convenient to do so. But there is much to be said for exhibiting all psychological variables as phenomena of demand. See P.H. Wicksteed, *The Common Sense of Political Economy* (London, 1910), Book II, Chapter IV, and "The scope and method of political economy in the light of the 'marginal' theory of value and of distribution," *Economic Journal*, vol. 24 (March 1914), pp. 1–23.

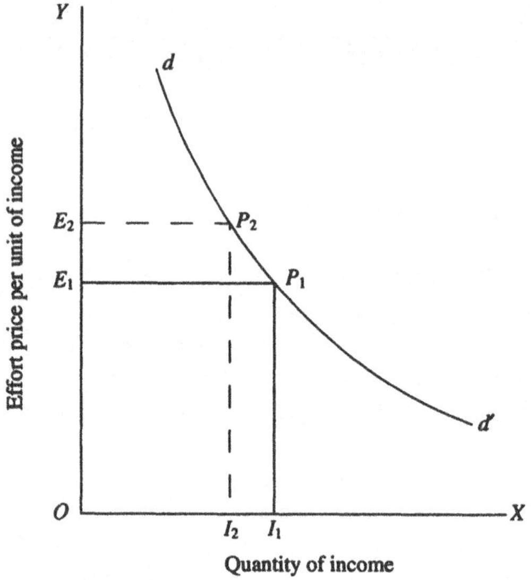

be shown by the difference between $E_1P_1I_1O$ and $E_2P_2I_2O$. If in this region dd' shows an elasticity greater than one this difference will be negative (i.e. less work will be done). If it is less than one the difference will be positive (i.e. more work will be done).

(*b*) The integral apparatus shows the same result with even greater clarity. Along OX we continue to measure quantity of income. Along OY, however, we measure the total amounts of effort which will be expended for different quantities of income. (That is to say, what was a rectangle on the unit apparatus has become a line on this apparatus.) Od is the total demand curve. The terms on which income can be obtained will evidently be an angular magnitude, the tangent of the angle $G_1\ OX$. Thus in the case depicted if the terms on which income can be obtained are represented by tan $G_1\ OX$ we get equilibrium at P_1 with OI_1, income earned for an expenditure of OE_1 effort.

Now suppose a tax imposed. We may represent this by swinging OG to the left. (To get OI_1 before, it was necessary to expend I_1P_1 effort. Now it is necessary to expend I_1Q_1. Equilibrium is re-established at P_2 with OI_2 income earned and OE_2 income expended. Since, in this region, Od shows an elasticity less than unity, OE_2 is greater than OE_1 (i.e. more work is done).

3. The propositions thus analysed are purely formal in character. They explain what will happen if the conditions of demand are of a certain nature. To discover what the conditions of demand are in any particular case, it is

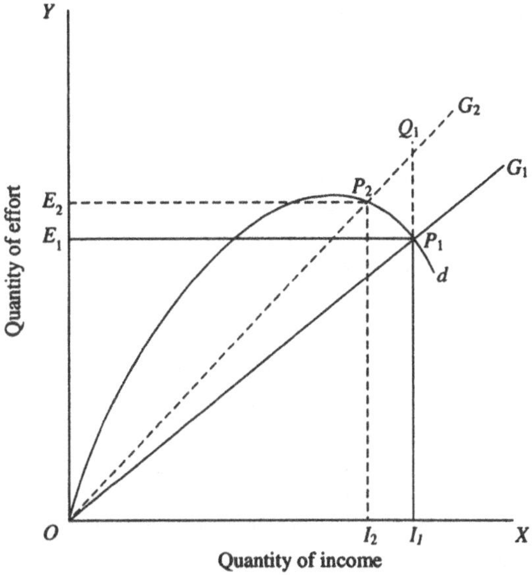

generally supposed that we must rely upon observation. We cannot predict *a priori* what the effects of a change in taxation or of a change in wage-rates will be; we must ascertain the probable elasticity of demand for income in terms of effort of the taxpayers or wage-earners concerned.

4. In recent years, however, propositions have been advanced which suggest that formal analysis enables us to predict that the elasticity of demand in the case of effort demand for income must always be less than unity – that is to say that the imposition of a tax will always have the effect of making a man work more, and a rise in his wage rates will always make him work less. If these propositions were true, they would obviously be of the highest *practical* importance – the effect on output of higher taxation need have no terrors for needy Chancellors of the Exchequer – and since they have been advanced by authorities no less eminent than Professor Pigou and Professor Knight, they clearly deserve the very closest attention.

5. The arguments of both the authorities mentioned involve in one form or another implicit appeal to the "law" or assumption of the declining marginal utility of units of income. Now *prima facie* it is difficult to see how this "law" or assumption justifies the inferences which appear to be based on it. *The assumption that, as income increases, the utility to an individual of additional units declines, justifies us indeed in inferring that the curve which exhibits the condition of demand for income in terms of effort will slope downwards, but it*

does not seem to justify the assumption that this curve must always cut a rectangular hyperbola negatively (i.e. that it must show an elasticity less than one at all reaches). The assumption or "law" lays it down that the final degree of utility diminishes, but it does not *prima facie* say anything about the *rate* of diminution.

6. But let us examine more closely the actual arguments concerned. Professor Knight's is the more general and will be taken first.

Professor Knight's argument concerns the effect of a change in wage rates. "In so far as men act rationally," he argues,[1] "... they will at a higher rate divide their time between wage earning and non-industrial uses in such a way as to earn *more money* but to work *fewer hours*." And he justifies this proposition by the following reasoning. "Suppose that at a higher rate per hour or per piece, a man previously at the perfect equilibrium adjustment works as before and earns a proportionately higher income. When, now, he goes to spend the extra money, he will naturally want to increase his expenditure for many commodities consumed and to take on some new ones. To divide his resources in such a way as to preserve equal importance of equal expenditures in all fields he must evidently lay out part of his new funds for increased leisure; i.e. buy back some of his working time or spend some of his money by the process of not earning it."

At first sight the argument appears overwhelmingly convincing, sufficient even to overcome the reflection of common-sense that, if it were true, it would follow that it would always be futile to offer rational men permanently higher wages if it was desired to elicit a permanently increased supply of work. But closer inspection seems to reveal a flaw. Professor Knight's argument assumes that the prices of the commodities constituting real income are unaltered. This is presumably true so far as money prices are concerned. But the relevant conception in this connection is not *money price* but *effort price*, and a change in the rate at which money income can be earned, money prices remaining constant, *constitutes* a change in the effort price of commodities. *The money price is the same but the effort price is diminished.* And, that being the case, the question whether more or less effort is expended on commodities is obviously still an open one. It depends on the elasticity of demand for income in terms of effort.

This may sound abstract, but if it is thought of in concrete terms, it becomes very simple. If real income be conceived as consisting of a flow of one commodity, say, bananas, and the process of producing bananas as an exchange of effort for income, then it is surely clear that, if for some reason the effort price

1. *Risk, Uncertainty and Profit* (Boston, 1921), pp. 117–18.

of bananas (real income) diminishes (a change equivalent to a rise in money wage rates), it is entirely a matter of elasticity of demand for bananas (real income) whether more or less effort is given for them, just as, if the money price of bananas changes, it is entirely a matter of elasticity whether more or less money is given for them.

The same objection can be put yet another way. In Professor Knight's example leisure is purchased by sacrificing income. We may therefore conceive – as he does – of a *real income price of leisure*. Now when the money rate of wages rises (commodity prices remaining the same) the real income price of leisure (the cost of leisure in terms of real income sacrificed) rises. And when the price of leisure (or anything else) rises it is not at all clear that more will be bought even out of an increased real income. Again it is all a matter of elasticity.

7. Professor Pigou's proposition[1] relates to the effect of a tax on the willingness to work of an individual. "Since a part of his income is taken away, the last unit of income will be desired more urgently than the last unit of income that would have been left to him if there had been no taxation. But the last unit of energy that he devotes to work will not affect him differently from what it did, consequently there will be a tendency for him to work a little harder. ..." Elsewhere this is put even more succinctly. "Since income is taken away from taxpayers the marginal utility of money to them is raised but the marginal disutility of work is unchanged. Hence, unless they are somehow impeded, they will increase the amount of work done."[2]

With very great deference it is submitted that this mode of argument proves much too much. This can be seen very readily if the argument be made completely general.

Suppose a man to be in receipt of a constant flow of exchangeable goods of any sort, say, corn. (The constant flow here is equivalent to the constant flow of disposable time which is assumed when variations in the supply of work are being considered.) Suppose that he is in the habit of exchanging some of this corn for a constant flow of some other kind of goods, say, coal (the constant flow of coal procured is equivalent to the constant flow of real income which can be earned by exchanging time for product). Suppose now that a tax is imposed which makes the price of coal higher (i.e. which makes the effort price of real income higher), would Professor Pigou acquiesce in an argument which ran as follows? The marginal utility of coal (real income) is now greater. But the marginal disutility of parting with corn (time) is unchanged.

1. *Economics of Welfare*, 1st edn (London, 1920), p. 593.
2. *A Study in Public Finance*, 1st edn (London, 1928), pp. 83–4.

He will therefore, unless impeded, part with more corn (time). Such an argument seems plainly fallacious: it implies that the elasticity of demand for *any* commodity is less than unity. But in what way is it different from the argument on which Professor Pigou is relying?

Is it not clear that the relevant circumstance in the case of the imposition of a tax or the raising of a price is the change in the terms on which exchange is possible? The marginal utility of real income (or the single good) changes with changes in the quantity possessed as before. It is the terms on which income (or the single good) can be obtained which alter and it is the magnitude of this change together with the rate at which the utility of income diminishes which determines the nature of the new equilibrium. The flaw in Professor Pigou's argument seems to be due to an ambiguity in the expression "marginal utility" used in this connection. If a tax is imposed the utility of the marginal unit of income will rise, but the utility of the income derived from a unit of work at the original point of equilibrium may rise or fall, for it depends on the rate of exchange as well as on the utility of the marginal unit.[1] When the price of anything rises, we are entitled, if we assume diminishing marginal utility, to infer that, in all but exceptional cases, less of the commodity will be bought. But we are not entitled to infer that more money (or more effort) will necessarily be spent on it.

8. If these considerations are valid we are left with the conclusion, reached earlier, that any attempt to predict the effect of a change in the terms on which income is earned must proceed by inductive investigation of elasticities. The attempt to narrow the limit of possible elasticities by *a priori* reasoning must be held to have broken down.

---

1. Mr. Hicks, to whom I am greatly indebted for assistance in framing the above criticism, has formulated the point symbolically thus:

If u = Utility of income earned,
v = Disutility of work done,
x = Amount of work done,
y = Amount of income received,

then in equilibrium $\frac{du}{dx} = \frac{dy}{dx}$ If the same amount of work is done, then $\frac{dv}{dx}$ remains unchanged, but $\frac{du}{dx}$ may vary in either direction; for $\frac{du}{dx} = \frac{du}{dy} \cdot \frac{dy}{dx}$. $\frac{du}{dy}$ must increase but $\frac{dy}{dx}$ must diminish, and the change in $\frac{du}{dx}$ will therefore depend on their relation, i.e. on the elasticity of demand for income. – QED

6 The Economic Works of Philip Wicksteed[1]

From *Economica*, vol. 10 (November 1930), pp. 245–58.

I

To the general public, it is probable that Wicksteed is known chiefly for his work as a classical and mediaeval scholar. For various reasons, some of which it will be our business to analyse later on, his work as an economist, although often expressly addressed to the generality of educated readers, has not received such extensive recognition. In this he has been unfortunate. Among professional economists his reputation has always been high: and as years go on it is likely to increase rather than to diminish. Nor is this reputation confined to this country. From the outset of his career as an economist, he received international recognition; and it would be difficult to find a really important work on pure economics written during the last twenty years which did not contain some reference to his work or some trace of his influence. His various books, never issued in large editions, have become extremely rare, and are greatly sought after, not only by the regular collectors of the literature of Economic Theory, but by the workday economist, endeavouring to provide himself with the indispensable instruments of his craft. An English economist, anxious to ingratiate himself with some American or continental colleague, could find no more certain claim to instant friendship than the gift of one of these much-prized volumes.

The beginnings of Wicksteed's interest in economics and his connection with the early Fabians, have been well described by Dr. Herford. The object of this article is to give some account of his main works in this field and to attempt a brief estimate of the significance of his various contributions.[2]

1. This article forms part of a chapter on Wicksteed's works as an economist which will appear in a biography by Dr. C.H. Herford, shortly to be published by Messrs. Dent [*Philip Henry Wicksteed: His Life and Work* (London, 1931)].

2. See the forthcoming biography referred to above. Dr. Bonar's Obituary Notice in the *Economic Journal*, vol. 37 (1927), p. 333, should also be consulted.

II

Wicksteed's first extensive contribution to the literature of modern economics was his *Alphabet of Economic Science*, a slim pocket manual which was published in 1888. The formative influence on his thoughts as an economist was Jevons. A copy of the second edition of the *Theory of Political Economy* which was purchased by Wicksteed in 1882 is in the possession of the present writer: and the marginal annotations on almost every page show how profoundly and how extensively he had meditated on its doctrines. In an earlier essay on the labour theory of value,[1] he had used the Jevonian theory to demonstrate the inadequacy of the classical and Marxian theories of value. The *Alphabet* was an attempt to restate and to elaborate positively its central guiding principles. The book is avowedly an introduction. Forty pages of careful mathematical illustration of the notion of limiting rates preface the attempt to apply this notion to the explanation of exchange values, and copious and minute illustrations accompany every step of the subsequent argument. In the history of theory, the book is perhaps chiefly notable for its introduction of the term "marginal utility" – a rendering of the Austrian "*Grenznutzen*" – as a substitute for the Jevonian "final utility," which, for obvious reasons, had tended to lead to confusions. But the book is not merely of historical interest. It still preserves considerable pedagogic value. Much as has been written on the subject it deals with since that date – not least by Wicksteed himself – it still remains one of the best available introductions to the so-called utility theory of value. Other introductions may be easier to read and perhaps more entertaining to the student. But none is more calculated to give him real grasp and comprehension of the subject. In broad outline, of course, nothing can be simpler than the general notion of diminishing marginal utility. But in closer application to the problems of commodity prices, the notion is apt to prove elusive, at least to the non-mathematician. And more than one economist of standing has been betrayed into grotesque misconstructions. It is the great merit of Wicksteed's book that, starting from a point at which no knowledge of the calculus is assumed in his readers, he succeeds in expounding the theory with such minuteness and precision, that misconstructions of this sort should be impossible for anyone who has read it with a normal degree of attention.

The book was an immediate success among economists. With one stride Wicksteed had secured a place in that esoteric circle whose pronouncements on pure theory command international attention. It was referred to approvingly

1. "The Marxian theory of value," *To-day*, vol. 2 (October 1884), pp. 388–409.

by Edgeworth and the great Pareto, most ferocious of critics, most uncompromising guardian of the sanctities of pure theory, gave it a prominent place in the bibliography of works on '*Economie pure*' which appeared in Part I of his *Cours*.* With the general public, however, it was not such a success. When the general public picks up an introduction to economic science, it expects to discover a handy guide to the solution of all the most controversial problems of the day – a few neat paragraphs about trade unions and wages, a chapter on trusts and big business, perhaps a diagram or two to lay bare the intricacies of the monetary system, all rounded off with a few sound generalisations about the future. But here was a book pretending to be an introduction, which started off with a series of graphs and algebraic formulae exhibiting the behaviour of falling bodies and the cooling of iron bars plunged into baths of cold water, and continued with exhaustive diagrammatic discussions of trivial household calculations, such as buying a coat or a loaf of bread, never saying anything which was short and snappy and simple. Small wonder that the hungry sheep, as usual, refused to feed, and continued to bleat to all the world that no nourishment was forthcoming in these pastures.

The preface to the *Alphabet* had promised that, if it proved to meet a want amongst students of economics, it should be followed by similar introductions to other branches of the science. This plan seems to have been abandoned. For the next work was one which by no stretch of imagination could be described as introductory or simple. This was the celebrated *Essay on the Co-ordination of the Laws of Distribution*, which was given to the world in 1894.

By the beginning of the 'nineties the centre of gravity in theoretical economics had shifted from the narrow problem of commodity value to the wider problem of distribution, or, as it is sometimes called, the pricing of the factors of production. Jevons and the Austrians had suggested a theory which as a first approximation might be held to elucidate the prices which could be secured for "ultimate commodities." The problem now was to decide in what proportions the prices were "distributed" between the different factors co-operating in the production of these commodities. It was this problem which the *Essay* was designed to solve. The solution offered was a form of what is sometimes known as the marginal productivity theory of distribution. If the product to be distributed is P, then to use Wicksteed's own statement, "the rates of participation in the product on which any factor K can insist ... will be dp/dk per unit and its total share will be $dp/dk\,.K$."[1]

---

* *Cours d'Economie Politique* (Lausanne, 1896–7).

1. *Essay*, p. 9.

How far this result had been reached independently of the work of others it is difficult to say. Just as, at the beginning of the 'seventies, the utility theory of value had occurred simultaneously to Jevons, Walras, and Menger, so at the beginning of the 'nineties, the productivity theory of distribution was "in the air" and different variants had been put forward by Marshall, Clark and others. It is certain that Wicksteed was acquainted with Marshall's work in this field, for there are footnote references to it in the *Essay*. But it is probable that his solution was reached as a result of his studies of Jevons, which were carried out before Marshall's *Principles* were published.[1] This is what seems to follow from Wicksteed's own account of his discovery,[2] and we may be sure that a man so scrupulously honest and so modest about his own achievements would have acknowledged the debt had it existed.

By the time the *Essay* was published, the idea that the notion of marginal productivity might play a part in the explanation of the price of the factors of production was becoming widely accepted among the more advanced economists. The same cannot be said, however, of the main proposition of the *Essay*, namely that if each factor is rewarded according to its marginal productivity the sum of the remuneration of each separate factor will exactly exhaust the product – in other words, that the marginal productivity analysis is a *sufficient* explanation of "distribution."[3] This bold generalisation has always been associated with the argument of the *Essay*, and it is true to say that, even at the present day, it remains the subject of lively controversy. Wicksteed himself, as a result of criticism by Mr. Flux and Pareto became dissatisfied with it, declared it to have been a premature synthesis[4] and in the *Common Sense of Political Economy* announced the proposition to be finally withdrawn. The grounds of his dissatisfaction, however, were technical and mathematical; it would be wrong to suppose, as has sometimes been done, that he renounced the productivity analysis in general.[5] Certainly the solution offered in its place in *The Common Sense of Political Economy* does not differ so noticeably from that of the *Essay* as to suggest that the earlier version was to be regarded as wholly misleading. And, so far as I understand

1. "On certain passages in Jevons's *Theory of Political Economy*," *Quarterly Journal of Economics*, vol. 3 (1889), pp. 293–314.
2. *Essay*, p. 43.
3. See, e.g., F.H. Knight, "A note on Professor Clark's illustration of marginal productivity," *Journal of Political Economy*, vol. 33 (1925), pp. 550–4; also H. Schultz, "Marginal productivity and the general pricing process," *Journal of Political Economy*, vol. 37 (1929), pp. 505–51.
4. Review of Pareto's *Manuale di Economia Politica*, *Economic Journal*, vol. 16 (1906), pp. 553–7, and *Common Sense of Political Economy*, p. 373.
5. It is worthy of note that Knut Wicksell expresses great surprise at Wicksteed's apparent recantation. See *Vorlesungen über Nationalökonomie* (Jena, 1913), Vol. I, p. 156.

them, the criticisms which have been made by Pareto and others relate to the nature of the assumptions made rather than to the internal logic of the argument. That is to say, if I am not mistaken, Wicksteed's proposition is not untrue; the only criticism to which it is exposed is that, in certain circumstances, its assumptions render it inapplicable. It is not so exhaustive as its author at first supposed. This is not a very grave defect in a new theory. We are none of us so near the goal as we tend to believe ourselves to be.

For sixteen years after the appearance of the *Essay*, Wicksteed published little on economic questions. A couple of reviews in the *Economic Journal*, on Jevons's *Principles*[1] in 1905 and Pareto's *Manual*[2] in 1906, constitute the sum of published utterances. But all this time his mind was revolving the terms of a synthesis wider than anything he had hitherto attempted, and in 1910 he published his *magnum opus* in this field, *The Common Sense of Political Economy*.

It is not easy in a short space to give an adequate idea of this work. The title conveys less than nothing. Indeed, never was a work of this kind more unfortunately named. It is not "common sense" in the ordinary sense of the term, and it is not *political* economy. It is, on the contrary, the most exhaustive non-mathematical exposition of the technical and philosophical complications of the so-called "marginal" theory of pure economics, which has appeared in any language. The only work with which it can be compared in this respect is Wieser's *Theorie der Gesellschaftlichen Wirtschaft* [1914], but even Wieser, like Marshall and other authors of 'systems,' really covers a much wider field, and does not enter into nearly the same degree of detail.

The aim of the book was twofold. On the one hand it attempted a systematic exposition of the Jevonian and Austrian theories, such that any reader commencing from no previous acquaintance of Economic Analysis would be in a position to achieve "an intimate comprehension of the commercial and industrial world." On the other, it involved an attempt "to convince professed students of Political Economy that any special or unusual features in the system thus constructed are not to be regarded as daring innovations or as heresies, but are already strictly involved and often explicitly recognised in the best economic thought and teaching of recent years."[3] As usual, Wicksteed made no claims to originality. Indeed he refrained from making claims which might very well have been made. But he did definitely hope that his work would compel recognition of the degree to which economics had been changed by the discussions of the last forty years. "I believe," he

1. "Jevons's economic work," *Economic Journal*, vol. 15 (1905), pp. 432–6.
2. *Economic Journal*, vol. 16 (1906), pp. 553–7
3. *Common Sense*, p. 2.

said, "that the reconstruction contemplated by Jevons has been carried to a far more advanced point than is generally realised even by those who are themselves accomplishing it. Adhesion to the traditional terminology, methods of arrangement, and classification, has disguised the revolution that has taken place. The new temple, so to speak, has been built up behind the old walls, and the old shell has been so piously preserved and respected that the very builders have often supposed themselves to be merely repairing and strengthening the ancient works, and are hardly aware of the extent to which they have raised an independent edifice. I shall try to show in this book that the time has come for a frank recognition of these facts."[1]

The book is divided into three parts. In the first comes a systematic working out of the marginal analysis. This is introduced by an extensive analysis of the economics of household administration, in which the principles of what the Germans call *Naturwirtschaft* are exhaustively examined. This is followed by a minute exposition of the notion of margins and limiting rates of expenditure, unparalleled in the whole literature of modern economic theory for clarity and precision. "Nowhere," said the late Professor Allyn Young, reviewing the book for the *American Economic Review*, "is there so clear a (non-mathematical) explanation of the meaning of marginal significance, or so effective a refutation of those writers who have thought that the existence of indivisible goods puts insurmountable obstacles in the way of the marginal analysis."[2] The analysis then opens out to include the phenomena of money and exchange. The implications of the Economic Nexus in the *Verkehrswirtschaft* are expounded. Markets, Earnings, Interest are systematically examined, and finally, at a great height, the interrelations of distribution and cost of production are made the basis for an exhibition of the whole notion of economic equilibrium.

The second part of the book, which is described as "Excursive and Critical," consists of a series of special studies of technical problems of analysis. The notions of the diagrammatic representation of margins and total utility are investigated with a precision and minuteness which provides a significant contrast with the cursory treatment usually afforded these matters even in respectable textbooks. There follow special studies of the supply curve and markets, and an examination of the concepts of increasing and diminishing returns and their relation to the theory of rent, in which some of the subsidiary propositions of the *Essay on the Co-ordination of the Laws of Distribution* are expounded and developed. Finally, in Part Three, the general

1. *Common Sense*, p. 2.
2. *American Economic Review*, vol. 1 (March 1911), pp. 78–80.

system of analysis elaborated in the earlier chapters is applied to the elucidation of certain practical problems, Housing, Unemployment, Redistribution of Wealth, Taxation, Land Nationalisation, Socialism, and so on. The treatment here is less detailed, more discursive than before, the Lucretian passage which prefaces this part of the book suggesting perfectly its intention. "But this faint spoor suffices for an alert mind; so that thou thyself may'st come at all the rest. For just as hounds, when once they have found the true track, full often search out with their nostrils the lair of the mountain-roaming quarry, hidden though it be with foliage, even so may'st thou, in such things as these, see for thyself one thing after another, work thyself into the secret lurking-places and thence drag out the truth."

The book was the culmination of Wicksteed's life work in this branch of knowledge. Into it he poured all the subtlety and persuasiveness, all the literary charm of which he was capable. It is a masterpiece of systematic exposition. It is the most complete statement of the implicit philosophy of economic analysis which has been published in our day. But with all these great merits, it did not succeed in attracting the notice of the general educated public and even among professional economists it has not exerted the influence which might have been expected.

Why is this?

Three reasons I think are to be discovered. In the first place there was the misfortune of the name, which I have already discussed. It did not succeed in attracting the general public. And many economists, I imagine, having learnt from bitter experience what is usually to be expected from works which profess to treat economic problems in a "common-sense" manner, have been positively deterred from investigating its contents. I well remember as a student, unaware as yet of Wicksteed's high repute among the inner circle of the craft, feeling definitely that a work which devoted seven hundred pages to a "common-sense" exposition of theorems which I already knew to be highly intricate and technical, was "extra-marginal" so far as *my* reading time was concerned.

Partly, I think, on account of its length. It is a weighty book, and although the exposition is most exquisitely organised, the nuances of argument most delicately fluted, yet it cannot be denied that it is possible that at times it may drag a little, may become a trifle *langweilig*. I do not find this myself, but it must be set on record that this was the impression it produced on so sensitive and so learned a critic as the late Professor Allyn Young.

But mainly, I think, what failure there is must be attributed to the nature of the task which Wicksteed set himself. Wicksteed lived at a time when it was still thought necessary for economists to write mainly with the general public in view. Economics was still a subject which was read and discussed in the clubs. The result was that at every point the economists' wings were clipped.

Whenever the use of a technical term or a reference to the periodical literature of the science would have simplified and sharpened the argument, the exposition had to be loaded with recapitulation and periphrases which only tended to hinder its progress. It is notorious that Marshall's great work on *Principles* suffers from this deficiency. But Marshall's *Principles* is high technicality itself compared with Wicksteed's *Common Sense*. Marshall, at least, permits himself the luxury of footnote discussions, a mathematical appendix and copious reference to the classics. Wicksteed goes serenely on, even in the most controversial sections, almost as though no other economist had ever written. Moreover, Marshall was professor in one of the great centres of economic study, where every shade of technical implication would be daily sifted out from his smooth flattened prose by tutors learned in the more esoteric oral tradition of the School. Wicksteed was an isolated classical scholar and extension lecturer, respected indeed by fellow economists, but with no regular pupils or assistants to make explicit the intimate affiliations of his thought. In such circumstances the only sure path to recognition was to keep to the tradition of the *Essay*, reserve his best thoughts for the expert public of the journals, and leave to professors, secure in the comfortable eminence of academic chairs, the thankless task of enlightening the general reader. But the preacher in Wicksteed died hard and he chose the more arduous endeavour.

III

Wicksteed's place in the history of Economic Thought is beside the place occupied by Jevons and the Austrians. The main stream of economic speculation in this country in the last forty years has come *via* Marshall from the classics. By this I do not mean that it shows no advance on the classics. That, of course, would be absurd: it has made the most superb advances. The judgement relates merely to tendencies. Marshall's position was essentially revisionist. He came, not to destroy, but to fulfil the work of the classics. Wicksteed, on the other hand, was of those who, with Jevons and Menger, thought that "able but wrongheaded man David Ricardo" had "shunted the car of Economic Science on to a wrong line, a line on which it was further urged towards confusion by his equally able and wrongheaded admirer John Stuart Mill;"[1] and that complete reconstruction was necessary. He was not a revisionist but a revolutionary. I have cited already the passage from the

1. Jevons, *Theory of Political Economy*, 3rd edn (1910), p. 1.

preface to the *Common Sense* in which he says that the time has come to recognise that modern economics is not a reconstruction of the old, but a new and independent edifice. The same point of view is very strongly presented in his review of Sir Sydney Chapman's *Political Economy*.[1]

The difference is perhaps very largely one of emphasis and *conception* of theory, rather than in the *substance* of theory itself. But none the less it modifies materially the presentation of theory by representatives of the Schools concerned. In spite of a very real agreement on the broad outlines of analysis, there is a world of difference between the "*look*" of Marshall's *Principles* and Wicksteed's *Common Sense of Political Economy*, Wieser's *Theorie der Gesellschaftlichen Wirtschaft*, or Schumpeter's *Wesen und Hauptinhalt der Theoretischen Nationalökonomie* [1908]. Nor must the degree of fundamental agreement be exaggerated. There are differences in the central core of theory. This is specially noticeable in the theory of costs – Marshall, and (up to a recent date) most of his followers, insisting that costs in the last analysis were something "real" and absolute, Wicksteed and the Austrians denying that they were anything but foregone alternatives. No doubt, in part, this difference of theory was due to a difference in ultimate assumption concerning the nature of the conditions of economic equilibrium.[2] But in part it was due to an ultimate difference of opinion concerning what psychological comparisons were *relevant* in the determination of *any* equilibrium. So far as this was the case, time, I think, has decided in favour of the revolutionaries. The conception of real costs as displaced alternatives, which Wicksteed so eloquently expounded, is now accepted by the majority of theoretical economists, though even now its implications are not always fully grasped.[3]

But it would be a great mistake to regard Wicksteed as merely a disciple of Jevons and the Austrians. He was much more than that. He was an independent and original thinker. Even where he expounded the main elements of the utility theory it is safe to say that he touched nothing which he did not make his own. Nor was his own position one of stationary equilibrium. He was continually reformulating and improving. I have mentioned already his willingness to jettison his original theory of distribution. An equally interesting example of this tendency is to be found in the comparison of the utility theory

---

1. *Economic Journal*, vol. 23 (1913), pp. 72–5.

2. I have tried to exhibit this difference of assumption as between Marshall and the Austrians elsewhere. See my article, "On a certain ambiguity in the conception of stationary equilibrium," *Economic Journal*, vol. 40 (June 1930), pp. 194–214 [above, pp. 59–78].

3. For a superb application of the Austrian theory of costs to the examination of certain theories of fluctuation, see F.A. Hayek, *Geldtheorie und Konjunkturtheorie* (Vienna, 1929), Chapter II.

expounded in the *Alphabet* and the Utility Theory of the *Common Sense*. Superficially the two theories are the same, and no doubt they do belong to the same family. But a closer inspection will reveal important points of difference. The *Alphabet* starts from the idea of the rate at which total utility is increasing. The *Common Sense* from the positions on the relative scale of preferences which marginal units of different commodities occupy. In the *Alphabet* the utility relevant to the determination of value is treated as if it were something absolute and measurable. In the *Common Sense* the sole relevance of *relative* utility is emphasised and the idea of *measurability* has given place to the idea of *order*. In the *Alphabet* the analysis is definitely "one-thing-at-a-time." In the *Common Sense* the emphasis of the simultaneity of the determination of all values is continuous. And so one could go on. There is no feature of the presentation which does not bear evidence of reformulation and improvement.

Apart, however, from his services as exponent of the general theory of equilibrium, there are certain particular contributions for which Wicksteed will always be remembered. I have discussed already his studies in the theory of distribution. Whatever the ultimate decision as to the truth or falsehood of the particular theorem he advanced with regard to the adequacy of the productivity analysis, there can be no doubt that economists owe him a high debt of gratitude for having focused attention on this aspect of the problem. It is not always those who are finally right who make the greatest contributions to progress.

A second contribution which must always be associated with his name is his famous demonstration of the reversibility of the market supply curve.[1] The general proposition that the reservation prices of sellers are in the ultimate analysis demands, was one which he continually reiterated with varying shades of emphasis. "What about the supply curve that usually figures as a determinant of price, co-ordinate with the demand curve?" he asked in his address as President of Section E of the British Association in 1913 – an address which epitomises many of his most characteristic doctrines.[2] "I say it boldly and baldly: There is no such thing. When we are speaking of a marketable commodity, what is usually called the supply curve is in reality the demand curve of those who possess the commodity; for it shows the exact place which every successive unit of the commodity holds in their relative scale of estimates. The so-called supply curve, therefore, is simply a part of

1. See *Common Sense*, pp. 493–526, and "The scope and method of political economy in the light of the 'marginal' theory of value and distribution," *Economic Journal*, vol. 24 (March 1914), pp. 13–16.

2. "The scope and method of political economy in the light of the 'marginal' theory of value and distribution," *Economic Journal*, vol. 24 (March 1914), pp. 1–23.

the total demand curve ... The separating out of this portion of the demand curve and reversing it in the diagram is a process which has its meaning and its legitimate function ... but is wholly irrelevant to the determination of the price."[1] It is safe to say that no one who has followed through his beautiful diagrammatic analysis of this proposition, and realised its wider implication that *all* psychological variables can be exhibited as phenomena of demand acting on fixed stocks of products or factors of time, will deny that the whole of the analysis of economic equilibrium has received thereby a transforming elucidation.[2]

Finally, in the realm of technical contributions, we must notice his analysis of the relation between the marginal productivity theory of distribution and the Ricardian theory of rent. The discovery that the rent analysis of the classics is the productivity analysis with, as Edgeworth put it, the relationship between dose and patient reversed, was, of course, not peculiar to Wicksteed. By one of those singular coincidences which seem to characterise the progress of our science, the idea seems to have occurred almost simultaneously to at least three writers in the early 'nineties, Wicksteed himself, J.B. Clark, and the much-neglected H.M. Thompson, author of *The Theory of Wages*.[3] But of the demonstrations of this proposition, Wicksteed's was incomparably the most precise and convincing; and, at the present day, a teacher who wishes to convince some recalcitrant student of the truth of this doctrine cannot do better than refer him to the classic reformulation which is to be found in Part II, Chapters V and VI of *The Common Sense of Political Economy*.

IV

But apart from these technical contributions and far transcending them in general importance come Wicksteed's elucidations of the implications for

1. For a very elegant demonstration of this last possibility in relation to the problem of hours of labour, see Wicksell, *Vorlesungen über Nationalökonomie*, Vol. I, p. 159.

2. It should be noted that the same general point of view was enunciated independently by Professor [H.J.] Davenport in his *Value and Distribution: a critical and constructive study* (Chicago, 1908), and further elaborated in his *Economics of Enterprise* (New York, 1913). Nothing that has been said in praise of Wicksteed's work in this connection should be understood as derogating from the merits or the helpfulness of Professor Davenport's exposition, for which, indeed, when he came to know it, Wicksteed had himself a very profound admiration. See his review of Davenport's *Economics of Enterprise*, *Economic Journal*, vol. 24 (1914), pp. 421–5.

3. See *Co-ordination of the Laws of Distribution*, pp. 18–20, J.B. Clark, "Distribution as determined by a law of rent," *Quarterly Journal of Economics*, vol. 5 (1980–91), pp. 289–318; H.M. Thompson, *The Theory of Wages* (London, 1892), Chapter IV.

social philosophy of the results of the theory of economic equilibrium – particularly those discussions of the nature of the economic relationship which are to be found in the chapter of the *Common Sense* entitled "Business and the Economic Nexus."[1] This, if I read him correctly, was the feature of his work to which he himself attached greatest importance, and it is for this above all that he deserves to be remembered. Yet, curiously enough, no aspect of his teaching has been more completely neglected. The reason is not far to seek. In England, at any rate, the average economist, secure in the tradition of an empirical approach to his subject-matter, is apt to be impatient of inquiries which linger on implications and modes of conception. The man in the street, egged on by the inexpert practitioners of other branches of the social sciences, may reproach him for an ingrained materialism and an assumption of a simplicity of motive unwarranted by the complexity of the situation to be analysed. But such reproaches leave him indifferent. He knows in his bones that they are unjust. He knows that, unlike his traducers, he is in possession of analytical instruments which do genuinely elucidate the understanding of complicated social relationships, and he is apt to regard with impatience those semi-metaphysical inquiries which harp on ultimate assumptions. The instinct, no doubt, is a healthy one, and has saved us from the torrents of empty methodology which at times have threatened entirely to submerge economic analysis elsewhere. None the less not all inquiries of this sort are empty, and it may be successfully contended, I think, that by their researches in this field a small group of economists – Wicksteed and Knight in English-speaking countries, Schumpeter and Mises in Central Europe[2] – have raised the whole discussion of equilibrium analysis on to an entirely new plane – a plane on which Economics is seen to be a discussion not of the nature of certain *kinds* of behaviour arbitrarily separated off from all others, but of a certain *aspect* of behaviour viewed as a whole. It is perhaps too early to evaluate the individual contributions to this stream of thought, for the movement is by no means exhausted, but when the final history comes to be written, I think it will be found that Wicksteed's exhaustive examination of the "economic relationship," and his insistence that this and not the pseudo-concept of the "economic motive," is the chief sociological preoccupation of economic analysis, will be seen to be by no means the least important contribution.

---

1. The curious should consult a tract entitled *Getting and Spending* [London, 1888], reprinted for private circulation from *The Inquirer*, 1888, for an earlier and much inferior statement of Wicksell's position in this respect.

2. See in particular [F.H.] Knight's essay on "The limitations of scientific method in economics" in *The Trend of Economics*, ed. Rexford G. Tugwell (1924), pp. 229–67; Joseph Schumpeter, *Das Wesen und der Hauptinhalt der theoretischen Nationalökonomie* (Leipzig, 1908); and Ludwig von Mises, *Die Gemeinwirtschaft: Untersuchungen über den Socialismus* (Jena, 1922), Part II, Chapter 5 [The nature of economic activity].

V

Such in broad outline was the main achievement as an economist of this noble and penetrating intellect. It is an achievement of rare distinction. Economics in England can boast a long succession of devoted and dispassionate practitioners. There have been none more devoted or dispassionate than Philip Wicksteed. It has been said that his work was detached and remote from reality. In a sense this is true. He was the purest of pure economists – always occupied with the general, always searching for the one in the many. He tried to erect a structure of principles which should be valid for all time and all conditions. His work is indeed destitute of statistical tables and discussions of contemporary business structure, but it is informed throughout by continuous regard for the intimate texture of conduct. There are many economists who have had wider contacts with the life of their times, there are many who have had a greater range of immediate practical usefulness: there are few who have done more to bring economics as a science into relation with life as a whole.

V

7 Economic Notes on Some Arguments for Protection[1]

From *Economica*, vol. 11 (February 1931), pp. 45–62.

The case for the tariff, as it is argued at the present day, is usually based on one of three types of argument – simple fallacies of composition, misconceptions of old theories, new (or apparently new) analysis. At this period of the twentieth century there is no need to discuss the first of these classes. The usual argument for safeguarding – Protection is good for this particular industry; Protection is therefore good for industry as a whole – is a good example of this type and, although it would be a relief if one could be sure that its manifest illogicality were apparent to .001 per cent. of the electorate, it is clearly not a subject of interest to professional economists. But the second and third types of argument have greater speculative attractions and it is the object of these notes to take a few typical specimens, and submit them to further analysis.

I

I turn first to misconceptions.

(1) The fundamental argument for complete freedom of trade is that it permits the maximum territorial division of labour. Under free trade the different parts of the earth's surface can be put to the uses for which, having regard to the conditions of demand, they have the maximum suitability. Free trade, that is to say, is the condition of the maximum productive efficiency, the condition of the maximum satisfaction of consumers' demand. It is conceivable that in the interests of defence or in the interests of aesthetic valuations not formulated in consumers' price bids – a demand for a countryside permanently devoted to arable farming, or what not – the inhabitants of certain areas or indeed of the world as a whole, might resolve to forgo some advantages of productive efficiency. Such a choice, if deliberately taken, would be outside the scope of economic analysis. Free Trade is not an end in itself; it is a means to an end.

1. A paper read before the London Economic Club, Tuesday, November 11th, 1930.

(2) These advantages are not limited to specialisation within particular areas. The wider the market the greater the specialisation. The greater the specialisation the wider the market. The mechanism of relative costs and prices may be trusted to keep territorial specialisation, equally with other kinds of division of labour, within the limits of the greatest attainable efficiency. There is no sanctity in the areas delimited by national frontiers. This fact is not always clearly realised. A continental friend who was visiting this country recently tells me that while over here he was frequently assured that in a modern state of reasonable dimensions it does not matter greatly what industries are fostered. 'In a little state like —,' it is said, 'of course you have to be careful. But in England ...' This argument seems to lack substance. We know that *within* national areas business men take the greatest pains to erect their factories at the point of greatest convenience. It is said that Ford's experts spend months calculating freightage, etc., from possible sites before deciding on a purchase. It is surely utterly unreasonable to suppose that considerations which are elementary prudence when choosing between sites unseparated by political frontiers, should cease to be relevant just because the accident of war or a royal marriage has caused a customs line to be drawn between the sites concerned. Nor should we underestimate the significance of such economies. Taken singly they may not always seem of very great importance. Cumulatively they make the difference between an efficient and an inefficient organisation of production.

(3) It is sometimes thought that these advantages cease if labour and capital are not completely mobile between different national areas. But this is to fail to realise the true nature of the main classical analysis. It is true that the ideas of *laissez faire* and *laissez passer* have intimate philosophical affiliations. It is true that *laissez faire* in the sense of free movement of *products* between different areas is only accompanied by the greatest benefit if, at the same time, there is free movement of *factors*. – To transfer labour from centres of low to centres of high productivity must always conduce to a greater total output, unless the tendencies to multiplication of the inhabitants of one particular part are incurably greater than those elsewhere. But it is not true that in a world in which *laissez passer* is not present, *laissez faire* as regards exchange is not desirable, either for persons or for the inhabitants of different segregated areas. Whether I can go to the point of greatest absolute productivity or not, it is always in my interest to do that in which, in my present position, I have the greatest comparative advantage. We entirely fail to realise the great strength of the free trade position if we do not realise that it was precisely to deal with the state of affairs prevailing where labour and capital were not freely mobile, that the classical theory of comparative costs was first elaborated. Nor has the strength of that analysis been in any way diminished by the fact that in more modern times we have come to think of costs in terms of foregone opportunities, rather than in terms of effort sacrificed. Professor Knight and Dr. Haberler have abundantly

shown that, conceived in this way, the doctrine of comparative costs becomes more rather than less convincing than in its earlier versions.[1]

(4) There are various so-called "exceptions" to this theory which are admitted more or less freely by analytical economists, the so-called Infant Industry argument based on intricate assumptions with regard to the behaviour of the cost curve in time,[2] the Terms of Trade argument and the argument for measures against spasmodic dumping being perhaps the chief. But, save in the case of the Terms of Trade argument – which very few think to be widely applicable in the case of manufacturing nations – it would not be admitted that these arguments were arguments for a tariff.[3] To establish a case for restriction of complete *laissez faire* is not to establish a case for particular administrative expedients. To ascertain that occasionally an operation for appendicitis is necessary is not to establish that the appendix is best removed with a chisel. This fact is often overlooked in popular discussions of this matter, and arguments which establish the negative conclusion that *laissez faire* may not in certain cases lead to the most satisfactory results are made the pretext for the crudest arguments for a tariff. The Infant Industry argument in particular has continually been abused in this manner.[4]

(5) Such, stripped of misconception, is the theory on which the main analytical argument for free trade is founded. There still remain certain misconceptions of its implications with which it is necessary to deal before proceeding to more complicated matters.

---

1. See Frank H. Knight, "A suggestion for simplifying the statement of the general theory of price," *Journal of Political Economy*, vol. 36 (June 1928), pp. 353–70; Gottfried Haberler, "Die Theorie der komparativen Kosten und ihre Auswertung für die Begründung des Freihandels," *Weltwirtschaftliches Archiv*, vol. 32 (1930), pp. 349–70. For an alternative statement of the same fundamental principle, see Bertil Ohlin, "Die Beziehung zwischen internationalem Handel und internationaler Bewegungen von Kapital und Arbeit," *Zeitschrift für Nationalökonomie*, vol. 2 (1931), pp. 161–99.

2. It is important to remember that if the infant industry argument is to have any validity at all, it must appeal to the possibility of achieving the widest kind of "external economy" – the creation of a tradition of industrial discipline and the like. It is perhaps worth observing, too, that the mere fact that, in course of time, a certain district could produce a certain article "*as well as*" another district where its manufacture is already established affords no justification for its establishment there. Its establishment can only be justified if it can be shown that at some point in the future it will have comparative advantage *and* that, after that, the gain, discounted at compound interest, will be such as will more than outweigh the sacrifice involved in beginning.

3. On attempts to deal with dumping by means of a tariff see the article by Professor [Arnold] Plant, "The anti-dumping regulations of the South African tariff," *Economica*, Vol. 11 (February 1931), pp. 63–101.

4. It is worth observing that Mill, who perhaps was more responsible than any for giving respectability to this argument, himself protested bitterly against the uses to which it had been put both in Australia and America. See *The Letters of John Stuart Mill*, ed. H.S.R. Elliott (London, 1910), Vol. 2, pp. 154–5.

(*a*) We may notice in the first place that nothing in the theory suggests that it ceases to be applicable, if to the limitations of economic activity due to natural obstacles there are super-added further limitations of a legal or institutional nature. It is sometimes thought that, if one country has a more rigid code of labour legislation than another or a heavier system of taxation, the desirability of concentrating productive effort on the points of greatest comparative advantage ceases. This is fallacious. Labour legislation may or may not increase efficiency. But even if it does not, there is no reason why, within the limitations it imposes, we should not buy and sell in the best markets. If it is ill-conceived it will diminish production. But production will be still further diminished if it is maldistributed by tariffs.

(*b*) But, secondly, it is often argued that the competition of goods produced elsewhere by low-wage labour may render the free trade presumption inoperative. If it did, it would put a stop to trade altogether not only between national areas, but also *within* them. For we live in a world in which labour incomes are by no means equally divided. In our own case, we should exclude the goods made by the rest of the world save America, Canada, and one or two other high-wage countries, while America, Canada, and the others would exclude the goods coming from us. The same paralysis would ensue within national areas. If exchange were confined to equal income groups the whole structure of modern industrial society would collapse. The low-wage labour argument entirely ignores the most obvious implications of the theory of comparative costs. Wages are not the *cause* of trade: they are the *result*. Where there is not obvious monopoly, low wages mean relatively low productivity, high wages relatively high productivity. For centres of high productivity and low productivity to refuse to trade with each other simply involves that their respective physical products will not receive so high a valuation and that their physical efficiency will be lowered.[1]

(*c*) But of course – and this is my third point – this is not in the least to argue that the rise of industries elsewhere may not prove injurious to the interests of the inhabitants of a particular area. There is nothing in the theory of comparative costs which suggests that free exchange is always accompanied by *advancing* real incomes on the part of each party concerned. All that it implies is that, where it is practised, real incomes will be *higher than*

---

1. On all this see Nassau W. Senior, *Three Lectures on the Cost of Obtaining Money* (London, 1830); J.E. Cairnes, *Some Leading Principles of Political Economy newly expounded* (London, 1874), pp. 355–407, and *Essays in Political Economy, theoretical and applied* (London, 1873), pp. 1–50; F.W. Taussig, *Free Trade, the Tariff and Reciprocity* (New York, 1920), pp. 48–94. If wages are artificially out of equilibrium the theory becomes more complicated, but it would be absurd to deny that, broadly speaking, it remains applicable. With all the artificial rigidity in modern wage structures it still remains true that productivity is the *main* determinant. It is fundamentally important in judging such matters to preserve some sense of proportion.

otherwise they would have been. If cooks become efficient lecturers in economics that may be a bad thing for me. But it does not follow that, because I am poorer, I should cease to buy in the cheapest market open to me or cease to sell the services I am best fitted to perform.

(*d*) Fourthly, it is sometimes held that the existence of surplus plant and material equipment generally within a given area is an argument for the abandonment of free exchange in respect of those things which the equipment could produce. This again is a misapprehension, and only the artificial separation of land from other forms of capital in the Ricardian analysis has prevented its general recognition as such. No economically educated person would argue that, because it does not pay to cultivate a piece of vacant land under free trade, it would therefore increase the social dividend to impose a tariff which would make such cultivation profitable. It was the whole burden of the Ricardian analysis that recourse to worse lands was a sign of poverty rather than riches: that to produce at home on poor lands rather than to procure by way of exchange food produced elsewhere at lower cost was economic folly. The same analysis applies to other material equipment. The plant is there: if at the prices prevailing it does not pay to use it, then it is best that it should go out of "cultivation."[1] It is possible, in the very short run and conditions which are not briskly competitive, to think of remote cases in which this presumption does not hold. If, for instance, there is "slack" in the domestic establishments but, owing to unwillingness to incur new expenses on marketing or to risk the disturbance of local monopolies, the producers concerned are not producing to the full, it is conceivable that a tariff which excluded foreigners from the home market would have the effect of permitting a reduction of costs which might in certain circumstances be passed on to the consumer. But the practical importance of such exceptions is negligible. In the last analysis they depend upon the assumption that the entrepreneurs in question are *afraid* of more active competition and hence display an inertia which prevents the full competitive equilibrium being achieved. To make cases of this sort the excuse for protective tariffs would be merely to perpetuate evils which in the long run foreign competition may be expected to cure.

II

(1) But what about surplus capacity in men? Does all this hold when we are affected with unemployment? There is no need for us to subsidise derelict land or derelict machines. We have to subsidise derelict men. Does not this

1. On all this see Haberler, *op. cit.*, especially pp. 364–70.

vitiate the free trade argument? This brings me to the second half of my discussion – the new (or apparently new) arguments for a tariff. For unquestionably it is the fact of unemployment which dominates the present discussion.

(2) May I commence by enunciating a platitude? The main object of economic policy is not to cure unemployment: it is to increase the social dividend. If by curing unemployment that end is accomplished, well and good. If the cure involves measures inimical to the increase of the dividend its desirability is more dubious. We know perfectly well that a general impoverishment would make us all work harder. It is yet to be shown that more work in this sense is in any way desirable.

(3) Now it is sometimes alleged that, before the war, when discussing the tariff problem, economists overlooked unemployment. I do not believe this accusation is really justified. It is true that in the more mathematical formulations of the pure theory of economic equilibrium it was found convenient to assume that the factors of production were in continuous employment. But no one – least of all the mathematicians – suggested that this was any more than a convenient first approximation. Unemployment due to industrial change, unemployment due to general business fluctuations – these were clearly recognised and discussed.[1] The reason why in the discussion of the tariff problem they were not more emphasised is simple. Much emphasis in this connection would have been misleading. Before the war, even if at any time considerable unemployment existed, there was sufficient flexibility in the industrial system for it to be reasonable to assume that, within a period that could not be described as unreasonably long – four years let us say – the difficulty would have disappeared. The tariff problem is essentially a long period problem. Only children or interested parties assume that tariffs once imposed are likely to come off quickly. In considerations relating to long period policy, clearly the short period disturbance is an irrelevant circumstance.

(4) But in the post-war period, in this country, the price and income system has lost this flexibility. At the same time it has had to sustain a series of abnormal shocks. As a result there has been continuous unemployment, and on top of this we now have the world slump with price-cutting and wage-cutting everywhere.

(5) Now it is not necessary to consider here the problem of the slump unemployment. When the slump goes a substantial proportion of the unemployment

1. It is wrong to assert, as is sometimes asserted, that it is only since the war that the existence of unemployment has been made the foundation of an argument for Protection. The recommendation of a 10 per cent. general Revenue Duty on all imported manufactures which was made by the minority of the Royal Commission on the Depression of Industry and Trade in 1886 – to take only one example – was based explicitly on this argument. See C. 4893–1886, pp. 15–17. The whole Report is an excellent corrective to the view that there is much new under the sun in fiscal controversies.

which came with it will go too – not all, if wages elsewhere are cut and ours remain rigid, but at least a substantial proportion. No one but a madman or a politician would attempt to cure a trouble of this sort which is essentially world wide and transitory by an expedient which is essentially local and permanent. What we have to consider is the so-called permanent unemployment which existed before the slump and which may remain with us after the slump is over.

(6) Continuous unemployment of this character is obviously the result of a disequilibrium between wages, prices, and productivity. The obvious remedies therefore are improvements in productivity or greater flexibility of wages. In the months before the slump, productivity showed signs of increasing. But wages remained rigid. And, since the slump, in spite of a fall in prices of almost unprecedented rapidity, the rigidity has persisted. Undoubtedly it is despair at this rigidity which has driven many who have hitherto been free traders into the ranks of the protectionists.

(7) At this point it is necessary to remove a misapprehension. If you talk to a city man, nowadays, he will tell you that the reason he supports proposals for a tariff is that a tariff will lower real wages and *so* reduce unemployment. This argument is fallacious. The fact that real wages are lowered by a tariff does not in the least imply *in itself* that the profit maker is benefited, that employment increases. If I am manufacturing, say, shoes at a price which involves no profit, the fact that the money wage which I pay my workmen procures them less bread, tea, clothing, etc., does not in the least improve my position. My position will only be improved by a reduction of costs, or a rise in the price of boots, or an increase in my volume of sales. If the price of boots is raised by the introduction of a general tariff, that very circumstance may lower real wages in so far as the price of boots enters into the cost of living. But it is the change in the profit margin, not the lowering of the purchasing power of money wages which benefits my position. It is true that a tariff will almost inevitably have the effect of lowering real wages. It is true that it may be conceived as an attempt to *get round* rigid money wages.[1] But the lowering of real wages is only incidental to its main operation.

(8) The main purpose of a tariff conceived as an instrument for the cure of unemployment is, as Mr. Hawtrey has said, to permit the luxury of a local inflation without incurring the immediate disadvantages thereof.[2] Other

1. In a very striking passage in the Liberal Yellow Book it is even described as "a surreptious method of raising the cost of living and lowering the standard of life" (Liberal Industrial Inquiry, *Britain's Industrial Future* [London, 1928], p. 58). This language is, however, open to the accusation that it grossly misrepresents the intentions of the protectionist; it should therefore be avoided.

2. R.G. Hawtrey, *The Economic Problem* (London, 1926), p. 289. See also *Good and Bad Trade, An Inquiry into the Causes of Trade Fluctuations* (London, 1913), Chapter XVIII, for some exceedingly illuminating observations on this aspect of the problem.

things being equal, it can only operate as a stimulus to business if it permits an expansion of credit. The view, that cutting off an import creates as much unemployment as it causes new employment, is still valid unless it is assumed that credit is capable of further expansion without causing an outflow of gold.[1] In this respect, the argument for protection is on all fours with the more sophisticated arguments for expenditure on public works.

---

1. If this proposition presents any difficulties perhaps the following diagrams will facilitate its acceptance. The dotted lines indicate the flow of money; the unbroken lines the flow of goods.

I IMPORT PROHIBITED: EXPORTER UNEMPLOYED.

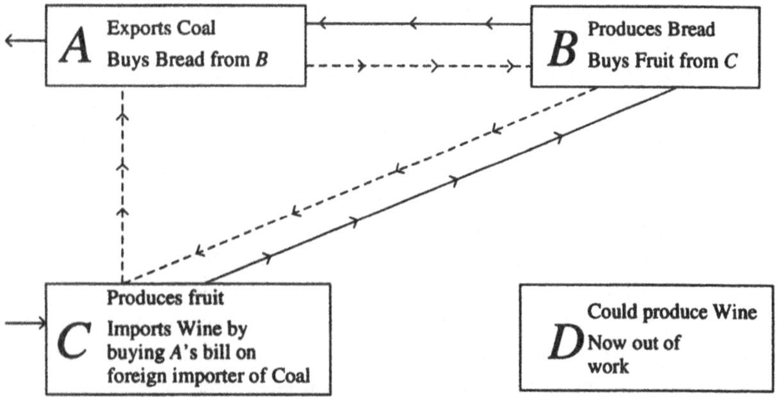

II IMPORT PERMITTED: HOME PRODUCER UNEMPLOYED.

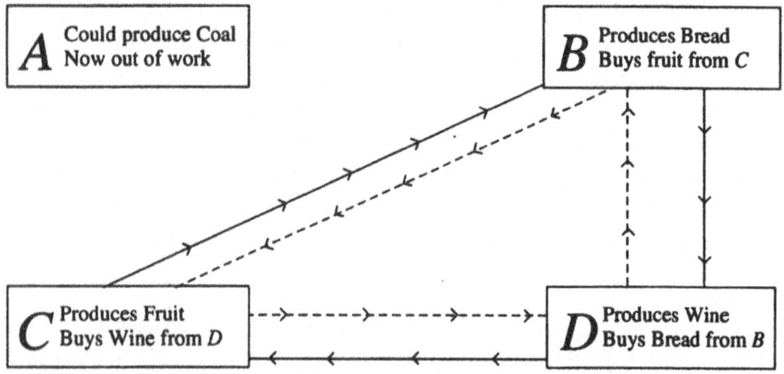

Unless there is an extension of credit or an increase in the velocity of circulation, unemployment persists. The suggestion mentioned by Professor Pigou (*Unemployment* [London, 1914], pp. 43–4) that the exporters will be employed by the persons taken into employment is only valid on these assumptions. Otherwise, it leaves out of account the producers who used to sell to the exporters.

(9) It is important that this should be realised. For, if it is not, the essential feature of the argument is apt to be overlooked. It is clear that, conceived in this way, the tariff is essentially of the order of shock tactics. Its beneficial effects – if it has any – are traceable to its *impact* rather than to its *endurance*. The fact that a tariff is *in* existence is no more safeguard against unemployment than the existence of permanent state activities like the Post Office. It is only its *coming into* existence which makes any difference. If tariffs therefore are to be a permanent cure for unemployment, we must raise our tariff walls every time there is a trade depression.

But are they even likely to be a temporary cure? This demands closer attention both to the assumptions of the theory and the state of the facts.

(10) Now it is perfectly true, as we have just seen, that in pure theory a case can be constructed in which circumstances are such that in the very short run a general protective tariff would have the effect of "curing unemployment." If there existed complete willingness on the part of the Unions to see money wages remain constant in the face of rising prices, then it is theoretically possible that a tariff by increasing prices and permitting an extension of domestic credit might reduce unemployment.

But it is important to notice the assumptions of this proposition – money wages constant, while prices rise. In fact, these assumptions are not likely to be justified. Money wages (particularly those on a cost of living basis) are not likely to remain constant in the face of rising prices. Hitherto in the history of the world, when Protection has been afforded to an industry or group of industries, the workers concerned have not refrained from demanding a share of the loaves and fishes. There seems no reason to suppose that in the future their practice in this respect will be different.

(11) But putting this on one side for the moment, how far should we regard the increase in employment in certain industries, which would probably follow the imposition of a tariff, as a net gain? The answer is not encouraging. A substantial proportion of the present volume of unemployment is in export industries which, for obvious reasons, are incapable of being assisted by a tariff. A tariff on imported coal will not assist the British coal industry to recover foreign markets. A tariff on cotton cloth would not foster the sale of this product in the hostile bazaars of the East. Nor would our shipyards benefit from a veto on the import of foreign ships. But not only will these industries not be assisted by a tariff: there is reason to suppose that they would be positively injured. And this in two ways.

(*a*) In the first place they will be injured because our foreign customers would be injured. If we refuse to buy from people abroad, then, *other things remaining the same*, people abroad are less capable of buying our products. For reasons which it is difficult to fathom, in certain quarters recently, this elementary generalisation, the *pons asinorum* of international trade theory, has come to be regarded, either as an exploded fallacy or as an irrelevant truism. Fallacy it certainly is not. The balance of payments must balance, and this is only one way of saying that it must do so. Nor is it easy to see why it should be regarded as an irrelevant truism. It is said that the "other things being equal" (which, to escape contumely, I have underlined) conceals the all-important possibility of lending more abroad. It may be agreed that this is a possibility. But it may be denied that it is very important. Suppose a tariff is imposed which reduces our imports by £50,000,000 a year. It is possible that in the very short run this falling off in the buying power of our foreign customers might be made good by short lending to the countries concerned. It is conceivable even that it might be financed merely by a transfer of floating balances standing to the credit of the exporting countries. But, obviously, this could not continue indefinitely. Every year there would be this deficiency of buying power. Short lending would have to be replaced by long. Now it is possible for really intelligent people to differ both about the difficulty and the desirability of increasing our long term export of capital. But it seems hard to believe that there can be much difference of opinion about the desirability or indeed the likelihood of continuous long term lending to repair the damage done by our own refusal to import. I can imagine one answer to this objection, the answer, namely, that we should lend more *elsewhere*. I do not think that in any case this answer would be valid. But it would be an answer which would be entirely illegitimate if it were put forward by those who are continually urging upon our notice the "organic nature" of trade connections and the great difficulty of extending exports anywhere.

(*b*) But leaving demand out of account altogether and concentrating only on the supply side, it is equally important to realise that Protection would injure the export industries by bringing about a rise in their costs. It has been emphasised already that if domestic prices are raised, then wages are likely to follow. If this does not show itself directly in export labour costs, it will have an indirect effect on the prices of the various services the export industries are compelled to use. Moreover, if the tariff is general, the raw materials used by many export industries would become more expensive. Nor would its restriction to articles classed as "wholly or mainly manufactured" do more than limit the damage. A substantial volume of commodities falling into this class are the raw materials of important export industries. No doubt it is possible to argue that these difficulties could be circumvented by a system of drawbacks. Those who take such arguments seriously may be referred to the discussion of these systems in the standard works on the subject.[1]

1. See e.g. T.E. Gregory, *Tariffs: A Study in Method* (London, 1921).

(12) It is fairly clear that *some* damage would be inflicted on the export industries by *any* tariff. Of course, a small tariff would not inflict so great a damage as a large one. Analytical economists who are also free traders must not be thought to be indifferent to this consideration. It would be difficult to be wildly alarmed about the probable effects of a one per cent. general tariff. It would not, however, be irrelevant to observe that the plea that it would "only be a little one" is not new in modern tariff history. It has been heard before.

(13) It is equally clear that many of the present advocates of Protection in this country would not mind doing damage to the export trades.[1] The export trades, it is said, are doomed to contraction anyway. Why worry if we accelerate the process? The important thing is the stimulation of new industries, the development of the home market. This reasoning does not carry *prima facie* conviction. It may be that in the future the plight of the export industries of this country will be worse even than it is at present. I do not myself think that this is bound to be the case, but it is certainly not inconceivable that it may happen. But that does not seem any reason for anticipating matters. It will not be a good thing if in time to come other people put a lower valuation on our products. The burden of proof still rests with those who urge that we should go out of our way to induce changes which otherwise might never occur.

(14) But let us waive these objections for the moment. Let us assume that we are prepared to 'cure unemployment' regardless of the effects on export. Even so, the attempt to do so by means of protective tariffs is open to a very grave objection. For surely if it is desired to increase employment by stimulating industry, it is also desirable to increase it by stimulating the *right* industries, that is to say those industries in which our comparative advantages are greatest. Now this is precisely what the protective tariff fails to do. For, obviously, by definition, it stimulates those industries which need protection, those industries, that is to say, in which our comparative advantages are most questionable: the industries in which our comparative advantages are unchallenged would receive no direct benefit. Unless we are to abandon all idea of a "proper" apportionment of the factors of production, these are not the industries which should be encouraged. One of the main industries to be encouraged by a general protective tariff would be arable farming. Yet judged by every test of present prices and costs and the probabilities of technical change in the future, both here and elsewhere, this is perhaps the last important industry which it would be desirable artificially to stimulate.

---

1. See e.g. a very illuminating letter from Mr. John Strachey in *The Nation and Athenaeum*, January 3, 1931.

(15) So much for Protection as a cure for existing unemployment. If the analysis developed above is valid, it seems unlikely that the highly problematical advantages which might conceivably accompany its impact would be held to outweigh its very obvious disadvantages, particularly in view of the almost inevitable permanence of tariffs and the probable transience of our present troubles. If the cure of present unemployment were everything, surely few reasonable men would recommend so drastic and crude a therapy.

But it is not everything. And it is now necessary to take account of a subtler form of these arguments which suggests not only that a tariff would cure our present unemployment, but that the existence of a tariff in future would avert the occurrence of more unemployment of a sort similar to that from which we are conceived to have been suffering in the past. I refer, of course, to the argument elucidated by Mr. Keynes in his recently published *A Treatise on Money*.[1] This is so important that it merits a separate section.

III

(1) It is a perilous undertaking to expound the high mysteries of any part of the *Treatise on Money*. Fortunately, this part of Mr. Keynes's doctrine is less novel than the rest, and permits of rough restatement in the terms of classical analysis.

The argument, as I understand it, all turns upon the alleged difficulties of varying in an upward direction the size of our export surplus. If we wish to lend more abroad, argues Mr. Keynes, then we can only do so if the export surplus is increased. The mere fact that we wish to lend more abroad and that we attempt to make the loan does not, in his opinion, save in very exceptional cases, have any direct influence on the trade balance. The direct consequences of attempts to increase foreign lending are pressure on the exchanges, a tendency to a drain of gold, and an upward movement of Bank Rate.

Now, before the war, argues Mr. Keynes, this process was usually enough to cure the situation. With the tendency to a rise in Bank Rate there was tendency for contraction of credit. With the tendency to contraction of credit there was a tendency to a fall in prices. With the tendency to a fall in prices there was a tendency to a fall in wages and other incomes. Exports tended to

1. (London, 1930), Vol. II, pp. 184–9. It is perhaps desirable to emphasise that, in all that follows, I shall be criticising this particular argument and not Mr. Keynes's general position – whatever that may be. An economist is not to be described as a protectionist because he believes in the possible validity of one theoretical argument for protection, and there is nothing in the whole *Treatise on Money* which would render the suggestion that Mr. Keynes wished to group himself with the current advocates of protection anything but grossly improper.

increase and equilibrium was restored with the creation of an appropriate export surplus – an appropriate *favourable* balance of trade – to use the Mercantilistic term he has resuscitated.[1]

But since the war the position has altered. The rigidity of money wages is a new factor in the situation. Nowadays, when there is pressure to lend abroad, the Bank Rate rises as before – or at any rate there is a tendency to a contraction of credit. But the further effects are different. Since money wages are rigid, all that happens is that the rise of Bank Rate frustrates itself, as it were, in unemployment. At the same time the capital market at home is thrown into disequilibrium. The money rate of interest is above the natural or equilibrium rate of interest. "Savings," therefore, are in excess of "Investment." The result is waste and persistent depression. This is the position in which we have been since 1925: and since England is an old country and the tendency in the future will be to attempt to lend more rather than less abroad, it is a position which is likely to grow worse instead of better.

How, then, is the situation to be cured? The flexibility of money wages, according to Mr. Keynes, is not likely to be restored. Hence there are only open two alternatives. Either we curtail the volume of foreign investment by imposing differential taxation or other minor inconveniences similar to those in vogue in France at the present moment. Or we impose a protective tariff which will limit the amount we buy from other people, and thus enable us to sell more exports on credit. The first proposal is to be preferred, but it involves certain obvious difficulties. Mr. Keynes is therefore "coming round" to the view that there may be something to be said for the second expedient.

(2) Such is the argument. What are we to say as to its validity? As an explanation of certain of the short period difficulties which may arise in a country in which wages are sticky and the monetary situation is abnormal – as it was here during the period of the restoration of the gold standard – there are elements in the theory which are important and useful. But it is as a normal long period theory of capital transfer that it must be judged; and, from this point of view, it is clear, I think, that there is an initial presumption against it. It would surely be an odd thing if the transfer of capital which is accomplished so simply and expeditiously *within* the boundaries of any customs area were to be accompanied by so devastating a series of consequences whenever it is

1. It would be a mistake to identify Mr. Keynes's desire to increase the favourable balance of trade with the general run of theories concerning the trade balance, current in the eighteenth century. According to Professor Viner, Sir James Steuart, who wrote in 1767, is "the only mercantilist who even cites the desirability of investment abroad as one of the reasons for desiring a favourable balance." See Jacob Viner, "English theories of foreign trade before Adam Smith," *Journal of Political Economy*, vol. 38 (June and August 1930), pp. 294–301 and 404–57.

attempted to vary the volume of lending *across* the customs areas. Did not long experience make him easy on this head – to parody Hume – what a fund of gloomy reflection might oppress Mr. Keynes as he computed and magnified the fluctuations in the volume of lending between Cambridge and London. "And, no doubt, had the Heptarchy persisted in England, the legislature of each State had been continually alarmed by the fear of a wrong balance; and as it is probable that the mutual hatred of these States would have been extremely violent on account of their close neighbourhood, they would have loaded and oppressed all commerce by a jealous and superfluous caution."[1]

(3) Moreover, from the point of view of pure theory, it is equally clear that the argument presents certain difficulties. Mr. Keynes is treating the amount which a country can lend abroad as *residually* determined, as profits used to be in the old classical analysis, and wages in the system of Francis Walker. Now if there is one common characteristic of modern analysis it is that in pure theory *nothing* is regarded as residually determined. Every quantity in the equations of equilibrium has a right to be regarded as being simultaneously determined with every other quantity – the equilibrating process being conceived as one of reciprocal causation.

(4) But it would be wrong to rest content with these *a priori* presumptions. For, pure theory notwithstanding, if certain economic quantities are notoriously sticky, we are justified, in short period analysis, in regarding certain other quantities which adapt themselves to them as being, as it were, in the nature of residues. The question, therefore, which we have to answer is whether Mr. Keynes's belief that in the modern world the export surplus is so insusceptible of change is actually justified. Is it in fact true, even in the short run, that the trade balance is not a function of what is being lent?

(5) Historically, I do not think it is open to question that the answer is in the negative. I know no case in the pre-war history of normal trade where the transfer problem alone was the cause of serious difficulties. Of course it is not part of Mr. Keynes's present argument that it was. He only contends that circumstances are now quite different. Still, wages were not perfectly plastic in the pre-war period, yet so far as I am able to discover the export surplus accommodated itself to fluctuations in the volume of foreign lending with great rapidity and little disturbance.[2]

1. *Essays, moral, political and literary*, eds T.H. Green and T.H. Grose (London, 1875), Vol. I, p. 335.

2. It is interesting to notice that in the chart given in Dr. C.K. Hobson's *The Export of Capital* (London, 1914), p. 222, on which are recorded fluctuations in employment, the export surplus and public issues for foreign investment, there is no obvious correlation between employment and the difference between foreign issues and the export surplus. I would not press this very far as no doubt the figures of public issues are by no means the whole story. But the apparent absence of correlation is at least worthy of notice.

(6) Much more convincing, because they relate to a later period and because they concern a case where the difficulties of transfer might be supposed to be greatest, is the evidence of the recent German trade statistics. Ever since he wrote *The Economic Consequences of the Peace* [1919] Mr. Keynes has been telling us that the creation of a German export surplus of any substantial size is wellnigh out of the question. It is clear that his present anxiety with regard to the future position of this country is merely a transfer of his apprehensions about Germany to the sphere of more general theory. It is therefore a not insignificant circumstance that since the flow of American funds into Germany began to fall off, an export surplus has been developing strictly according to the predictions of Mr. Keynes's opponents. Of course, the present position is abnormal. Not too much importance must be attached to events of so short a duration. But it is at least a combination of circumstances which calls for explanation if it is to be shown to be irrelevant to the general theory of transfer.

(7) So much for facts. But facts in themselves are not always good guides to prediction. Moreover, it would be wrong to argue that the verdict of facts was at present unmistakable. In the last analysis, therefore, we are bound once more to have recourse to more general theoretical considerations.

Now I think it would be wrong to deny that Mr. Keynes is right when he argues that rigidity of money wages makes every adjustment more difficult. Clearly he is right here. Clearly the fact that wages are rigid is an incentive to make transfers which otherwise would not be attempted. Nevertheless, I think he very greatly overestimates the inflexibility of the export surplus in modern conditions. I think this for two separate reasons.

(*a*) In the first place I think he always tends to underestimate the import side of the equation. The fact that a loan is raised for abroad, or that reparation taxes are paid, deprives domestic payers of spending power. Some of this spending power would be spent on imports. The situation is, therefore, to that extent automatically eased. I do not suggest that Mr. Keynes overlooks this entirely; I only suggest that he continually underestimates its magnitude.

(*b*) On the export side, I think he makes two mistaken assumptions.

(i) In the first place he assumes that the elasticity of demand for the exports of a manufacturing country is low. There seems no reason to suppose that this is the case. Competitive manufactures are likely to be in highly elastic demand. The more competitive the supply, the more highly elastic the demand for any part of it. This is a legitimate theoretical objection. I do not think recent German experience contradicts it.

(ii) But even if it were legitimate to assume that demand were comparatively inelastic, it would be wrong to assume that transfer was thereby made impossible. For it is a fundamental error to assume that the conditions of demand for export are unaffected by the fact that transfer is to be made. It is not merely a matter of the slope of the demand curve. It is a question of the movement of the demand curve as a whole. If I lend a man £100 out of a fixed income that means that immediately my demand curves are moved to the left – at any price I demand less – while his demand curves are pushed to the right – at any price, he demands more. Mr. Keynes would admit that this is so when individuals are making transfers in the same currency, but he argues that it is almost out of the question that international transfers should be made in this way. I confess this seems to me mistaken. I see no reason why, as money is collected and handed over in one centre, there should not be an immediate expansion of credit against that money in another centre. No doubt there are technical exchange difficulties. No doubt if the exports of the lending country are not suitable there is some long period transfer problem. I am very far from wishing to argue that in the majority of cases transfer is possible without some price movement.[1] But I do not believe that the difficulties are anything like as great as Mr. Keynes would have us believe. A technical problem no doubt can arise in the very short period. But the probability of its persistence has yet to be demonstrated.[2]

(8) I see no reason then to assume that even in the modern world the difficulties of international capital transfer are of the order of magnitude suggested by Mr. Keynes. And I see no reason, therefore, to follow him when he suggests that it might be desirable, either to limit the volume of foreign lending by interfering with the City, or to facilitate it by interfering with trade. Only the most overwhelming evidence of the probable persistence in normal times of a transfer problem of the very gravest difficulty could be held to justify such measures. That evidence, I contend, has not been submitted.

(9) Moreover, it may be questioned whether, for a community in our position, the effects of a tariff would be an easement even of the transfer problem. It is common ground that transfer is easiest when the loan is spent in the

1. I do not understand this to be the view of either Professor Ohlin or of Dr. Haberler, each of whom has expressed the view that Mr. Keynes's pronouncements on the transfer problem overstress the difficulties and overlook certain theoretical probabilities. See their discussion of this matter in recent numbers of the *Zeitschrift für Nationalökonomie*: – Gottfried Haberler, "Transfer und Preisbewegung," vol. 1 (1930), pp. 547–54, and Vol. 2 (1931), pp. 100–2; Bertil Ohlin, "Transfer und Preisbewegung," vol. 1 (1930), pp. 762–5.

2. Nothing that is said in these notes with regard to the economic possibilities of transfer must be regarded as affording any ground for minimising the grave political difficulties of the payment of Reparations. The fall of gold prices has imposed upon Germany a burden considerably heavier than that which was in the minds of the experts who were responsible for the passing of the Young Plan. At the same time, the general depression of trade has greatly intensified the budgetary difficulties of the Reich. Small wonder, if in times like these, the payment of Reparations, however feasible from the strictly economic point of view, encounters a psychological resistance, upon which all present arrangements may very well be shattered.

lending country. Now from what has been said already, it should be clear that one of the immediate effects of a tariff must be to raise domestic prices and costs. If the costs of the export industries are raised, there will be a tendency for their prices to rise also and to the extent to which this happens – to the extent to which the prices of *potential* export goods are raised – the incentive to spend the proceeds of any given loan in this country is obviously diminished. This seems to provide an *additional* reason for rejecting the proposal.

8 Consumption and the Trade Cycle[1]

From *Economica*, vol. 12 (November 1932), pp. 413–30.

I

The object of this paper is two-fold. Firstly, it examines critically certain theories which attribute trade depression to a deficiency of consumption. Secondly, it indicates very briefly and very tentatively what seems to me to be a more correct view of the relationship between consumption and the downward turn of trade. Neither the criticisms nor the constructive suggestions make any pretentions to originality. I have simply tried to adapt to the subject which I have chosen views which, if not yet universally accepted, today command the adherence of economists of standing in many different parts of the world.[2] In doing this, however, I have endeavoured to avoid the use of unfamiliar terminology. This has imposed considerable limitation on the attainment of complete precision, but, for various reasons, it seemed worth attempting.

II

1. To commence, then, with criticism. It is the essence of the so-called underconsumption theories that, under a capitalistic order of society, an insufficient amount is spent on consumption. Hence, it is argued, it is impossible for any

---

1. The substance of a paper read before Section F of the British Association at York, September 1st, 1932.

2. Besides the well-known works of Professors Mises and Hayek, the following may be consulted: Gottfried Haberler, "Money and the business cycle," in *Gold and Monetary Stabilization*, ed. Philip Quincy Wright (Chicago, 1931); Costantino Bresciani-Turroni, "Kapitalmangel und Währungsstabilisierung," *Die Wirtschaftstheorie der Gegenwart*, ed. Hans Mayer (Vienna, 1932), Vol. 2, pp. 391–403; J.R. Hicks, *The Theory of Wages* (London, 1932), Chapters IX and X; and Richard von Strigl, "Die Produktion unter dem Einflusse einer Kreditexpansion," *Schriften des Vereins für Sozialpolitik*, vol. 173 (1928), pp. 187–211.

long period to market goods at a profit. This contention is common to all such theories, but, in the detailed arguments involved, certain differences are apparent. For purposes of analysis, therefore, we may divide such theories further according as they involve an absolute or a relative deficiency of spending for consumption. Thus, on the one hand, we have theories which assert that the absolute amount spent on consumption tends to be insufficient. Into this group fall the views of those who urge that a stable consumers'-goods price level is essential to continuous prosperity. On the other hand, we have those theories which assert rather that it is the amount spent on consumption relatively to the amount invested which is at fault. Into this group fall the theories of Mr. J.A. Hobson. I propose to examine each of these groups separately.

2. Before doing this, however, I wish to devote some attention to a theory which goes beyond any of these and asserts not merely that the capitalist machinery does not result in enough being spent on *consumption*; but that it inevitably results in not enough being spent on the *product of industry in the gross*. I refer to the theory of Major C.H. Douglas. I select this theory for critical examination, not from any desire to select what some would regard as an easy target, but because it so happens that such an examination brings out, more vividly than any other way I know, the significance of certain propositions which seem to me to be very important in the general universe of discourse I have chosen. I do not know any writer on these subjects who enunciates so distinctly the exact opposite of what seem to me to be correct views on these matters.[1]

3. Major Douglas bases his diagnosis on a survey of factory costing. Take any article of factory manufacture, he says – a nut and bolt, for example. Part of its cost consists of wages, salaries and other payments to the recipients of ultimate income; but part consists of raw material charges, factory upkeep, and similar "overheads." The sums distributed as current *income*, therefore, are not sufficient to purchase the current output. Now what is true of one factory is true of all. It follows, therefore, that, throughout the entire economic system, there is a continuous deficiency of income to purchase the product – a deficiency which, if not made good by the continuous issue of paper money, must necessarily lead to chronic bankruptcy and confusion.[2]

1. Since writing the above I have had the privilege of seeing a manuscript by my friend, Mr. E.F.M. Durbin, in which the views of Major Douglas are criticised on somewhat similar lines. I should like to make it clear that Mr. Durbin had reached his conclusion quite independently. Mr. Durbin's analysis is much more exhaustive than mine and should be consulted by all who are interested in this type of theory. [The manuscript was the draft of *Purchasing Power and Trade Depression: A Critique of Under-consumption theories* (London, 1933). Durbin dedicated the book to Robbins who read and commented on the draft in the early autumn of 1932.]

2. *Economic Democracy* (London, 1920), pp. 56–8.

4. Such is the diagnosis on which this theory is based. In the past, public criticism of this theory has concentrated rather upon the obvious weakness of the inflationist propaganda with which it is associated than upon the fundamental logical fallacy which lies in the diagnosis itself. This is unfortunate. It is easy to see that if credit were issued on the lines suggested, the condition of the area in which the experiment was made would soon be as bad as that of Germany during the worst stages of inflation. But this leaves the logic of the argument unaffected. To refute a theory, it is not sufficient to show that its consequences are dangerous: it is necessary also to show that its logic is defective. Fortunately, in the instance we are considering, this is not difficult to do. The fallacy consists in a misapprehension of the conditions which make capitalistic equilibrium conceivable. It is perfectly true, as Major Douglas urges, that in such a system the sums distributed in any period as ultimate incomes – wages, salaries, etc. – are insufficient to purchase the product of industry of the same period, *if "product" be understood to mean the output of all financially independent productive units at all stages of the productive process* – the gross product in the sense in which the term is used in the statistics of the Census of Production.[1] But, *so far from this being a cause of disequilibrium, it is, in fact, an essential condition if any kind of equilibrium is to be preserved.*

5. This proposition can be very easily demonstrated. Let us consider a system which is in stationary equilibrium (i.e. a system in which no net saving is taking place). Now, it should be clear that only in very special circumstances is it compatible with the requirements of equilibrium that the recipients of net money income in any period should be in a position to purchase the whole product of industry during that period. Indeed, save in the special case of vertical integration all round, it can only be so when production is of what may be called the hand-to-mouth or single-stage variety. If the various consumption goods brought to market are each produced in one short operation with the aid of no "produced means of production," then, in any

1. The history of this conception is interesting. Introduced by Smith, it played an important part in the classical system until Mill's rejection of the wage fund theory in the 1870s. From that time it passed into undeserved neglect. Profesor Cannan, writing early in the 1890s, could find in it only "a ridiculous total" (*A History of Theories of Production and Distribution in English Classical Political Economy from 1776 to 1848* [London, 1893], p. 77). Later, Professor Irving Fisher rehabilitated it as a concept of monetary theory: "So far from being ridiculous, this total is the work of exchange done by money – the 'societary circulation' of Newcomb" ("What is capital?," *Economic Journal*, vol. 6 (December 1896), p. 534). The significance and theoretical utility of the concept is fully recognised in Professor Taussig's *Wages and Capital* (New York, 1896), but unfortunately that work did not always receive the attention it deserved and, in consequence, it is only quite recently that the importance of the classical conception has once again come to be recognised.

equilibrium situation, it is true that the amounts paid to their makers and the owners of the natural resources from which they are made will be equal to the value of the total product. In such circumstances, the value of the gross product and the net product will be identical. But once there exists "vertical" division of labour, production is divided into more than one stage. Unless there is complete vertical integration in every line of production, this means that the aggregate of money payments made in any unit period will be greater than the aggregate of payments to ultimate factors of production. That is to say, the value of the net product and of the gross product are no longer identical. The sums paid out for them are no longer identical. Some of the money paid out in each stage constitutes net income. But some goes to replace capital purchased from an earlier stage. We get an exact notion of the process if we think of the picture presented by the Census of Production statistics. The baker pays out wages, but he also buys flour to replace his stock. The miller pays out wages, but he buys wheat to make good his sales. And so on and so forth. At each stage there are costs which are not income.

Now, no doubt, in any computation of the net income, these elements in the gross income cancel out, leaving us with figures of net income which, in a stationary state, should correspond to computations of net income made on the income-tax assessment plan. But this is not to say that they are negligible from the point of view of equilibrium theory. On the contrary, they are most important. For in order that the system may continue in equilibrium – other things being the same – it is essential that they should continue as before. The condition of equilibrium is that the net income of the factors of production should be equal to the value of consumers' goods produced and that the payments between the earlier stages (the elements in the gross income which cancel out) should continue in such a way as to keep the value of capital constant; i.e. other things remaining unchanged, should themselves be unaltered in volume. Thus the complaint that the net income is insufficient to purchase the gross product is doubly absurd. It is unnecessary that it should be so if equilibrium is to be preserved. And it is undesirable that it should do so if the system is not to run down. If those payments which are not net income did not continue to be made, "many-stage production" in financially independent forms could not profitably persist.

6. We may perhaps see this second point more clearly if, for a moment, we allow ourselves to suppose that the tacit requirements of Major Douglas's critical diagnosis were actually to be fulfilled. Suppose that the incomes of the factors of production during any period were to be raised so as to equal the value of the gross product, offered for exchange during that period. What would this imply? Simply that the whole fund of free capital (amortisation quotas and working capital) had been turned into income: that the entrepreneurs had been compelled to pay out all that they receive "over the counter"

as wages, salaries, dividends, etc.[1] What would be the result of this? Clearly, unless the recipients of the extra income at once reinvested the increase, there would occur all the phenomena of the severest form of economic crisis. The prices of consumption goods would rise; but the prices of intermediate products, raw materials, machines, etc., would collapse for, by hypothesis, the free capital which constituted the demand for such products would have been transferred. Of course, such an extreme state of affairs is not likely to occur in practice. But if wages are above the equilibrium point it is possible for something disquietingly like it to begin to make its appearance.[2] In any case, the illustration should make clear the fundamental points overlooked by Major Douglas that equality of net and gross income is incompatible with the requirements of equilibrium under capitalist conditions and that the failure of the distributive machinery to secure this equality is not to be regarded as a disequilibrating factor.

7. Thus in the case most favourable to Major Douglas, the completely stationary state, his argument breaks down completely. If real accumulation is to take place – that is, if the system is to be "progressive" – the refutation applies *a fortiori*. For, in such circumstances, the gross income must *exceed* the amount spent on consumption goods by *more* than the difference between the gross income and the payments to the ultimate factors of production: it must contain a quantity equivalent to the amount of net saving. If accumulation is to take place, there must be abstention from using all the productive power available to produce a constant flow of real income in the present. Some current money income must be spent in ways which will yield real income only at some point in the future, other things remaining the same. To shift the proportion between gross income and net income in favour of net income, is simply to diminish the flow of saving.

8. It is time to proceed to underconsumption theories proper. In this connection, I turn first to those theories which attribute trade depression to a failure of the amount spent on consumption to reach a certain absolute figure – the figure which, in the given circumstances, would keep the price level of consumers' goods stable.

---

1. On the entrepreneur's place in distribution, see Taussig, *Wages and Capital*, especially Chapters I–VI. It has been said that Professor Taussig's book still smacks of the Wage Fund. On this, the appropriate comment is, not so much worse for Professor Taussig's book, but so much better for the Wage Fund Theory. I would make so bold as to assert that, at the present time, the whole drift of economic thought on these matters is towards a rehabilitation of these much-derided but little-understood propositions.

2. See Friedrich A. Hayek, "Kapitalaufzehrung," *Weltwirtschaftliches Archiv*, Vol. 36 (1932), pp. 86–108; also Hicks, *Theory of Wages*, Chapters IX and X.

Fortunately, it is not necessary to linger long in this neighbourhood. Although, in the last few years, there has crept into popular discussions the assumption that this view is universally accepted among economists, in fact the true state of affairs is almost precisely the contrary. In modern times, there have been few economists of standing who have not gone out of their way actually to refute it. The belief that there is nothing detrimental to the smooth working of the economic machinery in the changes which result in a consumers' goods price index falling with increased productivity, is not the esoteric creed of a handful of "sadistic deflationists" – as is sometimes suggested nowadays. It is the view which has been held by the majority of the men who have made modern monetary theory in English-speaking countries what it is – Marshall, Edgeworth, Taussig, Hawtrey, Robertson, Pigou.[1] That a belief that prices cannot fall without causing depression should be able to co-exist with the overwhelmingly convincing demonstration of the contrary proposition in nearly all the standard works on the subject is a most disquieting revelation of the gulf which still exists between scientific knowledge and popular opinion.

The refutation of the view in question is very simple. It is clear that there is nothing inimical to the profitability of a particular undertaking if the prices of its products fall *pari passu* with its costs. Now the price level is simply a statistical average of the prices paid for particular products. If, therefore, the prices of particular products may thus fall without difficulty, then there is nothing in their compilation into index numbers in government offices or elsewhere which need lead to industrial disaster.

It is sometimes said that this argument ignores the existence of fixed interest charges and other similar obligations. It cannot be emphasised too often that this objection is fallacious. In so far as industrial costs are concerned, it is plainly a begging of the question. The argument is that, *if* costs have fallen, prices can fall without loss of profitability: it is obviously beside the point to say that *some* costs have not fallen. So far as Government Debt is concerned, the objection has more plausibility, for it is true that, in such circumstances, the "real value" of each pound's worth of debt has risen. But it is not true that the "real burden" rises. By hypothesis, the fall in prices is due to increased productivity. Hence there is a larger product out of which to pay the larger

1. See, *e.g.*, Marshall's evidence before the Gold and Silver Commission of 1887 (*Official Papers by Alfred Marshall*, ed. J.M. Keynes [London, 1926], pp. 17–195); F.Y. Edgeworth "Thoughts on monetary reform," *Economic Journal*, vol. 5 (September 1895), pp. 434–51; F.W. Taussig, *The Silver Situation in the United States* (New York, 1893); A.C. Pigou, *Industrial Fluctuations*, 2nd edn (London, 1929); D.H. Robertson, *Money*, 2nd edn (London, 1928); see also Ludwig von Mises, *Geldwertsstabilisierung und Konjunkturpolitik* (Jena, 1928); and Gottfried von Haberler, *Der Sinn der Indexzahlen* (Tübingen, 1927).

interest. All that happens is that the bond holders, etc., share in the general increase of prosperity. This may or may not be ethically desirable. But it imposes no friction on the smooth working of the economic mechanism. The real burden of debt increases in the way suggested only when the price fall is due not to increased productivity but to absolute deflation.[1] If the price fall is due to increased productivity then the existence of fixed charges involves no modification of the fundamental proposition: a price fall of this nature has no inherent tendency to bring with it industrial depression.[2]

9. I now come to the second group of theories I have to criticise: the theories, namely, which attribute the coming of trade depression to a *relative* deficiency of the amount spent on consumption. The theories I have just examined assert that the collapse comes because the amount spent on consumption fails to reach a certain absolute magnitude. The theories I now wish to contemplate make no such assertion. They assert rather that it comes if the proportion between the amount spent on consumption and the amount invested falls below a certain point; a state of affairs which might come about on a stationary or even a rising price level of consumers' commodities. It is this view which is the central contention of the theory of the trade cycle which has been advanced by Mr. J.A. Hobson.[3]

Before commencing to examine his theory, however, one word of warning is perhaps necessary. The underconsumption theory as developed by Mr. Hobson and others has nothing to do with Mr. Keynes's theory of the

1. Haberler, *op. cit.*, pp. 112 ff.

2. Mr. Dennis Robertson and others have put the matter much more strongly and have suggested that, if prices *do not* fall in this way, there will be a disturbance of equilibrium. Mr. Robertson's pronouncement is so important that I venture to quote it at some length. He says: "The events of the last eighteen months ... have confirmed rather than shaken me in the belief that the maintenance of an even rate of industrial progress, difficult enough in any case, will be rendered more difficult still if the world commits itself to the view that, however great the improvements in technical efficiency, prices ought never to fall. Looking back, it becomes, I think, more and more arguable that the great American 'stabilisation' of 1922–9 was really a vast attempt to de-stabilise the value of money in terms of human effort by means of a colossal programme of investment in buildings, motor-car plants, etc., which succeeded for a surprisingly long period, but which no human ingenuity could have managed to direct indefinitely on sound and balanced lines. It becomes plainer, too, I think, that the disastrous slump in the prices of many foodstuffs and raw materials has been in part, at any rate, a nemesis for ill-considered efforts (greedy in the case of low-cost producers, pathetic and futile in the case of high-cost ones) to hold up prices in the face of falling costs. If the business man's psychology jibs at swallowing the moderate price falls dictated by increasing productivity, he renders himself more and not less liable to suffer the catastrophic price falls due to industrial dislocation and crisis – that is my case." (D.H. Robertson, "How do we want gold to behave?" printed in Royal Institute of International Affairs, *The International Gold Problem* [London, 1931], p. 45.)

3. *The Physiology of Industry* (London, 1889), *The Evolution of Modern Capitalism* (London, 1894), *The Industrial System* (London, 1909), *The Economics of Unemployment* (London, 1922).

cycle, although in recent discussions it has sometimes been identified with it. Mr. Keynes's theory of the cycle, it is true, invokes at one point an excess of "saving." But "saving" in the Keynesian terminology is essentially a monetary concept. In Mr. Keynes's view the difficulty arises when the monetary savings are not turned into real investment, whereas in Mr. Hobson's view it arises because that real investment is excessive in relation to real consumption. For Mr. Keynes, one way out of the slump would be a revival of investment; for Mr. Hobson, this would simply make matters worse.

10. By a curious irony of history, the central argument on which this theory is based depends upon concepts similar in kind to those of the celebrated doctrine of maximum satisfaction. At any given moment, argues Mr. Hobson, there is a proportion between spending and investing[1] which will make the social income of utility, over time, a maximum. In an inequalitarian society, this proportion is likely to be overstepped. The existence of rich people with saving habits imposes, as it were, upon capitalist society the deprivations and difficulties of a persistent Five-Year Plan. In an inequalitarian society, therefore, there will be periodic gluts due to oversaving and underconsumption.

11. Now the first thing to observe about this argument is that it involves the assumption that the utilities experienced by different economic subjects can be aggregated. That assumption, as I have argued recently elsewhere,[2] I believe to be totally unwarranted. Direct comparisons of individuals' experiences must, necessarily, involve arbitrary postulates entirely out of place in causal analysis. They belong to the sphere of ethics or aesthetics rather than to the sphere of positive science. On purely methodological grounds, therefore, I should be inclined to hold this argument invalid. A concept which has no scientific status can hardly be allowed to form part of a scientific explanation.

12. But, in adopting so radical a procedure, I am quite aware that I cannot expect by any means unanimous support. For the sake of argument, therefore, let me assume that the conception of social aggregates of utility is logically permissible. Even so, I can see nothing in economic analysis which would justify the inference that the failure of such an aggregate to reach its maximum through time has any *causal* significance for the relations between production and consumption. Quite apart from the fact that it is impossible scientifically to determine what that maximum is, there is no justification for

1. I use the term "investing" rather than Mr. Hobson's "saving" in order to leave no doubt about the "real" nature of the phenomena he is contemplating.

2. See my *An Essay on the Nature and Significance of Economic Science* (London, 1932), Chapter VI, Paragraph 2.

the view that its attainment or non-attainment is anything but a matter of complete indifference to the machinery which either brings about, or fails to bring about, equilibrium between supply and demand in the different parts of the economic system. For this machinery is governed, not by the movements of aggregates of social utility, but by the relationships of particular prices and costs – which, in turn, are governed not by *social* but by *individual* valuations. Equilibrium of exchange is possible between Dives and Lazarus even if (according to some systems of ethics) the aggregate of social utility would be greater if the initial distribution between them were less unequal.[1]

13. But if we examine this mechanism of prices and costs, we find nothing to lead us to suppose that any one proportion between investing and spending is more favourable than another to the preservation of stability. Provided that there is no inflation and "forced saving" – provided that the system as a whole is flexible – until the volume of accumulation is such as to make the marginal productivity of capital fall to zero, there is no reason to suppose that, with any given ratio between investing and spending, the relationship between prices and costs will be such as to make disposal of the product unprofitable.

We can see this most clearly if we revert to the point at which we left our examination of the arguments of the advocates of the fixed price level. The profitability of a productive operation is not a matter of the absolute prices at which its products can be sold: it is a matter of the relationship between these prices and its costs. Now if we assume a constant population,[2] it should be clear that investment is essentially a cost-reducing process. It increases productivity – *that is to say*, it reduces the cost per unit of output. Different degrees of investment make possible different degrees of cost reduction. When the total volume of accumulation is small, the increase of productivity – that is, the reduction of costs – due to an additional increment of investment, will be relatively large. When the total volume of accumulation is great, other things having remained the same, the increase will be relatively small (Law of Diminishing Returns). But until the rate of interest, which depends ultimately upon the difference between prices and costs in different

1. It is a curious paradox that Mr. Hobson, who has done so much in his time to undermine belief in any kind of 'invisible hand,' etc., should in his fluctuation theory proceed from the assumption that the proportion between saving and spending which maximises social utility – whatever that is – should also be that proportion which would ensure the smoothest running of a system governed by the price mechanism. The system only works if it is just! If the system of Marx can be called "inverted Hegel," can we not with justice describe this aspect of Mr. Hobson's system as "inverted Bastiat?"

2. This assumption excludes merely "horizontal" extensions to capital equipment to keep capital per head constant.

stages of production,[1] falls to zero, we are not entitled to assume that the increase of productivity has ceased; that is to say that the gap between costs and prices has been obliterated.

14. Now we know that, in fact, the rate of interest (using that term in the broadest sense) has never dropped to zero. We know that there are strong *a priori* reasons relating to supply of capital which make it extremely improbable that, in an individualistic society of men with limited lives and limited interest in posterity, it should ever fall to zero.[2] Beyond this, we are confronted with the stubborn fact that perhaps the most obvious and invariable concomitant of the break in prosperity is not the *lowness* of interest rates but their *rise*. And, quite apart from the strong theoretical case which (as I shall argue in a moment) can be constructed to show why this must be so, this is surely what one would expect. It is easy enough to see that a rise in the rate of interest must make the continuance of many enterprises unprofitable; it is extremely difficult to see why a fall in the rate of interest – such as would be the result of increased saving – should do harm to anyone except, perhaps, to those who live by lending. A fall in the rate of interest makes possible all sorts of enterprises hitherto unprofitable. Why then should it be regarded as a cause of depression?

15. It is sometimes thought that the tendency to a (relative) fall in the price level of consumers' commodities, which must accompany an increase in saving, is bound to make production unprofitable. This belief, however, is based on a failure to perceive that such a fall is necessary if the purpose of saving is not to be frustrated. The purpose of saving is to secure a greater provision for the future by abstaining from so great a present consumption as might otherwise have been possible. This means, essentially, that more factors of production must be devoted to production for the future, less to production for the present. If it were possible to augment the income of the future without this shift – other things, of course, remaining the same – then saving would be unnecessary. But in order that the shift from production for the present to production for the future may be brought about, it is necessary that production for the present should be made relatively *less* and production for the future relatively *more* profitable – just as, if more corn and less rye is required, the relative profitability of corn and rye production must alter in favour of the former.

1. See R. Torrens, *The Principles and Practical Operation of Sir Robert Peel's Bill of 1844 Explained, and Defended against the objections of Tooke, Fullarton, and Wilson* (London, 1848), pp. 132–3; E. von Böhm-Bawerk, *The Positive Theory of Capital* (London, 1891), Part VII; Frank A. Fetter, "Interest Theory and price movements," *American Economic Review*, vol. 17 Supplement (March 1927), pp. 62–105; and Friedrich A. Hayek, *Prices and Production* (London, 1931), Chapter III.
2. See Gustav Cassel, *The Theory of Social Economy* (London, 1923), pp. 247–8.

The tendency to a fall in the prices of consumers' goods is one of the essential parts of this process. To attempt to prevent it would be to frustrate the act of saving – just as to subsidise rye in the circumstances contemplated would frustrate the change in the direction of consumers' demand.

16. If this analysis is correct, then there is no reason to believe that trade depression is brought about by a deficiency of consumption – either absolute or relative. In fact, this is too weak a statement. Not only is there no reason to attribute depression to a deficiency of consumption; there is, on the contrary, considerable reason to believe that the coming of depression is due to the fact that consumption has become excessive in relation to the productive operations to be carried out. This brings me to the positive part of my paper.

III

1. In entering upon this part of the paper, may I emphasise once more what I said at the beginning, namely that what I am about to say is not intended to be a complete theory of the trade cycle. I do not know a complete theory of the trade cycle, and if I did it would obviously be impossible to develop it in the short space at my disposal. All that I wish to do is to suggest very sketchily a view of the part which may be played by fluctuations of consumption at one very critical phase of the cycle and to draw attention to certain facts which seem to give countenance to this theory.

2. Let us start by assuming a system in stationary equilibrium – i.e. a system in which there is no net voluntary saving. We have seen, in our examination of the Douglas Theory, that in such a state of affairs the total volume of money payments at any moment – the gross income – will be much larger than the total of net money incomes or the value of the net output of consumers' commodities. There will be a whole structure of payments which, in any computation of the net value of output, will cancel out but which in the given state of industrial organisation – vertical division of labour – are necessary to keep the system in equilibrium.

3. Now let us assume that, for some reason which we need not investigate, there takes place in this system an extension of the effective circulation. We need not stipulate whether this takes place by way of note printing or credit creation. It is sufficient for our purpose to assume that an inflation takes place.

4. If production were on a hand-to-mouth basis, that is to say, if there were no processes of production involving appreciable periods of time and "vertical" division of labour, the effect of such an inflation would be relatively simple. In hand-to-mouth production, the net income and the gross income are identical. By definition, therefore, they would move together. Some people would be in possession of spending power not released by the sale of

goods; these people would be able to secure more goods than their less fortunate neighbours. Since more money in the aggregate would be spent on goods, there would be a rise in the "general level of prices." That is all.

But when we are contemplating, as it were, a *three-dimensional* system in which production takes time and is organised into vertical stages – a system in which gross income and net income are not identical – we are not at liberty to apply this analysis without modification. For whereas, in a system of hand-to-mouth production, the full effects of the inflation or deflation will be immediate and can be responded to immediately, under many-stage production they will not work themselves out until the new money has circulated through the entire system. That part of the gross income which is not net income may change before net income changes and *vice versa*. Some prices will be affected before others; and, under the stimulus of such partial effects, there may occur changes in the technical direction of production which would not occur if the total effects took place instantaneously. It is these changes that we now have to investigate.

5. We may assume that the new spending power is made available by way of producers' credits. That is to say, there will be an addition to the supply of free capital available at the moment of inflation. (Since we are contemplating a stationary society, this supply of free capital will otherwise consist exclusively of the amortisation quotas and replacement funds of the different enterprises.) Such an increase will have the result that the rate of interest will be lowered. Indeed, it is through the lowering of the rate of interest that the new spending power is likely to be made available.

To whom, then, will the new spending power go? Clearly, to those entrepreneurs who are most affected by a lowering of the rate of interest – the entrepreneurs who are prepared to initiate those time-consuming, long-lasting processes of investment, which were excluded before by the limitations of the capital supply – by the former height of the rate of interest. To put it loosely: the new money will tend to go to entrepreneurs in the constructional industries and to the industries catering for those industries.

As the first effect of the increase in the circulation, therefore, we should expect to see a rise in the prices of the various goods involved in such processes. We should expect a rise in the price of such raw materials as coal and iron, and machines of the sort capable of facilitating these more capitalistic forms of production. There would be a tendency, too, for labourers and other "original factors" to be bid away to these jobs. (In a stationary society, the change of relative labour supply would involve a shift; in an "advancing society" – as Cassel has shown[1] – it is probable that some at least of the

1. See *Theory of Social Economy*, pp. 537–47.

relative change would be brought about by the greater absorption of new recruits into the industries undergoing expansion.)

6. But this is not the end of the matter, for although the new spending power may be spent in this way at first, yet, as it works its way through the economic system, it will affect other prices. As the additional spending power becomes net income, it will be spent on consumers' goods. The old proportion between the net income and the gross income tends to be restored. This will cause a rise in the prices of consumers' goods. But – and this point is fundamental – this will tend to reverse the changes initiated by the fall in the rate of interest. The relative profitability of producing consumers' goods will tend to be restored. The producers of such goods will bid for labour, etc., against the producers of producers' goods. Wages, etc., will rise still further. This means that, other things remaining the same, labour costs, etc., in the various branches of industry rise too.

Now this movement of labour costs, etc., must have the effect of upsetting the calculations of profit of the entrepreneurs who have embarked upon the new processes of production, made profitable by the fall in the rate of interest. According to their calculations, the new processes were profitable provided that a certain proportion only of their expenditure was devoted to the remuneration of labour. But now, by the rise in labour costs, they are compelled to exceed this proportion. What is to be done? Clearly, ask for more credit. Probably for a time this request can be granted. But if the new dose of inflation is to be similarly effective in the new situation, it must be proportionately larger than the previous doses. Clearly, if only for banking reasons, this cannot go on for ever. Sooner or later, a halt must be called. But, as soon as this happens, those undertakings which have arisen in response to the fall in the rate of interest are in difficulties. Competition between them and the other entrepreneurs drives up the rate of interest and the rise in this rate makes unprofitable the continuation of the new processes. To put the matter in Professor Cassel's terminology, the available supply of capital disposition is insufficient to take up the supply of real capital coming forward at profitable prices. The boom in the constructional industries, etc., collapses.

7. What happens to consumption while all this is taking place? Let me reformulate my argument – this time in terms of relative movements, so as to make it fit more closely the phenomena of an advancing society. At the outset, since the addition to the supply of money capital is due to no curtailment of consumers' spending, there is no tendency to a fall in the prices of consumers' goods. On the contrary, since relatively more factors of production are being devoted to the production of producers' goods, there will be a relative curtailment of supply coming forward and, therefore, a tendency to a rise. (Contrast this effect of "forced saving" with the effect on the price level of consumers' goods of voluntary saving.) Further, as the new spending

power becomes income, if there is no change in the relative disposition to spend and to save, more will be spent on consumers' goods and their price will again tend to rise. It is, indeed, this tendency to a *relative* rise in the price level of consumers' goods which, together with the rise in the rate of interest, brings the constructional boom to an end. It increases the relative profitability of processes of production which compete with those industries which depend on low interest rates for their continued existence.

8. It is interesting to compare this view with the theories of Mr. J.A. Hobson, which we have already examined. The two theories are identical in that they postulate an over-development of the constructional and allied trades. They differ fundamentally, however, in their interpretation of its causes. On Mr. Hobson's view, this over-expansion is due to voluntary saving. On the view I have outlined, it is due to what is sometimes called "forced saving" and it is the *cessation* of this process which brings about the collapse. Moreover, on Mr. Hobson's view, the only remedy for such a state of affairs would be a *diminution* of voluntary saving – i.e. an increase in consumption. On the view I have put forward, the situation can be saved only by such an *increase* of voluntary saving – i.e. a *diminution* of consumption – as will sustain the demand for producers' goods which the artificially lowered rate of interest seemed to make it legitimate to expect.[1] On Mr. Hobson's view, we "starve in the midst of plenty" because we do not demand enough; on the view I have suggested we "starve" rather because we seek to pluck the fruits of prosperity before they are actually ripe.

9. Such a view will appear paradoxical to many. It appears particularly paradoxical, I believe, if one has been in the habit always of thinking of the demand for producers' goods as being *derived* from the demand for consumers' goods. Such a conception is, of course, perfectly valid in its proper context and is of fundamental significance in the subjective theory of value. But it is all-important to realise that, although this is true *through time*, yet, *at a moment of time*, the demand for consumers' goods and the demand for producers' goods are not *complementary* but *competitive*. If I want more provision for the future, I must make less provision for the present. If this were not so, saving would be unnecessary.

10. This, in very brief outline, is the view I wish to suggest of the part which may be played by consumption during the upper phase of a trade cycle. How does it tally with the facts?

There can be little disagreement as to the movements of the capital market during the period in question. It is notorious that a boom in the constructional

1. See Strigl, *op. cit.*, pp. 201–3.

industries is accompanied by a considerable expansion of credit. It is equally notorious that the coming of a crisis is marked by increasing stringency and a sharp rise in money rates. On all this, the standard works provide ample information. The actual movements of consumption, however, are more inaccessible; reliable information here is harder to obtain. But it has been observed by many, notably by Spiethoff[1] and, more recently, by Bresciani-Turroni,[2] that what appear to be representative items of consumption show a tendency to increase in volume for some time after the collapse has set in. It is notorious, too, that, during the first eighteen months of the present depression, consumption was remarkably well maintained. The relative prosperity of the retailer during this period was one of the most remarkable features of a world plunging deeper and deeper into depression.

Absolute increases, however, are deceptive; for so many adjustments have to be made before they can be regarded as symptomatic of main tendencies. More important, I think, is the movement of prices. Here we have a phenomenon which has definite causal significance, and at this point, fortunately, the evidence is not so defective.

It is a fact which has long been recognised that, at the beginning of a slump, when wholesale prices are falling, retail prices are often still tending to rise. This fact is often attributed to the existence of a "lag." I do not deny the existence of "lags" on the supply side, but it is at least arguable that the phenomena in question are to be explained, at least in part, in terms of a tendency for consumers' demand to be sustained. More suggestive still, although it is, of course, simply another way of exhibiting the same fundamental fact, is the movement of the relationship between the prices of consumers' goods and the prices of producers' goods. There can be little doubt that the change of this relationship in favour of consumers' goods is one of the invariable concomitants of a crisis.[3] The crash begins just at that time at which the prices of consumers' goods begin to rise relatively to the price of producers' goods. I do not urge that this *proves* anything, for, of course, statistics by themselves do not prove anything. Proof, if it is forthcoming, is a question of the logic of the theory and the correspondence of its assumptions with the facts. But I do urge that figures of this sort are significant and I hope that, in the future, it will be possible to carry this kind of analysis considerably further.

---

1. Arthur Spiethoff, "Krisen," *Handwörterbuch der Staatswissenschaften*, 4th edn (Jena, 1925), Vol. 6, pp. 19 and 34.
2. "Kapitalmangel und Währungsstabilisierung," *Wirtschaftstheorie der Gegenwart*, Vol. 2, pp. 391–403.
3. In this connection, it may be useful to refer to a chart, published in *Die Wirtschaftskurve 1924*, no. 1 (February 1924), p. 25, showing the movement of this relationship during that laboratory experiment of an inflationary boom – the depreciation of the mark.

11. At this point I must break off my argument, not merely because I have already taken too much time, but also because, to be perfectly frank, there are so many things in the further course of the cycle which I do not feel capable of explaining. The whole question of the secondary phase of the depressions, still more, the mechanics of recovery, seems to be in an even less satisfactory state than the question of the boom and the collapse. To what extent it is possible to save any of the forced savings from the wreckage, to what extent it is possible for a recovery to take place which does not contain within itself the seeds of further depression, these are matters on which I do not feel that it is possible to pronounce with any feeling of certainty, in the present stage of knowledge.

12. But there is one thing, I think, which is tolerably clear. And with this I will end. If there has been a disturbance of the kind I have indicated – a misdirection and a wastage of capital – that means that, for the time being at any rate, the equilibrium level of factor prices – the level which will secure, in time, anything like full employment of the different factors – is lower than it would have been. If, in such circumstances, the market is not relatively free, if labour incomes and other factor prices are rigid, then it is almost certain that a state of affairs has arisen which begins to approximate to the Douglasian ideal when final incomes absorb more than the value of the final product. Such a state of affairs implies not merely that the factor markets are not cleared; it involves further a tendency to consumption of capital – a tendency which may merely mean a less rapid rate of accumulation but which may well become – as we have seen in Central Europe – an actual encroachment on the accumulation of the past.[1] If this is so, then I suggest, without any wish to be paradoxical or alarmist, that it may be well to consider very carefully the desirability of the various measures for "maintaining purchasing power," which are popular in so many quarters at the present time. It may prove to be no accident that the depression in which most measures have been taken to "maintain consumers' purchasing power" is also the depression of the widest extent and most alarming proportions.

---

1. See Nicholas Kaldor, "The economic position of Austria," *Harvard Business Review*, vol. 11 (October 1932), pp. 23–34; Oskar Morgenstern, "Kapital- und Kurswertänderungen der an der Wiener Börse notierten österreichischen Aktiengesellschaften 1913 bis 1930," *Zeitschrift für Nationalökonomie*, vol. 3 (1932), pp. 251–5; E. Welter, *Die Ursachen des Kapitalmangels in Deutschland* (Tübingen, 1931).

9 Remarks Upon Certain Aspects of the Theory of Costs[1]

From *The Economic Journal*, vol. 44 (March 1934), pp. 1–18.

The Theory of Costs is not one of those parts of Economic Analysis which can properly be said to have been unduly neglected. It has always occupied a more or less central position, and in recent years it has been the subject of a quite formidable body of new work. There is, indeed, no part of his subject about which the contemporary economist may legitimately feel more gratified, either as regards the quality of the work which has been done or as regards the temper in which it has been undertaken. Yet, in spite of this, the present state of affairs in this field is not altogether satisfactory. The various problems involved have been tackled by different sets of people; and the conclusions which have been reached in one part of the field have sometimes a rather disquieting appearance of incompatibility with conclusions which have been reached elsewhere. No doubt some of this apparent incompatibility is real. It is not to be expected that here – any more than elsewhere – economists should have reached finality. But some of it is probably illusory; and if, in discussing these matters, we were to state more decisively the problems which we are attempting to solve, and the assumptions on which we proceed, it seems likely that not only should we be able to clear up our outstanding real points of difference more quickly, but that, in the course of doing so, we should also discover that many of them depended essentially upon subtle differences of object and assumption, hitherto insufficiently stated. At any rate, it is in the belief that this would be so that these very tentative remarks are put forward.

The paper falls into four parts. In the first, I discuss the fundamental nature of costs; in the second, the relation between this conception and the

1. A lecture delivered before the Nationalökonomischen Gesellschaft, Vienna, April 7, 1933.

Marshallian supply curve; in the third, the relation between costs and technical productivity. I conclude with some notes on cost variation through time.

I

I start, then, with fundamentals. The conception of costs in modern economic theory is a conception of displaced alternatives: the cost of obtaining anything is what must be surrendered in order to get it. The process of valuation is essentially a process of choice, and costs are the negative aspect of this process. In the theory of exchange, therefore, costs reflect the value of the things surrendered. In the theory of production they reflect also the value of alternative uses of productive factors – that is, of products which do not come into existence because existing products are preferred.[1] Such is the conception of costs first systematically developed by Wieser[2] and made familiar in English-speaking areas by Green, Wicksteed, Davenport, Knight and Henderson.[3] Following the usage of Pantaleoni[4] and many others, we may refer to it for short as Wieser's Law.

---

1. This somewhat roundabout way of putting matters is deliberate. The money costs of production in any line of industry are a reflection of (*a*) the value of factors of production wholly specialised to that line of production (Wieser's "specific" factors) and (*b*) the value of transferable ("non-specific") divisible factors in other uses. It is in regard to these latter ingredients that Wieser's propositions have special relevance.

2. Friedrich von Wieser, *Uber den Ursprung und die Hauptgesetz des Wirtschaftlichen Werthes* (Vienna, 1884), pp. 146–70; *Natural Value* (London, 1893), pp. 171–214; "Theorie der gesellschaftlichen Wirtschaft," *Grundriss der Sozialökonomik* (Tübingen, 1914), pp. 61–4, 73–81, 142–6; also the juvenile work, "Uber das Verhältnis der Kosten zum Wert," *Gesammelte Abhandlungen* (Tübingen, 1929), pp. 377–404.

3. See David I. Green, "Pain-cost and opportunity-cost," *Quarterly Journal of Economics*, vol. 8 (January 1894), pp. 218–29; P.H. Wicksteed, *The Common Sense of Political Economy* (London, 1910), p. 373; H.J. Davenport, *Value and Distribution: a critical and constructive study* (Chicago, 1908), pp. 551–2, and *The Economics of Enterprise* (New York, 1913), pp. 106–49; F.H. Knight, *Risk, Uncertainty and Profit* (Boston, 1921), p. 92, and "Some fallacies in the interpretation of social cost," *Quarterly Journal of Economics*, vol. 38 (1924), p. 582; H.D. Henderson, *Supply and Demand* (London, 1922), p. 162.

4. Maffeo Pantaleoni, *Pure Economics* (London, 1898), p. 184.

It is probably true to say that, at the present day, the broad outlines of this conception are generally acceptable.[1] The work of Wieser's successors in this field – in particular the various writings of Professor Mayer – have brought home to us all its central importance as a unifying principle in the structure of modern analysis. And, in the sphere of applied economics, it becomes more and more clear that many of the most urgent problems of the day can be understood only in the light of the knowledge that it furnishes.[2]

---

1. It is sometimes held that Wieser's Law is only true of a state of affairs in which the supplies of the factors of production are fixed. If these supplies are flexible, it is urged, then the disutility principle – the concept of real cost as real pains and sacrifices – comes into its own as an independent principle of explanation. (See F.Y. Edgeworth, *Papers relating to Political Economy* [London, 1925], Vol. 3, pp. 56–64; D.H. Robertson, *Economic Fragments* [London, 1931], p. 21; Jacob Viner, "The doctrine of comparative costs," *Weltwirtschaftliches Archiv*, vol. 36 (1932), pp. 411 ff.) The objection is plausible but it is not ultimately valid. Even when we are contemplating a situation in which the total supplies of the factors actually used in production are flexible, it is quite easy to show that Wieser's Law is still applicable. Variations in the total supply of labour in productive industry are accompanied by variations in the amount of time and energy which is available for other uses. Variations in the supply of land in production are accompanied by changes in the supply of land put to consumptive uses. Variations in the supply of capital are accompanied by variations in present consumption. All economic changes are capable of being exhibited as forms of exchange. And hence, as Wicksteed has shown, they can be exhibited further as the resultant of demand operating within a given technical environment. (See Wicksteed, *Common Sense of Political Economy*, especially Book I, Chapter ix; also Franz X. Weiss, "Die Moderne Tendenz in der Lehre vom Geldwert," *Zeitschrift für Volkswirtschaft. Sozialpolitik und Verwaltung*, Vol. 19 (1910), p. 518; and K. Wicksell, *Vorlesungen über Nationalökonomie* [Jena, 1913], Vol. I, p. 159.) It has been said that this becomes impossible if account be taken of the so-called other advantages and disadvantages of different occupations. Professor Viner, in the article cited above, has urged this particular objection. The difficulty, however, seems to be capable of a simple solution. If the other advantages and disadvantages are treated as joint products, the Wicksteed constructions can still be maintained.

2. An example should make this quite plain. The introduction of improved methods of production sometimes has the effect of causing the price of the particular line of product concerned to fall below costs of production, and observation of this fact has often led to the belief that, therefore, the mechanism of free markets is incapable of dealing with the effects of scientific invention. But what does such a situation imply? Prices are below costs; the products fetch less than the amounts which have to be paid for the factors which produce them. But why is this? If the factors were completely specialised to the line of production in question – *i.e.* if they had no mobility – then, in a free system, their prices would fall automatically with the fall in the prices of their products. There could be no lasting disparity between prices and money costs. But the costs of transferable factors, according to Wieser's Law, are a reflection of their value in other possible uses. If, therefore, in one line of production, costs of production are higher than prices, this means, under our assumptions, that there are factors of production in that line which are more urgently demanded elsewhere – that the change in technique creates a new equilibrium of factors. As the transfer takes place under the pressure of the costs disparities, there will be movements of prices and costs tending to a restoration of profitability. It follows, therefore, that, if technical progress is accompanied by more extensive disequilibrium, the causes must be sought outside the area covered by our assumptions; the market is not free, the monetary mechanism is not functioning properly. There is nothing in the institutions of exchange as such which makes technical progress necessarily self-frustrating. This conclusion, which follows directly from Wieser's Law, is surely a conclusion of considerable practical importance.

But there is one matter on which there is not yet full agreement. It relates to the precise *mode* in which the displaced alternatives are to be conceived. Wieser's usage is clear. They are to be conceived in terms of *values* – in terms of the values of the goods of the first order displaced. "The cost of production of one thing," said Wicksteed, "is the marginal value of another thing."[1] This is the sense in which it has usually been understood. In recent years, however, it has been suggested in some quarters that they should be conceived in terms of technical *quantities* – in terms of the quantities (as distinct from the values) of the goods of the first order which might have been produced. This is the procedure suggested by Professor Knight in his "Suggestion for Simplifying the Statement of the General Theory of Price."[2] He invokes Adam Smith's parable of the beaver and the deer and concludes: "In sum, the cost of beaver is deer and the cost of deer is beaver, and that is the only objective and scientific content of the cost notion." The same procedure is adopted by Dr. Haberler in his recent article on the Theory of Comparative Cost.[3]

Now there can be no doubt that there is much that can be said for this suggestion. The conception of costs as technical displacement has an objectivity and precision which is in itself an advantage. It has none of that elusiveness which seems to inhere in concepts involving subjective valuation. Moreover, it is true that in equilibrium the values of goods produced with common factors of production and variability of technical coefficients are necessarily in harmony with their displacement cost ratios. It has been well known since the time of the classical economists that this was the case with the products of simple unskilled labour. This is, of course, the moral of the parable of the beaver and the deer. It is the achievement of Professor Knight and Dr. Haberler to have shown that the same generalisation can be extended to cover the case of production with more than one factor of production. If the amount of a commodity produced by a combination of factors of production is not the same as can be procured by devoting the same combination to the production of something else and procuring the first commodity by way of exchange, then clearly, if the conditions of production are technically variable, there will be evoked movements which tend to bring about this harmony.

So far so good. The argument seems overwhelmingly convincing. But on closer inspection certain difficulties present themselves. In the first place, it is important to recognise that there are wide areas where the conception of costs

1. *Op. cit.*, p. 382; see also P.N. Rosenstein-Rodan, "Grenznutzen," *Handworterbuch der Staatswissenschaften*, Vol. 4, pp. 1198 ff.

2. *Journal of Political Economy*, vol. 36 (June 1928), pp. 353–70.

3. "Die Theorie der komparativen Kosten und ihre Auswertung für die Begründung des Freihandels," *Weltwirtschaftliches Archiv*, vol. 32 (1930), pp. 349–70, especially the note on p. 358.

as technical displacements has clearly no application. This is the case if the productive process involve fixed technical coefficients. The imputation problem (and hence the cost problem) here can only be solved in value terms. Costs of production in value terms can and will change with changes in demand.[1] But the idea of changes in technical displacements in this instance has no meaning. The same is true where we are considering commodities produced with different factors of production. If *A* and *B* are produced with *n* and *m* and *C* and *D* with *p* and *q*, there will exist exchange ratios *between* members of the first group and members of the second, but it is impossible to conceive of technical displacement cost ratios save *within* them. There may be an exchange ratio between *A* and *D*, but when *A* is produced there is no technical quantity of *D* sacrificed. Yet there will certainly exist costs of production in the value sense.

Moreover – and this is even more important – it is the central requirement of any theory of cost that it shall explain the *actual* resistances which production in any line of industry encounters; that it shall explain to us the influences determining the elements of which account is taken by those responsible for production. Now, there can be no doubt that these influences are of the nature of valuations. The isolated producer thinks of the sacrifice he is making by not producing something else. The entrepreneur in the exchange economy thinks of the prices he has to pay for the factors of production. In each case, although – as with all valuations – there may be in the background a technical condition, yet the final determinant is not merely technical. The isolated producer thinks not merely of the quantity of goods he gives up, but of their place on the relative scale, compared with the place on the relative scale of the goods he acquires. The price which the entrepreneur pays for the factors of production he uses is determined not by the *number* of products which they can produce elsewhere, but by the value of such products. Indeed it is most highly improbable that he knows at all the number of products which can be produced elsewhere. All that he knows are values of the factors of production, which are, of course, reflections of the value of other products. If we reflect upon the way in which equilibrium is established, it is surely obvious that it is

1. We can see this most clearly if we contemplate an extreme case. Suppose a state of affairs in which two commodities are produced by the aid of two classes of factors of production – the factors entering into the manufacture of the two commodities in proportions which are different for each commodity. (For example, *PA* involves $2x$ and $1y$ and *PB* $1x$ and $2y$.) Now suppose a shift of demand. The relative scarcities of the factors and of the products will change. The cost of production (in money terms) of the commodity whose manufacture involves the higher proportion of the factor which has become relatively scarcer will rise. The cost of production of the commodity whose manufacture involves a higher proportion of the factor which has become relatively less scarce will fall. There is no movement of technical displacements which corresponds to this.

only through regard for cost in the value sense that any harmony between technical displacements and prices can be conceived to come about. It is only in equilibrium that such a harmony exists. In a state of disequilibrium, prices, costs and displacement ratios may all be different. If we do not keep these things conceptually discrete, we cannot understand the actual process of equilibration. This is not merely true of the Austrian approach. The condition that prices shall be equal to cost of production in the value sense is as essential a condition of equilibrium in the Walrasian system as the condition that marginal products shall be proportionate to factor prices.

For both these reasons, therefore, because there are whole areas where technical displacements are not conceivable, and because it does not focus attention on the actual process of price formation, I conclude that the conception of costs as quantities of goods foregone is not acceptable. No doubt the technical conditions of production play an important part in determining the conditions of equilibrium. But to make the cost concept purely technical is to deprive it of important analytical functions and to run the risk of misunderstanding. We shall see that a very similar procedure underlies some of the deficiencies of particular equilibrium analysis.

But this brings me to the second part of my paper: the relation between this general conception of costs and the Marshallian supply curve.

II

According to Wieser's Law, costs of production under competitive conditions are a reflection of the value of the alternatives which are displaced in order that the goods in that line of production may be produced and appropriated by the ultimate consumers. That is to say, they are essentially a reflection of the strength of excluded demands – demands both for the specific factors specialised to such lines of production and the non-specific factors capable of employment elsewhere. It seems to follow that, in the normal case, at the point of equilibrium, just as demand price will be decreasing, so will cost be increasing. This is quite obvious in the case of equilibrium of two commodities. To push production beyond that point would involve a product of diminishing relative utility – that is, a sacrifice of increased relative utility. I do not think that the situation is fundamentally changed when we consider many commodities. Nor do I think that, in this connection, it is necessary to take account of the possibilities of unusual utility functions. To move in any direction from a position of equilibrium is to encounter increased resistance: this is the fundamental conception.

But if this is so, what are we to say of the constructions, so familiar in the Marshallian system of what is sometimes called – in my opinion not very helpfully – "partial equilibrium analysis": the supply curve parallel to the *x* axis, and the supply curve with a negative inclination? At first sight we seem to be faced with a complete contradiction. Here are constructions which, if *they* are valid, seem to point to a definite rejection of our fundamental conception, while if *it* is valid, seem themselves to be doomed to be rejected. Nor are we in any way reassured when, turning to post-Marshallian criticism, we find it stated on high authority that, for the analysis of competitive conditions – and, of course, it is competitive conditions which are in question – constant cost is to be regarded as the normal and increasing cost as the quite exceptional condition.[1] We seem to have discovered a major inconsistency in the very centre of the corpus of pure economics.

Now in circumstances of this kind, before concluding that it is necessary to make a complete break with one or other of the apparently conflicting usages, it is always advisable to inquire more closely into the implicit assumptions on which they proceed. Again and again in the history of economic thought, the apparent contradiction between different usages has come to be seen to rest not upon deficiencies of logic on the one side or the other, but upon differences of assumption concerning the problem to be solved. This was notoriously so in the case of the historic disputes regarding the Theory of Rent.[2] A similar difference can, I think, be shown to underlie part at least of this apparent contradiction in the Theory of Costs.

For if we look more closely at the constructions in question, it becomes fairly clear that they are appropriate to the investigation of fundamentally separate problems. The general propositions regarding costs which spring from Wieser's Law are essentially a description of the conditions of equilibrium. They answer the question, what would happen to costs if, from a position of equilibrium – *other things remaining equal* – it were attempted to increase or diminish production in any particular line of industry. The constructions which we associate with particular equilibrium analysis, on the other hand, deal with what would happen if *other things were varied*; *i.e.* if production were to be increased in response to an increase in demand. That is to say, that they are essentially germane to a Theory of Variations. They relate not to forces which maintain equilibrium once it is established, but rather to the differences between one equilibrium position and another.

---

1. P. Sraffa, "The laws of returns under competitive conditions," *Economic Journal*, vol. 36 (December 1926), pp. 535, 550.

2. I have attempted to indicate some of the more important of such cases in an article entitled "On a certain ambiguity in the conception of stationary equilibrium", *Economic Journal*, vol. 40 (June 1930), pp. 194–214 [above p. 59]. The present paper is to be regarded as essentially a continuation of the same train of thought – but applied to a wider area than the simple analysis of final equilibrium.

Once this is realised the apparent contradiction which we have been considering vanishes. If other things do not change and it is attempted to increase the supply of a certain product, from the point of equilibrium, then it is natural that costs should rise, for the increase must be brought about by the use of factors which are more urgently demanded elsewhere. But if other things change – if, for instance, there is an increase in the demand for this line of product – then an increase of production to meet it need not encounter such an increased resistance. The change in the data which is characterised by the increase in demand here must be accompanied by a diminution of demand elsewhere, and this may be such as to release factors of production in such measure as to permit the necessary extension at constant, or even at diminishing cost. Once the data change, there is no presumption that an increase in output of a particular kind must be accompanied by more than proportionately increased outlay.

There is, therefore, no fundamental incompatibility between the implications of Wieser's Law and the constructions of "particular equilibrium" cost analysis. But it still remains to decide what degree of validity is to be attributed to these constructions in the actual connections in which they are most frequently employed.

If what I have been urging is correct, it seems clear that we cannot regard the Marshallian supply curves as serving the exact purposes of any causal explanation. They are rather to be regarded as providing schemata of certain possibilities of price variation. *If* the demand varies in this way and *if* the cost varies in this way, then it is implicit in these assumptions that the price will change in this way. They provide, as it were, a convenient shorthand note of different ways in which particular changes may be regarded. According to Edgeworth, "movement along a supply and demand curve of international trade should be regarded as attended with rearrangements of internal trade: as the movements of the hand of a clock corresponds to considerable unseen movements of the machinery."[1] It is the implication of what I have already said, that this too must be the way in which we should view the supply curves of the theory of domestic values, if our usage is not to be out of harmony with the more precise implications of general equilibrium analysis. They are notes of the implications of given changes of the general conditions of demand *and* supply, even though one curve is not shifted.

1. *Papers Relating to Political Economy*, Vol. 2, p. 32. Of course, this usage of the integral curves, which assumes other commodities besides those registered on the co-ordinates to be produced in the economy under consideration, must be distinguished from the use of similar curves under the assumption that only two commodities are capable of coming into existence. There are objections to the use of such an apparatus, well known to all readers of Pareto, but it is arguable that if Marshall had proceeded on these lines he would have been much more reluctant to adopt his compromise constructions than in fact he was.

If this is true, it follows that the construction in question must have a very limited validity for the analysis of the ultimate conditions of equilibrium. Its essential function is to facilitate the examination of what happens when certain conditions are varied. The assumption which underlies its use in descriptions of final equilibrium, that all possible variations outside the particular industry or market under consideration may be neglected, is essentially incompatible with the assumptions upon which any exhaustive description of such conditions must necessarily be based. This, indeed, is only another way of putting the point which has already been made. The assumption that the factors of production have an infinitely elastic supply leads to a concentration on the purely technical features of the situation which *necessarily* misleads when the conditions of final equilibrium have to be determined. The objection made earlier to the Knight–Haberler method of treating technical displacements as equivalent to value costs, applies much more strongly to a treatment of value costs which proceeds as if only technical determinants were relevant. It is quite true that, in a condition of competitive equilibrium, the prices of factors common to different industries are the same for the different industries concerned. But this is one of the *results* of the equilibrating process. It cannot be assumed to be a *condition* which would necessarily persist, were the other relations in the equilibrium disturbed. Yet this, of course, is the implication of a "constant cost" supply curve which is prolonged on either side of the point of equilibrium intersection.

Now, no doubt, once we get away from the hypothesis of pure competition, there are many problems in which the technical element is so predominant that, for certain purposes, constructions which focus attention upon such elements are permissible and helpful. It is well known that this is so in the case of the theory of monopoly. Recent work suggests that it is so in the case of the analysis of imperfect competition.

But such uses have their limitations. It is clear that they may be very definitely misleading when it is a question of deciding the significance for the economic system as a whole of one equilibrium position as compared with another. As I have argued elsewhere,[1] I am of the view that most investigations of this sort beg other, more fundamental, methodological questions. But, putting this on one side, it is surely clear that constructions which depend on the assumption that other things elsewhere remain unchanged, must necessarily lead to false conclusions when it is a question of estimating the total significance of changes which, by definition, *cannot* be unaccompanied by changes elsewhere.

---

1. See my *An Essay on the Nature and Significance of Economic Science* [1st edn, London, 1932], Chapter vi, Para. 2.

A simple example will make this clear. In the analysis of monopoly, for certain purposes the apparatus of intersecting demand and supply curves provides first approximations which are acceptable. But in any attempt to discover the significance for the economic system as a whole of monopoly in any line of industry it is open to very grave objections. For the assumption on which it proceeds – the assumption that other things remain equal – is incompatible with the most obvious implication of monopolistic restrictions; namely, the assumption that, since the number of factors employed in the monopolised industry is different from what would otherwise have been the case, their productivity in price terms *must necessarily be different*. It is illegitimate to argue that this change is of the second order of smalls. It may be of the second order of smalls for the monopolist's price policy. It may be of the second order of smalls in each of the other branches of industry affected; but for all the other branches of industry taken collectively it must be of a magnitude comparable in the universe of discourse – the "social" effect of the policy – with the magnitude of the primary variation. The objection, it will be noted, is almost exactly symmetrical with the fundamental objection to the use of the concept of consumers' surplus.

The case I have chosen is, of course, a very simple one. I should be very sorry to be understood as suggesting that those who use the apparatus I am discussing more frequently than I would care to do, are likely to be unaware of the proposition it exemplifies. But experience of the controversies of the last twenty years does, I think, suggest that the use of supply curves, rather than the apparatus of general equilibrium analysis, in discussing questions of this sort, carries with it dangers which may entrap even the subtlest and acutest intellects. There is a passage in the late Professor Young's critique of Professor Pigou's former position with regard to diminishing return industries[1] which has always seemed to me to be especially significant in this respect although, curiously enough, it has not attracted as much attention as other parts of the article. "The problem as a whole, it seems to me," he says, "is one to which the general theory of the diminishing productivity of individual factors is appropriate rather than the curve of marginal supply prices."[2]

1. A.C. Pigou, *Wealth and Welfare* (London, 1912), pp. 172–9.

2. Allyn A. Young, "Pigou's Wealth and Welfare," *Quarterly Journal of Economics*, vol. 27 (August 1913), p. 676 *et seq.* See also F.H. Knight, "Some fallacies in the interpretation of social cost," *Quarterly Journal of Economics*, vol. 38 (August 1924), pp. 218–29. Professor Pigou's retraction of his original proposition is to be found in the second edition of *The Economics of Welfare* (London, 1924), p. 194; Edgeworth's endorsement of this retraction in his review of this volume, "The revised doctrine of marginal social product," *Economic Journal*, vol. 35 (March 1925), pp. 30–9.

A fallacy which ensnared both Edgeworth and Professor Pigou is one which must necessarily be regarded as peculiarly deceptive. But I doubt very much whether they would have been thus ensnared if, instead of approaching the problem from the point of view of the intersecting curves of particular equilibrium analysis, they had started from the marginal productivity theorems – the example *par excellence* of the general equilibrium approach.

III

I hope I have said enough to make clear my view that there are profound dangers in any approach to the cost problem which identifies cost with the merely technical or which treats costs as if only technical influences were significant. It is, therefore, with an easy conscience that I can advance to an examination of certain aspects of the relation between costs and productivity in the technical sense.

There is no need for me to detain the reader with an examination of those variations of technical productivity which lead to increasing supply price. This is one of those parts of economic analysis where there is little ground for disagreement on purely analytical considerations. Dr. Sraffa, who is sceptical of the importance of the conception, bases his scepticism avowedly upon empirical grounds. Cases where one line of production utilises so large a proportion of the total supply of any factor of production that changes in the demand for the product will bring about changes in its price, he thinks, are rare. This view is, apparently, shared by Professor Knight. Whether or not one regards this as having *prima facie* plausibility, depends in part, I think, upon one's views on the classification of the factors of production. It sounds much more plausible if one thinks of two factors of production than if one thinks of many. But, in any case, no analytical issue is at stake.

But, on the other hand, when we come to those technical conditions which lead to diminishing supply price we find a very different state of affairs. The broad considerations involved in the discussion of imperfect competition and monopoly are, perhaps, not open to serious question. But the problems of diminishing costs under competition are still the subject of dispute and it is interesting to linger a little in this region.

We have seen already that if demand for a particular commodity increases, it may be accompanied by changes in demand elsewhere such as to cheapen the factors of production in the line of production in question. This is a possibility which emerges from general equilibrium theory, but it is not the possibility with which I wish to concern myself in this connection. What I want to do rather is to concentrate upon the possibility of cost reductions which are due to the operation of technical factors.

Now, at the present time it is generally agreed that, under purely competitive conditions, such reductions must be the effect, in the first instance, of the operation of external economies. That is clear even if, with Marshall and Mr. Shove, we recognise that the operation of external economies may be accompanied by changes in the optimal size of firms which themselves involve cost reduction. Unless external economies are operative, the technical influences making for diminishing costs will exhaust themselves before the first point of competitive equilibrium is reached. The influences making for cost reduction must be *outside* the firms whose costs per unit are under observation.

So far so good; but now the question arises why the external economies operate only as the scale of production increases. Clearly, the answer is that it does not pay to initiate the enterprises from which they spring until the demand for the ultimate produce is of a certain size. The doctrine of external economies, as Young emphasised, is merely one way of introducing into analytical constructions the old Smithian doctrine of the advantages of division of labour. It is one of the most familiar platitudes of this doctrine that the wider the market the wider the division of labour which is made possible.

But this does not completely answer our question. For we still remain in the dark concerning the reason why the advantages of division of labour must wait upon extensions of the market. Why cannot the various cost-reducing divisions take place *ab initio*, but *each on a smaller scale*? If we put the question in this way, the answer is obvious. For technical reasons they cannot be on a smaller scale. The quantities of factors which are exploited in a progressive division of labour are *indivisible* below a certain absolute size. Division of labour, external economies, depend upon demand conditions which render indivisible potentialities of production profitable.

But to solve the question in this way is only to find ourselves confronted with another. We have explained the possibility of diminishing costs in this sense by invoking the existence of indivisibility in the methods of production. But the assumption of competition seems to preclude the existence of indivisible factors; in a fully competitive situation, the factors of production must be capable of infinite division – or, in practical terms, of such degree of divisibility as to preclude the existence of any increasing return combination, using the term in its technical sense. How then, as the market enlarges with a general increase of factors of production, can we assume indivisibility to be exploited?

The answer is, I think, to be found in the distinction between actual and potential uses of factors of production. It may very well be the case that, given the total conditions of production, productive factors are sufficiently divisible in all the uses to which they are put for the situation to be regarded as competitive. But it is quite possible, at the same time, that some of these factors have *potential uses of a different sort* which, because of their technical indivisibility, are not exploited until the system as a whole, or large parts of it, has expanded. This, I believe, is a proposition which throws light, not only on the questions we are discussing, but also upon wider questions of localisation and general population theory. Let me try to explain what I mean.

Let me start with the simplest possible example. Among a group of independent producers of some simple product there may be one producer who has special skill at – shall we say – marketing. As a marketer he is greatly superior to the others. As a producer of the simple product he has equal skill. But his skill as a marketer cannot be satisfactorily employed unless there is a certain minimum quantity of marketing to do. Until demand has reached that point, therefore, he appears in the system as a provider of units of simple homogeneous undifferentiated labour like the rest. The competitive situation is stable. But beyond that point he emerges in a new rôle. He is now another factor of production – hitherto not appearing in the equations of equilibrium. At first, of course, in this situation he may be in a monopolistic position. But until the point at which it paid to employ him in this way the situation was fully competitive.

The example I have given is one which can be supposed to occur under conditions which, to all intents and purposes, may be regarded as *a*capitalistic – that is, a condition in which production has not yet become, in important senses, roundabout: conditions in which there is little vertical division of labour. But, of course, it is under more fully developed capitalistic conditions that the phenomena which it typifies become important. As capital accumulates, and demand increases, it pays to combine original factors of production, hitherto used in other ways, to produce technically indivisible means of production – machines, means of transport, and so on, which hitherto, because of their indivisibility, have not figured in the realised system of productive combinations at all. (If we think of the way in which capital accumulation has made possible the utilisation of indivisible transport systems, we can see how important considerations of this sort must be in any theory of localisation.) It is clear that the advantages of roundabout production are essentially the advantages of this vertical division of labour and that another way of describing them is to say that they consist in the progressive exploitation of potential methods of production excluded in less expanded systems by their technical indivisibility.

It is in this sense, I take it, that we are to interpret the theory of increasing returns developed by the late Professor Allyn Young in his presidential address to the British Association.[1] And it is worth noting, as he showed, how

1. ["Increasing returns and economic progress," *Economic Journal*, vol. 38 (1928) pp. 527–42.] I ought perhaps to state explicitly that this merely my own interpretation. It is not a transmission of any esoteric oral tradition. My own views on these matters spring chiefly from reflections on the remarks on the variations of productivity in [Fred] Taylor's *Principles of Economics* (Ann Arbor, 1911), pp. 141–2.

the phenomena in question escape the apparatus of particular equilibrium analysis and, indeed, involve changes which are quite incompatible with its assumptions. Granted the assumption of the Youngian analysis, we can see how diminishing costs can be regarded as *implicit* in a situation which is actually competitive. But we see, too, that such developments are to be regarded as being much more probably the function of the development of many industries than of one of them. We see too – and this is, perhaps, the more important point – that the diminution of costs here contemplated is essentially the product of vertical division of labour – that is, of the disintegration of industries. Neither of these things is compatible with the implications of the supply curve. This seems to constitute a presumption that the use of this instrument in the analysis of variation may well involve a concentration on the insignificant exception to the neglect of what, both from the point of view of theory and practice, must be regarded as the typical and significant cases.

IV

So far in this paper, the propositions I have discussed have, for the most part, dealt with variations of costs in terms of what has been well called comparative statics. That is to say, they consist essentially of a comparison of two states of equilibrium, and an investigation of the causes of difference. The demand for a group of products increases so that in the new equilibrium position factor prices and costs of production are different, and so on. They do little to elucidate the actual process of change – the path followed through time between one equilibrium position and the other.[1] This is notoriously the field of theoretical economics in which least has been done and in which most remains still to do. In concluding this survey, therefore, it seems appropriate to add certain remarks on this matter.

It is not necessary, in this connection, to expatiate on the significance of the Austrian contribution to this theory. It is clear that, in the characteristically

1. The distinction between these two stages of the theory of variations is not often clearly recognised in the English and American literature. It is, however, very clearly stated by V. Pareto (*Manuel d'economie politique* [Paris, 1909], p. 147), and it has recently been the subject of important studies by Mayer, Rosenstein-Rodan and Schams. See Hans Mayer, "Der Erkenntniswert der funktionellen Preistheorien," *Die Wirtschaftstheorie der Gegenwart*, ed. Hans Mayer (Vienna, 1932), Vol. 2, pp. 147–239b; P.N. Rosenstein-Rodan, "Das Zeitmoment in der mathematischen Theorie des wirtschaftlichen Gleichgewichtes," *Zeitschrift für Nationalökonomie*, vol. 1 (1930), pp. 129–42; Ewald Schams, "Komparative Statik," *Zeitschrift für Nationalökonomie*, vol. 2 (1931), pp. 27–61. See also my article on "Production" in the *Encyclopaedia of the Social Sciences*, ed. E.R.A. Seligman (New York, 1934), pp. 462–7.

Austrian constructions, we have a technique which is pre-eminently suited to the explanation of the phenomena of movement. On the demand side, the conception of the dependent use (*abhängige nutzen*); on the supply side, the conception of the displaced alternative – here we are dealing with elements which are the actual focus of attention of the economic subjects through whom changes come about. No one who has followed Wicksteed's exposition of the continuous relevance of Wieser's Law to the explanation of change[1] can doubt that the main instrument of explanation in this field has already been devised.[2]

These things are well known. Rather than linger in this neighbourhood, it is more profitable to turn once more to the Marshallian system. For here we have theories in which propositions which are true and helpful are not altogether disentangled from ways of expression which sometimes give rise to misapprehension.

The Marshallian doctrine of short and long period price is essentially an attempt to provide a theory of price change in terms of the length of time which is taken to overcome various technical obstacles on the supply side. The relative specificity – to use Wieser's term – of productive factors means that the immediate response to a change in the conditions of demand or supply is not necessarily a response to an ultimate equilibrium position. To take Marshall's own example: in the short period, a change in the demand for fish will be met by an increased output from existing fishermen and a more intensive use of fishing gear already in existence. In the long period, however – I use Marshall's own words – "the normal supply price ... is governed by a different set of causes, and with different results."[3] Capital and labour come into the industry or leave it; the fixed equipment involved is augmented or depleted. In the sphere of cost theory, this leads to the distinction between prime and supplementary expenses; in the sphere of distribution theory, to the distinction between quasi-rents and interest.

Now there can be no doubt that this doctrine contains much that is most valuable and important. The distinction between the immediate and more distant effects of a given change in demand, the imposition of a small tax, and so on and so forth – this is one of the most significant distinctions of the

1. *Common Sense of Political Economy*, Book I, Chapter ix.

2. It is significant in this connection that, historically, the Austrian theories are said to have sprung from Menger's inability to explain the short-term fluctuations of produce and stock markets in terms of the classical generalisations. It is clear that, for the most part, the classical theories are to be regarded as theories of comparative statics (in the sense explained above) with the differences between successive states of equilibrium explained in technical terms. The wage fund theory in certain aspects has, of course, a more dynamic character.

3. *Principles of Economics*, 8th edn (London, 1920), p. 370.

theory of variations, and it is one of Marshall's most conspicuous achievements that it has become universally recognised. None the less, as it stands, it is by no means immune from criticism. In particular, two criticisms suggest themselves.

In the first place, it may be suggested that it is liable to give rise to considerable misapprehension if one speaks, as Marshall does in the passage I have quoted, as if the causes operating in the long run are different from the causes operating in the short. Given a change in the data and the other fundamental conditions – including, as we shall see, what other people think about the data – the process of price change through time is determinate. The path followed by price, the rate and magnitude of the change, is determined by the total situation. Although the effects of the different conditions operative may *show themselves* at different points in the path, it is misleading to speak as if, from the moment of change onward, they were not each in operation. When the demand for fish increases, if it is supposed that the increase will be permanent, there is not an interval which elapses before the "long period tendencies" begin to operate. They *operate* from the beginning, but, owing to their nature, their *effects* are not manifest until some time has elapsed. It is therefore arguable, I think, that to have different labels for the discussion of long and short period effects here is liable to veil the essentially continuous nature of the economic process. Short period and long period theory in this sense do not explain different processes. They explain different *sections* of the same process. It would be absurd to suggest that this was not known to Marshall. But it is none the less true that his particular mode of expressing himself has sometimes led to its being overlooked by his readers.

Secondly – and this criticism is more substantial – here too, as in other Marshallian constructions which we have examined, it may be objected that the emphasis tends to have too technical a complexion. No doubt, the technical obstacles to change, the resistances through time, are fundamental. But it should be clear that, given the range of technical obstacles, the obstacles that will actually be encountered in any process of adaptation depend essentially upon *estimates* of the permanence of the change to which the adaptation is a response. The change which is expected to last for a short period invokes responses essentially different from the responses which are evoked by the change which is expected to be permanent. What are prime, and what are supplementary expenses depend essentially upon the length of time over which a change of output is expected to be operative. Thus, if by long period we understand a period long enough for final equilibrium to be reached, we can say that the length of the period is not only a function of the magnitude of the technical obstacles but also of the expectations entertained by the producers. The time it takes for an industry to become adapted to a permanent shrinkage of demand depends in part upon the rate of physical depreciation.

But it depends, too, upon the length of time taken by producers to become convinced that the change is permanent.

It seems, therefore, that, in a complete theory of costs, the part played by the estimates of the future of the various producers concerned will play a larger part than it plays in the original Marshallian doctrine. But, if this is so, then a further change is probable, which will necessarily bring this part of cost theory into more intimate relations with the other parts of the theory of change. There are certain cases of changes in data where different degrees of foresight on the part of producers have little effect save on the rate of adaptation. A single-line change of demand for consumers' goods in a system otherwise in even balance may be a case of this sort. Here, perhaps, the old single-line methods of cost analysis may be sufficient to explain the total movement. But there are other cases where the different estimates on the part of producers will themselves bring about further changes in the general situation: a simultaneous falling off of demand for the products of a large group of industries, as at the turn of a trade cycle, is an instance. Here, not merely the immediate policy of the producers concerned, but the future course of the general oscillation will be, in part at any rate, determined by expectations of the kind here discussed. And here, single-line analysis is patently inadequate. If the cost problem here is to be handled properly, it must be dealt with in conjunction with the theory of economic fluctuations. It is probable that the extraordinary sterility of much contemporary thought on the problems of overhead costs and surplus capacity is due to the fact that this junction has not yet been satisfactorily effected.

10 Remarks on the Relationship Between Economics and Psychology[1]

From *The Manchester School*, vol. 5 (December 1934), pp. 89–101.

1. The relationship between Economics and Psychology is not a matter which has ever given rise to much dispute among economists. Indeed, it is not a matter to which economists in general have devoted very much attention. The literature of the subject, such as it is, is largely the work of men who have been ignorant of Economics but anxious, for various reasons, to discredit its conclusions. If one wishes to discover what the great economists have thought on this matter, one must look to their practice and their occasional *obiter dicta*, rather than to any systematic work on the subject.

The reason for this is not far to seek. As I shall argue, there is no very intimate relationship between Economics and Psychology, and no very important propositions depend upon a correct determination of what relationship there is. I have never heard of an economist who was really interested in his job of thinking out new propositions in economic analysis, or of applying analytical knowledge to the elucidation of concrete situations, who was held up in his work by a lack of knowledge of this kind: and I cannot believe that such a one has ever existed. The people who have worried about such matters have had other ends in view.

Nevertheless, there is some justification for the inquiry. For, although, as I shall argue, Economics is almost entirely independent of any particular kind of Psychology, there can be no doubt that it deals in considerations which may be designated as *psychological* (or, more properly, as *psychical*[2]) and the clarification of this distinction may prevent certain misapprehensions and

1. The following essay was first read as a paper to a small circle composed chiefly of members who were not professional economists. I have preserved the spoken form in order to make quite clear its very modest pretensions. It in no way aspires to be regarded as a systematic treatment of the subject.

2. I owe this correction to my friend, Mr. H.W.B. Joseph.

serve to shed new light on the significance of certain accepted propositions. It is with this very limited objective that I venture to present this paper.

2. My first task is to describe the present status of what I have called the psychological elements in Economics. I can do this best by means of an historical retrospect which, incidentally, will enable me to recall certain matters which will be relevant to the discussion at a later stage.

The central object of economic enquiry – theoretical or applied – is the disposal of scarce goods. Human life is such that the things we want to do (the ends) are incapable of complete realisation, in the time and with the materials (the means) at our disposal. Hence, willy-nilly, we have to chose between one thing and another: and the choice of one thing involves the sacrifice of others. All the characteristic problems of Economics – market price, the rate of interest, the value of money, cyclical fluctuations, etc. – prove, in the last analysis, to have this characteristic in common, that they relate to human activities viewed as a distribution of scarce means between the various objectives of conduct. Theoretical Economics discusses the abstract forms of this distribution; Applied Economics concrete situations and problems in terms of these general categories. There are different ways of putting this into formal definitions but, at the present day, I do not think that there would be much disagreement regarding the substance of this description.

Such has been the general pre-occupation of Economics since its inception. But, of course, the modes of explanation which have been adopted by different economists have not remained constant. On the contrary, they have undergone what is, broadly speaking, a process of continuous development. One of the main characteristics of the process is the change in the position of the psychological factor.

There is no need, in this connection, for us to linger over the theories of the Physiocrats. It is the eternal fame of Quesnay and his school to have perceived the existence of a certain order and continuity in social activities. As Schumpeter has put it, they discovered the circle of economic activity – the interconnection of economic phenomena. But it cannot be said that they went far to explain it. Quesnay's *Tableau Economique* may be the first description of an economic equilibrium; but it is schematic rather than explanatory. It indicates one of the formal characteristics of equilibrium – the balance of income and expenditure – but it does nothing to show the nature of the forces which may be held to determine such conditions. And it certainly lays no stress on any psychological factors.

The first system of which we need seriously take account is, of course, the classical system, which is to be found *par excellence* in the works of Ricardo. Here is a body of propositions which was, in the truest sense, both explanatory and systematic. Whatever deficiencies may have been revealed by subsequent discussion, for certain purposes many of its propositions are still almost indispensable.

Now it is sometimes said that the classical system rested essentially upon the assumption of a world of economic men, buying in the cheapest market and selling in the dearest, oblivious of anything but self-regarding considerations. This view rests on misapprehension. For certain purposes, in the first approximation the classics undoubtedly did assume that in market dealings the aim was to maximise money profit. But they never argued that this was necessarily the case. In the second approximation, they developed a doctrine which definitely assumed the contrary: the Smithian doctrine of the tendency to equality, not of money receipts, but of total advantages. And it can be shown that most of their characteristic propositions in this field depended, not on the assumption that the money incentive was *everything*, but merely that the money incentive was *something* – which is surely not an unreasonable assumption when one is investigating the phenomena of the market.

Paradoxically enough, the one psychological assumption which they did make was of an entirely different nature – an assumption which depicted mankind not as a set of passionless calculating machines, but rather as the prey of overwhelming animal instincts, whose evil effects were only to be resisted by institutions and personal habits of the utmost possible austerity. I refer, of course, to the Malthusian Theory of Population. No one has understood the work of the classics who has not appreciated the significance of this generalisation. It explains their attitude to practical questions. It explains, too, the surprising certainty with which, in their most abstract analysis, they pushed through to conclusions which, at first sight, seem almost to have a material rather than a formal significance. It is one of the most characteristic differences between the classical and the modern systems that this doctrine which might, perhaps, with justice, have been described as psychological, has fallen completely out of the picture.

If we leave the Malthusian doctrine on one side, the most striking feature of the classical system is the *absence* of psychological elements. The Malthusian assumptions apart, the main features of the classical analysis were predominantly *technical* in character. The Law of Diminishing Returns, the Labour Theory of Value, the Theory of Comparative Costs, the Ricardian Theory of Rent – all served the main purpose of explanation by invoking technical concepts: the rate of variation of production, the labour time necessary for production, different degrees of fertility of soil – and so on and so forth. Even the Malthusian Theory in its palmiest days, played its main part in the theory of value and distribution *via* the technical concept of the amount physiologically necessary to secure the maintenance and reproduction of labourers. As is well-known, this was modified later. Subsistence became a psychological minimum. But the main psychological element explicitly assumed in the famous "stationary state" was the indisposition to accumulate below a certain minimum rate of profit. As can be readily seen from Mr. Edelberg's recent re-statement of Ricardo,[1] all the other chief elements of explanation were essentially technical.

Now, of course, it can be argued that many of the propositions of the classical analysis, assumed implicitly those psychological elements and constructions which, in the modern view, would be necessary to make them valid. Professor Knight has shown, for instance, that the celebrated parable of the beaver and the deer which was used by Adam Smith to demonstrate the labour theory of value, needs only to be re-stated in slightly different terms to make it valid in the universe of discourse it postulates.[2] Nevertheless, it is clear that, *as they were stated*, many of the classical propositions omitted to explain what we now see to be, in some respects, the primary conditions of any system of economic relationships, the influences operating on the demand side – the psychological elements in the system. The technical elements, which they stressed, were, no doubt, elements of which account must be taken in any system of analysis. But, taken by themselves, they were insufficient to determine the relationships to whose formulation they helped to contribute.

We can see this quite clearly if we take the example to which I have already alluded. In the Smithian example of the exchange of beaver and deer, it is permissible to concentrate attention on the technical conditions on production only on the assumption that these technical conditions are not variable. If we may assume that it always takes twice as long to catch a beaver as to kill a deer, then perhaps it is legitimate to neglect the psychological elements determining immediate valuations, etc., and proceed to argue that, in the long run, the ratio of exchange between beavers and deer will be two deer to one beaver. If it were not so, movements would be evoked which would tend to bring it about. But as soon as we drop this assumption – as soon as we assume that the time it takes to kill deer is a function of the number of deer killed, then clearly, unless we know the conditions of demand and the market, the equilibrium point cannot be determined. As there is no reason to assume fixed technical conditions of the kind invoked in the beaver–deer example, to be at all wide-spread, this means that, in the majority of situations, demand conditions cannot be neglected.

But, even if this were not so, exclusive concentration upon technical conditions would be very misleading. It might help us to *describe the conditions of equilibrium*; but it would not help us to explain how equilibrium *could be*

1. Victor Edelberg, "The Ricardian theory of profits," *Economica*, vol. 13 (February 1933), pp. 51–74.
2. Frank H. Knight, "A suggestion for simplifying the statement of the general theory of price," *Journal of Political Economy*, vol. 36 (June 1928), pp. 353–70.

conceived to be reached. In order that the technical production ratios may play the part assigned to them in this theory, it is necessary to assume that ratios of exchange – values – actually prevail in the market to guide productive effort. If you assume a random distribution of effort between beaver trapping and deer hunting, there is no reason at all to suppose that the ratio of exchange will be in harmony with the technical displacement costs. It is only when the market mechanism has been allowed to function and the ratio of exchange has enabled the producers to decide which is the best for them to do, that this harmony can be conceived to be established. Now the Labour Theory of Value tells us nothing about the formation of values when production are *given.* That clearly is a task which can be performed only by a theory which has taken account of the psychological side of valuation.

It is this shifting of the emphasis of theoretical economics which has been one of the main achievements of the work of the last seventy years. The classical economists had always recognised that, in order to be the object of exchange, a commodity must "have utility" – that is, must be the object of desire on the part of some member of the market. But beyond this they were unable to go. "Possessing utility," a commodity derived its value from the quantity of labour expended on its production, if it were capable of free manufacture; from a mysterious source which was called its scarcity, if it fell into the class of unproducible things like the pictures of Raphael or the autographs of dead boxers. There was no relation capable of precise explanation between the value of the good and its "utility."

And, of course, so long as the utility of a commodity was conceived as deriving from the *class* of commodities to which it belonged rather than from the precise use to which that particular unit was put, this *impasse* was bound to continue. There is no precise relation between the value of commodities and the "utility" of that class of commodities as a whole, irrespective of the uses to which they are put and the quantity in which they are present. It was not until it was perceived that the individual estimate germane to the determination of economic value, was not the estimate germane to the class, but the estimate of the significance of the actual use dependent upon the possession of particular units of the commodity, that the development of a value theory taking proper account of psychological elements was possible. Once this was realised, all the old paradoxes of value disappeared and the way was clear for a theory making subjective valuation its main foundation.

It is not necessary for me to plague you with a detailed description of this development. The main idea of marginal utility occurred to many economists working in different places round about the middle of the last century and in at least one case – that of H.H. Gossen – it was made the basis for systematic and extensive developments. But, for various reasons, these early discoveries had little or no effect. The incorporation of the psychological into the general body of accepted economic analysis had to wait until the appearance in the early 'seventies of the works of Jevons, Walras, and Carl Menger. From the work of these three men we must date the origin of the modern renaissance of theoretical economics.

But, in recognising this, it is very important that we should recognise too that their work provided only the beginnings. It is a great mistake to look upon the changes of the 'seventies as definitive and the whole development of the subsequent period as involving either minor refinements or the reintroduction of classical propositions on the supply side. On the contrary, many of the most important innovations since that time – the innovations, for instance, of Pareto and his followers – have consisted in the development of an apparatus capable of handling with much greater efficiency the complications of the psychological elements. To judge the modern economics by the formulations which are to be found in Jevons' *Theory of Political Economy*, path breaking as that work was in its day, is to risk falling into a serious misapprehension. Let me explain this in greater detail.

Let me take first the question of psychological foundation, for this is very germane to the question I have to discuss – whether there is any intimate relation between economics and psychological doctrines. It would be an easy thing, on the basis of a superficial inspection of Jevons and some of his English followers, to conclude that analytical economics was nothing more nor less than a series of corollaries of psychological hedonism. And it would be no far cry from this verdict to conclude that, since, in many quarters, psychological hedonism is regarded as discredited, analytical economics and all that depends upon it must share in the downfall.

The conclusion would be easy. But, in fact, it would rest upon a misapprehension. It is true that in the work of Jevons the marginal utility theory is developed on an avowedly hedonistic basis. It is true, too, that the celebrated Law of Gossen, the law of diminishing marginal utility, was propounded in the guise of a psychological law of satiation. But, in fact if we look at the parallel developments elsewhere, at the work of the early Austrians – Menger or Komorzynski for instance – we find just the same conclusions reached from a starting point which involved a definite repudiation of hedonism. It is no exaggeration to say that you could omit all those passages in Jevons which relate to the calculus of pleasure and pain, without any detriment to the main *economic* argument he is propounding.

Subsequent developments have made this clear. It is quite clear, at the present day, that the significant contribution of Gossen and Jevons was, not their hedonistic calculus, but the fundamental concept of the dependent use (the *abhängige nutzen*), which is quite independent of any hedonistic hypothesis. Gossen's Law in its modern formulation has lost any connection with the idea of satiation and embodies merely the incontestible platitude that, if the different uses of different units of a commodity offer unequal attractions, then they can be ranged in an order of declining importance. This seems to be a conception which is quite independent of any particular doctrine concerning the springs of human action.

It is not only in this respect that the Jevonian constructions have undergone revision and modification: other features have been reconstructed no less drastically. In the early days of the new theory, Jevons and others proceeded on the assumption that the "utilities" with which they operated were to be regarded as measurable – an assumption which, quite rightly, gave offence to philosophers. As a result of the work of Pareto and the younger Viennese School it has been realised that this assumption is totally superfluous. The theory of value which is to be found in more modern works is based, not on the assumption that utilities are measurable, but simply upon the assumption that they may be compared.[1] In its most remote ramifications, it involves nothing more than the assumption that the economic subject can judge whether the significance of *A* to him is greater than, equal to, or less than that of *B*. The Jevonian constructions, furthermore, proceeded on the assumption that the significance of any one commodity could be estimated independently of the amounts and the uses of other commodities: an assumption which, no doubt, had its uses as a first approximation, but which was manifestly insufficient to take account of processes of valuation which, in greater or less degree, take account of the system of ends as a whole. Here, too, the developments of the last thirty years have completely changed the position. It is the main purpose of the elaborate apparatus which has been devised by Pareto and, in more recent years, by Schönfeld and Rosenstein-Rodan, to take account of these and similar complications. Philosophers, who have an ingrained tendency to distrust the mathematical, do a grave injustice to modern developments of analytical economics if they accuse it of losing touch with reality. Paradoxically enough, it is just in order to be in a position to take account of situations of a degree of complication approaching that of the real world that these apparently remote abstractions have been devised.

At the present day, therefore, as a result of this process of development, you have a body of analytical economics which, while not ignoring the classical propositions regarding technique, takes equally into account the psychological elements in the disposition of scarce goods: a body of analysis, to use Pareto's words, which depicts economic phenomena as the inter-play of tastes and obstacles. Whether, recognising the priority, in a certain sense, of demand, we call this a subjective theory; or whether, attempting to devise a label which takes account of the psychological and technical elements, we

1. For the most systematic exposition from this point of view, see the important paper by J.R. Hicks and R.G.D. Allen, "A reconsideration of the theory of value," *Economica*, n.s., vol. 1 (February and May 1934), pp. 52–76 and 196–219.

call it dualistic, is a matter of words. The actual position is substantially as I have depicted it and I venture to suggest, in spite of some local disunity on semi-political questions such as monetary policy, etc., it is accepted by the overwhelming majority of present-day economists.

3. I now come to more controversial issues. As I have just indicated, there are few economists, who, at the present day, would reject any of the main features of the process of development I have outlined. All agree upon the insufficiency of the classical system. All agree on the necessity of taking into account most of the elements which I have called the psychological elements.

But there the unanimity ceases. In recent years, there have arisen voices urging a more austere attitude in regard to these elements. By all means, they say, let us take into account demand and let us do full justice to the complexities of demand in our system of curves and equations. But scientific method demands that we should leave out of account anything which is incapable of direct observation. Valuation is a subjective process and falls outside this region. We must, therefore, commence our analysis at that point at which valuation shows itself in action. Our theoretical constructions must assume observable data. The theory of value must be excluded from the theory of equilibrium.

It would be interesting to trace out in detail the rise of this tendency. Speaking broadly, I think, its origin is two-fold. On the one hand, it springs from the influence of behaviourism: from a desire to be in the fashion – a sure sign of intellectual sterility – or, on the other hand, as in the case of the School of Lausanne, it may spring simply from the aesthetic desire to secure the maximum possible austerity in analytical exposition.

But, whatever the occasion of this tendency, for it to become a general practice would, I am convinced, be a step in a backward direction. This for two reasons. The first is a reason of expositary effectiveness; whether it be aesthetically pleasing or no, we do, in fact, *understand* terms such as choice, indifference, preference, and the like in terms of inner experience. A theory which explains the pricing process in terms of scales of choice will not be *understood* in terms of externally observed behavour only. It will, quite inevitably, be linked up with introspective data. To ignore this, or definitely – in the interests of a false imitation of natural science – to attempt to suppress it, seems to me an altogether artificial position. No doubt, introspective data must be handled with especial caution. There are certain modes of procedure, such as the attempt to make quantitative comparisons, legitimate enough in the natural sciences, which are clearly illegitimate in this field. But, because some economists and some psychologists have exceeded what is methodologically permissible, to rule it out altogether seems to be a form of teetotalism inappropriate in scientific enquiry.

And in fact – and this is my second reason – when we come to look more closely at the assumptions of our analysis, we find, not only that it is inconvenient to treat these psychological elements as if they could all be observed from outside, but that, actually, it would be impossible to do so if we wish to explain the phenomena we set out to analyse. This is obvious as soon as it is stated specifically. It is clear that the most elementary process of price determination must depend *inter alia* upon what people think is going to happen to prices in the near future. Demand, that is to say, must be conceived not merely now – and thus afford the data for external observation – but also of a whole series of prices which people expect to prevail in the future. Such elements are not susceptible of external observation. Yet as Knight and others have shown, it is absolutely indispensable to take them into account if we are to understand at all the mechanics of economic change. It is quite easy to exhibit such elements as part of a general system of scales of preference.[1] But it is absurd to pretend that, in such circumstances, we take account only of observable data. How can we observe what a man thinks is going to happen?

4. If these considerations are correct, then it follows that there can be no question of excluding from economics its psychological elements. But it should be clear from what I have said already that the inclusion of such elements does not involve any close relation with systematic psychology. The elements in question are conceived in a purely formal manner. We make no assumption concerning their necessary content and, consequently, our conclusions are independent of the truth or falsehood of scientific doctrines which profess to explain this content. To explain why this man, in these circumstances, prefers fish to flesh; and that man flesh to fish; why to one love is more important than hunger and to another hunger than love – these are questions which, presumably, would be regarded by the psychologist as falling within his province. For the economist it is sufficient to assume that such preferences exist: his task is to examine their implications as regards the disposal of scarce goods.

But, it may be asked, when we descend from these austere regions of pure theory and investigate the disposal of particular scarce goods, in particular situations, are we not, in fact, making psychological investigations? Here again, the answer runs in terms of our former distinction. If we are attempting to ascertain the conditions of demand for fish in a particular market at a particular time we are indeed investigating psychological data. But we are not investigating them from the point of view of the psychologist. He wishes, presumably, to know why these things exist and to what law of psychic equilibrium, or psychic genetics they conform. We, on the contrary, wish to know simply *that* they exist in order to discover, in our own field according to the laws of our own science, what are the implications of such existence.

1. For an exact exposition of this procedure see J.R. Hicks, "Gleichgewicht und Konjunktur," *Zeitschrift für Nationalökonomie*, vol. 4 (1933), pp. 441–56.

But will not psychology assist us to discover such particular valuations – to say in *these* markets at *these* prices we shall discover fish to be preferred to flesh? It certainly has not done so in the past. Much as has been said by psychologists about the relevance of their studies to economics (and much has been said in their defence by economists with a livelier interest in other things). I have yet to meet the economist who used a text-book of psychology to assist him in investigations of this nature. And, on general grounds, I find it difficult to conceive development on these lines in the future. In recent years economists have done much work in the field of market analysis. An incredible deal of time and apparatus has been devoted to analysis of elasticity of demand for various products. If any significant psychological laws were to emerge in this field they would be much more likely to have emerged as a result of the efforts of economists than as a result of anything done by psychologists. Yet by now it is clear – it was quite clear to many of us from the outset – that such investigations can never lead to anything deserving the title of statistical laws. This is not in the least to minimise their importance, they do provide a rough basis for limited price predictions, in the area of collection, other things not changing greatly. But, in the last analysis, they provide not scientific laws at all but a particular way of writing history.

5. But finally, it may be asked, do not the generalisations of economics depend essentially upon a more general psychological assumption – upon the assumption of rationality? Is it not correct to describe the subject-matter of economics as the *rational* disposal of goods? And in this sense, cannot economics be said to depend upon another, and more contentious, kind of psychological assumption than any we have yet examined? This is a matter of some intricacy which deserves attention, not only for its own sake, but for the light it throws upon the methods of economics in general.

Now, in so far as the idea of rational action involves the idea of ethically appropriate action, and I think it is sometimes used in this sense in everyday discussion, it may be said at once that no such assumption enters into economic analysis. Economic analysis is "*Wertfrei*" in the Weber sense.[1] The

---

1. This proposition has been much questioned in recent years by certain English-speaking economists. But they have not yet shown that propositions involving "ought" are on the same logical footing as propositions involving "is." And, indeed, on examination, all their objections seem to resolve themselves into a fear that, if the scope of economics is thus defined, they may be precluded from discussing problems of social improvement from a normative point of view. But this apprehension is groundless. Nobody wishes to limit their freedom of action. Most of us think that it is very desirable that they should discuss such matters. All that is desired is that the logical division between the two types of propositions mentioned above should be clearly recognised. No one wishes to prevent a mathematician from discussing problems of good and evil. But he may bring the multiplication table into unnecessary discredit if he suggested that his views on ethics have the same logical sanction.

values of which it takes account are individual valuations. The question whether, in any further sense, they are valuable valuations is not one which enters into its scope. If the word rationality is to be construed as in any way implying this meaning, then it may be said that the concept for which it stands does not enter into economics.

But, in so far as "rational" is taken to mean merely "consistent," then it is true that an assumption of this sort does enter into certain analytical constructions. The celebrated generalisation that, in a state of perfect equilibrium, the marginal significance of divisible commodities is proportionate to their price, does involve the assumption that each final choice is consistent with every other, in the sense that if I prefer *A* to *B* and *B* to *C*, I also prefer *A* to *C*, and so on, that in a state of perfect equilibrium, internal arbitrage operations are excluded.

There is a wider sense, too, in which the conception of rationality can be understood as figuring in the discussions of the conditions of equilibrium. It may be irrational to be completely consistent as between commodities, in the sense I have described, just because the time and attention which such exact comparisons require are (in the opinion of the economic subject concerned) better spent in other ways. The marginal utility of not bothering about marginal utility is a fact of which account has been taken by all the chief writers on the subjective theory of value, from Böhm-Bawerk onwards. It is really not a recent discovery. It can be taken into account in a perfectly formal sense by permitting a certain margin (or a certain structure of margins) of inconsistency between particular valuations – the opportunity costs of internal arbitrage.

It is perfectly true that the assumption of rationality figures in constructions of this sort. But it is not true that the subject-matter of economics is limited to consistent action. Means may be scarce in relation to ends, even though the ends be inconsistent. Exchange, production, fluctuation – all take place in a world in which people do not know the full implications of what they are doing. Indeed, it is only in terms of irrational choice, that many of the more complex situations which economics has to study can be explained. The niggardliness of nature does not constrain only the actions of the wise.

The fact is, of course, that the assumption of rationality is simply one of a number of assumptions of a psychological nature which are introduced into economic analysis at various stages of approximation to reality. The perfect foresight, which it is sometimes convenient to postulate, is an assumption of a similar nature. The purpose of these assumptions is not to foster the belief that the world of reality corresponds to the constructions in which they figure but rather to enable us to study, in isolation, tendencies which, in the world of reality, operate only in conjunction with many others and then, by contrast as much as by comparison, to turn back to apply the knowledge thus gained to the explanation of more complicated situations. In this respect, as in so many others, the procedure of pure economics has its counterpart in the procedure of all natural sciences which have gone beyond the stage of collection and classification.

11 The Place of Jevons in the History of Economic Thought[1]

From *The Manchester School*, vol. 7 (April 1936), pp. 1–17.

I

William Stanley Jevons, whose centenary we commemorate, is not one of those economists whose merits have failed to achieve due recognition. In his own life-time his work on various practical questions gave him a reputation far transcending the limits of his own profession. Since his death he has been recognised universally as one of the most outstanding figures in the history of economic thought. Not merely as economist but also as logician, philosopher, reformer, he stands out as one of the most remarkable men of the age in which he lived. He is one of the great Englishmen of the nineteenth century.

Yet if one is asked precisely to define the exact nature of his achievement, the answer is not easy. He formed no school. He created no system. He died early, and few of his many brilliant ideas were worked out with the care and precision which, in our treacherous and elusive subject, alone can assure permanent validity. Marshall has said that he was a classic, in that he originated ideas which were capable of becoming the basis for long trains of systematic development.[2] Mr. Keynes has described him as a pamphleteer in that he flicked his ideas at the world, not waiting for their full elaboration.[3] Both verdicts are just. It is the totality of his achievements, the wide range of his

1. This paper was read before the Manchester Statistical Society on 27th February, 1936, and is reproduced here by kind permission of the Council of the Society.

2. *Memorials of Alfred Marshall*, ed. A.C. Pigou (London, 1925), p. 374. An author "is not for me classical unless either by the form or the matter of his words or deeds he has stated or indicated architectonic ideas in thought or sentiment, which are in some degree his own, and which, once created, can never die but are an existing yeast ceaselessly working in the Cosmos ... I incline to regard Petty and Hermann and Von Thünen and Jevons as classical, but not Mill." Marshall's verdict is especially significant. His earlier estimate of Jevons' place was by no means so favourable. See the *Academy* review reprinted in *Memorials*, pp. 93–100.

3. *Essays in Biography* (London, 1933), pp. 188 and 211.

activities, the fertility of his imagination, the marvellous lucidity and attack of his expository style, rather than the perfection of any one of his constructions, which gives him his place in history.

II

Jevons' main contribution to theoretical economics is to be found in his *Theory of Political Economy* [1871].[1] The posthumous *Principles of Economics* [1905] is a fragment – and a rather disappointing fragment at that. The *Primer of Political Economy* [1878] and the *Money and the Mechanism of Exchange* [1875] are elementary text books – devoted chiefly to descriptive matter: what theory they contain has no particular novelty. But the *Theory of Political Economy* is a great seminal work.

To appreciate its historical significance it is necessary to go back a little. In the years following the publication of Mill's *Principles of Political Economy* in 1848 a certain stagnation had overtaken the world of economic thought. The classical ferment had ceased to work. Yet the classical system, beautiful as it was, was incomplete. In default of new constructions, it was inevitable that attention should be drawn more and more to its deficiencies. It was inevitable that, if analytical economics failed to fill the gap, appeal should be made to other principles. In Germany, the sterility of theoretical speculation led to a definitely anti-theoretical reaction. It was not to be expected, said the

---

1. Jevons has been fortunate in the critics of his theoretical work. At the present day there is a wealth of important commentary available for the serious student. The following are especially valuable:

A. Marshall, "Mr. Jevons' theory of political economy," *Academy*, 1 April 1872, reprinted in *Memorials of Alfred Marshall*, pp. 93–100. See also Appendix I to the *Principles of Economics*, 8th edn (London, 1920), pp. 813–21.

E.H. Darwin, "The theory of exchange value," *Fortnightly Review*, vol. XVII (1875), pp. 243–53 (a defence of Jevons against Cairnes).

F.Y. Edgeworth, *Mathematical Psychics: An Essay on the Application of Mathematics to the Moral Sciences*, London School of Economics Reprints of Scarce Tracts on Economics and Political Science No. 10 (1932), Appendix V, "On Professor Jevons' formulae of exchange."

P.H. Wicksteed, "On certain passages in Jevons's *Theory of Political Economy*," *Quarterly Journal of Economics*, vol. 3 (1889), pp. 293–314, reprinted in *The Common Sense of Political Economy and Selected Papers and Reviews on Economic Theory* (London, 1933), Vol. II, pp. 734–54.

K. Wicksell, *Uber Wert, Kapital und Rente*, London School of Economics Reprints of Scarce Tracts on Economics and Political Science No. 15 (1933), pp. 20 ff.

A.A. Young, "Jevons's theory of political economy," *American Economic Review*, vol. 2 (1912), reprinted in *Economic Problems New and Old* (Boston, 1927), pp. 213–31.

F.H. Knight, "Relation of utility theory to economic method in the work of William Stanley Jevons and others," in *Methods in Social Science. A Case Book*, ed. Stuart A. Rice (Chicago, 1931), pp. 59–69.

leaders of the Historical School, that abstract analysis should yield knowledge of a living and developing social reality. The true instrument of sociological research was not analysis but history. In England this reaction never went so far. The classical system had been further developed and – what is seldom sufficiently recognised – the historical reaction over here was inspired, save perhaps in the case of Cunningham, by a much greater sense of proportion. Still the reaction was considerable. Cliffe Leslie may have been justified in protesting that Jevons was mistaken in suggesting that he wished altogether to abolish the deductive part of Economics.[1] But it is quite clear, as he went on to admit, that he regarded the urgent want of the time as induction and viewed with great suspicion long trains of deductive reasoning. There can be no doubt that this was typical of an important tendency. Some of the liveliest minds of the time were beginning to distrust theory or to lose interest in it; and with the exception of Cairnes, the representatives of the classical tradition seemed to lack the intellectual vigour to defend their methodological position.

In such an atmosphere, the *Theory of Political Economy* was at once a challenge and a portent. Its author was a man who had already won a public reputation by the excellence of his work in applied economics. The tract on the *Serious Fall in the Value of Gold* [1863] and the more ambitious *Coal Question* [1865] satisfied the most rigorous criteria of the anti-theoretical school. Indeed, as we should expect, the methods which he had devised in this connection – the systematic use of index numbers and logarithmic curves – were infinitely superior to anything devised by the traducers of theory. Yet here was a work by the same author in which the necessity for general theory was proclaimed with the utmost emphasis and which itself was devoted almost entirely to curves and equations having no precise quantitative content. It was true, said the author, that the widest possible development of separate specialisms was desirable. "There will arise various sciences, commercial statistics ... systematic descriptive economics, economic sociology and fiscal science. The whole subject is too extensive, intricate and diverse that it is absurd to suppose that it can be treated in any single book or in any single manner." But at the same time a general theory was indispensable. "As all the physical sciences have their basis, more or less obviously, in the general principles of mechanics, so all branches and divisions of economic science must be pervaded by certain general principles. The establishment of such a theory is a necessary preliminary to any definite drafting of the superstructure of the aggregate science."[2] Beyond this, and outraging

1. T.E. Cliffe Leslie, *Essays in Political Economy*, 2nd edn (London, 1888), p. 72.
2. *Theory of Political Economy*, p. 17. Throughout this paper the references are to the 4th edn (London, 1910).

even the feelings of some of the supporters of the classical methods,[1] it was contended that such a theory must necessarily be mathematical. "Our science must be mathematical," it said, "simply because it deals with quantities. Wherever the things treated are capable of being greater or less, there the laws and relations must be mathematical in nature. The ordinary laws of supply and demand treat entirely of quantities of commodity demanded or supplied and express the manner in which the quantities vary in connection with the price. In consequence of this the laws are mathematical. Economists cannot alter their nature by denying them the name: they might as well try to alter red light by calling it blue." If it were only for its apology for the mathematical method, which, as Allyn Young has remarked, is probably still the best statement of the matter,[2] the *Theory of Political Economy* would still be memorable.

But it was not merely as a vindication of abstract methods that the book was a challenge. In that respect indeed it could be regarded as a continuation of the main tradition. It challenged also the content of existing theory. There is no doubt that Jevons believed that his discoveries were completely revolutionary. "In the last few months," he had written to his brother eleven years before, "I have fortunately struck out what I have no doubt is the true theory of economy, so thorough and consistent that I cannot now read other books on the subject without indignation."[3] And at the conclusion of his book, there is a celebrated plea against the "Noxious influence of Authority" as represented by "David Ricardo, the two Mills, Professor Fawcett, and others who have made the orthodox Ricardian School what it is,"[4] so vigorous that it can only have sprung from the most overwhelming conviction. At the present day, with the superior lights of more than half a century's development to guide us, this attitude may seem extreme. From our point of view, the development of theory may seem in some ways to have been much more continuous. But it is clear that, to Jevons, his book seemed almost a complete break with the tradition.

And indeed there can be no doubt that his great idea, the idea that the origin of the objective exchange values of the market was to be traced to the subjective valuations of individuals, was very revolutionary. However much we emphasise the continuity of analytical tradition, we must admit that the vindication of this idea has shifted the whole emphasis of analysis in such a way as to deserve the name of revolution.

---

1. See, *e.g.*, the protest of Cairnes, *The Character and Logical Method of Political Economy*, 2nd edn (London, 1875), pp. 4–5.
2. "Jevons's theory of political economy," *American Economic Review*, vol. 2 (1912), reprinted in *Economic Problems New and Old*, pp. 213–31.
3. *Letters and Journal of W. Stanley Jevons, Edited by his Wife* (London, 1886), p. 151.
4. *Theory of Political Economy*, pp. 275, 277.

There are three aspects of this shift of emphasis which it is desirable to underline explicitly.

In the first place it puts the individual – the economic subject – in the centre of the analytical picture. It has been said that the mercantilists are preoccupied with gold, the classical economists with goods and the modern economists with men. Like most short statements about history, this puts too sharp an edge on it. Of course, it is not true that the classical economists regarded goods as having value without possessing utility; and we know that they were passionately preoccupied with the conditions of human improvement. But it is true that they tended to take the demand side as unimportant and in consequence got into all sorts of analytical difficulties. And it is true that they never even attempted to go behind demand to the more fundamental subjective valuations that underlie demand, that they moved all the time in the world of goods without enquiring concerning their significance to the individual. The subjective theory of value changed all that.

In the second place, just because of this change, the new theory provided the basis for a far-reaching unification of the concept of the very subject matter of economics. My friend, Professor Hayek, has stated that Menger, Jevons' great contemporary, was the first to base the distinction between free and economic goods on the idea of scarcity.[1] I confess I find it hard to believe that some of the earlier English writers at least, even if they did not use the actual term scarcity in this connection, had not some inkling of the distinction in question. But no one who has perused those passages in which the classical writers were wont to preface their exposition of the theory of value with distinctions between goods which derive their value from scarcity and goods which are capable of indefinite multiplication, will question for a moment that the classical analysis left considerable room for doubt on this matter.[2] The subjective theory of value changed all that too. All goods which are limited in relation to demand, all goods, that is to say, whose marginal units possess specific importance, are economic goods and have value. The question of their mode of reproduction is a minor question of technical coefficients.

In the third place, as regards the actual causation of value, the subjective theory, did as it were, stand the classical explanation on its head. According to the classical economists, granted that commodities possessed utility, their

1. *The Collected Works of Carl Menger*, Vol. I, ed. F.A. Hayek, London School of Economics Reprints of Scarce Tracts on Economics and Political Science no. 17 (1934), p. 13.

2. In the classical theory of distribution only land is specifically designated as scarce. There is no ultimate scarcity of labour: only the scarcity of food (which derives from the scarcity of land) limits its indefinite multiplication.

value was determined by their cost, that is to say, by the value of the factors of production which went to make them. According to the subjective theory, given the quantities of the factors and their technical substitutability, their values (and hence the cost of production of particular commodities) must be regarded as determined by the preferences of the economic subjects.[1] These were not merely different ways of putting the same thing, to be reconciled by emphasis on "mutual determination." Save in the case of land, the classical economists did not recognise the influence of demand on the prices of the factors of production, still less on costs. The theory of distribution was separate from the theory of value. In John Stuart Mill's system, it was even prior to it. In the post-Jevonian treatment, whether Marshallian or Austrian, it is simply its most general case. Goods would have value if there were no such thing as production, provided only they were scarce. The process of production has significance only in so far as it modifies the possibilities of choice.

All this and much more must have been surging vaguely in Jevons' head when he made the passionate challenge I have quoted. Yet it would be wrong to say that it was all clearly worked out in his book. If Jevons were to return to earth and to examine an up-to-date version of the theory of value such as we find, e.g. in Messrs. Allen and Hicks' recent essay,* he would find indeed that the fundamental substance of his central idea – that the ratio of final degrees of utility is proportionate to the ratio of exchange – remained. But he would find many – perhaps to him sometimes disconcerting – changes in formulation.

He would find, for instance, that the link with psychological hedonism which he went to such pains to establish – he prefaced his theory of utility with a theory of pleasure and pain – had been not merely ignored but even deliberately repudiated. Modern economics has followed Menger rather than Jevons here. We do not draw curves with ordinates of absolute utility; we express the significance of one commodity in terms of another at different margins. The idea of measuring utility cardinally tends more and more to disappear. Nor do we conceive of the diminution of relative utility in terms of psychological logical satiation. Jevons illustrated his theory to his brother by means of a dinner table illustration. "The decrease of enjoyment between

1. This way of putting things is designed to sidetrack the objection of those who object to describing the conditions of supply of factor services (as distinct from the total potential quantity) as determined by demand. The fundamental distinction is between the preferences of the economic subjects whether as consumers or producers on the one hand, and the technical conditions on the other.

*J.R. Hicks and R.G.D. Allen, "A reconsideration of the theory of value," *Economica*, n.s. vol. 1 (February and May 1934), pp. 52–76 and 196–219.

the beginning and end of a meal may be taken as an example."[1] We would avoid doing this. We consider merely the diminishing substitutability of one good for others, in regard to the whole hierarchy of prospective uses – again a Mengerian rather than a Jevonian construction. There is no theory of pleasure and pain in modern economics; we are concerned simply with the logic of choice.

He would find too that his theory had acquired much greater generality. We no longer think of the marginal utility (significance) of a good as dependent only on the quantity of that good we possess. We think of it as depending on the quantities of all the commodities in our possession. The accusation that the utility analysis is "atomistic," that by regarding the significance of marginal units of particular commodities as dependent on the supply of those commodities alone it ignores the "organic" inter-connections of our system of values, is irrevelant to modern analysis. Since the time of Edgeworth we have learnt to make utility a function of all the goods concerned. The indifference curve technique which we owe to Edgeworth, Fisher and Pareto[2] has been developed for this specific purpose.

But with all this, the fundamental discovery remains. The principle laid down as far back as 1862 in the paper presented to the British Association, that it is the marginal increment whose valuation is significant, is the basis of all subsequent development.

III

It is interesting to observe how Jevons fared in the attempt to apply this theory in detail and to develop a theory of distribution which should be consonant with its main requirements.

He was not very successful in elaborating a satisfactory theory of exchange. His celebrated equations of exchange[3] certainly showed one condition of

1. *Letters and Journal of W. Stanley Jevons*, p. 151.

2. It is desirable to emphasise the debt to Fisher. I do not think that it is sufficiently appreciated that his *Mathematical Investigations Into the Theory of Value and Prices*, first published in 1892, contains nearly all the innovations in this connection which we are accustomed to regard as characteristically Paretian.

3.
$$\frac{\phi_1(a-x)}{\psi_1(y)} = \frac{y}{x} = \frac{\phi_2(x)}{\psi_2(b-y)}$$

where a and b represent the quantities of two commodities initially held by the two economic subjects, x and y the quantities exchanged and ϕ_1 and ψ_1 and ϕ_2 and ψ_2 final degrees of utility to the economic subjects concerned.

equilibrium, namely that, in equilibrium, for each party to the exchange, final degrees of utility must be proportionate to price. This is right enough so far as it goes – on the simple assumptions Jevons was making. But it does not explain the formation of price under competitive conditions; and the so-called Law of Indifference and the very clumsy device of the "trading bodies" do not really help. The idea of relating marginal utility to demand at a price is due to Walras rather than Jevons.[1] And it was Edgeworth[2] who finally worked out the exact conditions which must be fulfilled if the price, the ratio of exchange, is to be completely determinate.

He was even less successful in developing a theory of distribution which should be coherent with his general theory of value. The very stern review of the *Theory of Political Economy* which Marshall wrote for the *Academy* is just, at least in this respect. He nowhere shows any real appreciation of the interdependence of the various elements determining the prices of the factors of production. Time and time again he seems to be on the brink of the modern theory. He sees that wages can be treated as rents.[3] He sees that the earnings of fixed capital are susceptible of a rent analysis.[4] He insists that wages and rents are determined by the size of the produce. But he does not develop a general productivity theory.[5] He accepts the classical theory of land rent without developing its implications as regards productivity: and, following the bad example of Walker, he treats wages as a mere residuum. All of which is very disappointing. For the idea that the value of ultimate commodities comes from their utility leads directly, as Menger emphasised, to the idea that the value of factors of production depends on the value of their products. All that is needed is the development of a technique for identifying marginal products.

But there is one section of his distribution theory which, I think, has often received less than justice. I refer to his theory of capital and interest. There is no doubt that he himself attached great importance to it. In the paper presented to the British Association it receives an emphasis equal to that accorded to the marginal theory of value itself, and there is evidence in his

---

1. The conception is clearly stated in the first memorandum presented by Walras to the Academy of Moral and Political Science in 1873, reprinted in the *Theorie Mathematique de la Richesse Sociale* (Paris, 1877).

2. See especially the illuminating and sympathetic critique of Jevons in *Mathematical Psychics* (London, 1881), Appendix V.

3. *Theory of Political Economy*, Preface, p. 1.

4. *Ibid.*, p. 1 and Appendix II.

5. Indeed there are places where he definitely denies the possibility of attributing to each factor its specific contribution to the product. See, *e.g.*, *The State in Relation to Labour* (London, 1882), p. 91.

letters that he regarded it as being of almost co-ordinate importance.[1] But it suffered from its association with the rest of his distribution theory. Marshall saw the defectiveness of its setting. But he did not realise its intrinsic originality; and it was shamefully misunderstood by Böhm-Bawerk who certainly ought to have known better.[2] The misunderstanding was probably enhanced by Jevons' own habit of repudiating connection with the classical writers.[3] So that, even at the present day, there are many who have not appreciated the importance of his contribution here.[4]

The substance of the theory is that the rate of interest is *inter alia* a function of the time for which factors of production are invested before yielding their final product. The essence of capitalistic production is resort to roundabout processes which yield a higher – that is, a more desired – product than more direct methods, but which necessitate a period of waiting before the yield of investment accrues. Capital is, therefore, to be defined as that which enables us to undertake such processes – in Jevons' view, "the aggregate of those commodities which are required for sustaining labourers of any kind or class engaged in work." And the rate of interest is the rate at which the product is increased as the period of production is extended, divided by the total product.[5] It is thus time which is the central figure in the picture. This comes out very clearly in a letter which Jevons wrote to Edgeworth in the last year of his life – a letter which, curiously enough, seems hitherto to have completely escaped attention.

---

1. *Letters and Journal of W. Stanley Jevons*, p. 155. There is an interesting passage in a letter to his sister written as early as 1859, in which the whole doctrine is anticipated: "I think you do not duly appreciate the comparative importance of preparation and performance, or perhaps, as I may illustrate it, of capital and labour. You desire to begin and hammer away at once, instead of spending years in acquiring strength and skill, and then striking a few blows of immensely greater effect than your unskilled ones, however numerous, would be. We enter here into one of those deeply-laid and simple propositions of economy which I hope some day to work out in a symmetrical and extensive manner hitherto unattempted even by Mill and Adam Smith." The discovery of the Jevonian theory of capital is thus anterior to the discovery of the marginal utility theory.
2. Böhm-Bawerk's error is sufficiently exposed by Wicksell, *Uber Werte, Kapital und Rente*, pp. 118–9.
3. He admitted kinship with Ricardo (*Theory of Political Economy*, p. 222) but denounced the wage fund theory most emphatically (p. 268). And in his *Principles of Economics* he goes out of his way to criticise Mill's fundamental propositions respecting capital in a most unsympathetic manner. (pp. 120–33.)
4. As usual Professor Taussig is outstanding amongst English-speaking economists for having got things in their proper perspective. See his very just appreciation and criticism in his *Wages and Capital*, published as long ago as 1896 (reprinted by the London School of Economics, 1932).
5. "If $F(t)$ be the product and $F'(t)$ the rate of increase, the rate of interest is $F'(t) \div F(t)$." (*Theory of Political Economy*, p. 246.)

"I have read your remarks on capital with care and interest: you will excuse my saying that you seem to be still deep in the fallacies of Mill. I fear you have not yet approached to a comprehension of my theory of capital as involving solely the element of time. I now see that the whole theory of the matter is implied in the expression for the rate of interest as given on p. 266 of my 2nd edition, some of the other expressions may be misleading. Indeed, as long as you speak of 'capital,' instead of capitalisation I think you are pretty sure to go wrong."[1]

If that does not constitute a fairly strong claim to be regarded as one of the founders of the modern theory of capital I do not know what does. There is no doubt that it is not set out with very great clarity. In the *Theory of Political Economy*, as distinct from the letter and the posthumous fragment, there are formulations of the capital concept which will bear too wage-fundish a complexion to be wholly free from objection. In all sorts of ways, the exposition is incomplete and incorrect. But the main formula is there. The essence of the use of capital is time. And the formula for the rate of interest, though framed on exceedingly narrow assumptions is correct. It is substantially the same as Wicksell's.[2]

Now, of course, this theory, much more than the subjective theory of value, is still to be regarded as an open question. It is quite clear that in the form propounded by Jevons it is in many respects too simple. It neglects compound interest, which is a phenomenon which itself vitiates the idea of the causal significance of any single average period of production.[3] It fails to provide a solution of the problem of durable goods. It considers only labour and not the vast multiplicity of different kinds of factors of production which in any full treatment of the problem must be worked into the picture. All this is painfully

1. *Letters and Journal of W. Stanley Jevons*, p. 439. There is an equally trenchant passage in the fragment on capital, reprinted as Appendix II to the 4th edition of the *Theory of Political Economy*: "To avoid confusion of ideas we ought not to speak of capital, but of capitalisation. Capital, if it consists of concrete wealth, is simply a theory and involves no idea of time: whereas we can have no reference to the use of capital without introducing time as the essence of the matter." (p. 295.)

2. In his essay on Jevons' *Theory of Political Economy*, cited above, Allyn Young urges that the Jevonian theory of interest is to be regarded as an incomplete marginal productivity theory. This, I think, is correct. But the essence of the marginal productivity theory, as it seems to me, is its emphasis on the interdependence of factors – the marginal products are partial differentials – and this is conspicuous by its absence in the Jevonian theory. The essence of capital theory, on the other hand, is its emphasis on the productivity of lengthy investment, and this Jevons emphasises. Hence, while I should say he perceived the main thing about capital theory, he was still some way off the central feature of the general marginal productivity theory of distribution.

3. See F.A. Hayek, "On the relation between investment and output," *Economic Journal*, vol. 44 (June 1934), pp. 207–31.

clear from recent controversy on the matter. But I confess that in my judgment, the critics of this theory have not really grasped its significant bearing. They pick away at unrealistic deficiencies in the first approximation and think that they have vitiated the central idea. It is, indeed, very easy to pick holes in almost any existing formulation of this theory of capital and interest. But I do not believe that anything which has been said, or indeed, that can be said, will vitiate the central notion that the essence of capitalistic production is the use of factors in processes which only yield their fruit after the lapse of time, and that the rate of interest is determined on the technical side by differences between the productivity of factors used for longer and for shorter processes. And that was the central thesis of the Jevonian theory of capital.

IV

I have lingered over Jevons' contribution to pure theory because it is there, in my judgment, that his work has greatest contemporary interest and significance. But a sketch of his significance as an economist would be ill-drawn, however slight it was, if it took no account of his work in the fields of applied economics and economic policy. For there was no field in which his touch showed greater evidence of sheer genius than in his capacity for handling facts, for marshalling large bodies of statistical evidence in a clear and succinct manner, and in extracting the utmost significance from them. Indeed, there have been some – I am not sure that Marshall was not one of their number[1] – who have held this to be his most conspicuous claim to fame. And if it is true – as I believe it is – that the occurrence of really great ability in applied economics is even rarer than ability in pure theory, then this claim may well be supported. For there have been few who have showed more ability here than the author of *The Serious Fall in the Value of Gold*.

But at the same time, by its very nature, the *substance* as distinct from the *method* of work in this field must have a more ephemeral significance than the discovery of general principles. The one remains, the many change and pass. The detailed facts of the fleeting day change and a new generation is confronted with new data. Of the many investigations which interested Jevons, most have ceased to have significance, save as history. We are left with the example of a method so fresh, so lively, so powerful that even when the substance it deals with is dead, we can contemplate its form with profit.

1. See the letter to Jevons, reprinted in *Memorials of Alfred Marshall*, p. 371.

Jevons' most important incursions into these fields were three, his investigation of the trend of prices in the fifties and sixties; his investigation of the coal question; and his investigation of the trade cycle. There were many others, the investigation of seasonal pressure in the money market, the census of the gold coinage, the match tax, for example, which would have brought fame to a lesser man. But in his work they are of smaller importance. In one of these major investigations he was completely right; in one as right as it is possible to be, predicting over more than half a century; in one, so far as we can see, quite wrong.

He was dead right about the movement of prices. *The Serious Fall in the Value of Gold* is one of the most beautiful investigations in applied economics ever made, and its contentions have been vindicated up to the hilt by subsequent researches. He was right about the increase of prices as against those who said that no increase had taken place. He was right as regards its probable limits, as against those who held that the increase in the supply of gold must lead to a catastrophic inflation.

We cannot speak so decisively about the contentions of the *Coal Question*. It is clear that many of Jevons' estimates have been found to be defective.[1,2] It is clear, too, that, at the present day, the prospect of a considerable decline in population renders many of his fears much less urgent. But his main thesis, that the rate of increase of the middle of the last century could not be maintained without rising costs of production, was surely correct. And he was correct, too, in supposing that, as time went on, the competition of other sources of supply of coal would become increasingly difficult to meet. Of course, the fact that we have reached a period of competitive difficulties does not prove that these difficulties are all of the kind that Jevons predicted. Some are pretty obviously not. But can it really be denied that some at least of our troubles have been due to the growing age and inaccessibility of some of our older coalfields?

It is in regard to the investigation of the trade cycle that we have to record Jevons' one comparative failure. It might have been hoped that, as the author

1. On all this the comments of Sir Alfred Flux should be consulted in the edition which he edited (3rd edn, London, 1906).

2. There is one analytical error in his arguments which has some practical significance. He argued that it was analytically wrong to suppose that the discovery of substitutes for coal could ever result in a slower rate of consumption on the ground that the demand for coal was on the same footing as the demand for labour, and the discovery of substitutes for labour had always, in the end, increased the demand for it (*Coal Question*, 3rd edn, pp. 140 ff). But this is not certain, it is only true if the elasticity of demand is high. It is not excluded *a priori*, that the discovery of ways of economising fuel may lead to a diminished rate of consumption.

of by far the best pure theory of capital that had up to then been propounded, and that as a member of your society which, as Mr. Ashton has recorded, was the scene of some of the best work in the early investigations of business fluctuations, he would have proceeded to solve this problem, too. And, if we look at the *Serious Fall in the Value of Gold* there is one passage which does, indeed, offer the highest promise of fruitful developments. "The remote cause of these commercial tides," he says, "seems to lie in the varying proportion which the capital devoted to permanent and remote investment bears to that which is but temporarily invested to reproduce itself."[1] 'There surely you have a text which neither Robertson nor Hayek would be ashamed of – a jumping-off point for nearly all that is most exciting in the modern theory of the trade cycle.[2] Unfortunately it was not to be. Having ascertained the existence of the cycle – there was nothing very new about this – and having thrown out this path-breaking suggestion, Jevons was beguiled into attempting to establish a correlation between the fluctuations of trade and certain astronomical phenomena – the sunspot cycle – using the price of corn either in England or in India as the connecting link! There is really little that can be said for this construction. The cycles did not always fit; two of the biggest crises of the century fell outside the series. The sunspot cycle was revised; and the list of crises was found to be so elastic that it was possible to revise it too.[3] Few authorities take Jevons' periodicities very seriously now. In any case the methodological basis of the whole speculation was weak. It is quite possible that there may exist rhythms of temperature or solar activity affecting crop yields and economic activity generally. But is there any probability that they are the only disturbing forces? Is there any evidence that only this kind of shock can be transformed into cyclical fluctuation? How much better if, instead of chasing this statistical will-o'-the-wisp, Jevons had settled down to give a solid account of the way in which "variations in the proportion between fixed and circulating capital" can give rise to crises and the many ways in which these variations can be occasioned.[4]

1. *Investigations in Currency and Finance*, 2nd edn (London, 1909), p. 24.
2. The passage is quoted by Hayek as an anticipation of recent views on this matter in an historical appendix to the second edition of *Prices and Production* (1935), p. 102.
3. Professor Wesley Mitchell's comment may be quoted: "Jevons had an admirably candid mind: yet in 1875, when the sunspot cycle was supposed to last 11.1 years, he was able to get from Thorold Rogers' *History of Agriculture and Prices in England*, a period of 11 years in price fluctuations, and when the sunspot cycle was revised to 10.45 years he was able to make the average interval between English crises 10.466 years. To get this later result Jevons purposely left out from his list of crises 'a great commercial collapse in 1810–11 (which will not fit into the decimal series)'; he also omitted the crisis of 1873, and inserted a crisis in 1878 which other writers do not find" (*Business Cycles*, 2nd edn (New York, 1927), p. 384).
4. The account in the *Primer* is fresh and interesting, but has no theoretical interest.

There is one other of Jevons' suggestions in these fields which deserves notice even in the wide survey we are taking. In the *Theory of Political Economy* he suggested that by the examination of trade statistics it should be possible to discover the demand functions for particular commodities, as Gregory King had attempted to do in regard to the price of corn. He was quite aware of some of the limitations of such functions when obtained. "The subject is too complex to allow of our expecting any simple precise law. Nevertheless, their determination will render economics a science as exact as any of the physical sciences – as exact, for instance, as meteorology is likely to be for a very long time to come."[1] He did not follow up the suggestion, save by one or two very sketchy examples, and it is arguable that even with all the qualifications he made he was too optimistic of results. Nevertheless, he is to be held as one of the chief pioneers of such attempts to make closer the relation between statistics and the general theory of value.

V

Jevons' interest in the application of economic theory was not limited to the investigation of the relations of facts; he was intensely interested in the prescription of policy also. His lively imagination was continually playing upon the leading problems of the day – bimetalism, ideal money, and management of posts and telegraphs, the position of married women in factories, trade unions and industrial co-operation. And he touched nothing that he failed to invest with new interest.

Most of these issues are now dead. But the general issue of the place of the state in economic life is, if anything, more urgent than ever. As we should expect, this was not an issue which Jevons neglected. The opening chapter of *The State in Relation to Labour* contains a long discussion of the question whether we can frame general criteria of the desirable limits of state activity – a discussion which I fancy has had great influence on the subsequent thought on this subject. The conclusion is reached that no such criteria are possible. Jevons examines the desirability of non-interference in regard to the conditions of labour. He has no difficulty in showing that there are cases – the use of dangerous machinery is a case in point – where there seems an obvious utilitarian justification for bringing about certain results by direct regulation rather than by leaving them to be secured by the slower-moving forces of the market. From these and similar considerations he reaches the conclusion that

1. *Theory of Political Economy*, p. 147.

there are no general rules – that every case must be examined separately. "The outcome of the inquiry is that we can lay down no hard and fast rules, but must treat every case in detail on its merits. Specific experience is our best guide or even express experiment where possible, but the real difficulty consists in the interpretation of experience. We are reduced to balance conflicting probabilities of good and evil."[1]

I confess I find this very unsatisfactory. It is easy enough to see why it was written. The Duke of Wellington, reviewing his troops, is reported to have said, "I don't know what impression these make on the enemy; but by God, they make me afraid." It is easy to see that Jevons, the enlightened utilitarian, must have felt much the same, reviewing the way in which popular advocacy of economic freedom, then, as now, was wont to prejudice a good cause, by opposition to measures which were obviously expedient, and by appeal to dogmas which were obviously indefensible. It is easy to understand the strong urge to repudiate all that. As against that wooden view of social life which sets up dogmatic rights to unlimited freedom of the individual and dogmatic limitations of government authority, without regard to their utilitarian justification, the Jevonian case is unanswerable; and it can hardly be better stated. But as the last word on the principles of industrial legislation, it is surely most inadequate. We do not believe that we can prescribe, out of the blue, detailed forms of industrial legislation which shall fit every conceivable state of industrial technique, and every conceivable type of population. But we do believe that there are certain analytical principles which must be invoked if we are correctly to analyse each case on its merits. And we do believe further that, given the general structure of different forms of society, and given a knowledge of what people want, it is not impossible to frame rules about the desirability of different types of action. We are really not always compelled to start from scratch whenever we are confronted with new proposals.

Now, of course, it is highly improbable that if things had been put this way Jevons would have made any objections. He states very clearly that he is considering the relation between science and practice, not the status of scientific generalisations themselves. He is very careful to say that "all effects of the proposed act, whatever be their remoteness or uncertainty, must be taken into account. There may be collateral or secondary effects which will not be apparent for years to come."[2] It is obvious that such effects cannot be detected save with the aid of analytical principle. And he goes out of his way

1. *The State in Relation to Labour*, p. 6.
2. *The State in Relation to Labour*, p. 6.

to say "in order to prevent the possible misapprehensions into which a hasty reader might fall, I may here state that I am a thorough-going advocate of free trade,"[1] which is a position he could only have reached by considerations very much transcending the merits of particular cases. But I do not think it is unfair to state that the net effect of his discussion here, however unintentional, is certainly to leave the impression that all questions of practice are completely open questions, and that there are no rules of any degree of generality which social science, combined with the utilitarian norms, may enable us to devise. Yet if this were to be regarded as the last word on the subject it would surely be very much to be regretted. Whatever may have been the case in Jevons' day, it is certainly not true today that the claims of general rules are over emphasised. We do not need any exhortation to be empirical. On the contrary, indeed, it is the lack of any body of generally recognised rules which constitutes one of our main difficulties. We have got into the most dreadful muddle dealing with each case "on its merits." No doubt this is because we have neglected to observe that this involves considering "the remoter as well as the more immediate consequences of action" – the Jevonian precepts might have seen us through if only they had been faithfully interpreted. But, as Jevons himself urged, the suitability of precepts can be tested experimentally, and we have had a long period of experimentation. Today, at least, it seems that if we are to get out of our present difficulties it will be, not by dispensing with general rules, but by seeking to reconstruct them on a sounder basis. Today, at least, we render homage to Jevons, not as destroyer, but as creator, not as one who loosened the hold of the old rules, but as one who, by his general services to economic science, prepared the way for a more rational formulation of the new.

---

1. *Ibid.*, p. 13.

12 How to Mitigate the Next Slump

From *Lloyds Bank Limited Monthly Review*, vol. 8 (May 1937), pp. 234–44.

I

If we take the summer of 1932 as the turning point, it is now getting on for five years since the bottom of the last depression. And although there is yet no reason to expect a severe break in the present run of prosperity, prudent men are beginning to ask themselves how long the good times will last and whether it is not possible to take action now which will mitigate the severity of the next depression when it comes. It is to the examination of certain aspects of this latter question that the present paper is directed. The title has been chosen very deliberately: I think it may be possible to mitigate depressions: I do not believe that, in the present state of knowledge, it is possible altogether to eliminate them. The scope of the discussion, too, has been deliberately limited to certain financial problems. On the stabilising effect of general measures for the revival of international trade and investment I have argued before in this journal.*

II

It has long been a maxim of prudence that, to avert a slump, it is necessary to avert the boom. If this is to be interpreted as implying that recovery must never be allowed to develop, there are doubtless many who would take exception to it. But if it means merely that it is desirable not to let recovery get out of hand, then surely it must be generally acceptable. It is a problem on which there is as yet no general agreement, whether recovery of any kind can be generated without at least some misdirection of investment which may be disadvantageous later on; and there would certainly be many views on the question

* 'The problem of stabilisation,' *Lloyds Bank Limited Monthly Review*, vol. 6 (April 1935), pp. 207–18.

at what precise point these mistakes became seriously important. But there can surely be little disagreement that, when a point has been reached at which prices begin to rise rapidly and shortages of labour and raw material are prevalent, the time is certainly due for the expansive process to be restrained. Only when the system is in a state of collapse and when idle capacity and idle labour abound, can a general expansion of credit be regarded with comparative equanimity.

Now this means quite definitely that, once this point has been reached, a continuance of the régime of cheap money which has accompanied the previous depression is dangerous. If money is kept cheap by deliberate manipulation in the face of a rising investment demand and rising costs and money incomes, then mal-investment of the kind which sooner or later leads to a bad crash is deliberately encouraged. There is no need to be a fanatical adherent of any particular brand of trade cycle theory to believe this. There is no need to believe that all depressions necessarily come the same way. It is only necessary to recognise what has always happened in the past when such conditions have been present. The collapse of a boom of this kind has always been followed by depression. If such a collapse is to be avoided, the régime of cheap money must not be artificially prolonged. A point comes when the rate of interest must be allowed to rise: to foster the idea that money can remain indefinitely cheap is to do a bad service to stability. And there is much to be said for the belief that a small rise early will cause less disturbance and difficulty than the much greater rise which is necessary later on, if inflationary conditions develop.

III

I hope that what I have just said will make it quite clear that I am no friend of the view which holds that we can dispense with the use of the discount rate as an instrument of stabilisation. In my judgment it is an indispensable instrument, an instrument which we must at all times be prepared to use with speed and vigour if the circumstances appear to call for such action. I think that cheap money conditions which are prolonged beyond the period when investment is naturally stagnant, are likely to breed bad investments. And I think that at the present time we should be prepared to see money rates rise rather than permit a further expansion.

Nevertheless, I think that those who attribute all the difficulties of our present position to a failure on the part of the authorities to bring the period of cheap money to an end at a much earlier date, scarcely do justice to the complexities of the situation. There is a sense in which they are right. We should have been in a more balanced condition now if recovery had taken place at a higher level of money rates. But it is not a sense which would have justified severe measures of contraction earlier on. Let me try to explain what I mean.

The extreme cheapness of money in London in the last four years has not been due to any one simple cause. It has been due partly to operations which were thought necessary in order to carry through the conversion [of 5 per cent War Loan to $3\frac{1}{2}$ per cent in June 1932]. It has been due partly to the inflow of foreign funds. It has been due partly to the shrinkage of foreign trade and investment.

Now in so far as the cheapness of money was due to the exigencies of the policy of conversion, it is no doubt legitimate to describe it as artificial. It has long been clear to those who took a long view that, both here and in America, the expansion of credit of the early years of this decade had provided the basis for a general expansion which might prove eventually difficult to control. But to attribute the peculiar conditions of the market only to this factor is to get things quite out of perspective. The stoppage of foreign investment, the shrinkage of international trade and the inflow of funds to London are factors quite as important. And, if we have regard to these factors, we must see that it was almost inevitable that money should have been unusually cheap during this period. While such conditions persisted and while the activity of the home market had not passed the point which, at an earlier stage, could have been regarded as normal, it was inevitable that the rate which equated the demand for loanable funds with the supply coming forward should have been abnormally low.

If this was so, then surely it would have been demanding a totally wrong policy to urge that credit should be generally contracted. There may have been much to be said for a little deflation of the gilt-edged market: certainly there was everything to be said for the utmost support necessary to prevent a further fall in the sterling exchanges. But, for the greater part of the period we are discussing, there can be no doubt that to raise rates generally would have involved a thorough-going policy of contraction. And that would have been inappropriate. The right policy surely was to extend the so-called principles of expansionism to the field of international trade and investment, to take measures which, by producing revival in the foreign sphere, would cause rates naturally to harden and so bring the market under control – not to contract the supply of credit but to produce a larger and a better balanced demand. We may blame the British authorities for their great timidity in this respect. We may urge that if they had shown greater initiative in restoring healthy conditions for international trade and investment, many of the present difficulties of the world, both economic and political, would never have developed. But to urge that *at that time*, in the absence of such measures, a higher level of rates was appropriate is, in my judgment, gravely to oversimplify the position.

But this period has now passed. The cheap money has taken effect. Investment has increased. Recovery has set in elsewhere. And on top of all this there has been launched in many countries vast programmes of public spending for rearmament. Prices are rising. In many parts of the system, the machine is working to capacity. These things are a danger signal. If, in such circumstances, the attempt is made to keep rates down, we are asking for trouble. It is highly improbable that long-term rates can be prevented from hardening. But the situation in the short-loan market is so abnormal that much slack may still run out before rates here come into line. How exactly to deal with this is a technical problem, the solution to which must necessarily change from moment to moment. But the principle is clear. If the boom is not to get out of hand, there must be no more credit expansion. Increased investment demand from whatever quarter must be met out of increased saving. If not, then rates must rise. This may mean not merely passive acquiescence in a changed situation, but also, in the short-term market at least, an active policy to keep the effective supply of credit from increasing.

IV

No matter how resolutely we attempt to curb the boom it is unlikely that we shall succeed in producing a state of affairs in which prosperity lasts for ever. To believe that this can be done is to live in a fool's paradise. The question therefore arises whether there are not other measures which may be prepared against the day when bad times come. We may well believe that the break is the consequence of mistakes made earlier on which have to be rectified. We may believe that, after a certain point, attempts to prevent it coming only serve to make things worse. But we should surely welcome any measure which, without giving rise to further maladjustment, would mitigate that secondary deflation which, following on the first liquidation, turns many sound positions into bad ones.

Now if such measures are to be not merely panic expedients, but measures designed with a view to healthy long-run development, we can lay down certain broad criteria which it is essential that they should satisfy. It is necessary that they should do nothing to disturb confidence: deflation is essentially a product of shaken confidence, and emergency measures which disturb confidence still further do more harm than they do good. It is necessary that they should be properly timed: if they come too soon they may merely stave off necessary liquidations and so prolong the agony: if they come too late they serve merely to stoke up a boom which has already started – as with the public expenditure on armaments at present. It is necessary that they should not figure so large in the expectations of business men that they actually become the mainspring of recovery: if they do there is danger that when they cease depression will once more begin – again we may draw a moral from the rearmament expenditure.

Such criteria, it is clear, go far to condemn the shock tactics which it was so fashionable to urge at the bottom of the last depression. The proposals for grandiose borrowing for *ad hoc* public works, which were put forward in various quarters, had much to commend them to the unreflecting; to oppose them was to court much unpopularity and misunderstanding. But, judged by these tests, they fail. They would have affected confidence at a time when the utmost stability was necessary if the conversion operations were to go through successfully. They would have come into operation at the wrong time. If public works of this kind are not to be incredibly wasteful, they may take anything up to one or two years to prepare: they would therefore have come into operation just when the forces of recovery were fully in motion, and they would have produced a distorting effect on business expectations. Like the armament expenditure, which in many countries took their place, they would have tended to *become* "the recovery," and the prolongation of the boom would have been contingent on their further continuance – to the infinite disorder of the whole system of public finances. If those who urged this sort of thing still desire recovery *à la* Hitler, they should say so. The thing has been tried out elsewhere and it does not seem that our position here is in any way inferior for its absence.

But to condemn ill-considered policies of this sort, is not to rule out all measures of counter-cyclical public investment – useful as it may be for propagandist purposes to suggest that it does. During the last depression it was very easy for the exponents of any project for wasting public money to pose as the only stabilisers and to represent the sceptics as "sadistic deflationists." For the fact is that, once a slump has begun, to start planning counter-cyclical measures is to lock the stable door when the horse has bolted; almost every measure which is conceivable is subject to grave disadvantages. But this is not to say that there are no measures which can be effective if planned sufficiently far in advance. Indeed, there is reason to suppose that there exists ready to hand the means for carrying out a policy which, without wasteful expenditure or enlargement of the sphere of governmental economic activity, might exercise a valuable damping influence.

In the modern world a substantial proportion of the total annual investment is constituted by investment by central and local government authorities. Opinions may differ as to the desirability of certain items of such expenditure. But on the necessity for some government expenditure on roads, bridges, drainage, civic buildings and such-like developments, there can be no question. If such things are not done by governments, they will not be done at all or they will be done very badly. For better or worse, therefore, we are confronted with a situation in which the proportionate importance of government expenditure is considerable.

Now, other things being equal, it is good business to borrow when rates of interest are easy and the prices of materials and services are low. We, therefore, make no unorthodox demand when we ask that policy should be directed to securing that, so far as is convenient, public investment of this sort should be planned so as to be slack during times of boom and more active during times of slump. If, during times of boom, public authorities were to slacken their borrowing, and if, during times of slump, they were to speed it up, there would develop a rhythm of activity which might do much to counter-balance the ups and downs of private investment. No doubt we should not claim too much for such a policy. It is not always possible to space out public expenditure in this way. It would be very foolish, for instance, in the interests of stabilisation, to postpone the building of an urgently-needed fever hospital. There is probably much public expenditure of the type of which this is an instance. But there does seem a margin within which more deliberate spacing is possible, and it seems thoroughly desirable that an attempt should be made to take advantage of its existence. During time of boom, central governments, and still more local government authorities, should be postponing avoidable development expenditure and preparing plans for setting such expenditure in motion when the bad times come again.

Such policy will always be useful. At the present time it is perhaps more needed than usual. At the present time we are entering on a boom which has been, as it were, superimposed on a boom. We are committed to additional public expenditure just at a moment when, on any theory of the trade cycle, additional public expenditure is most inappropriate. The resources of the capital market are already beginning to be extended. When the full impact of rearmament expenditure is felt they are likely to be strained. At the same time, the direction given to industry by the demand for war materials is bound to lead to developments which will be unprofitable when the present demand has passed. In such circumstances the policy here advocated would serve a double purpose. By damping down public expenditure on things other than armaments, it would ease the strain on the capital market and diminish the temptation to resort to unsound methods of finance. By deferring such expenditure till the time of depression, it would prepare a store of sound projects of development which could take up some of the deflationary slack in the capital markets when private investment holds back. There is certainly nothing very risky about such a policy. It is the very minimum of common prudence.

But are we doing anything about it? The policy is not new. It was first propounded, if I am not mistaken, some years before the war, by Professor Bowley in his evidence before the Poor Law Commission. And despite much diversion of opinion about other policies with which it has often been confused, it has had the steady support of the great majority of expert opinion ever since. Yet I doubt very much whether there has ever been any very serious attempt to carry out this type of planning. In fact, I doubt whether there even exists the machinery whereby the local authorities, whose actions are, of course, pivotal in this matter, can be systematically kept in step. Certainly if there does, the results are not very conspicuous. Any day at the present time one may open one's newspaper to discover it recorded with obvious approbation how this or that local authority has just approved a new programme of borrowing for projects "left over from the last slump." But this is exactly what they ought not to be doing. They ought to be closing down borrowing and preparing projects for the slump which is to come. Is it so remarkable that some of us are still somewhat sceptical of the capacity of governments to plan in the sphere at present occupied by private business, when they seem so lamentably unable to plan in a sphere where only governments can do anything?

V

We have seen already that it is a cardinal maxim of successful crisis policy that nothing should be done which is disturbing to public confidence. It follows, therefore, that it is fundamental that the budget should be properly balanced. This may sound very old-fashioned in a world of New Deals, of mounting public indebtedness and of a general belief that what is prudent in the conduct of ordinary business has no relevance to the conduct of government. In fact, however, nothing that has happened in recent years has done anything to discredit the rule that, for business to be healthy, there must be confidence in the solvency of governments. Prudent borrowing for essential public investment may, as we have seen, be a valuable means for combating deflation. But a budget which is seriously unbalanced may easily mar its practicability.

But budgetary equilibrium does not just happen. It is something that must be deliberately planned. And in times of depression, as we have seen abundantly recently, it is often peculiarly difficult to achieve. There is a tendency for certain sorts of revenue to decline and a tendency for certain sorts of expenditure to increase.

These tendencies are particularly obvious in the sphere of unemployment relief. Most states nowadays make some provision for the relief of unemployment. But when trade is bad the amount to be relieved increases. At the same time, under the systems of financing such relief now very often in vogue, contributions tend to fall off. Unless special provision is made, there is an automatic tendency towards an unbalancing of the public accounts, just at those times when, for the sake of business confidence, it is most desirable that the public accounts should be balanced. Yet, if the scale of relief is not excessive, to solve the problem by the reduction of relief is to frustrate the purpose for which it is instituted.

For this reason it seems desirable to make provision against the deficits of depression by building up reserves in times of prosperity. The finances of relief should be so arranged that in times of rising revenue and falling expenditure there arise surpluses at least equal to the deficits which are to be expected in times of falling revenue and rising expenditure. The good times should pay for the bad.

All this is the veriest platitude of traditional financial orthodoxy. And, although sound policy is never very popular, there is reason to suppose that, at present at any rate, public opinion is not unfavourable to such developments. It is well known that, since the recent reforms, an attempt is being made to run the British Unemployment Insurance Funds on these lines. It is not impossible to conceive an extension of the principle to certain other forms of public relief.

Unfortunately this does not altogether solve our problem, at any rate so far as trade cycle policy is concerned. The policy of accumulating a surplus in time of boom and using it in time of depression may be a solution of the budgetary problem. But it does not necessarily exercise a stabilising effect on business. Indeed, it may work in the opposite direction. It may accentuate the boom and intensify the slump. If the surplus which has accumulated in time of boom is invested in bills and securities, that tends to keep interest rates down and so to exaggerate the upswing. If to realise this surplus in time of depression these bills and securities are thrown on the market, that tends to keep interest rates up and so to make the downswing deeper.

Here, then, we have a substantial problem. If we do not accumulate a reserve but instead allow the budget to become unbalanced during depression, we run the risk of disturbing confidence. If we do accumulate reserves in the boom and then realise our investments in the slump, we run the risk of disturbing rates of interest. Is there no way of escape from this dilemma? I think a way can be suggested.

The root of the difficulty, as we have seen, lies not in the accumulation of a reserve but in the method of investing and realising it. If, instead of *investing* the surplus as it accrued, it was *hoarded* in some appropriate form, the effect would be quite different. As the reserve was accumulated, there would be a tendency to a contraction of spending; as it was spent, a tendency to expansion.

But is not this just the type of influence for which we have been searching in this article? In times of boom it is desirable that there should exist influences damping down the expansion. In times of depression it is desirable that there should be influences arresting the contraction. If public relief funds were managed on the financial principles we have already indicated; and if, instead of being invested, they were hoarded in some form or other, then, not only would they satisfy the canons of financial prudence, they would also play some part in the stabilisation of business. As the boom increased, so, automatically, money would be hoarded. As the depression deepened, so, automatically, hoarded money would be paid out. There would be some loss of interest, it is true. But, if the stabilisation were at all extensive, this loss would be more than offset in the long run.

In recent years the advocates of emergency borrowing in times of depression have sometimes sought to justify their policy by appeal to Bagehot's rule to pay out freely in time of crisis. The analogy is plausible. But it breaks down in an important particular. *Bagehot's rule assumes the existence of a reserve*: it does not advocate the progressive creation of public debt. Is it not possible that, by using the mechanism of public relief in the manner which has been suggested, we may employ a method which may more justifiably claim the authority of Bagehot – a method which, within the limits of financial orthodoxy, will give us all the advantages claimed for the method of emergency borrowing without the obvious dangers which the advocates of such methods so persistently overlook?

I put the suggestion in the form of a question. For the details of the problem are intricate; and it is most unlikely that I have perceived all the snags and the difficulties. I have purposely refrained from discussing the question in what forms the reserves should be hoarded; in gold, in deposits at the central bank or in deposits with other institutions. For this is a highly technical question whose solution must depend on detailed considerations of time and place. It may be that it can be shown that there are overwhelming difficulties here. It may be, too, that it could be shown that, in circumstances which are probable, the saving by way of stabilising influence would be less than the loss of interest on investments. On none of these matters would I pretend to any position of certainty. Nor would I claim for the proposal that it would necessarily do very much. This is not another cure-all. But we are not yet so well equipped with safe methods of mitigating depression that we can afford to neglect to examine any new opportunity that presents itself. It is because this particular opportunity, which exists ready to hand in our present institutional mechanism, has not yet received as much discussion as might have been expected, that I venture to draw attention to it.

that there should be influences arresting the movement. If public relief funds were managed on the financial principles we have already indicated, and [illegible]

[illegible]

13 Live and Dead Issues in the Methodology of Economics

From *Economica*, new series vol. 5 (August 1938), pp. 342–52.

I

1. The purpose of this note is a very humble one; it is an attempt to eliminate certain causes of unnecessary confusion. In the last ten years much has been written both by professional economists and by laymen on the methodology of economics. Some of this as it seems to me, has been concerned with live issues – with issues, that is to say about which intelligent men may well differ even when they have become fully aware of each other's premises. But some of it seems to rest upon misunderstanding and to relate to issues upon which there is no real dispute once the question is clearly stated. This note merely attempts to separate out some of these issues, particularly those that relate – or are thought to relate – to the vexed question of the status of realistic studies – to separate the quick from the dead in order that we may not any longer be encumbered by the latter. I hope that the absence of references will not be misunderstood. It would be easy enough to indicate the authorship of the misconceptions which are mentioned; and in certain cases the temptation has been strong. But I cannot help thinking that the purpose of the note is better served by deliberately refraining from assigning responsibility for what may seem to be obvious error. The issues are intellectual, not personal.

II

2. To deal first with dead issues. That the object of economics is to understand reality is not a proposition which is likely to be questioned by any economist. Indeed, if this had not actually been questioned by others, an apology would be necessary for stating anything so obvious. It is possible that, in the course of discussions of the exact nature of some of the postulates of pure theory (see paragraph 5 below) phrases may have been used – the "logic of choice", "deduction from the nature of the economic", for instance – which, to those who are not acquainted with the exact context of the discussion, may suggest

something else. But whatever may be the impressions of laymen, I cannot conceive the economist whose aim is not to understand reality; and I do not think that the whole literature of economics could furnish any fair quotation which could be adduced to show the contrary. As I myself have been pilloried as a sort of scientific antichrist in this connection, perhaps the following quotation from one of my own works may not be thought to be inappropriate: –

> "It is a characteristic of scientific generalisations that they refer to reality. Whether they are cast in hypothetical or categorical form, they are distinguished from the propositions of pure logic and mathematics by the fact that in some sense their reference is to that which exists, or that which may exist, rather than to purely formal relations.
>
> "In this respect, it is clear, the propositions of economics are on all fours with the propositions of all other sciences. As we have seen, these propositions are deductions from simple assumptions reflecting very elementary facts of general experience. If the premises relate to reality the deductions from them must have a similar point of reference.
>
> "It follows, therefore, that the belief often expressed by the critics of economics, that it is a mere system of formal inferences having no necessary relation to reality, is based upon misconception. It may be admitted that our knowledge of the facts which are the basis of economic deductions is different in important respects from our knowledge of the facts which are the basis of the deductions of the natural sciences. It may be admitted, too, that, for this reason, the methods of economic science – although not the tests of its logical consistency – are often different from the methods of the natural sciences. But it does not follow in the least that its generalisations have a 'merely formal' status – that they are 'scholastic' deductions from arbitrarily established definitions...
>
> "It follows, too, that it is a complete mistake to regard the economist, whatever his degree of 'purity', as concerned merely with pure deduction. It is quite true that much of his work is in the nature of elaborate processes of inference. But it is quite untrue to suppose that it is only, or indeed mainly, thus. The concern of the economist is the interpretation of reality. The business of discovery consists not merely in the elucidation of given premises but in the perception of the facts which are the basis of the premises."[1]

1. *An Essay on the Nature and Significance of Economic Science*, 2nd edn (London, 1935), pp. 104–5.

I do not think that the terminology of this passage is very felicitous. I can see all sorts of live issues concerning method lurking about the hinterland of certain sentences. But I do not think it is a very live issue to discuss whether its author believed that, in some way or other, it was his duty to study the real world.

3. I do not think that the issue is much livelier concerning the nature of that aspect of reality which economists have to study – the so-called question of scope.

In recent years, following Menger, some of us have canvassed the claims of definitions which explicitly draw attention to that fundamental limitation of goods in relation to wants which is the condition of the existence of conduct having an economic aspect. Economics, we have suggested, is essentially the study of the disposal of scarce goods and services.

This suggestion has not met with universal acceptance. But the difference between this and other definitions now current is not a very serious matter. It is probable that those who do not find this definition acceptable would prefer some such definition as that of Professor Pigou who regards economics as concerned with conduct which can be brought into relation with the measuring rod of money. As I have explained elsewhere, I myself feel that this suggests an unnecessary restriction of the subject matter of economics to a certain institutional setting. But this is a very minor point indeed. We surely can all agree that, in order that conduct may be brought into relation with the measuring rod of money, it must concern goods and services which are scarce. Whether we define the actual subject matter of study in terms which cover all institutional settings (the "scarcity" definition) or limit it to those settings with which we are most preoccupied (the "exchange" definition), is not a matter about which sensible people will waste many precious moments.

The only question with regard to the scope of economics which can be said to be in any sense alive, is the question whether economics, as such, can be said to include judgments of what is good or bad in the world of relative scarcities, as distinct from judgments of what exists or what might be conceived to exist. Here at least there is some appearance of difference. To many of us it seems that there is a definite difference of status between the proposition, for instance, that a market tends in a certain direction and the proposition that it is good that it should so tend. The one seems to be a judgment of fact – a proposition of what I should call economic science – the other a judgment of value – a proposition of what I should call ethics or social philosophy – and I should have thought that such a difference was fairly well established. But, in recent years, there have been some who have urged that the distinction should not be made. Economics, they say, should include both judgments of fact and judgments of value. Those who say otherwise are condemning it to a position of triviality and insignificance.

At first sight there seems complete deadlock. In fact, however, it usually turns out that those who adopt this latter attitude, are concerned not so much with problems of definition as with problems of conduct or deportment. They think that the economist will sacrifice opportunities for usefulness if he abstains from excursions into social philosophy and (apparently) they think that if such excursions are not dignified by the title, economic science, he may feel precluded from making them. The warning may be necessary. But the psychology may be questioned. To me at least, it seems difficult to believe that recognition of the distinction between the two kinds of proposition will prevent any man of spirit from being interested in both; and I certainly think that there is considerable utility in realising that the kind of test to which we may appeal in the one case is not available in the other. (I can prove by well-known methods of research that Professor *X* has devoted scarce time to controversy with Professor *Y*; but the proof that it was a good thing that he should have done this, rests on a different kind of argument.) I should, however, be the first to agree that the economist who thinks that his subject is capable of being used as a basis for policy without further appeal to social philosophy is cherishing a naïve delusion. My innocent remark that "equilibrium is just equilibrium" meant exactly that. And if I found anyone who could not pluck up courage to indulge in the relevant social philosophising unless he were permitted to call it economics, I should regret the inhibition as tending to mislead the laity. But I should not make it the subject of great lamentation.[1]

4. We have just seen that it is not disputed that the object of economics is to understand a certain aspect of reality. It is equally undisputed that, in order to understand reality, reality must be studied. Here again, if it were not for the misunderstandings of the recent past, an apology would be due for emphasising the obvious. I do not think that there is a single professional economist living who would dispute that the appropriate method of economics is the construction and development of hypotheses suggested by the study of reality and the testing of the applicability of the results by reference back to reality. There will obviously be legitimate differences of opinion concerning the reliability of particular forms of deduction and induction. And as we shall see later on, there are differences between the social sciences and the natural sciences, both in regard to the nature of the material handled and in regard to the reliability of the results of empirical tests, which may easily give rise to problems about which reasonable men may hold very different views. But on the

1. If the resuscitation of the old term Political Economy were acceptable as a rough description of this type of speculation, I think that perhaps we might agree even upon terminology.

necessity for the combination of deduction and induction, of theory and realistic studies, there is no dispute among sensible people. In a subject so wide as economics it is natural that there should develop some division of labour, that some should specialise on the more theoretical developments, some on description and verification. But it is not true that those whose interests are predominantly theoretical take a view of their functions any different from the view of his functions taken, let us say, by the theoretical physicist.

It is no more true that, in the majority of centres of study, the theoretical branches of our subject are cultivated at the expense of the applied – often as outside opinion may assert the contrary. On the contrary, it is probably true to say that, in the past, the development of pure theory has lagged behind because of the greater prestige of studies having more immediate relevance to practice. And because of the exigencies of the teaching programme in the relatively small departments of economics, characteristic of many British Universities, there is not much time for excessive concentration on pure theory. It is only in a few privileged centres that any considerable division of labour has proved to be possible; and even here the extent to which it actually goes is capable of grotesque exaggeration.[1]

What is true, of course, is that there is not yet nearly enough quantitative investigation of the applicability of the conclusions to which recent theoretical developments have given rise. Recent speculation has shown us a vast range of possibilities: until we have much more quantitative knowledge about the real world, we have to rely chiefly on hunch to say which possibility is probable. As Mr. Keynes has well put it: "Before we can either perfect our theory or apply it with safety to practical issues, there is another kind of knowledge which we need to increase: – namely, exact quantitative information concerning contemporary transactions ... The collection and arrangement of comprehensive statistics is of vast importance 'in order to eliminate impressionism.'"[2]

To do this, however, two conditions are essential – willingness on the part of governments and the business world to provide access to the facts, and sufficient endowment of faculties of economics to provide the computing and collecting assistance which such types of work necessarily involve. Unfortunately, in Great Britain at least, neither of these kinds of assistance

1. Thus for instance, at the London School of Economics, of some twenty-five members of the Economics Departments, not more than three or four can be regarded as predominantly specialised on pure theory.

2. *A Treatise on Money* (London, 1930), vol. 2, p. 407. It is curious that the author of this passage and the distinguished contribution to the applied theory of money in which it occurs, should have recently been singled out for public censure for "unscientific" methods of procedure.

has very often been forthcoming. But on the necessity for such developments there is not, and there has not been, any disagreement whatever.

III

5. There are, however, two questions, apt to be confused with this, on which disagreement is still very lively.

The first of these relates to the exact logical status of certain of the more general assumptions on which pure economics is based. It is well known that much of the structure of pure analysis depends upon assumptions of a very general character – the so-called economic principle, the assumption of an order of preference, etc. Now concerning the status of these assumptions there exist very lively differences. One school of thought regards them as essentially rational principles which are given *a priori* and which, while they show themselves in experience, yet require no appeal to experience to demonstrate their ultimate validity. Another, while not disputing the wide generality of their applicability, regards them as being derived from experience and having the same provisional status as the more obviously empirical assumptions. The former view has been very powerfully urged by Professor Mises and Dr. Bernardelli, the latter by Dr. Kaufmann and Mr. Hutchison among others; and dispute is still very active.

Now this is a matter of fundamental philosophical interest; and it is by no means to be regarded as settled by off-hand reference to fashionable beliefs regarding the logical status of the principles of the natural sciences. There could be no worse example of *a prioriism* in methodology than the calm assumption that what may be true of one branch of knowledge is necessarily true of others, without detailed examination of the body of knowledge which it is desired to classify. There are very fundamental epistemological questions involved here; and he would be a bold man who would regard the problems of epistemology as settled. I myself would confess to real doubt on the issue; and in the work alluded to above I have tried – in the first edition unsuccessfully, in the second, I hope, with greater, if not complete, success – to use a terminology which steers clear of the ultimate questions involved.

But whatever may be the truth about this most difficult question, it must be insisted that its interest lies outside economics. It is philosophical rather than practical. Whether we think that the main assumptions of the pure theory of choice rest upon observation or upon *a priori* knowledge, we all agree about the main conclusions. If they rest upon *a priori* knowledge then, to that extent they are certain. If not, even so it would still be agreed that the facts of experience corresponding to these particular assumptions are so general that they may be treated *as if* they were certain. Only one who knew nothing about pure economics could contend that the assumptions in question have been insufficiently tested.

Moreover, whatever the solution of the problem, its effects on practice would be very little. For no one has contended that conclusions drawn from the so-called *a priori* principles can be applied to the interpretation of particular cases without the use of supplementary assumptions whose foundation is obviously empirical and whose applicability must therefore be the subject of continual verificatory tests. If the widest claims of *a prioriism* were generally admitted, the necessity for continuous empirical study would not be in the least diminished.

6. There is, however, another issue which at first sight has a greater bearing on practice. It concerns the exact significance to be attached to the results of certain kinds of observation. Since probably it is misunderstanding of the implications of this controversy which has led to most of the current misconceptions concerning the status of realistic studies, it is perhaps desirable to deal with it in rather greater detail.

Let me try to make precise the exact nature of the methodological issue: its implications for practice will then become fairly obvious.

It will be generally agreed among those who have given serious attention to the facts that, whatever their exact logical status, the assumptions of what is usually called pure theory permit a considerable elaboration of deductive reasoning, which, with judicious choice of supplementary assumptions, can usefully be applied to the interpretation of a very wide field of phenomena. Whether, as some think, they are based upon rational principles or whether they are based upon experience so general that it is difficult to conceive situations to which they do not apply, these principles, like the principles of classical mechanics, are for practical purposes to be regarded as having an applicability which, if not ubiquitous and permanent, is at least sufficiently widespread to make it superfluous to bother much about them, each time they are involved. We should all agree that the mythical Schmoller student who, after five hundred pages of statistical investigation, decided that the price of pork in the Eastern District of Berlin in the years 1895–1900 was "determined by supply and demand", had been wasting his time.

We are also in agreement that, if we are to go much beyond qualitative generalities, we need further information of a much more specialised character. On the assumption of normal demand conditions we can deduce, for instance, interesting propositions about the *direction* of probable price change. But to arrive at knowledge about the *magnitude* of change we need information about elasticity.

There is no disagreement, therefore, about the desirability of statistical knowledge here. If the mythical Schmoller student had given us information about elasticity we should all agree that he would not have been wasting his time. But there is disagreement about the interpretation of the significance of such information once it is procured. Some think that by sufficient statistical investigation of this sort we can discover permanent quantitative laws and in this way put economics on the same footing in this respect as the natural sciences. Others – I count myself of their number – are doubtful of this. They think that there are reasons inherent in the nature of our subject matter why this hope is vain. To quote Professor Pigou: –

> "Even if the constants which economists wish to determine were less numerous, and the method of experiment more accessible, we should still be faced with the fact that the constants themselves are different at different times. The gravitation constant is the same always. But the economic constants – these elasticities of demand and supply – depending, as they do, upon human consciousness, are liable to vary. The constitution of the atom, as it were, and not merely its position, changes under the influence of environment ... This malleability in the actual substance with which economic study deals means that the goal sought is itself perpetually shifting, so that, even if it were possible by experiment exactly to determine the values of the economic constants to-day, we could not say with confidence that this determination would hold good also of to-morrow."[1]

No doubt even here it would be very unwise to push scepticism all the way. It may be that, although some of the "constants" are liable to rapid change, so that statistical findings which are valid to-day are no longer valid to-morrow, others have a rather more long-lasting validity. Examples will readily occur to those familiar with the econometric literature of recent years. Nevertheless I think there is a real divergence of opinion here which probably ultimately involves deep-seated differences concerning the place of consciousness in the universe.

But – and this is the point which is so often misconceived – whatever view we may take on this issue, our views on the desirability of bigger and better realistic studies are certainly not affected unfavourably. Indeed, if we take – as I take – the more sceptical view, our view of the importance of such studies will be enhanced rather than diminished. Popular inspection of recent methodological discussion of these matters has jumped to a conclusion which is precisely the opposite of the truth. If we are really convinced that we have, as it were, continuously to rediscover the magnitude of some of our constants, then how much more urgent, how much more obligatory, are the

1. *Economics of Welfare*, 3rd edn (London, 1929), pp. 9–10.

claims of continuous investigation. The chemist or the physicist may indeed hope that within a finite time, he, or at least his descendants, may have discovered *all* the necessary empirical information – applications thenceforward to be a matter of tables and formulae. But for the economist if he wishes – as we all wish – to go beyond mere qualitative generalisation, there can be no such hope. Day by day, in Sisyphus-like activity, he must discover his coefficients anew.

IV

7. I conclude with one reflection of a rather wider nature. The term methodology, as it is used in connection with economics, has come to cover two distinct, though perhaps related, fields of discussion. On the one hand it covers discussions concerning the way in which our investigations should be conducted – the problem of method in the narrow sense – on the other hand, discussions concerning the nature of the subjects studied and the significance and logical status to be attached to the results achieved.

Now it has always seemed to me that it is the second of these groups of topics which, at our present stage of development, offers problems of real intellectual interest. Now that we have a great mass of detailed studies which, we are convinced, mean something, it is surely useful to try to ascertain exactly what is their general field of reference and what degree of significance can be attached to their results. It is useful both for purposes of systematisation and for purposes of application. To know the ultimate nature of our subject matter is to be in a position, as Marshall would say, to perceive the one in the many and to establish relationships between propositions hitherto regarded as discreet. To know the logical status of our conclusions is to be in a position to apply our knowledge and to establish fruitful relationships with other fields of research.

The first group of topics, questions relating to procedure, has always seemed to me to offer much less scope for interesting or fruitful speculation. To discuss the method appropriate to a particular enquiry which one is about to undertake is a useful and often enthralling occupation. But, at this distance from Galileo and Newton, to discuss the method of any science *in vacuo* does not seem particularly necessary or entertaining. Perhaps there was a stage in the history of economics when this needed to be done; although I am inclined to believe that the main interest of the methodological discussion here has always been in the other field. But for practising economists, at any rate in England, this is surely a closed question. We all agree that in general we need both induction and deduction, observation and theoretical system; and that the important thing is to suit the method to the job. I can conceive that, from time to time, in regard to whole groups of topics, some emphasis one way or the other may be needed. In regard to recent developments of the theory of money, for instance, it may be salutory to emphasise the need for verification; in regard to historical studies of certain secular trends, it may be useful to press for more precise statement of the hypotheses which it is desired to verify. But in general, surely, the thing is sterile. Only in discussion of the significance of our results, do considerations regarding the respective rôles of different methods present problems of sufficient general interest to warrant separate discussion.

It is no accident of personal predilection, I suggest, that in the classification attempted above, both the live issues (paragraphs 5 and 6) are questions relating to the logical status of our assumptions or our results, whereas the issue of method in the narrow sense (paragraph 4) is to be found in the catalogue of issues that are to be regarded as essentially dead.

14 Interpersonal Comparisons of Utility: A Comment

From *The Economic Journal*, vol. 48 (December 1938), pp. 635–41.

In the course of his interesting paper on the "Scope and Method of Economics,"* Mr. Harrod raises once more the question of the status of interpersonal comparisons of utility. I do not wish directly to controvert any of his statements on this matter. But it occurs to me that a short account of the genesis of the views which I have put forward, and which form the subject of his friendly comment, might at once elucidate the nature of our differences and make clear to those who rejoice in the spectacle of disunity how very slender the practical implications of these differences actually are. I must apologise in advance for the personal nature of the argument. I am under no illusion concerning the interest of my intellectual difficulties in so far as they are purely my own. But, in so far as they can be regarded as typical, a brief explanation may perhaps facilitate mutual understanding.

My own attitude to problems of political action has always been one of what I might call provisional utilitarianism. I am far from thinking that thorough-going utilitarianism *à la Bentham* is an ultimate solution of any of the major problems of social philosophy. But I have always felt that, as a first approximation in handling questions relating to the lives and actions of large masses of people, the approach which counts each man as one, and, on that assumption, asks which way lies the greatest happiness, is less likely to lead one astray than any of the absolute systems. I do not believe, and I never have believed, that in fact men are necessarily equal or should always be judged as such. But I do believe that, in most cases, political calculations which do not treat them *as if* they were equal are morally revolting.

It follows, therefore, that when I came to the study of economics, I had the strongest bias in favour of a utilitarian analysis. The delicate balancing of gain and loss through intricate repercussions of policy which I found in such works as [Pigou's] *Economics of Welfare*, fascinated me; and I was powerfully attracted by the proposition, urged so forcefully by Edwin Cannan and others,

---

* *Economic Journal*, vol. 48 (September 1938), pp. 383–412.

that recent developments of the theory of value could be invoked to demonstrate the desirability of the mitigation of inequality. When I look back on that frame of mind, I find it easy to understand the belief of Bentham and his followers that they had found the open sesame to problems of social policy.

But, as time went on, things occurred which began to shake my belief in the existence of so complete a continuity between politics and economic analysis. I never thought of abandoning my provisional utilitarianism as a working political philosophy. But I began to feel that there were profound difficulties in a complete fusion between what Edgeworth called the economic and the hedonistic calculus. I am not clear how these doubts first suggested themselves; but I well remember how they were brought to a head by my reading somewhere – I think in the works of Sir Henry Maine – the story of how an Indian official had attempted to explain to a high-caste Brahmin the sanctions of the Benthamite system. 'But that,' said the Brahmin, 'cannot possibly be right. I am ten times as capable of happiness as that untouchable over there.' I had no sympathy with the Brahmin. But I could not escape the conviction that, if I chose to regard men as equally capable of satisfaction and he to regard them as differing according to a hierarchical schedule, the difference between us was not one which could be resolved by the same methods of demonstration as were available in other fields of social judgment.

This led me to a re-examination of the propositions of the text-books. It did not take long to see that the "law" of diminishing marginal utility, assumed by Cannan and others in the analysis of inequality, differed from the "law" of the same name invoked in the analysis of exchange and that the difference was precisely the introduction of this assumption of equal capacity for satisfaction. I did not see so quickly that the same assumptions were involved in most pronouncements relating to movements of the social dividend. But, gradually, reflection on the tariff problem and such-like matters forced me to this view. I found that this attitude was already maintained by a great number of continental writers: and further research on index number problems only strengthened my conclusion. Mr. Harrod very properly draws attention to the fact that, if we do not make the assumption of equal capacity for satisfaction, we are precluded from asserting that the repeal of the Corn Laws tended to increase the general welfare. In lecturing upon these subjects for many years, I have continually used this self-same illustration. By the time I came to write the book to which Mr. Harrod has referred, I had acquired the settled habit of classifying the propositions of traditional political economy according as they did or did not involve this particular assumption.

Having reached this stage, however, I was confronted with a further question. The assumptions of the propositions which did not involve interpersonal comparisons of utility were assumptions which had been verified by observation or introspection, or, at least, were capable of such verification. The assumptions involving interpersonal comparison were certainly not of this order. "I see no means," Jevons had said, "whereby such comparison can be accomplished. Every mind is inscrutable to every other mind and no common denominator of feeling is possible." Would it not be better, I asked myself, quite frankly to acknowledge that the postulate of equal capacity for satisfaction *came from outside*, that it rested upon ethical principle rather than upon scientific demonstration, that it was not a judgment of fact in the scientific sense, but rather a judgment of value – perhaps, even, in the last analysis, an act of will? Ought it not to be made clear, for instance, that theories of public finance which went beyond tracing the effects of given measures on prices, quantities produced and such-like measurable magnitudes, and which attempted to sum social gain or loss, were not, strictly speaking, economic science? The analysis of the effects of a small tax on particular prices and quantities of particular products would rest upon scientific demonstration. But according as Maine's Brahmin or Bentham, Hitler or St. Paul, laid down the postulates of interpersonal comparison, the valuation of these effects in terms of social welfare would be different.

The answer seemed obvious. The distinction existed. It ought to be recognised. But I confess that at first I found the implications very hard to swallow. For it meant, as Mr. Harrod has rightly insisted, that economics as a science could say nothing by way of prescription. It could say whether a certain course of action could lead to a desired end. It could judge the consistency of different policies. But, in itself, it passed no verdict of good or bad. It was not possible to say that economic science showed that free trade was justifiable, that inequality should be mitigated, that the income tax should be graduated, and so forth. I attached high importance to these propositions; and the realisation that I could not claim for them scientific justification was profoundly antipathetic.

Further thought, however, convinced me that this was irrational. I was bound to admit that what I was doing was simply to carry one stage further a very common and almost universally accepted practice. All economists recognised that their prescriptions regarding policy were conditional upon the acceptance of norms lying outside economics. All that I was doing was only to recognise that, in a field of generalisations hitherto thought to involve no normative elements, there were in fact such elements concealed. The traditional political economy, for instance, had taught that free trade increased social wealth. It had fully recognised that the prescription, built on this analysis, that free trade was a good thing, was contingent on the assumption that an increase of wealth was to be desired: if defence, for instance, was more than opulence, free trade had to go. All that I proposed to do was to make it clear that the statement that social wealth was increased, itself involved an arbitrary element – that the proposition should run, *if* equal capacity for satisfaction on the part of the economic subjects be assumed, *then* social wealth can be said to be increased. Objective analysis of the effects of the repeal of duties only showed that consumers gained and landlords lost. That such an arbitrary element was involved was plain. It seemed no less plain, therefore, that, here as elsewhere, it should be explicitly recognised.

Moreover, when I came to ask myself how much persuasive force was really lost to the principles of action which I valued so highly, I could not resist the conviction that my initial perturbation had been unnecessary, and even somewhat ridiculous. Of course I could see that, if I could prove scientifically that men were equally capable of happiness, that would be a great help in arguing with people who wished to treat them as if they were not. But although I had looked upon certain deductions from concealed assumptions of equality as scientific, I had never thought of claiming that particular status for the assumption of equality itself. If Maine's Brahmin had told me that members of such and such a caste or race were eligible for taxation ten times as heavy as others, since they were only one-tenth as capable of true happiness, the strength of my resistance would not have rested on belief in the social law of diminishing marginal utility. The belief that that helped could only rest on the prospect of putting up a smoke-screen of technical jargon to terrify an ignorant antagonist – surely not a very creditable manoeuvre. Why should one be frightened, I asked, of taking a stand on judgments which are not scientific, if they relate to matters outside the world of science? To recognise the claims of science in fields where scientific method was applicable was one thing; to attempt to claim scientific sanction for judgments of questions not capable of scientific proof was another. The one was an obligation on rational man; the other, the stratagem of spiritual uncertainty. Was it not only the timidity of an age which had lost all confidence in ultimate values which led us to attempt to claim "scientific" justifications for attitudes which in the nature of things could not be justified (or refuted) by appeal to laboratory methods?

Arrived at this point, it was not difficult to see certain positive advantages in the course I had felt compelled to follow. It did at least make it possible to keep a whole range of intellectual questions free from squabbles concerning philosophical matters. I had no objection to philosophical squabbles. But it did seem to me that great harm had been done by their intrusion into spheres where they were completely irrelevant. It might be necessary to discuss the political philosophy underlying the prescriptions of the theory of public finance. But it was completely futile to discuss the political philosophy underlying the positive theorems relating to the effects on prices and quantities produced of the imposition of small taxes. Yet, because of failure to separate out clearly normative and positive elements, this kind of discussion was continually arising. No one who had ploughed through the turgid mass of German work in this field could doubt the desirability of keeping philosophy in its proper place.

At the same time it seemed to me that, if this procedure were adopted, the due place of philosophy in the general scheme of social studies would be all the better emphasised. Once it was recognised how completely neutral were the findings of economic science, it would surely leap to the eye how necessary it was, if these findings were to be applied to human improvement, that they should be supplemented by political philosophy. In the past, it seemed to me, a failure to recognise the arbitrary element in certain of the findings of traditional Political Economy had been conducive to too facile a use of these findings in framing prescriptions for action. The achievement of wealth seemed so obviously desirable that it was a temptation to imagine that the propositions of economics could be translated forthwith into prescriptions for action without much further regard for considerations of political philosophy. I was not at all desirous of preventing economists from giving prescriptions. I was, indeed, fully convinced that, if a man tried to talk much about the ultimate questions of politics without a knowledge of economics, it was something of a miracle if he talked sense. But I felt that anything which brought out the necessity for independent and systematic study of the ends which prescriptions based on economics might serve, had profound pedagogical and practical advantages. The postulate of equal capacity for satisfaction, for instance, about which all the trouble had arisen, needed much more refinement if it were to be applied sensibly: it was possible, indeed, that an equalitarian postulate involving no reference to satisfaction might prove in the end to be more suitable. At the London School of Economics, where I was trained, and in the Oxford School of Philosophy, Politics and Economics, where I was teaching when I did most of my thinking about these things, this necessity was recognised in the structure of the curriculum; it seemed to me that what I was doing was simply to give it further emphasis. I confess I was very surprised when I found myself held up as advocating for economists the impossible and sterile virtue of never attempting to apply their conclusions – rapt astronomers of the social universe deigning no aid to navigators in search of the desired haven. All that I had intended – and it was certainly possible to cite the most explicit statements to this effect – was that they might better realise the exact connection between the normative and the positive, and that their practice as political philosophers might be made thereby more self-conscious.

This is a long story about the genesis of two or three pages in an essay that was written some time ago, and which was never expected to be the subject of much discussion. And if it were a matter of personal defence against all the accusations of imbecility, social indifference and even sinister interest which have been made against their author, I certainly should not have thought it any more worth while writing now than at any time in the past. But I am distressed that anything that I have said should give rise to recurrent dispute which suggests to the outside world a disunity among economists which I am persuaded does not exist: my essay was meant to defend economics from lay misunderstanding, not to provoke new confusion. Looking back, I do not feel that I have much to retract. I still cannot believe that it is helpful to speak as if interpersonal comparisons of utility rest upon scientific foundations – that is, upon observation or introspection. I am perhaps more alive than before to the extraordinary difficulties surrounding the whole philosophy of valuation. But I still think, when I make interpersonal comparisons (as, for instance, when I am deciding between claims affecting the satisfactions of two very spirited children), that my judgments are more like judgments of value than judgments of verifiable fact. Nevertheless, to those of my friends who think differently, I would urge that, in practice, our difference is not very important. They think that propositions based upon the assumption of equality are essentially part of economic science. I think that the assumption of equality comes from outside, and that its justification is more ethical than scientific. But we all agree that it is fitting that such assumptions should be made and their implications explored with the aid of the economist's technique. Our dispute relates to definitions and to logical status, not to our obligations as human beings. In the realm of action, at any rate, the real difference of opinion is not between those who dispute concerning the exact area to be designated by the adjective scientific, but between those who hold that human beings should be treated as if they were equal and those who hold that they should not.

15 Inquest on the Crisis

From *Lloyds Bank Review*, new series no. 6 (October 1947), pp 1–27.

It may be remembered that, when Mr. Churchill addressed the House of Commons on the morrow of the Munich Agreement, the first thing he emphasized was that we had suffered a major defeat. Similarly in any review of the present economic crisis, the first thing that must be stated is that we are the victims of a dreadful catastrophe. So far the weather has been so good and the issues involved have been so technical that it has almost seemed that, despite much fluttering in high quarters, the average citizen has tended to regard the breakdown of the experiment in convertibility and the virtual exhaustion of our dollar resources as a matter of comparative indifference. But this state of opinion cannot persist. As the winter comes on, as our rations are cut and our amenities (such as they are) abolished, we shall all realize only too vividly that, for the urban inhabitants of a tightly-packed island, such as our own, to be caught with an adverse annual balance of payments of some six hundred millions sterling, and inadequate reserves to cover it, is no minor incident. It is the biggest disaster in our long economic history.

How has this come about? We cannot undo the past. We cannot call back the wasted dollars. But we can perhaps learn from experience. It is still perhaps possible to rehabilitate our affairs and restore our fallen prestige. But only on one condition – that we understand aright the events of the last two years, both the mistakes and the misfortunes, and so shape our course better in the difficult months ahead. At any rate it is in the hope that this is so, and with no desire to indulge in futile recrimination, that the following pages are written.

I THE EXPEDIENCY OF THE LOANS

The root problem, as I see it, is why our dollar resources have vanished so quickly. How comes it that loans which were expected to last five years should have been nearly used up in just over a twelvemonth? It is this question, surely, which focuses the issues relevant to policy.

There is, however, a school of thought which would push the inquiry one stage further back. Why should we have borrowed at all, it is asked. Since painful adjustments had to come, would it not have been better to have faced them, back in 1945 with our war controls still in being and the sense of emergency still active, than to have propped up an unstable position for another two years while our controls disintegrated and our sense of purpose was lost? What have the loans done but confirm us in bad habits and vain expectations?

The question is not unnatural; the argument is not wholly irrelevant. It is true that at the present time, with the loans practically exhausted, we are not much nearer equilibrium in our balance of payments than we were in July, 1945, with the loans still in prospect. Indeed in some respects, as we shall see, our present position is inferior. We are moreover burdened with a not inconsiderable debt charge which will last for fifty years.

Nevertheless, I do not believe that it was wrong to seek foreign assistance; and I do not believe that history will regard the decision to do this as one of the decisions for which the present Government can justly be blamed. In 1945, as a result of what we had done during the War, our income from investments abroad was down and our export trade was severely contracted. In prospect it seemed likely that our balance of payments would be even more adverse than it is likely to be at present. But at the same time the markets of the world were clamouring for our goods; and although it was always doubtful how long this state of affairs would last and how much we could expand our exports without encountering difficulties of sale, yet it was clear that, for the time being, we had a wonderful opportunity to establish ourselves while the going was good and, given prudence in domestic policy, a fair chance of closing the gap in the balance of payments without an undue lowering of our standard of life. To do this, however, required time. For purely technical reasons it was not possible to expand exports to the required extent without a breathing space. Men had to be redrafted. Materials had to be re-allocated. Factories had to be re-tooled. Processes of production taking time had to be started from the beginning. There was no hope of closing the gap at once without either a most drastic limitation of imports or borrowing from abroad.

In such circumstances, in my judgement, recourse to foreign assistance was not only natural but prudent. If, in this way, there was a reasonable chance of balancing our foreign account without further cuts in consumption, already grievously reduced by war, then surely it was sensible to take it. It is all very well to say that, if the government was not prepared to take the measures necessary to take advantage of the breathing space, then it should not have borrowed. That can very well be conceded. But it is unusual for governments to assume that they will not have the courage of their convictions or the intelligence to carry them out; and expert advice which proceeded on this assumption would be severely limited in scope. Moreover, it is not at all clear that the heroic contraction of consumption which would have been necessary, had we refrained from seeking assistance, would have been possible without damage both to productivity and morale. It is part of our problem at the present time that, because of a similar unbalance, just such a restriction may be forced upon us; and I have yet to meet anyone of sense who did not view the prospect with grave apprehension. It would be hard to find any responsible person who would not be glad of some further measure of assistance to help us out of our difficulties. There are few, this side of the Iron Curtain, who hope that the Marshall "plan" will break down.

Hence, despite all the sound and fury of those who job backwards, I shall continue to assume that the main question we have to answer is, not whether it was wise to borrow, but rather why, having borrowed, we so quickly found ourselves in so parlous a position? Why have we run through the loans so rapidly?

II THE INCIDENCE OF MISFORTUNE

Any answer to this question which is to do justice to the complexity of the facts and to the very real difficulties of the situation must take account not only of policy at home but also of developments abroad. And since, as I see things, the strictures on policy must be severe, it is all the more necessary to emphasize at the very outset the considerable extent to which the conduct of policy has been embarrassed by external misfortunes which it was not within our power to control. Whatever we may think of policy, we must all admit that we have had very bad luck indeed.

The most conspicuous of these misfortunes has been the rise in the price of primary products. Since the ratification of the American Loan Agreement, the level of import prices has risen from 203 to 245 (1938 equals 100). Of course, taken by itself, this figure exaggerates the difficulty. The level of export prices has not remained constant: it has risen from 196 to 227. But since this is less than the rise in import prices, there is a disadvantage on balance which means that, in order to be able to pay for any given volume of imports, we have to increase our exports more than would otherwise be the case. In any event, the rise in import prices means a fall in the purchasing power of the loan, a shrinkage in the breathing space which it made possible. This danger was always feared by British experts and, I suspect, by some Americans, and it must always be a matter of regret that it did not prove possible to persuade the United States Administration to ask Congress for a bigger sum. But, apart from still greater efforts for a larger loan – which certainly would not have been a very popular policy at the time – it is difficult to see what could have been done to avert it. The rise of primary product prices is a world development quite beyond the power of this government to control. Incidentally, it is somewhat futile spending much time blaming others. There may have been some hard bargains by state monopolies. But in the main the rise of prices is the inevitable consequence of shortage. Given the demand, it is not the suppliers who are keeping prices up, but the absence of other suppliers coming forward. As Edwin Cannan once remarked, to blame sellers for shortage is like blaming a congregation that its numbers are too few.

In the same category of external misfortune must be put the drain upon our resources caused by the persistent unsettlement of the world and the consequent necessity for extensive overseas expenditure on the maintenance of armed forces and the provision of essential supplies. By this I do not wish to give a clean bill to every act of external policy in the last two years. No one who read Mr. Stamp's masterly analysis of the present situation in Germany, in the last number of this *Review*,* can hold us wholly blameless for the present state of affairs in that country. Nor in particular do I wish to give approval to the agreement with the United States whereby we shared the expenses of occupation in equal proportions; I cannot but believe that this was a grave error. But in general, surely, we must all agree that Mr. Bevin and our representatives abroad have striven manfully for world peace, and that if things have not turned out as we wished, the blame must lie not in our policy but in the dislocations and devastations of the War and in the policy of other powers. It is not British foreign policy which has divided Germany into sealed compartments and sought to make of Eastern Europe a closed economy. In any fair assessment of the causes of our present difficulties, these factors must be given full weight.

It should be clear, then, that both because of the shortage of primary products and the persistent failure to revive of important parts of the world, there have been drains on our resources which have greatly intensified the difficulties – which were always very great – of restoring our balance of payments before our external support was exhausted. It is not possible at this juncture to put a figure on the significance of these misfortunes. We need much more information than is yet available on the use of the loans before even the roughest estimate can be made. Moreover, in any such estimates there must always be a large element of unverifiable hypothesis. It is clearly inadmissible, for example, to assume that in more favourable circumstances all overseas government expenditure could have ceased overnight; and the amount that it is legitimate to assume away is necessarily in the nature of a guess. But if, for purposes of giving vividness and some order of magnitude to the argument, it were said that our difficulties had been increased by some fifty per cent., I would not say that the sense of perspective was radically erroneous.

---

* Maxwell Stamp, "Germany without incentive," *Lloyds Bank Review*, n.s., no. 5 (July 1947), pp. 14–28.

III THE CONDUCT OF POLICY

(a) A Mistaken Stricture

But when all account has been taken of bad luck there still remains a substantial residue of developments which can only be explained in other terms. If the unavoidable drafts on our resources were half as much again as the original estimate, it would still not be clear why loans which were expected to last five years should have been virtually exhausted in one and why in the second year of reconstruction, our external position was becoming worse than it was in the first. After all, it is not reasonable to assume that if external factors do not turn out as well as was expected, the position is essentially unmanageable. The adverse developments which have been noted above were apparent at a comparatively early stage and the absence of appropriate reaction, together with the general tardiness of our reconstruction, must surely be attributable to errors of policy. I do not think it is difficult to show what these errors were.

Before doing that, however, it is necessary to eliminate a possible cause of confusion. It is sometimes made a reproach to the British Government that the loan has been used for the wrong purposes. It is said that instead of spending it upon new machines and equipment for industry, as was intended, it has been 'frittered away' on consumption goods, food, films, tobacco and the like. In my judgement this accusation rests upon an essential misconception, not only of the actual purpose of the loan, but also of the general necessities of the situation. But because it has received wide currency, not only here but also in the United States of America, it is desirable to give it some attention.

Now I am very far from wishing to argue that our expenditure on imports, either as regards volume or composition, has been by any means immune from criticism. It may be that, having regard to the comparative smallness of our resources, we should have been even more careful than we were in relaxing the austerity of wartime standards – although if there be any among our American friends who are disposed to argue thus I would invite them to verify for themselves by practical housekeeping how small this relaxation actually was. I am fairly sure that, once the breakdown of coal had so obviously worsened the position, it was desirable there and then to impose some further restriction on imports. I can conceive that all along some things may have been imported which we should have done better to go without.

But on the general question whether, in the main, it was justifiable to import consumption goods rather than machinery, I hold that there can be no two answers. As we have seen already, our position at the end of the War was one of inability to pay for the imports which were necessary if consumption was not to be reduced. The purpose of foreign borrowing was to enable us to carry on while the volume of exports expanded. It was only natural, therefore, that in the main they should be spent on consumption goods. It may be that we should have been even more austere. It may be that there were certain items (such as films) of small proportionate importance, which could have been cut out or reduced. (It is clear that we could not have cut out tobacco without endangering the whole balance of our public finances). It may be that there have been some items of re-equipment which even in conditions of this degree of stringency, we should have strained ourselves still further to afford. But that we could have substituted machinery and equipment on a large scale for consumption goods or have restricted our purchases to the former categories, is a contention which, as I see it, can only be put forward on the basis of a complete misapprehension of the problem with which we were confronted. The main purpose of the loans was not new capital development on a large scale; it was to sustain the flow of necessary consumption goods until the process of reconversion put us in a position to pay for them out of our external earnings.

I conclude, therefore, that whatever incidental strictures can be passed upon our import programmes, our main deficiencies of policy are not to be found on this side. They are to be found rather on the side of export. There will be something to be said later on about a possible drain on the loans by way of capital transfers. But if we are first to concentrate – as we must if we are to establish a proper perspective – on our failure to bring our external balance *on current account* into a more satisfactory position, we must look not so much at our spending (which in the main was almost unavoidable) but at our sales (which were certainly not as great as they might have been) not at what we spent in order to maintain our consumption, but at what we did not produce in order to finance this expenditure. How comes it that in two years we had not put ourselves in a position to pay our way? It cannot be contended that it was any difficulty of marketing. That is a problem which may be very serious in the future. But since the end of the War the markets of the world have been clamouring for our wares: we could sell all that we produced. How has it happened, then, that we have not produced enough? That is the fundamental question we have to answer.

(b) The Shortage of Coal

The most obvious answer to this question is shortage of coal. The hold-up last winter lost us nearly six fateful months. The general shortage which has prevailed during the last two years, and which shows no sign of diminution, is a drag on our recovery the significance of which it is almost impossible to overestimate.

It would be tedious to elaborate in detail the nature of a factor whose paralysing influence is so manifest in every direction. But one point at least calls for special mention, the absence of coal for export. It is really amazing that this still attracts so little attention. In the past, both the power and the prosperity of this country have rested in a high degree upon substantial exports of coal. If we were exporting coal on the pre-war scale at the present time, we should be earning at least another £100,000,000 per annum – enough to cover our entire imports of grain and flour. The economy of much of Western Europe has depended on this margin of British coal; in its absence it staggers from crisis to crisis of underproduction. We talk glibly of the necessity of raising our exports as a whole by seventy-five per cent if we are to bring our balance of payments into equilibrium at something like a tolerable standard of import. Heaven knows this is likely to be difficult enough in any event. But in the absence of exports of coal, other exports – exports of goods, be it noted, with which the foreigner can dispense much more easily – must be increased by much more than seventy-five per cent. What is the change in our intellectual and moral climate – is it some deficiency of diet or some spiritual overstrain? – which brings it about that, not only the public in general, but even highly placed experts and ministers can talk calmly as if coal export was a thing of secondary importance, a transitory phenomenon of a past epoch which the wise man, trained by historic insight, may regret mildly but about which he will not bother himself unduly?

Now, it is obvious that one of the main reasons for the deficiency of coal supplies is a decline in output per head. With more equipment and with higher wages and with better working conditions, the miners are producing less per head than they did in 1939. If output per head were at the pre-war level our position would not be safe. But it would, nevertheless, be eased.

But output per head is not easy to control; and although it is impossible not to regard acquiescence in the change to the five-day week as an act of irresponsibility, yet if it were only a matter of failure to secure an increase in this elusive factor, the Government might well command as much sympathy as condemnation. But of course it is not. Aggregate output is a function not only of output per head, but also of aggregate numbers. The main burden of our strictures on the policy of the Government must be, not that they have failed to secure greater effort from the existing numbers of miners – after all, they have done a good deal of exhortation – but that they have failed to increase numbers sufficiently to offset the diminished will to work. It is, of course, not to be supposed that this would have been unattended with difficulty; there were (and still are) many obvious obstacles to overcome. But faced with the certainty that, in the absence of a sufficient increase in numbers, they were staking the fate of the nation – for nothing less was involved – upon the hope of increased output per head, it was certainly incumbent on them to do more than they have done. It is not a position which any British Government should accept that what has been possible for the French – recruitment abroad on a large scale – is somehow impossible for us. The failure since July, 1945, to make increase of the labour force in the mines a major objective of policy is an omission which history will not treat lightly. It is an omission which may yet bring us to chaos and near-starvation.

Last year, writing before the crisis of the winter, I wrote in this *Review* as follows:

> "If it were a mere matter of yet another winter of inconvenience to consumers and some slowing down of the rate of recovery which was very important for internal reasons, the comparative complacency of the public in this respect could at least be understood, if it were not shared. But, of course, much more than this is involved. The shortage of coal sets limits to the increase of exports. Unless, indeed, there is an expansion in coal production, it is difficult to see how our export drive can reach anything like its target. And in the present shortage of foreign exchange, any slowing down now may be quite disastrous. There will be no room for complacency if our dollars run short before our balance of payments is in equilibrium."*

I believe that when this was written some of my friends thought it too alarmist. I wonder if they think so still.

(c) Misdirection of Resources

The shortage of coal, although of pivotal importance, is not however, the only cause of our difficulties. Before the troubles of last winter, the rate of increase of exports was beginning to show signs of flagging, or at least was not proceeding with the speed which was necessary if we were to achieve the target before our foreign resources were dangerously low. This in itself may well have been partly due to the indirect drag of coal shortage. But there is reason to believe that there was more in it than that. There had developed a fundamental maldistribution of resources. If we are to understand how to get out of this present *impasse* it is essential to see what this means and how it arose.

If we look at the very interesting tables showing the size and distribution of the labour force at the end of last year, which are printed at the end of the *Economic Survey for 1947* (Cmd. 7046) one fact stands out very boldly: namely, that that part of industry which is devoted to production for export,

---

* "Economic prospects," *Lloyds Bank Review*, n.s., no. 3 (January 1947), p. 29.

although expanded substantially as compared with the pre-war level, was not expanded nearly enough to provide, at current levels of productivity, that increase of exports which was necessary if the balance of payments was to be brought into equilibrium without a severe limitation of desirable imports.

This fact, which is significant enough in itself, becomes even more impressive if it is considered in relation to the fact that the War sector (military forces and supply industries) had been reduced to about the pre-war level and that the volume of unemployment was unprecedently low. For it means that not only were the resources devoted to export insufficient but also that the resources liberated by the cessation of war had been reabsorbed by other activities. The redeployment of industry had take place. But it had taken place on the wrong lines. Other demands, other objectives, were absorbing resources which should have been devoted to procuring the wherewithal with which to pay for our imports. In 1945 it was possible for the expansion of exports to proceed by calling into activity resources, labour, capacity and materials, which were automatically released by demobilization and the closing down of production. By the end of 1946, the possibilities of this reserve had diminished to a prospective trickle. Given current levels of productivity per head – and in such circumstances to plan on the assumption of a large increase in that direction was to plan on the assumption of a miracle – the expansion of export could only take place by transfer from other forms of peacetime production.

In such circumstances the failure of exports to expand more rapidly is very easy to understand. There is no need to argue whether the drag came from man-power or materials; probably in some cases it came from one direction, in other cases from the other. The central fact is that the available scarce resources were to all intents and purposes fully employed and that too large a proportion were employed for purposes other than export. The labour, the timber, the steel, the fuel, the capacity which were available for production for export were less than would otherwise have been the case had less of them been absorbed elsewhere. The allocation was wrong. The less important had priority over the more.

How did this happen? A large share of the responsibility must be placed upon the vast schemes of development and capital expansion which have been undertaken by the Government and by business enterprise with the active encouragement of the Government. We have been suffering from a sort of economic megalomania. It has been assumed that we could not only expand our exports to the required level but also undertake programmes of social and business development quite without precedent in the inter-war period. The various programmes have been drawn up independently by different industries and different sets of experts, each concerned, not with what the economy could afford in terms of resources withdrawn from other sectors, but only with what would be technically desirable, were all other conditions favourable; and there have been no general directives adequate to keep them in proper proportion. There is a "need" for houses; let us therefore go ahead with all possible speed to construct the amount of house-room which the housing experts think could be produced. There is a "need" for re-equipment of heavy industry: let the order go forth that an ambitious and visionary programme will receive full encouragement. There have been many decisions of this kind and much disinterested zeal and self-sacrificing devotion to back them up. But there has been insufficient consideration of their significance in relation to the general allocation of resources; and when attention has been drawn to the inconvenient effects on other parts of the economy of decisions to go ahead with massive programmes in any one part, the disposition has been to assume that it would all come right in the end, or, if that was shown to be impossible at present levels of productivity, to assume that production all round could be increased so as to overcome the fundamental shortages.

The effect of all this has been to constitute a body of claims for resources for internal development far greater than was compatible with the attainment of the requisite degree of export expansion; and although doubtless, in the resulting confusion, many of these claims have not been satisfied – witness the "excessive" number of uncompleted houses – the net result has been that export expansion has fallen far short of what could actually have been the case, had the shortages created by these pressures not existed.[1] We can put this if we like another way. We can say that we have made plans for internal development so much in excess of what our own level of consumption leaves over that they could only be fulfilled by excessive use of resources drawn from abroad. We have had to draw upon the loans more quickly than otherwise would have happened because of our overambitious schemes of internal development. Thus, so far from it being true that the loans have not been used sufficiently for development, as distinct from consumption purposes, it can very well be argued that indirectly they have been used too much for this purpose. It is true that we have not imported the bricks and mortar and the engineering products from abroad. But we have used the loans to support the internal manufacture of these commodities and their use for capital development when we should have used them to promote a greater production for export.

1. Reference to the tables in the *Economic Survey* mentioned above shows that by December, 1946, whereas the labour devoted to export had only increased by 326,000, as compared with June, 1939, the labour devoted to Home investment (metals, building, engineering, etc.) had increased by 556,000.

In addition to the pressure on resources from centrally planned and centrally promoted schemes of development, there has been a more generalized pressure which has been due to the existence of excess spending-power diffused throughout the community. The War left behind it a large volume of pent-up accumulations, from war savings at the one end to abnormal company reserves at the other. The ultra-cheap money policy produced an appreciation of values tending greatly to encourage spending, not only out of income but also out of capital. Incomes have risen. The prices of important groups of commodities have been kept down by decree or by subsidy. The result has been a continual tendency for stocks to be used up and resources to be diverted to channels where production is not controlled and where, therefore, the desire for increased consumption can be gratified. We have not had a general inflation of prices: the controls have looked after that. But we have had (and are still having) a condition of suppressed inflation with many of the same effects on production and production for export as inflation old-style, and some evils of its own superadded – particularly as regards stocks and incentive. Readers of the last number of this *Review* who perused side by side the accounts of our own condition by Professor Hicks* and of that of Germany (where the suppressed inflation has gone much further) by Mr. Stamp, will not have failed to notice the alarming parallelism. Even the spivs who are blamed for so much – the convenient scapegoats of political incompetence – are not a spontaneous evil; they are an evil which makes its appearance whenever and wherever this kind of pressure is prevalent.

In making this diagnosis and in drawing the moral as regards our external position, we must not underestimate the difficulties with which policy has been confronted. The central mechanism which served us in such good stead during the War has lost effectiveness. The labour controls have gone – and despite much talk of a reinstitution of direction of labour they are not likely to be re-established in full rigour. The task of allocation is infinitely more complicated; and the allocation machinery is palpably inadequate to cover anything like the whole field. Those who reproach the Government for lack of physical planning, of the scale and the minuteness of the planning of the War years, show a singular lack of comprehension of the change in the nature of the problem and the conditions under which it has to be solved. I am no foe at this juncture to physical control where physical control is possible. But I do not believe that it is reasonable to contend there was ever much hope that our difficulties could be met satisfactorily by the unaided use of this type of mechanism.

* J.R. Hicks, "The empty economy," *Lloyds Bank Review*, n.s no. 5 (July 1947), pp. 1–13.

There was, however, one type of mechanism whose effectiveness was not diminished by the economic and political changes which the transition from War brought about. I refer to the financial mechanism. The control of national expenditure, both directly in the public sector and indirectly in the private sector, is a continuing responsibility of the Government equally with the safeguarding of the balance of payments. A great engine of fiscal administration in the narrow sense, unequalled throughout the world, has been built up through the years; and during the War, with the enlargement of our conception of the functions of public finance, there was superadded to it a mechanism for controlling investment in the larger sense and registering fluctuations in expenditure in general, in order that appropriate action might be taken to keep the development of the economy on lines deemed expedient. If due use had been made of this mechanism, if steps had been taken to keep internal investment and consumption expenditure within appropriate limits, I see no reason why, with due use of what other controls remained, the development of the economy could not have been kept on suitable lines and the disproportionate developments due to excessive expenditure have been checked.

Unfortunately, this has not happened. The development of financial policy and the development of economic planning as a whole have proceeded, or seemed to proceed, in separate almost watertight compartments. With the rise of external prices and the unexpected calls for government expenditure abroad making bigger and bigger calls upon our limited foreign resources, internal expenditure has been allowed to develop apparently without any regard to considerations of external equilibrium. I know no matter of peacetime policy on which in recent years the opinion of responsible professional economists has been more at one than on this. All schools have united in urging upon the Chancellor [of the Exchequer] the dangers of the situation and the urgent necessity of cutting our coat to suit our cloth. But like Pharaoh of old, with each successive warning the Chancellor has hardened his heart, has reproached friendly critics with wishing to bring about deflation, when all that they urged on him was to prevent inflation, and has proceeded, with sublime *insouciance*, on the assumption that the foreign balance and internal finance had nothing to do with one another.

But while final responsibility for policy must lie where it is constitutionally placed, it is only right to recognize that the climate of opinion in general has not been such as very often to call these particular aspects of policy in question. From time to time, it is true, the official Opposition has placed on record its general disapproval of the level of public spending. But when types of spending – the present housing programme, for instance – which are particularly exigent in their demands on our limited resources have come up for detailed discussion, the general tendency on the part of the Opposition has been for speakers to suggest that, had they been in office, they would have done not less but more than the Government. A most discreditable habit has developed of guying Sir Stafford Cripps for his very proper and courageous insistence that, at present, we cannot have both increased consumption and increased exports. And when the Chancellor actually decided to impose an increase in the tobacco duty, the Opposition, instead of applauding one of the wise and courageous acts of his regime,[1] streamed into the lobbies to vote against him. There have, of course, been honourable exceptions. But for the most part, in the last two years, political leaders on both sides have concentrated far more upon the search for popularity than upon the exposition of the facts of the situation. We have wasted our breathing space in a dream of cheap Utopias.

IV THE LEAKAGE OF CAPITAL

When we have explained the reasons for our failure to remedy our adverse balance on current account we have not, however, fully explained the catastrophe which has come upon us. For the using up of our external assets in the last few months has proceeded at a rate which cannot be reconciled with any known facts concerning our obligations on account of current purchases and current payments abroad. The statistics are indeed still veiled in some degree of mystery. But transactions which involved the using up of over £600 millions worth of external assets since the end of March cannot conceivably have been limited to transactions on current account. A leakage of capital on a colossal scale is the only explanation which fits the facts. Since we have thus lost amounts which, on a conservative estimate, could have financed, for many months to come, the imports of food which we now may have to go without, some further inquiry seems essential.

In popular discussion, hitherto, the disposition seems to have been to put all the blame on convertibility and the obligations in the Loan Agreement under which the experiment in convertibility was carried out; and since the rate of withdrawal after July 15th, when convertibility came into force, greatly exceeded the rate of withdrawal before then, it may well be that the arrangements which had been adopted in regard to that obligation must bear their due share of the blame. But to argue *simpliciter* that the convertibility obligation, by itself, was responsible for all that happened is completely to beg the question. For the obligation under the Loan Agreement, as under the

1. It was wise, of course, on the assumption that it would help to mop up internal purchasing power – which it is certainly doing; its virtues as a dollar saver are comparatively small. [The measure was taken in the Budget of April 1947.]

Bretton Woods statutes, to maintain convertibility *was not an obligation to maintain unlimited convertibility. It was an obligation extending only to the current account.* Now it is just the excess of the withdrawals over and above current account obligations which constitutes the problem to be investigated. I myself believe that, having regard to the general deterioration in our position, in particular to the rate at which our adverse balance was running, it was a mistake to attempt to maintain even this limited degree of convertibility. The possibility of such a situation had been well provided for in the loan agreement. Clause 12 of the loan agreement says that "each Government shall be entitled to approach the other for a reconsideration of any of the provisions of this agreement, if in its opinion the prevailing conditions of international exchange justify such reconsideration." I have little doubt that had this clause been invoked by the Government it would have found a sympathetic hearing from the U.S. Administration. But that is not the central problem. The central problem, I repeat, is how did it come about that, being obliged only to maintain convertibility on current account, we found ourselves in a position in which we were losing capital?

Now, on the information which so far has been made publicly available, precise answers to this question are not possible. The Chancellor gave many figures to the House of Commons. But he did not furnish anything which permitted a complete and systematic view of the situation. Indeed, it is doubtful whether at the time he himself was in a position to do so. For, whereas on that occasion he expressed the confidence that the August position would be more favourable, it was not more than a few days before he was compelled to come to the microphone and declare that he had lost more than another \$200 millions. We are still, therefore, very much in the dark. For this reason, in what follows I prefer to ask what seem to me to be relevant questions, rather than to pronounce on the answers with certainty.

The first question relates to the sterling balances. Were these under a control adequate to prevent an undue withdrawal? It is well known that the existence of large sums of liquid capital accumulated in London as payment for goods or services delivered for the most part during the War, and nominally capable of being withdrawn at the will of their owners, has long presented problems of the utmost technical and moral difficulty. It would be possible to write a treatise on this subject alone. But one practical consideration has long been clear amid the welter of casuistical issues and special circumstances: namely, that it would be fatal to allow them to be withdrawn suddenly or at a very substantial annual rate. On that consideration, which depends for its validity on no begging of the question whether the balances ought eventually to be repaid in full or not, but on the inescapable facts and potentialities of our balance of payments, it might have been assumed that all responsible opinion was united. But in fact we have witnessed during the last twelve months, from the Argentine agreement onward, the signature of agreements of bewildering easiness in this respect, both as regards prospective rates of repayment and as regards the amount of the balances to be regarded as free in the periods immediately ahead. If the rates of repayment in some of these agreements were to have been generalized, it almost seemed as if we might easily have been involved in annuities three times the amount of the annuities on the American and Canadian loans. While if we add up the amounts to be regarded as free in the months immediately subsequent to the agreements, we reach totals which, if withdrawn in a lump, would certainly have made the most substantial inroads on our dollar resources. Of course, we do not know what unwritten understandings lay behind these agreements. We do not know, moreover, to what extent, in the event, such understandings, if they existed, were honoured. But we are at least entitled to ask: as things have turned out, were these arrangements entirely satisfactory? Is there no reason to suppose that more drastic methods on our part, although doubtless galling to our pride and out of harmony with our traditions, would have better safeguarded our position and even the eventual security of our creditors?

But the accumulated balances of our wartime creditors were not the only funds which could leave London. There were very tight regulations on transfers to some parts of the world. It is not so certain that the regulations were so tight as regards transfers to others. It is therefore not unreasonable to seek further information regarding exchange control within the sterling area. Were the arrangements such as to preclude the transfer of funds to parts of this area where, perhaps, the peculiar conditions of trade or the lesser severity of the regulations made easier further transfers to parts of the world to which transfer from here was forbidden? Were they even such as to preclude transfers tending to increase the adverse balance on current account? It would restore confidence greatly if the Government could give a complete affirmative to this question. For the common gossip of the market and the logic of the known methods of regulation have given many to question gravely whether in fact there may not have been serious leakages in these directions.

This leads to a further question relating to the efficiency of our exchange control – and here I must ask my readers to pardon me if I appear to diverge into technicalities; there is indeed an unavoidable appearance of technicality but the issues involved are of great practical importance. The convertibility obligation, as we have seen, was an obligation to maintain not total convertibility but only convertibility on current account. This means in plain English that the foreigner was entitled to turn into dollars, if he pleased, not his capital but his current earnings. Now the question arises, was such a system viable unless some precaution existed against the sudden withdrawal not of *net* current earnings but of *gross*? – a danger which was particularly great whilst there existed the simultaneous possibility of sudden prohibitions on purchases from this country. Is it not inherent in the idea of current account convertibility that it should be worked through a system of short-period clearings of net earnings either way, rather than by a system which allows the foreigner, regardless of his own debts, all of a sudden one fine morning to demand dollar payment of the gross amount of current debts owed to him. This certainly was the way in which it has been supposed by many that the difficult and delicate system of current account convertibility would be worked. And since the Government allowed themselves to declare with such confidence that the arrangements made for meeting the obligation of July 15th were completely watertight, the possibility that other looser techniques might be adopted was not very widely discussed. Since so much money has been lost, we are entitled, I think, to inquire further concerning this question. We are entitled to ask whether there may not have been too great an inclination on the part of the Government to rely on mere gentlemen's understandings concerning how the right of withdrawal should be exercised, when the situation was one of such peril that the chief danger was not that the gentlemen might be offended if they were not treated as gentlemen but that those who were not gentlemen might take advantage of the privilege if they were treated as if they were?

Where so much is so dark and confused, it is difficult to feel any confidence that even one's questions are posed with a proper degree of precision. It may well be that, in these inquiries, there are phrases which, for one reason or another, fail to probe the essential points. But one thing is reasonably clear, and in any discussion of these matters it is desirable to keep it firmly in mind. An intolerable deal of money has disappeared like snow overnight and it has not gone, as it was intended that it should go, in payment for necessary imports. I confess that I find it difficult to see how this could possibly have happened had there not been serious errors of high policy, at least of the kind, if not of the exact definition, of these I have mentioned. If this is not so it should be made clear. For confidence has been severely shaken.

V THE FUTURE OF DOMESTIC POLICY

What is to happen now? This is not the place to provide a programme of action. But there are certain matters arising directly from the foregoing analysis which deserve emphasis in this connexion.

There seems little hope in the immediate future of avoiding a considerable contraction of imports. For all that is said in the popular press about the rallying of the rest of the world to help us, the fact remains that what help is likely to be forthcoming cannot possibly be a substitute for what we have been getting from the United States and Canada; and we have no longer the dollars with which to continue these purchases. It is conceivable that later on some fresh assistance may be forthcoming under the plans which have been discussed in Paris. But we should be foolish in the extreme if we were to count on this. We should be still more foolish if at this juncture we were to eat into our limited reserves, either of stocks or of foreign assets, in the hope that no contraction will prove necessary. If the thought that American help may be possible later on leads us to this kind of imprudence now, it would be better that we should put all thoughts of assistance out of our heads and concentrate on the realities of the situation. For, in any case, such assistance, if it is forthcoming at all in a year of presidential election, is not likely to be on such a scale as to enable us to live even as well as we have been living in the recent past.

But while some contraction of imports seems unavoidable, it is most important that we should keep in mind that the fundamental objective is not contraction but expansion. Despite all plans for an expansion of domestic food production, many of which I am convinced are based upon misconception of the possibilities and defiance of the rules of economy, it is an incontestable fact that we cannot hope to restore our standards of consumption, let alone our position of influence in the world, without an increase in the volume of exports. The expansion of exports now is as essential to our future power and happiness as was the expansion of munitions in the early days of the War.

If the argument of earlier sections of this paper is correct, two things stand out as essential *desiderata*.

First the production of coal must be increased and more must be made available for export. When I wrote about this problem last year and in the early months of this year, I suggested that the surest method of bringing this about was the recruitment and training of additional labour, if necessary from foreign sources – a suggestion which it was attempted to discredit by representing it as a proposal "to march 100,000 Poles to the coal face," just like that. I still think that a policy of additional recruitment is incumbent upon us. By all means let us get the existing labour force to work more – if we can. But do not let us allow the future of our industrial effort to depend on this uncertain aspiration. The Government has agreed upon the principle of foreign recruitment and a small trickle of such labour is actually under training or even at work in the mines. What is needed now is to conceive the policy in the spirit and on the scale in which it would have been conceived in wartime and to carry it out with the utmost expedition. There is no danger of overdoing it. The rate of wastage in the existing labour force is so great that there is no risk of an increase which will be superfluous later on.

Secondly, the inflationary tendencies of national income and expenditure must be arrested. The foregoing analysis indicates the line which action must follow. Programmes of capital development which are within the direct control of the Government must be reduced to more appropriate dimensions. This means sacrifices which will be very grievous, especially on the social side. But it is better even to have less accommodation, or less well equipped and commodious accommodation, than less food. But beyond this the general tendencies to excess expenditure must be checked. This is all the more urgent since the cessation of drawing on the loan will enormously increase the size of the potential inflationary gap. The appropriate instrument here is clearly budgetary policy. I suspect that, for the time being at least, the fall in values due to the collapse of the cheap money policy will be an adequate restraint over much of the field on the tendency to spend out of capital, although the position needs constant scrutiny. But the general inflationary pressure will persist, and to cure it, it will be necessary to budget for a very substantial surplus.

The means of attaining this surplus are to be sought on both sides of the account. On the side of taxation, I am inclined to think that the situation calls for a sharp increase in the purchase tax. If this is coupled with a promise that it will come down as the crisis is surmounted, it will serve three purposes. It will itself mop up superfluous spending. It will tend to provide saving by stimulating the postponement of purchases. Moreover, since it falls only on home sales, it should increase the incentive to export.

But the surplus must also be sought on the side of expenditure, not, it is to be hoped, by way of crude economy drives which bring anything and everything under the axe, but rather by way of carefully scrutinized reductions. This must necessarily raise the question of the subsidies which, as they are now administered, are a complete anachronism in our system of public finance. Introduced to stabilize prices when the level of wage rates was nearly ten points below the old cost of living index, they have continued in the same form, but in ever increasing proportions, while the level of wage rates has risen nearly forty points above. In such circumstances the argument that to reduce the subsidies substantially would cause widespread and intolerable distress is not really plausible. But to guard against hardship to those with families, it should be feasible, while still saving much, to provide some offset in the shape of an increase in the family allowance (perhaps some allowance for the first child), provided that this were part of a bargain that in the present emergency the change in the cost of living figure should not be made the basis for general claims for an increase of wage rates.

If in such ways it were possible to create a real budget surplus amounting to some five or six hundred millions, I am confident that there would take place an easement in our general position and prospects which might very well be truly spectacular. In urging this, I do not wish to be thought to be arguing that financial measures by themselves are all that is necessary in our present very desperate situation. To guard against all possible misunderstanding I would like to say explicitly that I am not in favour at this juncture of a general removal of the other controls; on the contrary, I am in favour of their vigorous and intelligent use. But I do argue that unless the over-all financial control is set right, the other controls are likely to be ineffective. In present circumstances, more than ever before, we need to create a situation in which what physical controls we can use are working with the stream, not against it. We need a position in which the tendencies of finance at home are not a drag upon the development of exports but positively work in its favour.

VI EXTERNAL RELATIONS

But what of our markets when the export goods are available? Hitherto, in the abnormal conditions prevailing we have found a ready market for all, or nearly all, that we could produce. But these conditions are already changing; and we cannot rely upon them to persist in future. In the absence of deliberate efforts to create sufficient elbow-room for trade, we may find ourselves with our industry at last ready to produce the requisite volume of exports, but insufficient buyers to take them off our hands.

This raises the much debated question of non-discrimination and the general policy of the Trade Charter. And here, at the risk of raising a hornet's nest, I would like to say that in recent discussion there have been signs that we are tending to lose our heads. In saying this I must not be understood as wishing to defend all the obligations of the Loan Agreement. In a world in which similar obligations were not to be accepted immediately by other countries, these imposed restrictions on our freedom of action which were difficult to accept and were indeed only acceptable at all as part of a bargain. What I am concerned to emphasize, however, is that before deciding that the whole principle of non-discrimination, applied with reasonable exceptions as adumbrated in the proposed Trade Charter, is contrary to our fundamental interest we should abstain a little from doctrinaire prepossession and inquire where that interest actually lies.

If we do this, I think, we shall discover a number of very relevant facts which have tended to be ignored just lately. To begin with, it would be very difficult, I believe, to show that so far we have been greatly embarrassed by the obligations we have already assumed. I can think of a few cases where complete liberty to discriminate in our purchases might have reaped some small advantage. But in the main the idea that great easements of our position would have been possible in this way is pure mythology. Where are the vast stocks of commodities which rest unsold because we have not been able to buy them on discriminatory terms?

But, of course, the main debate is concerned not with the past, but with the future. Shall we be able to do better for ourselves in future if the general presumption in favour of non-discrimination goes by the board?

Now, it may be freely admitted that if we could assume that everything else remained the same, that other countries with the power to retaliate remained acquiescent while we exploited discrimination to the full, it is quite conceivable that we might reap substantial benefits. It is certainly not a discovery of recent years that, in such conditions, discriminatory buying and reciprocal trade arrangements may bring advantages. But, of course, to conclude from this that a general abandonment of the principle of non-discrimination is to our advantage is completely to beg the question. It is really to show a fantastic conceit of ourselves and our power in the twentieth century to suppose that, if we were to embark on such a course, all the countries against which we might discriminate, having regard to our special difficulties and our special services to the world in the past, would bind themselves to a self-denying ordinance not to resort to similar measures and would stand by and take all the knocks. But if they do not practise such abstention, if they in their turn resort to similar practices, our prospects would become very difficult. With an export trade of peculiar vulnerability and a bargaining power in respect to primary products greatly inferior to what is commonly supposed, the likelihood is that we should be the losers and that our last state would be worse than our first. If anyone doubts this as a statement of probabilities let him read the two powerful articles by Mr. MacDougall in recent numbers of the *Economic Journal* (March, 1946 and March, 1947),* where the actual facts of our bargaining power and our trade position are faithfully set out and discussed. It is this kind of analysis which the advocates of discrimination have to meet, not, as they are inclined to urge, a set of doctrinaire and abstract prepossessions.

As a matter of fact, contrary to prevalent impressions, the question of the acceptability of the Trade Charter is not at all a question of the acceptability or unacceptability of discrimination in all its forms. For good or for bad, if it is examined as it is rather than abused *a priori*, the Trade Charter will be found to contain quite a number of provisions whereby, when certain conditions are satisfied, members are allowed to discriminate (balance of payments difficulties, common subscription to the I.M.F., scarce currency conditions, etc.). What is at stake is not a matter of discrimination or no discrimination but rather discrimination at will or discrimination according to rule. The practical issue therefore is this: Are we to be content with a limited right to discriminate agreed upon with those who might discriminate against us? Or do we attach so much importance to the right of unfettered unilateral action in this respect that we are willing to reject the Charter in its entirety, with all the possibilities of safeguards and new outlets for our exports which it undoubt-

* G.D.A. MacDougall, "Britain's bargaining power," *Economic Journal*, vol. 56, pp. 27–37, and "Britain's foreign trade problem," *Economic Journal*, vol. 57, pp. 69–113.

edly involves, and face the risk of retaliation at a moment when, in dire need of friendly support, we have overtly broken with the United States on a major project of reconstruction? A man must be far gone in doctrine if he plumps for this latter alternative without very grave reflection indeed.

Beyond this, moreover, there are even weightier arguments which justify some hesitation before adopting the complete change of direction in policy which is now urged upon us. If the search for a commonly acceptable commercial code breaks down and we begin to embark upon the policy of economic *bloc*-building, we run very grave risks of disrupting the Commonwealth. There has been much talk recently here in Britain about a Commonwealth Customs Union. It can scarcely have escaped observation that the response elsewhere has not been enthusiastic; and if we look at the facts of the world trading situation, rather than indulge in pipe dreams, it is easy to see that any attempt to build round this country a system which discriminates strongly against the United States – and that of course is what is really in question – is bound to impose the greatest strain on Commonwealth unity. The Canadians would almost certainly have to contract out. The position of South Africa is at least doubtful. India is definitely not interested. Even the Southern Dominions, bound as they are to this country by the most intimate trading relationships, would find the position embarrassing. It is one thing for us to defend the *status quo* as regards existing preferential arrangements and to insist that any modification here shall be part of an advantageous bargain. It is quite another thing to contemplate projects which threaten the solidarity of the English-speaking world for an economic gain which might very well be negative.

Most of the apparent strength of the case for discrimination rests upon the circumstances attendant on the present shortage of dollars. But I venture to suggest that if we dig a little beneath the surface we discover facts which point in a very different direction of policy. As I see things, the dollar shortage is largely to be attributed to three main factors: inadequate temporary assistance to ex-belligerent countries to tide them over the difficulties of the transition, inflationary internal policies and inappropriate exchange rates.[1] The first of these factors has been well discussed; how different the position would have been this year if UNRRA assistance had been continued or if a series of reconstruction loans similar to the loan to this country had been generally available to co-operative ex-belligerents. The second, inflationary internal policies, has been less discussed but its significance is plain; factors similar to those which have impeded the expansion of exports here have been operative on a large

1. It is surely a significant circumstance that, whereas dollar shortage was always predicted as a result of internal deflation in the United States, it has in fact appeared at a time when conditions in that country are the very reverse of deflationary.

scale in a great many other countries. But, so far, for reasons which are difficult to follow, the fact that the exchanges of many countries are plainly over-valued has attracted inadequate attention. Yet it is here, I believe, that there is to be found one of the main keys to the problem of restoring international equilibrium. If, for reasons of prestige or from inadequate conceptions of policy, a nation persists in maintaining rates of exchange quite out of relation to internal prices and costs, it is only natural that it should find itself in balance of payments difficulties. Of course, this is by no means the whole story of current disequilibria. But it is a part and an essential part which hitherto has tended to be suppressed. A great many of the more plausible arguments for discriminatory special arrangements would disappear overnight if appropriate adjustments, aided by appropriate short-term assistance, could be made in the exchanges.

By this I must not be understood to be advocating a change, here and now, in the value of the pound sterling: until there are encountered much severer difficulties in disposing of additional exports I should hold such a move to be ill-advised and premature. But there are other rates about which no such dubiety exists. It was one of the main purposes of the establishment of the International Monetary Fund to promote an orderly adjustment of the exchanges where fundamental disequilibria exist; and I am inclined to think that the time has come when its utilization for this purpose would be greatly in the common interest. How much more conducive to peace and prosperity would be resort to such adjustment, carried out by mutual consent under expert auspices and fertilized, let us hope, by new flows of temporary assistance, than the disorderly makeshift of discriminatory arrangements, economically fissiparous, subject continually to the perverse play of politics and tending to disrupt the diplomatic unity of the civilized world.

Yet we must be moderate in our expectations. We shall not see a return of prosperity to the world until political conditions are more settled. The most extensive reconstruction loans, the most careful financial policies, the most far-seeing adjustments of international trading arrangements, must all come to grief if present uncertainties continue. And continue they will until there are established more stable political groupings. This raises issues far transcending the scope of this paper and I will restrict myself to one observation. At the present time there is much talk of Western European Union. It is an idea which has many attractions, and before the War and long before the present discussions, I was one of its earliest supporters.[1] But much water has

1. The curious may care to consult my *The Economic Causes of War* (London, 1939) and a paper entitled "Economic factors and international disunity" in the World Order Symposium issued by Chatham House [Royal Institute of International Affairs, *World Order Papers, First Series*, September 1940, pp. 129–53].

gone under the bridges since then; and to me the overwhelming lesson of these years has been this: *in the two Great Wars of the twentieth century, Western Europe has failed to settle its problems unaided.* On each occasion the assistance of both the Commonwealth and the United States has been necessary. As I see it, having regard both to the economic balance of the world and to the intense political jealousies prevailing, there is no prospect of things being different in the future. By all means let us do what we can to consolidate the political and economic framework of Western Europe. But let us never forget that this must be conceived, not as an alternative to, but as part of, a larger consolidation of the Commonwealth, the Americans and Western Europe. We cannot hope to stabilize the world and safeguard the precious heritage of Western civilization on any less ambitious grouping. If this is true, it is very important. It may be an additional reason for some circumspection in external economic policy.

16 The Sterling Problem

From *Lloyds Bank Review*, new series no. 14 (October 1949) pp. 1–31.

It takes a lot to upset us nowadays. But the recent worsening of our balance of payments and the drastic devaluation of the pound have caused widespread bewilderment and anxiety. We were aware in a vague way that the position was not yet sound, that there was much to do before Marshall Aid came finally to an end in 1952. But the improvement last year, as compared with the disasters of 1947, had tended to conceal the essentially precarious nature of the contemporary position; and the fact that in 1949, with Marshall Aid still in full blast, our reserves should be dwindling at a rate which, if continued, would involve substantial cuts in consumption and widespread unemployment, has come as a severe disappointment. It is improbable that the great mass of the people yet realize at all the nature of the peril which threatens them: it is the nature of the system under which we live that it tends to insulate the man in the street from the premonitory symptoms of danger. But it is safe to say that the majority of informed opinion is now thoroughly disquieted. The fact that, for a second time, we have run into acute difficulties, while actually in receipt of massive aid from abroad, must surely suggest to serious minds in all parties that, however much we may have been the victims of bad luck, the implications of our own policies are in urgent need of re-examination.

It is in the hope of contributing to this process that the following notes have been written.

I FALSE SCENTS

Let us first try to clear our minds of false scents and inadequate explanations.

(a) The American Recession

There can be little doubt that one of the chief factors contributing to the recent decline of our reserves was the falling off of demand for colonial products, due to the cessation of inflation in America. It is not yet possible to give a quantitative assessment of this. But, when the figures are published, it will be very surprising if the decline in price of such commodities as cocoa and rubber does not stand revealed as one of the most significant single causes of our immediate embarrassments.

It is one thing to recognize this influence, however; it is quite another to jump to the conclusion that it is the only influence that we need take into account, still more that the whole blame for our present difficulties can be placed on American shoulders. For, in the first place, it is not the only influence. Quite apart from the decline in confidence which has been the by-product of rumours of trouble, it is unfortunately a fact that the volume of exports from this country has fallen and that the selling of our goods abroad is encountering rapidly growing difficulties. Not only in the dollar area, but in other quarters, the sellers' market tends to come to an end. The days when the inadequacy of our exports could be ascribed to difficulties of production rather than difficulties of sale are over. And, despite all that has been done, we are still far short of the wished-for goal.

It is, therefore, to get things quite out of proportion to regard the fluctuations of American demand as the sole occasion of our difficulties. It is even more mistaken to suggest that there is anything which reflects any special blame on the conduct of American policy in the extent to which these fluctuations have actually affected us. For what has happened so far in the United States cannot by any legitimate stretch of the meaning of words be regarded as a depression. There has been a cessation of inflation and a readjustment of certain prices – greatly to the benefit of American consumers. There has been a small falling off in the volume of production as compared with last year and some lag in the absorption of new recruits to the labour force. But there is still high prosperity in the United States; in all probability 1949 will be recorded as the second best year in American economic history. Whatever may be coming later on – and I make no prediction in these matters – it is just a sign of ignorance to regard what has happened so far as anything but a very minor recession. If our arrangements are so fragile that they cannot stand up to that without our whole future being jeopardized, then there is something very wrong with our arrangements: we are altogether too good to live. The member of parliament who recently attributed all our trouble to the inability of Congress to manage the American economy was not merely guilty of extraordinary ingratitude and bad manners, he also showed a lack of easily accessible information and an absence of knowledge of the world which must suggest grave doubts of his own ability to manage anything at all.

(b) External Misfortune Generally

For something of the same reason, it is not really very helpful to be always dwelling on our external misfortunes in general.

It is quite true that if we look around, it is not at all hard to compile a very respectable list of external circumstances whose absence would have been a material alleviation of the situation. Opinion may differ on the question whether before the War the general trend of trade was operating in our disfavour. But clearly there can be no question that our present difficulties owe their origin to the War and the dislocations and disturbances which have followed it. If our external assets had not been reduced, if we had not run into debt on an enormous scale, if the maintenance and increase of our capital equipment at home had not been sacrificed to developing the maximum striking power against the enemy, if we had not had to spend vast sums in policing various parts of the world, if other countries were in a position to pay us for what we sell in freely convertible currency, and if there had been no adverse turn in the terms of trade, how different the picture would be. It is possible to spend quite a long time attempting to assess the significance of these factors and dilating on their adverse effects.

But important as it is to know the nature of the misfortunes we encounter, it is no explanation of our present position just to list them and to leave it at that. For unless we are prepared to assume that the best possible policies are always automatically pursued, we must examine too the nature of the steps which have actually been taken to deal with these difficulties. We must ask whether they have been adequate to the occasion; we must even ask whether in some respects they may not have made things worse. When a ship encounters a storm, we do not immediately assume that it must be blown off its track. We ask what the captain has done. Has he shortened the right sails? Has he steered the vessel in the appropriate direction? We may indeed conclude that the elements are too much for him, that having done all that was humanly possible, it is yet unavoidable that the voyage should be disturbed. But we do not take this for granted. Ships are not built, navigators are not trained, on the assumption that only calm weather is in prospect. So, in considering the fortunes of the ship of state, we make things altogether too easy if we are content to assume that the mere enumeration of external misfortunes is a sufficient explanation of deviations from the desired course. We all know that a great many adverse incidents have happened in the last ten years. The question is, have we done all that was within our power to meet them?

Now it is on just this point that it may be suggested that the burden of proof is with those who suggest that we could have done no more. For *prima facie* the contention is most unplausible. It is now four years since the end of the War. During this time we have received advances from abroad on a scale never before known in economic history. It cannot be said that there has been no time for adaptation; nor that there has been no assistance from elsewhere to ease the strain. Yet, when last we were given the figures, the adverse balance was running at a rate as great as the rate prevailing shortly after the War. No responsible person will wish to under-estimate the very real difficulties which have made the transition period so much more arduous than at one time it was expected to be. But, in the face of these contrasts, it is surely hard to contend that there is not a case for enquiring whether in fact we have done all we could, or whether indeed some of the things which we have done have not proved to be additional aggravations of the position.

(c) Nationalization

In making this enquiry, however, it is necessary to remember that the policies which are under examination are policies which, directly or indirectly, affect the balance of payments, the problem under discussion. We are not making a survey of policy as a whole. There may have been many acts of policy in the last four years with which we disagree and whose ultimate influence on the economy we think to be likely to be bad. But, unless in the period concerned, they have adversely affected the balance of payments, they are not relevant to the discussion.

For this reason, in what follows, there will be nothing said about recent acts of nationalization. I will confess frankly that I have no love for what has been done in this connection. I do indeed regard it as having ominous implications for our progress in the future. But I do not believe that, so far, it has greatly affected the balance of payments. I should not adopt this attitude to all possible nationalizations; in my judgement, the nationalization of steel or insurance would have very direct adverse effects that way. But I do not think that this can be said of most of what has happened up to date, the nationalization of the Bank of England, transport, coal, gas and electricity.[1] I can understand the argument that the frame of mind which has led Ministers to concentrate so much of their own energies and – what is quite as important – the energies of the high civil service on these somewhat doctrinaire manifestations of policy, to the neglect of the more pressing and immediate problems of domestic and external equilibrium, is symptomatic of much that has gone wrong in this critical period. I should not quarrel with this contention. But it is a different thing from the contention that nationalization itself has had so far any very direct influence on the vicissitudes of the balance of payments. It is policy in this respect that is the subject of the present enquiry.

1. I should not wish to give so clean a bill to the abolition of the Liverpool Cotton Market.

II DIAGNOSIS

(a) The Export of Capital

If we start from the brute facts of the external accounts, the first item which is likely to suggest itself as a factor aggravating our difficulties, is the export of capital.

By this I mean either new investment or repayment of past debt. If we finance new construction abroad, if we extend the volume of short-term credits to overseas purchasers, if we allow existing sterling balances held in London to be run down, that is capital export; and, in present circumstances, that, directly or indirectly, is a strain on our resources additional to the strain of making payments for our own imports.

It is not very difficult to see how this happens. A direct strain arises if those to whom we lend or those who are claiming payment of sums left here in the past are allowed to turn their claims into gold or dollars. It should be clear that such operations must involve either a diminution of our own reserves or recourse to borrowing in hard currency. We sacrifice financial resources without any contemporary return in the shape of imports. The expenditure of gold and dollars is unrequited by goods and services.

Much the same thing happens, although the process may appear to be more indirect, if the sums lent or repaid are spent on our own exports. If we export a larger volume of goods on credit or if the export of constructional equipment is paid for by drafts on sterling balances here, that means in effect that, to that extent, our export activities have reaped no equivalent entitlement to imports. The exports are unrequited by corresponding goods and services.

It is sometimes argued, with great parade of esoteric technical information, that this parallelism between unrequited gold and dollars and unrequited exports is invalidated by the fact that some exports are specific, so to speak, to particular markets while, of course, dollars can be spent anywhere. The cloths that we send, let us say, to certain parts of the East, the machines that we make for particular development projects, are not marketable elsewhere. To argue, therefore, that, if they are paid for out of new loans or old balances, that involves the sacrifice of an equivalent amount of current earnings is said to be illegitimate.

The argument has some superficial attractiveness. But in fact there is very little in it. The specificity of certain ranges of exports may be freely admitted – although it is important not to exaggerate it. It is quite true that in many lines of export, even if the goods are not actually bespoken, they are adapted in one way or another to the requirements of particular markets. But it is very rarely true that the labour, the machines, the raw materials which went to make them are so highly specialized as to be incapable of being put to any other use which, directly or indirectly, could swell the total of requited exports. The cotton goods which are sold in a special market may be incapable of sale elsewhere. But the burden of proof rests with those who argue that the cotton out of which they are made, the spindles which spin the thread, the looms which weave the cloth and the labour, which is concerned at different stages of manufacture, cannot be used for anything else. And let it be remembered that it is not merely direct use for other export markets which exhausts the possibilities. If the products which can be made from the resources originally producing unrequited exports can serve at home as substitutes for other products made from resources which are capable of export production, the conclusion is the same: the unrequited exports involve a sacrifice of earning power in external markets. The fact that they are made means that we are allowing resources, which could earn the wherewithal to pay for our imports, to be used for new transfers or repayments of old debt abroad.

It is not easy to give the exact dimensions of this burden of capital export. But we know that it is large. The latest estimates for 1947 suggest that, on the most conservative accountancy, it was nearly £400 millions. (This was the year in which the Chancellor of the day described tentative queries whether something of the sort was not taking place as misinformed). Final figures for 1948 have not been published. But the provisional figures suggest something like £300 millions – significantly enough, not much less than the amount we were receiving by way of Marshall Aid. As for what has been happening recently, we know less. But two things are evident. First, that the increased rate of drain on the reserve seems considerably larger than anything which can be accounted for by current account transactions. Secondly, that there has been an increased rate of release of sterling balances. The recent settlement with India is a case in point.

These indications are serious. It is difficult to believe that the community at large is at all alive to their significance. They mean that we are using resources for capital export to a value of between a fifth and a sixth of our total imports, that at a time at which we have had to borrow abroad or solicit aid on a massive scale, we are in effect passing on a considerable fraction of the benefit in the shape of new loans or repayment of past debt. Whatever we may think of the justification of such a policy – and there will be much more to be said of this later – there can be no shadow of doubt that it has been a most substantial aggravation of the difficulties of our external account.

(b) Inflation

The second factor responsible for the increase of our difficulties is domestic inflation.

Now inflation is an ambiguous concept: and there are many ways in which different kinds of inflation may affect the economy. Perhaps the most obvious way and the way about which there is least controversy is its effect on prices and costs. Since the War, the level of retail prices has advanced from 148 (1938 = 100) to 179 and the level of wholesale prices from 166.7 to 228.6. We have no direct index of costs; but the Bowley Index of wage rates has moved from 154 to 193 and it is very difficult to believe that there has been any increase in productivity which goes at all far to offset this increase.

All this is tolerably well known; and, so far as the domestic scene is concerned, its consequences are sufficiently realized: the rise of wages, the increase of the general cost of living, the limping efforts of the salaried classes to catch up – these are recognized to be part of the inflationary process. In a vaguer way, those who give casual thought to these things must know that they are bad for our international position. It is customary even for Ministers to make some allusion to the disadvantages in external markets of a rising level of costs.

What is not generally realized, however, is the nature of the opportunity we have missed. Yet in fact it stands out conspicuously. In the period since 1945 prices and costs in the United States have also risen considerably. The B.L.S. Index of Commodities prices other than Farm and Food has risen from 123 in 1945 to 182 in May, 1949. We have only to reflect on the difference that it would have made to our competitive position if, while U.S. prices had risen to this extent, our own had remained relatively stable, to see what we have missed by inflation. The entire situation would have been different. What has to be done now by an extensive change in the rate of exchange, would have occurred automatically as a result of American inflation and our prudence. Throughout the inter-war period when doubts were expressed concerning our position in international trade, the one prime *desideratum* on which all of us were agreed was a rise in the American price level reflecting in some measure the favourable balance of payments. If anyone had told us that it had been revealed to him (authoritatively) in a dream that the American price level of goods other than Farm and Food would rise, as it has risen since the War, we should have sent out for drinks. We should have felt that we were sitting pretty. Well, they have risen in this way. But, because we have let ours rise too, we have to face a sterner form of readjustment. The decision to devalue the pound by thirty per cent, is a direct consequence of our failure to control internal inflation.

Considerations of this sort tend to put many of the phenomena of the general so-called Dollar Shortage in a light in which, so far, it has not been at all usual to contemplate it. There is much talk about this problem. Vast tomes of statistics are produced to exhibit its exact dimensions. The ingenuity of the experts is continually in operation to attempt to assess the precise weight to be assigned to the various circumstances adverse to the economies of Europe, Asia, South America and elsewhere which have made it harder for them to earn dollars. But the number of times on which mention is made of the fact that many of the economies concerned have allowed themselves to inflate even more than the United States of America is very much less frequent. Yet surely this must be regarded as one of the main features of the situation. No well-informed person will wish to deny the difficulties in which some (though not all) of the countries now suffering from dollar shortage were placed by the damages and dislocation of the War. But very extensive resources were at the disposal of most of these countries or were made available by relief grants or loans from the United States. If it had not been for the local inflations, it might still be that these funds would have been inadequate to establish full equilibrium yet awhile. But it is quite certain that they would have been much less inadequate than has actually proved to be the case. To discuss the under-supply of dollars without discussing the over-supply of the other currencies is to discuss Hamlet without the Prince of Denmark. To make the United States mainly responsible for what has happened, despite the rise in the American price level, the considerable reductions in the American tariff and the pouring out of dollars in the shape of loans and subsidies on a scale without precedent in time of peace, is a very shabby falsification of history.

To return to our own difficulties. The effects of inflation on the balance of payments are not limited to direct effects on relative prices and costs. Even where prices and costs are under control and are held steady by public regulation or private understanding, inflationary pressure is still an obstacle to the equilibrium of the balance of payments. For inflation is in essence a tendency to spend on consumption and development at a rate greater than the rate at which consumption and development goods are forthcoming, as measured at current prices. When this is taking place, there is a tendency to deflect for domestic purposes (either consumption or development) goods and services which otherwise would be available for disposal in export markets. It is not enough for prices and costs to be steady. It is not even enough for the exchange rates, at which these prices and costs are translated into terms of foreign moneys, to give reasonable scope for successful sales. If there is inflationary pressure, in the sense defined above, the volume of exports will tend to drop short of what is necessary, while the volume of imports, unless most rigidly controlled, will be continually tending to rise.

All this is tolerably well known by now, even if it is not always made the basis for ministerial decision. Since the crisis of 1947, it has not been a matter of serious dispute that, no matter whether there is budgetary equilibrium in the narrow sense, if there is not equilibrium in the general sense of a tendency for overall expenditure and output to be equal at stable prices, then the balance of payments must suffer.

What, however, is not so generally recognized is the probability that, at the present time, a process of this sort is still active. Our financial history in recent years seems to fall into three periods. There is first the period from the death of Keynes [in April 1946] to the great crisis of 1947. About the inflationary tendencies operative then, there is now no reasonable question. Under a Chancellor [Dalton] who could profess to be astonished at "the contrast between the great difficulty of the overseas position and the relative ease of the purely domestic financial position," there was a complete divorce between financial and general economic planning. We indulged in the crass folly of the ultra-cheap money policy; and consumption and investment were allowed to develop on such a scale that that part of the American loan, which was not being passed on by way of capital export, was used up long before it was anticipated, the development of exports being quite inadequate to reduce the gap to manageable proportions. There followed a period of retrenchment and reform. The investment programme was pruned. A real (as distinct from an illusory) budget surplus was planned and achieved. While all this was on a more modest scale than the advocates of this policy might have wished,[1] its success was at least equal to expectations. The sense of internal pressure slackened. The volume of export activity increased in a manner that was distinctly promising. This was the second phase of post-war financial history.

For the last few months, however, it appears that we have passed into a third phase, in which inflationary pressure is once more renewed. For some time it had been apparent that the mounting volume of public expenditure was likely to make grave encroachments on the Chancellor's ability to achieve a surplus. But the main political pressure, from the Right as well as from the Left, was all in favour of tax reduction, without specifying how it could be carried out without involving further inflation. Hence when the Chancellor produced a budget [in April 1949] in which these insidious and short-sighted pressures were resisted, the majority of economists were so relieved at his determination and so concerned to defend him against perverse criticism that they omitted to draw sufficient attention to the danger that the surplus for which he budgeted was very probably insufficient. Only Professor Paish and Mr. Tress kept their heads and, in a remarkable article in the *London and Cambridge Economic Service Bulletin* for May of this year which even yet has not received the attention it deserved, pointed out that, on the figures available, it looked as though the inflationary gap had reopened to dimensions of at least £100 millions *per annum*.*

1. Writing in this *Review* in October, 1947, I recommended a surplus of "five to six hundred millions" [above, p. 222].

* F.W. Paish and R.C. Tress, "The budget and economic policy," *LCES Bulletin*, vol. 27, pp. 42–8. [The Chancellor of the Exchequer was now Sir Stafford Cripps (since the resignation of Hugh Dalton in November 1947).]

Since then developments have begun to justify these gloomy prognostications. The unemployment figures by themselves would suggest strong inflationary pressure. A state of affairs in which, with a working population of over twenty millions, less than one quarter of a million are unemployed is certainly something very different from what one would expect of 'full employment' in the Keynesian sense with no tendencies to inflationary developments. When these figures are taken in conjunction with other developments these suspicions are greatly reinforced. During the summer there has been a marked contraction in the volume of exports. In a normal state of affairs it would be reasonable to expect that *for the time being* this would affect the unemployment statistics. That is not to say that the labour displaced would be permanently unemployed: only the ignorant or the malicious would suggest that this was a necessary consequence of the absence of inflation. But it would at least take a little time for the people concerned to find new jobs: and this would show itself in the figures. In fact this has not happened. The displaced labour has been reabsorbed almost instantaneously. There has been hardly a ripple on the pool. For the greater part of the summer indeed unemployment continued to decline. I see no way of accounting for this save on the assumption of a renewal of inflationary pressure. Professor Paish and Mr. Tress were right.

The reason for this is twofold: the growth in investment and the growth in public expenditure. Messrs. Paish and Tress came to the conclusion that "true net capital formation is likely to be something like £200 m. more this year than last." The budget estimates for 1949–50 were nearly £140 millions higher than the exchequer issues for the preceding year. The real surplus of 1948–9 which, it is now clear, was never really large enough to give our position the strength that it needs, bids fair to dwindle to proportions which are quite inadequate to finance the capital formation contemplated.

These changes are the result of policy. But let no one make the responsibility a matter of party recrimination. I have seldom heard any attacks from the Opposition on the volume of planned investment, especially when the most vulnerable form of investment, the so-called social investment, was under discussion. As for expenditure, all Oppositions attack expenditure. But, although there have been honourable exceptions, this Opposition, at any rate, has not avoided the inconsistency of attacking expenditure in general, while promising the maintenance or even the increase of most detailed items thereof. The vital issue at stake in a recent election was which of the two parties would provide the more houses. I have yet to learn that the Opposition candidate gave any reason for supposing that, although he would provide more, he would spend absolutely less. We have heard a good deal of the desirability of economizing on the food budget; but the Opposition has recently been at pains to inform us on huge posters that what is in mind is, not any increase in the price of food, but more economical buying and administration – which of course makes hay quantitatively of any but the most modest expectations in this connection. The fact is that since the War the majority of the community, whether Conservative, Liberal or Labour, have been living in a fool's paradise concerning what we can afford; and the majority of their leaders, whether Conservative, Liberal or Labour, have done little to correct the delusion. There are a few who, like Sir John Anderson and Lord Brand, have consistently warned us. If *they* care to say "I told you so" they will certainly be within their rights; for they have been shamefully attacked and misrepresented. But, for the rest, the less said about the past the better. Most have fallen short of the minimum survival standards of democracy.

(c) **Production and Incentive**

Let us turn for a moment to consider influences on production.

It follows from what has been said already that the volume of production has been insufficient to offset the increases that have taken place in money incomes. That indeed is one of the most intelligible descriptions of the fact of inflation: if production were to keep pace with money income, there would be no increases of prices in general and no general increases of costs. When we say, therefore, that there has been inflation (and, with inflation, the embarrassments which follow, other things being equal, in the balance of payments), we say that production has been inadequate in this sense.

But, of course, this is not to say very much. When there is no further reserve of capacity, production can only be increased by hard work and intelligence; whereas the volume of expenditure can be increased by ministerial directive. It would be a severe criterion of the efficiency of productive arrangements to demand that, whatever the follies of elected persons, the efficiency of production should be such as to wipe them out. What we want to know in this connection, therefore, is not why production has not offset financial mismanagement, but rather whether, in the circumstances, the volume of production has been all that it might have been expected to be.

Now on this point it is important to retain some sense of proportion. It may be said with some confidence that the alarmist reports, current in certain parts of the foreign press, of a vast falling-off in productivity all round are not true. I would not feel so confident that these reports were not justified in the case of certain industries – building, for example. But, by and large, I am fairly sure they are not true. I have not much faith in the general indices of production. But I do not believe that they go as wrong as all that.

Against this, however, when Ministers and official propagandists sound pæans of praise at our so-called "effort," when no less a person than the present Chancellor refers to it as "magnificent," I must confess that I am at a loss to understand their enthusiasm. It is true that the index of production is considerably above pre-war. According to the London and Cambridge Economic Service, the index for 1948 was 120, 1935–38 being about 108; in June this year it was 125. But the volume of employment is also above pre-war – exactly how much it is difficult to determine because of a change in methods of collecting statistics – which means that the increase in productivity per head, measured this way, is less; and of course it is productivity per head which matters. Mr. Aneurin Bevan, the other day, used a figure which suggested an eight per cent. increase. Assuming that this is correct, it is really not at all spectacular. If we are to maintain our position in the world, let alone make any progress, it is necessary to do much better than this. And when we leave the figures with their specious precision and look at facts which are known to all, the same impression emerges. When we reflect that this period of desperate emergency has been marked by the adoption of shorter hours and more holidays, the suspicion is reinforced, not merely that production has not been as great as might have been wished, but also that it has not been as great as it would have been legitimate to expect.

I wonder if anyone really doubts this in his heart? The five-day week is an amenity which is very desirable. But was it the happiest moment to adopt it when our reserves were depleted, when our assets were reduced and when, by common consent, a special effort was needed? Can anyone who has travelled abroad either in Continental Europe (where standards of life and capital equipment are inferior to our own) or across the Atlantic (where they are better) really maintain that in comparison we present the impression of an all-out struggle. The accusation that we are a castle of indolence is doubtless misplaced. But the claim that we are a hive of strenuous industry is also inaccurate. There is a certain mediocrity in what we do, an easy-going economy of effort, strangely out of harmony with the real perils of the situation.

In part this is probably a by-product of inflation. Inflation, of the degree to which we have been subjected, creates so intense a sellers' market for labour that, as in all intensive sellers' markets, there is a tendency for what is sold to deteriorate in quality. The threat of a possible rejection of what is offered ceases to operate. The possibility of dismissal has always been held to be an indispensable instrument of discipline in industry, in nationalized concerns equally with those under private ownership. But, if nothing is lost by losing a job, this sanction ceases its effectiveness. This may sound a hard thing to say; and by the unscrupulous it will doubtless be said to imply a plea for widespread deflation and unemployment. But this will be a gross misrepresentation. To argue that it is bad to be in a high fever is not to argue that the temperature should be several degrees below normal. We get the contemporary picture quite out of perspective if we suppose that an unemployment percentage below two represents a normal state of "full employment." On the contrary, it is one of the surest signs of a state of inflationary pressure. Few things can be more certain than that such a state of affairs cannot persist for ever. But, while it lasts, the same force which imposes a direct drag on the increase of exports at the same time damages the situation still further by undermining industrial discipline.

Beyond this, however, although still connected with the root trouble of excessive expenditure, comes the damage to incentive which arises from the present burden of taxation. This operates in various ways. I myself have little doubt that, at present levels, a high flat rate on income diminishes the will to work; when work is so highly taxed, there is a strong disposition to spend more time on the untaxed good, leisure, or at least to spend it on forms of work (e.g. jobbing gardening at the week-end) which escape the net of the tax collector. I think this is borne out by general observation, although, analytically, it is not certain. When, however, the rate of taxation rises with increasing income then the findings of analysis and observation are unequivocal. If the longer or the harder he works, the greater the rate at which he is taxed, a man will tend to work less. It is surely common experience that the increasing marginal rate of taxation is one of the chief disincentives of our day.

Such a disincentive, wherever it exists, is a day-to-day drag on productivity. But, on a long view, its effects are probably most serious in the sphere of enterprise. If a man or a company is confronted with the choice between routine operations, with a more or less predictable return, or a venture into the unknown, where failure means loss of capital and success the substraction by the tax gatherer of all but a small fraction of the gain, the temptation to continue with the *status quo* is strong. The point is so obvious that it needs no elaboration. But it is doubtful whether it is realized how damaging such a state of affairs can be in its cumulative effects. A society in which there is so strong an incentive against innovation and risky enterprise as there is in ours today, is a society which is in the gravest danger of falling behind in the increase of productivity. And to fall behind in the increase of productivity is just what we cannot afford today.

These considerations are especially relevant in a situation such as ours where one of the main *desiderata* is an increase in the volume of exports. Any drag on productivity is a drag on costs which, in turn, is a drag on export sales. But, over and above this, any deterrent to the taking of risks is a special deterrent to the search for new export outlets. It is a fallacy to suppose that increases of exports arise automatically, even if the situation be otherwise favourable. Export outlets are created by deliberate enterprise. The search for new markets is usually decidedly more hazardous than the cultivation of old ones. It is all very well for Ministers to get up at week-ends and make patriotic appeals to manufacturers to recognize the paramount necessity of exports. The experience of the last few years shows that manufacturers in this country are by no means deaf to such exhortations. But they are a poor substitute for the day-to-day incentive of possible extra gain. And it is just this incentive which tends to be deadened by a high marginal rate of taxation.

Speaking generally, it must surely be recognized that the conditions now prevailing in this country are the reverse of conducive to enterprise. At a time when we need enterprise and innovation more urgently than at any other period in our peace-time history, the whole tendency is to make the exercise of these activities more difficult. Everywhere the striking out of new paths is hampered by administrative control and legislative uncertainty; and these obstacles are but the sign and symbol of something deeper. With us, at any rate – I sense some change elsewhere – the spirit of the age is inimical to the spirit of enterprise: a levelling passion is abroad, restrictive of spontaneity. Distracted overworked men at the centre dictate and limit the activities of a periphery which becomes more and more apathetic. While this state of affairs persists it is not easy to be optimistic about the rate of increase of productivity in the future, and it is difficult to believe that it has not adversely affected our rate of recovery, and hence our balance of payments, in the past.

III REMEDIES

(a) Devaluation

The main action which has been taken by the Government to meet our present very serious difficulties has been devaluation of the pound from 4.03 dollars to 2.80.

Let me say at once that, subject to two very important *provisos* to be mentioned below, I believe this decision to be sound. I should not have said this while the sellers' market persisted in the world at large. While our deficiency of exports was a matter of production rather than of sales, in my judgement the balance of advantage lay in keeping the old rate. Doubtless this was not an unequivocal advantage; a lower rate of exchange would have meant a higher rate of profit in export business and hence a greater incentive to increase the volume of export production. Nevertheless, with the world in the state of confusion in which it then was, before any clear indication of competitive advantage and disadvantage had disclosed themselves, the dictates of prudence, it seems to me, lay in waiting to see how things turned out.

But once the sellers' market showed signs of disappearing and the extent of our competitive disadvantage in important markets became apparent, the balance of advantage shifted. It was fairly clear by the beginning of this year that the disparity in costs here and elsewhere was becoming such that only a change in the rate of exchange or a very severe deflation of incomes would serve to maintain the position we already held, let alone permit the further expansion of exports which is so urgently necessary. In such circumstances I have no doubt that it was right to choose devaluation. A change in the value of sterling is indeed a very serious and important step, not to be undertaken lightly. There is a great deal to be said for resorting to local contraction, rather than a change in the rate, when disequilibrium is of a minor order. But when the disequilibrium is large, then it is surely better to attempt to rectify it by a change in the rate, which leaves the internal income structure unaltered, rather than resort to contractions, which can only prove effective after long agonies of internal readjustment, if in the meantime they have not produced a *bouleversement* of the entire political and social structure. If I were to criticize anything in this connection, it would not be the decision to devalue, but the delay in coming to that decision, which must have cost us many millions of our all-too-scanty reserves. It is hard to understand the leisurely frame of mind in which these urgent matters have been handled.

I think it is right too that once this decision was made, it was decided that the cut should be of sufficient magnitude to give reasonable assurance that, provided always that certain other measures are taken and the advantage is not frittered away, the new rate can be held. Nothing would have been more disturbing than a movement which the world at large judged to be too small. In this connection, it must be recognized that since a large number of other countries have devalued with us, the effect of any given cut in our rate on our export sales in dollar areas is to that extent reduced, although to the extent that their devaluations put them in a better position to pay us in convertible currencies this may well be more than offset. Moreover, it must be remembered that, in all probability, the full measure of the difficulties which we are likely to encounter in international competition has not yet been revealed. It is well to have some margin in hand.

What has happened in the last few weeks is in effect almost the equivalent of an appreciation of the dollar, though without the disagreeable consequences for gold mines which that policy would have involved; and, for reasons which were most forcibly set forth by Professor D.H. Robertson in the last number of this *Review*,* on balance the change is to be welcomed.

* "Britain and European Recovery," *Lloyds Bank Review*, n.s., 13 (July 1949), pp. 1–13.

At any rate the burden of proof is with those who argue the other way. For let it be remembered that if it be argued that a downward movement of the rate of exchange of countries in disequilibrium would make things worse, the implication must be, other things being assumed to be equal, that an upward movement would make them better; and this does not seem to be plausible.

But all this is subject to the condition that the fundamental causes which have brought about disequilibrium cease henceforward to operate: that is to say, that inflationary pressure ceases and the export of capital is reduced to more appropriate proportions. If this does not happen any change in the rate of exchange will be in vain. If costs in this country continue to rise, or if the vast sums accumulated here as a result of the peculiarities of war finance continue to be withdrawn at a high rate, no change in the rate of exchange will save us. We shall continue to be in disequilibrium. Our reserves will continue to fall and within a measurable distance of time, we shall be forced to other policies by the sheer physical inability to buy what we need. But this process will involve short commons and widespread unemployment.

For this reason many of us would have felt happier if the change in the rate of exchange had been preceded by the other necessary changes in policy, retrenchment at home and some settlement of the problem of the sterling balances. At the present time we are in the position of a patient who needs two surgical operations, one easy, the other very difficult. The easy operation has been performed. But it will only be effective if it is accompanied by the other: and it is not sure whether the patient is going to submit himself to the second or whether, even if he is prepared to do so, the surgeons will have the nerve and the skill to perform it. Meanwhile, whether he knows it or not, he is in a position of extreme danger.

It is clearly incumbent on all of us, therefore, to try to think out exactly what is needed.

(b) Disinflation and Internal Finance

Let us look first at internal finance; if that is not in order, everything else is bound to go wrong. It is fundamental to take all traces of inflation out of the system; if that is not done the advantages of devaluation can be wiped out in a very few months or even weeks. It is desirable, too, to restore some greater degree of incentive to work and enterprise; for although the weakening of incentive does not show itself in immediate collapse, in the long run it must produce a further deterioration of our position in relation to more vigorous and efficient communities and so lead to further difficulties and further crises.

To do this it is necessary, in my judgement, to make reductions both in the volume of investment and in the volume of public expenditure.

So far as reductions in investment are concerned, I should like to make my position clear beyond the possibility of misunderstanding. I am no foe to investment. I accept the view which has been forcibly urged both by Professor Paish and Professor Viner,* that there are large sectors of our economy where in all probability the volume of investment has been less than would be considered desirable, having regard to reasonable expectations of progress. But this view is not incompatible with the view that the volume of investment in general has tended in recent years to be too large; there are branches of the so-called civil investment sector where I am sure that outlay has been too lavish. Moreover, it is not incompatible with the view that, in present conditions, there is not sufficient selectiveness in the investment process. In a time of capital scarcity, such as almost inevitably follows a great war, it is desirable that investments which yield quick returns should have priority over those whose return is longer maturing. It is more important to repair vehicles and rolling stock than to provide new roads or permanent way. I think there is considerable evidence that hitherto the investment programme has not been framed sufficiently with this principle in mind. To that extent, therefore, there will be elements in the present volume of investment which can rightly be regarded as dispensable – even though later on, when the capital scarcity has diminished, they may be very good investments indeed. What is needed is some general impersonal instrument of selection which will sort out the more urgently needed from the less.

For this purpose, I think the experience of the last few years tends to show that we cannot afford to dispense with the mechanism of the structure of interest rates. I am far from urging that this is the only instrument we should rely upon – there will be more to say about that a little later. Nor do I wish to over-emphasize its efficiency in all situations that are conceivable or in all parts of the economic system. But I would urge that experience of a time when interest rates have been held at levels quite out of relation with the contemporary scarcity of capital does suggest that the substitutes for higher rates to which we have recourse are not sufficient by themselves. I therefore come to the conclusion that, for the time being, in spite of its possible disadvantages in regard to public finance, it would be appropriate for steps to be taken to put the long term rate of interest up.

In this connection, I cannot forbear from alluding to what seems, at any rate at first sight, to be a palpable inconsistency in Government policy. Since the autumn of 1947 disinflation has been the accepted principle and, so far as the budget and the investment planning are concerned, some attempts, although inadequate, have been made to put this principle into practice. But

---

* Jacob Viner, "An American view of the British economic crisis," *Lloyds Bank Review*, n.s., no. 6 (October 1947), pp. 28–38.

in the narrower sphere of finance one looks in vain for parallel operations. The volume of deposits is clearly a matter which is completely within the control of the Bank of England; the joint stock banks at large are purely passive agents in regard to this total. Yet at a time when disinflation has been preached and (occasionally) practised elsewhere, a not inconsiderable expansion of bank deposits has been allowed. More surprising still, at a time when the reserve has been flowing out at a rate which was alarming to contemplate, there seems to have been no attempt to use the traditional instruments of monetary policy to prevent this happening. Many of us who listened to the Chancellor announce the most drastic devaluation in our history must have confidently expected that, before the end of his speech, there would be announced an increase in Bank Rate – a sign to the rest of the world that we had not only decided on a new value for the pound but that we were prepared to fight to defend it. But these expectations were not fulfilled. The nationalization of the Bank of England clearly precludes the attribution to that institution of independent initiative in policy; and the officials of the Bank must henceforward be regarded as possessing the same complete immunity from criticism as other members of the public service. But it is at least permissible to suggest that the Chancellor, who is now to be regarded as solely responsible for ultimate decisions regarding policy, has not as yet succeeded in bringing about so complete a harmony between his actions in different capacities as might be desirable in the public interest.

To charge higher rates when private enterprise borrows is obviously not enough. In the large sector of investment which is directly controlled by the Government, it is desirable that a similar selective principle should apply. Even where the Government does not have to pay higher rates on the funds at its disposal, it should judge alternative investment plans as though they were subject to this obligation. That is to say, it should reject the projects which do not promise a yield at least equal to the rate which is laid down as the criterion. Even in that sphere of social investment, where the computation of benefits in terms of cash is manifestly out of the question, it should be realized that the least urgent types of cases, which were sanctioned when easier conditions were assumed to prevail, must become extra-marginal now. Indeed, in my judgement, it is just in this sphere where the most considerable reductions are possible. There are many projects of civil development now in process or in contemplation which might well wait until we are faced, as we shall be later on, with the necessity to offset a spontaneous decline in investment.[1]

1. It is obvious, if these principles are applied, that there will be some cut in expenditure on housing. No pruning of the investment programme which took its job at all seriously could leave so extensive a branch of total investment untouched. In judging the significance of this it is important to realize that it need not imply a reduction in the number of dwellings. All that is necessary is that the standard should be temporarily lowered. This is not nearly so terrible as it sounds. I think it would be found that a return to standards, which, in the inter-war period, were considered quite acceptable, would release a significant amount of resources for other uses.

The extent to which it is necessary to cut investment, the extent therefore to which it is necessary to raise interest rates, obviously depends on the extent to which it is found possible to create a real surplus in the budget. The larger the surplus, the larger that is to say the volume of forced saving, the less the need for cuts in the investment programme. While sharing Professor Robertson's scepticism concerning the prudence of relying exclusively on the policy of the budget surplus as a substitute for the rate of interest, I am clear (as I fancy Professor Robertson is) that we cannot afford to dispense with this policy. The level of interest rates which just now would be necessary to prevent inflation, without a budget surplus, would be very unpleasant to contemplate. In our present predicament we cannot afford not to be eclectic in our financial policy.

But to create a budget surplus in circumstances in which, by common consent, the burden of taxation is at a level which itself is damaging to enterprise, it is necessary to cut expenditure. And if it is desired both to achieve a surplus and to permit some reduction of taxation it is necessary to cut expenditure even more. I am convinced that such cuts are necessary. The present volume of expenditure is one of the greatest threats to our recovery; and policies to which we are already committed bid fair to increase this burden. Disagreeable as it may be, we have to face the fact that we have tried to do too much too soon and that if we are not to endanger our hopes of further progress we must, for the time being, reverse the process until we are in a better position to afford what we hope to do. A considerable reduction of public expenditure has become a prime necessity of national safety.

For this reason, we must applaud the news that a serious attack is to be made on the general expenses of administration. It is indeed possible to exaggerate the economies which are possible in this direction. But it is not true that they are small.

Nevertheless this is not enough. We deceive ourselves if we suppose that the position can be made really safe by economies which involve no general changes in policy. It is only necessary to look at the composition of public expenditure to realize that this is so.

For this reason I cannot but deplore the type of all-or-nothing statement which is being made in many quarters, with regard to the social services. Even Sir Stafford Cripps, to whose realism and sense of public duty we owe so much, seems inclined to suggest that the present volume of expenditure on the social services is something completely sacrosanct, and that no policy of judicious economy here and there is possible without the ruin of the whole structure.

Such an attitude is surely unjustified. It is unjustifiable to contend that every item in this vast structure is equally indispensable. It is unjustifiable to contend that nothing can be cut without causing serious hardship and the collapse of all our hopes of improvement. It is not conducive to the calm consideration of the whole position, which is so essential if we are to extricate ourselves without the impairment of national unity, to argue that anyone who mentions the possibility of cuts in this connection is an enemy of humanity and progress.

Take, for instance, the example of food. It is just not true that extreme and extensive hardship would be caused if the prices of some of the subsidized commodities were allowed to rise a little. The arguments which are commonly employed in popular discussion of these matters are really an insult to our intelligence. In a community in which the expenditure on food is only a little more than a quarter of consumption expenditure in general, it is unreasonable to argue that there is not some margin for increases which do not cause grave hardship. Apparently it is necessary to remind ourselves that we are not still in the early days of the industrial revolution when a large proportion of the population really lived at the margin of subsistence. It may be that at the very bottom of the income scale there is a small group whose position would be embarrassed. But there are many ways of looking after that besides subsidizing the consumption of all of us: some change in family allowances, for example.

Or again, take the Health Service expenditure on which has reached such unexpected, such enormous, proportions. Is it really sensible to argue that nothing can be done here to relieve the strain which would not ruin the whole scheme? Surely not. On an earlier occasion Sir Stafford himself has hinted at the possibility of putting the scheme on a fee-paying basis. It does not need much imagination to see that a very modest innovation of this sort would greatly change the situation. It would yield a substantial sum to the exchequer: it would be a deterrent to frivolous visits. Yet who can contend that the majority of people would be gravely impoverished if they had to sacrifice the price of a few cigarettes any week that they called on the doctor?

Are these things impossible? I do not know; for possibility in this sense is a matter of will and persuasion. But two things are plain: first, that there exists a wide range of possible devices of the kind which have been cited above which, had we the will to adopt them, are at once administratively practicable and capable of bringing substantial easements to the budget without involving serious hardship; secondly, that if we do not do something of this sort our financial problem will continue to be unsolved and our position in the world at large will continue to be perilous.

(c) The Sterling Balances

Even if we put our internal finances in order and remove all traces of inflationary pressure from the system, our external account will still be under grave pressure, if the export of capital continues at the level of recent years.

To have to make exports (or to borrow abroad) to the tune of £300 millions a year or more to make possible new transfers or the repayment of old debt is a burden which we ought not to assume. It is a burden, moreover, which in all probability would never have been voluntarily assumed by the community at large if the community at large had known what it was doing. Public personages may from time to time boast of the vast assistance which we have rendered in this way in recent years; and unreflecting audiences may cheer. But if it were generally realized that thereby our own imports of food and raw material would have been jeopardized had we not found kind friends elsewhere to help us stagger on, it is hard to believe that the cheers would be very vigorous.

So far as new capital export is concerned, we may assume that there are means available to limit the volume of transfer. If interest rates were somewhat higher and if internal uncertainties were less, it is doubtful whether, in the present troubled state of the world, the volume of new capital that would voluntarily leave this country would be excessive. Even if this were not the case – and until the domestic prospect improves it would be dangerous to under-estimate the desire to move – existing mechanisms of control should be sufficient to keep the movement in check.

But the repayment of past debt presents another and very special problem, the so-called problem of the sterling balances. So long as there are outstanding the abnormally large balances accumulated during the War by governments and persons abroad, whose withdrawal is limited only by special arrangements made *ad hoc* at frequent special negotiations, so long will the situation have an incurable instability and uncertainty, utterly inimical to the restoration of more normal conditions. It is not only that with the type of temporary settlement which at present prevails in this field, our negotiators (i.e. the Chancellor and other Ministers concerned) seem chronically unable to refrain from making concessions which are obviously out of all relation to what is prudent – witness the amazing terms recently accorded to India – it is also that while there is this abnormally large volume of "old" sterling about in the world, it is almost impossible to make any real progress to the re-establishment of convertibility. Until this problem is settled on a more permanent footing, it is safe to say that we shall have to continue to endure exchange control of the most ferocious nature and that nevertheless our balance of payments will continue to be in jeopardy.

Now it is not to be denied that this is a very difficult and delicate matter. While we discuss it mainly on the plane of moral deserts and obligation we are not likely to get anywhere. From our own point of view, on this plane, the thing may appear to be simple. We did not incur the expenses, in respect of which these balances arose, for any narrowly selfish purpose. The money was spent in a common cause and we feel that it is unfair that we alone should bear the burden. There is something repugnant to the most elementary sense of equity that we should be endangering our whole position in the world, to repay monies whose expenditure made possible the victory of Alamein.

But this is only one side of the picture. There is no doubt that we hired the money, in the sense that we bought goods and services and paid for them in sterling. It is improbable that we should have got what we wanted on other terms. We feel that the money was spent in the common interest of humanity in preventing the domination of the world by Nazi and Japanese aggression. But it is gratuitous for us to assume that these feelings are necessarily shared by the creditors, not all of whom may have felt the same intense inner compulsion to sacrifice all rather than surrender. Moreover we must not let the difficulties of the moment obscure the fact that, in many cases, we, the debtors, are comparatively rich while they, the creditors, are absolutely very poor. It is not easy to believe that we can get very far while we merely bandy moral arguments with each other.

There are, however, practical considerations of a more generally compelling order of cogency. It is quite certain that not all the abnormal balances could be withdrawn at once without shipwreck of the whole structure of which they are part. If the attempt were made, we should be obliged to put up the shutters. It is also certain that we cannot repay at more than a very modest rate per annum – much more modest than the bountiful rates accorded recently – without imposing strains on conditions here which, when realized, would be thought to be intolerable. The present state of affairs just cannot last.

I conclude, therefore, that, although there should be no question of repudiation, there can be no obligation to repay at a rate which endangers our general stability. We must safeguard the interests of the whole body of creditors against the precipitate action of any group. This means in practice that, having made some more or less arbitrary segregation of the abnormal extra foreign balances accumulated during the War, we must quite definitely declare them to be inaccessible save at a certain rate, subject to waiver of the type prevailing under the terms of the first American loan, and only susceptible of modification in the case of those creditors who, like Canada and the United States, are prepared to regard the debts as being on a less commercial basis and make some definite scaling down.

Admittedly, a policy of this sort must give rise to all sorts of difficulties in centres which have based their plans on the prospect of a rapid withdrawal of the balances. It is to be feared that in certain centres something amounting to major investment inflation has been allowed to develop on the strength of expectations of this kind. Moreover, despite the fact that more rapid release creates intolerable embarrassments here at home, it cannot be denied that there are political considerations which make it very difficult to discontinue the process.

I have sometimes wondered, when listening to this kind of argument, whether an alternative settlement is not possible. Since so considerable a proportion of the yearly aid which we receive from the United States is passed on, directly or indirectly, to the sterling creditors, might it not be a good thing if, forgoing perhaps that amount of aid (which does not in fact accrue to our private advantage), we were to ask the United States to be directly responsible for a certain share of the balances and to make her own arrangements with the creditors concerning the rate of release. I used to think that it would be preferable, if we could settle this question ourselves. But I can see profound advantages in having it negotiated by a third party. I do not think United States negotiators would be so squeamish as ours in asking for some scaling down of the total amount; and, having regard to what they would have to offer, I do not think they would be so unsuccessful.

In any case, if the authorities of that much-pressed country feel that they have any further resources which they are prepared to devote to the furthering of a general international settlement, I can think of few ways of using money which would be likely to be more fruitful than this. It would break the logjam in the progress towards convertibility. It would promote development in areas where, in the absence of some such arrangements, development would certainly be retarded. It would open to United States traders markets from which at present, by reason of the necessities of our present policies, they find themselves shut out.

All this may be wishful thinking. What is not wishful thinking, however, is the contention that the state of affairs which has prevailed up to now in regard to these obligations cannot be allowed to continue. Two years ago when some of us ventured to draw attention to the dangers of the policy then in vogue in regard to the Sterling Balances, we were thought very wild fellows indeed. Today I believe the view that there must be some change is held by most serious-minded people.

IV INTERNATIONAL CONSIDERATIONS

I must not bring these notes to an end without one concluding reflection on international policy.

From time to time, since the end of the War, Ministers have stated that our ultimate objective in international financial and commercial policy is the restoration of multilateral trade and convertibility of currencies. At the talks this summer with American Ministers these sentiments have been reiterated.

Nevertheless it is hard sometimes to resist the impression that it is all more the repetition of a formula than the expression of a strongly-felt intention. We say we are in favour of these things; yet it is difficult to believe that our actions assume them as compelling necessities of policy: if it were so, we should surely have done more; we should have tried harder to recreate the conditions in which some progress towards the goal was possible. And when we pass from the pronouncements of Ministers to the small talk of political discussion it is impossible not to recognize large bodies of opinion which, so far from wishing to achieve this objective, in fact wish to move in exactly the contrary direction. Each successive crisis is hailed as providing the pretext for finally going back on our promises and seizing the occasion to build a different kind of world, a world of regional blocs, bilateral agreements, tied finance and discriminatory trading.

In this respect there is little to choose between the parties. On the Left, the impulse springs partly from a congenital dislike of the American economic system with its disconcertingly efficient free enterprise, partly from the feeling (which has much to justify it) that, in the last analysis, there is a certain incompatibility between multilateralism and convertibility and the type of planning which has been recently in vogue in this country. On the Right, it springs partly from motives of prestige – how desirable it would be to build up our *own* economic bloc – partly from the lingering influence of the old ideology of protectionism and preference. If the ghost of Ramsay Macdonald is a powerful influence deterring Labour Ministers from recognizing their plain duty in this crisis, the ghost of Joey Chamberlain is a powerful influence deterring Conservatives from recognizing the changed facts of the twentieth century.

But if we consider matters calmly and cast away doctrinaire prepossessions, it is difficult to avoid the conclusion that all this is very mistaken. The policies of economic regionalism and discrimination are not in our long-run interest, either economic or political. They may be plausible as the desperate expedients of a confused transitional situation. But if they are made the basis of long-term planning they are likely to complete the destruction of our general position in the world.

They are not in our economic interest for two quite distinct reasons. In the first place they are inherently unstable. I do not believe that anyone who has administered the system whereby we attempt to compel people to buy from us goods which they don't particularly want in return for promises on our part to buy from them goods which we don't particularly want, all in the interest of bilateral balancing, can believe for long in its ultimate survival value. The idea that we can build up stable connections whereby other countries continue to buy our relatively high-cost goods when relatively low-cost goods are available elsewhere, is a snare and a delusion. This is a danger which more and more is likely to force itself on our attention; there is so much talk about our difficulties in dollar markets that we tend to forget that difficulties in other markets are developing too and will continue to develop if we cannot maintain ourselves in international competition. In the immediate past it may have been possible to put up some justification for arrangements of this sort because of the over-valuation of sterling and other currencies *vis-à-vis* the dollar. In such circumstances there is a real argument for the case that arrangements which discriminate against dollar goods, may prevent a contraction of trade. But, with the general revaluation of currencies, this argument loses its justification; and the precarious nature of arrangements which are based on exclusion is likely to become more and more apparent.

In the second place, this type of policy is contrary to our interest because it is likely to provoke retaliation and to interfere with forms of co-operation which promise much more for the world. Just at the moment we hear a good deal about the consolidation, on a basis of exclusion of dollar goods, of Europe and the Sterling Area. But, quite apart from the fact that there are difficult clashes of interest between the countries concerned, it is too simple by half to believe that we can go very far along this road and expect either that the Americans will go on financing such operations or will show any enthusiasm for continuing to lower their tariffs. The fact is, as Sir Eyre Crowe recognized long ago in his celebrated memorandum on the basis of British foreign policy [in 1907], that the Empire or Commonwealth is an association which can only be held together on a predominantly *non-exclusive* basis. Any attempt, singly or in concert with a small group of Western European Powers, to make it a closed system is doomed to disaster from the outset. More than any other Great Power our economic interest in the long run must stand or fall with multilateralism.

But there are even more important political reasons why we should eschew these follies and continue on the course which we have adopted in common with America. Our supreme interest in this world is the preservation of peace and the safeguarding of the values of western civilization. The idea that this can be done without the closest and most continuous co-operation with the United States is silly. The idea that such co-operation can be maintained between two Powers or groups pursuing radically different economic policies in the international sphere is dangerous. The Americans have been very willing to make allowances for all the special devices which have been forced on us by the difficulties of the transition period. But if we were seriously to deviate from our promises to pursue identical final aims, it would not be long before we began to drift apart.

Let us hope, therefore, that the discussions which have recently taken place at Washington, if they have done nothing else, have restored our determination to let nothing come before co-operation between the United States and the Commonwealth. We must not allow ourselves to be deluded by the will-o'-the-wisp of the Third Force. To preserve the Atlantic Pact and to build upon it must henceforward be the chief objective of policy in the international sphere.

V CONCLUSION

For the moment, however, our main attention must be directed to preventing our economic position so deteriorating that what we do in the international field does not matter very much to anyone. These notes must end as they began. Our situation is very serious. While we are still receiving immense subsidies from the United States, we have reached a point at which our reserves are dangerously depleted. The policy which we have adopted to meet this situation, the devaluation of the pound, by itself is quite inadequate. Unless it is accompanied by other measures it may positively increase the danger. We are now in such straits that it is quite impossible to predict with any certainty whether we shall still be solvent in a few months' time. Our standard of living, our savings, our general position in the world, are in grave peril.

To remedy this no one solution will suffice. We need to operate on a wide front with a variety of expedients. But there is one measure without which all the rest will be in vain, the definite elimination of inflationary pressure. To stop inflation, to cut down excessive expenditure, that is the supreme need of the day. The technical difficulties of doing this are not great; in present circumstances there are abundant means of preventing unwanted deflationary developments. It is only our own states of mind which stand in the way of an expeditious handling of the situation; the obstacles are all psychological. Unfortunately, states of mind can be as intractable as any material obstacle. It is still an open question whether we shall have the sense and self-control to put our house in order in time or whether we shall only learn to do so through bitter experiences in which many of the things, which have hitherto made our society, for all its faults, more tolerable than most societies in human history, may well be irrevocably destroyed.

17 The Balance of Payments

The Stamp Memorial Lecture delivered before the University of London on 20 November 1951 (London: Athlone Press, 1951).

The Trust Deed which governs these lectures affords a wide choice of subject-matter. It requires that 'the lectures shall have as their subject the application of economics and statistics to a practical problem or problems of general interest and that the subject shall be treated from a scientific and not from a party political standpoint'. But beyond the letter of the Deed, there is perhaps implicit a further obligation, namely, to choose a subject which would have been congenial to the distinguished man whom the lectures commemorate. It is not a severe limitation; for little was alien to that vivid and versatile personality. But at least to those who knew him it must be an additional principle of selection.

I hope that the subject I have chosen, the problem of the balance of payments, will satisfy these criteria. It is undoubtedly a practical problem. It should be, even if it is not, a problem of public interest. There is certainly no danger that I shall treat it from a political standpoint; for, in this connexion, I must confess that I find the policies of all parties, as disclosed in their recent manifestoes, almost equally unrealistic and almost equally distasteful. And I hope that those who knew the late Lord Stamp will agree that it is a problem which would have interested him. Indeed, it is perhaps when we think of problems like this that we are most acutely aware of what we have lost through his untimely death [in 1941]. Had Stamp and Keynes been spared to us, with their commanding influence, both on public opinion and on the intimate shaping of policy, it is difficult to believe that our position would have been as precarious as it now is.

I PRELIMINARY ELUCIDATIONS

I have claimed that my problem is a problem of practical importance. But perhaps this is not a matter which can be taken completely for granted. For it is an important part of a very important English intellectual tradition that concern with the balance of payments as such is a superfluous preoccupation; and at first sight my intention may appear in sharp contradiction with this. What economist has not read with relish Hume's famous denunciation of the mercantilist outlook which, because of unnecessary fears regarding the balance of trade, 'loaded and oppressed all commerce by a jealous and superfluous caution'?* Nor was this attitude confined to the eighteenth or nineteenth centuries. As recently as 1931 my own teacher, Edwin Cannan, delivered a lecture entitled *Balance of Trade Delusions*, of which the peroration ran:

> Even so, we manage to carry on, and whether on or off the gold standard we certainly shall not benefit by reviving the three-hundred-year-old and long-ago exploded superstition that the balance of trade must be watched over and kept right by Parliament – a superstition which can only be ranked with the once equally widespread belief that witchcraft must be smelt out and witches burnt at the stake.**

At first hearing there seems something almost absurdly incongruous between such a pronouncement and experience since it was made. But in fact such an impression is most misleading. We forget entirely the work of the classical economists if we suppose that disturbances in the balance of trade were not one of their chief preoccupations. Think, for instance, of the disputes at the time of the Restriction of Cash Payments about the Report of the Bullion Committee (incidentally, reprinted in our own day by Cannan himself),*** or the furious intellectual duels between the Currency and Banking Schools at the time of the Bank Act of 1844. What was the core of these debates but concern with possible disequilibria in the balance of payments? What was the essence of the classical doctrine regarding the gold standard but prescriptions of policy which should prevent the balance from getting out of gear?

The fact is, of course, that the attitude, so vividly represented by Cannan's peroration, rests essentially upon an implicit assumption that certain other policies are being pursued and certain other policies are being avoided. *Provided* that sound money was available, *provided* that the law relating to banking prevented practices of over-issue, *provided* that public expenditure was financed without inflation, it was the classical view that there was no point in attempting to operate *directly* on the balance of payments: and a great deal to be said against it. It was in this sense and in this sense only that concern with the balance of payments was regarded as superfluous. This may have been right or wrong – there will be more to say about that later. But it was very different from the view that the balance of payments did not matter at all – that whatever internal policies were pursued, external relations would

* 'Of the balance of trade', *Essays, moral, political and literary* (eds T.H. Green and T.H. Grose, London, 1875), p. 335.

** Sidney Ball Lecture at Oxford (Barnett House Papers No. 15, London, 1931).

*** *The Paper Pound of 1797–1821* (London, 1919).

adjust themselves automatically. That is almost the exact reverse of the central classical tradition. There is no reason, therefore, for thinking that the earlier generation of economists would have been any less interested than we are in the recent history of the British Balance of Payments or would have regarded its present condition as any less a matter of practical concern.

II THE NATURE OF THE PROBLEM

I can perhaps best approach this problem by a brief excursion into very simple theory. We talk continually nowadays about difficulties with the balance of payments. What exactly do we mean by this? And how do such difficulties arise?

Now very often when we talk this way we are simply referring to ordinary accidents such as occur, not merely to the inhabitants of special areas which keep trading accounts, but also to any individuals or groups of individuals that we can think of. A block of investments loses its value; its owners are therefore that much less able to buy the things they would like. The demand for a group of products declines; the producers of those products therefore earn less and are to that extent less able to buy goods from others. These things may happen either to individuals or groups of individuals; and many of the things that we say about the difficulties in national balances of payments are exactly of this nature.

But, for this very reason, this mode of analysis does not take us very far. The so-called balance of payments crises which occur so frequently in the modern world may, or may not, spring from causes of the kind I have mentioned. But they certainly take a quite special form. When the earning power of an individual is cut, we may indeed say that this involves a balance of payments crisis for him, in the sense that, unless someone is prepared to lend to him, he will necessarily be unable to buy so much as in the past. We may use the same terminology in regard to the affairs of a group of individuals inhabiting some local government area, whose earning power has declined *vis-à-vis* the rest of the country – for instance, the inhabitants of a mining village where the mine is gradually being closed down. But in neither of these instances do we find any monetary difficulties as such, any special difficulty in procuring means of payment for those commodities which, with a curtailed income, it is still possible to buy. You can say, if you like, that the individuals in question suffer a sterling shortage in that their incomes are less than they were before. But you cannot say that they have any difficulty in getting notes from the bank against what money they have.

But this kind of difficulty is just what happens when there are balance of payments difficulties between nations with different currencies exchanging for one another at fixed rates. This is the essence of an exchange crisis in these circumstances. There are more demands for dollars than can be met by the available supply *at the rate prevailing*. Hence, in the absence of loans from abroad, a drain of gold from the reserves and the threat of a moment when the reserves are near exhaustion, when suddenly there are no means of paying for essential imports. All this may have its ultimate cause in one or more of the kinds of misfortune which I have mentioned already. But, in the absence of separate and unco-ordinated monetary systems, it could not take this form, nor could these special complications emerge.

Let us explore this conception a little more closely, for, if I am not mistaken, it takes us to the very heart of the matter. Let us suppose that the world is divided into two countries and that the only means of making payments both within and between these two countries are metallic coins of uniform denomination. There are no banks and no credit system. In such circumstances there is no reason at all to suppose that payments between individuals in the different countries will differ in any respect from payments between individuals in the same country: a payment out means that the individual or group of individuals has that much less to spend on other things – either at home or abroad; a payment in means the reverse. Individuals or groups of individuals may, of course, overspend, in the sense that they buy more than they sell, if they draw on reserves or get loans. If their earnings fall, they may be in real difficulties as regards their standard of life. But there is never any question of this bringing about monetary complications as such – a disequilibrium between supply and demand in the exchange market. For, by hypothesis, the monetary system is completely unitary.

Exactly the same thing would happen if, instead of one metallic money of uniform denomination, there existed side by side, as it were, two types of coin of the same metallic composition – always provided that both types of coin could be freely melted and freely exported. It is true that there would now exist a primitive foreign exchange market – where gold pounds, let us say, could be turned into gold francs. But, provided that the weight of the coins was the only difference, there could still be no question of monetary difficulties of the kind that we are investigating. One country might become richer, the other poorer, as a result of shifts of demand or shifts in relative productivity; and this might cause difficulties in the labour market and perhaps social unrest. But it is not to be supposed that the mere fact that the common metal in use was stamped into disks of different weight in the different countries could give rise to any difficulty in procuring either means of payment for anyone who was willing to offer the other.

Now change the picture. Install a separate credit system in each country, with separate central banks and separate treasuries each able to bend to their will the financial policy of these banks. At once the possibilities of the situation are

altered. Instead of the means of payment in each country being to all intents and purposes one system, there are now two systems with the possibility in each of independent tendencies in the levels of money income and expenditure. There is the possibility that income and expenditure in one country may be maintained at levels which bring it about that, at a fixed rate of exchange, there can persist an excess of demand over the supply of means of payment in the other money.

Now, of course, this need not be. If credit systems are managed so that the relative levels of income and expenditure in each country correspond roughly to what they would have been under a unitary system, then such difficulties will not emerge. (This, of course, was the intention, though by no means always the result, of arrangements under the gold standard.) But assume that this does not happen. Assume that the treasury in one country is borrowing at a rate which permits an increase of local expenditure more rapid than the increase of expenditure abroad and that there is no gain in relative productivity to justify this increase. Or, alternatively, assume that, if demand for the product of one of the countries falls off, then, for reasons of internal policy, the treasury there compels the central bank to take steps to replace, by a new creation of credit, the means of payment which otherwise would disappear. At once, in either of these cases, you have all the essentials of a modern balance of payments crisis. The seamless robe of a unitary monetary system is divided. Excess payments out involve no automatic reduction of spending power within. There is no presumption of any equilibrating mechanism. Equilibrium, if it occurs, is a matter of pure fluke.

Now, of course, there is nothing new about this analysis. In the essay from which I quoted earlier, Hume goes out of his way to allude to the credit system as a possible cause of disequilibrium. 'I scarcely know any method of sinking money below its level', he says, 'but those institutions of banks, funds, and paper credit, which are so much practised in this kingdom'. The Bullionist literature was in its essence a protest against a credit policy which had failed to keep internal spending at a level which would preserve the rate of exchange with other currencies unaltered. And whatever the crudities of the Currency School, it is clear that their protests and their constructive suggestions were based essentially upon an analysis which showed that, if internal expenditure were not kept in step with external conditions, difficulties in the exchange market would result. To say that because they rejected direct control of trade, the classical economists were blind to the problem of the balance of payments is to miss the central significance of what is perhaps the most permanent part of their system.

Let me pursue the analysis one stage further. It will now lead speedily to a point at which applications become possible.

It is a corollary of what I have just said that, given a fixed rate of exchange, there is always a level of internal prices and incomes at which the balance of payments would tend to equilibrium. It follows, therefore, that if there is disequilibrium, for any long period of time, this ideal level has been missed. The independent systems have not been co-ordinated so as to work as a single system. In this very important sense, therefore, we can say that disequilibrium in the balance of payments and a shortage of foreign exchange are *always* consequences of financial policy. This is not necessarily to argue that that financial policy was wrong; it is easy to conceive circumstances in which it might be sensible to follow such a course. It is to argue, however, that there is always a financial policy which would avoid this kind of trouble.

But at this point it is necessary to draw a further distinction, which I hope may bring some small comfort to those who have felt aggrieved by what you may think the one-sided rigour of my present conclusions. The persistence of external disequilibrium can always be attributed to a failure of financial policy. But it does not follow that the initiating cause is always financial. This is not implied in the least. The initial cause may be financial or it may be otherwise. It would be financial in this sense if there were a local expansion of income and expenditure not accompanied by a corresponding increase of output at home or some other favourable circumstance. It would be non-financial in this sense if there were some falling off in demand for our exports, or some loss of foreign assets, which involved a diminution in the supply of foreign exchange becoming available. In this second case, it would be the failure of finance to *react* to the changes in the real situation which was a condition of the persistence of the trouble; and in this sense the proposition that persisting disequilibrium is always the consequence of inappropriate financial policy would be true. But it would not be true to say that finance was the origin of the trouble, save in the very sophisticated sense that, if there were not separate financial systems, this particular kind of trouble could never emerge.

III THE SPECIAL STERLING PROBLEM

So much by way of general preliminaries. Let me now try to tackle the interpretation of our post-war history, with its persistent difficulties with the balance of payments and its acute crises at more or less regular intervals.

Now, in the course of this interpretation I shall be saying a good deal about our financial policy – or lack of policy. I should, therefore, like to begin by making it quite clear that I do not question for a moment the non-financial origin of many of our difficulties – using this phrase in the sense I have just tried to make clear. Our difficulties with the balance of payments undoubtedly spring in very large measure from adverse circumstances which are not, in the first instance, financial.

Having said this, I hope it is not necessary in this context for me to enter into any great detail. I must confess to a certain sense of desolation nowadays when I encounter yet again the hackneyed tale of misfortunes which we have heard so often from a thousand public platforms. For my purpose this evening, I am tempted to say with Macaulay that 'every schoolboy knows' that during the war we cut down our export industries to a bare minimum and that we sold substantial slices of our foreign property; that, when the war was over there were further drains on our purse in the shape of heavy relief and military expenditure; and that, since then, there have been still further acute embarrassments in the shape of steeply rising prices of essential imports and the losses we have suffered from the depredations of Dr. Moussadeq.*

Perhaps, however, there is another complication which deserves rather less perfunctory mention. The circumstances which I have already enumerated were certainly sufficient to set us a severe problem of adjustment. Our difficulties have been still further aggravated by the policies we have adopted in respect of debt repayment and capital export. While we were borrowing abroad on a gigantic scale and receiving, on top of that, extraordinary gifts in the shape of Marshall aid, we deliberately chose to repay old debt and to make new exports of capital on a scale which in fact, up to late in 1949, absorbed a very substantial proportion of our new borrowing and the free assistance we received. The wisdom of this course has always seemed to me highly questionable – especially in regard to debt repayment. I should never favour repudiation. But it has never seemed to me obvious, for instance, that we were under any special obligation to make very great sacrifices to repay at an extraordinary rate the debts incurred in the preparations for Alamein; and I have never found very convincing the argument that there were esoteric political reasons for such a course, unsuitable for public discussion, but shortly to be justified by gratifying improvements in our relations with the parties concerned. But, be that as it may, there can be no doubt that our general policy in this respect involved a considerable addition to the list of obstacles to our struggle towards equilibrium.

The list is a formidable one; and those who find in the misfortunes of economic life nothing but the play of perverse accident and bad luck – it is a frame of mind peculiarly congenial to whoever happens to be in power – can find ample grounds for self-deception in our history since 1945. But for those of us who are not in power and whose business it is to find causes rather than culprits, this mode of approach is insufficient. Undoubtedly the external difficulties have been severe. But this does not explain our failure to meet

* The nationalization of the Iranian oil refineries in March 1951.

them. We might well expect that they would affect our standard of living. But there is nothing in the nature of things which should lead us to expect that they should cause a persistent shortage of foreign exchange. It is surely a very poor view of the limits of policy and organisation to assume that we can only keep going when nothing untoward occurs. If a car fails to reach its destination, if it is continually running into the side, or if it is continually having to solicit hauls from passing lorries, we should not regard it as a sufficient explanation that the roads are not level and straight, that there are hills to ascend and corners to turn. And, indeed, when one examines this assumption in detail, it is sometimes a little difficult to conceive any circumstances in which, in present moods, we could be expected to prosper. American prices fall a few points; and we are compelled to devalue thirty per cent. American prices rise and we are again in the utmost embarrassment. In this frame of mind, surely, we postulate, as the condition of health and survival, a constancy of economic climate only realizable on totally air-conditioned planets. Therefore, before we resign ourselves to the view that we have done all that could have been done and that everything that has happened has been unavoidable calamity, it is desirable to inquire a little further concerning the mechanisms which have been operative and the policies that have been in vogue. Our inquiry is not limited to the problem why there have been disturbing influences. Even more important is the problem why these influences have not been met by a sufficient response.

To this problem, the theory which I have already developed affords the suggestion of a solution. If difficulties persist in the exchange market, there is a strong presumption that the internal financial conditions have been incompatible with the requirements of external equilibrium. And if we survey the policies which we know to have been followed, there seems strong confirmation of this presumption. I do not say that internal affairs have been managed with *no* regard to the external balance. That would be going too far. But it is at least clear that there has been more than one objective and that, where considerations of external equilibrium have clashed with domestic policy, they have usually had to go by the board. It is clear too that the traditional mechanism for securing harmony between internal and external conditions has been completely out of action. In so far as attempts have been made to adapt internal expenditure to the requirements of external balance, it has been *via* the budget and the direct control of investment, rather than through operation on the volume of means of payment available. The mechanism of monetary control has been out of action. The supply of money and credit has been almost completely passive to the so-called needs of business. The shades of Tooke and Fullarton have reigned triumphant in Great George Street.

Let me try to be rather more specific. It is not unfair to say that the frame of mind in which we entered the post-war period was very unfavourable to any reversion to pre-war financial policies in regard to external equilibrium. There were budgetary reasons for regarding with some apprehension a rise in the level of interest rates; and there were strong political prejudices (not confined to any one political party) against the disciplines of the gold standard. But at the same time the idea of a free pound, the idea of equilibration by continuous changes of exchange rates, encountered very general disfavour; it was, moreover, ruled out by our membership of the International Monetary Fund. There was, therefore, from the outset, the possibility of a conflict of policies. It must not be thought, however, that the connexion between internal and external conditions was altogether neglected; the pained surprise of a former Chancellor that the home trade was so good and the balance of payments position so difficult was probably unique among people in positions of responsibility. The guiding idea seems to have been that, if inflation could be held in check sufficiently, then probably the development of affairs at home and abroad would enable the fixed rate to be held. I imagine that this was the view which prevailed both in 1946, once the Keynes loan had been secured, and again in 1949, when the first attempt to maintain a fixed rate had broken down and a new start had been made by devaluation.

Such hopes were perhaps not entirely unreasonable. At the end of the war we had secured a promise of assistance which would enable us to hold the position without positive contraction, while our export trade expanded. American prices and costs were rising; had we succeeded in keeping stable our own level of prices and costs, it does not seem unplausible to argue that we might gradually have come into equilibrium by reason of the expansion elsewhere. That was a splendid opportunity missed. Similarly, in 1949 when devaluation had taken place, there was a position which offered hope in this respect. In the absence of further inflation, a thirty per cent devaluation, surely, gave considerable elbow room to re-establish external balance.

In the event, however, these hopes have been disappointed. The inflationary pressure has not been sufficiently checked. In 1946–47 there was the overt folly of the ultra-cheap money policy, which, together with some laxity as regards the export of capital, culminated in the crisis of 1947. Then, for a time, a determined effort was made and our hopes began to revive. But, in the winter of 1948–49, inflationary pressure again tended to become active; and the development of a very mild recession in the United States found us still so fundamentally weak that a major devaluation was necessary. Once more some initial effort was made to damp down the pressure; and in 1950 a most gratifying improvement took place. Then the coming of rearmament once more strengthened the incipient upward movement at home; and abroad it turned the terms of trade against us *via* the movement of raw material prices. A position existed, indeed, in which some positive curtailment of expenditure was desirable if external equilibrium was to be maintained. The measures which were adopted, however, fell far short of what was necessary; and today we are confronting a drain on our reserves as formidable as that of 1947 – out of balance this time, not only with the dollar area but also – a new development this – with the rest of the world as well.

From this record of failure I deduce two lessons. First that the method of adjustment through budgetary policy is subject to severe political limitations. In conditions such as have prevailed here since the war, with the old sources of saving curtailed by income redistribution, extraordinary budget surpluses were necessary if there was to be any hope of stability: and, although something was done in that direction, it was patently not enough. There are doubtless some who will attribute this to some exceptional lack of courage on the part of the governments that have been in power. For myself, I should be interested to discover whether more courage would have been shown by alternative governments. And anyway – it may be the baseness of middle-age creeping in – I confess I am beginning to have very slender confidence in a system where the maintenance of essential stability depends upon extraordinary courage and integrity on the part of *all* the governments *all* the time.

But, secondly, politics apart, does not all this experience show how clumsy and inadequate an instrument is budgetary policy, if operated by itself? I say nothing against policy of this kind in conjunction with other measures. Indeed I am sure that we cannot afford to dispense with it: in present circumstances, the rate of interest necessary to restrain outlay without a substantial budget surplus would be very inconvenient. But when it is a matter of maintaining external equilibrium in a situation in which conditions of external supply and demand are continually changing surely the probabilities are that budgetary policy *by itself* will only succeed as a matter of lucky accident. But that is the system upon which we have been relying. We have thrown overboard, as old-fashioned scrap, all the delicate mechanism of financial control which the experience of ages was gradually fashioning. In a situation where there is an obvious scarcity of capital, we have more or less frozen the interest structure. As for any regulation of the conditions of credit in accordance with the requirements of external balance, that has been the least likely thing in the world. In the circumstances, we have been perhaps lucky to get off as well as we have. If I may revert to my motoring simile, we have been attempting to drive our car through this difficult post-war country with the steering gear out of action, the wheels lashed rigidly in one direction, our only means of equilibration an occasional stop, every few months, for the wheels to be unlashed and turned at another angle – while ministers stand on the roof and deliver salutary exhortations.

IV CURRENT PANACEAS

What then are we to do? Before I proceed to draw the moral from what I have said already, it may perhaps be useful to pass in review certain popular solutions.

(a) Increased Production

Take first increased productivity. Once it is realized that there is a problem at all and that talk of difficulties with the balance of payments is not a mere political trick, it is a natural impulse to recommend an increase of productivity. To pay our way we must work harder and organize more efficiently; how often have we heard this injunction – and how little it has influenced our behaviour!

Now heaven forbid that you should think that I think poorly of increased production. I am sure that in present circumstances we need every ounce that we can get out of the machine. In certain industries, indeed, some increase is a prime condition of the success of any general policy. I can think of no single event which would do more to assist recovery than an increase in the production of coal. It is no exaggeration to say that an additional 20 million tons per annum would transform the possibilities of the situation – both here and in Western Europe. But on this subject I have been perhaps in danger of making myself a bore ever since the winter of 1946;* and in view of the approach of a severe fuel shortage this winter, it would be tedious to elaborate further.

Unfortunately, there is no guarantee in the nature of things that increased productivity by itself is likely to provide a permanent solution to our problem. For, first, we should note that an absolute increase of productivity, even at a comparatively smart pace, carries with it no necessary promise of any easement at all. If a parallel increase is taking place elsewhere and the movements of money income are also parallel, the position will be unaffected. To be effective the change must be not only absolute but relative. Our productivity must advance in relation to income more rapidly than elsewhere. This does not make the desirability of increase any the less – quite the contrary indeed. But it certainly suggests that to rely on increased productivity alone is to run the risk of serious disappointment.

But beyond this, it must be realized that there are many circumstances in which such a solution is not within the realm of practical possibility – even

* See pp. 209–12, 221.

supposing that productivity can be increased by mere exhortation. Let us suppose, for instance, an internal change in the value of money, in the shape of, say, a fifty per cent depreciation – not a wild supposition; worse than this has often happened. Is it really to be supposed that the most stupendous ingenuity, either of government or of business, could bring about an increase in productivity sufficient to offset this before the exchange market was hopelessly upset? Or suppose an extensive falling off in demand for a very important group of exports, such as the collapse of American demand for Japanese silk in the late twenties. Is it plausible to argue that increased productivity alone could re-establish equilibrium? Doubtless, in all such cases, to the extent to which productivity increases, the other changes which may be necessary are diminished in magnitude; and this makes increased production a prime *desideratum*. But to argue that in all circumstances it is the one thing necessary is to over-simplify almost to the point of childishness. And I would add, it does no benefit to the good cause of increased production if it is always being invoked as the god in the machine in cases where it is obviously insufficient.

(b) Direct Controls

But what about direct control, the system now in vogue? What about the regulation of the external balance through exchange control and the quantitative planning of imports and exports?

Again, before coming to my main point, I must guard against misapprehension. I will not conceal from you that I share the classical view that, as a rule, this is a cumbersome and superfluous policy. My Utopia does not lie in that prison-house. But I am far from believing that there are no circumstances in which policies of this sort are expedient; and indeed, in our position since the war I believe that some emergency measures of this sort have been unavoidable.

Thus, for instance, in present circumstances, I do not believe that all forms of exchange control could have been dispensed with. I have no particular liking for the way in which the control has been worked – which is extremely hard on migrating academics who wish to take the price of a low-grade dwelling-house to America, and extremely easy with certain former allies. I think that, if the problem of overseas debt had been handled differently, and if certain other desirable financial policies had been adopted, all this could have been run on a much lighter rein. But I cannot believe that, unless our reserve position had been very considerably stronger, we should have been prudent to dismantle the apparatus altogether.

Similarly, I have no desire to adopt a doctrinaire attitude to the quantitative control of imports. I have no love for these controls. I believe, with Professor

Meade, that in the long run there is nothing desirable that they can do which cannot be done by less clumsy methods. But I am far from thinking that there are no circumstances where they are not necessary as emergency measures. At the present time, for instance, when our reserves are in such immediate danger, there is a strong case for direct action on imports, while financial policy gets into action.

But having said all this by way of precluding misunderstanding, I now want to say very emphatically that, in my judgement, direct planning of the external balance is a policy with very severe limitations, even if it be judged solely by its effectiveness in this context and no regard be had to its other economic and political tendencies – which are nearly always bad.

For in the first place, although you can plan the quantities which you propose to import, you cannot plan either the prices you will have to pay or the amount which you can earn by export. It is the essence of international trade that the peoples of other countries are involved; and unilateral control over such transactions is in the nature of things impossible. That perhaps is one of the reasons why collectivists, from Plato onwards, have tended to be averse to international trade and to favour policies of autarky.

But, beyond this, there is the difficulty of administration. It is a fact of experience that direct control of this sort always tends to be behind the gun. The process of decision-making cannot be continuous. The plan cannot be altered from day to day. It is only when a crisis is on the way that action is taken – and that in circumstances when small adjustments are ruled out by the nature of the problem. Hence the vulgar spectacular nature of this side of economic life nowadays, with its big men flying about wildly in aeroplanes, its grandiose conferences, its last-minute compromises, and its penumbra of high politics even over consignments of canned meat and sardines.

These drawbacks are not imaginary. The difficulties of controlling external transactions directly are well borne out by our own experience. A perusal of official predictions is a most salutary check on any great optimism regarding our capacity to plan our lives in this way. In 1947, for instance, the predicted adverse balance was of the order of £350 million; in fact it was nearly twice this figure. In the present year we were warned that our surplus might disappear and perhaps incur a 'small' deficit; in fact we are tending to a deficit of something more like the 1947 magnitude. Nor do I think that this necessarily results from deficiencies on the part of those who prepare the estimates: some of the ablest members of the public service are concerned with these matters. The fact is that, in a world so subject to uncertainty as ours, global prognosis of this sort is impossible. It is like trying to foretell the weather for the next twelve months. Anyone who claims to be able to do so, should be automatically suspect. Hence all policy which is limited to adjustments at relatively long intervals is impotent. The thing is a snare and a delusion. When we hear, as we do from crisis to crisis, of great reliance on such plans, we should be alarmed rather than reassured; they carry with them a strong presumption that quite inadequate policies are in contemplation. What is needed in this connexion is not a pretentious attempt to map the unknowable and then to nail the economic system to this map until it is proved false, but rather some mechanism which from day to day is sensitive to change and produces adjustments to adverse movements when they are still small and do not call for heroic all-or-nothing measures.

FURTHER THOUGHTS ON POLICY

Where then is such a mechanism to be found?

The analysis which I developed earlier might seem to suggest that the obvious course was to revive a monetary policy which was conducted with a full regard to the external balance. When in surplus expand, when in deficit contract: there are many conceivable variants of mechanism; but that must be the chief rule of monetary systems which attempt to maintain external balance at fixed rates of exchange; and that is a rule which we must adopt ourselves, if the pound is not to drop still further.

In recent years, however, such systems have been very much out of favour. It is in any case somewhat alien to our post-war way of thinking that internal policy should pay heed to the international position – why should the realization of our dreams be broken by outside realities? But, beyond that, the argument which has done most to discredit such systems has been the argument that, to keep thus in step with developments elsewhere might mean the import of deflation and mass unemployment.

This argument is formally correct – and in certain circumstances the danger which it indicates might be a real one. But it is characteristic of the poor thought of our day that it has had most influence at a time when it was supremely irrelevant. Whatever the dangers to our position in the post-war period, the import of mass unemployment has not been one of them. There has been no deflation and mass unemployment in the United States; on the contrary, there has been one of the most intense and long-lasting booms in history. During this period at least, any adaptations which we should have had to make in the interests of equilibrium would have been adaptations, not to monetary, but to real changes. If we had had to contract it would have been, not because of deflation elsewhere but rather because real scarcities in a world of full employment compelled a contraction of our claims on world production.

Nevertheless, even in such circumstances, adaptations by way of changes in the volume of domestic expenditure may be painful. The rigidity downwards of the contract system is notorious. Adaptations upwards are all right. But an adaptation to a worsening may encounter all sorts of resistances. It is for this reason that in recent years there has arisen a powerful school of thought which favours the free exchange as a mechanism of external equilibration. Let us maintain freedom for internal policies of stability, it is said, and let what external adaptations are necessary come by way of movements in the rate of exchange rather than by movements in the volume of income.

There is much force in this position. Indeed, compared to the position of the muddleheads who think that you can do what you like internally and yet at the same time (without aid from America) maintain a fixed rate of exchange, it is enlightenment itself. Some of the most able, some of the most penetrating minds of our age have seen in such arrangements the monetary system of the future. The major work recently published by Professor Meade furnishes powerful arguments for this solution.*

Now I should be very sorry to argue that there are never conditions in which some movement of rates of exchange are preferable to internal contractions. When a system or group of systems has got badly out of line with the rest of the world, then there may be force in the argument that an alteration of exchange rates will cause less dislocation than internal contraction. If I am not mistaken, that was a very relevant argument in 1949.

But it is one thing to acknowledge that there may sometimes be a necessity for adjustments of this sort. It is quite another to accept them as the general mechanism of equilibration. The argument for occasional medicine is not the same as the argument for daily bread. And while I am far from wishing to show a closed mind on this exceedingly difficult question, I confess that I can think of certain considerations which make the picture somewhat less attractive than it seems at first blush.

In the first place, it seems to me important to remember that although a system of this sort may enable us to avoid some downward movements of income, it does not render unnecessary internal financial vigilance: it does not enable us to avoid some upward movements in interest rates and some overbalancing the budget, if external conditions become adverse. I am sure that this has not been overlooked by the high authorities I have mentioned; but I suspect that it is often forgotten by the general public. If there is no brake on expansion when the rate of exchange moves, the probable effect is simply that the rise in import prices is gradually diffused through the system and the beneficial influence of the initial change in the rate of exchange is frustrated. That is one of the things which has been happening to us recently.

---

* J.E. Meade, *The Theory of International Economic Policy, Vol. I: The Balance of Payments* (London, 1951).

It would be a delusion to suppose that the policy of the variable exchange permits completely painless adjustments.

But, secondly, and this comes even nearer home, the suitability of the system seems to depend in part upon the nature of the financial centre to which it is applied. It is easy to see that, for a small centre, the policy of the variable exchange may sometimes be the best way of establishing external balance. Certainly in such centres this device has often been used; and although some expectations have been disappointed and some wealth spilt, the stability of the world has not been greatly shaken. But, surely, new considerations are relevant when the same policy is proposed for a great financial centre, where other countries are in the habit of keeping reserves and whose money provides the medium in which an extensive volume of international trade is transacted. Here the movement of the rate of exchange is a much more serious matter. If it is a single discontinuous change, such as the devaluation of 1949, it is a major event in financial history. If it is a matter of day-to-day fluctuation, it creates new kinds of uncertainty.

Now this is exactly the position of London today; and it seems to me that any discussion of policy which does not take full account of these complications runs some danger of ignoring essential facts. I myself do not regard the existing sterling area arrangements as sacrosanct; I think we have made some sacrifices to these arrangements which are very hard to justify. But I do not think we should lightly assume that it does not matter if you break up the sterling area – that it does not matter to the world and that it does not matter to our interest. I am clear that without the sterling area, or some substitute for it, the economic life of the world would be even more chaotic than it is at present. I am clear too that, if London ceased to be a centre of international business, we should lose a good deal of other business as well, and the adjustments necessary to keep our balance of payments in order would be even more extensive and arduous. But it is not at all clear to me that the sterling area can be run, year in year out, on the basis of a fluctuating pound. I find it hard to believe that, for us, at any rate, all the problems of external economic balance are to be solved by movements of the exchange rate.

In this, however, I am quite prepared to admit that I may be wrong – at least as regards the distant future. I am much less disposed, however, to suspend judgement as regards the needs of the present situation. Here at least, I am quite definitely against any attempt to solve the problem by further alteration of the exchange. Given what had already happened at home and abroad, I was definitely in favour of devaluation in 1949. I should not be in favour of another devaluation in 1951. Nor should I be in favour of unpegging the exchange and allowing things to find their own level. Whatever may be advisable when internal politics are free from inflationary tendencies and when the rest of the world has full confidence in sterling, in present circumstances to abandon the rate (which only a few months ago was said to be too low) would seem to me an act of great unwisdom. And I am quite sure that it would be so interpreted in foreign markets on whose opinion, whether we like it or not, so much of our stability depends. I think we should fight for the pound at its present rate by all the means at our disposal; and among these means are the traditional mechanisms for control of the volume of credit. Therefore I welcome the steps which have recently been taken to put these mechanisms in operation – though I should be disingenuous if I let you believe that I thought that, as yet, we have gone nearly far enough along that road.

But that, I know, is a controversial view; and I would not end on such a note. What I hope is not controversial is the urgent necessity, by some means or other, of arresting the tendency to inflation which frustrates all our efforts towards recovery. We may perhaps still dispute about the means but, at this time of day, surely, we cannot still disagree about the end. Stop the inflation, stop it at all costs: that is the paramount need of the moment in the economic sphere. If we meet it (which we can do very easily, if only we have a mind to do so), we have still a future of high promise. If we do not, then I fear that our days are numbered, certainly as a great power, perhaps even as a stable society.

present circumstances to abandon the rate pegged only a few months ago [illegible]

18 The International Economic Problem

From *Lloyds Bank Review*, new series no. 27 (January 1953), pp. 1–24.

The following notes do not pretend in any way to be a detailed plan of action. But since, in the next few months, in consequence of the change of administration in the United States and the conclusions reached by the recent meeting of Commonwealth ministers, we are likely to be confronted with many international discussions and many plans of action, it seems worth while trying to get into some sort of perspective the main problems with which they will all be concerned. The fundamental standpoint is local and pedestrian. Each problem and each proposal is judged from the point of view of the U.K. interest; and that interest is estimated, not as it might be in a perfectly rational world, but rather as it is in the world of the present day with its manifold imperfections and its desperate irrationalities.

I POLITICAL ASSUMPTIONS

It is this mode of approach which leads me, in a survey which is primarily concerned with economic questions, to begin with a political proposition. It is this: that *the ultimate test of any proposal which emerges in the economic sphere is the question whether it is conducive to the political unity and strength of the Western Alliance and its associates*.

The reason for this is plain. For our generation at least the world is irrevocably divided. There is no reasonable hope of achieving peaceful co-operation with the Soviet *Bloc*; the one hope of avoiding actual war is that the countries of the West should be sufficiently strong and sufficiently united to make it obvious to the other side that there is no chance of success that way. But this means, not merely the co-ordination of defence, but also the elimination of causes of disunity; and some of these causes may be economic.

Now it is doubtless very easy to exaggerate the role of the economic factor in the generation of positive conflict. It is unlikely, for instance, that at the present day the United Kingdom and the United States would go to war with one another on account of obstacles to trade. But it is easy, too, to underestimate the degree to which the operation of such causes may prevent political unity. To imagine that year in, year out, the Western Alliance can be kept strong and effective between regional *blocs* which are barricading themselves against each other's goods and between which there is no personal intercourse save one-sided tourism and the special relations of staff officers and V.I.Ps. is to live in a fool's paradise. This is not to say that we shall not have to rub along in a situation which falls far short of perfection in these respects. But it is to say that it is silly to take more risks than are absolutely necessary: it is to say also that the nearer we can get to economic relations which are mutually harmonious the easier it will be to achieve the requisite degree of political unity.

II THE ALLEGED INEVITABILITY OF DISEQUILIBRIUM

But are such relations possible? Is it conceivable that the nations of Western Europe should achieve a trading position *vis-à-vis* the United States and Canada in which the equilibrium of their balance of payments does not depend on a continued flow of gifts and a barrage of quantitative restrictions against dollar goods? Before we can go further this question must be examined. For, of course, if the answer were negative, if no mutually satisfactory economic relations were possible, then the whole conception of international co-operation would be altered; and although the contention that it is negative has come chiefly from men of ill-will whom it is not worth while taking very seriously, chronic Americanophobes anxious for personal or political reasons to disrupt the Western Alliance, they are not its only supporters either at home or abroad. The belief that equilibrium is impossible between the dollar area and the rest of the world has sometimes been held by some of the most sensitive and generous minds on the opposite side of the Atlantic, anxious to persuade their fellow countrymen to acquiesce in the attenuated and artificial relations which they fear to be the most that can be hoped for in a world so constituted as ours.

It is my belief that these fears are largely, if not wholly, groundless; and that where it is possible to conceive the possibility of lasting disharmony, it is possible also to conceive the measures which would remove it. But to show this it is necessary to examine a little the arguments by which this position is supported. Under what conditions would mutually advantageous economic relations be impossible, or at least so politically hard of achievement as to be to all intents and purposes impossible?

Let us begin with the easy cases. We can all agree that if, every time the rest of the world showed signs of increasing exports to the United States, Congress were to impose additional obstacles to import, any hope of solving our problems that way would be at an end. It is a little difficult to swallow the claim that this truism, so excruciatingly obvious as to be scarcely worth mentioning, is a discovery of recent date, hitherto overlooked by the myopia of international liberalism. But there is no doubt that it is true.

Similarly, we can all agree that if the financial system in the United States were so inherently unstable that, at frequent intervals, aggregate expenditure showed a tendency to disastrous collapse, as in 1932–33, close association would have profound disadvantages. This is not to say that any tendency to moderate oscillation in those parts is a valid pretext for economic isolationism elsewhere; that is a very unconvincing position with which I have no sympathy whatever. But it is to admit that if there were a probability of the recurrence of strong deflationary tendencies in the United States, then many otherwise reasonable hopes would be frustrated. It is not easy to see what could be done about it – short of persuading the Americans to put their own house in order; for economic insulation is something which it is easier to talk about than to achieve. But certainly it would lend attractions to all sorts of policies which otherwise have little to commend them.

So far the discussion is on common ground. But now it is necessary to take account of an argument which cuts even deeper. Let us suppose that there exist instruments for restraining the increase of the U.S. tariff. Let us suppose, further, that there is no serious fear of deflation. Even so, say the pessimists, while productivity in the United States is so much greater than elsewhere and advances so much faster, equilibrium is improbable. The dollar problem, they say, is not a by-product of post-war dislocation and unwise fiscal policies; it is rather something inherent in the fundamental technical structure of the contemporary world which no financial policy which is politically feasible (or advisable) could hope to overcome.

What truth is there in all this? There is obviously nothing in the view that there are inherent disadvantages in trade as such between groups of different degrees of productivity. Quite the contrary indeed: the great principle of the division of labour is founded on just such differences; if there were no differences in productivity there would be no advantage in trade. And it is not difficult to show that, whatever these differences may be, there is always some relationship between money incomes in the groups concerned at which trade is mutually advantageous. If, for example, productivity in the United States were twice as high as elsewhere but incomes were only one and a half times as high, doubtless trade would tend to be one-sided. But supposing that, with productivity in the United States still only twice as high as elsewhere, money incomes were three times as high, then surely the currents of trade would tend to be reversed. This example is not intended to prove anything regarding the actual state of affairs at the present day. But it should suggest that trade relationships are a matter of relative costs and prices; and that if there is fundamental advantage in division of labour, then it is always conceivable that a relation of prices and costs could be achieved which would enable this advantage to be realized.

Now there is nothing in the notion of shifting rates of productivity or shifting conditions of international demand which upsets this principle. It is quite true that technical changes may bring it about that the potential position of the members of a national group is worse relatively and perhaps absolutely than it was before. But it still remains true that, whatever these changes, the situation can be better with trade than without it. The so-called principle of comparative advantage does not promise indefinite or continuous advance. It merely offers the opportunity of making the most of any given position – which, of course, may be merely making the most of a position which has seriously worsened. There is, therefore, nothing in the mere fact of differing rates of technical advance to upset the presumption of potential advantage in trade.

The difficulties, if difficulties there be, must therefore arise in the mechanism of adjustment. And indeed it is just here that it is not at all difficult to imagine circumstances in which an increase in the relative productivity of a national group, such as the United States, may impose serious and, indeed, intolerable inconvenience elsewhere. Suppose, for instance, that, as in the elementary examples of the text-books, the money supply of the world is fixed and that the modes of making payment in the various countries are also unvarying. In order that there may be equilibrium in trade, then, according to a well-known proposition of Ricardo's, it must be distributed between the different national areas in such a way as will reflect the differences of the values of the national products. Suppose now a shift in relative productivities; then, in order that equilibrium may be preserved, there must be a redistribution of the money stock so as to reflect the changes in the relative values of the national products. Now as the total money stock is fixed, this will involve an absolute increase of money income in the centres of increasing productivity and – and here's the rub – an absolute diminution in money income elsewhere. Obviously this may involve great difficulties for the centres where relative productivity has changed adversely. It is still ultimately an advantage for them to be in equilibrium with the rest of the world, for there is more to be got by participating in the international division of labour than by withdrawing from it. But the process of getting there may be intolerably painful.

Here, then, is the ultimate nightmare of the insulationists. And it may be freely conceded that, if the world were likely to work like this, there would be ground for their apprehensions. But, in fact, the conditions assumed are not very likely; and, in any case, they are quite unnecessary.

It should be clear from what has been said already that the essential condition for balanced trade is an appropriate relation between incomes in the different areas concerned; so that when the value of the product in one country increases relatively to the value of the product elsewhere, there is a shift in relative incomes. Now in the example given above – the example designed to make one's flesh creep – this shift takes place by expansion in one area and contraction elsewhere – as indeed it must, on the assumption of a fixed stock of money in the world and fixed habits of payment. But change this fundamental assumption and the whole appearance of things changes also. Remove the limitation that the money supply is fixed. Then it is easy to conceive a rate of increase which permits equilibrium to be reached without the pressure of contraction in the areas where productivity is advancing less rapidly. All that is necessary is for the increase in money supply to go to the centres where productivity is advancing more rapidly. Then the requisite change in the relation between levels of money incomes – the relative rise in the more rapidly advancing area – can come about merely by an increase there, incomes elsewhere remaining constant or advancing less rapidly.

The fact is that this bogey of a centre of superior productivity continually exercising a deflationary pressure elsewhere is only plausible if we assume monetary conditions which have seldom prevailed for any long period and which, in any case, need not prevail at all. How often in the course of modern history have the inhabitants of national areas been under the necessity of positive contraction of money incomes in order to get into international equilibrium – if they have not previously had a private inflation of their own? There have indeed been such cases; but it is difficult to believe that they are typical. The model is too static. The world does not work on the basis of a fixed money supply. If the conditions of equilibrium require relative shifts of the kind under discussion, there are many ways of bringing them about which do not involve the insulationist nightmare. To break the civilized world into two, to construct rival economic *blocs* within the area of the Western Alliance on the ground that this might conceivably happen, is not sensible. If we think that there is danger of its happening, the thing to do is to take direct steps to prevent it. But to act as if it were necessary is the limit of economic hypochondria.

But let us quit the realm of hypothesis and resume our findings by reference to fact. From what has been said already, it appears that there are three main possibilities which would frustrate any effort on the part of the rest of the world to get into equilibrium with the dollar area:

(*a*) A persistent rise in the U.S. tariff or other obstacles to trade *pari passu* with any potential improvement in exports to that area.
(*b*) An endemic tendency to severe deflationary collapse in the dollar area.
(*c*) A failure in that area for money income to rise commensurately with productivity.

To what extent have these theoretical possibilities been actual?

The answer is evident: they have no counterpart in the history of the post-war world.

(*a*) There has been no important rise in the U.S. tariff. Save for relatively minor lapses, the tendency has been downwards. The average level of the U.S. tariff today is considerably below what it was before the Hawley–Smoot tariff of 1930.

(*b*) There has been no tendency to catastrophic deflation in the U.S. economy. On the contrary, the tendency has been distinctly in the opposite direction. Since 1945 money incomes have risen more than productivity.

(*c*) It follows, therefore, that it is most improbable that the conditions of international equilibrium were such as to require a contraction of money incomes elsewhere *below* the levels of 1945. The trouble has been rather that, in the countries where the advance of productivity has been less than in the United States, the advance of money incomes has tended to be excessive. The conditions have been the reverse of the conditions of the insulationist's nightmare. Yet he continues to urge us to act as if it were true.

III THE LIMITS OF IMPERIAL PREFERENCE

If the foregoing arguments are correct the case for the formation of regional *blocs* loses much of its plausibility. If there is no inevitability of disequilibrium between the dollar area and the rest of the world, then we are still free to choose and the political presumption against more disunity than necessary, which was argued earlier on, continues to hold the field. But there remain other pleas for regional grouping which, not depending upon these arguments, deserve examination by themselves; in particular, there are the arguments for Imperial Preference which antedate the dollar problem by many a long day.

Now Imperial Preference is a fact. The preferential system is a going concern; and, whether or not we think the developments of 1932 were a particularly good thing, they are now part and parcel of our arrangements. There is no reason why they should be further modified or changed save in so far as there is clear advantage in such action – either by way of immediate gain to one or other of the parties concerned or by way of concessions secured in international bargaining. In a world in which high tariffs and other obstacles to trade are imposed by almost every nation, there is certainly no need to feel more guilty than the rest at arrangements which, if they restrict trade in certain directions, release it in others. And if the canons of international good behaviour are held to permit the formation of customs unions, there are few arguments in principle against the extension of preference. Each case must be judged on its merits and in relation to our general interest – which includes, of course, the maintenance of the political solidarity of the Commonwealth and the Western Alliance.

The question, therefore, is not one of principle but of fact. The idea of the development of the preferential system so as eventually to create a more or less integrated system of trade and finance for the Commonwealth was in itself a fine idea, an idea which has had a perennial fascination for many fine spirits. The question is: is it an idea which at the present day offers prospects of practical development?

In my judgement the answer is no. Whatever may have been possible a hundred years ago when the idea of an imperial Zollverein was first propounded, today the world has moved on and we deceive ourselves if we suppose that there is much hope in this direction. Here and there it is conceivable that there are gains to be made or existing positions to be consolidated. But in the main we are living in the past, pursuing the ghostly hopes of a vanished age, if we conceive the future of Commonwealth policy in these terms.

Consider first the possibilities of extension of the preferential system as regards trade. Is it not a significant circumstance that, outside certain circles in this country, there is very little support for this idea? The great Dominions are frankly Laodicean, if not actively hostile. Some hold fast to what preferences exist, others would not be unwilling to see them disappear. There is hardly any support for their extension. Indeed, it is clear that any very strong movement in that direction would introduce dangerous strains into Commonwealth relations.

The underlying reason for this is plain. There is no obvious advantage in such arrangements. Speaking broadly, it can be said that preferences offer attraction only if on balance the area within which they prevail is an *importer* of the commodities affected. But this is the reverse of the case with most of the staples in which the Dominions are interested. In this sphere the Commonwealth is on balance an exporter. It follows, therefore, that from the Dominion point of view the gain of special privileges in U.K. markets is liable to be offset by losses in markets elsewhere, and the game is not worth the candle. There are exceptions here and there. But in the main these have already been exploited to the full. The range of further advantageous bargains is small, even if we were not estopped from pursuing them by existing international instruments which are thought by most to bring advantage. It would be rash to say that it is non-existent; for there is usually something that has been overlooked. But it is not rash to say that it is not important, not in the least commensurate with all the emotions and all the rhetoric that have been expended upon its supposed existence.

When we turn to more comprehensive schemes of monetary and financial autonomy, the picture is even less promising. In this connection the first thing to note is that all such schemes necessarily involve the exclusion of Canada; for Canada is not now a member of the Sterling Area and it is not realistic to suppose that she could be induced to join. Now among the English-speaking members of the Commonwealth other than the United Kingdom, Canada is incomparably the most important, both in respect of wealth and of military power. Any scheme which, in the interests of Sterling Area solidarity and the provision of some counterpoise to other powers, pushes Canada further towards the United States would not seem to be particularly far-sighted. In fifty years Canada may have outstripped even the United Kingdom. How doubtful the wisdom of plans which proceed on the assumption of her exclusion from the Commonwealth which she may eventually lead!

But beyond this, such plans involve contradiction in that they assume developments which are impracticable, save on the basis of aid from outside. It is true that not all the advocates of these plans rely upon further aid; there are a few, more logical than their fellows, who argue against accepting a dollar more from the United States and Canada. But the majority of the advocates of an insulated Sterling *Bloc* are not prepared to urge the ardours and endurances, the severe restriction of local standards of consumption, which unaided development would involve. Now in the last few years the inhabitants of the North American continent have given more away than has been given at any other time in history. At the same time they have put up with much discrimination against their goods, in the belief that such measures were the product of a temporary emergency. But it is really not to be anticipated that they would continue their subventions and their loans at privileged rates of interest, if they were told that the purpose of it all was to build up an area from which they were to be permanently excluded.

In fact, as we have recently seen, there is little prospect that the other members of the Commonwealth will fall in with such schemes. There is now no serious ground for fear that the enthusiasts of Preference or the insulated Sterling *Bloc* will be allowed to make a damaging break-away. But for all that the prevalence of such ideas is a pity. They command the support of some of the most public-spirited and disinterested elements in our public life, who, however, will not see that to seek to preserve the Commonwealth in this way is to break it. And, because of this fixation, plans which are much more in our interest and in the interest of the Commonwealth at large tend to be ignored or even opposed. Infatuated with the visions of an earlier age, we are always hanging back, instead of giving a lead. We leave to others the initiative in the world of the future.

IV THE U.K. INTEREST IN COMMERCIAL POLICY

Much the same considerations apply to the more ambitious plans which are sometimes propounded for the creation of a great economic *bloc* comprising both the Sterling Area and Western Europe.

These plans have a much wider appeal than plans for the Sterling Area alone. The area is larger: there would seem to be ampler scope for new bargains and economies from larger markets. To the European Americanophobe they offer the possibility of building a counterpoise to the power of the hated North American continent; to the American Isolationist they offer the hope of getting rid, once for all, of commitments in the Old World and they do not arouse the same associations of Colonialism, 1776 and all that, which spring into action at any mention of Imperial Preference and the Sterling Area.

Nevertheless, in the last analysis, such plans do not offer much which can commend them from the point of view of the U.K. interest. I say nothing further at this juncture of their political imprudence, of the profound unwisdom which would push Canada still further out of the Commonwealth and which, in general, would tend to perpetuate an even greater degree of division than exists at present in the English-speaking world. But on economic grounds alone it is difficult to see the attraction. Who is to finance this combination? It has been difficult enough for the United Kingdom since the war to finance the needs of the Sterling Area; indeed, had it not been for the vast assistance received from North America, both by way of loan and by way of Marshall Aid, what has actually been done would have been quite impossible. Is it reasonable to suppose that we can carry the needs of Europe as well without imposing the most catastrophic limitations on our own development? Or is it really thought that an arrangement would be viable whereby the United States and Canada would take over the burden, year in year out, of providing for developments of which it was the avowed intention that they should never enjoy the usufruct?

It is clear that objections of this sort would not apply to the proposal which is sometimes ventilated, of forming a free or a freer trade union for the N.A.T.O. group, or rather the N.A.T.O. group enlarged to bring in the relevant colonial dependencies and such other members of the Commonwealth as are interested in the defence of the West. Here at last would be a grouping immune from the disadvantages which have been indicated in other plans. It would promote rather than hinder the political unity of the West. Its creation need involve no important sacrifices in respect of trade with the rest of the world. It would contain within itself sources of accumulation capable of providing for all the capital development which with available skills and personnel it would be reasonable to aim at. There would be a splendid future for such an area.

It is sometimes argued that such a grouping is undesirable in that it would involve inherent instability. The superior productivity of the United States, it is feared, would swamp all other productive enterprise in the area. This raises, of course, the question already discussed in Section II; and the exposure of the fallacy it contains provides what is perhaps one of the most vivid illustrations of the propositions there set forth. Suppose, just for purposes of argument, an extreme case – a completely unified area with internal free trade and a single monetary system. Is it not abundantly clear that the competitive strength of the industries in the different parts of the area would depend, everything else being given, upon the rates at which the local moneys were converted into the union currency when the conversion to a single money system took place? If, for instance, one dollar was converted into one unit of the new currency while a pound was converted into five, then doubtless in present circumstances a great many United Kingdom products would be hopelessly underpriced by products from the United States. If, however, the pound were converted into, say, two units, then it is probable that the boot would be on the other leg: many of the products of the U.S. would be out of the market. This is not at all to argue that so drastic an innovation is necessarily desirable, still less that the conversion rates mentioned by way of illustration are to be taken as any indication of present equilibrium rates between pound and dollar. It is only to show that if we were really to screw ourselves up to an experiment involving this degree of economic unification there is no reason to suppose that it need take place on terms giving a disequilibrating advantage to all products from North America.

But all this is very much in the air. If some responsible group in Congress or in the U.S. Administration were to propose anything so ambitious then I, for one, would hope that we should not be backward in seeking ways of bringing it about. Here and now, however, rather than speculate further on such projects, it is more profitable to enquire a little into the ultimate nature of our interest in any less extensive negotiations concerning the principles of commercial policy.

As I see things, two principles emerge:

(a) First, that we are profoundly interested in preventing any further rise in tariffs against our goods, still more, in securing a lowering of such tariffs. This follows clearly from our dependence on imports. The more markets abroad are restricted, the more difficult to secure by way of export the means to pay for necessary imports; the more markets are open the easier it is for us to pay our way. This, of course, is true for other countries as well. But it is especially relevant to policy in areas where dependence on sources abroad is especially great; for the United States ample markets abroad are not a matter of life or death, for the United Kingdom they are.

It follows that we have an especial interest in negotiations for tariff reduction. It is true that such negotiations involve give as well as take; and it is not true that the give in the shape of reductions of our own tariffs is necessarily merely a seeming sacrifice – free traders who argue that unilateral tariff reductions are *always* in the national interest are overstating their case; the case for multilateral reductions is liable to far fewer exceptions. But our interest in maintaining and extending markets is probably greater than that of any other major power. We should be the last to shirk the search for mutually advantageous agreements.

(b) But if this applies to tariffs, how much more does it apply to the more rigid obstacles to trade – quantitative restrictions and the like. I say nothing here against the wisdom of recent emergency measures taken to safeguard our own trade balance: when the patient is bleeding to death you do not eschew the use of the tourniquet. But it should be crystal clear that we, of all great trading nations, have most to lose if the use of such measures becomes permanent and universal. For in such an event there would be no hope at all of balancing our accounts by an expansion of exports: no cost reduction, no sales promotion, no alteration of the rate of exchange, would avail us. Surrounded by a Chinese wall of obstructions, our only way of getting into external equilibrium would be by curtailment of imports: and it is not difficult to think of quite possible circumstances in which the magnitude of the curtailment would be such as to involve really disastrous results, both to employment and consumption. A country specializing in the manufacture of high-grade specialities and luxuries, as we do, is peculiarly vulnerable to the effects of quantitative restrictions elsewhere; a generalization and perpetuation of recent Australian policy would knock us off our perch entirely and keep us permanently from climbing back. When, therefore, I hear alleged experts from our own area pleading for the superior advantages of quantitative regulation of trade, I tend to murmur, "*Deus quos vult perdere, dementat prius*". What degree of insanity is this which recommends to others the means of our own destruction?

If these principles are true it would seem to follow that strictly from the point of view of the U.K. interest, there is a good deal more to be said for the much abused G.A.T.T. than has recently been said in public – at any rate in this part of the world. It goes without saying that this is not a perfect instrument – who would expect perfection of a document negotiated between so many nations? It is quite probable that there are some respects in which it can be represented as cramping our own style in further negotiation; it would be rather surprising if this were not so. But agreements of this sort must be judged on balance; it is of their very essence to be in the nature of a compromise. And judged from that point of view, it seems probable that this particular agreement is very much in our interest. To have preserved this degree of order in international relationships, to have secured this degree of standstill in the upward movement of tariffs and to have secured so many movements downward – this is no mean achievement from the point of view of our interest. To throw it all overboard, to let the world be plunged once more in a free-for-all competition in raising obstacles to trade – this surely would be an act of folly.

Hence, in my judgement, failing some larger plan for the N.A.T.O. nations and their associates, we should make the maintenance of the G.A.T.T. arrangements a principle of policy. We should reaffirm our support of the general principle of approaching freer trade by bilateral bargaining within the rules of a mutual benefit club. We should resist attempts to abolish it. We should seek to consolidate its influence. We should support proposals for a further series of negotiations designed to reduce still more the existing obstacles to trade.

And if by any chance some American or other statesman, anxious to transcend the limits of speed possible on this pedestrian basis of detailed bargaining, were to propose big *ad valorem* cuts all round in existing obstacles, I should hope we should support that too. Unlike the U.S. in this respect, we are not in a position to give the world any spectacular lead by way of unilateral action; in present circumstances the risks would be too great. But it is the essence of our interest as a community dependent more than most on the existence and the opportunities of wide international markets, to support every attempt at clearance on a truly multilateral basis.

V INTERNAL FINANCE AND EXTERNAL EQUILIBRIUM

Trade policy, however enlightened, will not by itself bring equilibrium if finances are out of order. It is true that unilateral easements of obstacles will mitigate the degree of financial adjustment which may be necessary elsewhere; needless to say, a unilateral reduction of tariffs on the part of the U.S. would do much to ease the financial problems of Europe and the Sterling Area. It is true further that multilateral easements of the type discussed already will make it easier for financial policies to be effective; a general reduction of obstacles would almost certainly increase the effectiveness of cost reductions or alterations of exchange rates. But, in the last analysis, until financial conditions are under control trade policy is without a foundation.

It is indeed not easy to overstate the central importance of financial policy in this matter of international balance. For dispassionate study of the facts must surely reveal that it is the failure of financial policies which has been responsible for the persistence of our troubles – to be perfectly explicit, that it is the failure of the non-dollar centres to restrain their expansion which is responsible for their failure to get nearer to closing the dollar gap.

Let me guard myself at once against misunderstanding. I do not mean that the original disequilibrium was due to faulty financial policy. I have no intention of denying the critical significance of the war and the capital losses associated therewith, of the effect of the rise of prices and the adverse turn in the terms of trade, or of the strain imposed, particularly on the United Kingdom, by overseas transfers – which may or may not have been necessary. It is admitted that these and other circumstances created conditions in which a change in the relationship between dollar and other incomes was necessary; and that, in the absence of such a change, disequilibrium in the balance of payments was inevitable. To use the economist's jargon, there were "real" causes producing a dollar shortage. There is no dispute about this.

The contention concerning the rôle of financial policy relates, however, not to the *original causes* but to the *persistence* of disequilibrium. And here the position is plain. As has been argued above, the conditions of equilibrium demanded a change in the relation between the cost and income structures of the dollar area and of the countries affected by these real causes, that is to say, a relative rise in the dollar area. Now if money income and prices in the United States had remained constant, it would have been easy to understand any failure elsewhere to establish equilibrium. For in those circumstances, in order to maintain fixed rates of exchange there would have had to have been positive deflation elsewhere, and this would have been politically difficult and economically inadvisable. But this was not necessary. For prices and incomes in the United States rose smartly upwards; and in these circumstances what was chiefly necessary was that prices and incomes in the deficit countries should be restrained. As we all know, exactly the reverse movement occurred. Prices and incomes in the non-dollar area tended to rise – in many cases much more than prices and incomes in the dollar area. In such circumstances the persistence of dollar shortage was inevitable. Of course if this had not happened, if, that is to say, the financial expansion outside the dollar area had been restrained, it is impossible to be sure that full equilibrium would have been restored – though having regard to the magnitude of the rise in American prices it would certainly have been very astonishing if it had not. But while the relative movement has been as it has been, the burden of proof rests upon those who argue that there is any mystery about the persistence of dollar shortage.

If this is so, then obviously the first *desideratum* of policy for all countries affected with difficulties with their balance of payments is to stop inflation. There are many ways of doing this, both fiscal and monetary; and there is no simple rule as to which method is most expedient. In the light of experience since the war it is now coming to be agreed that both fiscal and monetary measures are necessary; monetary policies unassisted by fiscal measures involve levels of interest rates which may be highly inconvenient; fiscal measures unaccompanied by monetary control are apt to be insufficient and belated. And the trouble usually is that when governments have brought themselves to face the necessity for the one (whichever it is) they conveniently forget, or go slow with, the other. But whatever the technique, the important thing is to stop inflation – to make it a prime objective of policy that there shall be no financial expansion until there is equilibrium and strength in the balance of payments position.

In some cases this will not be enough. Where the local expansion has outstripped the expansion in the United States and where there has been no commensurate adjustment of the rate of exchange, then the mere cessation of inflation will not be sufficient to restore equilibrium. In such cases the appropriate policy is a change in the rate of exchange rather than positive financial contraction. Absolute deflation on a large scale is *not* (repeat *not*) recommended. The claim, often made by the opponents of financial stabilization, that it is impossible to maintain high levels of production and increased production without continually rising prices is inadmissible – its implications for the distribution of wealth and for social and economic stability generally are altogether too disastrous. But a policy of severe contraction when the situation could be redressed by a change in the rate of exchange is also inadmissible. It was to meet just such situations that there were inserted in the statutes of the International Monetary Fund the provisions for alteration of the exchange rates. A table of relative rates of inflation since 1949 makes it very obvious that there are centres where, sooner or later, advantage must be taken of these provisions. Relative inflation of 20 or 30 per cent. is not something which cures itself merely if prices are prevented from rising.

This recommendation of adjustment of exchanges which are obviously overvalued must not be taken to imply a recommendation of permanently floating rates all round. In spite of the high academic authority by which this proposal is sometimes supported, I find it hard to regard it as acceptable. It is easy to see that when rates are badly out of line, or other readjustments are necessary, circumstances may arise when some experimentation is desirable before final decisions are made regarding new parities. I say nothing against transitory measures of this sort, *provided the internal position has first been definitely stabilized*. But in general I am yet to be convinced that the dilemma is escapable that, when the general financial position is strong, free rates are usually unnecessary and that, when it is weak, they are apt to be a source of appalling danger. One thing at least must be agreed by all concerned: if the floating rate is to do what is claimed for it, it is absolutely imperative that any downward fluctuation shall be met by an increased curb on internal expansion – otherwise the danger of inflation is increased. Now it seems an odd thing, in a period marked conspicuously by the unwillingness of governments to impose curbs of this kind, that experiments should be recommended which make disaster even more certain if they don't. Or is it perhaps suggested that if the tipsy man is placed on the very edge of the abyss he is more likely to pull himself together and not fall over? Well, different people carry their drink differently; it would be rash to generalize about the probable outcome of all such experiments. But the history of free exchanges with weak internal finances does not afford conspicuous grounds for confidence!

VI CONVERTIBILITY

If these arguments are correct, the general aim should be the cessation of internal inflation and the adjustment of overvalued exchanges. At this stage, however, we encounter the question, what about convertibility? Ought internal stabilization to be followed here and now by a declaration that the pound is once more convertible? Or are there yet further conditions which need to be fulfilled?

This is a matter about which it is very important to keep our heads. There can be little doubt that if the pound is not eventually made convertible, its position as an international currency will suffer. If money cannot be placed in the Sterling Area in the full expectation that, if need be, it can be withdrawn with as little formality as is needed for withdrawing it from, say, Switzerland or from the United States, the flow of capital that is desirable for development will not occur. If the various members of the Sterling Area come to feel that when they have money in London – not merely in special accounts but also in any form in which it is convenient for them to hold it or invest it – they cannot be sure of retrieving it at will, they will tend to place their funds elsewhere. The path to convertibility may well be thought to be beset with danger, especially if we have regard to the volatility of funds created by fears of domestic policy and the international situation. Nevertheless, it would not be a prudent attitude to abandon the intention of achieving it or to postpone attempts in that direction to an indefinitely remote future.

But there is another attitude which is no less imprudent – the view which holds that we have only to stop inflation and the drain on the reserves to be in a position to declare the pound convertible forthwith. The friends of convertibility as a genuine goal should be as much on their guard against this as against the attitude which would abandon the goal altogether; for it is safe to say that if such an attempt were made before certain fundamental conditions are satisfied, it would be speedily reversed, and we should be further than ever from the wished-for goal.

The reasons for caution are various. In the first place come doubts regarding the future of our own balance of payments. At the moment all goes well and there is some net gain to the reserves. But in so far as this is not the by-product of sheer good luck – the recent turn of the terms of trade – it is a position which has been achieved at the expense of a degree of import restriction which we should not wish to sustain indefinitely. I see no reason in the figures to suppose that the present rate of exchange is inappropriate; I hope that policy will be directed firmly to maintaining it. But before I should be prepared to proceed further towards convertibility I should want to watch how it sustained some relaxation of restrictions. I should want to be sure that there was still reasonable hope of achieving a continuing surplus for a considerable time ahead. This scruple would apply even if the reserve were at a much healthier figure; there is no valid reason for sacrificing capital to maintain an untenable position.

But this brings us to the second ground for caution: the present inadequacy of reserves. It is one thing to argue, as has been argued above, for an internal policy designed to maintain a fixed rate of exchange. It is another to argue that such a policy is possible if the reserve is inadequate to the situation. This is not merely a matter of the need for a possible cushion to sustain imports while we are shifting exports on account of worsening in particular markets: it is a matter of a need for a reserve to sustain us in the event of an all over worsening due to some general slackening of demand. I am not here thinking of the possibility of a catastrophic depression in the United States; if that were to happen in present circumstances then, I am afraid, all optimistic bets would be off and we should have to start again. I am thinking rather of mild recessions of the kind which came in 1949 and might easily come again on a considerably larger scale. Now it may be possible to hope for international mechanisms which are some safeguard against such happenings; but we should be very sanguine if we were to rely upon the possibility of these arrangements and to expose ourselves to the dangers of such a contingency without adequate reserves of our own. I have no desire to throw cold water upon hopes with which I am fully in sympathy; but I should hold it an unjustifiable risk if we were to proceed much further towards convertibility until our reserves were very much greater than they are at present. If there are means of securing an adequate reinforcement by international negotiations which do not involve us in intolerable burdens in other respects, well and good, we can go ahead much faster. It is greatly to be hoped that all such possibilities will be fully explored; there may be great opportunities ahead. But if there are not then while not abandoning, either in words or in intentions, continued effort towards the ultimate goal, let us proceed with proper circumspection.

There is yet a further reason for extreme care in this respect: the possible action – or inaction – of other centres. If we declare convertibility while other centres remain to all intents and purposes inconvertible, then we expose ourselves to strains which at the present time do not arise and which, unless our position is much stronger than it is at present, might easily be much more than we could bear. If sterling becomes convertible then any centre at present suffering from a dollar shortage may easily be tempted to impose additional limitations on imports from the United Kingdom. Of course this is not inevitable; and convertibility might bring with it other compensating advantages. But once bit twice shy; it would seem an unwise policy to proceed to a unilateral declaration of convertibility when a multilateral declaration would make the position so much easier. Here again is a matter which is a suitable subject for international negotiation and in respect of which very helpful plans are conceivable. But if negotiation is without effect, that would be an additional reason for caution.

All this may seem a betrayal of the cause to those who hope from convertibility the immediate adoption of those practices which make possible its continuance, however great the strain which they impose. But this is not my hope. I confess freely that if I thought that a once-for-all decision of this sort would discipline us for ever into ways of good sense, I should find the prospect very attractive. But that is very unlikely to happen. Much more likely is the discrediting, for our generation, of the whole idea of convertibility. How much better to persuade governments to take the necessary measures first so that convertibility comes as the logical and advantageous conclusion of a policy that is not likely to be reversed.

VII STABILITY AND DEVELOPMENT

The measures which have been discussed so far should have the effect, if resolutely carried through, of restoring something like balance throughout the world, provided that expenditure in the large remains roughly stable, that is to say, immune from severe contractions and tending to advance as rapidly as the advance of population and production, but not more rapidly. But they do not, by themselves, ensure the fulfilment of this condition. They provide for relative, not absolute, stability.

Now there can be no doubt that, in this connection, a very special responsibility rests with the financial authorities of the United States. This is not because there is necessarily any special economic advantage in bigness as such, but merely because the volume of expenditure which they control is so large relatively to the rest. If the U.S. authorities manage to avoid severe contractions in aggregate demand and to keep the money incomes of the citizens approximately in step with their own increase of production, we may face this part of the future with reasonable calm. In such circumstances a severe collapse of aggregate demand elsewhere is unlikely, although, as we have seen to our cost, local inflations, with all that they imply for international unbalance, are not ruled out.

Nevertheless, this seems eminently a field in which international co-operation is desirable if it can be arranged. There is no *laissez faire* presumption here, no reason to suppose that, given modern credit systems, the unco-ordinated activities of central banks will necessarily lead to the best volume of aggregate demand throughout the world as a whole. Concerted attempts to achieve this ideal have therefore some presumption in their favour. Arrangements which would have the effect of minimizing irrational swings of expenditure would be very much in the general interest.

But where are such arrangements to be found? In recent months there has been much talk of plans for the stabilization of the prices of staple foods and raw materials. In principle there is nothing against such projects, provided that by stabilization is meant the evening out of short-period fluctuations rather than interference with long-period trends. But such aims are easier to postulate than to achieve. The path to stabilization is beset with dangers of restrictionism, and the consolidation of sectional interest. The predatory nature of men organized as groups of producers and backed by governmental authority, has to be seen close up at international conferences to be believed. Personally, having begun with a lively desire to see some experimentation on the lines of the buffer stock plans discussed in various quarters during the war, I have gradually come to entertain very limited hopes in this direction: the famous principle, "equal representation for consumers and producers" is usually the *façade* for a ramp. In present circumstances, if anything of this sort is to be attempted, I should have much more hope of action based upon the existing beginnings of arrangements for co-ordination of purchase of strategic materials. Here at any rate is a field in which, in the present state of the world, governments will almost certainly be led to operate, a field in which highly deleterious influences may arise if there is not some co-ordination of buying policy. Is there not good reason for trying to build upon what exists already – for trying to bring it about that the purchases of governments, so far from accentuating the ups and downs of markets, in fact have a damping effect?

But the main effort in the direction of general stabilization must be made in the sphere of finance. The logic of development would seem to point to central banking arrangements, if not for the world as a whole, at any rate for the Western Alliance and the free world at large. If there were no political boundaries this would be an easy matter. In a world in which the political divisions even within this group are unlikely early to disappear, it is a matter of much greater difficulty. Yet surely it is the goal to keep in mind. One money, one credit system for the free world – this would be the best means of securing the stability we need. The problem is to find practical ways of adapting existing institutions and existing habits so as to work gradually in this direction.

In this connection thoughts naturally turn to the existing international institution which was intended to serve this purpose: the International Monetary Fund. Now the best friend of that institution could hardly contend that hitherto it has fulfilled the high hopes which were held at its foundation. But before we decide that it is to be written off as a failure and some other institution put in its place, it is worth while asking whether there is no possibility of modifying its procedures and statutes so as to render it more effective.

The most patent deficiency of the Monetary Fund so far has been that it has not been used. Either because of the disinclination of some members to have recourse to it or because of the disinclination of the governing body to risk its funds, the volume of business has been negligible. To suppose that operations on this scale could ever provide an appreciable stabilizing influence in the world is to misconceive the nature of the problem. If nothing more than this is possible within this framework, then we may be sure that sooner or later the Monetary Fund will die.

Four things are necessary before the Monetary Fund can begin to perform the functions that are necessary, if something like central banking arrangements for the Western World are gradually to come into being.

First, there must be some modification of the absurd system of government whereby the most delicate, the most responsible business of the Fund has been conducted by a large board of directors or their alternates, sitting in almost continuous session. There must be reasonable provision for effective negotiation: some regard must be had to the maxim, so essential in financial discussions, that *you can't tell all the chaps all the time*. The conduct of affairs needs to be concentrated into the hands of a small number of trusted figures with full authority often to go ahead for weeks or months at a time with operations which they are under no immediate obligation to report to the governing body. This does not mean that no report is ultimately necessary: it only means a reasonable elbow room for conducting this sort of business the way it has to be conducted if it is to have any chance of success. The present system is altogether ridiculous; and if it continues nobody can complain if the really important decisions are made outside.

Secondly, the Fund needs more money. Certainly it has not been cramped in this respect hitherto. But that is because it has not been properly in action. If it is to discharge large functions of international stabilization, there must be a background of sufficient resources – of capacity to pay out freely as a lender of last resort. How this should be achieved is a technical problem of great delicacy. But, on the assumption that an attempt is to be made to use the Fund for these purposes, it would seem to be at least as hopeful a way of using some of the money that may be available for purposes of reconstruction as many other plans which have been taken quite seriously.

Thirdly, if there is to be more lending and borrowing then it is necessary to modify the requirement that the Fund and its officials should have no right to comment on the business of members and no right to take into account domestic policies when deciding on eligibility for credit facilities. The requirements to this effect written into the statutes, as is well known, very largely at the instance of the United Kingdom, were wrong. The idea that you can have an effective international credit institution without the power to say boo to a goose was not good sense. At the time it may have been necessary in order to induce governments to consent to co-operate at all. But it was backward looking rather than forward looking; and all the international co-operation that has achieved a ha'porth of good since that time has tended in the other direction. If the Fund cannot ask of its members the same willingness to submit to scrutiny and advice as the European Payments Union or N.A.T.O. its future is indeed dim.

Fourthly and above all, it is necessary that the two biggest partners in this enterprise should be resolved to make it work and be an instrument of common policy. Given goodwill and agreement on the part of the American and British financial authorities, a great deal which has seemed difficult in the past would at once become possible. In the absence of this attitude, it would be better to write the whole thing off and begin afresh on other lines.

Throughout these notes I have said nothing of military aid and international investment. This has been quite deliberate. So far as military aid is concerned, there is no reason to suppose that it will not go on in some shape or other, and will not play an important part in relieving fiscal strain in the countries concerned. But from the point of view of these notes, it is important that policy should not be based on this assumption. We should aim so to conduct our affairs that they are in equilibrium, whether or not we are securing special easement of military burdens. As for development in the wider sense, we have already the International Bank, alone among international institutions in having justified any reasonable expectations that may have been entertained when it was created. It is true that the amount it has lent has not been large as international financial transactions go. But it has been quite as much as it could have lent prudently. If, as time goes on, larger openings present themselves, beyond its present capacity to finance, the very fact that so far it has been careful and has only lent its funds after proper investigation rather than poured them out on the ill-considered schemes which have been pressed upon it, will make it easier, not more difficult, to arrange the necessary extensions of its facilities. For the rest, although the world badly needs development, I take the view that expenditure of this sort should be looked upon as a consequence rather than a cause of the establishment of reasonable international balance. Given confidence and a demonstration of the willingness and ability of the various governments of the free world to pay their debts and to provide for the reasonable treatment of funds which are invested within their borders, the provision of development finance should not be a matter of very great difficulty.

VIII POLITICS AGAIN – THE FUNDAMENTAL *DESIDERATUM*

But that brings us back to the political assumptions from which we started, although, so to speak, from the reverse direction. There it was a question of doing nothing in the economic sphere which would upset political solidarity. Here it is a question of action in the political sphere which makes harmonious economic development possible. For confidence will not be re-established, there will not be an adequate flow of international investment, there will be no stable economic progress, unless there is political stability in the world. And there will not be political stability in the world unless the Western Alliance is strong and united. Sufficient military power to resist aggression and sufficient political unity to maintain continuity of policy – these are not *alternatives* to economic stability and progress, they are its essential preconditions. If the West is strong and united, then everything else is possible. If it is not strong and united then there is no future at all. Unwise economic policies can upset political unity. But, in this most perilous epoch of Western Civilization, without military power and political solidarity any kind of economic policy is necessarily founded on sand.

19 Robertson on Utility and Scope

From *Economica*, new series vol. 20 (May 1953), pp. 99–111.

Like each of its predecessors, the latest addition to Sir Dennis Robertson's series of collected essays[1] is full of good things. Some of the papers on policy are indeed among the most important that he has ever written. It is difficult, for instance, to conceive anything more elegant or more closely packed with wisdom than the Presidential Address for 1947 to Section F of the British Association on "The Economic Outlook,"* and this is only the leading example of a whole series of contributions whereby Sir Dennis has not only contributed to our knowledge of the theory of policy in general, but has also diffused sweetness and light amid the anxious and bewildering problems of our day.

For professional economists, however, probably the leading feature of interest will be the lengthy paper which gives its title to the whole collection and which consists of a more or less systematic survey of recent developments in the theory of value and their relevance to our conception of the scope of economics. As this represents the considered judgment on these important subjects of the leading exponent now in harness of the main Marshallian tradition at Cambridge, perhaps a somewhat extensive commentary may not be thought inappropriate.

I

Let me begin with a brief summary of the main outlines of the paper. Broadly speaking, it falls into three parts.

The first (which consists of Section I of the paper) is devoted to a general picture of the outlook inherited by the author from the Cambridge tradition of his time and made explicit in Professor Pigou's *Wealth and Welfare* [1912] and subsequent versions thereof.

1. D.H. Roberson, *Utility and All That and Other Essays* (London, 1952).
* *Economic Journal*, vol. 57 (December 1947), pp. 421–37.

According to this outlook, the ultimate subject matter of economics is economic welfare. Changes in production and distribution are to be studied with a view to discovering their effects on economic welfare. Economic welfare is admitted as being only a part of welfare as a whole: but, while possible disharmonies are recognised, it is held that there is a presumption that what promotes the one will also promote the other, though not necessarily in like measure.

The foundation of this inquiry is a theory of individual behaviour, of which the law of diminishing marginal utility is the basic feature, utility in this connection being conceived as cardinally measurable. The propositions involved by this theory, conspicuously propositions relating to consumers' surplus, can then by a cautious process of aggregation be developed into a theory of social welfare, the essential assumption in this connection being the commensurability of the utilities experienced by different individuals.

After this introductory retrospect, the second part (which consists of Sections II, III and IV) discusses recent contributions to the theory of individual behaviour.

It begins with a brief exposition of the fundamental propositions of the famous Hicks–Allen article, "The Reconsideration of the Theory of Value."* These propositions evidently inspire the author with deep disquiet; for elsewhere, in another article reprinted in this volume, the famous "Revolutionist's Handbook," he refers to them as "The Hicks–Allen revolution, substituting marginal rates of substitution for marginal utility and threatening to reduce our discipline to utter sterility."

There follows a discussion of the attempt by Messrs. Samuelson and Little entirely to exclude psychological elements from the theory of value and to rely exclusively on observable facts. On the value of all this the author expresses considerable scepticism: "Was it worth while to go to such mountainous trouble to formalise in non-mental terms the behaviour of beings whom we have every reason to suppose to be equipped with minds?" If this is where the revolution leads us, he argues, how much better to be content with cardinalism, which, if postulating something in practice difficult to measure, is at least intelligible in terms of everyday experience and congenial to the universe of discourse of the real problems which we have to solve.

Having thus disposed of the behaviourists, the author returns to Professor Hicks and his attempts to rehabilitate consumers' surplus within the assumptions of ordinalism. These attempts are welcomed as a sign of grace and defended against certain critics. But it is suggested that, in going thus far, their author has

---

* J.R. Hicks and R.G.D. Allen, "A reconsideration of the theory of value," *Economica*, n.s., vol. 1 (February and May 1934), pp. 52–76, 196–219.

unconsciously come to occupy a position which seems to lie within the cardinalist fold. In this general connection, Professor Frank Knight's recent contributions are praised as tending to support the cardinalist position; but the constructions of Messrs. Morgenstern and Neumann, which definitely seek to measure utility in terms of degrees of uncertainty faced, are held to be unhelpful.

Finally, in the third part (which consists of Sections V, VI and VII) the author proceeds to deal with recent contributions to the theory of collective, as distinct from individual, welfare.

It begins with a defence of the concept of economic welfare – which is defined, not in terms of accessibility to the measuring rod of money but rather in terms of Edwin Cannan's "more material side of human happiness." The possibility of divergence between economic welfare in this sense and welfare in general is again stressed and, "partly for brevity and partly in the hope of craftily dispelling the notion that the phrase 'economic welfare' is bulging with ethics and emotiveness the author proposes as a substitute the term 'ecfare'."

The argument then embarks upon a discussion of Mr. Kaldor's suggestion for giving precision to the notion of an increase in aggregate productivity and of the various criticisms to which that has given rise. The opinion is expressed that most of these refinements have been more or less mutually destructive; and the author declares candidly his preference for the Pigovian treatment with its separation of the ideas of production and distribution which, he argues, "enshrines a basic truth which any group, and especially a national group in an acutely competitive world, will neglect at its peril."

This leads to a frontal attack on the refusal to allow interpersonal comparisons of utility. Here Mr. Little is picked out for commendation for his blunt assertion that such comparisons are possible. But, at the same time, the question is posed how he manages to do this if he is not prepared to admit cardinal measurements of individual utilities. "It is precisely because I agree with Little that we *do* want to, and believe that we can, make such interpersonal comparisons, and draw inferences from them about such important matters as taxation policy, that I find the claim of the Paretians to have proved the *redundancy* of the concept of cardinal utility so irritating. I don't mind being told that it is false – we can proceed to argue about that. But when I am told that I can go on believing it if I like but that it will not enable me to say or do anything which I couldn't say or do equally well without it, then I find it very hard not to get cross. For that seems to me quite patently not the case."

The paper concludes with a statement of the problems proper to be the subject of the attention of the economist, as conceived from this point of view. The opinion expressed in the Presidential Address to the Royal Economic Society [in June 1949] that the economist should move mainly on the economic plane as thus conceived is strongly reiterated. If, however, this is to be transcended, then the doubt is expressed whether much help is to be obtained from exhibiting the ultimate assumptions in the form of an all-embracing social welfare function "whose maximization would indicate that all our decisions have been those which the Archangel Gabriel, or perhaps only those which Uncle Joe Stalin, would have made in our place ... When we reach these regions of ultimate decision, I find it difficult to believe that mathematics has much to say that is not said more briefly in that aspiration of the Book of Common Prayer – that we may have a right judgment in all things."

My comments on all this will follow the same order of arrangement.

II

To begin then with the theory of individual behaviour.

On Sir Dennis's first point, the unhelpfulness of methods of explanation which seek to avoid all reference to mental events and to rely solely upon hypothetical observables, there is nothing for the present reviewer to do but express cordial agreement. Pure behaviourism has not proved a particularly helpful method in psychology proper. Why at this time of day, we should go out of our way to shackle ourselves with its self-frustrating inhibitions is not at all evident. It is perhaps true that in certain very simple cases of once-for-all choice, we can imagine behaviour curves constructed simply by exposing a collection of economic subjects to a sufficient number of alternatives and just watching their reactions as if they were mice in an experimental cage. On this basis, perhaps, without invoking the idea of a single thought going on in the heads of the persons concerned, we could reproduce descriptions of the conditions of equilibrium which in fact were first evolved in a much less sophisticated way. But as soon as we departed from these laboratory conditions we should be utterly at a loss to maintain the make-believe. How explain the phenomena of speculative markets without referring to anticipations of future events? How describe broad financial movements without contrast between plans and their fulfilment? It will surely come to be regarded as a paradox in the history of thought that, just at a period when the problems of economic dynamics were beginning to be successfully tackled by methods which can properly be described as extensions of the subjective theory of value, there should have developed a tendency to restate the statical foundations in terms which deliberately eschew any reference to the subjective at all.

Thus on the undesirability of hurling the baby out with the bath water, I am completely at one with Sir Dennis: I do not think that it is sensible to restrict our generalizations to observables and I see no objection to explanation in terms of assumed calculations and estimates. My difficulties relate to the nature of these calculations and estimates. Sir Dennis attaches great weight to the retention of the cardinal conceptions with which some at least of the better known versions of the subjective theory began – that of Jevons, for instance; I must confess to a certain preference for the ordinal conceptions characteristic of more recent formulations.

Some of Sir Dennis's more emphatic language in this connection is in the nature of an *argumentum ad hominem.* If you will not admit cardinal utility in the theory of individual behaviour, he urges, then you have no basis for interpersonal comparisons in the theory of social welfare. As may be suspected and as will be revealed in some detail later on in this review, I am perhaps not the man to be greatly moved by this particular argument. But I am sure that Sir Dennis would not wish us to decide the central issue on this argument. It may perhaps be true that the fate of certain theories of welfare economics depends upon the answer to the question whether individual judgments of utility are to be conceived in cardinal or ordinal terms. But it cannot be true that the answer to this question must be determined by the necessity to save these particular theories. That is a matter which must be settled on its own merits.

Now before entering into argument I would like freely to admit that, so far as the pure theory of value is concerned, I think that it is possible to make much too much of this question. There are certain matters of definition which are affected by its decision one way or the other – the definition of complementarity, for instance; and it is reasonably clear, even to a non-mathematician, that methods of algebraic exposition will be not inconsiderably affected – think of the almost indefinite proliferation of determinants which apparently the ordinal conception necessitates. But I cannot repress the conviction, whose confession doubtless will brand me once and for all as a Philistine, that when all is said and done the broad important outlines of the theory are not very seriously affected. Description of the conditions of consumer equilibrium in terms of equality between objective exchange rates and marginal rates of substitution happens to seem more elegant and more correctly stated than the older proportionality of exchange rates and marginal utilities. But it is surely wrong to pretend that it is an entirely different type of solution. To use the terminology chosen by their authors, the Hicks–Allen constructions are a reformulation; but they are not a revolution. If all that Sir Dennis were doing, were to exhort us not to lose our sense of proportion, I do not think that there would be much to disagree about.

But, of course, he is saying more than this. He is saying that, when we choose, we do so in virtue of estimates which are in principle quantitatively measurable rather than a mere ranking in an order of importance. And here, while I have no wish to make a fuss about a refinement which, in this context at any rate,[1] is perhaps of no great importance, on challenge, I must take the

1. *I.e.*, in the pure theory of value as opposed to welfare economics.

other side. I can think of choices which might be conceived in terms of some sort of quantitative measurement – the decision, for instance, whether or not to have a second helping of porridge – where it is perhaps not completely unplausible to assume reference back to some absolute quantum of sensual gratification which in principle might be measured. But in the main, when I introspect on these matters, I find judgments of a quite different nature. The kind of subjective valuation which lies behind an act of choice seems to me to be typified by the statement that I prefer this Rembrandt to that Holbein, where surely it would be fanciful and unrealistic to imagine some measuring rod applied to the degree to which each object lifts me above the zero of pleasure. Nor am I moved to take the olive branch extended by Sir Dennis when he exhorts us to reflect whether our differences may not be resolved by recognition of the difference between measurement in principle and measurement in practice. I suspect that there may be all sorts of ambiguities in the terminology of this dispute; I distrust the word 'measurement' and, lacking expert qualification, I am loath to set great store on the verbal distinction between cardinalism and ordinalism. But I feel pretty sure that there is a real distinction implied in the proposition which I learnt long ago from Professor Mises that *Das Werturteil misst nicht, es stuft ab, es skaliert.*[1]

Having said this, however, I must state a reservation. Professor Robertson, who has spent much time with the high authorities, informs us that to be an ordinalist you must refuse to believe in the possibility of the judgment of differences. That is to say, that while I may say I prefer *A* to *B* and *B* to *C*, I may not say that my preference for *A* over *B* is greater than my preference for *B* over *C*, for that involves the possibility of cardinal measurement. I confess that I find this very difficult to swallow. If it is true, then, while retaining my right to differ with Sir Dennis on the real nature of the judgment of value, I will cheerfully consent to be called a cardinalist. For I am quite sure that I can and do judge differences. The proposition that my preference for the Rembrandt over the Holbein is less than my preference for the Holbein over, let us say, a Munnings, is perfectly intelligible to me; but it does not seem to imply more than the capacity to recognize an order of importance of possible experiences. To relapse into abstraction, the fact that I can "find a point *B* between *A* and *C* such that the move from *A* to *B* is rated *just* as highly as the move from *B* to *C* does *not* seem to me to be 'the same thing as saying that the interval A–C is *twice* the interval A–B'," as Sir Dennis says the ordinalist asserts. This seems to me a *non sequitur*. The one judgment asserts equiva-

1. Ludwig von Mises, *Die Gemeinwirtschaft: Untersuchungen über den Socialismus*, 2nd edn (Jena, 1932), p. 93. [As translated by J. Kahane, 'Judgments of value do not measure: they arrange, they grade.' (*Socialism*, London, 1936).]

lence; the other implies the possibility of addition. To say that a particular Rembrandt and a Titian seem equally important does not seem to me to imply that I am saying that the Rembrandt *plus* the Titian will give me twice as much pleasure. And, surely, if it were true that the mere possibility of judgments of equivalence implied cardinal measurement, then the ordinalist would not have a leg to stand on anywhere; for the whole of this side of the theory of value rests upon the possibility of the quantification of such judgments in terms of the relation of different types of goods. But I suspect that the matter is all much more complicated than this. It is much to be wished that some authoritative ordinalist, such as Professor Hicks, would tell us (*a*) whether he regards as impossible the ranking of differences, as in my Rembrandt–Holbein–Munnings example above, and (*b*) whether, if the answer to this is in the negative, he regards such a ranking as necessarily implying cardinal measurement.*

III

Let us now turn to wider problems in the economics of welfare in general.

Here let me say at once that I should find it very hard to accept Sir Dennis's attempted rehabilitation of the "more material side of human happiness" as the best definition of the subject matter of economics; and I am very surprised to find it taking the place of the Pigovian "accessibility to the measuring rod of money," which, if not the same thing as the definition in terms of scarcity which I favour, differs from it only in a certain implied institutional restriction. I hasten to add that I do not regard this as a major doctrinal difference. For the best part of a quarter of a century Sir Dennis and I have been amiably discussing various problems of theory and practice without, so far as I am aware, our agreements or differences ever being influenced by this apparently quite fundamental difference of opinion concerning the definition of our subject. It is always easier to discuss the same things than to agree how to describe them; and for most purposes it is the discussion of particular problems which counts.

Still, if we are to discuss definitions, I must confess that I find it strange that Sir Dennis should argue so strongly for one which so obviously leaves out many of the things which, in his rôle as economist, he does, so to speak, every day of the week. By this, I am not referring to his exhortation to stick to our last and to refrain from invading other spheres; there will be something to say

* Hicks responded to the challenge Robbins set him with a note, "Robbins on Robertson on Utility," *Economica*, n.s., vol. 21 (May 1954), pp. 154–7.

about that later on. I am referring rather to his definition which, taken literally, certainly excludes activities which I am quite certain he would admit to lie completely within the most humble conception of the business of the economist – discussions of the national income for instance, a substantial portion of which consists of services and uses which cannot by the most drastic distortion of language be said to minister to the "more material side of human happiness" – symphony concerts, the duties of the Archbishop of Canterbury, military planning, philosophy tutorials, the ballet and so on. Why should the use of scarce resources to provide for the more material side of human happiness be deemed a legitimate object of study for economists, while the use of scarce resources for promoting the less material side should not?

It was difficulties of this sort, I well remember, which first led to my own discontent with this kind of definition. I had been brought up as – what I hope in most respects I still am – an admiring student of Edwin Cannan. I had read in the first chapter of his *Wealth* [1914] that the subject matter of economics was 'the more material side of human happiness' and had been expressly warned that this left out war and many other things which must not be regarded as wealth but rather as illth. And then, one day, having dutifully bent over backwards to make palatable this definition to my students, I was put to lecture on the economics of war and found that the general techniques of economics had much that was useful and illuminating to say about problems which had been specifically denied to be part of the subject matter. I note that Sir Dennis echoes Cannan's exclusions. And I cannot help asking how he and Edwin Cannan can have explained to themselves the peculiar accident of the universe which brings it about that the generalizations which, on their way of thinking, must be restricted to the analysis of those activities ministering to the more material side of human happiness, prove to have equal applicability to all sorts of other activities which their definition not only leaves out but rather, quite deliberately, *pushes* out. Surely, something has gone wrong somewhere.

In exactly the same way I find it difficult to accept Sir Dennis's distinction between welfare and economic welfare. Suppose that we are considering the erection of a cathedral. On Sir Dennis's view of our subject matter, we should presumably regard the fact that it is a convenient shelter from the rain and, if taken over by the Soviets, can be used as a granary, as its potential contribution to economic welfare, whereas the gargoyles on the porch and the towers are the servants of non-economic welfare. To my way of thinking this is not at all helpful. As I see things, the concept of welfare embraces many states of mind, some of a merely "sensual," some of a more "spiritual" nature; and, for some purposes, it may be interesting to sort them out into different classes. But the class "economic" will not be one of them. On this view, there are no economic states of mind. There are economic factors involved in the achievement of states of mind. But the states of mind themselves are not economic. Nor are the more "spiritual" states of mind necessarily any less dependent on economic factors than the less. Indeed, it may cost less in terms of scarce resources to put a roof on the cathedral and to instal hot water pipes, than to build the soaring spires and gorgeous canopies.

I have often asked myself how it was that definitions and distinctions which seemed to me so misleading should commend themselves to authorities so eminent and so acute as Edwin Cannan and Sir Dennis. After a good deal of pondering, I think I see a plausible explanation. Our states of mind depend, on the one hand, upon our wants and tastes and, on the other, upon the means available for their satisfaction. Now consciousness of want or objective is something essentially mental or immaterial: whereas the means of satisfying these wants or attaining these objectives can be described as "material" in that they are outside our minds, a part indeed of the external world. Now the study of wants as such or the modes of their change, is not part of the subject matter of economics, whereas the relations between wants and the scarce means of their satisfaction quite obviously is. If by a loose use of language this field comes to be called "the more material side of human happiness" then we speedily get into all the confusions and artificial classifications I have tried to point out. But it does not sound altogether unplausible.

In fact, I suspect this is what has happened. The more I con over what Sir Dennis has to say in this connection, the more I become convinced that what he is driving at is the distinction between ends as such and the relation between given ends and the scarce means for achieving them: and my impression is that if you substitute the phrase "means of welfare" for the phrase "economic welfare," in most places where it occurs, you will find that his argument proceeds as before but without all the difficulties which arise from the implication of his definition that only certain kinds of ends, the "more material," come properly within your purview.

But if this is so, then we ought all the more to resist, as tending away from possible reconciliation, Sir Dennis's proposed emendation of Professor Pigou's title. *The Economics of Welfare* is a title which in itself begs no questions. Whereas, if the above analysis be correct, *A Study of Economic Welfare* does. Nor shall we welcome as conducive to mutual understanding that very dubious and elusive entity "ecfare." We can agree wholeheartedly with its inventor that what economists have to study is the dependence of states of mind upon the availability of means rather than states of mind as such; and we can agree that states of mind can change for better or worse as a result of influences and tendencies which are right outside the scope of economics. But we must question whether this distinction, which is real and important, is best kept in our minds by a term which suggests that, in studying these means–ends relationships, we are also picking and choosing among the ends themselves.

IV

I turn now to the much debated question of interpersonal comparisons. I confess that I do this with some reluctance: so much has been written already. But I have a tiny olive branch up my sleeve; and it may serve some purpose to produce it.

Let us begin by re-stating the problem. Let us suppose that Sir Dennis and I are discussing the tastes and dispositions of our colleagues. There is no conceptual difficulty in comparisons of their relative valuations. If Sir Dennis thinks that, given his present provision with commodities and means of purchase, Professor *X* values a first edition of Ricardo more in terms of bottles of whisky than Professor *Y*, whereas I think the contrary, there is absolutely no difficulty in a friendly resolution of the dispute. We can form a little deputation and *ask* Professors *X* and *Y* or – if we are anxious to escape the contempt of the more astringent behaviourists among the younger generation – we can stealthily fix up a rather elaborate experiment in which Professors *X* and *Y* are exposed to the respective temptations of the commodities in question, and watch how they respond. On the basis of assumptions of this kind we can develop many of the main propositions of the general theory of value.

But now suppose that Sir Dennis and I differ concerning the absolute level of enjoyment which Professors *X* and *Y* would derive from the possession of the first edition of Ricardo. I say that I think that it is *X* who really gets most out of it whereas Sir Dennis thinks that it is *Y*. In this case no such definite means of resolving the difficulty are available. If we try asking, the probability is that we shall be jointly involved in reproaches of impertinence. "What, compare *my* refined delight in this superb item with the vulgar complacency of that fellow," sniffs Professor *X*. "That effete snob may say what he likes," bellows Professor Y, "but in fact my poor treasures mean more to me than he has ever felt about anything." There is no objective means of settling the dispute.

Let us remind ourselves of the classical passage in which Jevons sets forth the doctrine of non-comparability: it will serve to focus in more sedate language the difficulty I have just set forth. "The reader will find," says Jevons, referring to his theory of value, "that there is never in any single instance an attempt made to compare the amount of feeling in one mind with that in another. I know no means by which such comparison may be accomplished. The susceptibility of one mind may, for what we know, be a thousand times greater than that of another. But provided that the susceptibility was different in a like ratio in all directions, we should never be able to discover the difference. Every mind is thus inscrutable to every other mind and no common denominator of feeling seems to be possible." (*Theory of Political Economy*, 3rd Edition [1888] p. 14.) And he goes on to demonstrate that the theory of value does not need such comparisons.

Now it is the essence of Sir Dennis's position that we do in fact make such comparisons. It is all very well to say that they are impossible, he argues, but in fact they are made continually. Every time we try to make an equitable division of goods, among the factors taken into consideration are the respective capacities for enjoyment of the possible recipients. This happens when the head of the family is serving out dinner. It happens in a more exalted sphere whenever we are discussing distributive justice. Whatever may be the difficulties of making them, such comparisons are actually made.

But this does not really resolve the issue. Presumably no one will dispute that we do make statements of this sort. The question is, are they statements which are capable of verification either by observation or experiment? The occasion of the hypothetical dispute outlined above was the making of such comparisons, and the problem was how to judge between them, if the comparisons made by one person happened to differ from the comparisons made by another.

At this point, let me produce my tiny olive branch. In the past, comparing judgments which are capable of objective verification with judgments which are not so verifiable, I have sometimes put my point in the form of a comparison between judgments of fact and judgments of value. Mr. Little takes me to task for this usage. We should regard the judgment that one man was angrier than another, as a judgment of fact, he argues. Why should not the judgment that one man is happier than another, fall into the same category?

Now there is never much point in disputes about mere words. I think it could be argued that, because of the unavailability of objective tests, there was an element of the subjective in statements about anger. But, provided Mr. Little and Sir Dennis will agree that the kind of judgment here differs as regards verifiability from the kind of judgment with which I have contrasted it, I agree to accept rebuke for using the term judgment of value in a way they dislike, and to remain quiet, and indeed in a sense acquiescent, when they say they are making judgments of a certain kind of fact. In any case I would emphasize that to say of a judgment that it is a judgment of value does not mean that it is a merely arbitrary judgment. I don't know how values arise in the world or how we come to perceive them. But I am sure that judgments of value are an essential ingredient of purposeful action. And I like to think that when we argue about them, although we cannot test our results in the way in which we can test purely scientific arguments, we are not merely arguing to decide who is to be master of the world.

Having said this, however, I must go on to maintain that the propositions involving interpersonal comparisons which Sir Dennis wishes to defend, rest ultimately upon assumptions which are essentially *conventional* in character. When, for purposes of discussion of, let us say, the effects of progressive taxation, we assume that the economic subjects are equally capable of deriving satisfaction from equal increments of income, we are certainly not even pretending to be talking about facts. If we were trying to make statements about the facts of the situation, I suspect that most of us would say that people are not equal in this respect, that their capacity differs enormously. But that, of course, would be neither here nor there. For good or for bad, what we are doing in this connection is to make statements about the logical implications of certain conventions which, at bottom, are *political*. It is as though we had said, society will not be just, or it will not run so as to yield good results, unless we act *as if* the citizens were equally capable of satisfactions. I don't urge that this is always a sensible thing to say; I can conceive all sorts of reasons why this procedure is not always as helpful as is often thought. But I do urge that this is what in fact is being done. And I do urge, further – and here I come back to Sir Dennis – that this exploration of the implications of political conventions is something which is skies apart from the kind of analysis employed in the pure theory of consumers' behaviour. Sir Dennis seems to think that, unless they are all of a piece, the whole structure of thought collapses. I would argue rather that in the pure theory of value we do better without the conventions; and that in any theory of general welfare, instead of pretending to proceed within the same universe as that of the theory of value and distribution, we do far better to introduce our supplementary assumptions explicitly and attempt to vindicate them for what they are – conventions imported into applied economics from the sphere of political philosophy.

V

But this brings me to the last point I wish to raise in this already too protracted commentary.

Throughout all the detail of Sir Dennis's strictures, there runs a recurrent motive – the apprehension, namely, that the cumulative tendency of recent reformations is greatly to diminish the utility of our subject. The abandonment of old-style measurability,[1] the rejection of the distinction between economic and other forms of welfare, the recognition that the Jevonian "gulf" is only to be bridged by a convention imported from elsewhere, these changes, he fears, threaten "to reduce our discipline to utter sterility" and make it impossible for us to give advice which is helpful about anything.

1. Attentive readers will please note the adjective. I leave to others, more expert than I am, the question whether the kinds of order that we recognize may not, in some sense, be said to be measurable.

I do not share this view. I admit that there is practical usefulness in the contrast between changes in production – or, better said, productive power – and changes in distribution; and as one who in the past has expressed scepticism of the possibility of making judgments here without the importation of conventional elements, I have welcomed recent contributions which have rendered this scepticism unnecessary. I am indeed a little surprised that Sir Dennis is not more sympathetic to these contributions; for their explicit purpose is to put the contrast to which he attaches so much importance, on a firmer conceptual basis. I should be very sorry to say anything which might cause Mr. Kaldor the slightest embarrassment; but since his original suggestion of the compensation test was made by way of criticism of something I had said, it is perhaps not inappropriate for me to say that I have always thought that it was a very helpful idea. I would not suggest that it is likely to be very helpful in practice. But it is always a good thing to get our ideas straight: and to be able to define clearly the conditions under which we can speak of a change involving a change of productive power, is surely something to be welcomed.

But suppose that this was not established. Even so, I should still find it hard to agree with Sir Dennis's fears. Why should it vitiate the utility of a scientific discipline to admit that it cannot anywhere be used for purposes of *appraisal* without invoking criteria which come from outside? Is it a reproach to classical mechanics that *by itself* it furnishes no ultimate prescriptions for civil engineering? Is it not sufficient that, in its humble way, it can be held to provide knowledge which is *relevant*, if these ultimate aims are to be satisfactorily carried out? Similarly with economics. *By itself* the knowledge it provides may furnish no means of choosing between social objectives. But if it can provide knowledge which is relevant to this choice, that is enough. And that, surely, is not in question. How much of what is said in the rest of this invaluable book really stands or falls on the cardinal measurement of utility or on the objectivity of interpersonal comparisons?

Against this Sir Dennis might urge that a man who wished to be helpful in civil engineering would almost certainly fail if he knew nothing but classical mechanics, and that an economist who wishes to be helpful on policy will be unlikely to achieve his aim if he knows nothing but economics as restricted by modern reformulations. On this there must be full agreement. But how remedy the situation? Sir Dennis would seek to endow his economist with a wider, although limited and appropriately diffident, authority derived from within economics itself. I feel that this hope is vain and that it is far better from the outset to look elsewhere for the measuring rods of appraisal. Sir Dennis has a more ambitious conception of what economics itself implies but would confine the economist to that sphere. I incline to a narrower view of what can be got out of economics alone and exhort the economist, if he hopes to be at all useful, deliberately to look outside.

Here, as elsewhere, it is important not to exaggerate the practical significance of all this. Sir Dennis's peroration contains a superb summary of the considerations outside economics, as he conceives it, which are relevant to final judgment; and it is difficult to believe that any change in definitions and primary conceptions could make more penetrating or more piquant the quality of his analysis and advice on particular problems. But there is, I suspect, a pedagogic issue which is not entirely unimportant. The masters of our subject in modern times, from Alfred Marshall to Sir Dennis himself, have all been men whose educational background included much more than mere economics and who invoked history and politics with authority. I confess that it has sometimes occurred to me that, for students, too exclusive an attention to the subject as Sir Dennis describes it, may sometimes run the danger of consequences which we should all agree to be unfortunate – immediately, despite the warnings of introductory chapters, a naïve belief that most, if not all, of the solutions to modern problems were to be found within its ambit; and later, when disillusionment has supervened, a habit, most disconcerting to one's fellows, of rediscovering the most crashing truisms of politics and history and leaping from the bath, so to speak, with Archimedean enthusiasm, running naked through the city recommending them stridently to all and sundry.

Is this altogether fantastical? I do not think it is, even though the induction be a trifle Baconian. But I would not like to conclude without emphasizing that in this instance, as in all the others I have touched upon in these comments, it is only with reserve and some trepidation that I express views which may diverge from those of the wisest and most eminent practising economist in this country.

20 Schumpeter's History of Economic Analysis[1]

From *The Quarterly Journal of Economics*, vol. 69 (February 1955), pp. 1–22.

I

The contents of this large and (physically) very heavy volume are correctly indicated by its title. It is not a history of theories of policy; nor is it a history of economic systems; these matters are discussed only in so far as they throw light on the central subject – the evolution of those techniques of thought which enable us to describe and explain the economic aspects of reality. The plan falls into five parts. Part I (pp. 3–50) is devoted to a vindication of the autonomy of the subject and a discussion of its relations with other branches of knowledge. Part II (pp. 51–378) traces developments from the beginnings in Greco–Roman times to the promulgation in the last half of the eighteenth century of the Physiocratic and Smithian systems. Part III (pp. 379–752) deals with the period 1780 to 1870, so covering the English Classical school in its full development. Part IV (pp. 753–1138) takes us down to 1914 "and later," and ranges far and wide over the evolution of analysis since the Jevonian revolution. Part V (pp. 1139–84) is a fragment and deals in a sketchy way with certain very recent developments.

The genesis of this most ambitious enterprise lies a long way back. The monograph, *Epochen der Methoden- und Dogmengeschichte*, which as a young man Schumpeter contributed to the Tübingen *Grundriss der Sozialökonomik* [in 1914], had at once taken its place as incontestably the best short introduction to its subject; and several attempts had been made to induce its author to consent to an English translation. But he always held these at arm's length, declaring himself to be desirous of making some revision before allowing such a version to appear. Eventually, in 1941, when he had finished his *Capitalism, Socialism and Democracy*, he embarked upon

1. Joseph A. Schumpeter, *History of Economic Analysis*, edited from manuscript by Elizabeth Boody Schumpeter (New York: Oxford University Press, 1954).

this task, apparently conceiving it as a convenient side line to his main concern of preparing a major work on theory. Gradually, however, his interest developed; and thus for the last nine years of his life, so Mrs. Schumpeter tells us, it became a dominating preoccupation.

At the time of his death, his labors had resulted in the work which is embodied in the present volume. But the materials were far from their present form: they were scattered in many manuscripts in many places, some typed and corrected, some only typed, some merely in longhand. We owe it to Mrs. Schumpeter, devoted to this task through a prolonged illness even to the last weeks of her life, that the manuscripts have been assembled in their present form – a coherent, if not finally completed, book. The story of this reconstruction is itself almost a minor epic. The annals of our profession abound with the examples of wives whose unselfishness has made possible their husbands' books; and more than one wife has successfully supervised the publication of posthumous works. But it is doubtful whether there is any parallel to such a labor as this – a shining example of what comradely devotion can achieve. It is quite true that the book is not finished in the sense in which the author would have finished it had he lived to see it through the press. A few chapters are unwritten; several are unfinished. Occasionally even sentences tail off without a conclusion – the editor conceived her "editorial task to be the simple one of presenting as complete and accurate a version of what J.A.S. actually wrote as possible but not attempting to complete what he had not written." But, as with the Leonardo *Adoration* in the Uffizi, the grand proportions are there: and if some details are unfinished and others lacking, if here the perspective is only indicated by a sketch and there alternative versions blur the outlines, yet it is essentially an integral creation, to be judged and enjoyed as a whole.

II

There were many reasons why Schumpeter should have been peculiarly well fitted for an enterprise of this sort. He was born and brought up in one of the most brilliant and cultivated societies of Europe before the decline, at that time one of the chief centres of speculation in theoretical economics. As a young man he had travelled widely and studied in many other places; he had personal contact with many of the founders of modern economic analysis elsewhere. He had thus exceptional opportunities for appreciating the unity in apparent diversity of different traditions and different schools of thought. His experience, moreover, was not wholly academic. He had some knowledge of the world of affairs, both of politics and of business, although, if common report is to be believed, his achievements in these fields were not of any conspicuous excellence. He thus approached his subject with that modicum of practical experience without which, although it is no integral part of the subject, so much economic analysis is apt to be sterile. Then, in his middle age, when still at the height of his powers, a great American university had called him to a position, remote from these temptations, with exactly the right combination of academic duty and leisure, in which, all passion spent – or nearly spent – these powers could express themselves without distraction.

There were gifts, too, of intellect and temperament reinforcing these environmental advantages. He had a first-rate mind. He had himself made contributions of distinction to the corpus of modern analysis. Unlike many who have written on the history of this subject, he knew what it was about from the inside; he spoke with the authority of a high practitioner. He was, moreover, an excellent expositor and showman; in our profession, with the single exception of Keynes, he was probably the best talker of his generation. Then, although he was not incapable of the slightly feline dig, he was essentially fair and good-tempered. Himself the product of many streams of influence, his whole intellectual bent was eclectic – an excellent thing in an historian of thought. Indeed, it is arguable that at times this quality was present almost to excess; there are places in this book where the distribution of praise is on so lavish a scale that it is hard to suppress a feeling of being present at some very high-grade get-together at which the exceptionally knowledgeable chairman is almost too meticulously careful not to leave unmentioned any guest, however humble. Finally, with all his erudition, he was no pedant. He felt none of that compulsion often felt by men of high ability to see good only in one line, no matter what else is excluded. He knew enough of the world to know why some men of sense are irritated by economics; but he knew so much of economics that he knew too at what stage this irritation ceased to be justified. All of which, it must be agreed, constituted quite exceptional qualifications for writing the history of analysis.

Let it be said at once that the result, slightly unfinished as it is, is something which is without serious rival. The history of economic analysis has attracted some very first class talent: some of the contributions – such works, for instance, as Professor Viner's *Studies* or Mr. Sraffa's *Ricardo** – are outstanding in the scholarship of historical studies in general. But for the most part the work of high excellence here has taken the form of special studies rather than general history. There is very little that is absolutely first class in this sphere and nothing that will stand comparison, either in respect of scale or insight, with this work of Schumpeter's. This is

* Jacob Viner, *Studies in the Theory of International Trade* (New York, 1937); Piero Sraffa, ed., *The Works and Correspondence of David Ricardo*, 11 vols (Cambridge, 1951–73).

a really serious and mature treatment of the subject. And, although every expert reader will probably find something to grumble about in the parts which deal with the periods or authors he knows best, yet taking things in the large, it is safe to say that it will be a long time before it is displaced as the leading work in its field. Whether at the same time it is a good introduction is a matter of greater dubiety. If one has some familiarity with the material discussed, it is not easy to decide whether all the copious references and allusions are necessarily well suited to convey a clear picture to the beginner. My own guess would be that very frequently they are not. But this is no criticism of the book on the plane on which it elects to move. The right way to begin to acquire a knowledge of the subject is to read the original texts themselves. Reading about them, pondering comments on their significance, comes later; and it is at this stage that Schumpeter comes into his own. And if any beginner, not knowing his way about, is in need of a compendious guide, he can always read the *Epochen* – now at last fortunately available in translation.

If this verdict is correct, if here at last we have something which can be regarded as a standard work on its subject, it follows that criticism must be concerned chiefly with matters of particular perspective and detail. That, indeed, in the main is the substance of what follows. But before thus closing up to the canvas, it is perhaps worth asking whether there are no critical comments to be made of its general appearance and execution.

In my judgment there are two – not, I think, of such importance as seriously to detract from the total achievement, but still perhaps deserving to be put on record.

First, I must confess that I find it hard to resist a certain impression of undue length. By this, I hasten to say, I mean no derogation of its aim or its merit as a treatise on the grand scale – despite the canons of a somewhat short-winded age, there *is* a certain virtue in bigness, provided that it is proportionate to its object. I refer rather to a certain tendency to discursiveness, a certain lack of control of the impulse to elaborate, which at times at least seems to be excessive. I suspect that this book could have been a couple of hundred pages shorter with advantage. This is perhaps partly due to the unfinished state of the manuscript: a final revision would almost certainly have involved a slimming process here and there – it would be unfair not to take this into account. But partly it is probably due to a more fundamental cause; I suspect that Schumpeter's literary habits did tend to over-elaboration – think, for instance, of the *Wesen und Hauptinhalt* – or even, dare I say it, of *Business Cycles*.* I ought perhaps to add that I do not think that the result is

* *Das Wesen und der Hauptinhalt der theoretischen Nationalökonomie* (Leipzig, 1908); *Business Cycles* (New York, 1939).

boring; the many long summer days that I have devoted to reading these 1184 pages have been most agreeable. It was always pleasant to hear Schumpeter hold forth, even if now and then his points were a little otiose. But prolixity is a fault, even though it may sometimes be a fault on the good side; and I think that this book is a little prolix.

Secondly, I suspect that now and then there is a tendency to overemphasis and even to paradox in connection with certain reputations. This is not an easy point to make, since, taking the book as a whole, one of its chief merits is its excellent perspective. Moreover, it may well be that some differences with Schumpeter here are irreducible differences of temperament and local affiliation. Nevertheless, I do think that from time to time there are errors of this sort, so that, so to speak, certain figures suddenly pop out of the canvas and lose relation with their surroundings. Thus, for instance, on page 465 in the course of a well-merited eulogy of von Thünen we are surprised to read that "If we judge both men exclusively *by the amount of ability of the purely theoretical kind* that went into their work, then, I think Thünen should be placed above Ricardo or indeed above any economist of the period with the possible exception of Cournot." Now, of course, arguing about class lists at this level is not a particularly profitable occupation: and arguing about von Thünen in particular is highly esoteric. But surely there is something wrong about a judgment which, leaving aside von Thünen, even on Schumpeter's somewhat specialized criterion, would place Cournot above Ricardo. Cournot was certainly a highly talented man whose formulations of the demand function and the theory of monopoly were contributions of absolutely first class importance. But let us apply the good Austrian test of the so-called loss principle. Suppose the theoretical contributions of Ricardo and Cournot to be alternately withdrawn – which would involve the greater impoverishment? Can there really be any hesitation about the answer? Certainly the relative amounts of space given to the work of these two authors by Schumpeter himself would seem to leave no doubt about it. Similarly, later on in the book, we find pre-eminence in his period assigned to Walras rather than to Marshall[1] – although it must be said at once that Schumpeter has many fine things to say about the latter. Again, I cannot but feel a certain artificiality of emphasis. Undoubtedly Walras was a great economist, perhaps among the greatest. But is it really to be argued that the loss of his contribution, outstanding though it was, could outweigh the loss of Marshall's? We may agree that Walras had a raw deal during his life and is probably not sufficiently appreciated even in our own day. But I submit it is to get our perspective wrong if, in the laudable effort to rehabilitate him, we rate him as high as all that. But more of this later.

1. *Op. cit.*, p. 827.

III

Part II, where the history really begins, runs from Plato and Aristotle to the physiocrats and Adam Smith. It is easy to see the advantages of this arrangement. The vision of streams of fragmentary pieces of economic analysis springing from the treatises of moral philosophers and the *ad hoc* utterances of administrators and pamphleteers and culminating in the eighteenth century in the discovery of the system in economic life, is a fine one and opens up grand perspectives. But to exhibit it without a break in time has two disadvantages: it tends to minimize the degree of achievement in the eighteenth century discovery of system: Quesnay and Adam Smith (and Cantillon before them) were not just two more moral philosophers or pamphleteers. And to have a break after Adam Smith but not before tends to suggest a certain divorce between the *Wealth of Nations* and the Classical writings of the nineteenth century which may foster misunderstanding; the unity of the English Classical school, either as regards analysis or as regards policy, is not to be understood save in the light of a common acceptance of the general outlook of Adam Smith. In the *Epochen* there were two parts covering this period: Part I, *Die Entwicklung der Socialökonomik zur Wissenschaft* which dealt with the philosophers and pamphleteers, and Part II, *Die Entdeckung des Wirtschaftlichen Kreislaufs*, which, as its name implies, dealt with the discovery of the economic system. I am inclined to think that for the main purpose of the book, although perhaps not for the treatment of such subjects as money and interest, this arrangement was superior.

So far as the philosophers and pamphleteers are concerned, the treatment seems to me to be in the main well proportioned and just. I say this with some reserve, since so far as the scholastic writings are concerned, I have never lived with the original texts long enough to form more than the broadest impressions; and there are a great many aspects of the mercantilist literature about which I still find it very hard to make up my mind. It is quite clear that the rejection of most of this literature as worthless was a gross error: if the classical economists have suffered from overcrude interpretations of their point of view, it must be admitted that they themselves were guilty of the same kind of unfairness in regard to their predecessors. But I am fairly sure that more recent interpretations, either by members of the Historical school or by Keynes, tend to err in the opposite direction: the theory of the barrenness of money did not rest upon a liquidity preference theory of interest, nor did emphasis, in a régime of advancing prices, upon the accumulation of treasure necessarily rest upon dread of deflation. In spite of a certain love of paradox and of the *recherché*, Schumpeter treads very delicately here. I suspect that some of those who know best these branches of the literature would tend to the view that his interpretations were still too charitable; and there is doubtless much scope for dispute about particular interpretations. But in general his treatment must command respect: if it is not a final verdict, it provides at least agenda for grown-up talk.

On the eighteenth century developments I find him less impressive. He has none of Hume's feelings about the physiocrats – very much the contrary indeed;[1] and he provides an account of Quesnay's position which I venture to say is much more impressive and very much more intelligible than anything that that very gnomic expositor ever wrote himself. But he still leaves one reader at least with the feeling that, individually and as a group, they have sometimes been overpraised and are indeed overpraised by him. Doubtless the *Tableau Economique* can be construed to stand for an idea of great power and importance – though I fancy that there is more jobbing backward in this interpretation than we are often prepared to admit. But it is surely a significant circumstance that among the rest of the group the scientific aspect of the *Tableau* had hardly any influence; it was an object of worship, the symbol of a cult rather than a stimulus to further development. If profundity of thought and scientific detachment are the qualities to be valued, the work of Petty and of Cantillon seems to me to be on a much higher level.

As for the treatment of Adam Smith, I am inclined to regard it as one of the few real lapses in the book. There can be little doubt that Adam Smith was one of Schumpeter's blind spots. In an earlier, though not so much earlier, essay, he describes Smith's achievement as a "'burst into publicity' – the *Wealth of Nations* was not more than this."[2] And in the present volume he actually says that nobody who had not read them would credit the author of the *Wealth of Nations* with the power to write the posthumously published essays.[3] It would be possible, of course, to quote sentences which in themselves convey high praise. But I do not think that it is open to question that the general impression which is left by the treatment of Adam Smith is one of slightly patronizing, slightly derogatory debunking – the man was a good systematizer of other people's ideas, an excellent expositor, lucky in his period, whose "very limitations made for success."[4] Why this was so, whether it was because of Smith's coolness about Political Arithmetic – he "took the safe side that was so congenial to him"[5] – or whether it was because of some chemical disaffinity of temperament – "a fact which I cannot help considering

1. "They are, indeed, the set of men the most chimerical and arrogant that now exist, since the annihilation of the Sorbonne ... I wonder what could engage our friend, M. Turgot, to herd among them." *Letters of David Hume*, ed. J.Y.T. Greig (Oxford, 1932), Vol. II, p. 205.

2. "Professor Taussig on wages and capital," *Explorations in Economics: notes and essays contributed in honor of F.W. Taussig* (New York, 1936), p. 213.

3. *Op. cit.*, p. 182.

4. *Ibid.*, p. 185.

5. *Ibid.*, p. 212.

relevant, not for his mere economics, of course, but all the more for his understanding of human nature – that no woman, excepting his mother, ever played a role in his existence,"[1] – it is difficult to say. But the existence of some nonrational inhibition is incontestable. It is not the first time that a scholar with Schumpeter's background has been baffled and irritated by the unpretentious clarity and restraint of eighteenth century English moral philosophy.

IV

Part III, which occupies nearly four hundred pages, contains the fullest and most systematic account to be found anywhere of the Classical system in its full development. For this much gratitude is due. But I have some reservations about matters which are not altogether unimportant.

First a matter of background influence – the role of Utilitarian moral philosophy. I am inclined to think that Schumpeter got this all wrong. I am not thinking here of his description of this outlook as "the shallowest of all conceivable philosophies of life;"[2] that can conceivably be overlooked as a lapse into Neo-Hegelian cliché which might perhaps have been expunged in a final revision. I am thinking rather of his suggestion that the Utilitarian background was to be conceived as confined to Bentham and the two Mills.[3]

This seems to me very questionable. I would have said rather that the background of the entire school, from its beginnings in Hume's *Essays* right through to Cairnes and Sidgwick, was through and through Utilitarian – and this stands even for Adam Smith whose explicit moral philosophy had a somewhat different complexion. In my judgment it is a mistake to regard Bentham and the Mills as *the* characteristic English Utilitarians. They represent – or at least Bentham and James Mill represent – a peculiarly severe and idiosyncratic version of a general outlook which, from a philosophical point of view, has had much more persuasive advocates both before and since.[4] And the habit of judging actions and policies by their consequences rather than by reference to some intuitive norm, which is the salient characteristic of this outlook in contrast to that of the continental metaphysicals, was common to almost all the English speaking economists of the age. The contrast is well exemplified in Nassau Senior's conversation with the de Broglies:

---

1. *Ibid.*, p. 182.
2. *Ibid.*, pp. 133 and 407.
3. *Ibid.*, p. 408.
4. Schumpeter's footnote (p. 408) in which he tries to rescue Sidgwick from this classification is not one of his happier efforts.

"This led us to talk of Bowood and from Bowood we went to Bentham. The Duke had never seen his Bowood correspondence: indeed he seemed to be little acquainted with his works. The Prince knew more of them but admitted that he had not studied them accurately.

Prince de Broglie – There are valuable hints in them as there must be in the works of a man of diligence and originality, but they scarcely repay the labour of mastering a system based on error.

Senior – Do you reject then utility as the foundation of morals?

Prince de Broglie – Certainly I do. It is generally rejected in France.

Senior – And what do you substitute?

Prince de Broglie – Our innate feelings of right and wrong."[1]

It might be argued, of course, that Senior was just the neutral interrogator, as he so frequently was in his conversations. But I am pretty sure that in this instance this interpretation would be wrong. The question, what is to be done if we reject considerations of utility, is typical of the attitude of the main tradition of English political economy. I hasten to add that I fully agree with Schumpeter that the logical coherence of their analytical propositions does not stand or fall with this background.[2]

Next comes a matter of position and influence. It is Schumpeter's contention – or at least, so it appears at a certain stage of his argument – that Ricardo's influence has been overstressed, that there were no conspicuous Ricardians save James Mill, McCulloch, and De Quincey, and that, by the beginning of the thirties, the school had spent itself and was no longer a living force. There were the Ricardian socialists, of course, there were Marx and Rodbertus – and Rossi! But the main stream of English Classical analysis had emancipated itself from this influence. This is a point of view which recently has had some support in other quarters. It is, therefore, perhaps deserving of more thorough examination.

A great deal of the paradox in this position begins to vanish if we are prepared sufficiently to narrow our concept of what the Ricardian position was. Of course, if we interpret this position as chiefly involving the assumption of an absolute standard of value, on the lines attacked by Bailey,[3] and the peculiar doctrine regarding the relation between "wages" and "profits" (i.e.,

1. Nassau Senior, *Conversations with M. Thiers, M. Guizot and other Distinguished Persons during the Second Empire* (London, 1878), Vol. II, p. 176.

2. Painful experience compels me to register the hope that the above piece of historical diagnosis will not be taken as a manifesto of personal affiliation. Personally, I am content to be something of a pluralist in moral philosophy. I think a utilitarian calculus is quite a good first approximation to many of the workaday problems of social policy. For the ultimate problems of personal conduct I am much less disposed to regard it as helpful.

3. It is more than doubtful whether Ricardo would have pleaded guilty to this indictment.

proportionate wages and proportionate profits) which from that day to this have been such a stumbling block to correct interpretation, it is perhaps just to say that it died with James Mill – with De Quincey's *Logic* as a very belated posthumous progeny – and we can even bring ourselves to stomach the astonishing proposition that J.S. Mill was not really Ricardian.[1]

But this surely is an intolerable restriction. A juster definition, I suggest, would leave the influence of Ricardo over a very wide field quite dominant throughout the whole of the Classical period. It was a stroke of expository genius, on Schumpeter's part, to make Senior's fundamental propositions the peg on which to hang his central analysis of the Classical position. But how much of Senior's work would have seen the light in the form in which it did, were it not for the influence and example of Ricardo? It is true that at many points Senior is critical of Ricardo. But where else in his book does Schumpeter restrict the significance of the term "influence" to slavish reproduction? What is relevant in this connection is not whether the analysis of value and distribution of Senior and J.S. Mill – not to mention money and international trade – followed Ricardo in all respects but whether it conformed to the type of analysis of which his works are the archetype. I cannot help thinking that, once he had released his paradox, Schumpeter would not really have disputed this position. At any rate by page 677 we find him arguing, apropos of the theory of rent, that "so great was Ricardo's success that even some writers who adopted Say's scheme in other respects, inserted into it a Ricardian treatment of rent without betraying any symptom of logical discomfort."[2]

In this connection I am inclined to suggest that much too much can be made of some of the things said at the celebrated evenings of January 13th and April 15th, 1831, at the Political Economy Club at which the question was debated "What improvements have been effected in the Science of Political Economy since the publication of Mr. Ricardo's great work: and are any of the principles first advanced in that work now acknowledged to be correct." A recent writer[3] in *Economica* has made the account of the proceedings given in Mallet's diary a reinforcement for a diagnosis of rapid decline of Ricardian Economics. In fact, however, Mallet's account is by no means decisive on this point. The general conclusion, at the end of the second meeting, seems to have been that "Ricardo is a bad and obscure writer, using the same terms in different senses: but that his principles are in the main

1. *Op. cit.*, p. 529.
2. The writers were Roscher and J.S. Mill.
3. Ronald L. Meek, "The decline of Ricardian economics in England," *Economica*, n.s., vol. 17 (February 1950), pp. 43–62.

right."[1] What is perhaps, however, even more significant and what has apparently escaped Dr. Meek's attention is that Torrens, who on this occasion was the ringleader of the anti-Ricardians, subsequently repented of this attitude and published one of the most candid retractations in the history of economic discussion. I do not think that this covered his critique of the Ricardian search for a measure of value: he continued to give praise to Bailey. But it certainly covered the rest. The Introduction to the *Budget* is largely an attempted vindication of Ricardo on profits and a disavowal of earlier strictures on this doctrine and on the theory of rent. "Some of the commentators on the doctrines of Ricardo appear to have fallen into the misconception that, in altering his nomenclature, and in modifying his principles as varying circumstances required, they refuted his theory of profits. In this censure I include myself."[2]

I now come to a number of more detailed points. In his discussion of population theory, Schumpeter gives the impression that the law of diminishing returns had nothing to do with the original formulation of Malthusian doctrine. This view, of course, has very formidable supporters. No less an authority than Edwin Cannan, who was so seldom wrong on his texts, gave it a classic form in his dictum that "to imagine that the *Essay on the Principle of Population* was ever based on the law of diminishing returns is to confuse Malthusianism as expounded by J.S. Mill with Malthusianism as expounded by Malthus."[3] Nevertheless, I do not think that he was right. Admittedly, the mere comparison of geometrical and arithmetical potentialities of increase does not itself necessarily involve this relationship. But the idea underlying the comparison is of the same order of conceptions; and it is surely no mere coincidence that in another connection Malthus was one of the first to formulate the so-called law. This, of course, has been perceived before and, indeed, is clearly the basis of the view which is attacked by Cannan; up to this point, perhaps, the issue might be regarded as undecided. But the textual evidence seems to indicate otherwise. It is true that there is no mention of diminishing returns in the *first* edition of the *Essay*. I am not so clear, however, that this can be asserted of the second edition, where, on page 7, we are told that "in proportion as cultivation extended, the addition that could yearly be made to the former average produce must be gradually and regularly diminishing."

1. Centenary Volume of the Political Economy Club (London, 1921), p. 225.
2. *The Budget: On Commercial and Colonial Policy* (London, 1844), p. xxxvi.
3. *A History of Theories of Production and Distribution in English Classical Political Economy from 1776 to 1848* (London, 1893), p. 144. In my salad days, in a *festschrift* for Cannan, I echoed this view very strongly. The curious may consult "The optimum theory of population," *London Essays in Economics: in Honour of Edwin Cannan*, eds T. Gregory and H. Dalton (London, 1927), pp. 104–5.

What, however, seems to me decisive is the language of the *Summary View of the Principle of Population*, the extract from his article in the Supplement to the *Encyclopaedia Britannica* which Malthus issued in 1830.

"It has already been stated, that while land of good quality is in great abundance, the rate at which food might be made to increase would far exceed what is necessary to keep pace with the most rapid increase of population which the laws of nature in relation to human kind permit. But if society were so constituted as to give the fullest scope possible to the progress of cultivation and population, all such lands, and all lands of moderate quality, would soon be occupied; and when the future increase of the supply of food came to depend upon the taking of very poor land into cultivation, and the gradual and laborious improvement of the land already cultivated, the rate of the increase of food would certainly have a greater resemblance to a decreasing geometrical ratio than to an increasing one. The yearly movement of food would, at any rate, have a constant tendency to diminish, and the amount of the increase of each succeeding ten years would probably be less than that of the preceding."[1]

Clearly this is not a very strict formulation. But at least it makes it very difficult to maintain that there was no connection in Malthus' mind between his ratios and diminishing returns to labor applied to land. The good sense of the matter seems to be admirably expressed by Dr. McCleary when he says that "although Malthus did not explicitly base his arithmetical ratio on the law of Diminishing Returns, the concept of diminishing returns was present and influential in his mind."[2]

I find myself equally unable to agree with Schumpeter upon an important aspect of the Ricardian theory of value. On pages 600 and 601 he has a long disquisition on Ricardo's perversity in opposing the supply and demand theory for the explanation of long-run values, contending that he was "completely blind to the nature and the logical place in economic theory of the supply and demand apparatus ... had he but stopped to ask *why* exchange values of commodities would be proportional to the quantities of standard labour embodied in them, he would, in answering this question, have found himself using the supply and demand apparatus by which alone (under appropriate assumptions) that law of value can be established."

Now there can be no doubt that Ricardo had himself to thank for a great deal of the misunderstanding which has arisen in this connection. To have written a whole chapter *against* the supply and demand theory, without

1. *Op. cit.* Reprinted in D.V. Glass, *Introduction to Malthus* (London, 1953), p. 139.
2. *The Malthusian Population Theory* (London, 1953), p. 111. This excellent essay may be strongly recommended as the sanest study of this highly controversial subject. It is worth observing that Dr. McCleary's view has the support of the high authority of Marshall.

defining more clearly exactly wherein lay the nature of his opposition, was simply asking for trouble. Moreover, it is clear that once we get away from the very peculiar basis of the Ricardian theory, there is a wide sense in which the cost of production which may be opposed to supply and demand as an explanation of normal value, is itself determined by the forces underlying supply and demand for factors and their products; the special theory which sidetracks all this proves to be based on intolerably restrictive assumptions. Nevertheless, the idea that while he accepted supply and demand as determining market values, he ignored their operation in the determination of natural values is a complete mare's nest, despite the very high authority, from Senior onwards, by which it has been supported. This is conclusively shown by the very *Notes on Malthus* to which Schumpeter refers us; the relevant note stands out half a mile:

"Mr. Malthus mistakes the question – I do not say that the value of a commodity will always conform to its natural value without an additional supply, but I say that the cost of production regulates the supply and therefore regulates the price."[1]

V

Part IV, 1870–1914 (and later) is in effect a review of modern economic theory since Jevons and, in my judgment, is the best thing in the whole book. These were the developments, which were most congenial to Schumpeter's own temperament, and it was here that his roving eclecticism and the conciliatory side of his character showed themselves to their best advantage. The story is told both in terms of persons and of theorems. The leading personalities are reviewed; some of the sketches here are astonishingly felicitous: for instance, I do not think that Böhm-Bawerk and his contribution have ever been more persuasively depicted. The general character of theoretical developments in different fields is set forth. A special chapter is devoted to elucidating the contents of equilibrium analysis with the *Elements* of Walras playing the part here which, in the section on the Classical theorems, was allotted to Senior's four propositions. There are special studies of the evolution of the idea of the production function and the vicissitudes of the theory of utility, and a separate chapter on money and cycle theory. If any enquirer wishes for a unified account of what modern theory (not merely to 1914 but, as the title says in brackets, "and later") has been about, it is here for him to read.

1. *Notes on Malthus*, Sraffa edn of *Works*, Vol. II, pp. 48–9.

Perhaps the most admirable feature of all this is its cumulative demonstration of the underlying unity, amid apparent diversity, of all this speculative activity. Schumpeter excelled at this. It was his real conviction, as I think he once said, that there are fundamentally no schools nowadays, but only good economists and bad economists, and he brings this out with extraordinary sympathy and force in regard to the work of this period. Perhaps from time to time this is overdone. There was, for instance, more at issue in the controversy about real costs than Schumpeter is willing to concede – though I should be perfectly prepared to agree, and indeed to argue, that it can chiefly be resolved into a question of appropriate approximation. Again the undeniable hostility of the Lausanne school to any form of partial equilibrium analysis, however safeguarded and qualified, was a very real barrier between members of that group and their colleagues elsewhere; and their intransigence in that respect, I should say, quite as much as the blameworthy indifference of the outside world, was one of the chief reasons why the good side of their work had to wait so long for recognition. But in the main the assertion of a common subject matter and common methods is sound and it is no small service thus so definitely to have distinguished the wood from the trees.

In this general perspective perhaps the least satisfactory feature is the treatment of Marshall. This is a delicate and difficult matter to elucidate: delicate, since I am fully aware that the main criticisms in this notice may be represented as defenses of a local tradition, difficult, since in many respects Schumpeter writes so well about Marshall – how refreshing, for instance, it is to see it clearly recognized that markets peculiar to individual firms are one of the important features of Marshall's analysis.[1] Nevertheless there are misconceptions and criticisms on which some comment seems to be called for.

Perhaps the best method of approaching the core of discomfort here is by way of examining Schumpeter's contention that Marshall was ungenerous, that he did not pay sufficient tribute to the originators of some of his most fundamental ideas.[2] It seems to me that there is very little in this. I should not be prepared to contend that Marshall was always an altogether agreeable character; he was obviously a bit of a Turk at home and his behavior to Sidgwick on one occasion certainly calls for explanation.[3] But there is really

1. This could perhaps with advantage have been reinforced by explicit quotation of the paragraphs of the *Principles of Economics* (8th edn [London, 1920], pp. 841–50) in the mathematical appendix where the distinction between marginal revenue and price is very clearly set out, together with reasons for neglecting it in analysis of the more competitive part of the field. And if, at this juncture, our author had been in a more hortatory mood, he might have pointed out that, besides being set out very clearly in Cournot, the description of monopoly equilibrium in terms of equality between marginal revenue and marginal cost was even used in such a popular textbook as S.J. Chapman's *Outlines of Political Economy* [London, 1911] (p. 177).

2. *Op. cit.*, pp. 838 ff.

3. See *Henry Sidgwick: A Memoir*, by A.S. and E.M.S. (London, 1906), pp. 394–6.

no evidence at all that he did not handsomely acknowledge the debts of which he was conscious. His references to Cournot and von Thünen probably did more than anything else to revive and spread the reputation of these authors and his solicitude for the position of Ricardo even comes under rebuke from Schumpeter. It is true that he wrote a severe review of Jevons. But there is no reason to doubt his own explanation that he was angered by the treatment of Ricardo and disappointed by the fragmentary nature of the *Theory*. Elsewhere he paid ample tribute to the lively and powerful intelligence of its author.

In this connection it is perhaps worth quoting from a manuscript note which is reproduced in the *Memorials*; it gives a more vivid account of a state of mind than any amount of secondhand conjecture. "I looked," wrote Marshall, "with great excitement for Jevons' *Theory*: but he gave me no help in my difficulties and I was vexed. I have since learned to estimate him better. His many sidedness, his power of combining statistical with analytical investigations, his ever fresh honest sparkling individuality and suggestiveness impressed me gradually; and I reverence him now as among the greatest of economists. But even now I think that the central argument of his *Theory* stands on a lower plane than the work of Cournot and von Thünen ... [M]y youthful loyalty to him [Ricardo] boiled over when I read Jevons' *Theory* ... I have a vivid memory of the angry phrases which would force themselves into my draft, only to be cut out and then reappear in another form a little later on, and then to be cut out again."[1] This is not the utterance of an ungenerous spirit.

A similar quotation may serve to indicate his position regarding Dupuit, another victim of neglect, according to Schumpeter. "The notion of an exact measurement of Consumer's Rent was published by Dupuit in 1844. But his work was forgotten; and the first to publish a clear analysis of the relation of total to marginal (or final) utility was Jevons in 1871, when he had not read Dupuit. The notion of Consumer's Rent was suggested to the present writer by a study of the mathematical aspects of demand and utility under the influence of Cournot, von Thünen and Bentham."[2] This surely is complete enough recognition. Schumpeter speaks of "footnotes in the wrong place."[3] But this footnote is just where it should be – after the exposition of the doctrine of Consumer's Surplus in the text. He might have asked with greater cogency why it was omitted in later editions. But the charitable solution here would rest upon Marshall's conceptions of the exigencies of a textbook in

1. *Memorials of Alfred Marshall*, ed. A.C. Pigou (London, 1925), pp. 99–100.
2. *Principles*, 2nd edn (London, 1891), p. 184.
3. *Op. cit.*, p. 840.

popular use; and when one thinks of the way in which Marshall consistently underplayed his own originality, seeking to present the most pathbreaking constructions as notions assumed implicitly by the masters of the past, it is reasonable to assume that he did not attach overwhelming importance to the acknowledgment on all possible occasions of all possible patents.

There remains the question of his attitude to Walras, to whom reference in the text of the *Principles* is very sparse and that not at all on the main Walrasian contributions. Here we reach considerations much more important than scientific etiquette and the presence or absence of a magnanimous disposition. We have to consider the nature of the respective contributions of the men concerned and Marshall's probable attitude towards that of Walras.

Now there can be no doubt whatever, as Schumpeter himself acknowledges, that Marshall was fully seized of the conceptions of general equilibrium. The attempt, sometimes made by members of the Lausanne school, to oppose a supposititious Marshallian partial equilibrium system to a Walras-cum-Pareto general equilibrium system just will not bear examination. The opening chapters of Book VI (Preliminary Survey of Distribution) together with the famous Note XIV in the Mathematical Appendix are essentially the presentation of an approach as ambitious in its scope and vision as anything presented by Walras, although much more concise in expression. The idea that there can have been anything particularly novel to Marshall in the Walrasian equations is not at all plausible. He certainly knew about utility theory and, as we have seen, he had acknowledged his sources – which were not Walrasian. The influence of demand on the pricing of productive services, explained in terms of the net product and marginal product principles, was a central feature of his own system. Explanation of interest, and hence capitalization, in terms of the productiveness of permanent capital instruments and the discount on the future restraining their supply, was equally prominent in his thought; and the filling out of this statical theory by a cash balance approach to the theory of money had figured prominently in his evidence to the Gold and Silver Commission – some time before Walras had fitted it into his own system. Charged with neglect of the Walrasian contributions, I am sure that Marshall would have defended himself in this manner.

But if asked why nevertheless he did not make more specific reference to their treatment by Walras, I am inclined to think that he would have moved to the offensive. He did not make more specific reference to the Walrasian treatment of these problems, he would have said, because that treatment was on lines with which he was very much out of sympathy. This lack of sympathy arose for a variety of reasons.

First, there was no obvious practical use in this way of setting things forth. "Prof. Edgeworth's plan of representing U and V as general functions of x and y," he said in relation to a different but not dissimilar problem, 'has great attractions to the mathematician; but it seems less adapted to express the every-day facts of economic life than that of regarding, as Jevons did, the marginal utilities of apples as functions of x simply."[1] Marshall, who wanted to use his theory of demand for statistical applications, would tend to be impatient with the complications of the Walrasian functions, and probably felt that, in the first approximation at least, for suitably chosen commodities, they could be neglected.

But, secondly, there was a deeper reason which he himself has set forth very explicitly. On his view the important problems of theory were not problems of describing stationary equilibrium – which was altogether too easy – but rather problems of describing change and development. And while, doubtless, here the statical method was appropriate enough, nay, even indispensable, mathematical methods of presentation tended to become intolerably complex and – what is more to the point – to emphasize the wrong factors. "It would be possible," he said – obviously with Walras and others of that school in mind, but, with characteristic reticence, omitting derogatory explicitness – "to extend the scope of such systems of equations ... and to increase their detail, until they embraced within themselves the whole of the demand side of the problem of distribution. But while a mathematical illustration of the mode of action of a definite set of causes may be complete in itself, and strictly accurate within its clearly defined limits, it is otherwise with any attempt to grasp the whole of a complex problem of real life, or even any considerable part of it, in a series of equations. For many important considerations, *especially those connected with the manifold influences of the element of time* (my italics), do not lend themselves easily to mathematical expression: they must either be omitted altogether, or clipped and pruned till they resemble the conventional birds and animals of decorative art. And hence arises a tendency towards assigning wrong proportions to economic forces: those elements being most emphasized which lend themselves most easily to analytical methods."[2] He goes on to say that nevertheless "in discussions written specially for mathematical readers it is no doubt right to be very bold in the search for wide generalizations." But the general disinclination is writ large – and with Marshall it cannot be ascribed to any lack of aptitude for this kind of analysis.

I am not here concerned to defend this attitude. I am concerned only to explain it. I think myself that it was a great handicap for those of us who had to learn our economics from Marshall's *Principles* that he left so much unstated in the way of statical foundations. We have had laboriously to redis-

1. *Principles*, 8th edn, p. 845.
2. *Ibid.*, p. 850.

cover for ourselves theorems and implications with which he was completely familiar all the time; and this has taken up too large a part of our lives. In this respect at least his passion always to be intelligible to businessmen and practically helpful to the world at large, has been a hindrance rather than a help. But I do think that, whether he was right or wrong in this respect, the underlying attitude which I have tried to make explicit, provides quite a sufficient explanation for the absence of much reference to the Walrasian system. He felt no personal debt in respect of those propositions of Walras with which he was in harmony: and for the rest I suspect that he definitely felt that the emphasis was either superfluous or in the wrong direction. The hypothesis of lack of generosity or of a desire – Schumpeter actually goes out of his way to suggest this – to 'uphold the national tradition' against the wretched foreigners,[1] seems quite uncalled for.

What I think is perhaps even more surprising is Schumpeter's failure here to perceive more clearly the true nature of Marshall's contribution. In estimating the relative merits of Walras and Marshall – it is he who started this hare, not the reviewer – it is not enough to compare their achievements and priorities in the analysis of stationary systems. On this plane, perhaps, there is not much between them; as we have seen there is no doubt that Marshall had all the main theorems and some of the priorities. The point is rather that Marshall did so much more. The characteristic features of the Marshallian system, the analysis of the time element, the doctrine of short and long period normal price, quasi-rents, the dynamic theory of money and credit, the study of growth and decline, are all in a sphere which begins, so to speak, where the Walrasian system tends to leave off. Marshall himself protested against the notion that the central idea of the *Principles* was statical;[2] his claim was that it was "concerned throughout with the forces that cause movement," and that "its keynote" was "that of dynamics, rather than statics," and this claim was surely justified.

It might have been thought that this was a feature which would have made special appeal to Schumpeter, whose own central contribution had been so much in the theory of development: and there are passages, notably where he deals with Marshall's theory of monopoly, where such an attitude emerges. But on more fundamental conceptions, there was, of course, a very deep cleavage. It is not true, as Schumpeter seems at one place to suggest, that Marshall attached no significance to the innovating function of entrepreneurship:[3] quite the contrary indeed. Book VI and the historical sections, both of

1. *Op. cit.*, p. 840.
2. *Principles*, 8th edn, p. xix.
3. *Op. cit.*, p. 892–3.

the *Principles* and of *Industry and Trade*, pay great attention to such factors. But viewing things in the large and not abstracting from the facts of fluctuation, he was inclined to emphasize the continuity of things – *Natura non facit saltum* was the motto of the *Principles* – whereas we know that Schumpeter's conception of the world involved much more of discontinuity and seismic convulsions.

VI

Part V, which is supposed to deal with the most recent developments, is a mere fragment – a series of first drafts which doubtless would have been completely remodelled had their author lived to finish them. Indeed, if the aesthetic unity of the book were the criterion, I should say that their inclusion was a mistake; though as a series of indications of the trends of Schumpeter's thought they were possibly worth preserving. The Introduction consists largely of the syllabus of a rather elementary course delivered at Mexico City. Chapter 2, on "Developments Stemming from the Marshall–Wicksell Apparatus" breaks off almost before it has begun. Chapter 3 on "Economics in the 'Totalitarian' Countries" seems almost pointless for the little it manages to scrape together; and Chapter 4, if it were intended to make very high claims for the progress of dynamics and business cycle research, falls considerably short of achieving its object. This is especially true of the short section on econometrics; after all that has been said earlier in the book about the prospect of placing economics on a more exact basis by research of this type, this jejune report has a distinct effect of anticlimax.

The only chapter which has any pretensions to move on the same level as the rest of the book is Chapter 5 on "Keynes and Modern Macroeconomics." This chapter is as interesting for its overtones as for its explicit content. It is clear that the spectacle of much contemporary Keynesianism inspired in Schumpeter a distaste that must have been almost physical. It is clear too that he was profoundly shocked by Keynes's occasional indifference to scholarly considerations, his eccentric, and frequently unjust judgments of his predecessors, and his obvious ignorance of much earlier work that was very relevant to his subject – deficiencies which, indeed, are inexcusable in smaller fry but which somehow or other do not seem to matter so much with him. His reaction to the man himself, too, was very ambivalent; there seems to have been something in Keynes that alternately attracted and repelled him. But in this chapter he has made a great effort to be fair. The influence of Keynes is acknowledged, his stimulating effect on thought, especially the thought of the young, is emphasized. A handsome tribute is paid to his qualities as economic adviser. And while the assumptions of his theory are set out in a form in which an obvious light is thrown on its limitations, I do not think that any point that is made in this connection is unfair or invalid. Certainly the conclusion that the Keynesian paradoxes hold chiefly in a state of deep underemployment and that when the appropriate corrections are made for conditions of fuller employment, the theory becomes much more "Classical" in general content and implication, is one which would almost certainly have been accepted by Keynes himself – at least in his latest period.

None the less, I doubt if this is a chapter which will satisfy many. It certainly will not satisfy those who hold extreme views on either side: the extreme Keynesians will be content with nothing less than 100 per cent idolatry, the extreme anti-Keynesians with nothing less than excommunication with bell, book and candle. But the satisfaction of more middle views is very doubtful. The thing does not really come to life. There is little to which exception can be taken.[1] The general perspective is not seriously wrong. But it is as though the effort to be fair, the desperate resolution to say nothing that was not just and right, has used up all the author's vitality and penetration. The portrait is not incorrect. But the life has gone. This judgment may be too severe – after all, the chapter is an uncorrected fragment. Nevertheless, I cannot suppress the feeling that however extensive and finished the treatment, it would still have shown the same characteristics.

But I must not end on a note which might suggest any subtraction from the high praise of this book as a general performance which I gave at the beginning of this review.

The last time I met Schumpeter was on a river picnic in the middle thirties. He had turned up unexpectedly from the United States on the day of our annual seminar outing at the School; and he was immediately co-opted as an honorary member, so to speak, and pressed into joining the excursion. It was a lovely day in June; and, as we glided down the Thames between Twickenham and Datchet, I can still see him, cheerfully ensconced in the prow of our ship, surrounded by the eager spirits of the day, Nicky Kaldor, Abba Lerner, Victor Edelberg, Ursula Hicks – Webb, as she then was, the

---

1. There is one very bad error of detail on p. 1171 where the outlook of the earlier pages of *The Economic Consequences of the Peace* [1919] is represented as anticipating, at least in regard to England, the author's views on saving – "the arteriosclerotic economy whose opportunities for rejuvenating venture decline while the old habits formed in times of plentiful opportunity persist." This is just not true. The outlook here is exactly the contrary – the war has shaken the institutions which fostered a high rate of saving, "The war has disclosed the possibility of consumption to all and the vanity of abstinence to many" (p. 22), the consequences for the future of capitalism may be disastrous. If anyone doubt this version, he may be referred to the following pronouncement from a *Manchester Guardian Reconstruction Supplement* (Aug. 17, 1922), written only shortly after. "In order to keep our heads above water, the national capital must grow as fast as the national labour supply which means new savings at the rate of £400,000,000 to £500,000,000 per annum."

master-organizer of the party – the four fingers and thumb of each hand pressed against those of the other, discoursing with urbanity and wit on theorems and personalities. So I conceive of this book, a splendid excursion down the river of time, with good talk and magnificent vistas.

21 Notes on Public Finance

From *Lloyds Bank Review*, new series no. 38 (October 1955), pp. 1–18.

I INTRODUCTION

The following notes on certain very general aspects of the problems of public finance are not specifically related to the more technical details of our present budgetary position. In so far, however, as the accession to power of a new government [in May 1995] is a moment when the wider implications of policy may be legitimately conceived as due for consideration, they may perhaps be thought to have some practical relevance. That, at any rate, is their intention. I have the feeling that we are apt to take for granted certain tendencies of contemporary financial policy and to dismiss the prospect of any substantial change as impracticable. My main object is to show that this attitude is uncalled for.

II THE IMPORTANCE OF PUBLIC FINANCE

The first point I want to make is the importance of public finance.

By this I do not mean merely the importance which has been traditionally associated with it for constitutional or personal reasons. Needless to say, the provision and expenditure of public money is a matter of great constitutional significance; and anything which affects our pockets on the scale on which they are affected by modern taxation is a matter of great personal concern. What I have in mind much more in this connection is the positive rôle which is played by the system of public finance in the general working of the economy.

This shows itself in two ways. We are gradually getting used to the idea of the budget as an instrument of over-all stabilization. If the economy is tending to depression we look to measures of public finance to help to reverse the tendency; if it is tending to boom we look for some fiscal curb. It is greatly to be hoped that the revival of monetary policy, which had been so foolishly neglected in the years immediately after the war, will not lead us to abandon these expectations. It is perhaps possible to imagine a world in which the business of stabilization could be left entirely to monetary measures. But the world we inhabit, with its rigidities and insensitive spots, demands a more eclectic treatment. The need for the use of the budget as a stabilizer is a need which has come to stay.

But beyond this we have to take account of public finance as an influence on the long-term evolution of the economy. By this I do not mean merely the use of public funds to finance particular industrial schemes or to encourage particular developments. Doubtless that plays a part – and in some countries an important part. I mean rather something much more far-reaching than this: I mean the general influence of the system of public finance on enterprise, accumulation and the distribution of income and property.

In a vague way, of course, we acknowledge this influence. We spend a great deal of time discussing the influence of taxation on enterprise – with singularly little result. But do we sufficiently appreciate the much more tangible influence of taxation on general social and economic structure? Do we fully realize the way in which the appearances of the material and social world are changed and moulded by the influence of public finance? It is doubtful.

Yet if we consider what actually happens this influence is very obvious. Any man over fifty, who pauses to reflect, knows at once that the world of today is changed almost beyond belief from the world in which he grew up as a boy – the look of town and country, the way we live, the texture of social relations, the distribution of influence and power. Some of this is due to technique – the automobile, the aeroplane, the radio – some to the general growth of wealth and population, some to the shattering impact of war. But any attempt to enumerate the main formative influences which left out the influence of taxation and its effects on relative demand would be very incomplete. In the sphere of policy, indeed, the influence of the tax system is probably greater and more continuous than any other.

We can see this very vividly if we consider alternative forms of policy. In the politics of recent years, the intention to produce change has been quite deliberate. We have had various kinds of control. We have had widespread measures of nationalization. Yet compared with the relentless, ubiquitous influence of the tax machine, these things sink into insignificance. I would not argue that it is a matter of indifference whether certain industries are, or are not, collectively owned and managed; the disadvantages of a form of industrial organization which seems at once insusceptible to control by other organs of the State and yet a continuous liability to the Exchequer if anything goes wrong, seem to me to be not inconsiderable. Yet the difference which is made to the distribution of wealth and to social relations generally by, for example, the replacement of the old marks "G.W.R.", "L.N.E.R.", etc., by the omnibus "British Railways", counts for very little compared to the operation of death duties and income tax. In the revolution of our time it is the tax machine which is the principal revolutionary agent.

If I were asked to sum up in a word the salient characteristic of this revolution, I should choose the word collectivism. "We are all socialists now", said Sir William Harcourt, when he introduced the death duty principle [in 1894]; and he spoke better than he knew. There are naturally many other ways of conceiving the changes: the equalization of income is an important aspect, of which there will be more to say later. But in the end, I think, it is the collectivist tendency which is dominant: the tendency to shift more and more the sources of initiative to the central government and its organs. Even the equalizing tendency, as it works under the present system, has chiefly this significance. True, it redistributes income; but it also destroys independent sources of power. It leaves more to be done by government.

Now let me say at once that I do not think that all aspects of this tendency are bad. Up to a point I have no objection to Sir William Harcourt's description. Many of the extensions of the functions of the State which we have witnessed in our time seem to me to be necessary and desirable, in particular all those which serve positively to create greater equality of opportunity. But ideally I would wish these extensions to take place in a *milieu* in which there were sufficient checks and balances to prevent them becoming predominant, so that although the *absolute* area of state activity had increased, it had not increased *relatively*. But, of course, the collectivism of this country in this day and age has not been of this nature. While, thank heaven, we are still far from the limiting condition in which there is only one property owner and one employer, we have gone some way along that road. There can be no doubt that the power of the State, relatively to other social elements, has greatly increased. And this seems very much to be regretted.

How far is this to be regarded as inevitable? To what extent are the influences which have brought it about to be regarded as inescapable? It is to the exploration of these questions that the main body of this inquiry is directed.

The arrangement dictates itself. The influences with which we are concerned spring, partly, from the sheer weight of taxation, partly from the peculiar nature of the tax structure. It will be convenient to follow this order.

III THE WEIGHT OF TAXATION

To begin then with the weight of taxation.

It would be wrong to say that this is the cause of all the trouble; it will be one of the main contentions of these notes that, given the *amount* to be raised, it makes a great deal of difference *how* it is raised – that the nature of the tax structure is very important indeed. But it is nevertheless true that, if the amount were less, differences of structure would also be less important. In this sense, it is right to regard a good many of our difficulties as springing from the large amounts, in relation to the totals of national income, which the tax system is called upon to provide. Certainly, a good many of the problems with which the beautifully written Report of the *Royal Commission on the Taxation of Profits and Income* [Cmd. 9474, 1955] is concerned would diminish greatly in significance were it possible for us to return even to immediately pre-war proportions of public expenditure.

What are the hopes of reducing this burden?

To get our ideas straight on this very vital question, it is essential to clear our minds of *clichés* and wishful thinking. There are still a great many people who lift up their voices in public who are under the impression – or who at any rate succeed in creating the impression – that there are vast easements to be secured by some general process of what they call "economy". If only some great Chancellor would arise, they seem to argue, who would nerve himself to exhort a spendthrift and complacent bureaucracy to "*cut out the waste*", all would be well; and, alas for the vanity of human wishes, Chancellor after Chancellor disappoints them.

Now we must not quarrel about words in this connection. Doubtless there are senses of the words "economy" and "waste" which would oblige us to treat such exhortations with respect. In so far as we are spending more than we can easily bear, the situation may be said to call for economy. In so far as the money which is spent one way, could more profitably be spent some other way, the expenditure may well be described as wasteful. There is undoubtedly much need for economy and much money wasted in these senses.

But if these words are taken to refer, as the context usually implies, not to broad questions of policy but to the costs of administration, it is safe to say that they are empty and misleading. There are no economies conceivable, there are no wastes in the sphere of administration, whose achievement or elimination would affect very substantially the present problem of the dead weight of taxation.

In saying this I do not mean to say that all administration is "economical", that there are no examples of "waste" anywhere in the system. That would be absurd. I am sure that bad patches exist and that there is always room for improvement. What I mean is simply this, that the costs of the administrative machine are so small in relation to the other objects of expenditure that to focus attention on them, rather than on the costs which are the result of policy, is to get the picture totally out of perspective.

Consider, for instance, the vote of the Ministry of Agriculture and Food. The aggregate amount for the current year is over £300 millions, of which no more than £16 millions are the costs of the machine, the rest being accounted for mainly by subsidies. Thus, if all the administration could be done for nothing, or by the Minister himself and a couple of secretaries, we should still be left with expenditure which is 95 per cent. of the present vote.

There are indeed real problems of economy and real problems of cutting out waste – problems which involve sums which are really appreciable in relation to the total volume of expenditure. But these problems arise, not in the sphere of administration but in the sphere of policy, a sphere for which the much-abused race of administrators has no responsibility. Nothing could be more conducive to cynicism than the spectacle of members of Parliament working themselves into a fury of righteous indignation about some delinquency of administrators, involving perhaps a few thousands and then, sheep-like, trooping into the lobbies to endorse policies which involve the expenditure of many millions.

What, then, are the prospects of economies in the sphere of policy?

Here to get a sense of proportion it is desirable to divide the problem into broad sections.

Clearly there can be no question of reduction in the matter of War Pensions or interest on the National Debt.

Defence expenditure is obviously reducible. But it is profoundly to be hoped that, until there are much more tangible signs of a will to peace elsewhere than have yet been forthcoming, there will be no relaxing here. The enormous expenditure under this head is, of course, one of the main reasons for the change in the proportion of public expenditure to national income since the inter-war period. But since it is this expenditure which hitherto has helped to save us from the fate of the Iron Curtain satellites, it is surely a part of the burden which should be borne without complaining.

There remains, therefore, the sphere of expenditure on domestic objects. Here there is an area of statutory benefits in respect of some kinds of social insurance which presumably is to be regarded as politically – and, I would say, ethically – inviolable. Beyond this, as Mr. Gaitskell showed with his token scheme of a shilling for prescriptions, there is a certain room for manoeuvre, even in regard to welfare expenditure; and in the sphere of subsidies, there is a very appreciable margin indeed. I wonder whether many people whose pockets are not immediately affected really believe that the present volume and objects of agricultural subsidies make any kind of economic sense.

Nevertheless, politics and vested interests being what they are, a man would be sanguine indeed who would venture to predict any very substantial lightening of the burden from deliberate reductions of policy. Of the scope for such lightening there can be no doubt. But it is only in the shadow of dire catastrophe that we should be likely to do it on any very extensive scale.

Much more hopeful in the long run is the easement which may come with a gradual increase in the volume of production. If production increases at a modest rate, and if on balance we do not increase our present commitments, then a quite substantial shift in the proportionate burden might be expected. In this connection, I would like to draw attention to a very interesting article which has recently appeared in the *District Bank Review*, from the pen of Mr. Alan Peacock.* In this article Mr. Peacock shows that, on the assumption of an increase of production of two per cent. per annum, even if we make an allowance for the increase in social expenditure at present rates due to increases of population, or changes in age composition, by 1964 government expenditure as a percentage of gross national product could have fallen from the 34 per cent. of 1953 to 29 per cent., and by 1979 to 22 per cent.

These are very substantial reductions and the rate of increase of production assumed is very cautious. But the underlying assumption is critical: namely, that we do not change the real rates of present commitments. Over the years, a substantial easement is attainable without any positive cuts; all that is necessary is to mark time where we are, not to increase the rate of commitment in one line unless it can be diminished commensurately in another. This is not very much to ask. But whether this degree of self-restraint can be expected of future governments is anybody's guess. Personally, I should be very unwilling indeed to bet heavily on no net increase. But I should be disagreeably surprised if what increase there is should be so large as to wipe out the whole of the possible relief.

IV THE PRINCIPLES AND PRACTICE OF PROGRESSION

Any relief of this sort, however, lies some way ahead in the future. At present, failing reductions in expenditure due to major changes of policy, any hope of making the tax system work in a less collectivist direction lies in changes in the tax structure.

Let us look at this, first, in regard to the taxation of income.

From the point of view of these notes, an inquiry into long-run social and economic effects, the salient feature of our income tax is its high rate of progression.

Now it seems to be commonly accepted nowadays that there should be some degree of progressiveness in the tax system. Why there should be this agreement is not altogether easy to see. The argument for the kind of progression which arises from the mere fact of an exemption limit is, of course, very plain: even the most strenuous supporters of the principle of proportionate

---

* "The future of government expenditure", *District Bank Review*, no. 114 (June 1955), pp. 27–41.

taxation have been willing to concede that their principle should not come into operation until a minimum of subsistence had been provided for.

But, beyond this, the grounds for agreement that, as income increases, it should be taxed more than proportionately, are not at all obvious. It is all too plain that the principle of progression necessarily involves very awkward anomalies; the grievous position of authors, artists and others with highly fluctuating incomes is a case in point. And the intellectual arguments which are usually cited in its favour are, to put it very mildly indeed, by no means unequivocal – the famous application of the minimum sacrifice principle is surely the hedonistic calculus at its most unconvincing.[1] Nevertheless, most of us – including the present writer – do agree in a vague and woolly way that some degree of progression is desirable – and it would be otiose to argue over-much here with this particular manifestation of the *Zeitgeist*.

But to agree that *some* degree of progressiveness is desirable does not involve agreement with *all* scales of progression. And I think that it is about time that someone who is not deeply involved personally, having chosen a different way of life, should say bluntly that the higher reaches of our own progression are quite indefensible save upon avowedly confiscatory theory. So far as earned income is involved, they constitute a discrimination against enterprise and ability such as has never before existed for any long time in any large-scale civilized community. Certainly they are not dictated by the needs of revenue: the upper rates of surtax could be just cancelled without creating any very severe budgetary problem. The most that can be said in their defence is that they were brought into existence at a time of crisis when they did not seem – and indeed were not – inappropriate to the needs of the situation and that, now that that crisis has passed, they have continued to exist because those who rule over us have been afraid to challenge the purely demagogic arguments by which they are usually supported.

Public criticism up to date has tended to be concentrated upon the effects of these rates on incentive. These are not effects whose significance I have any disposition to minimize. The arguments which do that have always seemed to me to be singularly futile. Of course, it is quite true that a substantial amount of the more conspicuous work of the world is done from

1. If any reader, not being a fanatical egalitarian, should think that these sentiments are too sceptical, I should like to draw his attention to a remarkable essay, recently published by two members of the Chicago Law School – *The Uneasy Case for Progressive Taxation*, by Walter J. Blum and Harry Kalven, Jr. (Chicago, 1953). Messrs. Blum and Kalven have no axe to grind: their book is a perfectly dispassionate examination of a case, with no very clear conclusion emerging. But they certainly succeed in showing how extremely superficial has been most of the argument up to date on this extremely important question; and, incidentally, they show, too, how to conduct a very difficult economic and ethical investigation without becoming involved in jargon or obscurity.

nonpecuniary motives. It is true, too, that experience shows that when men in responsible jobs are remunerated by salaries which do not fluctuate with effort, a substantial proportion can be relied upon to do their work with competence and zeal – though there is also a proportion who do not. But to argue that, where income does fluctuate with effort and enterprise, there is no disincentive from high marginal rates, does not seem to me to make sense. If we would not argue that it made no difference if the marginal rate is 20s. in the pound, so that there was *no* reward for additional risk and effort, why should we contend that the position is so radically changed when the residue from a pound's worth of earnings was 6d. or 1s.?

But important as may be the incentive effects of extreme progression, they must surely take a second place beside the more general effects on economic and social structure. It is indeed a surprising circumstance that these are not more widely realized. We are told that under the present system, the number of *net* incomes (i.e. incomes after tax) over £6,000 a year is now less than two hundred; and the suggestion is that the revolution of which this is a symbol is to be regarded as an unequivocally good thing.

To me the verdict seems a much more difficult business. Perhaps this is due to some personal inhibition. But I must confess that the circumstance that it is now virtually impossible to build a fortune like Lord Nuffield's does not fill me with any particular enthusiasm. On the contrary, I can see several grounds for regarding it with some apprehension.

Is it a particularly good thing, I ask myself, that there should no longer be any substantial blocks of individual wealth whose owners can defy fashion, foster minority causes and give succour and support to the eccentric and the unpopular? Are we really very glad that in future so few private persons will be in a position to commission the building of architecturally pleasing dwellings of any considerable size or to support on a large scale independent institutes of learning? Do we regard it as a specially fortunate circumstance that benefactions of the kind which gave the nation the Courtauld pictures and the Courtauld Institute should, in future, be virtually out of the question; and that what support is given to the arts and culture, not to mention the universities, should have to come, if it comes at all, from central or local government? I am far from thinking that, in the old days, the provision made by the owners of private wealth for the general cultural needs of the community was all that might have been wished; and that there was no need for supplementation by public money. Quite the contrary. But a situation in which there are no sources of initiative save at the centre seems to me at least as unsatisfactory as a situation in which the decentralized sources are inadequate.

But the consequences of levelling to this extent are not limited to the world of learning and culture: they inform the whole texture of our social and economic structure. The fact that it has become so difficult to accumulate even a comparatively small fortune must have the most profound effects on the organization of business; and it is by no means clear to me that these results are in the social interest. Must not the inevitable consequence of all this be that it will become more and more difficult for innovation to develop save within the ambit of established corporate enterprise, and that more and more of what accumulation takes place will take place within the large concerns which – largely as a result of individual enterprise in the past – managed to get started before the ice age descended? Some of this may be technically inevitable – though a good deal that is said about technical inevitability is ill-founded. But if we are not deliberately working for a time when everything is taken over by the State, is it to be regarded as desirable that it should be so tremendously accelerated by the incidence of a tax system which is the result not of the ineluctable laws of physics, but of very easily modifiable votes of the House of Commons?

Or, to put the question in blunter terms, if our ideal is not universal collectivism but rather property-owning democracy, are we content with a tax system which is working all the time the other way?

V THE TAX ON MARRIAGE

It is very unlikely that this state of affairs will last for ever. The degree of inequality of net income in this country at the present day is something which, so far as I know, is much less than in any large-scale society at any time in history. Having regard to the great differences in the value of the product of different kinds of effort and enterprise, it seems intrinsically improbable that so great a levelling will be maintained; and this consideration is reinforced when we think of the eventual political outcome of a system of equality of opportunity in which so high a percentage of the latent talent is given adequate opportunity for all the development of which it is capable – in conditions where all have a chance, the argument against differentiation of reward tends to lose at least some of its force. But all this is looking very far ahead. At the present time, a direct reduction of the progression of the surtax is likely to be a very slow starter.

But this does not mean that all hope must be deferred of any mitigation of the effects of the system. While a substantial reduction of the general progression of the surtax might encounter considerable resistance, a reform of the present system as it affects marriage and the family would probably secure extensive support.

The position under our present tax laws of married persons with independent incomes which add up to more than a certain figure is an anomaly to which attention has frequently been drawn: they would be better off if they lived together without being married. This, of course, is a direct effect of progression; under a strictly proportionate tax, it would be a matter of indifference whether incomes were aggregated or not. It is a somewhat surprising circumstance, in a community professing respect for the institution of matrimony, that it has been tolerated for so long. For it is in fact a direct tax on marriage – to be more precise, on marriage among the rather better off middle classes.

The Report of the Royal Commission devotes some attention to this problem. But it is perhaps questionable whether its arguments here have the force and cogency which they have in so many other directions.

The Commissioners first point out that this anomaly does not affect all married persons and that it is not until aggregate incomes reach certain levels that the tax on marriage begins. This is true, and, as a corrective of loose statements, is doubtless very much in order. But from the ethical point of view it does not seem to go very far. The tax remains a tax in the instances where it is levied; and it is surely not a very creditable feature of a tax system that it discriminates between income groups in respect of incentive or disincentive to marriage.

The Commissioners then go on to assure us that it is very doubtful whether the effect of the tax in positively encouraging what they call "more casual associations" is in fact at all extensive. Probably this is true, though, in the nature of things, supporting evidence must have been very hard to obtain. As a people we attach great importance to the married state and we are prepared to make great sacrifices to achieve it. But it is difficult to see how the failure of a policy to produce a certain effect, because of strong resistant moral factors, can be regarded as being in itself a very convincing vindication of the moral status of that policy; we may be gratified that the citizens have not been deflected from virtue by the operation of a certain penalty, but we do not, for that reason, regard the penalty as justifiable. We may be confident that the Commissioners would have condemned in the strongest possible terms a subsidy to "more casual associations." Yet the distinction between immunity from a tax and eligibility for a positive subsidy, though real, is hardly so great as to warrant complete reprobation in the one case and comparative lack of concern in the other. Nor, from the ethical point of view, does it seem that matters are made any better by a warning that the rectification of the anomaly would be expensive to the Exchequer; the greater the expense of rectification, the greater the tax upon marriage.

It is my submission, however, that we should not be content with mere rectification by abolishing aggregation. There is an opportunity here for an innovation of policy which would give marriage and the family a place in the tax system corresponding to our continual lip-service to the national importance of these institutions. Under the American system, roughly speaking, husband and wife may aggregate their incomes and then each be taxed upon a half of the aggregate. Under the so-called "quotient" system prevailing in some other countries this process of aggregation and division is extended to the family, with each child counting as a certain fraction of an adult for purposes of division. A system of this sort solves at one stroke, so to speak, the double problem of eliminating some of the injustice of progression and of providing allowances for children in some measure proportionate to the expenses of the income group into which they are born – a counter-agent to the differential birth rate. The fact that arrangements of this kind are actually in force elsewhere should at least give pause to any tendency to dismiss the suggestion as frivolous. Why should a nation which professes to regard the family as the essential foundation of society not do more to give recognition to that status in its system of public finance? And is there any reason to suppose that change on these lines would be opposed to popular sentiment?

VI THE DEATH DUTIES

If there is anything at all in the argument of the last section, it would seem to suggest that there is ample scope within the system of the income tax for changes which would foster the decentralized, as opposed to the centralized, influences in our society. The same kind of scope reveals itself if we turn to the field of the death duties.

There can be little doubt that the taxation of property passing at death, as practised at present in this country, is one of the most powerful instruments of change that has ever operated in a great society. This influence is gradual and, save from the point of view of the persons immediately concerned, unsensational. We do not realize from day to day or from year to year what is happening. Yet the relentless working of the estate duty, at its present level of graduation, is such that, within the lifetimes of many now living, the greater part of the great accumulations of the past will have been taken over by the State and the day of the large inheritance will be no more. The great country houses now derelict or used as offices by public boards are an impressive symbol of a process which is ubiquitous.

Now, to use the transition from one generation to another as a means of bringing about social change is, if imposed change be desired, as civilized and as comparatively painless a method as can well be imagined; and it has had the blessing of some of the greatest of our social philosophers. "Would you follow the counsels of equality without contravening those of security", wrote Bentham, "wait for the natural period which puts an end to hopes and fears – the period of death". John Stuart Mill thought a progressive income tax an outrage – "a tax on industry and economy" imposing "a penalty on people for having worked harder and saved more than their neighbours"; but he was prepared to do the most drastic things with inheritance. Any law of inheritance is a very artificial thing: there is no *prima facie* case against "interference" in this field.

But it is a profound error to think that all interferences must work the same way. This is demonstrably untrue. A system which enforces a rigid primogeniture will produce a very different kind of society from a system which enforces a mathematically equal division among members of the family. A partial confiscation of estates passing at death will produce very different results from rules which tend to their division among a number of inheritors.

Now, what is true of the law of inheritance in general is also true of taxation in particular. Different systems will have totally different results. There is all the difference in the world between a system which taxes the estate as a whole on a steep basis of graduation and a system which applies the same graduation, not to the estate as a whole, but to the portions which are received, according to the disposition of the testator, by the legatees. The one system tends to the obliteration of property, the other to its wider diffusion.

The first of these systems, the system which taxes the estate as a whole, is the system under which we now live. And there can be no doubt that if it is desired to bring about a state of affairs in which the degree of inequality due to inequality of inherited property is at a minimum, it works most powerfully in that direction. Although we do not fully realize it, it has already changed the nature of our society most extensively and, if it continues to work at the present rate, it will have changed it altogether before more than two or three generations have elapsed.

But will it have changed it in a desirable way? That is the great question. And, so far as I am concerned, the answer is, quite definitely, no. I have no objection to measures affecting inheritance which tend to remove the more extreme manifestations of inequality. But I have great objection to a system which simply appropriates property, uses the proceeds for current expenditure, and leaves more and more of the functions which used to be discharged by property to be discharged, if they are discharged at all, by the State. The present system is through and through collectivist in its ultimate tendency; and while fully admitting the need for extensive collectivist functions in any well constituted society, I view the prospect in which the collectivist leviathan is confronted only by dependent individuals as a condition which we should seek to avoid.

Contrast the working of this system with the working of a system which differs from it, not necessarily at all in the rate of graduation, but in the unit to which it is applied: the *legacy* rather than the *estate*. Here the tendency is not to obliteration but rather to division. The principle of progression in this context provides a positive incentive to diffusion. On present rates, a man disposing of an estate of £200,000 would pay nearly twice as much tax if it were bequeathed in a lump as if it were divided in four equal proportions. The effect of such a system, over the years, would be a society almost different in kind, as regards the ownership of property, from the society produced by the working of the estate duty. And from my point of view it would be a much better society, much more robust and independent, much more capable of decentralized initiative, much less liable to mass hysteria and mob movements. It would be a practical realization of some of the ideals, not of a collectivist, but rather of a distributivist society.

Let no one say that such a system in impracticable. For, as we should all know, the rudiments of such a system did actually exist in our own tax system for a very long time. Up to a short time ago, the British death duties included both estate and legacy duty. It is true that, in course of time, the legacy duties had become comparatively unimportant and were probably a great nuisance to the Board of Inland Revenue. But under the chancellorship of Sir Stafford Cripps, the legacy duties were abolished [in 1949]. The estate duty, with its remorseless destructive influence, was left to dominate the scene.

From the point of view of these notes, this was exactly the wrong kind of reform. It was the estate duty which should have been abolished and the principle of the legacy duties made the sole principle of the system. Admittedly, this would have involved a rather more expensive apparatus of administration. But this would have been as dust in the balance beside its beneficial effects in other directions. It is true, too, that it would have involved a loss of revenue. But since the death duties at their present height must be principally paid out of sales in the capital market, any deficit this created would have had no general disequilibrating influence. The present death duties are a form of tax which can be reduced without serious fear of inflation.

It was doubtless very logical for Sir Stafford Cripps, who was a convinced over-all collectivist, to abolish this form of taxation and to give the estate duty sole sway. It is not plain to me that it is equally logical for the same system to be maintained by those whose Utopia lies in the opposite direction.

VII PROFIT-SHARING AND SHAREHOLDING

A reform of the death duties on the lines just indicated would be a powerful influence tending towards a property-owning democracy. But it would not be a cure-all. It would only manifest its effects over time. And it would not do anything to change the position of those who at present are propertyless and have no expectations from the propertied.

Now, one of the most urgent problems of the day is somehow or other to give a greater number of people a sense of interest in the nation as a going concern. In a society which is not completely authoritarian there will always be a good deal of sectional bickering about the size of shares in the division of the product; and it is possible to get much too agitated about such inevitable manifestations. But the situation today in which there is the most palpable misapprehension on the part of large sections of the community about the amount that there is available for distribution, still more the conditions under which that amount may be increased, is a genuine cause for concern.

Now it is quite obvious that nationalization is no cure for this frame of mind. Whether or not nationalization brings technical advantages not obtainable in other ways is a matter which is perhaps still open to discussion. But the idea that the workers in nationalized industry have any closer realization of the connection between effort and output and the amount that can be withdrawn from the common pool without involving the enterprise concerned in loss, has been disposed of by the march of events. It may be an exaggeration to say that the workers in a nationalized industry have less sense of responsibility than workers elsewhere. But it would certainly be quite absurd to say that they have more.

To meet this situation the claims of profit-sharing are often canvassed. If the workers in an industrial establishment are given a direct share of profits, it is urged, they will come to have a sense of solidarity with its interests and some understanding of its problems. The solution of the class struggle is the extension of this kind of arrangement.

I would not question that there is a good deal to be said for this position. A great volume of experience seems to suggest that in establishments where genuine profit-sharing schemes have been introduced and where it has been possible to persuade the wage-earners that this was no mere device for upsetting the normal process of wage-fixing, relations between management and workers have very greatly improved. It has even been suggested that in a certain constituency at the recent general election a substantial number of wage-earners were moved to change their political allegiance on the ground that the nationalization with which their firm was threatened would upset the arrangements for profit-sharing.

Nevertheless, profit-sharing is not a radical solution. An entitlement to a share in profits on this basis is not property. It cannot be bought and sold. It does not carry with it a liability to loss. It involves no proportionate voice in control. There is an essentially *ex gratia* element in it all. A profit-sharing democracy is not necessarily a property-owning democracy.

I do not think it is at all desirable to attempt to remedy these deficiencies by introducing an element of compulsion. The idea of compulsory profit-sharing creates more problems than it solves. It rides roughshod over the rights of existing shareholders. Its incidence and its benefits are unequal as between companies with different degrees of financial gearing. There is no common rate of sharing which is appropriate to all types of industry. It involves privilege without responsibility and confers none of the reserve power of real property. I should regard the introduction of compulsory profit-sharing as likely to do much more harm than good.

If we ask ourselves what is the ideal solution to this problem from the non-collectivist point of view, the answer is obvious: the workers should themselves own equities. The solution to the lack of responsibility and solidarity which comes from an insufficient diffusion of property is a greater diffusion of property. There is nothing wrong in the property system itself. The result of the evolution of many ages, it solves a great many economic and social problems which otherwise would be insoluble. The trouble is that it is not yet sufficiently widespread. It is not necessary that everyone should be a property owner or that all ownings of property should be equal. But it is highly desirable that more people should own property.

If this is so, it has a very immediate bearing on the problem under discussion. If the owners of industrial undertakings feel moved to take deliberate steps to bring their workers into more intimate association with the prospects of their company and with the prosperity of industry in general, the best thing for them to do is to make their distribution in the form of shares. They should seek on a large scale to make equity owners of the workers. An unconditional share in the equity, rather than a conditional share in the profits, is the appropriate solution to many social and industrial problems.

Now – and this brings us back to the main contention of these notes – this is a development which can be either greatly impeded or greatly facilitated by tax policy. Hitherto, I do not think it can be denied that the tax laws have been so many obstacles to be circumnavigated. Imaginative schemes on these lines have had to be shelved because the liability to tax, in some form or other, made the scheme either inoperative or unattractive. But there is nothing in the nature of things why this should continue to be so. It is easy to think of a number of ways in which the bias should work in the opposite direction and, so far from deterring distributions on these lines, the tax system positively favour them.

It is, of course, very easy to think of objections. Certainly, any attempt to change the law in this way would have a rough passage at the hands of the defenders of the logic of the existing tradition. Why should companies fortunate enough to be in a position to carry out such schemes receive the added benefit which would be provided by deliberate stimulus through tax reductions? Why should workers who receive such distributions be exempt from the obligation to regard them as income? And so on and so forth. To all of which the answer is that the gain from inconsistency in this respect is judged to be vastly more significant than its disadvantages. For this is not a mere matter of a year-to-year assessment of tax liability: it is a matter of deliberately producing an important shift in the property structure and an important gain in social and economic solidarity. As we have seen already, there is nothing particularly neutral in the operation of the present tax structure. Relentlessly, year by year, it is pushing us towards collectivism and propertyless uniformity. Why then should we not begin to use it to produce change in another direction?

22 Thoughts on the Crisis

From *Lloyds Bank Review*, new series no. 48 (April 1958), pp. 1–26.

I

One of the many troubles about our present financial difficulties is the complexity of the intellectual issues involved. To the superficial observer, at least, the crisis of last autumn blew up in a comparatively clear sky: how many professional prophets predicted anything like what actually happened? Moreover, even if, with wisdom after the event, we piece together the various influences immediately operative, how much agreement do we find concerning the longer-run tendencies operative? Was the inflation of the demand-pull or the cost-push variety? To what extent is the trouble to be attributed to the deficiencies of monetary policy as an instrument or is it true to say that the instrument had not been appropriately applied? These and such-like questions beset any attempt at diagnosis of the crisis.

When we turn to prescription, the position is no less complicated. Was a seven per cent. Bank Rate justified as a crisis measure or was it simply the last resort of a conventional misapprehension of the situation? Is a ceiling on advances an appropriate control of the volume of money? Was there no alternative to cuts in investment? How are all these measures to be conceived in relation to developments in the outside world? And in any case where do we go from here? Is inflation really an evil and, if so, how far are we prepared to go to stop it? Is a centrally controlled wages policy an appropriate remedy? What should be our attitude to the question of the reserve? It is to problems of this sort that we need at least a provisional answer before we can make up our minds on even the smaller issues of day-to-day policy. Small wonder that at the present time there is more confusion, more division among men of knowledge and goodwill than perhaps at any time in post-war history.

It is not my belief that I know all the right answers to these tremendous questions. Anyone who has participated continuously in public discussion of such matters over any long period of time – in my case, more than twenty-five years – must, if he is candid, admit to many occasions on which he has made mistakes and the strong probability that he may make other mistakes in the future. We are all in the same boat in this respect. But if we are to make any progress at all we must go on exchanging opinions and seeking to set forth, with mutual respect and toleration of other points of view – commodities in somewhat short supply in certain quarters recently – the ultimate reasons for our own attitudes. At any rate, it is in the hope that in this way we may eventually come to greater agreement that I venture to offer these very fragmentary and very imperfect reflections.

II THE CAUSES OF THE CRISIS

Let me begin with the immediate causes of the crisis.

The first point which deserves to be made is a negative one: this was *not* a crisis of the current account. Despite the embarrassments of the ill-conceived Suez adventure, in the first half year we were running a surplus on balance of payments account at the rate of £250 millions per annum; and the indications are that for the full year the surplus was probably of the order of £200 millions. The belief that it was the trade figures which were to blame was ill-founded. It is true that a surplus of £200 millions per annum is not all that might be wished. If we are to play our part in overseas development and, at the same time, achieve a reinforcement of the reserves commensurate with our external obligations, something more like £450 to £500 millions is desirable. Still, the fact that it fell short of the ideal does not turn a quite respectable surplus into an alarming deficit. The true causes of the trouble have to be looked for in quite a different direction.

There can be no doubt that for some time prior to the crisis the position of sterling in the foreign exchange markets had been under some suspicion and the holders of sterling had been apt to be apprehensive of the slightest adverse movement. It is probable, however, that the immediate occasion for the beginning of the run was the partial devaluation of the franc which, perhaps because it was only partial, inevitably gave rise to expectations of further changes. There were rumours of an upward revaluation of the mark and all sorts of vague talk of a general realignment of European currencies.

In such circumstances it was only to be expected that sterling should come under pressure. There was no likelihood that sterling would appreciate in any such realignment and some possibility, to put it mildly, that it would depreciate in terms of the stronger currencies, the mark and the Swiss franc. Now, whatever may be the moral obligations of British nationals when confronting such prospects, there is obviously no obligation on foreigners to expose their funds to loss or to forgo the opportunity of gain. Some movement out of sterling was, therefore, almost inevitable.

In the general position of London ever since the war, such movements tend to have a snowball tendency. The reserves are so small in relation to our external liabilities that, if there is a significant downward movement, all sorts of holders, who would not normally have wished to move, begin to think that perhaps it would be better to get out before things get very much worse. This mood tends to spread. Creditors, who have payments due to them in sterling, withdraw their money earlier than would otherwise have been the case. Debtors, who have payments to make, defer payment as long as they can in the hope that it will cost them less in the end. Pure speculation begins to play its part and extensive bear positions are created. If the reserves were larger, the danger of this kind of development would be to that extent less. With a really adequate reserve, the capital account could sustain substantial withdrawals without the danger of a run.

* * *

But, even with the reserves at such a low level as ours since the war, the situation is not necessarily unmanageable. There is room for much difference of opinion concerning the policies adopted last autumn. But one thing surely has been demonstrated: that a run of the kind which was taking place can be stopped, if sufficiently strong action be taken. And if action is taken sufficiently soon, and if there exists a general expectation that it will be carried to any lengths requisite to reverse the drain, then, as likely as not, very severe action will not be necessary. This is not a universal rule. It is not difficult to think of external drains which could not be dealt with in this manner. But in general it is true that, where there exists general confidence in the determination of the authorities concerned to adopt the policies necessary to safeguard whatever reserve there is, then a cumulative deterioration of the situation is unlikely.

This takes us to the very heart of the trouble last year. Rightly or wrongly, there was no confidence. There was no confidence in the willingness of the financial authorities to take action to safeguard the reserve. And, more fundamentally, there was no confidence in the willingness of the government to pursue policies which would mean that the reserve was not continually in danger. As we have seen already, it was not true that the current account was in any immediate danger. But it was true that it was feared very generally that policies were dominant which would bring just this danger about. The failure to restore a position which had begun to deteriorate two years earlier, the continuation of inflation and the prospect of rising levels of public expenditure, all contrived to produce an expectation of further deterioration. And when such expectations are prevalent they tend to bring their own realization.

Thus, while the immediate occasion of our troubles last autumn was provided by external events not within our immediate control, the cause of their magnification and the apparent unmanageability of the situation was a general belief in the weakness of our own internal policy. It would certainly be wrong to argue that, if there had been no internal weakness, there would have been no alarms and excursions regarding France and Germany. But if the internal position had been strong, these alarms and excursions would have been very much easier to deal with. And the root cause of our weakness, of our failure to accumulate a sufficient reserve and to achieve a position in international trade strong enough to be immune to the impact of international rumour, was the continuation of internal inflation.

It is, therefore, to the examination of this situation that we must now turn.

III THE CAUSES OF INFLATION

Let us begin by reminding ourselves of what had actually happened. If 1950 be taken as 100, by the autumn of 1957 the cost of living index had risen to 143. This shows an average rise of nearly $6\frac{1}{2}$ per cent. per annum. During the same period in Germany, prices rose to 115, or by 2.2 per cent. per annum, and in the United States to 118, or by 2.7 per cent. per annum. Nor was there any pronounced tendency for this movement to cease. Since early in 1955 various measures of restraint, including a credit squeeze of sorts, had been in operation. Yet in the twelve months from August, 1956, to August, 1957, the rise in prices was still as much as 4 per cent. The fact that, with a rate of inflation so substantially higher than in the two other great industrial countries mentioned, our balance of payments was not in a much poorer condition, must indicate a very considerable degree of undervaluation in 1949 when the sterling parity was altered. But, obviously, such elbow room has its limits. It was not unreasonable, therefore, for both foreign speculators and observers nearer home to feel that, if the inflation continued in this manner (i.e. at a greater rate than elsewhere), then there was grave trouble ahead.

What was the prime cause of this tendency? Did it arise on the side of demand or on the side of costs? If it was a demand inflation, the operative factors were an urge to business expansion born of the prospect of good profits, a situation in which liquid funds were plentifully available to business, either in their own reserves or in capital markets where the terms of borrowing were very much lower than the prospects of profits. If, on the other hand, the upward pressure on prices is conceived to have originated on the side of costs, the significant factors in the situation would have been a continued pressure of the trade unions to better their relative position, and it would have been a continued rise in wage-rates which, in spite of apprehensions of diminished profits, compelled producers continually to raise their prices. Clearly, both explanations are conceivable. The question is, which fits the facts?

From my point of view, for the greater part of the post-war period it is the explanation in terms of the pull of demand which has the greater plausibility. If the prime movement had been on the side of costs, the prospect of profits would have been continually threatened, the index of wage-rates would have tended to rise faster than the index of weekly wage earnings, the volume of vacancies would have tended to fall below the level of applications. And these things did not happen. For the greater part of the time, profit prospects were good, earnings were rising faster than wage-rates, and the volume of vacancies remained higher than the volume of applications. As I see the picture, the rise of wage-rates was, for the most part, the *consequence* rather than the *cause* of the situation. The demand for labour was so strong that, even if the trade unions had been much weaker, it is probable that a similar movement would have taken place. Indeed, paradoxically enough, it might have been more accentuated: the cumbersome process of collective bargaining tends to take longer than the operations of freer markets.

Towards the end of the period and at the present time the picture tends to change. It is probably true to say that, when you put the brake on a demand inflation you are then confronted with the danger of a cost inflation. If the trade unions have got into the habit of cashing in on the demand inflation every spring, then very naturally they will tend to go on trying to do so for a time even though the increase of demand has slackened. They will continue to press for increased wage-rates; and now, if inflation proceeds, it can be described as having its origin on the side of costs.

This explanation also seems to me to fit the facts of recent history. The penultimate phase of the U.K. inflation begins in 1954 with the lowering of discount rates and various budgetary easements, notably the change in investment allowances. An investment boom of full dimensions develops. Then in 1955 sundry checks begin to be applied, the first credit squeeze, the autumn budget and so on; and the prospects of profit, although still pretty good, become less attractive, the disparity between the rise of earnings and wage-rates begins to diminish, the gap between vacancies and applications narrows ... Inflation from the pull of demand tends to diminish. Inflation from the push of costs becomes more likely.

* * *

All this is obviously very controversial: there are many observers of the situation, whose judgement I respect, who would differ considerably in emphasis, giving more weight throughout to the push of costs, less to the pull of demand, than I find appropriate. But on one point I hope we should all be agreed; namely, that none of this could happen if there were a sufficiently strong control of the supply of money (i.e. cash plus bank deposits). By this I do not wish to beg the question whether such a control is itself desirable – there will be much more to say about that later on. Nor do I argue in the least that the supply of money is the *only* factor governing the volume of expenditure: it is almost humiliating at this time of day to have to insist that any form of the quantity theory held by any reputable economist in the last two hundred years has taken account of the demand for money (expressing itself *via* velocity) as well as of the supply thereof. All that is contended is that, if the supply of money is adequately varied, the other influences on expenditure can be offset so as to prevent inflation.

But if this is so, how did it come about that in all these years the inflation was allowed to continue? It cannot be argued, at any rate since the return of the Conservative government in 1951, that the authorities were opposed to the use of monetary policy *per se*. In the early years after the war, under the Labour government, this may have been so: at any rate a positive monetary policy was not pursued. But since 1951 all that was supposed to have been changed: the return to monetary policy was claimed as one of the positive achievements of the change of régime. And, in the first crisis of that period, monetary policy had indeed some effect. Yet inflation reasserted itself: and when, since the summer of 1955, there was some show of control by way of monetary policy, the results, at least until the drastic measures of last autumn, were not all that might have been wished. It would be going much too far to say that the credit squeeze and the other monetary measures which accompanied it had *no* effect – a case could be made out for the view that by the winter of 1956–7 they were beginning to work. But it is quite obvious that up to last autumn they had not stopped the inflation.

At least three reasons can be given for these disappointing developments.

In the first place, come the deficiencies of fiscal policy. The budgets of 1954 and 1955, with their changes in investment allowances and tax reductions, definitely tended to an increase of general expenditure. And thenceforward, until the Thorneycroft budget of 1957, it must be noted that very little was done to bring the surplus above the line into a non-inflationary relation with the below-the-line deficit.

Now, monetary policy, properly conceived and executed, can be a very powerful means of stopping an inflation. But if fiscal policy is tending the other way, then the strain put upon monetary policy is to that extent greater: even tighter conditions are required. And that, clearly, was one of the governing circumstances. With their fiscal measures – or lack of measures – successive Chancellors tended to undo what they were trying to do with the discount rate and credit policy generally. It is easy enough to understand and indeed to sympathize with the motives. The long-run arguments in favour of reduction of some taxes are very strong indeed. But reductions of taxation, unless accompanied by reductions of expenditure or by the substitution of other taxes, are apt to have an inflationary influence. And this is one of the things which has been happening since 1954.

Secondly, given the task to be accomplished, then, even on the assumption that the machine was in good working order – an assumption to be questioned in a moment – it seems clear to me that what monetary measures were adopted were both too little and too late. The theory of monetary policy does not say that *any* raising of interest rates, *any* tightening of the credit base, is sufficient to curb over-all expenditure, however strongly it is developing: it says that *some* level of interest rates, *some* curtailment of the credit basis may be relied upon to have that effect. And what these critical levels are varies obviously with the general tendencies of the system, and the time of the operation. A small touch on the brakes at an early stage may be more effective than greater pressure later on. If there is an over-all budgetary deficit, then the optimal level of interest rates will be higher than if there were an over-all budget surplus.

But here too the evolution of policy was the reverse of what was required. At the time of the budgetary easements in 1954, interest rates had recently been lowered. Throughout the ensuing months, as the inflation gathered strength, monetary policy was further eased. Then, when rates were eventually moved up, the movement was so small that, even if the machine had been working properly, it would have been very surprising if it had been effective. At each stage, when change came it seemed to be wrung out of the authorities long after outside opinion had formed the conclusion that it was necessary. Clearly, this is a matter on which there can be much argument in detail. But I do not think it unfair to say that, until the autumn of last year, nothing that was done in this sphere gave the impression that it was likely to succeed.

* * *

All this, I suspect, would be true even if, as I have assumed hitherto, the machinery of control had been working as it is supposed to work in the standard textbooks – if, that is to say, the Bank of England, through its discount rate and its open market operations, had had effective control of the volume of credit. This brings us to the third reason for failure.

For, in fact, it is now pretty clear that the control was no longer working according to the standard model. It has been demonstrated by Professor Sayers[1] and by the editor of this journal[2] that the immense volume of floating

1. "The determination of the volume of bank deposits: England 1955–6", in *Central Banking after Bagehot* (Oxford, 1957), pp. 92–107.

2. [W. Manning Dacey], "The floating debt problem", *Lloyds Bank Review*, n.s., no. 40 (April 1956), pp. 24–38.

debt now outstanding introduces a complication into the situation which is not dealt with in the textbooks. To all intents and purposes the Treasury bill has become the equivalent of money: and, with the Treasury bill issue in other hands, the control of the credit base by the central bank is necessarily weakened. The application of the lever no longer automatically applies the brake. A detailed explanation of the events of recent years in these terms is still a matter of considerable obscurity: only the Bank of England is in full possession of the necessary information – and that information has never yet been made public. But, speaking broadly, it is clear enough that in recent years there have been times when, because of government borrowings on short term, the Bank has no longer been in a position to control the situation. At a time when too exclusive a reliance was being placed upon monetary policy, the apparatus thereof was defective. The braking mechanism, so to speak, was in continual danger of failing to grip. And on several occasions it did fail.

But this brings us to the events of last autumn.

IV THE NATURE OF THE CRISIS

Memories tend to fade of events which were unpleasant. To see what happened in proper perspective it is desirable to remind ourselves of the situation with which we were confronted.

The central fact of this situation was the drain of reserves. For many weeks before September 19th, gold and dollars had been pouring out of the country at a rate rising to £100,000,000 a month. At the lowest point of the crisis the reserve had fallen to $1,850 millions. That is to say, at the then rate of withdrawal, there would have been a total exhaustion within a matter of months. But, of course, long before this, as the process proceeded, the rate would have increased: there would have developed a veritable *sauve qui peut*. The plain fact was that, if nothing had been done, either devaluation or a repudiation of current obligations was a virtual certainty within a few weeks.

Now, it is a matter of fairly general agreement that, if there is what the Bretton Woods statutes call a "fundamental disequilibrium" in the external relations of a financial centre, then devaluation may be an appropriate remedy. If prices and costs in any area have got so out of line with prices and costs elsewhere that, to restore equilibrium at fixed rates of exchange, a general deflation of local rates of pay would be necessary, then it is better to alter the rates of exchange. This is true whether the disequilibrium is due to deflation elsewhere or to inflation at home. If deflation elsewhere is the cause, there is not much occasion for argument: there is no reason to import deflation. But the same is true if domestic inflation has been the culprit.

Inflation of this sort is an evil: but so too is deflation. Rather than endure the damages of long drawn-out unemployment and loss of production, better operate on the foreign exchanges.

But the crisis last autumn was not a crisis of this nature. As we have seen already, it was not a crisis on the current account. It was the capital account which was in difficulties. And here the trouble was due to a fear of devaluation or a fear that further inflation would upset the current account and so make devaluation necessary.

In such circumstances it would probably be more or less generally agreed that devaluation would have been totally inappropriate. It would have robbed our creditors. It would have made our imports more expensive. It would have strengthened the tendencies to internal inflation. It was, therefore, entirely inadvisable as a voluntary policy; and to have sat still doing nothing and watching devaluation forced upon us would have been an abject failure of government.

For similar reasons, I cannot believe that on this occasion any good purpose could have been served by letting the rate float. The policy of the floating rate is an acutely controversial matter and it would be idle to claim that there is any general consensus of opinion about it. But I think that it would be generally agreed that a moment of extreme weakness is not the moment for making such an experiment. The rate would certainly have plunged downwards, precipitating further withdrawals and, in the absence of countervailing measures, provoking further internal inflation, eventually justifying a permanently lower rate – the so-called ratchet effect. Although in general I prefer the system of fixed rates with the possibility of agreed adjustment *à la* Bretton Woods, I would not rule out the use of the floating rate on any possible occasion: a depression of the 1929 intensity in the U.S. might well create a situation in which for a time it was advisable to let the rate take the strain. But the situation in September last year was not at all like this and, in my judgement, a floating rate would only have made things worse.

As for the repudiation of current obligations which would have been involved by the re-imposition of full exchange control and the blocking of the sterling balances, surely it would have been both dishonourable and inexpedient. It would have been dishonourable since these balances have been left here on the definite understanding that they would be available whenever required. In the years immediately after the war there was a case, which I, for one, thought very cogent, for imposing some restraint on the release of the abnormal accumulations of wartime. But that is ancient history: for the most part, the war-time balances have been run down; the present balances have been deposited since then. To close down on them without putting up a fight would be the most flagrant failure to keep faith with our clients. It would be inexpedient too: whatever we may think of the eventual future of the sterling area, whether we foresee for it a glorious future or whether we think it will eventually give way to other arrangements, we surely do not wish to see it liquidated overnight with all that that would imply. But that is what the blocking of balances and the reimposition of all-over exchange control would involve.

But if all these courses were rejected, what remained? In my judgement, at least, the course which was actually adopted: a clear announcement that the rate of exchange was not to be changed, backed up by the announcement of measures which should prove unmistakably to the world at large that the inflation was not to be allowed to continue.

The formula is simple enough. But there can be no doubt that its application involved greater hazards than would have been present earlier on. It is safe to say that, up to last summer, at almost any time in the preceding six years, the government could have stopped the inflation without running any risks that really mattered. To stop a small local inflation when the rest of the world economy is running at a high level involves no danger of subsequent deflation. But again and again we refused to grasp the nettle. With an unemployment percentage continually lower than anything recorded in peace-time history, we let fears of totally imaginary dangers inhibit the very mild measures that would have been necessary. But now the position was beginning to change. A recession was developing in the United States. Should we not be imposing our anti-inflationary measures at a time when there was at least a risk that anti-deflationary measures would become necessary a little later on?

As I see things, the danger was – and is – a real one. The possibility of a deepening of the U.S. recession was not imaginary. But neither was the possibility of a total collapse of sterling. And the one danger was certain and near at hand, while the other was still remote and conjectural. Moreover, it is difficult to believe that, if our crisis had been allowed to intensify with an eventual immobilization of the reserves and free funds of the sterling area, there would have been any substantial alleviation of the troubles of the world at large – quite the contrary indeed. Hence the common sense maxim of dealing with dangers one at a time as they materialized was still applicable. The order of the day was to save the pound. If there was a world depression by next summer and the pound had been saved, perhaps we could do something to help. But if the pound had collapsed and London was immobilized in the splints and bandages of a post-crisis exchange control, that would be out of the question. In such circumstances, to refuse to stop our own inflation because later on deflation might come elsewhere would seem to be about as sensible as refusing, when the house is on fire, to call the fire engine on the ground that there may be floods later on.

V THE POLICIES OF THE EMERGENCY

Now for a few brief comments on the measures actually adopted – the raising of the Bank Rate and the limitations on advances and expenditure. I will also add a word on the absence of any further limitations on consumption.

(a) The Raising of the Bank Rate

To begin with the Bank Rate. From my point of view the surprising thing about this episode is, not that it happened but rather that so many people were surprised that it happened – and among these, not merely everyday citizens, to whom the proceedings of a great capital market are perhaps inevitably always something of a mystery, but also professional dealers whose livelihood depends upon an intelligent understanding of these matters. I am sure that an observer from Mars who, before, his visit, had worked up his knowledge of mundane financial crises by a short study of how the majority of central banks have behaved in the majority of past financial crises, would not have been at all surprised. Yet here were people who had been in the business all their lives to whom the bare possibility does not seem ever to have occurred. No wonder they were a little upset.

Now, it may be admitted at once that the effectiveness of movements of the Bank Rate as a sole means for controlling the total volume of expenditure may very justly be called in question. It is certainly arguable, as I have argued above, that the powers of the Bank in our own time have been gravely impaired by a distended volume of short-term government debt: and that, for that reason, an effective control of the money supply demands more drastic and comprehensive measures. There will be a good deal to say about this later on.

But this is not to say that as a crisis measure, a raising of the Bank Rate is to be regarded as ineffective. It is, of course, not true that such a movement, carrying with it, as it does, a corresponding movement of conventional rates on borrowing and lending, not to mention strong psychological effects on the security markets, has *no* effect on the volume of internal expenditure – even though it be arguable that such effects can be as well produced by other, less expensive means. And, internal effects apart, it would surely be quite absurd to argue that it has no effect on the movement of funds into and out of the country. It has a direct effect *via* the cash incentive: it increases the advantages of leaving money here or bringing it in, it diminishes the relative attraction of other places. The indirect effect is even more important: it is a signal to all and sundry that the integrity of the currency is to be preserved. Whatever the deficiencies of our present machinery, it is an important fact that the members of other financial centres tend to regard the movement of money rates as an index of policy. To them the raising of the Bank Rate here is a sign that the pound is to be defended.

I wonder how many of those who have been most critical since this measure was taken in fact would have been prepared at such a moment to forgo these advantages. With gold and dollars pouring out at catastrophic rates, would it not have been just a trifle purist to have abstained from the use of an instrument which again and again in the past had been proved to have the effect of arresting this kind of drain? I do not think many of the critics would have wanted to devalue. Some, perhaps, would have argued for complete exchange control, though it is doubtful if at the same time they would have welcomed the consequences of such a régime – a complete break-up of the sterling area. But, if such expedients were not acceptable, it is not easy to see any practical alternative to what was actually done. Or is it to be argued that the drain would have come to an end of its own accord – as the result of speeches by ministers assuring the world at large that in fact everything in the garden was lovely?

(b) The Limitation on Advances

If this argument is correct, Bank Rate is still an indispensable weapon for dealing with an acute crisis. For dealing with a secular tendency to inflation, however, it is not a particularly suitable instrument. For this purpose it is desirable to adopt other measures for limiting the flow of expenditure.

So far as the banking system was concerned, the measure which was actually adopted was the imposition of an upper limit on the aggregate of advances. Each of the clearing banks undertook not to exceed in the present twelve months the average level of its advances in the preceding year. There were small modifications of detail for particular lines of credit. But this in substance was the broad policy adopted.

Now, conceived as a crisis measure, to be adopted at short notice with the minimum of resistance from all immediately concerned, there is probably a good deal to be said for this device. It has precedents in past policies. It requires no legislation or statutory regulations. And, despite the strictures which I shall develop shortly, it cannot be said to be without effect; there would not be so much grumbling if this were in fact the case.

Nevertheless, conceived as a policy for the longer period, still more if conceived as an expedient to be adopted whenever this kind of danger emerges, it is open to considerable criticism. It bears unequally upon different banks, according to the different lending policies which they have been pursuing. It tends to paralyse financial competition, which in the long run must be a very bad thing. And, as a partial control, it does not really go to the root of the matter. The root of the matter is control of expenditure as a whole.

But to do this the fundamental *desideratum* is control of the supply of money. Given over-all control at that end, there can be adaptation to all sorts of vagaries of expenditure in particular sectors. Given an absence of such control, there can be no guarantee that control in one sector will not be frustrated by the absence of control elsewhere. This is not to say that, even if the supply of money is under control, there may not arise a need for supplementary special controls. But it is to say that, if it is not under control, the whole system is liable to get out of hand.

Now, as already emphasized, the disquieting feature of the recent situation was that the money supply was not under effective control: the excessive volume of short-term debt has weakened the hand of the central bank. The monetization of debt has made the Treasury rather than the Bank of England the arbiter of the total volume of cash plus deposits. The needs of short-term borrowing rather than the needs of the system for cash and credit have been liable to disturb over-all stability.

In more normal circumstances the appropriate remedy for such a situation would be funding. The volume of Treasury bills should be reduced until there is no threat to the complete control of the credit base by the Bank of England. It is true that this would involve some increase in the annual debt charge. But to keep this charge down by techniques which endanger the future of the pound is not sensible policy. An increase would be a small price to pay to regain control of the credit base and hence of aggregate demand in general.

Unfortunately, in a financial crisis such operations are not necessarily practicable. Throughout the greater part of the year the position had been becoming more difficult in this respect. After years of passive acquiescence in lending in a deteriorating standard of value, the investor had gradually become aware of what was happening and was demanding progressively higher returns on fixed interest securities. The Church of England and the learned societies had led the way; and now the man in the street had tumbled to the fact that if you lend for a money return of 4 per cent. per annum net and the value of money is falling at the same rate, then you are lending at a zero rate of interest. The run on the pound intensified the difficulty. It is safe to say that, in August and September of last year, orthodox funding on a scale necessary to re-establish control of the credit base would have been quite out of the question.

In such an emergency there seems to me strong argument for some extraordinary measure which, by operating on the liquidity position of the banking system shall impose limits on its total lending. If action can be taken at this end, then there need be no paralysis of competition, no wooden interference with different modes of doing business. But the credit base as a whole can be brought under effective control.

* * *

In public discussion, the device most favoured for accomplishing this has been compulsory variation of minimum liquidity ratios. On the assumption that, in modern conditions, it is the liquidity position, rather than the cash reserve, which ultimately governs the supply of money, it is argued that powers should be taken to require the observance of minimum liquidity ratios and that these ratios should be varied according to the requirements of general policy. This is not the same as the existing provision of the banking law in the U.S. under which the Federal Reserve Board has the power to vary minimum cash reserve requirements; although it has sometimes been mistaken for this, it is a more comprehensive requirement. But it is a device of the same type conceived in relation to the exigencies of our own system.

In principle, there seems little objection to such a regulation provided it is regarded as an emergency expedient. But there are technical difficulties which are often overlooked. The actual liquidity position of the banks varies from week to week; and, since the effects on investments and advances of such changes are multiple, it would be necessary to make very frequent changes in the prescribed ratio. Moreover, these changes would have to be by small fractions, not easy to judge and not easy to justify to the public.

Much superior in my judgement is the plan which was recommended as far back as August, 1956, by Messrs. Paish and Alford[1] and again by Messrs. Alford and Edey as the crisis was developing,[2] namely, the imposition of a fixed liquidity ratio – or one varied at comparatively long intervals – plus a revival, for the duration of the crisis, of the system of Treasury Deposit Receipts (T.D.Rs.) whereby the banks are required from week to week to keep an appropriately varying volume of assets in a form which is definitely illiquid. Such a method is capable of doing all that is claimed for the system of variable liquidity ratios but with much greater refinement and precision. The appropriate variations in the supply of money are now secured *via* the variations in the volume of T.D.Rs. rather than the variation of the liquidity ratio. The principle of the operation is the same.

Let me hasten to add that, in my judgement, in being regimented in this manner the banks would have a real grievance. Their business would be being interfered with because of a situation created not by their policy but by the policy, or rather lack of policy, of the government. But I do not believe that this kind of interference would be more damaging to their business than

1. "How interest rates cut spending", *The Banker*, vol. 56, pp. 476–87.
2. "Home finance", *London and Cambridge Economic Bulletin*, n.s. no. 23 (September 1957), pp. ix–x.

the interference to which they are now subjected under the present arrangements of the credit squeeze: and if there were some definite understanding that the regulation was to be regarded definitely as transitory, to be relinquished as soon as orthodox funding on an adequate scale was once more practicable, I do not think that the grievance would be intolerable.

It may well be that the occasion for this sort of thing is even now passing. As the prospect of inflation wanes, the possibilities of orthodox funding become more extensive. Nevertheless, it seems to me that there is perhaps some utility in thus spelling out the principles of alternative measures even if on this occasion they prove to be no longer applicable.

(c) The Limitations on Expenditure

Finally, we may note the proposed limitations on expenditure.

This is so political a subject that it is not easy to say much about it that is not right outside the sphere of economics in any sense whatever. How much the country will stand in the shape of reduction here, what it would be prudent politically to exempt there, to what extent discredit will arise if a gesture is not made in this direction – these are not questions on which the economist who does not care to transform himself into Adam Smith's "crafty and insidious animal", the politician, has very much to say. Two comments, however, are perhaps permissible.

The first is that, in the context of what was actually proposed, the term reduction is misleading. The celebrated "cuts" were prospective. Extra expenditure which had been projected was to be forgone. Doubtless, this was very important. Increases on the scale which had been contemplated would have imposed still more strain on the system; and we must not underestimate the political effort apparently necessary to impose even this degree of restraint. Nevertheless, if we are to use words accurately, not *reduction* but *standstill* was the more appropriate description.

The second comment is that, in the subsequent discussion, the nature of the margin for manoeuvre has been often misconceived. To judge from leading articles and correspondence in the press, it would appear that there were immense savings available if only ministers would order a naturally spendthrift and wasteful public service to be more careful all round. But this is a pathetic and dangerous delusion. Doubtless there is always a little waste even in the best regulated establishments; and perhaps there are a few hundred thousands to be gained by general cheese-paring on small items which are unable to defend themselves and which, on intrinsic merits, perhaps even deserve some increase. But all the main reductions possible involve, not administrative, but political decisions, and major decisions at that; and decisions on matters of this sort are the decisions which most ministers of most parties tend to shirk. Perhaps they are right. Perhaps some wisdom, invisible to those not in the fray, prevents them from steps which would disintegrate, not only their own peace of mind, but also the fabric of society. But if this is so, then standstill, or a slower creep forward, is the most we can hope for in the sphere of public expenditure; and in respect of what has been done recently we should be grateful for small mercies.

(d) The Absence of Limitations on Consumption

The criticism is sometimes made of the measures adopted last autumn that their main incidence fell almost wholly on investment. The raising of the Bank Rate, the ceiling on advances and the "cuts" in public expenditure all tended to have their main effect, directly at least, by restraints on the volume of investment.

The immediate answer to this, I suppose, is that, in an inflationary situation, the cutting of investment is the cutting of investment for which no corresponding savings were planned. If the disposition to save had been adequate, then there would have been no danger of inflation.

Nevertheless, in a situation in which so much is artificial, I see no particular reason to believe that the existing volume of savings is, in any sense, optimal; and I see no objection in principle to applying restraints on consumption in order to ease inflationary pressure. If, in such a situation, there were available tax variations which, without damaging the incentive to work or to save, could have restrained pressure at the consumption end, then in my judgement there would be good ground for imposing them.

The trouble is to discover appropriate and practical methods – particularly when the crisis blows up in an inter-budgetary period. I confess that I see no good grounds for still further variations in a purchase tax system which is already sufficiently arbitrary and discriminatory. If there existed a general sales tax in its place – still more, if there existed a general sales tax *plus* general exemption allowance[1] such as has been proposed by Professor Paish – I would say that the circumstances of last autumn provided a copy-book case for the use of variations both of the rate and the exemption allowance, as counter-inflationary influences. Unfortunately, such expedients do not exist and it is not possible to improvise them overnight.

Equally efficacious, and perhaps politically no more difficult to impose, would be variations in the contributions of employers and employed to the

1. To be effected by a distribution of coupons entitling each citizen to a certain volume of tax-free purchases.

social insurance funds. This plan, invented by Professor Meade, was blessed by both parties in the Coalition White Paper on Employment Policy.* After the war, the essential machinery was actually built into social insurance legislation by the Labour government; and there can be no doubt in principle that comparatively small variations here could have powerful countervailing influence either against inflation or deflation. Unfortunately, the machinery was never used by those who installed it; and probably at the present time, there is a good deal of political and administrative dust in the works. I still think, however, that it is a very good plan and that on some future occasion it should be tried – either one way or the other.

VI PROBLEMS OF THE FUTURE

And now what? There can be no question that, whether or not they were the best that could be conceived, the measures actually adopted last autumn have stopped the run. Since September 19th the reserves have been mounting again – not perhaps quite as rapidly as might have been hoped, but nevertheless unmistakably and strongly upward. There have been various signs that confidence is not completely re-established – the downward flicker following the very hostile reception of the Cohen Report,* for instance – and the prospect of divided counsels and political dissension in the future gives rise to legitimate apprehension. But, for the moment, the atmosphere of crisis has passed and we can look round a little.

The first question which naturally arises is how we now stand in relation to developments in America. Has the contraction there reached a point which is so liable to infect us with similar tendencies as to warrant a complete reversal of policy here? Are we confronted with a major depression in the world at large against which it is a prime necessity for us to take independent internal action?

The enquiry is serious; and, as I have indicated already, I think that it deserves to be taken seriously. I should, therefore, like to make it quite clear that it is my view that if the contraction in the U.S. were to assume the dimensions of a major depression, it would be incumbent upon us to adopt insulating measures. I do not think that this would be at all easy; it is quite possible that present rates of exchange would have to be sacrificed in the process. But it seems to me plain that, in the event of such a development, such policies would be necessary.

* Cmd. 6527, May 1944, Appendix II.

* *First Report of the Council on Prices, Productivity and Incomes*, February 1958.

If, however, this does not happen, if the American contraction is arrested before it goes into something really severe, then I think any attempt on our part to take the initiative would not only be premature but also dangerous. The pound is certainly not yet strong enough to risk the impression of a renewal of inflation. Anything which tended now to raise our prices and costs while the rest of the world was consolidating at a lower level would be a renewed embarrassment. And from the point of view of the world at large, we should certainly do no one a good service by a policy which once more threatened the position of sterling. Clearly, we must avoid unnecessary severity. The object of the present exercise is to strengthen the pound and prevent expenditure rising faster than productivity; and, as the danger to the capital account diminishes, there will be no need to prolong measures which were specifically suitable for dealing with that particular difficulty. But to go beyond such relaxations would be risky. This is very unfortunate. It would be very gratifying to be in a position in which we could afford to take the initiative in stimulating a world revival. But to be able to do that now we should have put our position in order earlier. With a strong reserve all sorts of things would have been possible that with a weak reserve are a source of peril.

Now, I do not profess to know what is going to happen in America. Where expert opinion on the spot is so sorely divided, it is surely to set a high value on one's powers as a prophet to pretend to predict from a distance. I confess I find it hard to believe that, in an election year with so many shots in the locker, the Administration and Congress will be content to witness a dangerous deterioration. But such things have happened before and I would not be sure. What seems to me to be fairly clear is that there have been no developments yet which, in our special and highly peculiar position, would call for extraordinary action. I hope myself that the U.S. Administration will redouble its efforts to put the gears in reverse: I wish, for our sake, that they had done so earlier. But I see no immediate call for such action here. The situation calls for unceasing vigilance, and if things get very much worse we may find ourselves the other side of the looking glass where all sorts of rules are reversed. But so far I do not think this has happened. For us at least – although not, I suspect for the U.S. – the maxims of prudence still have a positive sign.

* * *

Assuming this to be correct, let us enquire a little further concerning the nature of these maxims. Assuming that events elsewhere do not compel a drastic change, how should we wish our own development to proceed? What are the fundamental objectives of policy in regard to expenditure and the price level?

It should be clear in the first place that these objectives do *not* include deflation – policies designed to produce a positive contraction of incomes or the price level. It should not be necessary to labour this point. But I am afraid that experience proves that it is. It has become almost a habit, recently, among certain writers and speakers, that if a man argues against *in*flation, he should be at once denounced for recommending *de*flation. I suppose that, in most cases at least, one ought to treat this as if it were sincere: the subject is difficult and tempers are easily aroused. But deflation is certainly not the only alternative to inflation. It is perfectly possible – and until recently I should have thought that it would have been assumed to be the most natural attitude – to be opposed to both and to regard some sort of over-all stability as the objective. At any rate, despite popular oratory, I have yet to meet any responsible person who wishes to impose a positive deflation. To stop inflation, that is the objective: and to talk of deflation and mass unemployment, when the cost of living index has only just stopped rising and the unemployment percentage is still lower than in most other countries of the world and at most times in modern history, is simply to darken counsel.

But do we really want to stop inflation? I suppose there are very few politicians who would admit to wanting it to continue. But a great many act as if they were prepared to tolerate such an outcome; and there are certainly others, not so directly connected with politics, who are definitely prepared to argue as if it were something which we ought to put up with. In modern conditions, it is contended, while of course hyper-inflation is to be avoided, a creeping inflation is to be accepted as the condition most conducive to growth. To make stable money the objective is to risk stagnation and unemployment.

I find this position unacceptable. I do not in the least deny that the process of *stopping* an inflation may involve some temporary check to production and employment: if you are swerving towards a precipice, some temporary slowing up is the price you have to pay for re-establishing a safer direction of motion. But I know no reason which would lead to the conclusion that smart rates of growth and high levels of employment are impossible on a steady price level. In the recent history of Germany, for instance, there is ample evidence disproving this view.

But suppose there are strong trade unions and an incessant pressure for wages rising faster than productivity, is not this expectation vitiated? Do there not then exist conditions in which growth can be sustained only at the expense of some degree of inflation?

The question is grave and so is the answer. If, for any long period, wages rise faster than productivity, then the alternatives are either unemployment and diminished production or continuous inflation. It is, of course, possible to conceive that some small increases of wages can be financed out of profits without serious reactions on employment. But the statistical limits are small;

and it is to treat the subject with less seriousness than it deserves to assume that there is any long-lasting solution in this direction. Exactly the same problem would exist were all industry nationalized and all profits appropriated by the State: if wage-rates rose faster than productivity, the main alternatives would be unemployment or inflation.

But are we right in assuming that such a development is inevitable? I see no ground for a pessimism as deep as this. As I have argued above, I do not believe that the greater part of the inflation which has taken place already is to be explained in these terms. On my conception, up to recently the rise of wages has usually been the *result*, not the *cause*, of the general inflation. When the demand for labour in most parts of the economy so much exceeded the supply, the trade union leaders would have had to be angels not to cash in on the situation. If they had not been there, it is improbable that the rise would have been much less.

But now the situation has changed. For the time being, at least, the demand inflation is at an end. The funds out of which it was financed are under more control – at least, let us hope they are. And the question what in the new conditions will be the policy of the leaders of the unions is not yet solved. I am not one of those who believe that much good is to be expected from mere exhortation to any section of the community; if I had been a trade union leader during the last few years I should have become positively neurotic at the barrage of appeals to my patriotism, social solidarity, sense of decency, and so on and so forth. But it is not at all obvious to me that trade union leaders are so indifferent to their own interest as to persist long in policies liable to create unemployment, if inflationary finance is not there. This is not to say that I should expect the ending of a period of inflation to be free of friction or that I believe that people in such positions are incapable of mistaking for a time where their true interests lie – the trade unions of this country for years have clung to restrictive practices which in the long run help no one. But it would surely be very short-sighted policy for any government to assume that such responsible bodies are incapable of learning from experience and to base policy upon the assumption that they will always react one way whatever the general state of the economy.

Whether this be true or not, my conception of the duty of governments in this connection is clear. It is not the duty of governments to make the maintenance of employment the be-all and end-all of policy, regardless of what happens to the value of money. It is their duty rather to maintain conditions which will make a high level of employment compatible with a stable value of money. They should not say we guarantee employment whatever demands are made in respect of wage-rates; they should say rather we will try to maintain such a volume of expenditure as, given an income-level rising with productivity, will maintain a high level of employment. If they do this, then, in a free society at any rate, it is for trade unionists and all the rest of us to decide how we react as regards the prices we put on our own particular products.

This, clearly, is a controversial view. There are many who hold that salvation lies in a much more authoritarian direction. Control of wages from the centre, plus some measure of dividend limitation, is the solution they favour. My solution is in quite conscious opposition to this. I do not think that experience elsewhere suggests that in the absence of deliberate monetary stabilization, a general wage control is likely to be successful; and, if monetary stabilization is attempted, such a control seems to me unnecessary. I have no desire at this time of day to see the whole apparatus of independent trade unionism, which has performed such valuable services in the past, sacrificed in so dubious an enterprise. I think it is more compatible with the principles of a free society that we should be free to make mistakes and to learn from them than that we should be clamped down by a system of regulation from the centre which, if experience elsewhere is anything to go by, is itself no less liable to error.

* * *

To return, however, to the theory of continuing inflation, perhaps the ultimate criticism here is that the thing is extremely unlikely to work out as planned. I should be willing to concede that, *if* there could take place an inflation of, say, $\frac{1}{2}$ or even 1 per cent. per annum, and that *if* this could go on unperceived and unanticipated, then there might be important advantages. There would be a mild reinforcement of the power to accumulate in the shape of higher money earnings on the part of companies and employers. There would be elbow room for the process of collective bargaining to make small mistakes of rate-fixing without causing unemployment. Against this, there would be some injustice to the owners of fixed interest-bearing securities and the recipients of incomes which are only adjusted at long intervals. But experience of periods of mild gold inflation tends to suggest that on balance there would be substantial prosperity.

But all this depends upon the assumption that the process is unanticipated and, until it has happened, unperceived. If, after a time, people become alive to what is happening, still more if they come to assume that a certain decline in the value of money is one of the necessary concomitants of accepted policy, then they will adjust their plans accordingly and none of the beneficial by-products of unperception will be present. Lenders will not lend, save for a higher rate of interest. Contracts will not be concluded, save with a margin allowing for the expected rate of depreciation. What is more, after a time, the difficulties will be cumulative. The fear of inflation tends to create more inflation. Most of the paper inflations of history were gradual to begin with: but they ended in something not at all gradual.

All this would apply to a community without external economic relations or where the external factor was relatively unimportant. Where, however, external relations loom large in the economic structure, as they do in ours, the effects of inflation are apt to be much more immediate and much more serious. If the inflation is not only absolute but relative, if, that is to say, it is greater than any such movement which is going on elsewhere, then the effects on the balance of payments show themselves very quickly. It is not a matter of danger in the long period, it is a matter of danger in a very few months. And this, of course, is particularly germane to our situation. I can imagine a mild inflation in the United States proceeding without over-much difficulty for several, perhaps for many, years. I cannot conceive such a development in this country. If we go on inflating, and if our inflation is greater than is going on in important countries elsewhere, then – as indeed we know from the recurrent crises of the post-war period – the effect is likely to be sharp and sudden. And I do not think our peculiar system, with its world-wide ramifications depending essentially on a particular kind of understanding and confidence, can stand an indefinite succession of crises.

But that brings me to the last point which I wish to make in this already overlong paper. For the next few years at least, an objective, second only in importance to the avoidance of inflation or deflation, must be the strengthening of the reserve. With our capital account in its present condition, our reserves are quite inadequate. We are trying to be bankers for a large part of the world; but we are not prepared to keep a reserve large enough to preclude crises of confidence. In such conditions rumours which, were the reserves at all adequate, would exhaust themselves in light gossip, tend to start major convulsions. The position is not permanently viable: and it should be a major objective of policy to put it right.

It is sometimes said that this is impossible. We have done all we can since the war and yet there is no improvement. The only way in which the reserve position can be improved is by some gigantic international operation. Failing this, we should set our sights at a lower target and resign ourselves to the mediocrity of our position.

This argument seems to me to lack substance. I am no foe to international action in regard to this problem; and I would greet with enthusiasm action of the kind suggested by Sir Oliver Franks in his recent annual statement [as chairman of Lloyds Bank]. But I do not agree that, if international action is slow in developing, there is nothing that we can do to help ourselves. I cannot see any justification for this, either in theory or experience. Other countries have increased their reserves. Why should not we? What is so different in the condition of Germany and ourselves that while, on balance, our reserve has not increased at all since the summer of 1950, in the same period the German reserve has mounted from $260 millions to some $4,000 millions? Doubtless there are many inessential differences which can be cited one way or the other. But the main difference, I submit, is that the Germans have had the will to do this thing and we have not. And let no one say that this has been accomplished at the price of poverty and stagnation. Between 1950 and 1957, while our real output per head has increased by about 15 per cent., the German has risen by nearly 60 per cent.

Is it not the bankruptcy of statesmanship and national morale to argue that this sort of thing is impossible for us?

23 Hayek on Liberty[1]

From *Economica*, new series vol. 28 (February 1961), pp. 66–81.

I

This is a very ambitious book. "It has been a long time," says the author, "since that ideal of freedom which inspired modern Western civilization and whose partial realization made possible the achievements of that civilization was effectively restated"[2]. It is such a restatement which is here attempted. The range covered is extensive: social philosophy, jurisprudence, economics and politics are all summoned to make their contribution to the main theme and a broad historical perspective informs the whole. In a revealing passage Professor Hayek explains that, although he still regards himself as mainly an economist, he has "come to feel more and more that the answers to many of the pressing social questions of our time are to be found ultimately in the recognition of principles that lie outside the scope of technical economics or of any other single discipline."[3] It is with such principles that this book is chiefly concerned.

The argument falls into three parts. The first deals with fundamentals: the nature of liberty, its value and its relation to other notions and objectives – responsibility, employment, equality and majority rule. The second is devoted to a conception which the author regards as quite pivotal to the constitution of liberty, namely, the rule of law, its essential characteristics and its vicissitudes in time and place. The third, which is entitled "Freedom in the Welfare State," consists of a series of applications of the principles thus developed to problems of contemporary policy: the place of Trade Unions in a free society, Social Security, Progressive Taxation, Housing and Town Planning, Agriculture and Conservation, Education and Research, and so on. A postscript entitled "Why I am not a Conservative" brings the whole to a conclusion.

---

1. *The Constitution of Liberty*, by F.A. Hayek (London: Routledge & Kegan Paul, 1960).
2. *Ibid.*, p. 1.
3. *Ibid.*, p. 3.

Let it be said at once that the result of all this is a book which certainly rises to the high plane of the matters with which it elects to deal and which, by reason both of the depth of its analysis and the width of its learning, must surely take an honourable place among the standard works on the subject. Nor is the tone less impressive than the content. The issues discussed are intrinsically controversial and the author obviously attaches great importance to his conclusions; yet the theme is set forth with studied moderation and the appeal is to reason rather than to emotion. It cannot be said to be easy reading; the arguments, although clear and well marshalled, demand frequent pauses for reflection. Nor is it likely, even with those who are in general sympathy with the position it adopts, to command continuous assent; considering the extraordinary difficulty of the problems involved, it would be surprising if it did. But it is a book which must be taken seriously; it is not to be disposed of by guying occasional judgments. Indeed, it may be said to be a test, not of its quality but of its readers, that even where it arouses most disagreement, there at least it should command respect.

If, therefore, in what follows, the emphasis seems to dwell on points of difference, that must be taken as springing, not from any lack of warm admiration for the work as a whole, but rather as a tribute to the spirit in which it is written and a testimony to its thought-provoking power. I have written as I should talk if we were having a friendly discussion in the staff seminar here [LSE], as we have done so often in the past.

II

Professor Hayek's conception of liberty, like that of the great liberal thinkers of the past, runs in terms of absence of arbitrary coercion. In Sir Isaiah Berlin's useful classification[1] it is the negative conception. Some coercion there must be in order to provide a sanction for the framework of law which creates the possibility of liberty. But, beyond that, it is of the essence of liberty that the individual should be free from constraint by others and that, in relation to the law, he can adjust his conduct as he does to impersonal natural limitations.

All this is excellent and has seldom been argued with greater persuasive power, especially in relation to the rival "positive" conceptions. Professor Hayek has little difficulty in exposing the essential confusion involved in bringing under one heading the freedom involved by the absence of coercion and the so-called freedom from want which is said to flow from a certain

1. See his notable Inaugural Lecture, *Two Concepts of Liberty* (Oxford, 1958).

level of real income. The limitations imposed on us by nature and technique are not the same as the limitations imposed on us by other men: and although resounding oratorical effects may be achieved by assuming that they are, yet nothing but confusion in thought and action can be the consequence. Nor is any good purpose to be served by describing liberty as a state of affairs conducive to inner freedom or to the realization of the best self; this also can open the door to all sorts of muddles and worse. It is hard enough to realize liberty in the traditional liberal sense without it being loaded with all sorts of extraneous and often contradictory associations.

Matters become more difficult, however, when political liberties are concerned. Professor Hayek would have us draw a sharp line between liberty in his sense and the right to vote; and it is not at all difficult to see why he does so. There may be much personal liberty under despotism – historically this has often been so – whereas political democracy resting on the right to vote may quite easily go totalitarian – for which there are also many historical and contemporary instances. Nevertheless, I venture to submit that not to be allowed to participate in making the law under which one has to live, to be prevented, if necessary by force, from entering the polling booth, must surely be described as a deprivation of liberty. The voteless citizen of mature years, however free in other respects, must be regarded in this respect as suffering a discriminatory exclusion; and if we have regard to the way in which the absence of the right to vote has resulted in other discriminatory exclusions, especially where women or coloured people have been concerned, this cannot be dismissed as a trifling matter. A full realization of liberty, in terms of Professor Hayek's general conception of absence of coercive constraint, must therefore involve the liberty to vote. That this carries with it liberty to destroy other liberty is undeniable; and we may agree with J.S. Mill and Professor Hayek that, for this reason, popular government carries with it very grave dangers. But this is just one of those paradoxes of life which are not to be eliminated by restricting the connotations of terminology.

There is a further matter in respect of which I do not feel that Professor Hayek's definitions completely catch the spirit of his general analysis. In his conception, the absence of coercion depends essentially upon the existence of known rules equally applicable to all. His discussion in this connection is one of the most impressive features of his whole argument: the case for the rule of law, divested of the misconception which marred Dicey's classic treatment, is presented with a weight of historical learning and logical force which can only be described as masterly. But is this the whole of the story? Cannot law in this sense be oppressive and restrictive? Must we not distinguish between a liberal rule of law and others?

Professor Hayek is not unaware of this question. "It is not to be denied that even general, abstract rules, equally applicable to all, may possibly constitute severe restrictions on liberty," he says. But he goes on to minimize the difficulty. "When we reflect on it," he continues, "we see how very unlikely this is. The chief safeguard is that the rules must apply to those who lay them down and those who apply them ... and that nobody has the power to grant exception. If all that is prohibited and enjoined is prohibited and enjoined for all without exception ... little that anybody may reasonably wish to do is likely to be prohibited." And he urges that it is "significant that religious beliefs seem to be almost the only ground on which general rules seriously restrictive of liberty have ever been universally enforced".[1]

I am afraid that I do not find this very reassuring. For reasons which I do not follow, Professor Hayek seems to think that "most such restrictions imposed on all" are "comparatively innocuous beside those likely to be imposed on some." This perplexes me. I am quite prepared to admit that discriminatory restriction may be more hateful than restriction which is general. But I should have thought that some of the most repellent restrictions in history had been religious; even in twentieth century societies some of the prohibitions regarding, say, contraception and divorce, which in some countries are enforced in the name of religion, are only one degree less odious and contemptible than racial discrimination itself. Moreover, even if communism is not to be described as a religion, many of its prohibitions are generally applicable; and I should scarcely have described these as just "irksome," the adjective which Professor Hayek uses for his own somewhat quaint example – the Scottish Sabbath.

III

One of the most interesting sections in Professor Hayek's treatment of fundamentals is that in which, following a train of thought developed in his Dublin Lecture of 1945, *Individualism, True and False*, he distinguishes between what, in his view, are true and false theories of liberty.[2] The one, typified by the thought of the Scottish philosophers Hume, Adam Smith and Ferguson, he describes as empirical (or occasionally anti-rationalist): it finds the essence of freedom in spontaneity and the absence of coercion. The other, typified by the thinkers of the French Enlightenment, Rousseau and the Physiocrats, and, somewhat surprisingly, the nineteenth century English Utilitarians, he describes as rationalist: it believes freedom to be realized and attained only in the pursuit of an absolute collective purpose. The one conceives of reason as acting within a framework of institutions and morals, the product of more or

1. *Op. cit.*, pp. 154–5.
2. Reprinted as Chapter 1 of his *Individualism and Economic Order* (Chicago, 1948).

less unconscious evolutionary experiment. The other conceives of an independent antecedent human reason that invented these institutions or at least, by a fiction, sanctioned them, and by which they can be judged as a whole. The one leads to true liberty: the other very easily turns into its opposite.

I have no doubt that much of this is very true and very important. From the positive point of view, the recognition of an order in society which has not been planned as a totality is clearly fundamental; and never has the path-breaking significance of the great eighteenth century discoveries in this respect been better set forth than in Professor Hayek's luminous exposition, itself the source of many new insights. As he develops the conception of a spontaneous organization which is not only a sorting out of comparative aptitudes and technical advantages, but also a means of utilizing and developing a heritage of knowledge never capable of being grasped as a whole by any of the participants in the process, the time-honoured theme of the advantages of the division of labour assumes a new aspect; and propositions that have been repeated more or less parrot-wise for a hundred and fifty years acquire a meaning and depth seldom before realized. I would venture to pick this out, together with his earlier papers on similar topics, as one of Professor Hayek's most enduring contributions to our subject.[1] Nor is the negative emphasis of his analysis less relevant to the main theme. The belief that society owes its origin to rational deliberation on its shape as a whole is manifestly false. The belief that it is within the power of reason to re-shape society at one go is a dangerous delusion – the fallacy of holism against which Karl Popper has argued so powerfully. To ignore those aspects of social relationships and institutions which are the result of spontaneous adaptation rather than deliberate authoritarian contrivance is often to miss the most powerful and beneficial elements. To initiate change without paying due heed to them is to risk failure and sometimes much worse than failure – social disaster. The difference between British and French history in this respect may perhaps be conceived as in some measure an exemplification of this danger.

Nevertheless, I have some reserves in this connection, both regarding the manner of formulation and the substance.

First, as regards manner, I must confess to a certain disquiet at finding the position to which, on the whole, I incline, described as an *anti*-rationalist position. Doubtless, if rationalism is to be conceived solely in terms of Descartes and his influence, there is good historical justification for so describing the opposition; furthermore, both in this chapter and elsewhere, Professor Hayek is careful to distinguish this "anti-rationalist" opposition to the false use of reason from irrationalism – rejection of reason in its proper

1. *Ibid.*, pp. 1–32.

sphere. Nevertheless, I cannot help thinking that it is a term which is likely to be misunderstood and, if for that reason only, should be avoided.

Moreover – and here perhaps we approach a little nearer to substance – while I am largely in agreement with this emphasis on the importance of the non-rational element in social habits and institutions, I confess to a certain fear that, with the less sophisticated, such an emphasis may topple over into indiscriminate acceptance and admiration. After all, not all institutions and habits which survive are to be regarded as beneficial; some at least are unmitigated evils which to treat with respect were absurd. It is certainly not a "rationalist fallacy" to subject them to critical scrutiny. In this connection, I find a very significant contrast between Hume and Burke, whom Professor Hayek tends to bracket together. Hume usually seems to me to be about right: he certainly recognizes the limitations of reason in respect to the origins of institutions and morals; yet he never hesitates to use it where it is appropriate in criticizing the extent to which they satisfy the test of public utility. Whereas Burke, for all his wisdom and insight, which no man of sense would wish ever to deny, not infrequently lets his sense of the majesty of the past degenerate into what I, at least, should regard as indefensible conservatism. It is all very well for Professor Hayek to claim him as a Whig; doubtless, even to the end, there were strong traces of that tradition. But it was not the Whig in Burke which became the bible of the European reaction and it was not the Whig which was the legitimate subject of Peacock's entertaining satire. Speaking broadly, I would say that Professor Hayek's emphasis on the spontaneous and non-rational origin of important elements in the social order is of quite fundamental importance for the liberal outlook, but that it is liable to become the foundation of an illiberal mysticism rather than "true" liberalism unless it is understood that such elements are subject at all times to critical scrutiny from the standpoint of the requirements of public utility.

But this brings me to a much more fundamental point. I must admit that I have always found the greatest difficulty in accepting Professor Hayek's disposition to classify the nineteenth century English Utilitarians with his "false" Continental Rationalists, and I feel that this is apt to lend support to illiberal uses of Professor Hayek's main position. I say this with diffidence, for there are few men living from whom I have learnt so much of the history of thought as I have from Professor Hayek; and I know that his position in this respect has been held by other high authorities.[1] Nevertheless, I cannot persuade myself that it does justice to the facts: no one would seriously suggest that, for all its crudities and, if you like, errors, the thought of Bentham and the Mills

1. *E.g.*, Harold J. Laski, *Political Thought in England: Locke to Bentham* (London, 1920), p. 21, where Rousseau and Bentham are conjoined under a common generalization.

as regards epistemology did not stand foursquare within the tradition of English empiricism – as opposed to rationalism – and I should have thought that the onus of proof must lie very heavily with those who, *as regards political philosophy*, would wrest it out of a similar place in a closely allied tradition. Moreover, I will confess unashamedly that I do not think that the main drift of nineteenth century English Utilitarian thought tends to a liberalism which, in any sense intelligible to me, deserves the appellation "false".[1] As the issue here is of some importance both as regards the history of thought and as regards fundamental social theory, I trust that an explicit statement of the grounds of difference will not be thought out of order.

It is not difficult to make out a case for Professor Hayek's classification. If we compare the writings of the nineteenth century English Utilitarians with those of the eighteenth century philosophers whom he designates as "true" liberals or individualists, there can be no doubt that we find considerable differences, at any rate so far as Bentham and James Mill are concerned – J.S. Mill and Sidgwick[2] present a more complicated appearance, which I should have thought on balance to be less favourable to Professor Hayek's case. There are differences of style and there are differences of substance. There is a truculence and acerbity about the enunciation of fundamental principles by Jeremy Bentham, for instance, which is far removed from the tentativeness and urbanity of the formulations of David Hume. And the criticism of laws and institutions is far more radical: Hume on the whole was not discontented with things as they were, Bentham was a zealous reformer. Moreover, it has often been suggested that the calculus of utility as set forth by the Benthamites might ultimately prove an argument for collectivist rather than individualist measures, both in the sphere of public finance and in regard to the organization of production.[3] At first sight, therefore, it does not seem implausible to class Bentham and his disciples with the zealots of the French Enlightenment rather than with the calm philosophers of our middle Georgian age.

But to do this seems to me to mistake superficialities for substance. For the critical division in social philosophy, both in the eighteenth and the nineteenth centuries, is surely between those who judge laws and institutions in

1. In this connection, see also Sir Roy Harrod's important critique of the earlier version of Professor Hayek's classification: "Professor Hayek on Individualism," *Economic Journal*, Vol. 56 (1946), pp. 435–42.

2. The unsupecting reader will, I fancy, be a trifle surprised to find the noble and temperate Sidgwick in Professor Hayek's heretics' gallery. But here he is on p. 419 where his *Elements of Politics* (1891), although recognized to be "in many respects an admirable work," is stigmatized as "already strongly tainted with that rationalist utilitarianism which led to socialism."

3. See, for instance, A.V. Dicey, *Law and Public Opinion in England during the Nineteenth Century* (London, 1905), pp. 303–10.

terms of conformity to an abstract scheme of rights, deduced in some way or other from the principles of pure reason, and those who judge them in terms of the utility of their consequences – the judgment being, of course, in terms of rational analysis but the ultimate criterion, as both Hume and Bentham showed, being something outside reason. It is the division between those who cry "let justice be done, if the skies fall," and those who would regard the falling of the skies to be one of the consequences which must be taken into account before it is decided whether a particular action or a particular framework of action is, or is not, just. It is the division between those who argue that the specification of a good society is something which can be set out in a few well-chosen propositions, based on "the nature of things and of men"[1] and applicable at all times and all places, and those who argue that the conditions of life being complex and the ultimate criteria of the good being feelings rather than reasons, no such simplicity is possible.

Now so far as this division is concerned, there can be little doubt that Bentham and those who were influenced by him are to be classified in the same group as Hume and the other eighteenth century utilitarians, and therefore in a group opposite to Professor Hayek's "false" rationalists. We know that, in the historical preface to the second edition of the *Fragment on Government*, Hume is singled out by Bentham himself as the source of his phrase, the principle of utility:[2] and, although the style and mode of exposition differ radically, both in their specific affirmations and in their rejections, the substantial identity of view between these two thinkers is remarkable. Hume found the "sole origin" and justification of property to be public utility.[3] So did Bentham. Hume mocks gently at the concepts of "rationalist" politics and declares that with "the writers on the laws of nature you will always find that, whatever principles they set out with, they are sure to terminate here at last and to assign, as the ultimate reason for every rule they establish, the convenience and necessities of mankind."[4] Bentham, embarrassed by his election as an honorary citizen of revolutionary France, declares natural rights to be nonsense, "natural and imprescriptible rights, rhetorical

1. See, for instance, the conversation between Mercier de la Rivière and Catherine the Great quoted in my *The Theory of Economic Policy in English Classical Political Economy* (London, 1952), p. 35.

2. We know also the celebrated footnote to Chapter 1, Para. 36 of the same work, in which, after referring to the demonstration in the *Treatise of Human Nature* of the proposition "that the foundations of all *virtue* are laid in *utility*," Bentham goes on: "For my own part, I well remember, no sooner had I read that part of the work which touches on this subject, than I felt as if scales had fallen from my eyes. I then, for the first time, learnt to call the cause of the people the cause of virtue."

3. *Concerning the Principles of Morals, Essays, Moral, Political and Literary* (ed. T.H. Green and T.H. Grose, London, 1875), Vol. II, pp. 179 and 183.

4. *Ibid.*, p. 189.

nonsense – nonsense upon stilts."[1] Why, it may be asked, is the one to be classified as a "true" individualist, the other with the "false" individualists whose absurdities he so drastically condemned?

Professor Hayek makes much of an allegation that "Not Locke, nor Hume, nor Smith, nor Burke, could ever have argued as Bentham did, that every law is an evil for every law is an infraction of liberty."[2] On this, I suggest that the appropriate comment must be that neither would Bentham – in the ultimate sense of Professor Hayek's argument, that is to say in the sense of a *net* evil. Surely it is clear that in the Benthamite calculus every law has a double aspect, the pain (evil) it inflicts by coercion and the pleasure (good) it permits by preventing other pains. Good laws are laws which result in a surplus of pleasure, bad laws a surplus of pain.[3] In the broad context of his thought, the quotation is decidedly congruous with this interpretation; but fortunately we have Bentham's own words on the subject in language so definite and so astringent as to leave little room for doubt. In the *Manual of Political Economy*, expatiating on the significance of taxation, he points out first that a tax is a subtraction from the pleasures of the taxed. He then goes on to say that "It would, however, be a gross error, and an extremely mischievous one, to refer to the defalcation thus resulting from the mass of liberty or free agency, as affording a conclusive objection against the interposition of the law for this or any other purpose," and then, broadening the horizon of generalization, "Every law which does not consist in the repeal or partial repeal of a coercive law, is itself a coercive law. To reprobate as a mischief resulting from that law, a property which is the essence of all law, is to betray a degree of ignorance one should hardly think possible on the part of a mind accustomed to the contemplation of any branch of the system of the laws – a total unacquaintance with what may be called the logic of the laws."[4] It is difficult to believe that Locke or Hume or Smith or Burke would have disagreed with this.

It might be argued, I suppose, that the Greatest Happiness Principle which figures so prominently in the Benthamite facade, is just another formula on all fours with the fundamental declarations inspired by the "rationalist" outlook. But this would be a misapprehension. The "rationalist" declarations claimed definite status as the foundations of social order. *They were ultimate*

1. *Anarchical Fallacies, The Works of Jeremy Bentham* (ed. Sir John Bowring, 1843), Vol. II, p. 501.
2. Hayek, *op. cit.*, p. 60. The quotation from Bentham is from Hildreth's translation of *The Theory of Legislation*, 4th edn (1882), p. 48.
3. "The *evil* produced is the outgo, the *good* which results is the income." (*The Theory of Legislation*, p. 32.)
4. *Works* (ed. Bowring), Vol. III, p. 34.

solutions – "all you know on earth and all you need to know." The Utilitarian formula, by contrast, offered simply a *criterion by which particular solutions could be judged*. The one offered a simple list of rights and duties applicable to all societies: the other a principle by which the detailed prescriptions of particular codes and systems of law might be put to a general test. It is perhaps arguable – though, in my judgement, the thing has been somewhat overdone[1] – that Bentham himself did not pay enough attention to the lessons of history. But any suggestion that it was ever believed by him that the adoption of his principle would automatically churn out a code which was universally valid regardless of local or historical differences, cannot survive even the most cursory inspection of the *Essay on the Influence of Time and Place in Matters of Legislation*.[2]

Moreover, it is getting things very much out of proportion to think of Bentham as primarily concerned with the elaboration of a general formula. His major achievement, the achievement which entitles him to rank among the great thinkers and benefactors of mankind, was in the sphere of applications. And his method – which J.S. Mill happily named "the method of detail,"[3] the method, namely, of treating wholes by splitting them up into parts – was the main characteristic of his work. In practice, the famous calculus served chiefly as a rough reminder that, when judging particular laws and institutions, it is necessary to take into account their influence, positive and negative, on *all* the individuals likely to be affected. It is hardly possible to think of a contrast more complete than the contrast between the exhibitionist rhetoric of a Rousseau and the painstaking examination of detail of a Bentham.[4]

As for the extreme radicalism of Bentham's approach, particularly in his later years – his antipathy to Blackstone, his jeers at the "Matchless

1. Largely as a result of the picture painted by J.S. Mill at the time of his maximum reaction from Benthamism. But Mill did not know Bentham until Bentham was a very old man; and there is good reason to suppose that in all sorts of ways he subtly misconceived the master. See Charles Warren Everett, *The Education of Jeremy Bentham* (New York, 1931).

2. *Works* (ed. Bowring), Vol. I, pp. 170–94.

3. John Stuart Mill, *Dissertations and Discussions: political, philosophical and historical* (London, 1859), Vol. I, pp. 339–40.

4. In this connection it may be of interest to quote Bentham's own comment on the contrast. "The first business, according to the plan I am combatting," he argues, "is to find and declare the principles, the laws of a fundamental nature; that done, it is by their means that we shall be enabled to find the proper laws of detail. I say no: it is only in proportion as we have found and compared with one another the laws of detail, that our fundamental laws will be exact and fit for service ... What is the source of this premature anxiety to establish fundamental laws. It is the old conceit of being wiser than posterity – wiser than those who will have had more experience." (*Anarchical Fallacies. Works* (ed. Bowring), Vol. III, p. 494.) I should have thought that this last comment would have been especially congenial to Professor Hayek; for what is it but an application to the future, of his own justification of the evolution of law in the past?

Constitution" – here no doubt we have an attitude which may well be thought to be, in some respects at least, the exact opposite of Burke's. But it is not for that reason to be classified as untrue to the spirit of liberalism. For on this matter the verdict of history is clearly on Bentham's side. The legal and institutional abuses which were the target of his criticism were real abuses. The reforms which flowed from his efforts and those of his followers were lasting improvements. Why then should we describe as a "false" liberalism the critical analysis and the constructive imagination on which they were based? Indeed, I will confess that, from my point of view, if this were falsity, the "true" liberalism of some of their predecessors, including Hume, could have benefited by a slight infusion. If any unsophisticated reader, carried away by the cogency and authority of Professor Hayek's argument, is led to think of Benthamism in its main historical aspects as something which is to be bracketed with the pseudo-logic of the more Messianic social creeds, let him read some cold description of pre-Bentham legal proceedings and institutions in the United Kingdom. Let us hope that the shock he will get will not lead him into the opposite error of imagining that all reforms are possible overnight and that it only needs a little ingenuity to purge the system of all anomalies without harm to anyone or anything. But at least he will see another aspect of the subject which demands due consideration.[1]

There remains only the tendency to collectivism alleged to be implicit in the Greatest Happiness Principle. Now there can clearly be no denying that some utilitarians, from William Thompson onwards, have been thoroughgoing collectivists – though, I suspect, they have been the exceptions rather than the rule – and attempts have often been made to justify some collectivist measures by appeal to utilitarian principle. But it seems hard to blame all this on Bentham and his friends. If Professor Hayek is thinking of progressive taxation, he will find the pseudo-law of diminishing social utility clearly

1. Professor Hayek must forgive me if, in this connection, I contrast his attitude with that of Acton whom he admires so much. According to Professor Hayek, "Bentham and his Utilitarians did much to destroy the beliefs which England had in part preserved from the Middle Ages, by their scornful treatment of most of what until then had been the most admired feature of the British constitution." And (this, incidentally, well illustrates Professor Hayek's peculiar pejorative use of the word "rational"), "they introduced into Britain what had so far been entirely absent – the desire to remake the whole of her law and institutions on rational lines ..." (p. 174). According to Acton: "A century ago it was well known that whoever had an audience of a Master in Chancery was made to pay for three, but no man heeded the enormity until it suggested to a young lawyer that it might be well to question and examine with rigorous suspicion every part of the system in which such things were done. The day on which that gleam lighted up the clear hard mind of Jeremy Bentham is memorable in the political calendar beyond the administration of many statesmen." (Quoted by C.K. Ogden in the Introduction to his edition of *The Theory of Legislation* [1931].)

adumbrated in an *obiter dictum* of Hume,[1] and some justification for the progressive principle itself in Adam Smith's remarks on the taxation of houses[2] – whereas an indictment almost as severe as his own is to be found in J.S. Mill's *Principles*.[3] As for the main principle of economic organisation, can there really be much doubt that Bentham was in the main an individualist? I should have thought that his repeated insistence, even against Adam Smith,[4] that adult individuals were the best judges of what knowledge was relevant to their immediate action would have been specially acceptable to anyone stressing, as does Professor Hayek, the importance of the division of labour in this respect. And even though J.S. Mill, as is notorious, was willing to regard himself as a socialist as regards small-scale experiments in co-operative ownership and organization, it must always be remembered – what is nearly always forgotten – that nowhere in the literature is there a more tremendous warning of the evils of over-all collectivization than in the well-known passage in *Liberty*.[5] It is true that Bentham and his followers were not doctrinaire individualists, in, say, the manner of Herbert Spencer. They recognized that there were conditions of society when economic paternalism was justifiable. They recognized too that there were cases where, external economies or diseconomies being conspicuous, some form of collectivist control was sanctioned by the test of utility; and not believing themselves to be in complete possession of all relevant social knowledge, they were not opposed to all experiments in collectivist organization. But in this, surely,

1. *Op. cit.*, p. 188: "It must be confessed that whenever we depart from this equality we rob the poor of more satisfaction than we add to the rich."

2. "It is not very unreasonable that the rich should contribute to the public expense, not only in proportion to their revenue, but something more than a proportion." (*An Inquiry into the Nature and Causes of the Wealth of Nations*, ed. E. Cannan [London, 1904], Vol. II, p. 327.)

3. *Principles of Political Economy with some of their applications to social philosophy*, ed. W.J. Ashley (London, 1909), p. 808.

4. See especially *The Defence of Usury*, Letter XIII (*Works* (ed. Bowring), Vol. III, pp. 20–9), especially the following which I should have thought to be almost quintessential Hayek. "Is it endurable that the legislator should by violence substitute his own pretended reason, the result of a momentary and scornful glance, the offspring of wantonness and arrogance, much rather than social anxiety and study, in the place of the humble reason of individuals, binding itself down with all its force to that very object which he pretends to have in view? Nor let it be forgotten, that on the side of the individual in this strange competition, there is the most perfect and minute knowledge and information which interest, the whole interest of a man's reputation and fortune can engender, on the side of the legislator, the most perfect ignorance."

5. *On Liberty* (Blackwell edn [Oxford, 1946]), p. 99. "If the roads, the railways, the banks, the insurance offices, the great joint stock companies, the universities and the public charities were all of them branches of the government, if in addition the municipal corporations and the local boards, with all that now devolves on them, become departments of the central administration, if the employees of all these different enterprises were appointed and paid by the government, and look to the government for every rise in life; not all the freedom of the press and popular constitution of the legislature would make this or any other country free other than in name."

they were only talking good sense and good economic analysis. I see no reason whatever why, for these reasons, the most devoted believer in liberty should deny them the title of "true" individualists or force upon them classification with Cartesian rationalists.[1]

IV

The final section of Professor Hayek's book is entitled "Freedom in the Welfare State." I am inclined slightly to regret this title since I doubt the expediency of bringing all the subjects discussed under this kind of blanket classification. I suppose that the words "Welfare State" do stand for something which, in contrast to the picture of an earlier age, does have some kind of meaning. But, as the contents of this section themselves show, as soon as we come to look at what are regarded as characteristic features we find that, to discuss them intelligently, they have to be split up and treated separately. Thus, for instance, the problem whether special legal privileges for trade unions are or are not desirable from the liberal point of view is something which is skies apart from the problems of state-aided education. True that in a formal textbook of the old-fashioned type they would both perhaps figure in the section on the functions of the state. But, so far as I can see, that is about all.

I submit that this is something more than a mere verbal quibble. For it seems to me that much confusion is caused by argument in terms of such vague hold-all descriptions. The question, "Are you, or are you not, in favour of the Welfare State?" is, in my conception, the sort of question to which a reasonable man should refuse a simple answer. For, surely, from almost any conceivable point of view, the answer must be that one approves of some things and disapproves of others. Yet discussion is frequently posed on this plane, both by those who expect a favourable reply and those who expect the reverse. And I cannot help feeling that Professor Hayek, who will be

1. Professor Hayek very rightly lays emphasis upon the Cartesian influences on his "false" individualism. I cannot help wondering whether in deciding to put Bentham among the Cartesians, he did not perhaps forget what Jeremy himself had to say about the philosopher in question and his habits of thought. Appropriately enough it occurs in the analysis of Article I of the Declaration of Rights. "*Whatever is, is* – was the maxim of Descartes, who looked upon it as so sure, as well as so instructive a truth, that everything else which goes by the name of truth might be deduced from it. The philosophical vortex-maker – *who, however mistaken in his philosophy and his logic was harmless enough at least* (my italics) little thought how soon a part of his own countrymen, fraught with pretensions as empty as his own, and as mischievous as his were innocent, would contest with him even this his favourite and fundamental maxim by which everything else was to be brought to light." (*Anarchical Fallacies, Works*, ed. Bowring, Vol. III, p. 499.)

suspected by at least half his reviewers of being "against" the welfare state, runs the danger by his choice of title of having his detailed arguments discussed, not in terms of their merits, but rather in terms of some equally wide (and misleading) description of their tendency as a whole. And that, I think will be a very great pity. For, whether you agree with him or not on the various subjects under consideration, he has always something to say which deserves respectful consideration.

Let it be said at once that this is by no means always negative. It is true that there is vigorous criticism, some of it of very great force: I personally should find it impossible to refute the main criticisms of special privileges for associations of producers, trade unions or otherwise; the exposure of the crass inequity and diseconomy of rent restriction, one of the meanest of all demagogic expedients, seems to me quite unanswerable; and I think that there is much more in the strictures on progressive taxation, at any rate extreme progression, that many of the critics will concede. But, as befits one who derives so much from the great traditions of English Political Economy – not only of the eighteenth century but also of the nineteenth – Professor Hayek's attitude is not one of *laissez-faire* in the sense of leaving nothing to government but the functions of the night watchman. Side by side with his critique of *étatiste* policies, there are developed a series of alternatives which, set out in a more systematic form, might well be regarded as liberal agenda for state action. Thus, for instance, following J.S. Mill, he states powerfully the case for compulsory education and, with various reserves – some of which I find difficult to follow – he favours some state assistance for those who are unable to afford it. But, again following J.S. Mill, whose grave warning is the motto of his chapter,[1] he sees serious dangers in an exclusive provision of educational services by the state; and he gives positive blessing to the proposal which has been put forward by Milton Friedman and others[2] that parents should be given vouchers covering the costs of education, which they could then hand over to schools of their choice. Opinions may well differ, even among liberal thinkers, concerning the value or the practicability of particular items of the Hayek agenda, and it is very easy to think of directions in which they might be extended. But, cumulatively, they form a programme which those who have the cause of individual freedom at heart could do well to ponder seriously.

1. "A general state education is a mere contrivance for moulding people to be exactly like one another, and the mould in which it casts them is that which pleases the predominant power in the government, whether this be a monarchy, a priesthood, an aristocracy or the majority of the existing generation." (*On Liberty*, p. 95.)

2. See, for instance, the interesting article by Mr. J. Wiseman ["The economics of education"] in the *Scottish Journal of Political Economy*, vol. 6 (1958–9), pp. 48–58.

Having said this, however, I should be highly disingenuous it I were to conceal the fact that there are aspects of Professor Hayek's approach in some of these connections about which I have very considerable hesitation: I find some of his treatment one-sided; and I doubt very much the justification of some of his more extreme apprehensions.

I can illustrate both these kinds of difficulty from his discussion of the problems of social security. On these he has some things to say which seem to me both true and important. I find very impressive his plea that a part, at least, of the deductions from earnings which now form so conspicuous a feature of certain social security systems of Western Europe might well have been left in the hands of the earners to invest in private insurance policies more adapted to their own conceptions of need, and I have an instinctive sympathy with his dislike of centralized systems which in the nature of things cannot develop more than a limited degree of flexibility and, in the absence of continual vigilance, are liable to considerable abuses. I see much to be said for the view, so powerfully developed by Mr. Hagenbuch,[1] that if our hope is that the members of the poorer classes shall eventually enjoy the present standards of the middle class, it is desirable to frame our institutions so as to allow the development of middle class habits of independence; and I am inclined to believe that some of our present practices in regard to social security may tend in the other direction.

But I cannot regard all that has happened with the degree of disquiet which it so obviously arouses in Professor Hayek; if I think of the system I know best, that of the United Kingdom, my reaction is much more mixed. I agree that the weight of our taxation is an embarrassment – though I am far from thinking, as I suspect Professor Hayek does, that we are in a state of economic decline. I agree too that the degree of progression where the higher incomes are concerned is both unfair and unwise. But it is surely a great mistake to blame all this on our social legislation. Whether the conceptions be good or bad, I should have thought that they could be easily afforded, were it not for the magnitude of our expenditure on defence; and while, in the present international situation, I have no desire to see that cut, it seems to me that to lay all the blame on the social services for any resulting complications, is to get things quite out of proportion. Similarly, with extreme progression – the contribution made here to substantial redistribution is small. The social security system and social services in general could go on more or less as at present, even if a Chancellor of the Exchequer should pluck up enough courage to decree that no one should be taxed more than, say, three-fifths of his marginal income.

1. "The rationale of the social services," *Lloyds Bank Review*, no. 29 (July 1953), pp. 1–16.

Moreover, there is a positive side, which I should have thought, on any calm assessment of the position, needs bringing into the picture. It may very well be that some liberties have been curtailed which we should wish to retain and that some habits have been fostered which we should wish to discourage. But I cannot believe, even on a very long-run assessment of values, that, in what is perhaps a blundering way, we have not achieved considerable positive good. I confess that when I look at social conditions in contemporary Britain, with its well-fed, healthy and essentially decent and humane citizens and their children, and draw the contrast with what, as a young man, I knew 40 years ago, I do perceive a most solid and substantial improvement. Much of this, the greater part doubtless, is due to the growth of wealth, the product of the despised system of free enterprise. But I do not think it can reasonably be denied that some of it is due to what has been done through the state in the sphere of social services, ill-conceived as some of the mechanisms and some of the benefits may be urged to be. And when I look to all the difficult and anxious problems to come, I suspect that although we have scrambled some eggs which we may find it hard to unscramble, yet the improvement which has been achieved is not just something improvidently snatched from the future, but something which, on balance, will make it easier to go forward as a reasonably harmonious community.

But this brings me to my second scruple in this connection. I cannot suppress the conviction that Professor Hayek is somewhat too apt to extrapolate his apprehensions of evil and to assume that deviations from his norm lead cumulatively to disaster. I say this with reserve for I think that some of the criticisms which were made on this score of his *The Road to Serfdom* [1944] were both ill-informed and unfair; there certainly have been tendencies in history which have led to catastrophe; and those who judged his analysis of the influences leading to the growth of national socialism on the continent in terms of the evolution of Anglo-Saxon institutions exhibited an outlook which was definitely parochial if it was not actively malicious. What disquiets me is not the contention that this sort of thing *may* happen but rather any assumption that it almost certainly *must*. For instance, in my judgment Professor Hayek is justifiably critical of some contemporary arrangements regarding old age pensions and apprehensive of the difficulties which may arise should the burden be greatly increased. But why should he argue as if these were at all likely to lead us to social disintegration and the concentration camp? This seems to me to be one of the less probable outcomes of the evolution of our institutions in this respect. There are some interventions, such as attempts at individual price-fixing in wartime, of which a tendency to spread may be fairly confidently predicted. There are others, such as some kinds of taxes and subsidies, or some experiments in government ownership and control where, the causal mechanisms involved being much more complicated and indirect, no such predictions are safe. And, in general, I am bound to say that, whatever may be the case in particular instances, any absolute scepticism regarding the stability of all mixed economies seems to me to have little basis in either logic or history.

The fact is, I suspect, that, when it is a question of diagnosing what we believe to be present evils, we economists are particularly liable to the temptation to drive home our points by warnings which go considerably further than the circumstances of the case would in fact justify. The appendix to Sir John Sinclair's *History of the Public Revenue* (3rd edn, London, 1803) contains a most salutary list of unfulfilled predictions of imminent catastrophe by English economists; and it would be very easy indeed to bring it up-to-date. The moral of this, of course, is not that we should sit back and say nothing or pursue only the more unreal problems of pure theory – it is very arguable that the fact that we have avoided disaster so far and done pretty well on the whole is partly due to the willingness of so many people to stick their necks out and utter warnings. It is rather that, rejecting, as we do in others, historicism with its bogus apparatus of inevitable trends and improbable cycles, we are under a special obligation to see that we do not fall into the same error ourselves when we have a case to argue. I am very conscious that I have sometimes done this myself. And I should be lacking in candour if I did not say that I think that on occasion the very strong arguments of this most sincere and important book are weakened by such a tendency.

V

This review is already too long. But I should be sorry to bring it to a close without emphasizing once more that any criticisms which I have felt impelled to make must not be interpreted as detracting from the liveliest appreciation of the qualities of this book as a whole. It is a work which surely no one with even a bare minimum of magnanimity and sense of what is fine can read without gratitude and admiration – gratitude for a splendid contribution to the great debate, admiration for the moral ardour and intellectual power which inspired it and made it possible.

plicated and indirect—no such predictions are ever valid. In general, I am inclined to say, that, whatever may be the case in particular instances, any [illegible]

24 The International Monetary Problem

From *The Journal of Political Economy*, vol. 76 (July–August 1968), pp. 664–77.

I

The thesis I shall attempt to maintain in this paper is that the international monetary problem is essentially political in nature. I shall argue that it arises from tendencies which are very deep-seated in the life of modern states; that these tendencies are not all to be regarded as necessarily perverse or sinister in intention or indeed in outcome; and that therefore the solution, or, better said, the solutions, to the problem must be themselves political. These are propositions of great generality, and for the most part their supporting argument will move on the same plane. I hope, however, that there will be some morals and some incidental observations more immediately relevant to contemporary reality.

II

To begin with the nature of the problem: It would be taking the subject too easily to rely on its definitional implications. There is indeed profound significance in the fact that the problems we have to discuss owe their origin to the organization of human society into separate sovereign states and that this organization is, in some sense of the word which we all understand – even if we cannot make this understanding precise – to be regarded as political rather than economic. It is true, too, that these problems, problems of transfer and of balances of payments, are essentially problems of money changing which arise only when there are different, usually national, moneys to be exchanged. You can have problems of inter-area disparities of income, of mobility, and of investment within single-money areas; but you have the problems we are discussing only where there is more than one money. Yet while the existence of separate national moneys is a necessary condition for the emergence of these problems, it is not an inevitable cause, and examination of the other conditions that must be present if problems of this sort are to arise takes us right to the heart of the subject.

Consider a world organized into separate nations with different national moneys of different names and different metallic values but in which all payments, national and international, are made in coins of a single metal which is meltable, mintable, and exportable at will. In such a world, clearly, our problems do not arise. There are exchange markets. There exists the possibility of deviations of exchange rates from the metallic parities. But the freedom to melt, mint, and trade internationally in the fundamental metal means that these deviations will be confined within narrow technical limits. If there is no suspension of these freedoms, then to all intents and purposes a single standard still exists. The problems of the exchange markets are mere technicalities.

The position is not changed if we relax the assumption of pure specie payments and allow the use of notes and checks, provided we stipulate that there be 100 per cent metallic cover for every credit instrument in use. The difference between this system and the pure specie system is, of course, only a difference of commercial convenience. One cannot say it is exactly the same as the pure specie system, since no doubt the mere fact of convenience makes some difference to the volume of trade; the fact that you can pay with a $10 million check rather than be obliged to take the same amount around in sacks of coin or gold bars presumably has some effect on commercial habits. But there is no reason to suppose that the mutual relationships of the various national moneys will be affected.

Once the assumption of 100 per cent cover is relaxed, however, the situation changes radically. Paper credit is now not automatically the same as its nominal metallic equivalent; the substitution ratio need not therefore be unity. The various states cannot confer the quality of legal tender outside their own areas, and this in itself may give rise to short-term transfer problems. But beyond this, and ultimately more important, there are now, by hypothesis, as many potentially independent centers of initiative as regards the supplies of national purchasing power as there are different national authorities – a state of affairs excluded by the assumptions of pure specie payments or their paper equivalent. This means that there is now no guaranty whatever that the different money supplies will act together as if they were one; the likelihood that they will not is very great. But if this happens, then there will be disequilibrium in the markets for foreign exchange, difficulty in the maintenance of fixed parities, and all the troubles which we have come to associate with the idea of the international monetary problem.

Now in most cases these troubles could still be avoided if the various centers of independent supply were all to adopt rules of policy such that local expansions or contractions were similar to what would be the case were there only one source of supply in existence. This would not necessarily solve the liquidity problem; you can conceive sudden occasions of discontinuous transfer which would break any reserve supporting a multiple credit system. But apart from such catastrophes, the possibility of the maintenance of international equilibrium this way is easy enough to conceive in abstraction, and there can be little doubt that what there has been – and is – of reasonably stable international monetary relations at fixed rates of exchange has been due to the practice from time to time of rough approximations to this sort of policy.

But the difficulties are formidable. To begin with, there are difficulties of conception. If we assume, as I explicitly assumed just now, that all centers of supply are committed to this policy, then the rules of the game are comparatively simple: there should be expansion when gold flows in, contraction when it flows out. (There can be some subtlety of formulation here according to the assumptions regarding reserve systems and their relation to the total money supply, but for our purposes this can be neglected.) But suppose that comity of policy is broken. Suppose that one center pursues a different policy – a policy, let us say, of local expansion not warranted by any increase in the international value of its products. Other things being equal, this will mean a loss of reserves here and gains elsewhere. Now if comity of policy were operative, a gain of reserves in any center should involve local expansion; this would be the way in which any increased value of local products in the world market would be translated into the higher incomes which this increase justified. But if the gain of reserves is due to unjustified expansion elsewhere, there seems no similar obligation. Why should the receiving centers import inflation from elsewhere? The same query applies, with perhaps greater emotional appeal, to the reverse situation. If a loss of reserves is due to unwarranted local contraction elsewhere, there is surely no obligation to allow the movement to spread.

Thus, even given the will on the part of the majority of monetary authorities to focus their policies on the preservation of international equilibrium, the defection of a small number can enormously complicate the formulation of rules of policy.

But the difficulties here are not merely difficulties of conception. Beyond these – and this is where the political factor comes in – there are likely from time to time to be differences of policy. There is no guaranty that independent sovereign states will wish to sacrifice their independence in financial policy and subordinate all alternative possibilities of initiative to the preservation of international monetary equilibrium. The power to pursue independent policies is there. It is running counter to all knowledge of modern political communities, whether democratic or dictatorial, to suppose that sometime it will not be used, and recent history tells us that it often has been so used.

Now it is sometimes assumed that all such manifestations of independence necessarily imply policies which from every point of view are to be regarded as reprehensible. And I would agree that up to date most of the more conspicuous episodes of this sort have been eligible for this condemnation. The majority of cases of chronic balance of payments difficulties have been due either to a faulty choice of exchange rates at an earlier period or to policies of financial expansion unwarranted by internal rates of growth – policies as inimical to distributive justice at home as to stability of the exchanges abroad. Clearly, an area which allows persistent inflation of its internal prices and costs has no grounds for complaint if its balance of payments tends persistently to be in deficit. To avoid offense to other nationals, I will cite as an example the recent history of the United Kingdom. But it would not be difficult to find other instances from the history of nearly all European nations.

But other policies are conceivable. Suppose that important areas are suffering from strong deflation. Other things being equal, if a policy of maintaining fixed exchange rates prevails elsewhere, this means that the deflation must spread. Would it necessarily be thought unreasonable if the authorities of an area thus threatened elected to fall out of step and to maintain internal demand? But if such a policy is pursued, then clearly there will be a tendency for imports to exceed exports and thus for pressure on the exchanges. Similarly, if there is inflation elsewhere and attempts are made to prevent it from spreading, the systems thus acting will tend to accumulate gold and thereby run the risk of being accused of unneighborly behavior. But would such accusations be rationally justified?

The same point can be put with even greater generality. We know that even in a completely closed system, there is no guaranty that the movement of money and credit will be in any sense optimal unless they are definitely managed to that end.[1] But in a world of open communities, there is still less probability that the un-co-ordinated activities of each will lead to any sort of desirable aggregate movements. In the absence, therefore, of co-ordinating arrangements, to expect that the different authorities should *never* adopt independent policies of their own would be to expect something intellectually indefensible and politically unnatural.

III

This brings me to the idea of floating rates. Confronted with the tendencies I have been discussing, some observers have been led to offer a very radical

1 It might be decided in such a system that the probable movements of gold supply constituted the least evil of all practical regulators, though for such a policy to be rational, it would have to be the result of conscious choice or acquiescence.

solution. It is obvious, they say, that independent policies will persist whether we like them or not. Nationalism is here to stay, and all attempts to superimpose an international system are doomed to failure. Why not face the facts and, instead of wasting time on half-baked expedients such as the IMF or modifications therefor, admit that the right solution in the modern age is for each center to pursue what internal policies seem appropriate and to allow freely fluctuating rates of exchange to settle its external economic relations? I suspect that some such arguments, doubtless modified in the case of the more responsible by postulation of the need for international co-operation in regard to capital movements, underlie the attitude of a majority of economists today, at least in the English-speaking world. They are therefore deserving of careful and respectful consideration.

Let me begin by a clarification of intentions. In what I have to say in this connection, I shall be evincing considerable skepticism concerning both the desirability and the practicability of this policy as a general solution to the international monetary problem. But there are certain positions which I shall *not* be adopting, and I should like to repudiate them specifically.

In the first place, I shall not be arguing that a floating rate is never capable of bringing a balance of payments into equilibrium. I shall indeed argue that a floating rate carries with it certain political dangers which may render it incapable of producing this effect. But on the plane of pure analysis, nothing is further from my mind than to argue that a floating rate in a world otherwise stable, backed up by appropriate internal measures, may not be an efficient instrument of equilibration. There was a time in which it was fashionable to argue that international elasticities of demand were likely to be so low as to defeat this end. The advocates of physical control of everything were sure that nothing less than a universal regime of quotas would keep the world on an even keel. I do not know whether any wisps of this miasma have survived the powerful statistical or analytical criticisms it has received. I only wish to make it plain that it is not part of my intellectual outlook.

Second, I do not wish to question the appropriateness of the policy of the floating rate in every conceivable set of circumstances. On the contrary, I find it easy to think of many circumstances in which I should regard a floating rate as either harmless or even positively beneficial. If an important currency, such as the dollar or the pound, were to be pushed off its existing fixed parity, I can easily believe that it would be advisable *for the time being* to let the rate float in order to avoid the error of restoring a fixed rate at an inappropriate level. If I were confronted with the problems of some small economy, largely dependent on the export of one type of commodity, yet internally with a very sticky income structure, I should be far from arguing that to let the exchange rate, rather than the income structure, take the shock of fluctuations in world prices would be a foolish policy, even in the long run. I am really not at all doctrinaire about practical action in specific instances. What I am concerned with here, however, is not the floating rate as an occasional expedient, but rather floating rates as a general solution to the international monetary problem. Having regard to the volume of heavyweight support for such a solution, from my great friends Milton Friedman and James Meade outward and downward, I do not think it can be contended that this is an imaginary or unworthy target.

At the outset, we may perhaps agree that it is not a completely ideal system. It is essentially a concession to political nationalism. We should not wish to institute it where separate nationalities do not exist – to have a series of floating rates with all the opportunities for upsets and arbitrage between separate moneys in each of the states of the Union. I know that there have been heroic attempts to elaborate a concept of optimum currency areas within which adjustments take place by factor movements and between which adjustments are made by movements of the rate of exchange. But although I am sure we are all acutely conscious of the real problems presented by the existence of stagnant patches within national economies, I doubt that many of us would be prepared to tackle them by creating all the complications of separate state or local government area currencies. Better interlocal subsidies and incentives to interlocal movement. It is only where there are separate sovereign states that the idea begins to make sense, but since there is precious little connection between the extent and shape of most modern national areas and what would be in any sense optimal from the point of view of economic integration, it does not necessarily make very good sense even in that context. Only the fact that the national states are there makes it really worth extensive discussion, so that even if it is workable as a *pis aller*, it can hardly be described as ideal.

I hope, though I am not so sure of this, that there would be some agreement that it is not a particularly liberal system. It is true that the idea of a freely fluctuating price for foreign exchange has a liberal flavor; it certainly sounds more liberal than the clutter of restrictions on capital movements and travel which advocates of Schachtian systems would impose on us. But the flavor is deceptive. To maintain such a system, it is necessary to impose a most illiberal restriction, namely, the prohibition on the inhabitants of each separate area against making contracts in any medium other than the local currency. For clearly, in a world of freely fluctuating currencies, there would be a permanent incentive to make contracts in terms of the currency expected to fluctuate least. The tendency of a liberal system would be toward the elimination of the weaker currencies. This was to be witnessed in the world of the nineteenth century, when gold and silver circulated side by side. It was witnessed, too, in the world of currency instability following World War I, when the pound and the dollar became the units of account over a rapidly growing area of economic relationships. The fact that it does not happen today is due to deliberate legislation: a gold clause in contracts is not now enforceable at law in many countries. And if it were desired that freely fluctuating exchanges were to be the general mechanism of international economic equilibration, that system would have to be preserved in this way. I will not say that this is a conclusive argument against it, but it conforms ill to the presumptions of a system of free choice.

But these are ideological considerations. In a world in which few things are pure and most systems are something of a patchwork, the question of the desirability of proposals of this sort will be decided, not by whether they conform to some doctrinal pattern, but by whether they afford a practicable and tolerable solution to the problems with which they are supposed to deal. And it is on this plane that my skepticism is most active.

I will begin by ventilating certain doubts concerning the stabilizing effects of the floating rate on the position of individual economies. I hope I have already made it clear that I do not in any way wish to question the analytic possibility of such effects or their occasional occurrence in history. But it is a far cry from such an admission to the belief that this is the practical probability in the majority of cases. For it is an indispensable condition of the success of such a mechanism that internal financial stability be preserved. It has been shown again and again in theory and verified in practice that unless this condition is present, the result of a fluctuating rate will be destabilizing rather than the reverse. If a downward movement of a rate is accompanied by an internal expansion, there is a strong probability that unless the system concerned was in a considerable degree of under-employment, with considerable scope for cost reduction with expanding output, the effect of the downward fluctuation will be offset and the point of equilibrium will be still lower down – the famous ratchet effect.

Now I do not wish to assert that the adoption of a floating rate need necessarily carry with it a tendency to a looser internal discipline, and I know authorities, whom I respect, who would argue exactly the contrary – that the fluctuations of the rate would induce a closer regard for internal stability. But I am bound to say that my guess is that, in the majority of cases, the effect would be mainly the other way. The tendency would be to argue that now that the rate was free to float, the balance of payments would look after itself – that there was no longer any need for the hampering internal disciplines necessitated by adherence to a fixed rate. I repeat, it is not necessary that this should be so; there are austere exponents of the floating rate philosophy, Professor Meade for instance, who would be there to argue the policy of prudence. But I think they would be apt to argue in vain. The economists who behind the scenes are arguing in and out of season for cutting the pound loose are doing so, for the most part, just in order to be able to engineer a renewed expansion of money supply and spending. They would repudiate you if you argued that the one hope of making a lower rate of exchange work was to keep a firm hand on the brakes at home. This is clearly a matter of political judgment. For what it is worth, my own view is that a world of floating rates would witness more, rather than less, instability of internal economic conditions.

But this is not the main point. The main point is that, with the world constituted as it is, this thing is not going to happen. We are not going to see a world in which every national currency is free to fluctuate in terms of all the others. I have argued already that in the absence of co-ordinating influences, there are strong political forces making for disharmony in a world of fixed exchange rates. But I must now argue that there are also forces working across political frontiers which militate against the emergence, or at least the permanence, of a system of the kind I am discussing. Let us suppose for a moment that it came about that some world conference, if it ever achieved that kind of lucidity, were persuaded by Professor Friedman, or some other man of goodwill, to free all the foreign exchanges. What would happen? I think you can be reasonably certain that within a few weeks a great number of the smaller and weaker currencies would have been pegged once more to the stronger ones – the inconveniences of trade and the desire to maintain some stability in the world value of the reserves would lead to that. And I do not think it would be long before the central banks of the stronger areas began to get together to see what could be done to re-establish reasonable fixity of rates between the currencies for which they were responsible. If the fact of political independence constitutes an incipient centrifugal influence in international monetary relations, the interests of the majority of traders and bankers constitute, in contrast, an incipient centripetal influence.

IV

If these arguments are correct, it follows that we cannot hope to eliminate the political influences on international monetary relations by an all-round policy of laissez faire in the foreign exchange markets. The system would not stand that degree of freedom. Somehow or other there would be re-established relations of greater stability and, with their re-establishment, most of the problems of maintaining stability with which we are at present confronted.

But what are the possible alternatives? Still assuming the organization of the world into separate political units with separate centers of financial initiative and no organized co-ordination, what other remedies are proposed for the disequilibriums with which we are so frequently confronted?

The first remedy that is often proposed is the keeping of higher reserves. It is this which underlies the more sophisticated propaganda for the raising of the gold price; indeed, it is sometimes argued that any such raising at the present time should be accompanied by an undertaking not to make the increased reserves thereby created the basis for immediate credit expansion. But, of course, it is not only the advocates of a higher gold price who are in favor of higher reserves to meet the vicissitudes of international capital movements; there are many others who support it for perhaps better reasons.

Now, I am all in favor of higher reserves. In a world liable to ups and downs of confidence in different currencies, the existence of substantial reserves is a most important first-line defense against panic movements. It is one of the outstanding weaknesses of the financial position of the United Kingdom since the war, that, with all its quick external liabilities, the reserve has not been greater. Let me say at once that I do not blame the Bank of England for this weakness; I am sure that the authorities of that institution would have been only too glad to hold reserves two or three times their present magnitude. I blame rather the general policies of successive governments which, by tolerating, if not engendering, a more or less continuous pressure of excess demand, have made impossible the accumulation of adequate reserves that has taken place in other centers like France and Germany, whose position at the beginning of the period was not in any way obviously superior to that of the United Kingdom. I am clear that a financial center accepting the custody of balances from abroad should regard as a paramount duty the keeping of sufficient reserves to offset any probable sudden tendency to withdrawal.

But reserves, however adequate for this purpose, do not necessarily solve any but transitory problems of adjustment. The worsening of the balance of payments of a particular center, if it is due only to a bad harvest or to some short-term extraordinary expenditure abroad, may indeed be dealt with by a transfer of specie. And of course a transfer of specie from a dead reserve to a center where it is made the basis for a credit expansion will itself ease the problem of longer-period adjustment. But in the last analysis, if disequilibrium in the balance of payments is due to more fundamental and continuing influences, the existence of reserves is no substitute for adjustment of relative prices and costs. Failure to perceive this was one of the fundamental errors of Tooke and Fullarton, the leaders of the famous Banking School in the mid-nineteenth-century controversy. As against their opponents of the Currency School, they were doubtless right in insisting on the possibility of meeting short-period external drains by the existence of higher reserves, and it was a great pity that this part of their advice was not heeded. But in ignoring the necessity for relative expansion or contraction to reflect more fundamental movements, they were seriously wrong, and although the case of their opponents was to some extent vitiated by an undue emphasis on the necessity for fluctuation in the currency as distinct from the total flow of circulation, on the deepest plane of analysis it was right, and all experience since that time has tended to vindicate their main position. If a center losing reserves does not allow this loss to influence the flow of internal expenditure, then only a reversal of the cause producing the loss or the occurrence of a purely adventitious favorable movement elsewhere will prevent the continuation of the drain with all the possibilities of crisis that that may involve.

It is clear, then, that higher reserves are not enough. There must also be the possibility of adjustment. And if we are to rule out alterations of exchange rates, then there must be adjustment of relative prices and incomes.

Now I think it is possible vastly to exaggerate the difficulties which this would involve. Of course, if the authorities of any particular area sail right away on their own, with internal policies that leave relations with the outside world entirely to chance, then the chances are great indeed that, in the end, nothing but changes of the exchange rate will serve to put things right. But speaking generally, in a world in which money incomes in most areas are tending to rise and would still rise if such movements were limited to the reflection of increased productivity, the correction of disequilibriums need seldom involve more than a curb on increase where balances are unfavorable and an acceleration where they are favourable. The belief that the purchasing of an international standard necessarily involves continual resort to positive deflation over a major part of the field rests on excessive contemplation of purely static models. If the world money supply is increasing at a reasonable rate, it will be the exception rather than the rule for anything more to be needed than adjustment of relative rates of increase in the different areas concerned. A great deal of the argument against the 'rules of the game' of international standards, from Keynes in his more combative moods downward, has been more concerned with making the flesh creep than with the probabilities of the world situation.

Having said this, however, I should like to make it quite clear that in the modern age, at any rate, the "rules of the game" are not enough – which brings me back to the point I was laboring earlier. Let us suppose that the authorities of the leading nations of the world, having lived through so many crises brought about by non-observance of these rules, become reconciled to "orthodox" practice in this respect. Even so, the system suffers from a radical deficiency: *there is no central management of the money supply as a whole.* In the past, it was the implicit assumption of the theory of the international metallic standard that the rate of increase of such metals was a suitable ultimate control. I doubt that this was often justified – though it can be argued that in the absence of anything better it was the best assumption to make. But in the modern age, when the value of gold is so overwhelmingly dependent on monetary policy in the different leading centers and when the prospects of gold production are so uncertain and precarious, all this has worn too thin to carry conviction. Moreover, even if the future of gold were more certain than it is and a suitable rate of increase were assumed, it would not be good enough. For we are now apt to think – and who shall say that we are wrong – that a satisfactory monetary system needs management and that a mere guaranty of a non-deflationary annual supply of metal is an inadequate fulfillment of this need.

Hence, even in a world with ample reserves in the leading centers and a reasonable willingness all round to obey common rules of adjustment, the absence of co-ordinated regulation of the aggregate money supply is a serious deficiency in the system – a deficiency which may well be regarded by the various national authorities as justifying an ultimate reservation of the powers of independent action.

V

In the last analysis, therefore, only a surrender of sovereign power in this respect and its transfer to a supranational authority providing a single money can provide an ultimate solution to the international monetary problem. And since the surrender of sovereign power in regard to money creation would ultimately involve surrender of independent action in regard to many other aspects of policy, including military action on all but the smallest scale, this is not at all likely, at any rate, on a worldwide scale. The complete unification of world monetary arrangements could only be the consequence of still more far-reaching political arrangements. For the time being, at any rate, we have to jog along with inferior arrangements.

What form should these take? Still detaching ourselves from contemporary reality but assuming a world of independent centers of financial initiative, what arrangements should we wish to introduce to bring about some systematic co-ordination of policies?

As I see things, these arrangements should fall into three groups.

First, there should be provision for some pooling of reserves, such that centers under sudden severe pressure would be able to count on common support to allay panic transfers and to afford a breathing space for any needed adjustments. It would be necessary for the use of this common reserve to be hedged about by rules precluding resort to it merely as a means of prolonging policies which were leading to disequilibrium; and doubtless the framing and administration of such rules would be a matter of some delicacy. But I see no reason to suppose that the good sense of the leading central bankers of the world would be unequal to the solution of this problem.

Second, while there should be agreement to endeavor to maintain equilibrium at fixed rates of exchange, there should also be provision whereby rates could be varied by common consent if failure to keep in step had reached a point of fundamental disequilibrium, that is, a lack of balance that could be remedied at fixed rates only by very drastic measures of deflation – or inflation. Such a provision would not exclude resort to floating rates as a temporary measure, provided that there were agreement on the limits within which rates could vary. It would, however, exclude resort to floating rates as a permanent condition.

Third, there should be provision whereby the aggregate volume of purchasing power throughout the world would be managed in such a way as to avoid grave disturbance to economic activity from either shortage or excess. Clearly this would be the most difficult requirement to satisfy. A beginning might be made by agreements with respect to the variation of the common reserves available. In the end, however, nothing less would be adequate than something like an international central bank with powers to pursue active policies of expansion and contraction of credit, with the conscious aim of maintaining such levels of activity generally as are compatible with reasonable stability in the purchasing power of money.

It will not escaped your notice that the apparatus which I have just been deducing from the most general principles bears in important respects a close family resemblance to the actual apparatus of international co-operation under which we live – the International Monetary Fund. So far as the first two of my three desiderata are concerned, the provision of pooled reserves and the maintenance and adjustment of exchange rates, the description fits more or less exactly, save that in my formulation of the rules of adjustment there is greater explicitness concerning the possibility of periods of experimentation. There are, however, certain deficiencies in the constitution and powers of the Fund which so far have prevented it from conforming to what I should regard as the ideal type of this kind of compromise, and it is with some short indication of these that I wish to conclude this paper. It will further underline my contention that the main difficulties giving rise to the international monetary problem are largely political in origin.

First come deficiencies of constitution. The Fund was created at a time when a hazy idealistic universalism dominated the Anglo–Saxon milieu in which it was conceived, and, despite the provision whereby voting power is related in some degree to economic power and potential, it still suffers from the inherent defects to which this gave rise. Indeed, had it not been for the failure of the U.S.S.R. to honor its signature of the Final Act, it is pretty clear that it would have proved totally unworkable. For the fundamental need of this kind of international co-operation is not that it should embrace all and sundry, but that there should be firm understanding and an organization capable of swift and, if need be, secret action among the powers whose currencies are really significant in international trade. The real problem arises in their relations, not in the fringe phenomena; and it is only if they can achieve a modus vivendi that the splinter countries of the world have a stable focus of reference. Hence, although we are saddled here with a constitution that would be very hard to alter, and all the absurdities of subscriptions and voting rights in respect of currencies which hardly anybody wants to use, I welcome the emergence of the so-called Group of Ten as the nucleus of effective action and greatly hope that future developments will consolidate its ascendancy in the shaping of future policy.

Second, and more fundamentally important, come deficiencies in respect to my third desideratum – provision for the management of the ultimate credit base. No doubt it can be argued that the statute which permits a change in the price of gold, if sufficient support is forthcoming, can be classified under this heading. But this is a crude instrument capable of effective use only once or twice in a century, and then attended by the possibility of most disturbing side effects. I would not wish to be understood to be ruling it out in certain catastrophic circumstances. But I do submit that we need instruments much subtler and more responsive than this if we are to meet successfully the problems of modern credit systems. Nothing can be more certain than that, if something of this sort is not furnished internationally by voluntary co-operation between the leading financial centers, the different national authorities will themselves attempt the same thing severally, with all the possibilities of disharmony and confusion which independent action necessarily involves.

Now here is a problem involving genuine intellectual difficulties. What have been the needs of the world in this respect in the recent past? What are the probable needs in the future? These are not questions on which men of goodwill are necessarily united. There is real scope for sincere differences of opinion. For myself, I am inclined to support the position of those who argue that, in the recent past, there has been no need of additional liquidity. Although I can see that different verdicts are possible on the means whereby liquidity has been provided, I cannot believe that a period that has witnessed everywhere such a conspicuous fall in the value of money can seriously be said to have suffered from a significant deficiency of the credit base. But looking to the future, I change sides. The elasticity of the gold exchange standard seems to me to have reached its desirable limits, and, taking a moderate view of the probabilities of future gold supply and the prospective need for expansion of reserves, I see a clear case for innovation and reform. I will not expatiate here on the minutiae of alternative plans. But I am clear that the discussions of the last three years have been concerned with important technical problems.

Nevertheless, the center of controversy in this connection is surely not chiefly technical. To anyone who has followed the course of the recent debates with even the most cursory attention, it must be obvious that although there are doubtlessly genuine differences of opinion on particular matters of diagnosis and technique, the main points at issue are the degree of willingness to co-operate and the struggle for relative power. What is at stake in the argument between the United States and France in this connection is not nearly so much what technical form international monetary co-operation shall take as whether it shall take place at all.

All of this brings me back to the thesis with which I began this paper, namely, that in the last analysis, the international monetary problem is essentially a political problem and that eventually it can be solved only on the political plane; this in turn suggests a final reflection that, important though it is to snatch at any opportunity to solve these problems by measures of partial co-operation, in the end they will be solved only if we can achieve a greater degree of like-mindedness in overtly political aims. All the problems of economic relationships among the so-called Atlantic Powers could be solved quite easily if only there were a greater will to common political action and eventual political unity. And unless sooner or later such a will does emerge, I am afraid not only that the international economic problems will remain unsolved, but that what there is of a common civilization of the West will go the way of other cultural entities of the past which had no ultimate will to survive.

25 On Latsis's *Method and Appraisal in Economics*: A Review Essay[1]

From *Journal of Economic Literature*, vol. 17 (September 1979), pp. 996–1004.

I

In September 1974 there took place, at Nafplion in Greece, a gratifyingly small but distinguished conference of a somewhat unusual nature. Its object was to examine the general grounds of appraisal of the status and the progress of scientific theories, particularly with reference to the views of the late Imre Lakatos embodied in his conception of the Methodology of Scientific Research Programmes as developed in his notable contribution to the Symposium *Criticism and the Growth of Knowledge*, edited by himself and Alan Musgrave [5, 1970]. But instead of ascending into the stratosphere of pure speculation, the organizers of the conference decided to focus their principal attention on two fields, the history of physical science and economics respectively; and by concentrating on theories and progress in these subjects to bring greater concreteness to the discussion of the general problem. This volume, splendidly edited by one of the principal organizers and contributors to the conference, Dr. Spiro Latsis, embodies the papers contributed and evoked by the sessions devoted to economics. A companion volume, *Method and Appraisal in the Physical Sciences*, edited by Colin Howson [2, 1976], does the same thing for the other sessions. Together they are records of an occasion that I personally found more stimulating than any other conference I have ever attended.

The titles of both these books, although generally felicitous, are perhaps apt to give the impression that their content matter is concerned indifferently with the normative and the positive; and indeed the occasional appearance of

1. *Method and Appraisal in Economics*, ed. Spiro J. Latsis (Cambridge: Cambridge University Press, 1976).

versions of the more formal statements of the requirements of the Lakatos Programme may convey the same thought – historically the word methodology has been itself somewhat ambiguous in this respect. It is therefore a welcome circumstance that, in his Preface, Dr. Latsis should explicitly repudiate this interpretation and make it clear that, according to Lakatos, "the proper domain of philosophy of science is the appraisal of past achievements and *not* the rendering of heuristic advice" (p. viii). Appraisal may indeed involve examination of method. But it does not prescribe the mode of the evolution of thought.

The contributions to this symposium cover a wide field. Dr. Latsis introduces the subject and illustrates his theme by an illuminatory critique of the present state of the theory of the firm. Professor A.W. Coats and Professor Herbert Simon deal with aspects of the connection between Economics and Psychology. Professors Axel Leijonhufvud and Neil de Marchi deal, respectively, with Keynes and the Leontief paradox, and Professors Mark Blaug, T.W. Hutchison, and Sir John Hicks discuss wider aspects of the congruence of the criteria proposed and the history of economic thought. Clearly it would be impossible, in an article of this length, to survey in detail all the different aspects of these various contributions. I hope, therefore, that it will not be thought inappropriate if in the course of this review I mainly present my own views on the general problems involved with due reference to relevant points made by the distinguished authors.

II

The subject is Economics. Its generalizations cover any aspect of behavior that is conditioned by the existence of scarcity – scarcity of time, of productive powers, of goods and services of all types. So far as I know, the first approach to this conception occurs in Hume's discussion of property in his *Treatise of Human Nature* [3, 1874, pp. 261–62] and in various connections it crops up again and again in one form or another in subsequent literature – the idea that it only emerges in my youthful writing is erroneous. Whenever the objectives of conduct are various and the means of achieving them are limited, it is not difficult to see that it has a comprehensive application. Where there is no scarcity of the various kinds indicated, there is no behavior that has an economic aspect.

It has been objected that this conception is either too wide or too narrow: on the one hand there is a vast field of behavior influenced in one way or another by the fact of scarcity, which is of no particular interest; on the other hand there are many influences outside the spheres of markets and exchange, which economists should take into account. So far as width is concerned, it is quite true that much conduct having an economic aspect is extra-marginal as regards systematic study. But this is true of most other aspects of reality that are the subject of systematic investigations. In natural science, equally with social studies, we concentrate on problems of interpretation rather than examine just any phenomena that happen to strike our attention. As regards the accusation of narrowness, I suspect this rests on misapprehension due perhaps to undue preoccupation with the theory of exchange. In fact, explanation of the influence of scarcity extends far beyond the immediate incidence of catallactics: it covers questions of incentive, institutions, and indeed much of the legal framework of society, not to mention matters of indiscriminate, as well as of discriminate, benefit.

This brings me to the question of the relation of Economics to Psychology. Professor Coats gives an interesting account of the abortive attack by certain American economists, chiefly at the turn of the century, on mainstream Economics on the ground that it took no account of the published views of psychologists or indeed of psychological factors outside narrow conceptions of pecuniary interest – though whether this attack should be dignified as a methodological research program in the Lakatos sense is perhaps a matter on which opinions may vary. The fact is, of course, that, from a very early stage, psychological interpretations and elements have played a part in economic generalizations The first part of Adam Smith's famous chapter on differences in wages and profits in different employments where he deals with what he would call "natural" influences [12, 1976, ch. 10], makes it abundantly plain that tendencies to equilibrium in these connections are tendencies *not* to equality of money returns, but rather to equality of net advantages, including anticipated social esteem, subjective reactions to alternative occupations, and various attitudes to uncertainty. If one had to ask which part of Smith's detailed analytical system had survived into modern treatments, this would have strong claims to high priority.

Let me dwell a little on the position of uncertainty in economic analysis for, without calling into criticism Professor Simon's very interesting reports concerning the tests he has made of various kinds of reaction to uncertainty, I confess I am more than a little puzzled by his suggestion that what he calls substantive rationality has dominated the field of speculation up to a recent date. In this respect again, I would invoke the *Wealth of Nations* with its piquant account of the effect on recruitment to certain occupations of "the overweening conceit which the greater part of men have of their own abilities ... [and] their absurd presumption in their own good fortune" [12, 1976, p. 124]. In this connection I recall also that the third approximation in Irving Fisher's *Rate of Interest* [1, 1907], one of the greatest analytical works of the first half of this century, is specifically directed to the effects of comparative ignorance on the upshot of investment. Nor can I forget the profound discussion of the nature and effects of uncertainty in Frank Knight's brilliant *Risk, Uncertainty and Profit* [4, 1921]. I am naturally fascinated by the experiments in computational method on reaction to uncertainty by Professor Simon and his associates, but I should doubt if the results had more than limited *spatial and temporal validity* as illustrations of assumptions that have been built into general economic analysis for quite a long time. Professor Simon would not, I am sure, contend that they relate to the reactions of, say, present-day Eskimos and Melanesians, or Americans of the seventeenth and twentieth century – let alone the twenty-first century when it arrives.

Still crossing the t's and dotting the i's of the psychological elements in economic analysis, I cannot resist a slight gloss on Dr. Latsis's suggestion that my own outlook is confined to the assumption of rational conduct. This must certainly be entirely due to expository failure on my part: my early writing on such subjects offered many very legitimate targets. But if "rational action" means, as I think it should mean, *consistent* action, in the sense that, if one prefers *A* to *B* and *B* to *C*, then it is consistent to prefer *A* to *C* and inconsistent to prefer the contrary, I certainly do not hold that all action that is not vegetative must be regarded as rational in the sense that mutually contradictory preferences and policies on the part of single individuals or collections of individuals are ruled out. I think a good deal of the application of economics to practical policy is devoted to elucidation of just such situations. The fact that for certain purposes of pure analysis – a Walrasian equilibrium for instance – it is useful to assume rationality in the sense of consistency, certainly does not oblige us, at least from my outlook on our subject matter, to rule out all situations involving scarcity that do not conform to this assumption.

III

I now come to the essential similarities and differences between physical and economic sciences.

As regards the logical status of the respective propositions concerned, there can surely be no dispute in either case to Hume's distinction between *ought* and *is*. I certainly believe that in what I call Political Economy as distinct from pure economics (*i.e.*, the application to public policy of economic generalizations claiming scientific status)[1] there is, or should be, much normative appeal to matters of ethics or social philosophy involving judgements of

1. See my *Political Economy: Past and Present*, pp. 1–3, for an explicit justification of this terminology [10, 1976].

value rather than judgements of fact. But on the positive analysis of the implications for behavior of the fact of scarcity – Economics – I see no reason to recognize any difference between such generalizations and the generalizations of Physics or of Biology.

Nor do I claim that, as regards appraisal, there is an ultimate difference. Generalizations about physical or economic phenomena are essentially conjectures, capable of deductive development, but, while exposed to refutation by appropriate testing, incapable of final and definite proof. In this respect I am a convinced Popperean. I do not regard Lakatos's Methodology of Scientific Research Programmes as, in any important respect, contradictory to Popper's main contention. Indeed I would regard his prescriptions, his "hard core" propositions, his heuristic postulates, his "protective belt," and his insistence that broad programs of research should not be deterred by incidental failure as a distinguished spelling out of implications of the main body of Popper's contribution. I confess that while recognizing, in appropriate places, differences in stylistic emphasis in Popper's exposition, I do not regard these differences as constituting essential divergencies of outlook justifying the attribution to the author of inconsistent views within the central contribution. I should certainly regard it as a total misapprehension – which I am sure Lakatos would not have wished to propagate – to regard Popper as a *naive* falsificationist. Therefore personally I regard the broad conceptions of *The Logic of Scientific Discovery* [9, 1959] as generally applicable, whatever particular scientific discipline we practice.

This is not to say that in my judgement, there are no differences, arising from the nature of the subject matter, between the various Physical Sciences on the one hand and Economics on the other. The need for the so-called "hard core" of the assumptions of economic analysis to be buttressed by so many auxilary assumptions, explicit or implicit, if any development that is not ultimately banal is to be expected, seems to me to be an obvious difference. Beyond that, the possibilities of testing are so hedged about with both practical and intellectual difficulties as to constitute almost a difference in kind. The practical difficulties are obvious; the requirement of *ceteris paribus*, despite all sorts of ingenious techniques, is very exacting. But the intellectual difficulties are even more formidable. There is not only the continual change in the pattern of tastes and obstacles, presenting problems comparable to those that would exist in Natural Science if every time a relevant observation were made, the table of atomic weights had to be recalculated; there is also the further complication of the learning subject – Newton's apple did not change its habit because its behavior had been made the subject of generalized description, as a stockbroker might if quantitative laws of the response of fixed interest securities to various changes had been discovered. We should never forget that economic reactions, as distinct from physical reactions, are mediated by the existence of human minds capable of weighing alternatives and learning from experience, as Professor Machlup has so powerfully argued in his "If Matter Could Talk" [6, 1969, ch. 12]. I am definitely not saying that these complications inhibit *any* useful speculation about economic tendencies and relationships: on the contrary one cannot look at contemporary economic policy in most areas without realizing how useful a modest knowledge of Economics could be. But they certainly impose limitations on ambitions concerning precision and prediction outside fairly formal deductions from pretty obvious assumptions. For example, the proposition that the volume of spending cannot greatly exceed the volume of production without affecting the value of money may be regarded as helpful; whereas the statement that a given increase in such an excess will affect long-term interest rates by a definite percentage is highly dubious if not consciously fraudulent. No economist would admit that the more generally accepted propositions of his subject are *no use* in understanding economic relationships and movements. But at this stage of my life I am fairly clear that his claims should be limited, especially in the field of quantitative prediction.

IV

But now comes the grand question: how does the history of the subject stand up to our methods of appraisal?

I do not think that this question is as easy to answer as the parallel question in regard to Physical Science. As Dr. Latsis's discussion of the theory of the firm brilliantly shows, it is sometimes possible to isolate – or partly isolate – the evolution of particular theories and subject them to this kind of scrutiny. But, in the main, the interrelations of the elements in general economic systems are so close that detached appraisal has its limitations. I suspect that reservations of the kind I have in mind underlie Professor Blaug's masterly paper. It is certainly easier, at any rate initially, to adopt Sir John Hicks's method of a bird's eye survey of the real, or alleged, revolutions in the main body of theory: and this is how I intend to proceed.

We may begin with the Smithean system. The main object of the *Wealth of Nations*, in so far as it presented positive propositions rather than prescription, was to show how the division of labor was regulated by the extent and incentives of the market, and how the growth or decline of such a system depended on the degree of the division of labor and the accumulation or decumulation of capital. (I leave undiscussed Sir John's provocative revival of the suggestion that Smith's synthesis was "taken over" from the Physiocrats – if there is question of the main influences on the central Smithean system, I personally should be inclined to name Cantillon rather than Quesnay and his disciples.) I hope that it would be agreed that, in the general setting in which I have posed the appearance of the contents, it set the background for most of the questions that most economists have been discussing ever since.

I am not inclined to regard the contributions of Ricardo, important as they may be, either positively or negatively, in provoking further thought as constituting a "revolution" as regards the Smithean system *in general.* I would not wish to underestimate the development of *pure analysis*, in one sense of the word, which takes its rise from Ricardo's *Principles* [11, 1817]. But, given the path-breaking positions of Smith as regards the functions of markets and accumulation, I see Ricardo's propositions chiefly as attempted reformations of particular positions concerning value and distribution. I do not think that, when John Stuart Mill stated that he was attempting in his *Principles* a work "similar in its object and general conception to that of Adam Smith," he intended to convey the impression of a revolution, even though he went on to say that "the *Wealth of Nations* is in many parts obsolete and, in all imperfect" [8, 1848]. While there had been notable additions, conspicuously in the theory of international trade, there remained some of Smith's errors and many of his excellences in the development of nineteenth century Classical Economics.

Matters are different in regard to the so-called Marginal Revolution, whether one regards it as starting with the unjustly neglected anticipators of utility theory (D.H. Lloyd, Jules Dupuit, and Herman H. Gossen), or conspicuously with the developers of that line of thought (W.S. Jevons, Karl Menger, and Léon Walras). I am inclined to agree that the importance of minutiae of the alternative forms of approach to the psychological element underlying demand, although intellectually highly interesting, may have been overdone. But the fundamental change of emphasis regarding the analytical status of demand, not only for goods of the first order but for factor services and for the valuation of specific factors and indeed for free capital, eventually gave the substance of the theory of value and distribution a content radically different in important respects from the Ricardian developments of the Smithean system. Marginal rates of substitution, marginal productivity, marginal time preference, marginal rate of return over cost – these are conceptions, arising for the most part, though not entirely – think of J.H. von Thünen and A.A. Cournot – from the work of the fifty years after 1871, which are important ingredients in any present attempt to understand economic phenomena. And despite anticipations and various origins, it is not lacking in perspective to regard them as products of the Marginal Revolution. There are indeed elements of continuity with earlier analysis, as Marshall, rightly, never ceased to urge; but the look of the thing is different.

In all such developments the prime elements of the theoretical assumptions involved, though fundamentally important, are not such as to demand much complicated testing. I have in mind questions such as, other things being equal, are you capable of ranking anticipated satisfactions in a descending order of magnitude? Do you value such satisfactions according to their availability in time? Is it possible for you to gauge the degree to which the uses of different means of production are substitutable for your purposes? These are questions that should be asked and their meanings examined. But the tests involved are pretty simple. It is the complications that arise when such conceptions are amalgamated and applied to particular problems that are difficult to disentangle. And, as we have seen, any attempt to invest them with *permanent*, as distinct from momentary, quantitative values involves difficulties of a completely different order. Even so I am inclined to agree with Professor Hutchison that generally there has been insufficient testing in Economics. As regards the elementary conceptions, I imagine that diminishing returns might set in early to very protracted examination – and sometimes does. In more complicated constructions there is often an amazing naiveté as regards the availability of the specific facts essential for testing; and there are many parts of our subject, the areas that general theory shows to be indeterminate, where I am disposed to think that frank declarations of ignorance within limits may be a valuable supplement to any presumptions based on history or psychology, useful though these may be in particular instances.

There is one aspect of the original Smithean position that deserves special notice in this connection, both intrinsically and in regard to subsequent developments; namely his assumptions regarding aggregate demand and money and banking. His assertion that "what is annually saved is as regularly consumed as what is annually spent, and nearly in the same time too; but it is consumed by a different set of people" more or less assumed, in the absence of misbehavior by the states, or perhaps by banks, a tendency to overall equilibrium of supply and demand: and in this sense it was developed, at least by James Mill and Ricardo and (more doubtfully) by J.B. Say, on the last of whom nearly all the subsequent blame has somewhat unjustly been laid. Although charitable interpretations may be put on the underlying intellectual intentions in this connection, the general assumption was obviously not in accordance with the facts of a monetary economy: and despite Malthus and his followers, it was not until J. S. Mill's important essay on the *Influence of Consumption on Production* that this particular matter began to be treated in a manner more consistent with experience [7, 1844]. Meanwhile there were taking place in the field of finance, developments on the side of money and banking, themselves giving rise to new problems, at first not properly conceived, at least by Smith; and the more or less regular ups and downs of trade, typical of the years between 1815 and 1914, gradually attracted more systematic attention. What with these and the acute problems of inflation and deflation of the present century, the treatment of overall equilibrium and disequilibrium, which is almost taken for granted in the Smithean system, has assumed an entirely different status in the theoretical perspective of today. It is perhaps also to be noted in this connection that, in spite of the absence of consensus, there has been here at least a good deal of recourse to statistical testing of one kind or another.

Whether all this is to be called a revolution or not is perhaps a matter of words. I personally doubt if having regard to the variety of the geographical sources, the French, the German, and the English speaking worlds, and the times at which the various contributions appeared, including the profound insights of Henry Thornton at the beginning of the nineteenth century, this appellation is very suitable. I certainly think that Keynes's influence on public opinion and on policy *was* revolutionary; but, as the mists of controversy disperse, I doubt if the degree of discontinuity between his important theoretical contributions and those of, say, the great Scandanavians, not to mention Ralph G. Hawtrey and Dennis H. Robertson in this country and Milton Friedman and others in the United States, will be regarded as having the status of isolated innovation as is sometimes supposed. I am not clear that Professor Leijonhufvud would altogether agree about this; and I would freely admit that the developments of the last sixty years are perhaps still too close for us to feel sure that we give them their true place in the perspective.

V

Arriving at last at the ultimate question of the symposium – the use and validity of the Lakatos criteria for appraisal of the development of Economics – I think it is clear, as is demonstrated by the distinguished contributions of Dr. Latsis and Professor de Marchi, that there are episodes in the evolution of particular theories that can be very usefully analyzed on these lines. It is possible to think of other cases where this verdict might also apply – other episodes in the history of the theory of international trade, for example, and Irving Fisher's speculations on the theory of the relation between real and nominal rates of interest. And where this can be done without the appearance of forcing, it is obviously to be welcomed.

I confess however to some doubts about the application of this technique to the developments of branches of more general theory. This is not to abandon the ultimate criteria of logical consistency and the desirability of sophisticated and realistic tests. But it is to suggest that accounts of the evolution of such broad fields as, let us say, the theories of value and distribution, not to say general growth, if appraised on the formal lines of the Lakatos requirements, would involve a presentation of what actually happened, which would be difficult to recognize. Perhaps it might be good for our souls to make the attempt: I sometimes think that knowledge of the common postulates and experiences involved is apt to be taken too much for granted; and it is arguable that these should be more spelled out. But I do not think that ultimately evaluation of the logical status and explanatory power of the constructions concerned would be greatly altered. I think that most who took part in the Nafplion conference must have recognized the closer fit of the actual history of episodes in the development of physical science to the Lakatos scheme of appraisal than, with the possible exceptions I have mentioned, would often happen especially in the history of the broader developments of economics; and, without abating very warm tribute to the usefulness of the juxtaposition of our talks, I do not think that this was altogether an accident, although perhaps it suggests deficiencies of past practice.

In recording this provisional conclusion, let me once more reiterate that, in my opinion, it does not involve the abandonment of sincere belief in the not inconsiderable intellectual status and practical usefulness of the subject. But I do recognize its limitations, doubtless springing, at least in part, from the intrinsic differences from physical science, which I was at pains to set forth earlier in this paper. Thus, for instance, I should have little reserve in predicting that measures designed to restrict the level of rents of dwelling-houses below what would have emerged in a free market would result in an alleged "shortage" of houses; and an exposition of the grounds of this opinion would perhaps be boring in its simplicity – although a surprising number of public personalities appear not to know them or, if they do know them, effectively conceal this knowledge when they discuss policy in this respect. But if I were to venture beyond such a qualitative forecast and attempted to indicate the precise magnitude of the "shortage" resulting from the same measures in population areas with different recorded reaction times in the past, I might be doing something that had some limited local usefulness in time and space; but the grounds on which I presented such conjectures would be much more complicated and vastly more likely to be wrong.

In my judgement current appreciation of the real value of economic science has been too much influenced by excessive focus on its power to *predict* to the neglect of its wider power to *explain*. This emphasis runs two dangers. From the point of view of the lay philistine, the record is not good – the claims have been much too extensive and have often been just wrong. From the professional point of view, all generalizations that have not predictive power tend to be regarded as worthless, although some of the most profound insights into the nature of the economic system – the Walrasian analysis for instance – most palpably do not possess this power.

Now admittedly some prediction, usually of a non-quantitative kind as, for instance, my above example of the analysis of the effects of rent restriction, are certainly possible and useful. And more detailed *projections*, which do not claim to be forecasts of what will actually happen – *and emphasize this to the laity* – may sometimes be helpful in enabling administrators and entrepreneurs to make up their minds in choosing between various alternatives. But the broader speculations of our subject have a wider significance than that. Doubtless they are essential background – often overlooked – both to predictions or projections. But where these are not possible or attended with such reservations as to have little practical value, they still afford, or attempt to afford, a general picture of the structure of abstract relationships arising from scarcity under various institutional frameworks – exchange, production, capitalization, money and finance, and the ways in which they may change. Thus, while we may not be able to predict what form the future may take, we may attempt description in general terms of how economic systems work or may work and put our conjectures as well as we may to the test of present observation and past record. And such knowledge, as well as providing useful perspectives, may itself sometimes throw light on the solution of wider problems of social and political choice.

References

1. Irving Fisher, *The Rate of Interest: Its nature, determination and relation to economic phenomena* (New York, 1907).
2. Colin Howson, ed., *Method and Appraisal in the Physical Sciences: The critical background to modern science, 1800–1905* (Cambridge, 1976).
3. David Hume, *A Treatise of Human Nature*, ed. T.H. Green and T.H. Grose (London, 1874).
4. Frank H. Knight, *Risk, Uncertainty and Profit* (Boston, 1921).
5. Imre Lakatos and Alan Musgrave, eds, *Criticism and the Growth of Knowledge* (Cambridge, 1970).
6. Fritz Machlup, "If matter could talk," in *Philosophy, Science and Methodology*, eds Sidney Morgenbesser, Patrick Suppes and Merton White (New York, 1969), pp. 286–305.
7. John Stuart Mill, "The influence of consumption of production," in *Essays on some Unsettled Questions of Political Economy* (London, 1844), pp. 47–89.
8. John Stuart Mill, *Principles of Political Economy with some of their applications to social philosophy* (London, 1848).
9. Karl R. Popper, *The Logic of Scientific Discovery* (London, 1959)
10. Lionel Robbins, *Political Economy: Past and Present, A Review of Leading Theories of Economic Policy* (London, 1976).
11. David Ricardo, *On the Principles of Political Economy and Taxation* (London, 1817).
12. Adam Smith, *An Inquiry into the Nature and Causes of the Wealth of Nations*, eds R.H. Campbell and A.S. Skinner (Glasgow edn of the Works and Correspondence of Adam Smith, Oxford, 1976).

26 Economics and Political Economy

From *The American Economic Review*, vol. 71 Supplement (May 1981), pp. 1–10.

May I begin by saying what an honor I feel it to be asked to lecture before this distinguished assembly on a foundation designed to commemorate the fame of one of the most influential economists of the earlier years of your great association. May I also say what an intense pleasure it is to be chaired by my dear friend William Baumol, an excolleague and, since our first acquaintance, the source of so much learning on my part and continuous inspiration.

Let me start by a word or two about my title which may have seemed to some of you formidably all embracing. This, let me assure you, would be a misapprehension: my target is comparatively restricted. At the beginning of my career, in my salad days, I wrote a slender essay entitled *The Nature and Significance of Economic Science*; and from time to time its contents have been the subject of criticism and discussion. I have seldom made any comment on this but I have gone on thinking. Thus, when I was invited to give this lecture, it occurred to me, with your approbation, Chairman, that, at the approaching end of my career, it might be a good opportunity to gather together some reflections on the subject of that essay and perhaps to put things in such a way as to make peace with some of my critics.

My remarks will fall broadly into four main parts. In the first – very briefly, you will be glad to hear – I shall resume my position on the definition of the subject matter of Economics. In the second I shall discuss its status as a science. In the third I shall examine the attempt to give scientific justification to the normative propositions known as Welfare Economics. And in the fourth I expound my own conception of what I now call Political Economy. In conclusion I shall try to sum up the main contentions of these somewhat discursive reflections and to point a moral as regards teaching.

I

To begin with subject matter, the conception that I argued in my book was of those aspects of behavior which, in some way or another, arise from the existence of scarcity. Now I am not at all indisposed to accept, for purposes of after-dinner conversation, Jacob Viner's wisecrack that "Economics is what economists do." But this only shifts the question one stage further: what is it that they do? What is the object of their investigations?

I hope I do not need to say much about what, in my youth, was probably the most widely used answer to this question, namely *the causes of material welfare*. Quite apart from the precise meaning of this ambiguous term, it is an easy matter to show that there is an economic aspect to the choice between the causes of material and nonmaterial welfare. And since William Baumol together with Bowen, has written a very persuasive and extensive work on the economics of the *Performing Arts*, I think we must regard this conception as too narrow, and indeed misleading, and look elsewhere for a plausible description of the nature of our subject matter.

Much more interesting is the proposal put forward by my old friend and colleague, Fritz Hayek, to revive Archbishop Whately's proposal to rename our subject as the science of *Catallactics* (pp. 3–5), or the *Science of Exchanges*. I should certainly agree that, even where there is no market, the economic aspects of decisions and activities concerning scarce means and time can be regarded as the exchange of one state of affairs for another; and I think that this approach leads to very deep insights. But I do not think it makes sufficiently clear the conditions which lead to exchange, whether actual or implied.

But this, of course, is what the definition in terms of behavior conditioned by scarcity specifically does – scarcity being conceived as the relationship between objectives, either personal or collective, and the means of satisfying them. As you know, it first emerges in so many words in David Hume's *Treatise of Human Nature* (pp. 261–62) and it is made explicitly applicable to economic relationships in general in a famous chapter in Menger's *Grundsätze* where the limitation of goods confronted with conceivable demand is made the necessary condition of the activity of economizing. It covers exchanges and the institutional arrangements which arise in connection with this limitation.

Thus, coming back to Jacob Viner, I doubt very much that what economists do when they discuss what is, or what can be, the nature of such possibilities is not covered by this definition.

II

This brings me to the second division of my reflections. Let me say at once that I see no reason for denying to the study of the activities and institutions created by scarcity the title of science. It conforms fundamentally to our conception of science in general: that is to say the formation of hypotheses explaining and (possibly) predicting the outcome of the relationships concerned and the testing of such hypotheses by logic and by observation. This process of testing used to be called verification. But, since this way of putting things may involve an overtone of permanence and nonrefutability, it is probably better described, as Karl Popper has taught us, as a search for falsification – those hypotheses which survive the test being regarded as provisionally applicable. I am pretty sure that all the positive propositions of economics conform to this description. In this context, therefore, we may regard them as falling into the same category of knowledge as astronomy, physics, and biology – although, some may think, something of a poor relation.

But at the same time we must recognize that, within these logical criteria, the methods and problems of economic science are very substantially different from those of the so-called natural sciences. This springs from the fundamental circumstance that the subject matter is an aspect of human action and therefore must be conceived as including purpose. That is to say that our explanations must to some extent be *teleological*. This is not to argue with von Mises and some of his followers that we must regard human action, if not purely vegetative, as at all times *rational* in the sense that, given belief in the range of technical knowledge available to individuals or collections of individuals, action must be *consistent*. I confess that I have never been able to understand this contention: I should have thought that one of the main practical functions of economic science was to enable us to detect inconsistencies in plans, such as, for instance, simultaneous demands for low interest rates brought about by increases in the size of the credit base and a diminution of inflation. But, putting this conception aside, I would have thought that the contention that explanations of economic relationships must involve considerations of purposes, implicit or explicit, to be relatively noncontroversial.

Unfortunately this is not so. Influenced presumably by behaviorism in psychology, there are those who urge that in economics we must exclude any hypothesis which relies on conceptions which are not *directly observable* in the sense that they could be recorded as being perceived by the senses of an outside spectator and thus made the data of explanations of causal relationships.

I confess that I fail to see the necessity, or indeed the desirability, of the self-denying ordinance. I concede that, in the examination of simple markets, observations can be made which can be regarded as *revealing* preferences for action on the part of the persons concerned; and thus more or less determinate solutions achieved of the probable outcome. But I cannot believe that such considerations are in any way superior to those which go behind the observed dispositions to the psychological conception of *ordering* upon which the so-called subjective theory has been based in the past. And if we proceed to consider more complicated situations, I simply cannot conceive explaining to a visitor from another planet the ups and downs of a stock exchange without invoking the psychological element of expectations, not to mention error and the vagaries of fashion. According to my inadequate knowledge of physical science, I doubt whether its explanations are limited to elements which are directly observable. So long as the elements in the hypothesis are indirectly testable, they are surely scientifically admissable. Thus I ask why we, as economists, should impose on ourselves greater austerity than this?

There are, however, other differences of considerable significance between the nature of the subject matter of economics and most, if not all, natural sciences, namely, to use Paretean terms, the absence of constants both of tastes and of obstacles.

In natural science, once causal connections have been established, the quantitative relationships can usually be assumed to persist, other things being equal. It is not necessary to calculate the table of atomic weights every time particular explanations or predictions are attempted. Alas, this is not so in economics. Immense ingenuity may be devoted to establishing the conditions of demand for particular commodities; and these may sometimes help in making guesses for the future. But tastes change. A Minister of Finance would be ill advised if, in making estimates for tax purposes of the demand for cigarettes, for instance, he were to rely on computations which had been made ten years ago: he must keep himself up to date with current fashions and knowledge. The influence of the Reformation made no change in the forces of gravity. But it certainly must have changed the demand for fish on Fridays.

The same absence of persistence applies also on the side of obstacles. The human beings, whose behavior in regard to scarce goods and services is the subject of our study, are capable of learning: and learning affects conduct in various ways. Thus changes in knowledge concerning the reactions of matter in various contexts do not affect matter itself. But they may affect the possibilities of technology and therefore human action. Beyond this, knowledge concerning the results of such behavior can affect future behavior. An econometrician might discover a formula concerning the response of the Dollar Exchanges to given developments of monetary and financial policy; and if he kept it to himself, he might make a lot of money. But if he released it in the journals or the media, then it would be likely to become wrong: people would alter their financial dispositions according to the new knowledge and thus render the new knowledge erroneous.

For such reasons, quantitative prediction in economics is apt to be hazardous; much more hazardous indeed than predicting the weather. Time-series, if they have been properly collected, have status as economic history and they may serve an important role in testing explanations of the past. But, as a means of predicting the future, they are liable in various degrees to the vicissitudes of preferences and knowledge; and unless this is continually borne in mind, they can be seriously misleading.

This is not to say that suitably qualified propositions involving numbers should not be attempted; nor that some are less liable to error than others. Still less is it to argue that explanation of causes believed to be operating in the field of economic relationships is not a worthwhile branch of intellectual activity. There are a great many things which can be said in this connection; indeed I would say many of the most important propositions of the subject fall into the category where quantification is quite out of the question. All that is intended by the remarks I have just been making is to emphasize the differences between our subject matter and the subject matter of many natural sciences, and to draw attention to the appropriate limits which it must impose on our claims. And if, by any chance, my emphasis in this respect casts any doubt on the contention that ability to predict is the sole or necessary criterion of scientific activity, I should not feel unduly depressed. I do not think that the understanding of economic phenomena hitherto achieved, although palpably imperfect, is anything to be ashamed of.

Finally, it is important to recognize that the propositions of economics, as it has developed as a science, are positive rather than normative. They deal *inter alia* with values; but they deal with them as individual or social *facts*. The generalizations which emerge are statements of existence or possibility. They use the words *is* or *may be*, not *ought* or *should be*. There can be events or institutions having an economic aspect which we ourselves regard as ethically acceptable or unacceptable. But, in so far as the explanations of their causes or consequences are scientific, they are neutral in this respect.

It is sometimes questioned whether in the discussion of any social or economic relationships this quality of what the Germans call *Wertfreiheit* is attainable. No less an authority than Gunnar Myrdal has devoted a whole book to the argument that, explicitly or implicitly, all propositions of economic theory, all classifications of happenings having an economic aspect, must involve judgments of value. I do not agree with this position. I don't think that the proposition that, if the market is free and demand exceeds supply, prices will tend to rise, has any ethical content whatever. Nor do I concede that recognition of the consequences on investment of disparity between rates of interest and rates of return depends in the least on the political prepossessions of the economist who perceives it.

Needless to say I do not at all deny that, in the course of evolution of economics as we know it, there has been a good deal of intermixture of political and ethical discussion with the scientific discussion of fact and possibility. I shall shortly be discussing this matter further in the light of certain specific instances; and it will not appear that, *provided the logical difference between the two kinds of propositions is clearly kept in mind*, I am in the least hostile to the combination. In that youthful book of mine which evoked such fervid denunciation, I expressly denied that my position involved the view that "economists should not discuss ethical or political questions any more than the position that botany is not aesthetics means that botanists should not have views on the layout of gardens." On the contrary I went on to argue, "it is greatly to be desired that economists should have speculated long and widely on these matters." As you will see later on, my position today only involves a slight purely semantic modification of this pronouncement. I still hold that the distinction of the different kinds of propositions is inescapable and that we run the dangers of intellectual confusion on our own part and justifiable criticism from outside if we do not explicitly recognize it.

III

But this brings me to the next division of my subject – the status of Welfare Economics. And since, as you may suspect, my verdict is to be somewhat adverse, let me say at once that I would yield to no one in admiration of the intentions of this development and of the ingenuity with which its analysis has often been conducted. It would not be the first time in intellectual history that dedicated efforts have led to a confusion of claims; and nothing that I am about to say must be construed as contending that these efforts were not worthwhile.

The *raison d'être* of Welfare Economics is simple. How desirable it would be if we were able to pronounce as a *matter of scientific demonstration* that such and such a policy was good or bad. Take, for instance, the removal of a protective tariff. Given information about the elasticities of demand and supply of the immediate past, we can certainly make guesses, in price and income terms, about the gains to consumers and the losses to producers of the probable outcome. There are all sorts of scientific difficulties here which I have touched upon, or hinted at, already. But the guesses, such as they are, are on an objective plane. But as soon as we move to the plane of welfare, we introduce elements which are not of that order. As in the great work of Marshall and, still more, Pigou, we are assuming that comparisons between prices and incomes before and after the event can be made a verifiable basis for comparisons between the satisfactions and dissatisfactions of the different persons involved. And that, I would urge, is not warranted by anything which is legitimately assumed by scientific economics.

Let me at once guard against a misunderstanding which has often occurred in criticisms of this position. Of course I do not deny that, in every day life, we do make comparisons between the satisfactions of different people. When the head of a family carves up a turkey, he may take account of his estimate of the satisfaction afforded to different members by different portions; and, in more serious judgments of social relationships outside the family, whenever we discuss distributional questions, we make our own estimates of the happiness afforded or the misery endured by different persons or groups of persons.

But these are *our* estimates. There is no objective measurement conceivable. Let me remind you of the fundamental issue here by comparing two situations, one of which in my judgment falls *within* scientific economics as such, and one *without*. Suppose elementary barter: *A*, who has a bottle of whisky, has the opportunity of exchanging it with *B*, who has a classical record of, say, *Fidelio*. It should be quite easy to ascertain by asking the relative valuations of the objects concerned before exchange. *A* relates that the classical record is worth more to him that the bottle of whisky; *B* contrariwise. This at no point involves interpersonal comparisons of absolute satisfaction. But now suppose that *A* and *B* fall into conversation about their respective enjoyments and *A* says to *B*, "Of course I get more satisfaction than you out of music," and *B* vigorously asserts the contrary. Needless to say, you and I as outsiders can form our own judgments. But these are essentially subjective, not objectively ascertainable fact. There is no available way in which we can measure and compare the satisfactions which *A* and *B* derive from music. Intelligent talk? But that may be misleading. Facial expression? That too may be deceptive. Willingness to make sacrifices of other things? But that clearly shifts the emphasis to the satisfactions derived from other things; and we are left with the ultimate difficulty of interpersonal comparisons that, as Jevons put it, "Every mind is thus inscrutable to every other mind and no common denominator of feeling seems to be possible" (p. 85).[1] Jevons' emphasis may be a bit extreme; we certainly think we know what other people are feeling, though opinions notoriously differ in different cultural settings and between different people. But it is surely incontestable where scientific proof or measurement is in question.

In this connection it is interesting to note the quite explicit agreement of Bentham to the proposition I am arguing. Among the Bentham papers, there is a passage, cited by Eli Halévy, which makes it very clear that the author of the most rigid exponent of the so-called Felicific Calculus was under no delusion that interpersonal comparability was anything but a convention – a convention, it is true, which he regarded as essential to practical reasoning. "Tis in vain," he said, "to talk of adding quantities which after the addition will continue distinct as they were before, one man's happiness will never be

1. See also Philip Wicksteed, p. 68.

another man's happiness; a gain to one man is no gain to another: you might as well pretend to add twenty apples to twenty pears. Which after you had done it would not be forty of any one thing but twenty of each as there was before" (pp. 495–96).

Now recognition of this difficulty led Pareto to the suggestion that we could only say that a community was better off if, all tastes remaining constant, a change took place which improved the position of one individual or group of individuals without making any of the rest worse off.[1] Personally I can't see anything much wrong in this from a conversational point of view. But it is clearly a judgment of value.[2] If the remaining groups regard their position relatively, they may well argue that the spectacle of such improvement elsewhere is a detriment to their satisfaction. This is not a niggling point: a relative improvement in the position of certain groups *pari passu* with an absolute improvement in the position of the rest of the community has often been a feature of economic history; and we know that this has not been regarded by all as either ethically or politically desirable.

An extension of the Pareto criterion which appeared first in the English literature in Jacob Viner's discussion of the effects of tariff changes in his *Studies in the Theory of International Trade* (pp. 533–34), but which owes its vast repute to its rediscovery by Lord Kaldor and Sir John Hicks, is the so-called *Compensation Principle*. According to this principle, we can still say that a community is better off, despite the fact of a change involving gains for one person or group and losses for others, if out of the gains it would be possible to compensate the losses and still leave a benefit for the gainer or gainers.

Now it is obvious that, in order that such a statement can be made, it is necessary that the compensation should actually be paid. The fact that such compensation is *conceivable* is not sufficient: if it is not *actual*, the fundamental Paretean condition is violated that while the position of one person or group is improved, the position of all others is unchanged. All that we can do if compensation is not made, is to point to the change in the positions of the gainers and the losers which at once must raise distributional considerations quite obviously involving further, and more obvious, judgments of value than are implied in the original Paretean conception!

But supposing compensation is supposed to be paid, it is still germane to point out that the practical use of such judgments which it is legitimate to make on this basis, is incomparably less than the claims originally made for Welfare Economics with capital letters. I am not blind to the negative light

1. See Vilfredo Pareto, pp. 617–18.
2. This aspect of the fundamental Pareto proposition is well emphasized by Charles Rowley and Alan Peacock in their excellent book, pp. 7–25.

which the Paretean criterion must throw on the omission of externalities, positive and negative, and the problems to which they give rise; for instance, the desirability of appropriate fiscal incentives or disincentives. But I am clear that the inclusion of such factors must, in most cases, necessitate assumptions involving comparisons and contrasts of individual experiences. Still more is this true of any consideration of distributional questions. I am not against such discussions. As I shall shortly disclose I am emphatically in favor of them, in the hands of qualified persons and under appropriate labels. But with the best will in the world, I cannot help thinking that John Chipman and John Moore are right in their verdict that what they call the New Welfare Economics in an article of that name, has broken down in the strictly scientific sense and left us with the fundamental implications of the passage in Jevons which I have already quoted, namely that all recommendations of policy involve judgments of value.

IV

But this brings me to my last main division. Ought we to be afraid of such assumptions? Clearly there is much to be said against such austerity, at any rate from the point of view of our usefulness to society. Politics are much too important to be left to the politicians – Adam Smith's crafty and insidious animals – and, as was the intention of my original pronouncements on this subject, if they are aware of what they are doing and do not claim scientific authority for conclusions which clearly go beyond science, there is much to be said for the practitioners of scientific economics discussing such questions of policy. They may not agree on the extra-scientific elements in their arguments. But, provided the distinction is observed, there is everything to be said for the discussions of policy to be conducted by those who are aware of the objective implications of the values on which policy rests.

But manifold problems arise even here. Let us assume for a moment the explicit adoption as a postulate of Bentham's felicific calculus, namely interpersonal comparability, each subject to be treated as equally capable of satisfaction, and use that as a basis for recommendation.

Now I make no comment on the substance of this postulate. I personally do not judge that, in any scientific sense, people are necessarily equally capable of satisfaction – whatever that may mean. I readily agree that personal entitlement in equal situations to equal treatment by law is desirable; and I would go beyond that in saying that, in personal relationships, the treatment of one's fellows on a basis of equality answers my criterion of civilized behavior. But when we come to the kind of problems with which economists interested in policy are concerned, matters become more difficult.

Let us take, for instance, the problem of direct taxation. As Edgeworth showed – without, however, recommending the conclusion – the felicific calculus, applied simply to this problem of achieving the minimum aggregate sacrifice, would involve complete equality of income. But even the most hopelessly naive would hesitate to adopt this as a practical maxim of policy. Quite apart from the tangle of administrative problems of sorting out what should be regarded as equality of income in different circumstances, there arises the quite fundamental problem of incentive – should unequal contributions receive equal remuneration? I do not think we need go further than the experience of communist states to discover that so crude an application of the idea of equal capacity for satisfaction and equal rates of diminishing marginal utility of income is really not at all helpful.

Again let me revert to the example already mentioned when I was discussing Welfare Economics – the principle of compensation for improvements involving losses elsewhere. As we have seen, it must be agreed by all exponents of this principle that in order to satisfy the fundamental Paretean criterion, it is necessary that compensation should actually be paid. But very little reflection is needed to raise doubt whether this is a sensible principle. If an improvement has been made which damages the interest of producers whose output has previously been in greater demand, is it now desirable to make payments which may have the effect of preventing movement out of the group affected? Again the problem proves to be more complicated: the solution is not to be found by a simple formula. A dynamic society needs mobility. Or does it? Is compensation to be contingent on acceptance of direction of labor? Or is that an infringement of others' rights?

And so I could go on. The burden of my remarks at this point is that formulae based on the assumptions of either the old or the new Welfare Economics are unlikely to be helpful and may well miss the main point entirely. They give at once the impression of precise guidance and yet they leave out important relevant criteria. As I have urged elsewhere, they are to be regarded as a draughty halfway house. The name conveys an impression of value-free theory which it should be just our intention to avoid.

Fortunately the evolution of terminology in this sphere provides a method of eliminating such confusion. As I said earlier on, in its beginning the label Political Economy covered a *mélange* of objective analysis and applications involving value judgments. The first three books of the *Wealth of Nations* are chiefly devoted to analysis of the market economy and its vicissitudes through history; that is to say generalized *description*. The fourth and fifth are devoted to alternative systems of policy and the functions of the state: that is to say generalized *prescription*. And until even Jevons – and after – both subjects were included under the same label, although surely the difference between the title of J.S. Mill's essay "*On the Definition of Political Economy and on the Method of Investigation Proper to it*" and the title of his *Principles of Political Economy with some of their Application to Social Philosophy* indicates a clear perception of the difference. In the last hundred years, however, beginning conspicuously, perhaps, with Alfred and Mary Marshall's *Economics of Industry* (1879), we have come to describe the generalized description as *Economics* or *Economic Science*; and the label *Political Economy*, as implying judgments of value of which we do not wish to be accused, has tended to drop out of use.

My suggestion here, as in the Introduction to my *Political Economy: Past and Present*, is that its use should be revived as now covering that part of our sphere of interest which essentially involves judgments of value. Political Economy, thus conceived, is quite unashamedly concerned with the assumptions of policy and the results flowing from them. I may say that this is not (*repeat not*) a recent habit of mine. In the Preface to my *Economic Planning and International Order*, published in 1937, I describe it as "essentially an essay in what may be called Political Economy as distinct from Economics in the stricter sense of the word. It depends upon the technical apparatus of analytical Economics; but it applies this apparatus to the examination of schemes for the realization of aims whose formulation lies outside Economics: and it does not abstain from appeal to the probabilities of political practice when such an appeal has seemed relevant."

It should be clear then that Political Economy in this sense involves all the modes of analysis and explicit or implicit judgments of value which are usually involved when economists discuss assessments of benefits and the reverse or recommendations for policy. In particular it deserves to be noted that the whole business of choosing index numbers falls into this conception; and surely few improvements in procedure are more desirable than recognition of this fact. But, in general, the overt recognition of the extent to which the multiplicity of proximate criteria guiding considerations of policy involve judgments of value must be wholly beneficial.

The question therefore arises what should be the ultimate values guiding us in this field. The answer must necessarily be debatable: there is no agreement yet on the ultimate desiderata of the good society: consider for example the variety of opinions regarding the desirability of growth. Speaking personally, I see no objection to regarding utility in a very wide and non-quantitative sense as one of the principal criteria. As an illustration I would cite Hume's famous discussion of the circumstances in which the institution of property is, or is not, justified, in his *Enquiry Concerning the Principles of Morals*. And since I have earlier quoted Bentham's recognition of interpersonal comparisons as a *postulate* rather than a scientific possibility, I would like to say here that, in practice, his so-called felicific calculus, far from making quantitative estimates, was actually employed in Hume's sense – a matter of judging the arrangements of society *as a going concern* according as, in a broad way, they were likely to increase pleasure or diminish pain.

Thus for instance if I were today to respond to Roy Harrod's challenge how to judge the repeal of the Corn Laws, I should not attempt to justify it in terms of the gain of utility at the expense of the producers. I should not know how to do this without comparisons which, to put it mildly, would be highly conjectural. I should base my vindication on the general utility of the extension of markets and the resulting enlargement of liberty of choice. And, as I imagine Hume would have done, I should allow for specific exceptions and stipulate conditions of tolerable and intolerable rates of change.

But, even interpreted in Hume's sense, utility is not enough – at any rate to my way of thinking. There might be utility in the broad sense in the working of the institutions of a well-run slave state, and yet the assumptions behind my Political Economy would reject them. And this would not be for the reason that the attribution of utility to such institutions was wrong – though I suspect that empirically it would be. It would be for the far deeper reason – or principle you may call it – that *acts which are not free are not acts which are capable of having value in the ethical sense.* We do not regard the movement of a herd of cattle as falling under ethical categories any more than the heat of the sun or the furious winter's rages. Only where conditions of human freedom, in some sense or other, are present do such judgments have meaning.

But the conception of liberty itself involves complications. Liberty is not anarchy. It is not a free for all – often as it is said to be by those who hate it. The idea of individual liberty does not involve liberty to curtail other people's liberty. That is why the necessity of a framework of law and an apparatus of enforcement is an essential part of the conception of a free society. But this is no facile criterion. In this connection I would cite the work of the great man after whom this lecture is named. No candid reader of Richard Ely's famous *Property and Contract* can come away believing that the sections of the law with which it deals are capable of being inscribed on two tablets of stone, or that the weighing of considerations of utility, in the sense in which I have defined it, and of the claims of liberty as the essential of conduct coming under the categories of ethics, is an easy matter.

Thus both as regards utility and liberty we are eventually involved in questions relating to the coercive powers of government and the basis of consent. I have no doubt that in the discussion of such problems considerations of Political Economy are relevant. Consider, for instance, the whole range of Adam Smith's third function of the state: "the duty of erecting and maintaining certain public works and certain public institutions which it can never be for the interest of any individual, or small number of individuals, to erect and maintain, because the profit would never repay the expense to any individual or small number of individuals, though it may frequently do much more than repay it to a great society" (pp. 687–88). Indeed, without in any way subscribing to the so-called Marxian theory of politics, I suspect that such considerations must play a very large part in any articulate theory of the state, its evolution and its activities. I welcome the growing recognition of the duty of political economists to extend their systematic investigations in this sphere; and thus, in my conception at any rate, we have quite enough on our plate in this connection to occupy us for many generations to come.

V

Let me sum up the main points of these discursive reflections. As regards the subject matter of Economic Science, I adhere to its description in terms of behavior conditioned by scarcity. As regards its status as a science, I see no reason to deny its susceptibility to the usual logical requirements of a science, though I have emphasized the peculiar nature of its subject as concerned with conscious beings capable of choice and learning. I see no reason why we should be terrified into thinking that such analysis necessarily involves ideological bias. But beyond that, in the application of Economic Science to problems of policy, I urge that we must acknowledge the introduction of assumptions of value essentially incapable of scientific proof. For this reason, while not denying the value of some thought going under that name, I have urged that the claims of Welfare Economics to be scientific are highly dubious; and I go on to argue the lack of realism which is involved by some of the inferences which may be drawn from its assumptions. Instead I recommend what I call Political Economy which, at each relevant point, declares all relevant non-scientific assumptions; and I furnish some indications of the leading criteria and fields of speculation which should underlie this branch of intellectual activity.

One final word concerning the implications of this conception of the task of Political Economy. I venture to suggest that, as teachers of the subject, our instructions will be more fruitful if, side by side, they run parallel with suitable courses in Politics and History – Politics because it deals systematically with philosophical and constitutional matters which as regards Political Economy only arise incidentally; History, because while it certainly does not lay down laws by which we can foretell the future, it does give a feeling for the possibilities of action which confining our attention to the present certainly fails to convey. I fancy that such exhortations are more at home in my own country where excessive specialization in the first-degree stage, productive of one-eyed monsters, is too frequently the order of the day. But the general principle seems to me to be sound.

References

William J. Baumol and William G. Bowen, *Performing Arts – The Economic Dilemma* (New York, 1966).

J.S. Chipman and J.C. Moore, "The new welfare economics, 1939–1974," *International Economic Review*, vol. 19 (October 1978), pp. 547–84.

F.Y. Edgeworth, *Papers Relating to Political Economy*, Vol. II (London, 1925).

Richard T. Ely, *Property and Contract* (New York, 1914).

Eli Halévy, *The Growth of Philosophic Radicalism* (London, 1928).

R. Harrod, "Scope and method of economics," *Economic Journal*, vol. 48 (September 1938), pp. 383–412.

F.A. Hayek, *New Studies in Philosophy, Politics, Economics and the History of Ideas* (London, 1978).

J.R. Hicks, "The foundations of welfare economics," *Economic Journal*, vol. 49 (December 1939), pp. 696–712.

David Hume, *A Treatise of Human Nature*, vol. II (eds. T.H. Green and T.H. Grose, London, 1874).

David Hume, *Essays, Moral, Political and Literary* (eds. T.H. Green and T.H., Grose, London, 1875).

William S. Jevons, *The Theory of Political Economy*, ed. R.D. Collison Black (London, 1970).

N. Kaldor, "Welfare propositions in economics," *Economic Journal*, vol. 49 (September 1939), pp. 549–51.

Alfred Marshall and Mary Paley Marshall, *The Economics of Industry* (London, 1879).

Carl Menger, *Grundsätze der Volkswirtschaftslehre* (Vienna, 1871).

Gunnar Myrdal, *The Political Element in the Development of Economic Theory* (London, 1953).

Vilfredo Pareto, *Manuel d'Economie Politique*, 2nd edn (Paris, 1892).

Lionel Robbins, *An Essay on the Nature and Significance of Economic Science* (London, 1932).

Lionel Robbins, *Economic Planning and International Order* (London, 1937).

Lionel Robbins, *Political Economy: Past and Present, A Review of Leading Theories of Economic Policy* (London, 1976).

Charles K. Rowley and Alan T. Peacock, *Welfare Economics: A Liberal Restatement* (London, 1975).

Adam Smith, *An Inquiry into the Nature and Causes of the Wealth of Nations*, eds R.H. Campbell and A.S. Skinner (Glasgow edn of the Works and Correspondence of Adam Smith, Oxford, 1976).

Jacob Viner, *Studies in the Theory of International Trade* (New York, 1937).

R. Whately, *Introductory Lectures on Political Economy*, 4th edn (London, 1855).

Philip H. Wicksteed, *The Alphabet of Economic Science* (London, 1888).

Bibliography

This list of Robbins's published writings is organized in the following sections: Books (including books edited), Articles in Journals, Pamphlets and Reports, Chapters in Books, and Reviews in Journals. I have not included the numerous articles, reviews and letters Robbins contributed to newspapers and magazines: in his early years as a lecturer Robbins undertook a good deal of journalism; later he was a frequent contributor to periodicals such as *The Economist. The Spectator, Time and Tide* and, particularly in the 1970s, the *Financial Times*. I have indicated where Robbins himself reprinted his own articles but I cannot pretend to have sought or located *all* the many collections in which Robbins's articles have been reprinted. This bibliography also does not list the translations into many languages of Robbins's books.

Books

(1926) *Wages: An Introductory Analysis of the Wage System under Modern Capitalism* (London: Jarrolds).

(1932a) *An Essay on the Nature and Significance of Economic Science* (London: Macmillan). (1935) 2nd edn (London: Macmillan). (1984) 3rd edn (London: Macmillan).

(1932b) Philip H. Wicksteed, *The Co-ordination of the Laws of Distribution*, London School of Economics Reprints of Scarce Tracts on Economics and Political Science No. 12. (1992) Revised edn, with an introduction by Ian Steedman (Aldershot: Edward Elgar).

(1933) Philip H. Wicksteed, *The Common Sense of Political Economy and Selected Papers and Reviews on Economic Theory* (London: George Routledge & Sons Ltd). Introduction reprinted as 'Philip Wicksteed as an economist' in *The Evolution of Modern Economic Theory* (1970), pp. 189–209.

(1934) *The Great Depression* (London: Macmillan). (1976) (Plainview, NY: Books for Libraries Press).

(1934–5) Knut Wicksell, *Lectures on Political Economy*, trans. E. Classen (London: George Routledge & Sons). Introduction reprinted as 'Wicksell's *Lectures on Political Economy*' in *The Evolution of Modern Economic Theory* (1970), pp. 210–22.

(1937) *Economic Planning and International Order* (London: Macmillan).

(1939a) *The Economic Basis of Class Conflict and Other Essays in Political Economy* (London: Macmillan).

(1939b) *The Economic Causes of War* (London: Jonathan Cape). (1968) 2nd edn (New York: Howard Fertig).

(1947) *The Economic Problem in Peace and War: Some Reflections on Objectives and Mechanisms* (London: Macmillan).

(1952) *The Theory of Economic Policy in English Classical Political Economy* (London: Macmillan). (1978) 2nd edn (London: Macmillan).

(1954) *The Economist in the Twentieth Century and Other Lectures in Political Economy* (London: Macmillan). Chapters II–VIII reprinted as chapters II, VI, III, V, VIII, IX, VII of *Money, Trade and International Relations* (1971).

(1958a) *Robert Torrens and the Evolution of Classical Economics* (London: Macmillan).

(1958b) R. Torrens, *Letters on Commercial Policy*, London School of Economics Reprints of Scarce Works on Political Economy No. 14. Introduction reprinted as 'Torrens's *Letters on Commercial Policy*' in *The Evolution of Modern Economic Theory* (1970), pp. 92–6.

(1963) *Politics and Economics: Papers in Political Economy* (London: Macmillan).

(1966) *The University in the Modern World and other papers on higher education* (London: Macmillan).

(1968) *The Theory of Economic Development in the History of Economic Thought being the Chichele Lectures for 1966, revised and extended* (London: Macmillan).

(1970) *The Evolution of Modern Economic Theory and Other Papers on the History of Economic Thought* (London: Macmillan and Chicago: Aldine).

(1971a) *Autobiography of an Economist* (London: Macmillan).

(1971b) *Money, Trade and International Relations* (London: Macmillan).

(1976) *Political Economy: Past and Present, A Review of Leading Theories of Economic Policy* (London: Macmillan).

(1979) *Against Inflation: Speeches in the Second Chamber* (London: Macmillan).

(1980) *Higher Education Revisited* (London: Macmillan).

Articles in Journals

(For details of collections other than Robbins's own collections in which articles were reprinted, see *Chapters in Books*, p. 436.)

(1926) 'The dynamics of capitalism', *Economica* 6 (March), pp. 31–9. [Review article of Maurice Dobb, *Capitalist Enterprise and Social Progress*.]

(1927) 'Mr. Hawtrey on the scope of economics', *Economica* 7 (June), pp. 172–8. [Review article of R.G. Hawtrey, *The Economic Problem*.]

(1928) 'The representative firm', *Economic Journal* 38 (September), pp. 387–404. [Reprinted above, Chapter 1.]

(1929a) 'The economic effects of variations of hours of labour', *Economic Journal* 39 (March), pp. 25–40. [Reprinted above, Chapter 2.]

(1929b) 'Notes on some probable consequences of the advent of a stationary population in Great Britain', *Economica* 9 (April), pp. 71–82.

(1929c) 'Economic readiness for war', *Royal Engineers Journal* 43 (June), pp. 248–56.

(1930a) 'The present position of economic science', *Economica* 10 (March), pp. 14–24. [Reprinted above, Chapter 3.]

(1930b) 'On a certain ambiguity in the conception of stationary equilibrium', *Economic Journal* 40 (June), pp. 194–214. [Reprinted above, Chapter 4.]

(1930c) 'On the elasticity of demand for income in terms of effort', *Economica* 10 (June), pp. 123–9. [Reprinted above, Chapter 5.]

(1930d) 'The economic works of Phillip Wicksteed', *Economica* 10 (November), pp. 245–58. Also published in C.H. Herford, *Philip Henry Wicksteed, His Life and Work* (London and Toronto: J.M. Dent & Sons Ltd, 1931), pp. 228–47. [Reprinted above, Chapter 6.]

(1931a) 'Economic notes on some arguments for protection', *Economica* 11 (February), pp. 45–62. [Reprinted above, Chapter 7.]

(1931b) 'The economics of import boards: a criticism of Mr. Wise's proposals', *Political Quarterly* 2, pp. 204–23. Reprinted in *The Economic Basis of Class Conflict* (1939), pp. 182–210.

(1932a) 'The Ottawa resolutions on finance and the future of monetary policy', *Lloyds Bank Limited Monthly Review* 3 (October), pp. 422–38.

(1932b) 'Consumption and the trade cycle', *Economica* 12 (November), pp. 413–30. [Reprinted above, Chapter 8.]

(1934a) 'Remarks upon certain aspects of the theory of costs', *Economic Journal* 44 (March), pp. 1–18. [Reprinted above, Chapter 9]

(1934b) 'Remarks on the relationship between economics and psychology', *Manchester School* 5 (December), pp. 89–101. [Reprinted above, Chapter 10.]

(1934c) 'L'agriculture dirigée' [trans. François Radot], *Revue d'Economie Politique* 48 (September–October), pp. 1503–20. Reprinted in *The Economic Basis of Class Conflict* (1939), pp. 135–60.

(1934d) 'The planning of British agriculture', *Lloyds Bank Limited Monthly Review* 5 (November), pp. 458–69. Reprinted as 'The consequences of agricultural planning' in *The Economic Basis of Class Conflict* (1939), pp. 161–81.

(1935a) 'A student's recollections of Edwin Cannan', *Economic Journal* 45 (June), pp. 393–8.

(1935b) 'The planning of British agriculture – a rejoinder', *Lloyds Bank Limited Monthly Review* 6 (February), pp. 89–92.

(1935c) 'The economics of restrictionism', *The Banker* 33 (January), pp. 19–25. Expanded version in *The Economic Basis of Class Conflict* (1939), pp. 29–44.

(1935d) 'The problem of stabilisation', *Lloyds Bank Limited Monthly Review* 6 (April), pp. 207–18.

(1936a) 'The place of Jevons in the history of economic thought', *Manchester School* 7 (April), pp. 1–17. Reprinted in *The Evolution of Modern Economic Theory* (1970), pp. 169–88. [Reprinted above, Chapter 11.]

(1936b) 'The nature of national planning in the sphere of international business', *Amsterdamsche Bank N.V. Financial and Economic Review*, no. 47 (April), pp. 1–9. Reprinted as 'The nature of national planning', *Economic Planning and International Order* (1937), pp. 13–38.

(1936c) 'The consequences of economic nationalism', *Lloyds Bank Limited Monthly Review* 7 (May), pp. 226–39.

(1936d) 'Economic nationalism and monetary policy', *The Banker* 38 (June), pp. 192–7.

(1936e) 'The consequences of economic nationalism', *International Conciliation*, no. 323 (October), pp. 466–78.

(1936f) 'Miedzynarodowe regulowanie plac i czasu pracy' [trans. Jan Drewnowski], *Ekonomista* 36, no. 4, pp. 3–15. Reprinted as 'International Regulation of Wages and Hours of Labour' in *Economic Planning and International Order* (1937), pp. 158–83.

(1937) 'How to mitigate the next slump', *Lloyds Bank Limited Monthly Review* 8 (May), pp. 234–44. Reprinted in *The Economic Basis of Class Conflict* (1939), pp. 237–55. [Reprinted above, Chapter 12.]

(1938a) 'Live and dead issues in the methodology of economics', *Economica* n.s. 5 (August), pp. 342–52. [Reprinted above, Chapter 13.]

(1938b) 'Interpersonal comparisons of utility: a comment', *Economic Journal* 48 (December), pp. 635–41. [Reprinted above. Chapter 14.]

(1938c) 'The long-term budget problem', *Lloyds Bank Limited Monthly Review* 9 (April), pp. 158–67. Reprinted as 'The long-term budgetary problem' in *The Economic Basis of Class Conflict* (1939), pp. 256–77.

(1939a) 'The export problem', *Lloyds Bank Limited Monthly Review* 10 (July), pp. 214–27.

(1939b) 'The export problem: a reply to Mr. Glenday, *Lloyds Bank Limited Monthly Review* 10 (September), pp. 286–95.

(1947a) 'Economic prospects', *Lloyds Bank Review* n.s. no. 3 (January), pp. 21–32.

(1947b) 'Inquest on the crisis', *Lloyds Bank Review* n.s. no. 6 (October), pp. 1–27. [Reprinted above, Chapter 15.]

(1949a) 'The economist in the twentieth century: an oration delivered on the 53rd Anniversary of the foundation of the London School of Economics', *Economica* n.s. 16 (May), pp. 93–105. Reprinted in *The Economist in the Twentieth Century* (1954), pp. 1–17.

(1949b) 'The sterling problem', *Lloyds Bank Review* n.s. no. 14 (October), pp. 1–31. [Reprinted above, Chapter 16.]

(1949c) 'Full employment as an objective', *Comptes-rendus des Travaux de la Société d' economie politique de Belgique* no. 192 (December), pp. 6–22. Reprinted in *The Economist in the Twentieth Century* (1954), pp. 18–40, and in *Money, Trade and International Relations* (1971), pp. 41–65.

(1950) 'Towards the Atlantic Community', *Lloyds Bank Review* n.s. no. 17 (July), pp. 1–24. Reprinted in *The Economist in the Twentieth Century* (1954), pp. 170–97.

(1953a) 'The international economic problem', *Lloyds Bank Review* n.s. no. 27 (January), pp. 1–24. [Reprinted above, Chapter 18.]

(1953b) 'Robertson on utility and scope', *Economica* n.s. 20 (May), pp. 99–111. [Review article of D.H. Robertson, *Utility and All That and Other Essays*.] [Reprinted above, Chapter 19.]

(1954) 'Seis conferencias do Professor Lionel E. Robbins', *Revista Brasileira de Economia* 8 (June), pp. 9–232. Reprinted in English in *The Economist in the Twentieth Century* (1954), Chapter III–VII, and in *Money, Trade and International Relations* (1971), Chapters VI, III, V, VIII, IX, VII.

(1955a) 'Schumpeter's history of economic analysis', *Quarterly Journal of Economics* 69 (February), pp. 1–22. [Review article of Joseph A. Schumpeter, *History of Economic Analysis*.] Reprinted as 'Schumpeter on the history of economic analysis' in *The Evolution of Modern Economic Theory* (1970), pp. 47–72. [Reprinted above, Chapter 20.]

(1955b) 'Notes on public finance', *Lloyds Bank Review*, n.s. no. 38 (October), pp. 1–18. [Reprinted above, Chapter 21.]

(1955) 'The teaching of economics in schools and universities', *Economic Journal* 65 (December), pp. 579–93.

(1956a) 'Las opiniones de Robertson sobre la utilidad y el objeto de la economia', *Revista de Economia Politica* 7, no. 1, pp. 489–506.

(1956b) 'A letter from David Ricardo', *Economica* n.s. 23 (May), pp. 172–4.

(1956c) 'Opiniones del Professor Lionel C. Robbins sobre los estudios universitarios de economia y los problemas profesionales de su enseñanza', *Moneda y Credito* 59 (December), pp. 150–7.

(1957a) 'Packe on Mill', *Economica* n.s. 24 (August), pp. 250–9. [Review article of Michael St John Packe, *The Life of John Stuart Mill*.] Reprinted as 'The life of John Stuart Mill' in *The Evolution of Modern Economic Theory* (1970), pp. 97–110.

(1957b) 'Equality as an Objective', *Crossbow* 1 (Autumn), pp. 18–22. Reprinted as 'Equality as a social objective' in *Politics and Economics* (1963), pp. 73–90.

(1958) 'Thoughts on the crisis', *Lloyds Bank Review* n.s. no. 48 (April), pp. 1–26. Reprinted in *Politics and Economics* (1963), pp. 166–96. [Reprinted above, Chapter 22.]

(1959) 'The present position of economics', *Rivista di Politica Economica* XLIX (August–September), pp. 3–19.

(1961) 'Hayek on liberty', *Economica* n.s. 28 (February), pp. 66–81. [Review article of F.A. Hayek, *The Constitution of Liberty*.] Reprinted in *Politics and Economics* (1963), pp. 91–112. [Reprinted above, Chapter 23.]

(1965a) 'Recent discussion of the problems of higher education in Great Britain', *Public Policy*, vol. 14, pp. 203–20. [Pollak Lecture, Graduate School of Public Administration, Harvard University, 18 March 1964] Reprinted in *The University in the Modern World* (1966), pp. 17–39.

(1965b) 'Report on Robbins', by Lord Robbins and Boris Ford [interview], *Universities Quarterly* 20 (December), pp. 5–15.

(1966) 'Of academic freedom', *Universities Quarterly* 20 (September), pp. 420–35.

(1967) 'Malthus as an economist', *Economic Journal* 77 (June), pp. 256–61. Reprinted as 'Malthus in perspective', in *The Evolution of Modern Economic Theory* (1970), pp. 85–91.

(1968) 'The international monetary problem', *Journal of Political Economy* 76 (July–August), pp. 664–77. [Reprinted above, Chapter 24.]

(1971a) (with Donald MacRae, May Eppel, Maurice Freedman and Leslie I. Edgar) 'Morris Ginsberg: Five Memorial Addresses', *The Jewish Journal of Sociology* XIII (June), pp. 5–16.

(1971b) 'Unsettled Questions in the Political Economy of the Arts', *Three Banks Review* no. 91 (September), pp. 3–19.

(1972) 'Keynes Lecture in Economics: The International Monetary Problem', *Proceedings of the British Academy* LVIII, pp. 293–311.

(1979) 'On Latsis's *Method and Appraisal in Economics*: a review essay', *Journal of Economic Literature* 17 (September), pp. 996–1004. [Reprinted above, Chapter 25.]

(1981) 'Economics and political economy', Richard T. Ely Lecture, *American Economic Review* 71 Supplement (May), pp. 1–10. Reprinted in *An Essay on the Nature and Significance of Economic Science*, 3rd edn (1984), pp. xi–xxxiii. [Reprinted above, Chapter 26.]

(1982a) 'The IEA, 1957–81 – An Appraisal', *The Journal of Economic Affairs* 1 (July), pp. 201–4.

(1982b) 'The place of Jevons in the history of economic thought', *Manchester School* 50 (December 1982), pp. 310–25.

Pamphlets and Reports

(1941) *Economic Aspects of Federation* (London: Macmillan for the Federal Union Research Institute).

(1951) *The Balance of Payments, The Stamp Memorial Lecture delivered before the University of London on 20 November 1951* (London: Athlone Press, 1951). [Reprinted above, Chapter 17.]

(1952a) *The Internal Financial Situation in member and associated countries, Report by a Group of independent Experts* (Paris: Organisation for European Economic Co-operation).

(1952b) *Report of the Committee on the Export of Works of Art etc.* (London: HMSO).

(1954) *Export of Works of Art, First Report of the Reviewing Committee appointed by the Chancellor of the Exchequer in December, 1952*, Cmd. 9292 (London: HMSO).

(1955) *Report of the Committee on the Rebuilding of the Queen's Hall*. Cmd. 9467 (London: HMSO).

(1963a) *Higher Education, Report of the Committee appointed by the Prime Minister under the Chairmanship of Lord Robbins 1961–63*. Cmnd. 2154 (London: HMSO).

(1963b) *Export of Works of Art 1962–63, Tenth Report of the Reviewing Committee appointed by the Chancellor of the Exchequer in December, 1952*, Cmnd. 2174 (London: HMSO).

(1963c) *Address by the Special Visitor. On technology and economics and their relation to public policy, Commemoration Day 24 October 1963* (London: Imperial College of Science and Technology).

(1964) *London Opera Centre, Report of the Committee appointed by the Governing Body to investigate recent criticisms of the Centre* (London: Royal Opera House).

(1965) *Bentham in the Twentieth Century, Address to the Assembly of Faculties, University College, London, 16 June 1964* (London: Athlone Press). Reprinted in *The Evolution of Modern Economic Theory* (1970), pp. 73–84.

(1966) *Of Academic Freedom: An Inaugural Lecture under the 'Thank-Offering to Britain' Fund* [6 July 1966] (London: Oxford University Press for the British Academy).

(1970) *Jacob Viner 1892–1970* (Princeton, NJ: Princeton University Press).

(1972) *Technology and Social Welfare*, Joseph Wunsch Lecture 1972 (Haifa: Technion/Israel Institute of Technology).

(1973) *The International Monetary Problem, Second Keynes Lecture in Economics, 26 October 1972* (London: Oxford University Press for the British Academy).

(1974) *Aspects of Post-war Economic Policy* (Fifth Wincott Memorial Lecture), Occasional Paper No. 42 (London: Institute of Economic Affairs).

(1977) *Liberty and Equality*, Occasional Paper No. 52 (London: Institute of Economic Affairs).

(1980) *Objectives of Monetary Policy: Past and Present, The Second Mais Lecture* (London: City University).

(1981) *Dos Conferencias: Keynes como economista politico; la situacion economica, financiera y monetaria actual* (Buenos Aires: Fundacion Bolsa de Comercio de Buenos Aires).

(1982a) *The Mixed Economy* (Madrid: Editorial Moneda y Credito).

(1982b) *Stagflation* (Nankang, Taipei, Taiwan: Institute of Economics, Academia Sinica).

(1982c) *International Economic Relations* (Nankang, Taipei, Taiwan: Institute of Economics, Academia Sinica).

Chapters in Books

(For bibliographical details of the articles and extracts from books and pamphlets reprinted see *Books, Articles in Journals* and *Pamphlets*, p. 429–35 above.)

(1927) 'The optimum theory of population', *London Essays in Economics: in Honour of Edwin Cannan*, eds T. Gregory and H. Dalton (London: George Routledge & Sons Ltd), pp. 103–34.

(1930) Introduction to Harold E. Batson, *A Select Bibliography of Modern Economic Theory 1870–1929* (London: George Routledge & Sons Ltd), pp. vii–ix.

(1931a) Foreword to Friedrich A. Hayek, *Prices and Production* (London: George Routledge & Sons Ltd), pp. vii–xii.

(1931b) 'The case of agriculture', *Tariffs: the Case Examined*, by a Committee of Economists under the Chairmanship of Sir William Beveridge (London: Longmans, Green & Co.), pp. 148–69.

(1931c) (with G.L. Schwartz) 'Tariffs for revenue', *Tariffs: the Case Examined*, by a Committee of Economists under the Chairmanship of Sir William Beveridge (London: Longmans, Green & Co.), pp. 170–84.

(1931d) 'The economic works', in C.H. Herford, *Philip Henry Wicksteed, His Life and Work* (London and Toronto: J.M. Dent & Sons), pp. 228–47.

(1933) Introduction to Friedrich A. Hayek, *Monetary Theory and the Trade Cycle*, trans. N. Kaldor and H.M. Croome (London: Jonathan Cape), pp. 5–9.

(1934a) 'Production', *Encyclopaedia of the Social Sciences*, ed. E.R.A. Seligman (New York: Macmillan), pp. 462–7.

(1934b) Introduction to Ludwig von Mises, *The Theory of Money and Credit*, trans. H.E. Batson (London: Jonathan Cape), pp. 11–13.

(1936a) 'Memorandum on the fundamental reasons for increased protectionism', Joint Committee of the Carnegie Endowment for International Peace and the International Chamber of Commerce, *Separate memoranda from the Economists consulted by the Joint Committee on The Improvement of Commercial Relations between Nations and The Problem of Monetary Stabilization* (Paris: International Chamber of Commerce), pp. 27–43. Reprinted as 'The causes of increased protectionism' in *The Economic Basis of Class Conflict* (1937), pp. 107–34.

(1936b) 'The consequences of economic nationalism', in *International Conciliation: Documents for the Year 1936* (New York: Carnegie Endowment for International Peace), pp. 466–78. Reprint of article (1936c).

(1937a) 'The economics of territorial sovereignty', *Peaceful Change: An International Problem*, ed. C.A.W. Manning (London: Macmillan), pp. 41–60. Reprinted in *The Economic Basis of Class Conflict* (1937), pp. 81–106, and in *Money, Trade and International Relations* (1971), pp. 235–51.

(1937b) Foreword to Costantino Bresciani-Turroni, *The Economics of Inflation, A study of currency depreciation in post-war Germany 1914–1923*, trans. Millicent E. Sayers (London: Allen & Unwin), pp. 5–6.

(1938) 'Les méthodes d'observation économique et les problèmes de la prévision en matière économique', in Lionel Robbins, E.F. Wagemann, Leon Dupriez, José Vandelos and Verrijn Stuart, *Cinq conférences sur la Méthode dans les recherches économiques* (Paris: Libraire du Recueil Sirey), pp. 9–27.

(1939) Preface to Chi-Yuen Wu, *An Outline of International Price Theories* (London: Routledge), pp. xi–xii.

(1940a) 'Economic aspects of federation', *Federal Union: A Symposium*, ed. M. Chaning-Pearce (London: Jonathan Cape), pp. 167–86. Reprinted as *Economic Aspects of Federation* (1941).

(1940b) 'Economic factors and international disunity', in Royal Institute of International Affairs, *World Order Papers, First Series* (London: Royal Institute of International Affairs), pp. 129–53.

(1946) 'On the elasticity of demand for income in terms of effort', in William Fellner and Bernard F. Haley (eds), *Readings in the Theory of Income Distribution* (Philadelphia: Blakiston), pp. 237–44. Reprint of article (1930c).

(1949) 'Cannan, Edwin', *Dictionary of National Biography, 1931–1940 Supplement*, ed. L.G.W. Legg (London: Oxford University Press), pp. 141–3. Reprinted as 'A biographical note on Edwin Cannan' in *The Evolution of Modern Economic Theory* (1970), pp. 229–33.

(1952) 'Robbins on Wicksteed', in Henry William Spiegel (ed.), *The Development of Economic Thought: Great Economists in Perspective* (New York: Science Editions), pp. 700–17. Reprint of 'Introduction' to Philip H. Wicksteed, *The Common Sense of Political Economy* (1933).

(1955) 'Freedom and order', in Arthur Smithies and others, *Economics and Public Policy: Brookings Lectures 1954* (Washington DC: The Brookings Institution), pp. 131–57. Reprinted in *Politics and Economics* (1963), pp. 27–52.

(1956) 'The revolution of our time', in Anthony Lejeune (ed.), *Time & Tide Anthology* (London: André Deutsch), pp. 52–5.

(1957) 'A note on the formal content of the theory of international trade', *Contribuiçoes a Analise do Desenvolvimento Economico* (Rio de Janeiro: Livraria AGIR Editora), pp. 267–71.

(1958) 'The United States economic problem, 1957–77', in Committee on Economic Development, *Problems of United States Economic Development* (New York: Committee on Economic Development), Vol. I, pp. 169–76.

(1958) Foreword to Tapas Majumdar, *The Measurement of Utility* (London: Macmillan), pp. ix–x.

(1960a) [Oral evidence to Radcliffe Committee, 24 July 1958] QQ. 10190–10254, Committee on the Working of the Monetary System, *Minutes of Evidence* (London: HMSO), pp. 673–8.

(1960b) 'The aims of monetary policy and the means of achieving them', Committee on the Working of the Monetary Sytem, *Principal Memoranda of Evidence*, Vol. 3 (London: HMSO), pp. 211–19.

(1961) Foreword to Reghinos D. Theocharis, *Early Developments in Mathematical Economics* (London: Macmillan), pp. v–vi.

(1962) 'The present position of economics', *Guest Lectures in Economics*, eds. Elizabeth Henderson and Luigi Spaventa (Milan: Dott. A. Giuffre), pp. 31–46 Reprint of article (1959).

(1962) 'Monetary theory and the Radcliffe Report', *Guest Lectures in Economics*, eds. Elizabeth Henderson and Luigi Spaventa (Milan: Dott. A. Giuffre), pp. 87–109. Reprinted in *Politics and Economics* (1963), pp. 197–226, and in *Money, Trade and International Relations* (1971), pp. 90–119.

(1962) 'The economic functions of the state in English classical political economy', in Edmund S. Phelps (ed.), *Private Wants and Public Needs: issues surrounding the size and scope of government expenditure* (New York: Norton), pp. 94–101. Abridged version of sections (i)–(iii) of Lecture II, 'The Economic Functions of the State', *The Theory of Economic Policy in English Classical Political Economy* (1952), pp. 34–46.

(1963) 'The great depression', in Gordon Wright and Arthur Mejia, Jr. (eds), *An Age of Controversy: Discussion Problems in Twentieth-Century European History* (New York: Dodd, Mead & Co.), pp. 213–19. Reprint of Chapter I of *The Great Depression* (1933), pp. 1–11.

(1965a) 'The place of Jevons in the history of economic thought', *Economic Thought: a historical anthology*, ed. J.A. Gherity (New York: Random House), pp. 328–45. Reprint of article (1936b).

(1965b) [Memorandum of evidence], University of Oxford, *Commission of Inquiry, Evidence, Part 11, Individuals* (Oxford: Oxford University Press), pp. 172–80. Reprinted with Robbins's oral evidence to the Commission [30 November 1964] as 'Evidence presented to the Commission on Oxford University' in *The University in the Modern World* (1966), pp. 57–100.

(1966a) 'An economist looks at business', in John Jewkes *et al.*, *Economics, Business and Government*, Occasional Paper No. 8 (London: Institute of Economic Affairs), pp. 25–31.

(1966b) Foreword to *The Travel Diaries of Thomas Robert Malthus*, ed. Patricia James (Cambridge: Cambridge University Press), pp. vii–ix.

(1966c) 'Recollections of Clive Gardiner, 3', in *Clive Gardiner 1891–1960* (London: South London Art Gallery), pp. 13–15.

(1967a) 'Issues and alternatives' and 'Concluding observations', *Monetary Reform and the Price of Gold*, ed. Randall Hinshaw (Baltimore: Johns Hopkins Press), pp. 7–25 and 143–50.

(1967b) Introduction to *The Collected Works of John Stuart Mill, Vols. IV and V: Essays on Economics and Society*, ed. J.M. Robson (Toronto: University of Toronto Press), pp. vii–xii. Reprinted as 'Mill's *Essays on Economics and Society*' in *The Evolution of Modern Economic Theory* (1970), pp. 118–63.

(1967c) 'Regulation', *The Business System: Readings in ideas and concepts*, eds Clarence Walton and Richard Eells (New York: Arkville Press), vol. I, pp. 691–6. Abridged version of *The Theory of Economic Policy* (1952), pp. 34–46.

(1968a) Foreword to Harold Wincott, *The Business of Capitalism: A selection of unconventional essays on economic problems of the 1960's* (London: Institute of Economic Affairs), pp. xi–xii.

(1968b) 'The subject matter of economics', *Economic Anthropology: Readings in Theory and Analysis*, eds. Edward E. Leclair Jr. and Harold K. Schneider (New York: Holt Reinhart & Winston), pp. 88–100. Extract from *An Essay on the Nature and Significance of Economic Science* (1935), pp. 1–23.

(1968c) 'Reversing the engine', *Looking Forward to the Seventies: A Blueprint for Education in the Next Decade*, ed. Peter Bander (Gerrards Cross: Colin Smythe), pp. 23–30.

(1970a) Foreword to Milton Friedman, *The Counter-Revolution in Economic Theory* (First Wincott Memorial Lecture), Occasional Paper 33 (London: Institute of Economic Affairs), pp. 4–5.

(1970b) 'The place of Jevons in the history of economic thought', *Economic Thought: a historical anthology*, ed. J.A. Gherity (New York: Random House), pp. 169–88. Reprint of article (1936b).

(1972a) 'On the elasticity of demand for income in terms of effort', *An Anthology of Labor Economics: Readings and Commentary*, eds Ray Marshall and Richard Perlman (New York and London: Wiley), pp. 189–93. Reprint of article (1930c).

(1972b) 'Inflation: an international problem' and 'Concluding observations', *Inflation as a Global Problem*, ed. Randall Hinshaw (Baltimore: Johns Hopkins University Press), pp. 10–25 and 128–46.

(1972c) 'Chairman's Introduction' and 'Chairman's Summing Up', in *Inflation, Economy and Society*, IEA Readings No. 8 (London: Institute of Economic Affairs), pp. 3–8 and 127–30.

(1973a) 'Summing up: mergers and the legal framework', in G.C. Allen *et al.*, *Mergers, Take-overs and the Structure of Industry*, IEA Readings No. 10 (London: Institute of Economic Affairs), pp. 81–4.

(1973b) 'Remarks upon certain aspects of the theory of costs', *London School of Economics Essays on Cost*, eds J.M. Buchanan and G.F. Thirlby (London: Weidenfeld & Nicolson), pp. 19–41. Reprint of article (1934a).

(1974a) 'Causes, effects, developments' and 'Summing up', in L. Robbins *et al.*, *Inflation: Causes, Consequences, Cures: discourses on the debate between the monetary and trade union interpretations*, IEA Readings No. 14 (London: Institute of Economic Affairs), pp. 1–9 and 104–5.

(1974b) Foreword to Jack Embling, *A Fresh Look at Higher Education: European Implications of the Carnegie Commission Reports* (Amsterdam, London and New York: Elsevier Scientific Publishing Company), pp. ix–xi.

(1975a) 'Issues and choices' and 'Concluding reflections', *Key Issues in International Monetary Reform*, ed. Randall Hinshaw (New York: Marcel Dekker), pp. 11–27 and 145–57.

(1975b) Foreword to David Seckler, *Thorstein Veblen and the Institutionalists: A Study in the Social Philosophy of Economics* (London: Macmillan), pp. ix–xi.

(1978) 'Economists and trade unions, 1776–1977', in Lord Robbins *et al.*, *Trade Unions: Public Goods or Public 'Bads'*, IEA Readings No. 17 (London: Institute of Economic Affairs), pp. 5–16 and 19–20.

(1979a) Introduction to Roland Vaubel, *Choice in European Monetary Union* (Ninth Wincott Memorial Lecture), Occasional Paper 55 (London: Institute of Economic Affairs), pp. 4–6.

(1979b) 'Introductory remarks', Stephen C. Littlechild *et al.*, *The Taming of Government*, IEA Readings No. 21 (London: Institute of Economic Affairs), pp. xix–xxiii.

(1979c) 'The nature of economic generalizations', *Philosophy and Economic Theory*, eds. Frank Hahn and Martin Hollis (Oxford: Oxford University Press), pp. 36–46. Reprint of *An Essay on the Nature and Significance of Economic Science* (1935), pp. 72–9, 83–4, 86–9, 90–8, 100.

(1979d) 'The mid-twenties: an economist's view', in John Buxton and Penry Williams, *New College Oxford 1379–1979* (published by the Warden and Fellows in commemoration of the sixth centenary), pp. 112–19. Extract from *Autobiography of an Economist* (1971), pp. 111–19.

(1981) 'Questions and options', and 'Concluding reactions', *Global Monetary Anarchy: perspectives on restoring stability*, ed. Randall Hinshaw (Beverly Hills and London: Sage Publications), pp. 29–47 and 161–76.

(1983) 'On Latsis's *Method and Appraisal in Economics*: a review essay', *Methodological Controversy in Economics: Historical Essays in Honor of T.W. Hutchison*, ed. W.A. Coats (Greenwich Conn: JAI Press), pp. 43–54. Reprint of article (1979).

(1988) 'The Methods of Economic Observation and the Problems of Prediction in Economics' in D.P. O'Brien, *Lionel Robbins* (London: Macmillan), pp. 170–8. Translation of chapter (1938).

(1990) 'Hot Springs and after, May–June 1943', 'Bretton Woods, June–August 1944', and 'The Loan Negotiations and the ITO, September–December 1945' in *The Wartime Diaries of Lionel Robbins and James Meade, 1943–45* eds Susan Howson and Donald Moggridge (London: Macmillan), pp. 8–91, 156–220 and 221–48.

(1992) 'Economic notes on some arguments for protection', *Protectionism in the World Economy*, ed. Forrest H. Capie (Cheltenham: Edward Elgar), Chapter 4. Reprint of article (1931a).

(1995) 'An Essay on the Nature and Significance of Economic Science (Macmillan, London, 1932, pp. 98–105)', *The Foundations of Econometric Analysis*, eds David F. Hendry and Mary S. Morgan (Cambridge: Cambridge University Press), pp. 98–102.

Reviews in Journals

(1925) T.E. Gregory, *The Present Position of Banking in America, Economica* 5 (November), pp. 358–9.

(1926a) Stephen Mills, *Taxation in Australia*, and A. Ramaiya, *A National System of Taxation*, *Economica* 6 (March), pp. 111–12.

(1926b) Gustav Cassel, *Fundamental Thoughts in Economics*, *Economica* 6 (June), pp. 223–5.

(1926c) R.C. Mills and F.C. Benham, *Lectures on the Principles of Money, Banking and Foreign Exchange, and their Application to Australia*, *Economica* 6 (November), pp. 359–60.

(1927a) M.J. Bonn, *Das Schicksal des Deutschen Kapitalismus*, *Economic Journal* 37 (December), pp. 613–16.

(1927b) E. Mahaim, *L'Organisation Permanente du Travail*, *Economic Journal* 37 (December), pp. 638–9.

(1927c) J. Bonar, *The Tables Turned: A Lecture and Dialogue on Adam Smith and the Classical Economists*, *Economica* 7 (December), pp. 391–2.

(1928) Sir Alfred Mond, *Industry and Politics*, *Economic Journal* 38 (September), pp. 442–4.

(1929a) Sir Josiah Stamp, *Some Economic Factors in Modern Life*, *Economic Journal* 39 (June), pp. 248–50.

(1929b) Edwin Cannan, *A Review of Economic Theory*, *Economic Journal* 39 (September), pp. 409–14.

(1930a) Nassau W. Senior, ed. S. Leon Levi, *Industrial Efficiency and Social Economy*, *Economic Journal* 40 (June), pp. 272–5.

(1930b) Othmar Spann, *Types of Economic Theory*, *Economica* 10 (June), pp. 200–2.

(1931a) Dr Martha Stephanie Braun, *Theories der Staatlichen Wirtschaftspolitik*, *Economica* 11 (November), pp. 469–72.

(1931b) Fritz Machlup, *Börsenkredit, Industriekredit und Kapitalbildung*, *Economica* 11 (November), pp. 472–5.

(1932) James Bonar, *A Catalogue of the Library of Adam Smith*, Economica 12 (August), p. 365.

(1936) Ragnar Nurkse, *Internationale Kapitalbewegungen*, *Economica* n.s. 3 (February), pp. 108–9.

(1937a) Gottfried Haberler, *Der Internationale Handel*, and *The Theory of International Trade*, trans. Alfred Stonier and Frederic Benham, *Economica* n.s. 4 (February), pp. 102–5.

(1937b) *The Agricultural Dilemma, A Report of an Inquiry organised by Viscount Astor and Mr. B. Seebohm Rowntree*, *Economica* n.s. 4 (February), pp. 113–14.

(1940a) I. Berlin, *Karl Marx: His Life and Environment*, *Economica* n.s. 7 (February), pp. 93–4.

(1940b) Boris Souvarine, *Stalin: A Critical Survey of Bolshevism*, *Economica* n.s. 7 (February), pp. 94–6.

(1957) Frank H. Knight, *On the History and Method of Economics – Selected Essays*, *American Economic Review* 47 (June), pp. 397–9.

(1958) Donald MacDougall, *The World Dollar Problem, A Study in International Economics*, *Crossbow* 1 (New Year), pp. 43–44. Reprinted as 'MacDougall on the Dollar Problem' in *Politics and Economics* (1963), pp. 159–65.

(1959a) Per Jacobsson, *Some Monetary Problems – International and National*, ed. Erin E. Jucker-Fleetwood, *Crossbow* 2 (Spring), pp. 65–7.

(1959b) Lord Beveridge, *A Defence of Free Learning*, *Crossbow* 3 (Autumn), p. 72.

(1960a) Sir Dennis H. Robertson, *Lectures on Economic Principles*, *Economica* n.s. 27 (February), pp. 71–4. Reprinted as 'Robertson's *Lectures on Economic Principles*' in *The Evolution of Modern Economic Theory* (1970), pp. 248–52.

(1960b) Knut Wicksell, *Selected Papers on Economic Theory*, ed. Erik Lindahl, and Torsten Gardlund, *The Life of Knut Wicksell*, trans. Nancy Adler, *Economica* n.s. 27 (May), pp. 173–7. Reprinted as 'New light on Knut Wicksell' in *The Evolution of Modern Economic Theory* (1970), pp. 223–8.

(1960c) Richard K.P. Pankhurst, *The Saint Simonians, Mill and Carlyle: A Preface to Modern Thought*, *Economica* n.s. 27 (August), pp. 278–9.

(1961) Carl S. Shoup, *Ricardo on Taxation*, *Economica* n.s. 28 (August), pp. 326–8.

(1962a) William C. Lehmann, *John Millar of Glasgow, 1735–1801: His Life and Thought and his Contributions to Sociological Analysis*, *Economica* n.s. 29 (February), pp. 96–7.

(1962b) Jack Stillinger, ed. *The Early Draft of John Stuart Mill's Autobiography*, *Economica* n.s. 29 (May), pp. 202–4. Reprinted as Annex (i) to 'The Life of John Stuart Mill', *The Evolution of Modern Economic Theory* (1970), pp. 110–13.

(1962c) G.S.L. Tucker, *Progress and Profits in British Economic Thought, 1650–1850*, *Economic Journal* 72 (1962), pp. 374–6.

(1963) Mary P. Mack, *Jeremy Bentham: An Odyssey of Ideas, 1748–1792*, *Economica* n.s. 30 (May), pp. 196–7.

(1965) *The Collected Works of John Stuart Mill, Vols. XII–XIII: The Earlier Letters of John Stuart Mill 1812–1845*, ed. Francis E. Mineka, *Economica* n.s. 32 (November), pp. 458–60. Reprinted as Annex (ii) to 'The Life of John Stuart Mill' in *The Evolution of Modern Economic Theory* (1970), pp. 113–17.

(1966a) *The Collected Works of John Stuart Mill, Vols. II–III, Principles of Political Economy with some of their applications to Social Philosophy*, ed. J.M. Robson, *Economica* n.s. 33 (February), pp. 92–4. Reprinted as 'Mill's Principles of Political Economy in *The Evolution of Modern Economic Theory* (1970), pp. 164–8.

(1966b) Ronald L. Meek, *The Economics of Physiocracy: Essays and Translations*, *Economica* n.s. 33 (February), pp. 94–6.

(1966c) Emil Kauder, *A History of Marginal Utility Theory*, *Economica* n.s. 33 (August), pp. 347–8.

(1966d) John Rae, *Life of Adam Smith*, ed. Jacob Viner, *Economica* n.s. 33 (August), p. 349.

(1967a) John Stuart Mill, *On the Logic of the Moral Sciences*, ed. Henry M. Magid, *Economica* n.s. 34 (February), p. 90.

(1967b) R. Warren James, *John Rae, Political Economist: An Account of his Life and a Compilation of his Main Writings*, *Economica* n.s. 34 (August), pp. 335–7.

(1969) Mark Blaug, *Economic Theory in Retrospect*, 2nd edn, *Economica* n.s. 36 (November), pp. 442–3.

(1970a) John M. Robson, *The Improvement of Mankind: The Social and Political Thought of John Stuart Mill*, *Economica* n.s. 37 (May), pp. 194–5.

(1970b) *The Collected Works of John Stuart Mill, Volume X: Essays on Ethics, Religion and Society*, ed. J.M. Robson, *Economica* n.s. 37 (November), pp. 422–4.

(1971) D.P. O'Brien, *J.R. McCulloch: A Study in Classic Economics*, *Economica* n.s. 38 (August), pp. 321–2.

(1973) *Essays in Biography, Volume X of the Collected Writings of John Maynard Keynes*, *Economic Journal* 83 (June), pp. 530–1.

(1974) *The Collected Works of John Stuart Mill, Vols. XIV–XVII: The Later Letters of John Stuart Mill, 1849–1873*, eds Francis E. Mineka and Dwight N. Lindley, *Economica* n.s. 41 (August), pp. 336–8.

(1976) *The Collected Works of John Stuart Mill, Vols. VII–VIII: A System of Logic Ratiocinative and Inductive*, ed. J.M. Robson, *Economica* n.s. 43 (November), pp. 446–7.

(1977) *The Early Economic Writings of Alfred Marshall (1867–1890)*, ed. J.K. Whitaker, *Economica* n.s. 44 (February), pp. 91–2.

(1978) Susan Howson and Donald Winch, *The Economic Advisory Council 1930–1939: A Study in Economic Advice during Depression and Recovery*, *Journal of Economic Literature* XVI (March), pp. 114–15.

(1979a) *The Collected Works of John Stuart Mill, Vols. XVIII and XIX: Essays on Politics and Society*, ed. J.M. Robson, *Economica* 46 (February), pp. 89–106.

(1979b) James M. Buchanan, *Freedom in Constitutional Contract: Perspectives of a Political Economist*, *Economic Journal* 89 (September), pp. 683–4.

(1980a) Patricia James, *Population Malthus*, *Economica* 47 (November), p. 471.

(1980b) *Religious Thought and Economic Society, Four chapters of an unfinished work by Jacob Viner*, eds. Jacques Melitz and Donald Winch, *Economica* 47 (November), pp. 489–90.

(1980c) *The Collected Works of John Stuart Mill, Vol. XI: Essays on Philosophy and the Classics*, ed. J.M. Robson, *Economica* 47 (November), pp. 490–1.

Index of Names

Index of Subjects

SPRINGER NATURE

GPSR Compliance

The European Union's (EU) General Product Safety Regulation (GPSR) is a set of rules that requires consumer products to be safe and our obligations to ensure this.

If you have any concerns about our products, you can contact us on ProductSafety@springernature.com

In case Publisher is established outside the EU, the EU authorized representative is:

Springer Nature Customer Service Center GmbH
Europaplatz 3
69115 Heidelberg, Germany

The manufacturer's authorised representative in the EU is Springer Nature Customer Service Centre GmbH, Europaplatz 3, 69115 Heidelberg, Germany. If you have any concerns regarding our products, please contact ProductSafety@springernature.com

Printed and bound by CPI Group (UK) Ltd, Croydon, CR0 4YY
10/10/2026
02231228-0016